Advanced Assembly Language
The Peter Norton Programming Series

Who This Book Is For

Intermediate to advanced assembly language programmers who want to extend their programming expertise and add new performance to their programs.

What's Inside

- More than 100 ready-to-run programs that show the best ways to handle the keyboard, files and disks, graphics and the screen, the mouse, the math coprocessor, and more

- Expert tips on writing pop-up programs, using macros, interfacing to BASIC, FORTRAN, C, and Pascal, as well as interfacing to Windows

- A learn-by-doing approach to programming that shows code in action in a direct, highly readable style

About the Peter Norton Microcomputer Libraries from Brady

All of the volumes in the Peter Norton Libraries, written in collaboration with Peter Norton Computing, provide clear, in-depth discussions of the latest developments in computer hardware, operating systems, and programming. Fully tested and rigorously reviewed by the experts at Peter Norton Computing, these libraries deserve a special place on your bookshelf. These libraries are comprised of two series:

The Peter Norton Hardware Library gives you an insider's grasp of your computer and the way it works. Included are such best-selling classics as *Inside the IBM PC*, *Inside the Apple Macintosh*, and *The Hard Disk Companion*.

The Peter Norton Programming Library focuses on creating programs that work right away and offers the best tips and techniques in the industry. It includes *Advanced BASIC*, *C Programming*, *C++ Programming*, *QBasic Programming*, *Advanced DOS*, and more.

Advanced Assembly Language

Steven Holzner with Peter Norton Computing

Brady

New York   London   Toronto   Sydney   Tokyo   Singapore

Copyright © 1991 by Peter Norton
All rights reserved,
including the right of reproduction
in whole or in part in any form.

 Brady

A Division of Simon & Schuster, Inc.
15 Columbus Circle
New York, NY 10023

Manufactured in the United States of America

10 9 8 7 6 5 4 3 2 1

Library of Congress Cataloging-in-Publication Data

Norton, Peter
　　Advanced assembly language [computer file].

　　1 computer disk ; 5¼ in. + 1 v.
　　System requirements: IBM PC or compatibles; 640K; DOS 2.0 or higher; Microsoft Macro assembler (version 5.1) or Turbo assembler; monochrome or color monitor; 2 disk drives; printer (optional).
　　Title from book.
　　Not copy-protected.
　　Audience: Adult computer users.
　　Summary: A utility for writing working assembly language programs using assembler software. The text provides a functional approach covering keyboard, screen handling, and file handling, among other related topics. Assumes the user has some assembly language background.
　　1. Programming languages (Electronic computers)—Software. 2. Utilities (Computer programs)—Software. I. Holzner, Steven. II. Title.
[QA76.7]　　　005.4　　　91-7137
ISBN 0-13-658774-7

Contents

Introduction — xv
How This Book Is Organized — xv
What You'll Need — xvi

Chapter 1. Writing Our First Programs — 1
Our First Assembly Language Program — 3
Running Our First Program — 4
How to Make .COM Files — 5
    The Program Segment Prefix — 7
    The Data Area in .COM Files — 8
    The Procedure in the .COM File — 11
    Ending Your Program — 12
    Using More Than One Procedure in .COM Files — 13
    Finishing the Code Segment — 14
.EXE Files versus .COM Files — 15
    How Relocation Works — 16
    An .EXE File Shell — 17
    The Stack in .EXE Files — 19
    AT and .COM Files — 21
The Program Segment Prefix in Detail — 24
    The Disk Transfer Area — 27
    The Code in .COM Files — 29

Chapter 2. How to Handle the Keyboard — 31
Keyboard Input — 33
    INT 21H Service 1 Character Input with Echo — 33
    SMALL.COM Converts to Lowercase — 34
    INT 21H Service 6 Read Key without Wait — 36
    REPEATER.COM Repeats What You Type — 36
    INT 21H Service 7 Read Key with Wait — 37
    HOLD.COM Waits for a Password — 37
    INT 21H Service 8 Read Key without Echo — 38

v

vi ▶ Advanced Assembly Language

INT 21H Service 0AH String Input	38
String Instructions	39
MOVS, MOVSB, MOVSW, and REP	40
CMPS, CMPSB, CMPSW, REPE, and REPNE	42
SCAS, SCASB, and SCASW	44
LODS and STOS	46
INT 21H Service 0BH Check Keyboard Buffer	47
INT 21H Service 0CH Clear Keyboard Buffer and Execute Service	47
The BIOS Interrupts	48
BIOS INT 16H	48
All about Keyboard Scan Codes	49
Extended ASCII Codes	49
INT 16H Service 0 Read Key	50
INT 16H Service 1 Examine Keyboard and Read	50
INT 16H, Service 2 Read Status Byte	50
Inside the Keyboard Buffer	51
Circular Buffers	53
Using the Keyboard Interrupt	54
READEM.COM Reads Directly from the Keyboard	55
Chapter 3. Screen Handling	**59**
The BIOS Screen Handling Services	62
Services 2 and 3 — Set and Get Cursor Position	62
Screen Page Numbers	63
Screen Attributes	64
The Screen Buffer and Attribute Bytes	66
PRINT_IT.COM Prints All Possible Characters	68
Service 0EH — Teletype Write	73
Graphics	73
INT 10H Service 0 — Set Video Mode	73
Black and White versus Color	75
Palettes	77
CGA Background Color	78
High-Resolution CGA Mode	80
Service 0CH — Write Dot	81
The EGA	81

The Service 10H Functions	83
The VGA	84
From CGA to EGA to VGA	84
Using the DAC Registers in the VGA	86
VGA 16-color Modes	87
VGA-only 256-color Mode	88
Writing Graphics Images Directly in Memory	91
Writing to the Buffer in CGA Modes	91
CGA_PIXEL.COM — Direct CGA Buffer Use	93
Writing to the EGA/VGA Buffer	98
EGA/VGA Bit Planes	98
EGA_PIXEL.COM — Direct EGA Buffer Use	99

Chapter 4. Getting the Most from Files — 111

File Control Blocks	113
File Handles	113
The DOS File Handle Services	114
RUBOUT.COM Deletes Files	116
File Error Checking	118
DOS Error Codes	119
BACK.COM Copies Any File	121
The Second File Name	122
Writing the Data to File Two	128
Inside Files	132
File Records	132
Retrieving Data from Files	134
The Read/Write Pointer	135
Using the Read/Write Pointer	137
PHONE.ASM — A Database Program	137
Setting the Read/Write Pointer	142

Chapter 5. Using the Mouse — 147

Interrupt 33H	149
Getting Started with the Mouse	149
Initializing the Mouse	150
Displaying the Mouse Cursor	150
Getting Mouse Information	151

Reading the Mouse Queue	152
Handling the Mouse Cursor	154
The Alphanumeric Mouse Cursor	156

Chapter 6. Using the Disks 159
The Disk Drives in Your Computer	161
A Disk Sector by Sector	162
How the Boot Record Works	162
How the File Allocation Table Works	164
The Directory on a Disk	168
Logical Sectors and Tracks	169
Hard Disks and Partitions	170
DOSCHECK.COM Checks for DOS Booting	172
How Subdirectories Work	174
The BIOS Disk Support	177
INT 13H Service 1 Read Status of Last Operation	178
The DOS Services	181

Chapter 7. Writing Your Own Pop-up Programs 187
Writing Memory-Resident Code	189
How Interrupts Work	191
Intercepting Interrupt Vectors	192
The Get and Set Interrupt Vector Services of INT 21H	194
Getting the Old Interrupt Vector	194
Resetting the Interrupt Vector	195
Making Code Memory-Resident	196
Writing a Program That Can Handle Interrupts	198
Calling the Old Interrupt	200
Indirect Calls and the DD and LABEL Directives	201
Use This TSR Shell	204
Some Things You Can't Do	205
Some Things You Can Do	205
Intercepting the Keyboard Interrupt	207
The Key-intercepting .COM File Shell	209
SWITCH.ASM: A Memory-Resident Hot Key Program	211

Chapter 8. Truly Fast Math — 215

How Signed Numbers Work — 217
    The Sign Bit — 217
    Creating Your Own Signed Numbers — 218
    Two's Complement Numbers — 219
    The NOT and NEG Instructions — 220
    Signed Multiplication — IMUL — 223
    Adding with Carries — 225
    The SBB Instruction — 228
    Big Time Multiplying — 229
    Big Time Division — 230
    Computerizing Our Dividing Example — 233
    How Does Division Look in Code? — 235
    Comparing DX:AX and BX:CX — 236

Bit-by-Bit Manipulations — 238
    SHR and SHL — 238
    SAR and SAL — 239
    The Rotate Instructions: RCL, RCR, ROL, and ROR — 240
    Rotating through the Carry — 243

Converting between Bases — 244

Chapter 9. Using Macros and Advanced Directives — 251

Printing Out a Trial Message — 253
    Printing the Trial Message Directly — 253
    Subroutines — 255

Linking — 256
    Linked Subroutines — 259
    Using Data in FILE2 — 261

How to Use Groups — 262
    GROUPs and Different Segments — 265

Libraries — 266
    Library Commands — 267

How Macros Work — 268
    Passing Parameters to a Macro — 275
    Using % and & in Macros — 275
    The LOCAL Directive in Macros — 278
    Macro Libraries — 278

The EXITM Directive	279
IRP and IRPC	280
REPT	280
An Example Using Macro Directives	281
PURGE	282
Using Self-Redefining Macros	282

Chapter 10. Linking to BASIC, FORTRAN, C, and Pascal 285

How Calling Conventions Work	287
Linking to a Pascal Example	289
Using BP and Stack Frames	291
All about Functions and Subroutines	293
How to Return Values from Functions	293
Returning Big Values in C	294
Returning Big Values in BASIC, FORTRAN, and Pascal	294
Returning Data in Our Example	295
The BASIC–Assembly Interface	297
Passing Parameters in BASIC	299
Shortcut Parameter Passing in BASIC	300
The FORTRAN–Assembly Interface	302
Passing Parameters in FORTRAN	304
Shortcut Parameter Passing in FORTRAN	306
The C–Assembly Interface	307
Passing Parameters to C	309
Shortcut Parameter Passing in C	311
The Pascal–Assembly Interface	312
Passing Parameters to Pascal	313
Shortcut Parameter Passing in Pascal	314
High-Level Languages in General	315

Chapter 11. Using the 80×87 317

Getting Started with the Math Coprocessor	319
Adding Integers with the 80×87	320
Subtracting Integers with the 80×87	323
Multiplying and Dividing Integers with the 80×87	325
80×87 Integer Formats	327
80×87 Floating Point Formats	328

Normalized 80×87 Format	328
The 80×87 Instructions	331
F2XM1 — 2^X Minus 1	331
FABS Absolute Value	332
FADD Addition	332
FBLD Load BCD Number	333
FBSTP Store BCD Number	333
FCHS Change Sign	334
FCLEX Clear Exceptions	334
FCOM Comparison	334
The RECORD and MASK Directives	335
FDIV Division	338
FIADD Integer Add	338
FICOM Integer Compare	339
FIDIV Integer Divide	339
FILD Load Integer	339
FIMUL Integer Multiply	340
FINIT Initialize 80×87	340
FIST Store Integer	340
FISTP Store Integer and Pop Stack	340
FISUB Integer Subtract	341
FLD Load Real	341
FMUL Multiply	341
FNCLEX Clear Exceptions — No Wait	342
FNOP No Operation	342
FNSTSW Store Status — No Wait	343
FPATAN Arc Tangent	343
FPREM Partial Remainder	343
FPTAN Tangent	344
FSQRT Square Root	344
FST Store Real	345
FSTSW Store Status	345
FSUB Subtraction	345
FTST Test for Zero	346
FWAIT Wait	346
FXAM Examine	346
FXCH Exchange Registers	347
FXTRACT Extract Exponent and Significand	347

FYL2X Y — Log$_2$ X	347
80 × 87 Errors and Error Checking	348
Putting Error Checking to Work	350

Chapter 12. Using Microsoft Windows   357

Window Messages	360
WinMain — The Main Window Function	362
DecodeMessages — Where the Action Is	371
The Windows Definition File	403
Making MYWINDOW.EXE	403

Chapter 13. Introduction to OS/2   407

OS/2 Is Not So Different	409
The 80 × 86	411
Segment Selectors	411
Hardware Gates	412
Security Rings	413
How Multitasking Works	413
Communication between Programs	414
Writing an OS/2 Program	414
Dynamic Linking	416
An OS/2 EXE File Shell with DosExit	416
OS/2 Output (Vio and DosWrite)	420
The DosWrite Service	420
VioPopUp — Pop-Ups under OS/2	428
TAKE5.EXE — An OS/2 TSR	429

Chapter 14. OS/2 Presentation Manager Primer   435

Welcome to the Presentation Manager	437
OS/2 and the Mouse	437
Programming the Presentation Manager	438
Some Unpleasant Presentation Manager Surprises	438
Getting Started with the Presentation Manager	439
The Window Function	464
Reentrant Code in OS/2	465

Chapter 15. The Presentation Manager in Action — 477
The Gpi Functions — 479
GpiCharStringAt — 479
GpiSetColor — 489
Reading Keys in Presentation Manager — 498
Presentation Manager Graphics — 508
      GpiPolyLine — 518
Resizing the Window — 525

Appendix A. The BIOS and DOS Reference — 533

Appendix B. The OS/2 Reference — 583

Appendix C. Device Drivers and IOCTL — 599

Index — 611

Limits of Liability and Disclaimer of Warranty

The authors and publisher of this book have used their best efforts in preparing this book and the programs contained in it. These efforts include the development, research, and testing of the theories and programs to determine their effectiveness. The authors and publisher make no warranty of any kind, expressed or implied, with regard to these programs or the documentation contained in this book. The authors and publisher shall not be liable in any event for incidental or consequential damages in connection with, or arising out of, the furnishing, performance, or use of these programs.

Trademarks

Most computer hardware and software have trademarks or registered trademarks. The individual trademarks have not been listed in this book.

Introduction

In this book we are going to assume that you already have some assembly language background. Perhaps you've picked up the basics of assembly language on your own or perhaps you've read a book. In either case, we'll start here, at the level an introductory book might finish, taking for granted that you have a grasp of the essentials and that you want to learn more.

Introductory texts are good to get you started. But they are, after all, just the beginning. Introductory texts have no time for memory-resident code, no time for the 80×87, the VGA, macros, fast bit-by-bit graphics, or interrupt handlers. Usually, getting this kind of knowledge takes a more advanced book.

Despite the popularity of assembly language on the PC, there have been few advanced assembler books published — and even the introductory texts can be difficult to read. Too often, assembly language books are just dry catalogs of instructions, more like dictionaries than learning aids. Reading them is like trying to learn to fly by reading about plane construction.

There is no substitute for the real thing: seeing your code work. For that reason, this book will be as practical as possible and as filled with examples as we can make it.

Also, many introductory texts skim over the system resources — the BIOS and DOS services — without going into any real detail. Since it is essential that an assembly language programmer knows what the system resources offer, we will cover them fully. Appendix A is a reference section, including all interrupts from 0 to FFH, Appendix B includes the popular OS/2 service calls, and Appendix C covers the internal workings of device drivers for interested readers.

How This Book Is Organized

This book is organized functionally around the different parts of the machine — there are chapters on the disk drives, the display, and so forth. This functional approach works better than simple catalogs of instructions, which leave people without the ability to connect what they have learned into a working whole.

We cover the machine in some depth: EGA/VGA displays, keyboard handling, disk drive handling, and so on. Then we move on to more advanced software directions: Microsoft Windows, for example, and OS/2 (as well as the OS/2 Presentation Manager). We also work through advanced assembler features such as macros and interfacing to high-level languages. These topics can add a lot of power to your programming.

What You'll Need

Thoughout the book, we will use the Microsoft Macro Assembler Version 5.1 and DOS 4.0. If you have an earlier version of the assembler, you should probably upgrade it since Version 5.1 was revolutionary, and we're going to use many of its features. If you have the Turbo Assembler, TASM, everything we do will work there too.

Keep in mind that this is an advanced book and, for that reason, we will work at a pace a little faster than that of introductory books. Since our emphasis will be on writing working programs, we will start with the fundamental process of writing a program — where to use PROC, where to use ORG, whether you need a stack or not, and so on. Many beginning texts never actually include programs you can simply type in, so this is our best starting point. Let's begin there in Chapter 1.

Chapter 1

Writing Our First Programs

Writing Our First Programs

THE FIRST STEP toward seeing your code in action is being able to write programs. For that reason, this first chapter is devoted to a review of assembly language and a discussion of writing assembly language programs that work. Every piece of code you write will have to fit into a program of one sort or another to work at all, so this chapter will get us off the ground. In addition, a number of basic concepts, such as segments, will be reviewed here to get us going.

Our First Assembly Language Program

Let's start off with a program that you can simply type in and run. This demonstration program is a very simple one named PROTECT.ASM, and it acts very much like ATTRIB. It will change a file's attribute to read-only, which means that the file cannot be written to or deleted. The corresponding unprotect program, RELEASE.ASM, uses the same code except in the one line where the attribute is set. Both of these programs are small and are written to be made into .COM files. Assembling programs as .COM files rather than .EXE files makes them small and efficient in both code length and, therefore, disk space.

The details, the instructions, and the functions of this program will become clear later in this chapter when we cover the program segment prefix (PSP). What is important now is not the MOVs and INTs of PROTECT itself, but the way they are enclosed by the .CODE, PROC, and ENDP statements. The one line difference between PROTECT and RELEASE where different attributes (one to protect, zero to unprotect) are used is marked in Listings 1-1 and 1-2.

Listing 1-1. PROTECT.ASM — Protect Disk Files.

```
        .MODEL SMALL
        .CODE
        ORG     100H

PROTECT PROC    NEAR
        MOV     DX,82H   ;Point DS:DX to filename
        MOV     DI,82H   ;Start looking in PSP
        MOV     AL,13    ;Look for carriage return
        MOV     CX,12    ;Scan up to 12 letters
REPNE   SCASB            ;Find end of Input
        MOV     BYTE PTR [DI-1],0   ;Make string ASCIIZ
        MOV     AL,1     ;Function Code
→       MOV     CX,1     ;This is to protect
        MOV     AH,43H   ;Use Service 43H
        INT     21H      ; of INT 21H
        INT     20H      ;End the Program.
PROTECT ENDP

        END     PROTECT
```

4 ▶ Advanced Assembly Language

```
Listing 1-2. RELEASE.ASM — Unprotected Disk Files.
        .MODEL SMALL
        .CODE
        ORG     100H

RELEASE PROC    NEAR
        MOV     DX,82H     ;Point DS:DX to filename
        MOV     DI,82H     ;Start looking in PSP
        MOV     AL,13      ;Look for carriage return
        MOV     CX,12      ;Scan up to 12 letters
REPNE   SCASB              ;Find end of input
        MOV     BYTE PTR [DI-1],0  ;Make string ASCIIZ
        MOV     AL,1       ;Function Code
      → MOV     CX,0       ;This is to UNprotect.
        MOV     AH,43H     ;Use Service 43H
        INT     21H        ; of INT 21H
        INT     20H        ;End the Program.
RELEASE ENDP

        END     RELEASE
```

To enter PROTECT.ASM and RELEASE.ASM, type the code in with your word processor. In this case, name the two files PROTECT.ASM and RELEASE.ASM, respectively. To create PROTECT.COM, run PROTECT.ASM through these steps:

```
MASM    PROTECT;
LINK    PROTECT;
EXE2BIN PROTECT PROTECT.COM
```

The Macro assembler MASM will produce an object file named PROTECT.OBJ. The program LINK links this into an .EXE file, PROTECT.EXE. The linker will also produce a warning, indicating that PROTECT doesn't have a stack segment:

```
Warning: No STACK segment
```

.COM files don't need stack segments, however, so this warning is harmless. Even so, the linker still prints it out whenever it finds an .OBJ file without a stack segment. EXE2BIN (EXE to BINARY) converts PROTECT.EXE into PROTECT.COM. It is PROTECT.COM that we will run.

Running Our First Program

To protect a file named THISFILE.ASM from deletion or modification, all you have to do is to type:

```
C:\>PROTECT THISFILE.ASM
C:\>
```

THISFILE.ASM's attribute is now set to read-only, so that file cannot be deleted or overwritten. After creating RELEASE.COM, you can unprotect THISFILE.ASM with the corresponding command:

```
C:\>RELEASE THISFILE.ASM
C:\>
```

When the file is unprotected, you are free to delete or edit it again.

PROTECT uses DOS interrupt 21H to set the protection of a file; since DOS does most of the work, we can keep our program small. Now let's see how it works.

How to Make .COM Files

Except that it has no space for data, PROTECT is typical of .COM files. The most basic .COM file consists of one code segment enclosing one program. There is a skeleton, or shell, of a .COM file, outlining its basic parts in Listing 1-3.

Listing 1-3. .COM File Shell.

```
        .MODEL SMALL
        .CODE
        ORG 100H
ENTRY:  JMP PROG_NAME
        :
        Data here
        :
PROG_NAME PROC NEAR
        :
        :
        :
        Your program goes here
        :
        :
        INT 20H    ← Notice the Interrupt 20H used to finish the program
PROG_NAME ENDP
END ENTRY
```

The program's name in this example is PROG_NAME. By looking at the skeleton, you can pick out the various parts of PROTECT. As we go on, this original shell will become more elaborate and will contain not only more procedures (PROG_NAME is the only one used here) but also different segments.

6 ▶ Advanced Assembly Language

Let's work through this skeleton line by line. The first two directives set the memory model and define the beginning of the code segment:

```
→          .MODEL SMALL
→          .CODE
           ORG 100H
ENTRY:     JMP PROG_NAME
           :
```

The .MODEL directive sets the *memory model* for the program. We'll have more to say about memory models later, but for now you must know that to use the simplified segment directives like .CODE, we'll have to specify a memory model (we'll mostly use the SMALL model in this book). The memory model indicates the maximum sizes for the code and data parts of a program — and therefore the size of the addresses (one or two words) necessary to access items in them. For example, if your data section can be multiple segments in length, the assembler will have to use two-word addresses to reach data items. Here's how the memory models are defined:

Model	Means
TINY	.COM file format.
SMALL	All data fits in one 64K segment, and all code fits in one 64K segment. (This means that both data and code can be accessed as near).
MEDIUM	All data fits in one 64K segment, but code may be greater than 64K.
COMPACT	Data may be greater than 64K (but no single array may be), and code must be less than 64K.
LARGE	Both data and code may be greater than 64K, but no single array may be.
HUGE	Data, code, and data arrays may be greater than 64K.

NOTE The HUGE model is not available in the Turbo assembler, TASM.

In addition, everything we put into our programs will have to go into a segment of one sort or another because our code is constrained by the architecture of the 80×86. Addresses are always designated with two registers, such as CS:IP or DS:DX. To point to any address and fetch either data or code, two registers must always be set — a segment register and an offset register.

For that reason everything we do will be enclosed inside segments. The assembler will always know what segment we are referring to when we reference code or data this way. The .CODE directive informs the assembler that we are beginning the code segment. If we put in another segment directive (like .DATA or .STACK), the code segment automatically finishes, and the new segment starts.

The next line, ORG 100H, needs explanation as well:

```
        .MODEL SMALL
        .CODE
      → ORG 100H
ENTRY:  JMP PROG_NAME
        :
```

This line is included in .COM files but not in .EXE files. ORG tells the assembler where you are in a program; ORG 100H tells the assembler we will now be assembling code that is to start 100H bytes into the program. We do this in .COM files since we have to make room for the 256-byte (100H) program segment prefix (PSP), the program's header that DOS provides. This prefix always starts at CS:0000. The executable code for all .COM files always starts just after the PSP, at CS:0100.

The Program Segment Prefix

When DOS loads your .COM file, say PROTECT.COM, into memory, it sets up a program segment prefix, or PSP, for it. A PSP is also set up for .EXE files. However, with .COM files there is a special restriction: The PSP has to fit inside the one common segment. There is no such restriction with .EXE files, and we won't worry where the PSP is for them. All .COM files, however, must fit into one 64K space.

A typical .COM file in memory has a PSP from CS:0000 to CS:00FF, followed by the program at CS:0100. When the .COM file is loaded, all segment registers (CS, DS, ES, and SS) are set to the same common segment.

Even the stack, pointed to by SS:SP, has to be in the same segment. DOS sets up a stack for .COM files at the very end of the segment, and you should always take care not to overwrite this stack. In general, it is wise not to touch the last 256 bytes of the segment the .COM file has been given — addresses from CS:FF00 to CS:FFFF.

The PSP is 256 bytes long and provides our program with as much help as DOS can give. This includes information about what was typed on the command line and other items. It is because of the restriction to one segment that our code will be placed after the PSP in memory. For this reason, we put the directive ORG 100H into the beginning of every .COM file.

8 ▶ Advanced Assembly Language

The next instruction that the assembler sees after ORG 100H will be placed at CS:100H. This instruction is a jump:

```
            .MODEL SMALL
            .CODE
            ORG 100H
──▶ENTRY:   JMP PROG_NAME
            :
            Data here
            :
   PROG_NAME PROC NEAR
            :
```

If we want to store data in our .COM file, we usually put it right at the beginning. The reason for this is that it is best to define your data labels before you reference them. Since .COM files always execute the instruction at 100H first, we make this instruction a jump over the data and go to the main procedure (JMP PROG_NAME). This way, the data is left undisturbed. When a .COM file is run, the 80 × 86 will always be instructed to enter at CS:100H and will always jump over the data to start the program:

```
            .MODEL SMALL
            .CODE
            ORG 100H
  ┌── ENTRY: JMP PROG_NAME
  │         :
  │         The Data Area
  │         :
  └─▶PROG_NAME PROC NEAR
            :
```

Reserving space this way for our data is a little artificial, but it is convenient. It is the way .COM files are almost invariably written (some store the data at the very end of the program).

The Data Area in .COM Files

The assembler provides us with a number of ways of storing data, now that we've defined the data area. The data we want to supply our programs with can either be known ahead of time (like error messages or prompts that we want to type out) or not (like temporary storage for numbers our program is working on). In addition, the bytes or words that we set aside in memory can be given names so that we can reference those memory locations as variables in our program. The assembler converts those names into

Writing Our First Programs 9

addresses when it assembles the program. Here are some examples of data storage, listed from the common to the more rare:

```
            .MODEL SMALL
            .CODE
            ORG 100H
ENTRY:      JMP PROG_NAME
            APPLES  DB 3              ;One byte long, initialized to 3.
            ORANGES DB 5 DUP(0)       ;Five bytes, initialized to 0.
            STUFF   DB 1,2,3          ;Three bytes, set to 1,2,3, respectively.
            MESSAGE DB "Disk full$"   ;Ten bytes initialized with ASCII.
            ONEWORD DW ?              ;One word, not initialized.
            HRSINYR DW 24*365         ;This word set to the 8760 = 2238H.
            TWOWORD DW 2 DUP(ABCDH)   ;Two words, both initialized to ABCDH.
            BIG     DD ?              ;A doubleword - can store addresses.
            BIGGER  DQ "HI"           ;A QuadWord, two ASCII characters max.
            BIGGEST DT "HO"           ;Ten bytes.
PROG_NAME PROC NEAR
            :
            :
            :
```

When .COM files are loaded into memory, they are loaded at the first available address that is a multiple of 16 bytes (a "paragraph" boundary in memory) by COMMMAND.COM. CS, DS, ES, and SS are all set to the same value. The assembler treats labels as offsets from DS. Since DS is already set, we can just reference data labels defined in our data area like this:

```
            .MODEL SMALL
            .CODE
            ORG 100H
ENTRY:      JMP PROG_NAME
            APPLES  DB 3              ;One byte long, initialized to 3.
            ORANGES DB 5 DUP(0)       ;Five bytes, initialized to 0.
            :
PROG_NAME PROC NEAR
         → MOV     AX,APPLES
         → CMP     AX,ORANGES
         → MOV     ORANGES,AX
            :
```

If APPLES and ORANGES were in a different segment, we would have to set DS to that segment before referencing them. We could print out the "Disk full" message using DOS' string printing service, service 9, of Interrupt 21H by first pointing DS:DX like this:

10 ▶ Advanced Assembly Language

```
            .MODEL SMALL
            .CODE
            ORG 100H
ENTRY:      JMP PROG_NAME
            :
            MESSAGE DB "Disk full$"
            :
PROG_NAME PROC NEAR
        →   LEA     DX,MESSAGE
        →   MOV     AH,9
        →   INT     21H
```

"Disk full" would appear on the screen (the "$" is used by service 9 as an end-of-string marker, telling it when the string ends). The instruction LEA DX, MESSAGE loads the effective address (the offset address) of MESSAGE into DX. Since we are working in a .COM file, DS is already set to the one and only segment.

When the assembler assembles the code, it will automatically store an address for the label MESSAGE. For example, if MESSAGE is three bytes into the program, LEA would find that MESSAGE is 103H bytes from DS:0000, and MESSAGE would be replaced with the address 103H. The code actually generated in the .OBJ file would look like this to the 80 × 86:

```
LEA     DX,103H
MOV     AH,9
INT     21H
```

Besides bytes, of course, we can store words with Define Word (DW). The Define Doubleword directive (DD) is less frequently used, but it is still often used to store two-word addresses.

The remaining two directives, Define Quadword (DQ) and Define Tenbytes (DT), are used primarily to store either large numbers or floating point notation. For example, with DQ you can store integers up to a whopping 18446744073709551615. Although you can store arbitrarily long ASCII codes byte by byte with an expression like

```
MSG     DB      "Fatal Error!"
```

it is worth noticing that the largest ASCII argument you can give to DW, DQ, or DT is two ASCII characters. DB "AB" will produce the ASCII code for "A" and then "B" in your code. DW "AB", however, will produce "B" first and then "A" in 80 × 86's usual reverse order of low-byte, high-byte storage. (You don't have to worry if you don't know how this works — we'll cover it soon.) DQ "AB" will give you "B," then "A," and then three words of zeros. DT "AB" will give "B," then "A," and then eight bytes of zeros.

▶ **Writing Our First Programs** 11

> **NOTE** It is also worth noticing that although labels can be as long as you like, the assembler will only recognize the first 31 characters.

The Procedure in the .COM File

Let's continue down the .COM file shell with the procedure itself, which is the integral part of all .COM files:

```
    ENTRY:   JMP    PROG_NAME
             :
             Data here
             :
→   PROG_NAME PROC  NEAR
             :
             :
             Program code goes here
             :
             :
             INT    20H
    PROG_NAME ENDP
```

The directives PROC and ENDP define a procedure. In reality, PROC just defines a label, and the NEAR or FAR attribute associated with it (NEAR is the default) can be associated with any label as well. The procedure TEST

```
             .MODEL SMALL
             .CODE
             ORG    100H
    START:   JMP    TEST
             (Data)
             :
→   TEST     PROC   NEAR
             MOV    AX,1
             INT    20H
    TEST     ENDP
             END    START
```

could have just as well been constructed using a NEAR label (that is, one with a colon after it). This code will generate the same .COM file

```
             .MODEL SMALL
             .CODE
             ORG    100H
    START:   JMP    TEST
             (Data)
             :
```

12 ▶ Advanced Assembly Language

```
→ TEST:      MOV     AX,1
             INT     20H
             END     START
```

but using PROC and ENDP help keep order in large amounts of code.

In a .COM file, all procedures, including the main one, must be declared NEAR because a .COM file is limited to one segment. NEAR labels are intrasegment labels. A NEAR jump only uses the lower word of the label's address, the offset.

> **TIP** If you want more space than a .COM file allows, you can use .EXE files, which allow you to use multiple segments. For example, in .EXE files, you could use the label TEST PROC FAR and then call TEST from another segment (an intersegment jump). This way, you can expand the memory you control to practically all that is available.

Ending Your Program

The procedure TEST ends with INT 20H, the way our .COM files will usually end; this interrupt passes control back to DOS. Another common way of ending procedures is with the instruction RET:

```
             .MODEL  SMALL
             .CODE
             ORG     100H
START:       JMP     TEST
             (Data)
             :
TEST         PROC    NEAR
             MOV     AX,1
→            RET
TEST         ENDP
             END     START
```

When .COM files are loaded, the stack pointer, SP, is set to the top of the available segment, and then a word of 0000 is pushed, leaving SP at FFFEH. When you have a RET at the end of a program, the word of zeros is popped off the stack and put into IP. Control is then transferred to CS:IP (i.e., to CS:0000), the very first byte in the PSP. The first two bytes of every PSP, for any program, are always CDH 20H, machine code for INT 20H. RET at the end of .COM file therefore sends control back to the beginning of the PSP where an INT 20H is executed. This method is the same as including INT 20H at the end of your program.

In .EXE files, this word of zeros is not pushed onto the stack and, as we shall see, you have to put it on yourself at the beginning of each program.

Another way of ending programs that we will use applies either INT 27H or INT 31H, the terminate-but-stay-resident interrupts. Before finishing, we will load the address of the end of the program into DS:DX, and execute INT 27H or INT 31H. All the code from CS:0000 to the address DS:DX will then be held resident in memory by DOS. New programs that are to be run will be loaded in memory after the end of the resident program. In a very practical sense, we will be able to modify DOS this way.

> **TIP** Although INT 27H has been the most common way to load terminate-and-stay-resident programs, INT 21H, service 31H gives you an option that INT 27H does not: with service 31H, you can return an exit code that can be interrogated by a DOS-level program or a parent procedure.

Using More Than One Procedure in .COM Files

Frequently, we will want to break massive, unwieldy sections of code up into more reasonable and manageable sections. For this purpose, high-level languages like FORTRAN provide PROCEDUREs, SUBROUTINEs, and FUNCTIONs, but in assembly language we can only use another PROC. For instance, if we had a program that was to search all files in a given subdirectory for a particular string, it might look like the outline in Listing 1-4.

Listing 1-4. File Searcher Outline.

```
            .MODEL  SMALL
            .CODE
            ORG     100H
  START:    JMP     TEST
            (Data)
            :
  FIND      PROC    NEAR
  NEW_FILE:
→           CALL    GET_FILE
            [- Is the string we want in it? -]
            JE      YES
            JMP     NEW_FILE          ;No matches, get new file
  YES:      [- Print file's name -]   ;Match! Print filename
            INT     20H
  FIND      ENDP

→ GET_FILE  PROC    NEAR
            [- Find next file in the directory -]
            [- Read it in -]
            RET
  GET_FILE  ENDP
            END     START
```

14 ▶ Advanced Assembly Language

There we can safely put all the codes to find a new file on the disk and read it into a subroutine named GET_FILE. Whenever we need a new file to search, we only need to call GET_FILE. When we do, control transfers to the first line in the subroutine GET_FILE. The entire subroutine is executed, and the RET instruction at the very end sends control back up to the line right after CALL GET_FILE in the procedure FIND.

Finishing the Code Segment

The last thing we'll do in our skeleton .COM file is to finish the code segment. The assembler is expecting to see everything inside some segment, and it must also be told when we are through with a given segment. To close the code segment, we can use another segment directive, such as .DATA or .STACK, or we can use the directive END like this:

```
            .MODEL SMALL
            .CODE
            ORG 100H
ENTRY:      JMP PROG_NAME
            :
            Data here
            :
PROG_NAME PROC NEAR
            :
            :
            :
            Your program goes here
            :
            :
            :
            INT 20H    * Notice the Interrupt 20H used to finish the program
PROG_NAME ENDP
      * END ENTRY
```

This is the last directive to the assembler that we will give in this file. END tells the assembler to stop assembling, and the label ENTRY means that we want the 80×86 to enter the program at the label ENTRY (at 100H). The entry point is the location in the program of the first instruction to be executed.

There is only one entry point in any .COM or .EXE file. The location of a program's entry point is stored in the header of an .EXE file on disk, but in a .COM file, which has no header, it is always assumed to be 100H. In an .EXE file, you can set the entry point wherever you want it.

If you intend to make a file into a .COM file, you assemble and link it, and then pass it in the form of an .EXE file to EXE2BIN. If EXE2BIN does not find the specified entry point to be at 100H, it will give you the terse error message "File cannot be converted," which has given many programmers trouble. Using a line like END ENTRY and labeling the location at 100H as ENTRY solves the problem. When DOS enters at this point, it will immediately see the line:

```
ENTRY:   JMP PROG_NAME
```

> **TIP** As in most undertakings, now that you've seen it done there is little need to memorize the rules. If you want to write a .COM file, you can simply use the outline or shell we've developed. This is one facet of programming that deserves stress throughout the book. Once you've got a working framework, it can be made into a foundation for other projects.

.EXE Files versus .COM Files

The other type of directly executable file that DOS supports is the .EXE file. Let's say a .COM file has been loaded at address 1234:0000. When it runs, its code is limited to the region 1234:0000 to 1234:FFFF or 64K memory bytes. .EXE files, on the other hand, can be large and can spread code and data over several segments.

> **NOTE** It is worth noting that the .COM form is not even supported under OS/2; all you can use there are .EXE files, as we'll see later.

All jumps or calls in .COM files only need to know the offset that they are to jump to — the segment address never changes. For this reason, a .COM file is ready to run right after the EXE2BIN stage.

In .EXE files, however, there can be calls from segment to segment, and so these FAR instructions need additional information. In particular, FAR instructions inside .EXE files need to know the full segment and offset addresses they are to call or jump to.

When DOS loads an .EXE file, it can be put almost anywhere in memory, at any segment address. Therefore, DOS must relocate the code by fixing all FAR instructions to contain the proper segment addresses of their destinations. For that reason, a header is included at the beginning of every .EXE file. This header's length varies from file to file, but it is never less than the 28 bytes listed below.

Word starts	Explanation
00	Always 4D 5A. Marks this file as an .EXE file.
02	Remainder after dividing load module's size by 512.
04	Size of file in 512-byte pages.
06	Number of relocation table items.
08	Size of header in paragraphs (16 bytes).
0A	Minimum number of paragraphs required after loaded program.
0C	Maximum number of paragraphs required after loaded program.
0E	Offset of Stack in load module in paragraphs.
10	SP register loaded with this word.
12	Negative sum (ignore overflow) of all words in file (checksum).
14	IP register loaded with this word.
16	Offset of code segment in load module in paragraphs.
18	Offset of first relocation item.
1A	Overlay number. If no overlays used, this number is 0.

After these 28 bytes, the addresses of FAR instructions that must be fixed up are stored. In this book, we will only rarely have occasion to develop files so large that they need to use the .EXE format. We will discuss .EXE files further later (especially under OS/2 and in our chapter on linking to high-level languages), but mostly we will use the much more convenient and common .COM files. .COM files are often shorter and more compact. They keep everything under control because only your code is there. No extras are added by DOS in a header. This is the level at which you really have control of your PC. Nonetheless, we will have to use .EXE files at times, so let's review how they work and what the header contains.

How Relocation Works

Here's how the process of loading and relocating an .EXE file works: first, a Program Segment Prefix, a PSP, is built in the lowest available paragraph boundary. The first part of the .EXE file's header is read in and the size of the complete header is read from bytes 8–9. This size is stored in paragraphs, that is, in units of 16 bytes, rounded up. A 33-byte header would have a three stored here (33/16, rounded up).

The size of the actual code that will run, the *load module*, is found from the difference of the total .EXE file size (calculated from bytes 2–5) and the header size (already found in bytes 8–9). A segment, called the start segment, is found in memory such that there will be enough space to take the load module. After the load module is loaded into memory, the *relocation table* — the addresses of instructions in the load module that have to be modified — is examined.

For each instruction in the load module that needs to be fixed, there is a two-word address in the relocation table giving that instruction's location from the beginning of the load module. The instruction at that address is found, and the start segment is added to the address that the instruction already contains. This process continues until the code is fully relocated and the program is ready to run. All the FAR jumps and calls are set up properly at this point.

That's how relocation works. Although it is simple enough, it is still a complication that we would like to avoid, so we will use .COM files wherever we can.

An .EXE File Shell

Listing 1-5 shows an .EXE file shell. All the parts of this shell appear in almost all DOS .EXE files.

Listing 1-5. .EXE File Shell.

```
            .MODEL SMALL
            .DATA
            :
            Your Data Goes Here
            :

            .CODE
PROG_NAME   PROC    FAR
            PUSH    DS
            XOR     AX,AX
            PUSH    AX
            MOV     AX,@DATA
            MOV     DS,AX
            :
            The Program Goes Here
            :
            :
            RET
PROG_NAME   ENDP
            .STACK  200H

END         PROG_NAME
```

18 ▶ Advanced Assembly Language

In .EXE files, we are not limited to one segment, so we do not have to fit the data in after a jump at ORG 100H. In fact, we don't need a special instruction at ORG 100H at all, since an .EXE file can set the entry point to be anywhere (the entry point is stored in bytes 14–17 of the header). END PROG_NAME at the end of the .ASM file would, for example, set the entry point to PROG_NAME. In .EXE files, we can have a special segment for the data alone, and we can set that aside with the .DATA directive:

```
           .MODEL SMALL
→          .DATA
           :
           Your Data Goes Here
           :

           .CODE
PROG_NAME  PROC    FAR
           PUSH    DS
           XOR     AX,AX
           PUSH    AX
           MOV     AX,@DATA
```

All the data we will use in this program goes here, labeled as in .COM files, for example:

```
           .DATA
→          APPLES  DB      1
→          ORANGES DB      5
           .DATA
```

To work directly with these numbers, however, we have to be sure that the Data Segment register (DS), is set correctly and points to @DATA, which is the value that stands for the data segment as defined with the .DATA directive. This is one of the first things we will do in the code itself. It is, however, always advisable to keep the data segment first since the assembler should know the names of these labels before they are referenced in the program.

After the data segment comes the code segment:

```
           .MODEL SMALL
           .DATA
           :
           Your Data Goes Here
           :

→          .CODE
PROG_NAME  PROC    FAR
           PUSH    DS
           XOR     AX,AX
```

Writing Our First Programs

```
        PUSH      AX
        MOV       AX,@DATA
        MOV       DS,AX
        :
        The Program Goes Here
        :
```

When .COM files are loaded, all segment registers get set to the same value picked by the loader, COMMAND.COM. In .EXE files, the procedure is more complex. DS and ES are set to the segment of the PSP. Since you can place the stack anywhere you want, the stack segment's location in the load module is stored in the header (bytes 0EH–11H). SS and SP are loaded from this information, after the start segment is added to SS. Since the code and entry points are also up to you, CS and IP are loaded from values given in the header (bytes 14H–17H), after adding the start segment to CS.

The declaration of our main program is the same as in .COM files except that here the procedure must be declared FAR just as in .COM files it must be NEAR:

```
            .CODE
→ PROG_NAME     PROC      FAR
        PUSH      DS
        XOR       AX,AX
        PUSH      AX
        MOV       AX,@DATA
        MOV       DS,AX
        :
        The Program Goes Here
        :
```

The Stack in .EXE Files

In .COM files, the stack is all set up for you, and a word of zeros is pushed already. When you return to DOS with RET, control can jump to CS:0000, where there is an INT 20H instruction waiting. A RET at the end of a FAR procedure will pop two words off the stack (at the end of a NEAR procedure, only one would be popped). In .EXE files you have to prime the stack yourself, which is customarily done with these instructions:

```
            .CODE
  PROG_NAME     PROC      FAR
→       PUSH      DS
→       XOR       AX,AX
→       PUSH      AX
        MOV       AX,@DATA
        MOV       DS,AX
        :
        The Program Goes Here
        :
```

Since DS contains the segment of the PSP, it is pushed first. Next, AX is set to zero with the fancy instruction XOR AX,AX. XOR is the eXclusive-OR instruction; it works just like an OR instruction except that the result is zero when XORing two ones:

XOR	0	1
0	0	1
1	1	0 ←

Whenever you XOR any number with itself, zeros always meet zeros and ones always meet ones to give a net answer of zero. (MOV AX,0 could have worked here as well, but professional programmers often use XOR since it is faster.) After AX is zeroed, it too is pushed on the stack so that control will return to the first byte of the PSP, DS:0000.

DS is still set to the default value of the PSP, not to the data segment we have defined. To point DS properly, we use these instructions:

```
            .CODE
PROG_NAME        PROC      FAR
        PUSH     DS
        XOR      AX,AX
        PUSH     AX
    →   MOV      AX,@DATA
    →   MOV      DS,AX
        :
        The Program Goes Here
        :
```

After this, the program continues as usual and no differently from the ones we would write in a .COM file. The procedure PROG_NAME ends with a RET instruction and a PROG_NAME ENDP:

```
            .CODE
PROG_NAME        PROC      FAR
        PUSH     DS
        XOR      AX,AX
        PUSH     AX
        MOV      AX,@DATA
        MOV      DS,AX
        :
        The Program Goes Here
        :
    →   RET
    → PROG_NAME       ENDP

            .STACK   200H
    END     PROG_NAME
```

The final segment in our .EXE shell is the STACK segment. In .COM files, DOS sets up the stack for you, but in .EXE files you must do it yourself. Here we use the .STACK directive to set up a stack of 200H words:

```
.STACK 200H
```

After the stack segment, the .EXE file ends in the same way as .COM files end with an END statement pointing to the entry point. Unlike .COM files, as we have said, .EXE files can be entered anywhere and so the line END PROG_NAME

```
            :
            The Program Goes Here
            :
            RET
   PROG_NAME      ENDP
            .STACK 200H
→  END      PROG_NAME
```

does not have to point to an instruction at 100H. Since .COM files do not have the header that .EXE files do, it is assumed that .COM files will start right after the PSP in memory, at CS:100H.

The simplified segment directives .CODE, .DATA, and .STACK will be very useful for us, but we won't be able to use them all the time. Sometimes, we'll have to turn to the older SEGMENT and ENDS directives.

AT and .COM Files

If we want to use the BIOS data area at 0040:0000 in a .COM file, we need only to define a segment around it. For example, in a .COM file, such a declaration may look like the one in Listing 1-6 (below).

Listing 1-6. .COM File Shell Using BIOS Data Area.

```
     .MODEL SMALL
→ DATA_SEG       SEGMENT AT 40H
         ORG    6CH
   TIMER_LOW     DW    ?      ;Clock low word
   TIMER_HIGH    DW    ?      ;Clock high word
→ DATA_SEG       ENDS
         .CODE
         ORG    100H
   ENTRY:  JUMP  PROGNAME
```

Listing 1-6. .COM File Shell Using BIOS Data Area.

```
        :
PROGNAME    PROC NEAR
        MOV     AX,DATA_SEG     ;Set up DS.
        MOV     DS,AX
        ASSUME  DS:DATA_SEG
        MOV     CX,TIMER_LOW
        :
        :
        END     ENTRY
```

Here we are defining a segment named DATA_SEG and specifying that it begins at address 40:0000 with the AT directive. To use this data segment, we have to change the value in DS like this:

```
.MODEL SMALL
DATA_SEG        SEGMENT AT 40H
        ORG     6CH
TIMER_LOW       DW      ?       ;Clock low word
TIMER_HIGH      DW      ?       ;Clock high word
DATA_SEG        ENDS
        .CODE
        ORG     100H
ENTRY:  JUMP    PROGNAME
        :
PROGNAME        PROC NEAR
*       MOV     AX,DATA_SEG     ;Set up DS.
*       MOV     DS,AX
*       ASSUME  DS:DATA_SEG
        MOV     CX,TIMER_LOW
        :
        :
        END     ENTRY
```

Note in particular the use of the ASSUME directive: Every time we change the contents of a segment register and the assembler needs to know the new value, we must tell the assembler what that will be with an ASSUME (the assembler has to calculate offsets from that segment address, but, since the program is not actually running, it does not know what the segment value will be unless we tell it). We don't have to use ASSUME with the simplified directives .CODE, .DATA, or .STACK, since an ASSUME is already built into them.

The above program would make a perfectly acceptable .COM file. At first it seems to break the .COM file's restriction of only one segment. But that prohibition was really only against the need to relocate code. If you know precisely where the bytes in memory that you want to work with are, the .COM file can be assembled with the full two-word

▶ **Writing Our First Programs** 23

addresses of those memory locations already in the code. In such cases, there is no need for relocation.

In other words, when the program references TIMER_LOW in the above .COM file shell, the assembler sees that DATA_SEG is defined at 40H, and that TIMER_LOW is at ORG 6CH, so it can substitute 0040:006CH for references to TIMER_LOW immediately. No relocation will be needed later. As soon as we know where the data we want to operate on is in memory, such as the PC's internal timer, the screen buffer, or the interrupt vector table, we only have to define a segment around it and .COM files can reach them too.

TIP Among other things, the BIOS data area holds the bytes that define the state of the keyboard, like this:

Bit	State	Byte at 40:0017	Byte at 40:0018
0	Right Shift	1 → Key is pressed	
1	Left Shift	1 → Key is pressed	
2	Cntrl Shift	1 → Key is pressed	
3		1 → Alt Shift Pressed	1 → ^Num Lock On
4	Scroll_Lock	1 → On	1 → Key is pressed
5	Num-Lock	1 → On	1 → Key is pressed
6	Caps-Lock	1 → On	1 → Key is pressed
7	Insert	1 → On	1 → Key is pressed

You can change the keyboard state of the PC with these bytes. For example, using DEBUG, here's how to assemble a small program named TURNCAPS.COM that turns on CapsLock by ORing 40H, or 01000000B, with the status byte at 40:17:

```
C:\> DEBUG
     NTURNCAPS.COM
     A100
     MOV AX,40
     MOV DS,AX
     MOV BX,17
     OR BYTE PTR [BX],40
     INT 20
     <CR>
     RCX
     D
     W
     Q
```

The Program Segment Prefix in Detail

The Program Segment Prefix is one of the most useful things in assembly language programming. It is DOS' interface to your program. In both the file and disk handling of this book we will have something to say about the PSP. There's a diagram of it in Figure 1-1.

Byte #	0	1	2	3	4	5	6	7
	Int 20H		Top of Memory		For DOS Use	Bytes 5–9 contain a Long Call to DOS...		
	...Function Dispatcher		The Termination Address IP		CS		Break Exit Address IP	
	Break Exit Address CS		The Critical Error Address IP		CS			

```
              This area
              used by DOS                  5C
                                           ┌─────────────────────
                                           │ First Free FCB...
                                           │           6C
                                           │           ┌─────────
                                           │           │ Second Free FCB...
  80  ┌──────────────────────────────────────────────────────────
      │ Text typed after the program's name goes here...
      │                The
      │                  Default
      │                    Disk
      │                      Transfer
      │                        Area
 100  ├──────────────────────────────────────────────────────────
      │                   - Your Program -
      │                          :
      │                          :
```

Figure 1-1. The Program Segment Prefix (PSP)

We will assume that this is a PSP for a .COM file, so that the PSP starts at CS:0000. Let's take the time to work through the PSP byte by byte.

Byte 0 As we have already seen, the first word of the PSP is CDH 20H, that is, the machine code for INT 20H. This instruction, at CS:0000, is usually the last instruction your program will execute.

Byte 2 The two bytes at locations CS:0002 and CS:0003 together form a word that gives you the location of the "top of memory" in paragraphs; that is, the first segment not allocated to your program. A 2000H here would mean that the first available segment is 2000H, at address 2000:0000, or 128K. When a .COM file is loaded, it is allocated all available memory. The amount given to .EXE files depends on the minimum and maximum memory requirements, as given in the file's header. DOS keeps track of memory, and provides ways of allocating and deallocating sections of memory. If your program wants to load in other programs and run them, it must first make sure they will have adequate memory.

Bytes 5–9 These bytes make up the stored machine code for a far jump to the DOS function dispatcher. This is the subroutine that dispatches your INT 21H call to various subprograms of that interrupt. DOS may make use of this call, but we will not. If you ever take the time to unassemble (e.g., using DEBUG, CodeView, or some other debugger) any portion of INT 21H, you will find several far jumps to this same address. The two bytes starting at CS:0006 — part of the above five bytes — tells you the amount of free space left in the segment.

Byte 0AH At CS:000A there is a two-word address, stored as IP:CS. This and all following addresses in the PSP are stored in the typical IBM PC memory fashion. Words are stored with their low bytes lower in memory and high bytes higher. A directive such as DW 1234H, therefore, leaves 34H 12H in memory, not 12H 34H.

That means that the two words of an address are stored with the low word lower in memory (such as IP in CS:IP) and the higher word higher. An address such as the one for the DOS function dispatcher, which might be F00D:FFF0, would be stored as: F0 FF 0D F0. If you are not familiar with this reverse method of memory storage, it will take a little getting used to.

The two-word address at CS:000A is the Terminate Address. This is the address to which the computer will return when the program is finished. Starting as long ago as DOS 2.0, programs can load in other programs and run them. When such a subprocess is done, control should return to the program that loaded it, not directly to DOS.

> **TIP** Previously, programmers would change the Terminate Address themselves as a means of chaining programs together. When one program was done,

26 ▶ Advanced Assembly Language

> control would not go back to DOS, but to the next program. Don't be tempted by this procedure. Use interrupt 21H service 4BH (EXEC) instead, which will load and execute programs for you; going through DOS itself is far safer in this case.

Byte 0EH Following this address are two more addresses at locations CS:000E and CS:0012, also stored as IP:CS. The address at CS:000E is the Control Break Exit address. If you press a Ctrl-Break while your program is running, control will be sent to this address. If you want to add your own Ctrl-Break handler, you can change this address. You could, for example, add some diagnostics to your program that would be printed whenever a Ctrl-Break is typed.

Byte 12H The address stored at CS:0012 is the Critical Error exit address. This error handler is supposed to intercept and inform you of hardware problems. Usually, this means disk problems. The familiar message "Write Protect Error writing Drive A. Abort, Retry, Ignore?" comes from this error handler. If you want to handle errors yourself, you can change this address to point to part of your program's code. You will be able to tell what is wrong by the contents of the registers.

Byte 16H The part of the PSP from CS:0016 to CS:005C is reserved for use by DOS. Most of this area is set to zero when your program is first loaded, ready to be used.

Byte 2CH At CS:002C, you will find the segment address of the *environment string*. For example, if the bytes 08 09 appear here, then your environment string is at 0908:0000. The environment string tells you how the PC's environment has been set up.

For example, a copy of the last PROMPT (changing the PC's prompt from C>) or PATH commands are stored here. If you see a string like: PROMPT = tg in the environment string, you know that the prompt has been set up to display the time of day like this: 12:34:56>. PROMPT = pg will display the current directory. The default is PROMPT = ng.

The COMSPEC string is also part of the environment string. COMSPEC, the comand file specification, tells DOS where to find the file COMMAND.COM if it should need to load it in again. A string such as "COMSPEC=A:\" will appear there, and you can change it if you wish.

Byte 50H Also in the DOS reserved area, at CS:0050, are the bytes CDH 21H, or machine code for INT 21H. Just like the CDH 20H stored at CS:0000, DOS can easily issue an INT 21H interrupt this way.

Byte 5CH Two default File Control Blocks, FCBs, provided by DOS for your program, start here. One is at CS:005C and another is at CS:006C. Although DOS still supports the use of FCBs, they're all but dead; using *file handles* is now the preferred method of file handling (we'll only use file handles in this book). Nonetheless, a File Control Block can be to DOS what a filename is to us. When a file is opened, the current position in it, its length, its name, its type, and so on are all kept in the FCB.

DOS provides us with two free FCBs here in the PSP. If you type the name of any program with a filename following (such as "MASM TEST.ASM"), DOS loads MASM.EXE in and puts an unopened File Control Block for TEST.ASM at 5C in MASM's PSP. An unopened FCB consists only of the file's drive number and its name.

Byte 6CH If you have a program that can handle two files at once, such as "EDIT FILE1.TXT FILE2.TXT", DOS sets up an FCB for FILE1.TXT at CS:005C, and one for FILE2.TXT at CS:006C.

> **TIP** Opened File Control Blocks are longer than closed ones; if you open an FCB (that is, open the file), it takes up 37 bytes. Because the FCB at 5C overlaps the one at 6C, you should move the second one if you intend to use them both.

The Disk Transfer Area

Byte 80H. Half of the PSP, starting from CS:0080 and ending at CS:0100 — 80H or 128 bytes — makes up the *disk transfer area* or DTA. This is a default DTA, set up for you by DOS. When you read from the disk or write to it, data is often moved to or from the DTA by the system programs.

> **TIP** If you need more than 128 bytes in the Disk Transfer Area, you can reset the DTA's address to a larger buffer that you've set up with interrupt 21H service 1AH (which we will do later).

DOS rarely uses the DTA for disk reads and writes now; however, these reads and writes are internally buffered, so it does not have to rely on the DTA, which is a miniscule 128 bytes long. Even so, the DTA has other uses.

28 ▶ Advanced Assembly Language

Besides being a storage and work area for disk data, all the characters typed after the program's name (including the space) are loaded into the DTA so your program can read them. This way, the program can communicate with the person who uses it. For instance, if we typed: "MASM This is a test. This is ONLY a test.", the characters " This is a test. This is ONLY a test.‹cr›" — where ‹cr› is ASCII 0DH (also, note the leading space) — would appear in MASM's DTA, starting at offset 81H. The byte at 80H holds the number of characters typed.

Let's take another look at our earlier program PROTECT, which reads the file name we want to protect from the DTA:

```
            .MODEL  SMALL
            .CODE
            ORG     100H

PROTECT     PROC    NEAR
            MOV     DX,82H          ;Point DS:DX to filename
            MOV     DI,82H          ;Start looking in PSP
            MOV     AL,13           ;Look for carriage return
            MOV     CX,12           ;Scan up to 12 letters
REPNE       SCASB                   ;Find end of Input
            MOV     BYTE PTR [DI-1],0  ;Make string ASCIIZ
            MOV     AL,1            ;Function Code
            MOV     CX,1            ;This is to protect
            MOV     AH,43H          ;Use Service 43H
            INT     21H             ; of INT 21H
            INT     20H             ;End the Program.
PROTECT     ENDP

            END     PROTECT
```

PROTECT is a .COM file, so all the segment registers will be set to the same segment that holds the PSP. If you've typed "PROTECT THIS.FIL", the characters " THIS.FIL‹cr›" will appear in the DTA, where ‹cr› is an ASCII 13, 0DH.

Here is a DEBUG dump of PROTECT's DTA after the command "PROTECT THIS.FIL‹cr›" has been typed:

```
-D80
090F:0080  09 20 54 48 49 53 2E 46-49 4C 0D 00 00 00 00 00   . THIS.FIL......
090F:0090  00 00 00 00 00 00 00 00-00 00 00 00 00 00 00 00   ................
090F:00A0  00 00 00 00 00 00 00 00-00 00 00 00 00 00 00 00   ................
090F:00B0  00 00 00 00 00 00 00 00-00 00 00 00 00 00 00 00   ................
090F:00C0  00 00 00 00 00 00 00 00-00 00 00 00 00 00 00 00   ................
090F:00D0  00 00 00 00 00 00 00 00-00 00 00 00 00 00 00 00   ................
090F:00E0  00 00 00 00 00 00 00 00-00 00 00 00 00 00 00 00   ................
090F:00F0  00 00 00 00 00 00 00 00-00 00 00 00 00 00 00 00   ................
```

▶ Writing Our First Programs 29

We have to find the name of the file to protect. In PROTECT's code, we point to the first letter of the filename, "T", by pointing to offset 82H. 80H always holds the number of bytes typed, 9 of them here, and 81H holds the space typed after "PROTECT". PROTECT then searches with the instruction REPNE SCASB for the carriage return character, 13, and puts a zero in place of it. If you are not familiar with string searches such as REPNE SCASB, don't worry — we will cover them in a later chapter.

```
    PROTECT         PROC    NEAR
            MOV     DX,82H          ;Point DS:DX to filename
            MOV     DI,82H          ;Start looking in PSP
            MOV     AL,13           ;Look for carriage return
            MOV     CX,12           ;Scan up to 12 letters
  → REPNE   SCASB                   ;Find end of Input
  →         MOV     BYTE PTR [DI-1],0   ;Make string ASCIIZ
            MOV     AL,1            ;Function Code
            MOV     CX,1            ;This is to protect
            MOV     AH,43H          ;Use Service 43H
            INT     21H             ; of INT 21H
            INT     20H             ;End the Program.
    PROTECT         ENDP
```

Putting a zero byte after the filename makes the filename string into what is referred to as ASCIIZ (ASCII Zero) format. In this form we can pass the filename, "THIS.FIL"0, directly to INT 21H, Service 43H, which changes the file's attributes. To select Service 43H, we place 43H into AH and issue an INT 21H instruction:

```
    PROTECT         PROC    NEAR
            MOV     DX,82H          ;Point DS:DX to filename
            MOV     DI,82H          ;Start looking in PSP
            MOV     AL,13           ;Look for carriage return
            MOV     CX,12           ;Scan up to 12 letters
    REPNE   SCASB                   ;Find end of Input
            MOV     BYTE PTR [DI-1],0   ;Make string ASCIIZ
            MOV     AL,1            ;Function Code
            MOV     CX,1            ;This is to protect
  →         MOV     AH,43H          ;Use Service 43H
  →         INT     21H             ; of INT 21H
            INT     20H             ;End the Program.
    PROTECT         ENDP
```

The Code in .COM Files

Our discussion of the DTA finishes the PSP. An experienced assembly language programmer frequently makes use of the resources in the PSP.

> **TIP** Although IBM says that you are not supposed to work with any addresses in the PSP before 5CH, with care and practice, the whole PSP — as we've

> diagrammed it — is available to you. Programmers can work safely with any part of it they wish.

After the PSP is set up, the .COM file itself, the code, is loaded in memory. Since .COM files have no headers, the code in it is loaded verbatim. Finally, control is passed to CS:0100, and the program is on its own.

Now that the program, either .EXE or .COM, is fully loaded in memory, and we know what's available, we're all done with the general outlines of writing programs. Now let's concentrate on what goes in them by learning how to accept keyboard input in Chapter 2.

Chapter 2

How to Handle the Keyboard

Keyboard Input

As mentioned in the Introduction, the first part of this book is divided into sections that correspond to the various parts of the PC. For example, there is a chapter covering the disks, covering the screen, and one covering the mouse. In each chapter, we'll go through all the ways to work with that subsystem, which usually means we'll cover BIOS and DOS services first and then develop our own strategies later in the chapter.

In this chapter, we'll look at the ways that programs can accept keyboard input. We'll start with the usual methods, using the INT 21H or BIOS services. Afterward, we'll continue to the more in-depth method of using a program to read from the keyboard buffer directly, intercepting keystrokes as they are typed. This latter method is the way many professional packages work.

In this chapter, we will review the BIOS and DOS interrupts that have to do with accepting keyboard input; for more systematic coverage of the BIOS and DOS interrupts, or for reference, see Appendix A, which lists all the interrupts from 0 to FFH.

INT 21H Service 1 Character Input with Echo

Input	Output
AH = 1	AL = ASCII code of struck key
	Does Echo on screen

Note that this service checks for ^C or ^Break.

Interrupt 21H, service 1, is the most basic, beginning level method of reading in keystrokes. There are four DOS services that deal explicitly with character input: services 1, 6, 7, and 8. Here's a comparison of them:

INT 21H Service	Will Wait	^Break Seen	Will Echo
1	X	X	X
6			
7	X		
8	X	X	

To call service 1, you simply load a one into the AH register — selecting service 1 — and use an INT 21H instruction, like this:

```
MOV   AH,1
INT   21H
```

The PC will wait until a key is struck (or will read one key from what was typed ahead) and return the struck key's ASCII code in AL.

If AL returns 00, then a key requiring an extended ASCII code was struck. If this happens, you must issue another INT 21H service 1 (or 6, 7, or 8) call. This time AL will contain the second byte of the extended ASCII code of the struck key. For the moment, however, we are not anticipating the use of any function keys or any other keys that need extended ASCII codes, so we will put off their description until we cover BIOS INT 16H.

SMALL.COM Converts to Lowercase

Here's a short example that can readily be typed in with DEBUG. All SMALL.COM does is to read keystrokes, convert lowercase ASCII into uppercase ASCII, and then type the character back. To type the character back, we use INT 21H service 2 (covered in Chapter 3). This service types out the ASCII code in the DL register, so we have to load it properly. Just type this to DEBUG:

```
F:\>DEBUG
-NSMALL.COM       ← Call this file SMALL.COM
-A100             ← And start it at 100H
08F7:0100 MOV AH,1    ← Select INT 21H service 1
08F7:0102 INT 21H     ← Read the typed in character
08F7:0104 ADD AL,20   ← Add 20H = ASCII 'A' - ASCII 'a'
08F7:0106 MOV AH,2    ← Now use service 2 of INT 21H
08F7:0108 MOV DL,AL   ← And set up the DL register for it
08F7:010A INT 21H     ← Print out the small character
08F7:010C JMP 100     ← And jump back to the beginning
08F7:010E INT 20H     ← This INT 20H is only for form's sake.
08F7:0110
```

Whenever you work with DEBUG, it will assume all numbers you give it are in Hex. For example, to convert the byte ASCII 'A' (ASCII 65) into the small letter ASCII 'a' (ASCII 97), we have to add 32 (that is, 97 - 65) or 20H. In DEBUG, we type this in this way:

```
08F7:0104 ADD AL,20    ← Add 20H = ASCII 'A' - ASCII 'a'
```

DEBUG always assumes that we are using Hex notation. In addition, we can't use labels in DEBUG, since DEBUG is not really a full assembler. DEBUG assembles the

How to Handle the Keyboard 35

lines we give it line by line, however, so we can see the addresses we want to jump to. After we read in one capital letter and type back the small version, we want to jump up to the top of the program and start all over again. To do this, we will use a JMP instruction, which sends us back to the beginning of the program, CS:100, this way:

```
08F7:010C JMP 100        ; And jump back to the beginning
```

After typing our program in, let's check what we've written with the U instruction:

```
-U
08F7:0100 B401         MOV     AH,01
08F7:0102 CD21         INT     21
08F7:0104 0420         ADD     AL,20
08F7:0106 B402         MOV     AH,02
08F7:0108 88C2         MOV     DL,AL
08F7:010A CD21         INT     21
08F7:010C EBF2         JMP     0100
08F7:010E CD20         INT     20
        :
        :
```

We can see that our program takes up 16 bytes, from CS:100 to CS:10F. To write it out as a functioning .COM file, we load CX with 16 (=10H) and use the W instruction:

```
-RCX
CX 0000
:10
-
-W
Writing 0010 bytes
-Q
```

To make sure our file got written, we do a directory search:

```
F:\>DIR SMALL.COM

 Volume in drive A is DEVEL
 Directory of  F:\

SMALL    COM       16   2-24-86   8:43p      -16 Bytes
        1 File(s)     63488 bytes free
```

and then run it. After you type SMALL, SMALL will be loaded and run, but no prompt will appear. Any capital letters you type, however, will appear on the screen with the corresponding small letter next to them:

36 ▶ Advanced Assembly Language

```
F:\>SMALL
AaBbCcDdEeFf
```

We've made no provision for quitting SMALL.COM; by itself it would continue indefinitely, accepting capital letters and converting them into lower case. Fortunately, however, this DOS keyboard input interrupt service checks for ^C or ^Break, and so you can type either to quit.

INT 21H Service 6 Read Key without Wait

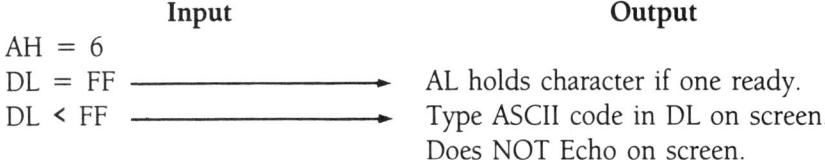

Note that this service does not check for ^C or ^Break.

This service is the direct console I/O service. Service 6 does *not* echo to the screen, nor does it wait for a character to be typed. If you load DL with FFH and call service 6 (i.e., load AH with 6 and issue an INT 21H instruction), AL will return the character that was typed, if one was typed, and the zero flag will not be set.

On the other hand, if no character is in the keyboard buffer, the zero flag will be set, and no character will be returned in AL. If the typed key has an extended ASCII code, AL will first return 00 and you must call service 6 again to get the second byte of the extended code (just like all the other DOS keyboard services).

If you load a character's ASCII code (not 0FFH) into DL and call service 6, that character's ASCII code will be printed out, making this a particularly versatile service. This service, however, does not check for ^C or ^Break.

REPEATER.COM Repeats What You Type

Let's write a quick example using this service called REPEATER.COM. REPEATER's job will be to read whatever character has been typed in and type it back out until a new character is typed. Service 6 is the only DOS keyboard service that returns characters but does *not* wait for you to type something in. If nothing was typed in, we want to keep typing out what we have been typing. The program appears in Listing 2-1 (below). Notice that since there is only one procedure in this .COM file, we did not even use the PROC and ENDP directives.

Listing 2-1. REPEATER.COM — Repeats Typed Keys.

```
        .CODE
        ORG     100H
START:  MOV     AH,6        ;We'll only use service 6 here.
TOP:    MOV     DL,0FFH     ;Read a character in.
        INT     21H         ;With INT 21H
        JZ      TYPEOUT     ;If there was NO character, type out old one.
        MOV     CL,AL       ;Store new character
        CMP     AL,'E'      ;Was it an 'E'?
        JE      FINISH      ;Yes, jump to the end of the program.
TYPEOUT: MOV    DL,CL       ;Type out the stored character
        INT     21H         ;Again with service 6
        JMP     TOP         ;And begin again.
FINISH: INT     20H         ;Finish up here and exit.

        END     START
```

Also, because service 6 does not check for the ∧C or ∧Break characters, we check to see if the typed character was an 'E' (for End). If so, we jump to the end of the program and quit.

This service is different from service 1 because it does not wait for you to type a character before returning, does not check for ∧C or ∧Break, and does not echo the typed character on the screen.

INT 21H Service 7 Read Key with Wait

Input   **Output**
AH = 7   AL = ASCII code of struck key
                NO Echo on screen.

Note that this service does not Check for ∧C or ∧Break.

This DOS service is very much like service 1, except that it does not echo characters on the screen and does not check for ∧C or ∧Break. It will, however, wait until you type a key.

> **TIP** Because it does not echo characters on the screen, you should use service 7 in the middle of games to type in a password, or in graphics modes where you do not want to disturb the display.

HOLD.COM Waits for a Password

Since it does not check for ∧C or ∧Break, we can even write a program called HOLD.COM that will not allow anyone to use your PC until they type in a three-letter password ("DOS"). HOLD.COM, in Listing 2-2 (below), is immune to ^C or ^Break (but it will not stand up to a reboot). If you run HOLD, the PC will simply wait until the three-letter password, "DOS" is typed.

Listing 2-2. HOLD.COM — Waits for a Password.

```
         .CODE
         ORG     100H
START:   MOV     AH,7            ;Here we will use service 7.
         INT     21H             ;Of INT 21H.
         CMP     AL,'D'          ;Was the typed letter a D?
         JNE     START           ;No, start over.
         INT     21H             ;Yes, get next letter.
         CMP     AL,'O'          ;Was this letter an O?
         JNE     START           ;No, start over.
         INT     21H             ;Get last letter.
         CMP     AL,'S'          ;An 'S'?
         JNE     START           ;Nope, start over.
FINISH:  INT     20H             ;Yes, finish up and exit.

         END     START
```

INT 21H Service 8 Read Key without Echo

Input	Output
AH = 8	AL = ASCII code of struck key.
	Does NOT echo the typed key.

This service checks for ^C or ^Break.

This service is the same as service 1, except that it does not echo the typed key on the screen. The only difference between this service and service 7 is that service 7 doesn't check for ^C or ^Break. If you want to use passwords, but also want to include ^C or ^Break checking, this is the service to use.

INT 21H Service 0AH String Input

Input	Output
AH = 0AH	Buffer at DS:DX filled.
[DS:DX] = Length of buffer	Echo the typed keys.

This service checks for ^C or ^Break.

Service 0AH was written to take buffered keyboard input. For the first time, we will have to deal with more than one key at a time, so we will also cover the 80 × 86's string handling instructions in this section.

How to Handle the Keyboard 39

Many parts of DOS itself use this service. To use service 0AH, we have to point DS:DX at an area in memory to be filled with keyboard input. The first byte of that area, the byte at location DS:DX, has to hold the (nonzero) number of bytes that the buffer can hold. If your buffer can hold 16 bytes, you make the first byte hold a value of 16.

The keys that are typed are placed in the buffer, starting at the third byte. The backspace key works as it should when you are typing, and mistakes that are erased never reach the final buffer. (If you have to load input buffers and make manual provisions for the backspace key, it can be very difficult.) The buffer will keep storing characters until the next to last byte is reached. If you try to type any more characters, besides a carriage return, the PC will beep with the familiar buffer-full beep. Please note that the buffer length stored in the first byte is the actual number of bytes the buffer can take, which excludes the first two bytes at DS:DX and DS:DX + 1. When you type a carriage return, input is ended.

When control returns from INT 21H, the second byte in the buffer will hold the number of characters typed.

> **TIP** If you plan to use service 0AH, you should know that the last character it returns will always be an ASCII 0DH, a carriage return. For example, if we typed "Testing...", our buffer would end up like this (note the carriage return at the end):
>
> ```
> DS:DX points here.
>     Number of bytes typed.
>  ↓      ↓   "T"  "e"  "s"  "t"  "i"  "n"  "g"  "."  "."  "."
>  10    0A   54   65   73   74   69   6E   67   2E   2E   2E   0D   00   00   00   00   00   00
>        ←─────────────────────────── 16 Bytes ───────────────────────────→
> ```
>
> This means that you should allow space for one more than the actual number of characters you want to receive.

String Instructions

There are many ways that assembly language excels in string handling jobs, most notably in string searches or comparisons. Since we will use these string instructions — MOVS, CMPS, SCAS, LODS, and STOS — later, and, since many introductory books do not cover them at all, they deserve our attention here.

The string instructions are so important to the 80×86 that the SI and DI registers have been set aside for them. String operations assume that as you move data, it moves from the address ES:[SI] to DS:[DI]; SI stands for Source Index, and DI for Destination Index. The string instructions increment or decrement these indices automatically.

MOVS, MOVSB, MOVSW, and REP

MOVS, or Move String, is the most elementary of string operations. All you must do is point DS:SI at the source string and ES:DI at the destination area and execute MOVS. To copy a string that is 20 bytes long from POINT_A to POINT_B, you could use the code in Listing 2-3 (below).

Listing 2-3. Code to Move a String from POINT_A to POINT_B.

```
        .DATA
        POINT_A DB "This is ONLY a test."
        POINT_B DB 20 DUP(?)

        .CODE
;Copy string of 20 bytes from POINT_A to POINT_B
        PUSH    DS              ;First set up ES (See below).
        POP     ES
        ASSUME  ES:@DATA        ;Tell the Assembler
        LEA     SI,POINT_A
        LEA     DI,POINT_B
        CLD                     ;Make sure we increment.
        MOV     CX,20D          ;Put 20 Decimal into loop counter.
AGAIN:  MOVS    POINT_B,POINT_A
        LOOP    AGAIN
                :
                :
```

One or two lines in that Listing 2-3 should be discussed. Since ES may theoretically be set to any value, and the strings we want to use are in the data segment, we first set up ES to point to data with these instructions:

```
        PUSH    DS              ;First set up ES (See below).
        POP     ES
        ASSUME  ES:@DATA        ;Tell the Assembler
```

Since segment registers cannot be loaded directly into each other, they usually must go through some all-purpose register (like this: MOV AX,DS MOV ES,AX). The stack is a way around that, and it is commonly used since each PUSH or POP assembles into only one byte of machine code.

The instruction CLD, or Clear Direction Flag, is an important (but often neglected) part of this type of code:

```
;Copy string of 20 bytes from POINT_A to POINT_B
            PUSH    DS                  ;First set up ES (See below).
            POP     ES
            ASSUME  ES:@DATA            ;Tell the Assembler.
            LEA     SI,POINT_A
            LEA     DI,POINT_B
            CLD                         ;Make sure we increment.
            MOV     CX,20D              ;Put 20 Decimal into loop counter.
    AGAIN:  MOVS    POINT_B,POINT_A
            LOOP    AGAIN
```

As soon as the MOVS instruction is executed, both SI and DI are automatically incremented. If you had used CLD's complement, STD (Set Direction Flag), both DI and SI would be decremented every time you use MOVS.

NOTE When you start a program, the direction flag is automatically cleared.

The MOVS instruction itself also deserves comment. When you move data, the 80×86 must know whether you intend to move bytes or words. When you use an instruction such as MOVS POINT_B,POINT_A, the assembler can check the declaration of both POINT_A and POINT_B. Since both have been declared with DB, the assembler knows that you intend to move one byte at a time. Instead of assembling this instruction into MOVS, the instruction is actually assembled into MOVSB, Move String Byte. Similarly, if you had declared POINT_A and POINT_B with DW, the Assembler would have used MOVSW, Move String Word, in the final code.

The string instructions come with a built-in loop instruction as well; REP stands for repeat. The same code as above could have been done this way:

```
;Copy string of 20 bytes from POINT_A to POINT_B
            PUSH    DS                  ;First set up ES (See below).
            POP     ES
            ASSUME  ES:@DATA            ;Tell the Assembler
            LEA     SI,POINT_A
            LEA     DI,POINT_B
            CLD                         ;Make sure we increment.
            MOV     CX,20D              ;Put 20 Decimal into loop counter.
    REP     MOVS    POINT_B,POINT_A
```

REP is a prefix for string instructions that turns them into one-line loops. Like LOOP, REP decrements the CX counter until it is zero.

We could have used the instruction MOVSB in this case. For instance, this code is also equivalent to that above (note that MOVSB and MOVSW take no operands, but you must set up SI and DI):

42 ▶ Advanced Assembly Language

```
;Copy string of 20 bytes from POINT_A to POINT_B
        PUSH    DS              ;First set up ES (See below).
        POP     ES
        ASSUME  ES:@DATA        ;Tell the Assembler
        LEA     SI,POINT_A
        LEA     DI,POINT_B
        CLD                     ;Make sure we increment.
        MOV     CX,20D          ;Put 20 Decimal into loop counter.
        REP     MOVSB
```

CMPS, CMPSB, CMPSW, REPE, and REPNE

CMPS also works with two strings at a time, like MOVS. A normal CMP is done comparing the bytes (or words) at DS:SI and ES:DI, the flags are set accordingly, and then SI and DI are incremented (or decremented, depending on the direction flag). For example, let's say we want to find where the difference in TRAVELOG_A and TRAVELOG_B are. Here's how they've been set up in the data segment:

```
.DATA
TRAVELOG_A      DB "I went to Ireland$"
TRAVELOG_B      DB "I went to Iceland$"
```

We could then find the first nonmatching byte with the code in Listing 2-4 (below).

Listing 2-4. Find Difference between TRAVELOG_A and TRAVELOG_B.

```
.DATA
TRAVELOG_A      DB "I went to Ireland$"
TRAVELOG_B      DB "I went to Iceland$"

.CODE
;Find first NON-matching byte in the two strings
        PUSH    DS
        POP     ES
        ASSUME  ES:@DATA
        LEA     DI,TRAVELOG_A
        LEA     SI,TRAVELOG_B
        CLD
        MOV     CX,18
→   REPE CMPS   TRAVELOG_A,TRAVELOG_B   ;Repeat WHILE Equal
        JNE     MIS_MATCH
MATCH:  MOV     AX,1
                :
                :
MIS_MATCH:
```

With this code we can search through the first 18 bytes of the strings. REPE CMPS compares the two strings, TRAVELOG_A and TRAVELOG_B, until two characters do

How to Handle the Keyboard 43

not match. REPE means repeat while equal. When two characters do not match, the flags are set to indicate that the elements being compared were not equal: we can take advantage of that with a JNE MIS_MATCH.

```
           MOV      CX,18
      REPE CMPS     TRAVELOG_A,TRAVELOG_B    ;Repeat WHILE Equal
→          JNE      MIS_MATCH
    MATCH: MOV      AX,1
```

If the branch to MIS_MATCH is taken, there was a mismatch in the strings. (DI and SI are incremented after all comparisons, however, so the address of the nonmatching bytes would be DS:SI-1 and ES:DI-1 when you reached the label MIS_MATCH.) If the two strings matched completely, CX would be 0, the flags would be set so that the JNE is not taken, and control would continue with the next line:

```
           MOV      CX,18
      REPE CMPS     TRAVELOG_A,TRAVELOG_B    ;Repeat WHILE Equal
           JNE      MIS_MATCH
→   MATCH: MOV      AX,1
```

This section of code finds when the first byte of two strings, STRING_A and STRING_B, *do* match:

```
    ;Find first MATCHING byte in the two strings
           PUSH     DS
           POP      ES
           ASSUME   ES:@DATA
           LEA      DI,STRING_A
           LEA      SI,STRING_B
           CLD
           MOV      CX,500
→   REPNE  CMPSB                             ;Repeat While NOT Equal
           JE       SAME_BYTE
    DIFFERENT:
           MOV      AX,1
```

Here we are using CMPSB, which takes no operands, and using REPNE, which means repeat while not equal. In this example, only the first 500 bytes can be compared for a match. The instruction CMPSW is just the same as CMPSB, except that it compares full words at a time.

SCAS, SCASB, and SCASW

The Scan String instructions are similar to CMPS, but instead of comparing two strings, these instructions compare a byte (in AL) or a word (in AX) to a byte or a word in a string. Let's make up an example that accepts input with INT 21H service 0AH and tells you the position of the first character "a" in the string. This program, FIND_a, will type out the position of "a" in a string, starting with position 0, for example, and the string "abcde" will give an answer of 0. FIND_a, in Listing 2-5 (below), is a simple program, and it can only handle input strings of up to 10 bytes, including the carriage return (since it has to return a single digit answer).

Listing 2-5. FIND_a.COM — Finds 'a' in Keyboard Input.

```
        .CODE
        ORG     100H
START:  JMP     FIND_a                  ;Make this a COM file.
STRING  DB      10,11 DUP(0)            ;Buffer, starting with 10 in 1st byte.
FIND_a  PROC    NEAR
        MOV     AH,0AH                  ;Select service 0AH.
        MOV     DX,OFFSET STRING        ;Set up DS:DX.
        INT     21H
        CLD                             ;Make sure DI increments.
        MOV     AL,"a"                  ;Scan for "a" by putting it in AL.
        MOV     DI,OFFSET STRING+2      ;Point to beginning of string.
        MOV     CX,10                   ;Scan up to 10 letters.
        REPNE   SCASB                   ← Repeat while NOT equal, Scan byte.
        JNE     OUT                     ;If no match, just exit.
        MOV     AH,2                    ;A match was found, print <cr><lf>
        MOV     DL,13                   ;<cr>
        INT     21H
        MOV     DL,10                   ;<lf>
        INT     21H
        DEC     DI                      ;Point to matching byte.
        MOV     DX,DI                   ;We want to print ASCII value of DI.
        SUB     DX,OFFSET STRING+2      ;Subtract offset of beginning of string.
        ADD     DL,"0"                  ;Add beginning of numerals in ASCII.
        INT     21H                     ;And type out answer.
OUT:    INT     20H     ;End the Program.
FIND_a  ENDP
        END     START
```

In FIND_a.ASM, we use the instruction REPNE SCASB, one of the most common string instructions, to locate the byte "a" in the typed-in string. If we had been looking for an entire word, say "apple," instead of just "a," we could have searched for the first character, "a," with REPNE SCASB and then added a REPE CMPSB instruction to check whether the characters following "a" are "pple."

A few things are worth noticing in this example. One is that we set up our keyboard input buffer using DB wisely, initializing the first byte to hold 10, our buffer length:

```
        .CODE
        ORG     100H                    ;Make this a COM file.
START:  JMP     FIND_a
     →  STRING  DB      10,11 DUP(0)    ;Buffer, starting with 10 in 1st byte.
FIND_a  PROC    NEAR
                :
```

Another new thing is our use of the OFFSET directive, which loads a label's offset from the beginning of the segment into a register. In the code, we reference the beginning of the input string with the address STRING+2:

```
                :
        MOV     AL,"a"                  ;Scan for "a" by putting it in AL.
     →  MOV     DI,OFFSET STRING+2      ;Point to beginning of string.
        MOV     CX,10                   ;Scan up to 10 letters.
REPNE   SCASB           ← Repeat while NOT equal, Scan byte.
        JNE     OUT                     ;If no match, just exit.
        MOV     AH,2                    ;A match was found, print <cr><lf>
```

If we had wanted to, we could have set up the data area this way:

```
        ORG     100H                    ;Make this a .COM file.
START:  JMP     FIND_a
     →  BUFFER  DB      10,0
     →  STRING  DB      10 DUP(0)
FIND_a  PROC    NEAR
                :
```

This would have still given us an unbroken string in memory of 12 bytes, the first one set to 10, the rest to zero. But we then could have referenced the beginning of the input string directly with the label "STRING" and could have simply said MOV DI,OFFSET STRING.

To use REPNE SCASB, we loaded the counter, CX, with 10. This means that if no match is found in 10 repetitions, control will pass on to the next instruction. If a match *is* found, control will also pass on to the next instruction (since REPNE means repeat while *Not* equal), so we have to distinguish between the two.

SCASB acts just like CMP in setting the flags, so if we found a match, the flags will be set as though a CMP between two equal items had just been done. If no match is found, the flags will have been set as though a CMP had been done between unequal items. In this case, we want to quit, so we test the result of our scan with JNE OUT, testing the last comparison done in REPNE SCASB:

```
                :
        MOV     AL,"a"                  ;Scan for "a" by putting it in AL.
        MOV     DI,OFFSET STRING+2      ;Point to beginning of string.
        MOV     CX,10                   ;Scan up to 10 letters.
REPNE   SCASB           ← Repeat while NOT equal, Scan byte.
        JNE     OUT                     ;If no match, just exit.
        MOV     AH,2                    ;A match was found, print <cr><lf>
```

If a match is found, we want to print its position in the string out (beginning with 0). We first send a carriage return (ASCII 13) line-feed (ASCII 10) pair using the DOS printing service, number 2. We first print a ‹cr›, then a ‹lf›, and finally find the position of the "a." (Recall that the REPNE SCASB left ES:DI pointing at the byte following the match, so it has to be decremented first.)

```
                :
REPNE   SCASB           ← Repeat while NOT equal, Scan byte.
        JNE     OUT                     ;If no match, just exit.
        MOV     AH,2                    ;A match was found, print <cr><lf>
        MOV     DL,13                   ;<cr>
        INT     21H
        MOV     DL,10                   ;<lf>
        INT     21H
      → DEC     DI                      ;Point to matching byte.
      → MOV     DX,DI                   ;We want to print ASCII value of DI.
      → SUB     DX,OFFSET STRING+2      ;Subtract offset of beginning of string.
      → ADD     DL,"0"                  ;Add beginning of numerals in ASCII.
        INT     21H                     ;And type out answer.
```

LODS and STOS

The last two string instructions of the 80×86 are the Load String (LODS) and Store String (STOS) instructions. The purpose of LODS is to load strings byte by byte from DS:[SI] into AL. STOS stores them byte by byte into ES:[DI]. After each move, DI or SI is increased. These instructions both provide quick, easy access to string manipulation and handling. As with all string instructions, even if you use an instruction like

```
START:  JMP     LOOK
        STRING1 DB      "Apple of my eye."
LOOK    PROC    NEAR
        LEA     SI,STRING1
      → LODS    STRING1
```

it will actually be put into the code as LODSB without any operands. In fact, the only reason that you have to include the name of the string STRING1 in the instruction above is so the assembler can check the attribute of STRING1 (it is BYTE) and use LODSB instead of LODSW. (The assembler always assembles STOS into STOSB or STOSW.)

STOS is an excellent instruction to use if you want to store a string and, at the same time, check for a particular character. Since each character in the string to be stored moves through AL, you can check it before storing it. With STOSB, you can move byte after byte from AL into memory.

This finishes our survey of the 80 × 86's string instructions; you should keep in mind that they are an important part of the ability of assembly language to deal with large quantities of data rapidly. We will have more use for them later in the book, but now let's continue with the available keyboard input services that DOS provides.

INT 21H Service 0BH Check Keyboard Buffer

Input	Output
AH = 0BH	AL = FF → Character ready.
	AL = 00 → Nothing to read in.

Note that in this service ^Break is checked for.

This DOS service is unique. Without actually reading a character, you can check and see if something has been typed. Its use is simple: all you do is load AH with 0BH and issue an INT 21H instruction. If a ^Break has been typed, the program is interrupted. If not, control returns from INT 21H and you can look at the contents of AL to see if there is a key or keys to be read in. If AL is 0FFH, there is something to be read in with one of the keyboard services. If not, AL is 0.

> **TIP** The utility of service 0BH is that with it you can use services 1, 7, 8, or 0AH without the usual wait. If you want to pick up characters and echo them on the screen, for example, you could use service 1, but only if you don't mind waiting until there is something there to read. On the other hand, with service 0BH, you can check and see if some key is waiting to be read from the keyboard buffer. Use service 1 if there is a key waiting.

INT 21H Service 0CH Clear Keyboard Buffer and Execute Service

Input	Output
AH = 0CH	Standard Output from the
AL = Keyboard Function #	selected service.

Note that ^Break is checked for.

DOS service 0CH clears the keyboard buffer and then will invoke a keyboard service (1, 6, 7, 8, or 0AH). You will have to wait until a key is typed because the first thing it does is erase keys typed ahead of keys in the keyboard buffer.

The use of this service is specialized, but, when it is called for, it is necessary. In particular, when crucial choices have to be made, it is important that typed-ahead bytes in the keyboard buffer are not interpreted as responses. When you type DEL *.*, for example, a prompt always comes up asking "Are you sure (y/n)?" Before this message is typed, the keyboard buffer is cleared to take care of characters that may already have been typed ahead. The same thing is true for the disk error message: "Error reading Drive:B Abort, Retry or Ignore?". FORMAT.COM also clears the keyboard buffer before asking "Format another (y/n)?"

After the keyboard buffer is cleared, the number in AL is read and that DOS service is executed. For example, if we had put a 0AH there, we would first have cleared the keyboard buffer and then executed DOS service 0AH, buffered input, just as if we had put 0AH into AH.

The BIOS Interrupts

We've completed the DOS interrupts dealing with the keyboard. There are still a number of BIOS interrupts to examine, however. In general, DOS provides services with more error checking and options, while BIOS provides the sturdy, low-level services that DOS itself is built on.

BIOS INT 16H

Input	Output
AH = 0	AH = Scan Code AL = ASCII code
AH = 1	Zero Flag = 1 → buffer empty
	Zero Flag = 0 → AH = Scan Code
	AL = ASCII Code
AH = 2	AL = Keyboard Status byte.

BIOS is the really low-level worker of the PC. An essential difference for us between BIOS and DOS is that most of the BIOS interrupts are *reenterable*. What this means is that if some program is executing a BIOS interrupt, another program can start to execute the *same* interrupt before the first program is done. This is not the case for DOS. If we reason, all keys leave two bytes in the keyboard buffer — an ASCII code and a scan code — and some keys' ASCII codes are zero. Those keys are represented by an extended ASCII code.

When one of the DOS keyboard services returns a zero in the AL register, the key that was pushed has no normal ASCII code, and you must reissue the same service call again to get a new number into AL, the scan code.

INT 16H Service 0 Read Key

BIOS INT 16H returns both the scan and ASCII code of a typed character. If you set AH to 0 before issuing an INT 16H instruction, INT 16H waits for a key to be typed if there are none waiting, and then returns the key's scan code in AH and its ASCII code in AL. If AL is 0, the key is an extended ASCII key, and the extended ASCII code is in AH.

INT 16H Service 1 Examine Keyboard and Read

If you select service 1, INT 16H examines the keyboard for you without altering it. If the zero flag is set on return, the buffer is empty and there is no key to be read. If the zero flag is set, AX is set just as it would be in INT 16H service 0; that is, AH contains the scan code and AL contains the ASCII code.

INT 16H Service 2 Read Status Byte

Finally, selecting service 2 before issuing an INT 16H returns the keyboard status byte in AL. This keyboard status byte is read directly from the BIOS data area at address 40:00. This area also contains the keyboard buffer. There is an immense amount of information in the BIOS data area, so let's take a look at it:

The BIOS Data Area

Address(es)	Contents
40:0000 - 40:0006	Addresses of RS 232 adapters 1–4
40:0008 - 40:000E	Addresses of printer adapters 1–4
40:0010	Equipment Flag (returned by Int 11H)
40:0012	Manufacturer's test mark
40:0013	Motherboard memory (in Kbytes)
40:0015	I/O channel memory
40:0017	The Keyboard Flags (see below)

▶ **How to Handle the Keyboard** 49

want to use DOS INT 21H services from a memory-resident program, we'll have to go to great pains to make sure that no other program is using INT 21H at the same time.

> **NOTE** OS/2, in contrast to DOS, *is* reenterable.

For example, if a program is in the middle of executing a BIOS interrupt when a memory-resident program takes control and tries to execute the same interrupt, there would be no problem. With DOS interrupts, however, this is a disaster. The machine is likely to crash. We will have more to say about this difference later in Chapter 7.

The BIOS keyboard interrupt, INT 16H, is one of the fundamental interrupts of the PC. Besides returning the ASCII value of a typed key, it also returns the character's *scan code*.

All about Keyboard Scan Codes

For each of the 83 (84 on a PC AT) or 101 keys on the PC's keyboard, there is a code called a scan code. This is the code the microprocessor in the keyboard sends to the PC when a key is typed. For example, the "A" key has an ASCII code of 41H and a scan code of 1EH. The "S" key, right next to it, has an ASCII code of 53H and a scan code of 1FH.

> **TIP** If you want a quick way of finding a key's scan and ASCII codes, you can use this short BASIC program (it's much shorter than the corresponding assembly language program), which reads directly from the keyboard buffer:

```
10    FOR I=1 TO 10:KEY I,"":NEXT I
20    DEF SEG = &H40
30    FKEY$=INKEY$:IF FKEY$="" GOTO 30
40    TAIL=PEEK(26):TAIL=TAIL-2:IF TAIL < 30 THEN TAIL = 60
50    CODE1=PEEK(TAIL):CODE2=PEEK(TAIL+1)
60    PRINT HEX$(CODE1) SPC(1) HEX$(CODE2) SPC(2);:GOTO 20:END
```

Extended ASCII Codes

There are more keys on their keyboard than there is space in ASCII to represent them, especially when you take into account Alt, Num Lock, and Control combinations. However, there is a unique scan code for every key or legal key combination. For that

How to Handle the Keyboard

40:0019	Numbers input with Alt key
40:001A	Location of Keyboard Buffer Head
40:001C	Location of Keyboard Buffer Tail
40:001E - 40:003D	Keyboard buffer
40:003E	Status of Diskette Seek
40:003F	Status of Diskette Motor
40:0040	Timeout of Diskette Motor
40:0041	Status of Diskette
40:0042 - 40:0048	Status Bytes of Diskette Controller (the NEC)
40:0049	Display Mode (see the section on Clock)
40:004A	Number of columns (40 or 80)
40:004C	Length of Video Regen. Buffer
40:004E	Starting Address in Regen. Buffer
40:0050 - 40:005E	Positions of cursors on screen pages 1–8
40:0060	Mode of the Cursor
40:0062	Active Page Number
40:0063	Address of current display adapter

Inside the Keyboard Buffer

Now we can pass into the real depth of keyboard handling on the PC: the keyboard buffer and INT 9. When you strike a key on the PC's keyboard, a complex sequence of events occurs. The keyboard is a peripheral like any other communication device such as the disk drive or speaker. As such, it communicates with the 80×86 though an I/O port. The keyboard itself is complex enough to have its own microprocessor on board, an Intel 8048 (or later processor). When you press one of the PC's keys, the 8048 generates a code depending on the key's position on the keyboard; this is the key's scan code.

This byte-long code is then stored in a register, and the 8048 generates an Interrupt 9. This interrupt works as discussed: an address is found at the correct interrupt vector, 0000:0024 (9 × 4 = 36 = 24H) and the code there (stored in ROM) is run. If your program has turned interrupts off with a CLI instruction

```
        MOV     DX,48A9H  ;Find I/O address
      → CLI               ;Don't let in interrupts now.
        REP STOSB         ;Move the data
```

then INT 9 cannot take place and typed keys are ignored. If interrupts are enabled, however, the byte scan code waiting to be read in is read through its own port, port

52 ▶ Advanced Assembly Language

60H. If it were not for this one line in BIOS: IN AL, 60H, the PC would be a useless machine.

Let's take a brief look (with DEBUG) at the beginning of the keyboard interrupt, interrupt 9. First, we must find the address at which its service routine begins, so we dump the interrupt vector at 0000:0024:

```
-D0:24        ↓   ↓   ↓   ↓
0000:0024  87 E9 00 F0-DD E6 00 F0 DD E6 00 F0          .i.p]f.p]f.p
0000:0030  DD E6 00 F0 DD E6 00 F0-57 EF 00 F0 47 01 70 00   ]f.p]f.pWo.pG.p.
0000:0040  65 F0 00 F0 4D F8 00 F0-41 F8 00 F0 59 EC 00 F0   ep.pMx.pAx.pYl.p
0000:0050  39 E7 00 F0 59 F8 00 F0-2E E8 00 F0 D2 EF 00 F0   9g.pYx.p.h.pRo.p
0000:0060  00 00 00 F6 F2 E6 00 F0-6E FE 00 F0 40 01 70 00   ...vrf.pn~.p@.p.
0000:0070  53 FF 00 F0 A4 F0 00 F0-22 05 00 00 00 00 00 F0   S..p$p.p"......p
0000:0080  07 0B E3 00 80 01 3A 05-42 02 06 06 70 02 06 06   ..c...:.B...p...
0000:0090  E2 04 3A 05 E0 13 E3 00-2E 14 E3 00 13 27 E3 00   b.:.'.c...c..'c.
0000:00A0  13 0B E3 00                                       ..c.
```

These bytes, 87 E9 00 F0, give us the address F000:E987, so we unassemble that address:

```
-UF000:E987
F000:E987 FB          STI
F000:E988 50          PUSH    AX       ← Store all registers
F000:E989 53          PUSH    BX
F000:E98A 51          PUSH    CX
F000:E98B 52          PUSH    DX
F000:E98C 56          PUSH    SI
F000:E98D 57          PUSH    DI
F000:E98E 1E          PUSH    DS
F000:E98F 06          PUSH    ES
F000:E990 FC          CLD
F000:E991 E8AA15      CALL    FF3E
F000:E994 E460        IN      AL,60    ← Read in the character.
F000:E996 50          PUSH    AX
F000:E997 E461        IN      AL,61    ← Read keyboard control port.
F000:E999 8AE0        MOV     AH,AL
F000:E99B 0C80        OR      AL,80
F000:E99D E661        OUT     61,AL    ← Reset keyboard for next character.
F000:E99F 86E0        XCHG    AL,AH
F000:E9A1 E661        OUT     61,AL
F000:E9A3 58          POP     AX
F000:E9A4 8AE0        MOV     AH,AL
F000:E9A6 3CFF        CMP     AL,FF    ← FF means the 8048's buffer is full.
-Q
```

Right before us is the actual line used to read in keyboard characters. The number read in this way is then compared with a lookup table, the scan code table, and ASCII values are found for those characters that have them. Some controlling characters get no further than INT 9 and do not leave any mark in the keyboard buffer at all. For example,

How to Handle the Keyboard 53

although keys like Shift, Alt, and Control produce INT 9's (all keys do), they just modify what comes next. BIOS keeps track of which one of these are active by checking the keyboard status byte at 40:0017.

After a key's ASCII code is found, it is put together with the key's scan code into the keyboard buffer. For each key that leaves anything in the buffer, two bytes appear.

Circular Buffers

The keyboard buffer itself is a set of 16 words in memory in the BIOS data area. These bytes are set up to be what is called a circular buffer. Since the reading and writing operations from and to this buffer are independent, circular buffering allows you to put in and take out keys easily. At any given time, one of these 16 words, called the *head*, is the position that the next character will be read from. Another, the *tail*, is the position that the next character can be written to. When keys are typed in, the tail advances. When you read one, the head advances. When either comes to the end of their 16-word range, they wrap around to the beginning again. A good model for this circular buffer is a ring of 16 words, with the head forever chasing the tail. Two more bytes in the BIOS data area hold the current addresses of the head and the tail.

When everything is read, the head catches up with the tail; the two are at the same address, and the buffer is empty. Conversely, if the tail wraps around and comes up from behind the head, the buffer is full.

> **TIP** The place to use circular buffers is when two parts of your program are producing and reading data at different rates. If you use a circular buffer, this problem is taken care of with the most efficient possible use of memory.

With DEBUG, we should be able to take a direct look at the keyboard buffer at 40:1E. In particular, we can examine it with the Dump instruction. Let's fill the buffer with A's and then examine it. To avoid having to type D0040:001E, which would fill the buffer up, let's do a Dump of 128 bytes before 40:1E so we only have to type D ‹cr› since Dump takes up just where it stopped. Here's how it looks:

```
-D0:39E         ← 128 Bytes before the keyboard buffer
0000:039E   00 00                                                ..
0000:03A0   00 00 00 00 00 00 00 00-00 00 00 00 00 00 00 00      ................
0000:03B0   00 00 00 00 00 00 00 00-00 00 00 00 00 00 00 00      ................
0000:03C0   00 00 00 00 E5 FE 00 F0-E5 FE E5 FE 00 F0 FF FF      ....e~.pe~e~.p..
0000:03D0   5D EF FF FF 40 00 3A EF-00 F0 06 00 00 00 01 00      ]o..@.:o.p......
0000:03E0   40 00 6F EC 00 00 43 E6-80 00 02 00 00 00 01 00      @.ol..Cf........
```

54 ▶ Advanced Assembly Language

```
0000:03F0  00 7C 21 E7 00 F0 46 F2-04 00 CF E5 00 F0 97 F2   .|!g..pFr..Oe.p.r
0000:0400  00 00 00 00 00 00 00 00-8C 03 00 00 00 00 00 00   ........<.......
0000:0410  BD 40 00 00 01 C0 00 40-00 00 38 00 38 00         =@.....@..8.8.
-AAAAAAAAAAAAAAAA             ← Fill the buffer with "A"
  ^ Error                     ← Which DEBUG naturally thinks is an error.
-D                            ← And now examine it.
0000:041E  41 1E                                              A.
0000:0420  41 1E 41 1E 41 1E 41 1E-41 1E 41 1E 41 1E 41 1E   A.A.A.A.A.A.A.A.
0000:0430  41 1E 41 1E 41 1E 41 1E-0D 1C 44 20 0D 1C 03 80   A.A.A.A...D ....
0000:0440  3A 00 04 00 00 0D 01 03-02 07 50 00 00 40 00 00   :.........P..@..
0000:0450  00 18 00 00 00 00 00 00-00 00 00 00 00 00 00 00   ................
0000:0460  07 06 00 B4 03 29 30 E6-0A 00 00 00 98 4D 11 00   .....)0f.....M..
0000:0470  00 00 FF FF 00 00 00 00-14 14 14 14 01 01 01 01   ................
0000:0480  1E 00 3E 00 00 00 00 00-00 00 00 00 00 00 00 00   ..>.............
0000:0490  00 00 00 00 00 00 00 00-00 00 00 00 00            .............
-Q
```

If you look at the ASCII part of the display you'll see our typed A's. Each A is stored as a 41H (its ASCII code) and a 1E (its scan code). At the end of the last A the carriage return we typed (i.e., AAAAAAAAAAAAAAAA‹cr›) is stored as 0D (=ASCII 13) 1C (its scan code). Finally, you can see our D‹cr› instruction. This last ‹cr› leaves us at the top of the buffer. The next key typed would be wrapped around, and stored at the beginning at 40:1E.

It is worth noting that although there are 16 words in the keyboard buffer, the buffer can only take 15 keystrokes before it is filled and you get beeped. The reason for this is that the tail word is where the next character will go. Let's assume the tail is right behind the head, and that there are 15 characters in the buffer. If the buffer took one more keystroke, the tail would advance and overlap the head. But an overlapping head and tail is the signal for an empty buffer. Since there is no way to distinguish a 16-character filled buffer and an empty buffer, BIOS allows a maximum of 15 characters.

In addition, when you type a key, the 8048 in the keyboard generates a scan code. When you release the key, a second scan code is generated (and another INT 9 is issued). This second scan code is the same as the original value plus 128 — this is the PC's signal that you have released the key. If it doesn't see this signal about half a second after receiving the original scan code, it will start to generate repeating characters (this feature is called typematic). If you are writing code that will intercept the keyboard interrupt, INT 9, it is important to know about this second call made after a key has been released. For this second call, though, the position of the head and tail do not change, so your program will be able to tell that no new characters were added.

Using the Keyboard Interrupt

It is possible to use INT 9 before BIOS gets to it. If you do it, you must interpret the scan code that comes in from the keyboard port. Usually, it is much easier to let BIOS interpret the scan codes and put the character into the keyboard buffer before working on it. After all, the scan code table that BIOS uses is large and it is hard to see a reason for duplicating all that in your code.

Since we have now seen the fundamentals behind the keyboard buffer, we should put it to work by introducing some code that uses the keyboard buffer directly. Let's write a short program to bypass the DOS and BIOS key-reading services and read keys directly from the keyboard buffer.

READEM.COM Reads Directly from the Keyboard

Reading directly from the keyboard buffer will be easy. First, we have to set up the memory model:

```
        .MODEL SMALL
        :
```

Next, we straddle the BIOS data segment with a segment definition like this:

```
            .MODEL SMALL
ROM_BIOS_DATA    SEGMENT AT 40H    ;BIOS statuses held here, also keyboard buffer

            ORG     1AH
            HEAD DW    ?                    ;Unread chars go from Head to Tail
            TAIL DW    ?
            BUFFER     DW    16 DUP (?)     ;The buffer itself
            BUFFER_END LABEL WORD

ROM_BIOS_DATA    ENDS
        :
```

Now we're free to set up our code segment. The first thing we do in the code is to load DS properly with the segment address of ROM_BIOS_DATA. Then we can check whether or not the tail and the head are at the same position. If they are, no key is waiting, and we should keep looping until one is:

```
            .MODEL SMALL

ROM_BIOS_DATA    SEGMENT AT 40H    ;BIOS statuses held here, also keyboard buffer

            ORG     1AH
            HEAD DW    ?                    ;Unread chars go from Head to Tail
            TAIL DW    ?
            BUFFER     DW    16 DUP (?)     ;The buffer itself
            BUFFER_END LABEL WORD
```

56 ▶ Advanced Assembly Language

```
ROM_BIOS_DATA   ENDS

        .CODE
        ORG     100H            ;ORG = 100H to make this into a .COM file

READEM  PROC    NEAR            ;The keyboard interrupt will now come here.
*       ASSUME  DS:ROM_BIOS_DATA  ;Examine the char just put in
*       MOV     BX,ROM_BIOS_DATA
*       MOV     DS,BX
GET_CHAR:
*       MOV     BX,HEAD         ;Point to current head
*       CMP     BX,TAIL         ;If at tail, no char waiting
*       JE      GET_CHAR        ;So loop until one is waiting
        :
```

If a key is waiting, however, it will be waiting at the buffer's head, which we have loaded into BX. We can just read that character and then clear the buffer like this:

```
        .MODEL SMALL

ROM_BIOS_DATA   SEGMENT AT 40H  ;BIOS statuses held here, also keyboard buffer

        ORG     1AH
        HEAD DW ?               ;Unread chars go from Head to Tail
        TAIL DW ?
        BUFFER      DW      16 DUP (?)      ;The buffer itself
        BUFFER_END  LABEL   WORD

ROM_BIOS_DATA   ENDS

        .CODE
        ORG     100H            ;ORG = 100H to make this into a .COM file

READEM  PROC    NEAR            ;The keyboard interrupt will now come here.
        ASSUME  DS:ROM_BIOS_DATA  ;Examine the char just put in
        MOV     BX,ROM_BIOS_DATA
        MOV     DS,BX
GET_CHAR:
        MOV     BX,HEAD         ;Point to current head
        CMP     BX,TAIL         ;If at tail, no char waiting
        JE      GET_CHAR        ;So loop until one is waiting
*       MOV     DX,[BX]         ;Get character
*       MOV     TAIL,BX         ;Empty the buffer
        ;------ CHAR IN DX NOW -------
        :
```

And that's it: we've waited until a key appeared, and then we've read it directly out of the buffer. Moving the head back to the tail then resets the buffer, and we're ready for the next character. We're left with the struck key in DX. The ASCII code is in DL and the scan code is in DH.

▶ How to Handle the Keyboard 57

We can check that character. If "Q" was typed, for example, we can quit the program and finish up. Otherwise, we just print the character on the screen. The full listing of READEM.COM is in Listing 2-6 (below).

> **NOTE** Note that the character is not printed on the screen just by typing it. It only goes into the keyboard buffer that way. It is up to us to type it out.

Listing 2-6. READEM.COM — Reads Keys from Keyboard Buffer

```
            .MODEL SMALL

ROM_BIOS_DATA   SEGMENT AT 40H   ;BIOS statuses held here, also keyboard buffer

            ORG     1AH
            HEAD DW  ?                   ;Unread chars go from Head to Tail
            TAIL DW  ?
            BUFFER      DW      16 DUP (?)       ;The buffer itself
            BUFFER_END  LABEL   WORD

ROM_BIOS_DATA   ENDS

            .CODE
            ORG     100H                ;ORG = 100H to make this into a .COM file
READEM      PROC    NEAR                ;The keyboard interrupt will now come here.
            ASSUME  DS:ROM_BIOS_DATA    ;Examine the char just put in
            MOV     BX,ROM_BIOS_DATA
            MOV     DS,BX
GET_CHAR:
            MOV     BX,HEAD             ;Point to current head
            CMP     BX,TAIL             ;If at tail, no char waiting
            JE      GET_CHAR            ;So loop until one is waiting
            MOV     DX,[BX]             ;Get character
            MOV     TAIL,BX             ;Empty the buffer
        ;------ CHAR IN DX NOW -------
            CMP     DL,"Q"              ;Was "Q" or "q" typed? (i.e. quit)
            JE      BYE
            CMP     DL,"q"
            JE      BYE
            MOV     AH, 2
            INT     21H
            JMP     GET_CHAR            ;Go back for a new character.

BYE:        INT     20H

READEM      ENDP

            END     READEM   ;END "READEM" so 80x86 will go to READEM first.
```

And that finishes our review of keyboard handling in the PC. We've gone from the high end to the low end, covering just about every way of reading keys in assembly language that there is (with the exception of new tricks we'll pick up later under OS/2 or Microsoft Windows). The next logical step after accepting keyboard input is to produce output, and we'll do that in the next chapter, Chapter 3.

▶ Chapter 3

Screen Handling

▶ Screen Handling

SCREEN DISPLAYS on the PC machines have gotten steadily better over time — a popular improvement. The original Color Graphics Adapter (CGA) could only display four colors at a time, with a poor resolution of 320 × 200 (320 vertical colums, 200 horizontal rows), and it flickered badly. The individual pixels on the screen were so large that they were better called squares than dots.

The other option, the Monochrome Display Adapter (MDA) didn't flicker, had good resolution, but it also didn't do graphics. All it uses are alphanumeric characters. With the introduction of other highly competitive machines, it became clear that graphics was an up-and-coming issue in hardware, and IBM eventually followed the lead.

In 1984, IBM introduced the Enhanced Graphics Adapter (EGA). The EGA can select 16 colors to display at once from a selection of 64, doesn't flicker, and has pretty good resolution, 640 × 350 (almost as good as the monochrome display, which has 720 × 350). In addition, the EGA could display anything that the CGA or MDA could — it even used the same character set as the monochrome screen. The improvement can be readily seen in the difference in memory size allocated to the CGA — 16K — versus the EGA — (up to) 256K.

Then in April 1987, along with the introduction of the PS/2, the Video Graphics Adapter (VGA) was born. The Video Graphics Adapter is built with an IBM chip and can do everything the EGA can do (and, in turn, the EGA can do everything that the CGA and MDA could do) and more. The tremendous expansion in the numbers of colors that can be displayed is the specific advance of the UGA. In a particular (low resolution) mode, the VGA can display 256 colors at once, chosen from a selection of 256K possibilities. This number is slightly qualified by the poor resolution in this mode: only 320 × 200. Other VGA graphics modes allow higher resolution display (such as 640 × 480) but with a correspondingly fewer number of available colors. In addition, there are many super-VGAs* and the XGA to choose from. Graphics and color on the PC and PS/2 had clearly become an important issue.

This chapter on screen handling and graphics will partly be an exploration of BIOS INT 10H because, for most purposes, it *is* screen handling and graphics on the PC at the assembly language level. Even the services of INT 21H that print on the screen (only alphanumerics) call BIOS to do it. BIOS is the software in ROM (augmented now by what is read in from disk), and it is the lowest level of support in your PC — even below DOS.

Of course, we can also reach the video buffer directly in memory. That's one of the advantages of working in assembly language. We'll do that too in this chapter, writing *directly* to the CGA buffer in high resolution mode and to the EGA/VGA buffer in 16-color mode. There's a lot going on in this chapter, so let's get started immediately with the BIOS screen handling services.

---

* For more information, see *Advanced Programmer's Guide to SuperVGAs* by Sutty and Blair (Brady, 1990).

The BIOS Screen Handling Services

We'll begin by examining the screen handling services and the ways that BIOS can put characters on the screen. For example, this is where we'll learn about colored characters, character attributes, and how to move the cursor around or scroll the screen. When we've finished with the screen handling services, we'll turn to graphics.

One thing you should know before we even begin unravelling the huge INT 10H is that you can't count on it to preserve the AX, SI, and DI registers. When we use it, we'll have to protect those ourselves. DOS would return those registers without a problem, but this is the lowest level of our machine — BIOS.

We'll begin with the first screen-handling services available. What could be more fundamental to screen handling than moving the cursor around? And that's what services 2 and 3 do.

Services 2 and 3 — Set and Get Cursor Position

Service 2 — Set Cursor

Set these things:
AH = 2
DH,DL = Row, column of new position (0,0 is upper left of screen)
BH = Page number (usually 0)

Service 3 — Get Cursor

Set these things:
AH = 3
BH = Page number (usually 0)

Returns:
DH, DL = Row, column of current cursor position.

There are two services here, service 2 and service 3. Service 2 sets the cursor position, and service 3 gets the current cursor position for you.

We'll use service 2 in our program PRINT_IT.COM very soon. This service gives you the chance to position the cursor where you want it on the screen. The cursor position is always given as coordinates like: (row, column). To set this position, just put the row and column numbers in DH and DL, respectively. The upper left of the screen is (0,0), and values increase from there, as shown in Figure 3-1 (below).

▶ **Screen Handling** 63

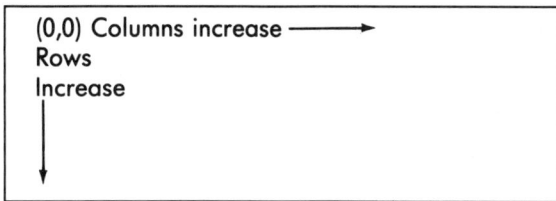

Figure 3-1. Screen Row and Column Numbering

Service 3 allows you to get the current cursor position. This is useful if you are writing, say, a pop-up program (see Chapter 7 on pop-up programs) and want to use an INT 10H service to write a notepad on the screen. With service 3, you can get the original cursor position (before you popped up) so that you can restore it later, after writing your notepad.

Screen Page Numbers

You also have to load the *page number* into BH to use these services. The page number takes a little more explaining: the video memory can be divided up in some video modes into *pages*. Although we will not deal with pages here, we must at least examine the concept.

Some video modes require more memory than others. If there is some unused memory in some particular video mode, IBM lets you use it as extra pages of screen display.

The CGA, when it is doing pixel-by-pixel graphics, requires 16K instead of the 4K it uses for its alphanumeric mode (as we'll see shortly). This memory is always available on the CGA card, and since it is enough to make up four full screens of text, IBM allows you to use pages in the graphics monitor when dealing with text. This is how pages were born.

Normally, all pages are copies of each other, and page 0 is displayed. With BIOS, though, it is possible to skip around and selectively write to particular pages. The default page is 0, and that's the one we will always use here (the use of pages is not common).

To use the cursor services, set the page number in BH to 0. If you want to set the cursor position, you can pass new coordinates to service 2 in (DH,DL). If you want to get the current position, service 3 will return it to you in the same way. We'll have the chance to set the cursor for ourselves later.

There is more to screen handling than just using the cursor. Besides working with the cursor, we can scroll the screen up or down (in OS/2, you can even scroll it sideways). This is done with services 6 and 7.

Services 6 and 7 — Scroll Active Page Up or Down

Set these things:

AH = 6 → Scroll up
 = 7 → Scroll down
AL = Number of lines to scroll (blank lines will be inserted). AL = 0 means blank the whole active window.
(CH,CL) = Row, column of upper left corner of scroll window.
(DH,DL) = Row, column of lower right corner of scroll window.
BH = Attribute to be used on blank line.

This is how scrolling is done in the PS/2 and PC. You can even scroll some small section of the screen independently, and it makes a startling effect. Here you set the scroll area's boundaries with (CH,CL), row, column of upper left corner of scroll window, and (DH,DL), row, column of lower right corner of scroll window. To scroll this window up, use INT 10H service 6. To scroll down, use service 7.

You can select the color of the new line yourself. This is our first introduction to color. To select the color in alphanumeric modes, you choose what is called the *attribute*.

Screen Attributes

The attribute is a one-byte long value that determines how the character you will be printing is printed. For example, you can select green characters on a blue background, or yellow characters on a red background.

When you set the attribute of the new line, every position in it is given the same attribute byte (even though there is no character there yet). This will determine what the characters that you print there will look like. That is, if you print new characters there, they will use the attribute already set for that line (it is also possible to set attributes character-by-character when printing, if you want to do it that way). An attribute byte is diagrammed in Figure 3-2.

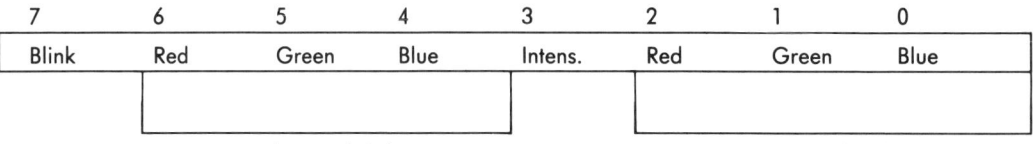

Figure 3-2. A Screen Attribute Byte

> **NOTE** Set bit to 1 to turn on that particular color.

One attribute byte is reserved for each position on the screen. By setting the attribute byte for a character, you can select the mix of red, green, and blue for both the foreground color (the color of the character) and the background color (the color of the rest of the screen). Also, you can set bit 3 for high intensity display, and bit 7 to make the character blink. A red foreground on a green background would have an attribute byte of 00100100B, or 24H, as shown in Figure 3-3.

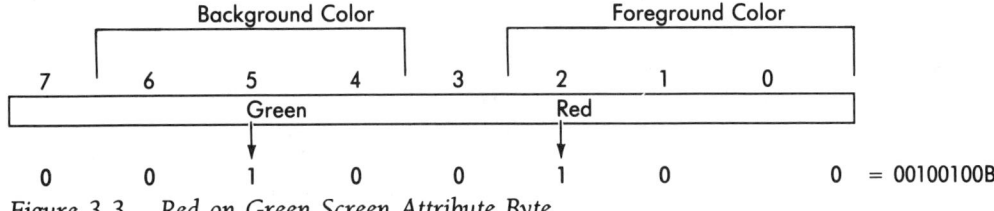

Figure 3-3. Red on Green Screen Attribute Byte

We will use the attribute byte character-by-character when we print out colored characters in service 9.

> **TIP** You can mix the colors in a screen attribute byte by adding the respective bit values together. Here are the bit values to add in forming your attribute byte:

Bit value	Color generated
1	Blue foreground
2	Green foreground
4	Red foreground
8	High intensity
16	Blue background
32	Green background
64	Red background
128	Blinking

For example, to get a normal setting of white on black, you would turn all the foreground colors (the letter itself) on this way: 1 + 2 + 4 = 7. If you wanted to make that high intensity, you would add 8 to give 15 = 0FH. If you wanted blinking reverse video in white, set all the background colors on, and add 128 to make it blink: 16 + 32 + 64 + 128 = 240 = 0F0H.

The Screen Buffer and Attribute Bytes

A character's ASCII and attribute bytes are stored in the screen buffer. This buffer, therefore, carries two bytes per character in alphanumeric modes. The bytes go like this: character, attribute, character, attribute, and so on. The first character in the buffer goes on the top left of the screen.

There are 25 lines (numbered 0 - 24) × 80 columns (numbered 0 -79) = 2,000 positions on the screen, so the screen buffer requires 4,000 bytes of memory (about 4K) to display a single alphanumeric page. In monochrome monitors, this memory starts at B000:0000, and in graphics monitors at B800:0000. For the EGA and VGA modes, this memory starts at A000:0000.

> **TIP** When the EGA or VGA is operating in a CGA mode, the video buffer starts at B800:0000, not A000:0000. In other words, in those modes, you should look for the video buffer there — not at A000:000. (The EGA or VGA does this to let it maintain compatibility with programs that address CGA memory directly.)

In graphics mode, things work similarly, but with pixels, not bits. In the CGA 320 × 200 mode, there are 320 × 200 = 64,000 pixels. In that mode, the CGA allows four colors, so each pixel needs two bits in memory; this means that the total CGA memory requirement will be 64,000 pixels × 2 bits/pixel / 8 bits/byte = 16,000 bytes. This is rounded up to 16K.

Say that we wanted to write directly to a monochrome adapter's (MDA) memory. We could use the DEBUG edit command like this:

```
A>DEBUG
-EB000:0000
B000:0000  20.  _
```

DEBUG will let us edit the byte at B000:0000, the first byte in the monochrome video buffer (use B800:0000 for a CGA or the CGA modes of the EGA or VGA). It tells us that this byte is currently a 20H = 32 = the ASCII space character. We can type our own value, which will appear directly after the "." — let's use ASCII 41H (= 65 = the ASCII "A" character):

```
A>DEBUG
-EB000:0000
B000:0000  20.41   - Type 41
```

Screen Handling   67

Follow this with a space, and DEBUG will skip on to the next byte, and the "A" will appear on the screen:

```
A>DEBUG
-EB000:0000
B000:0000  20.41   07.
-Q
```

This is the attribute byte of the first screen position. Let's change it from normal video (attribute 7) to blinking reverse video (attribute F0H), followed by a space bar, and then a <cr> to quit editing:

```
A>DEBUG
-EB000:0000
B000:0000  20.41   07.F0   20.  ← type a <cr>
-Q
```

This enters a flashing "A" on the screen, writing directly to the monochrome video buffer, as shown in Figure 3-4.

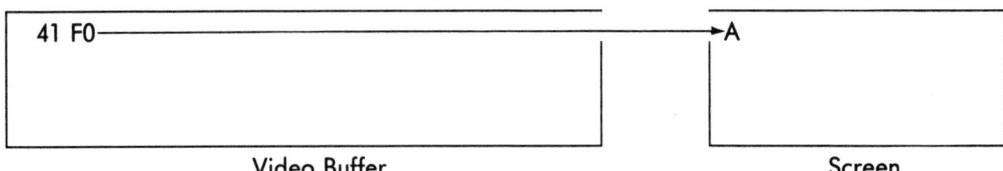

Figure 3-4.   *The Flashing A in the Video Buffer*

For each screen location, both an ASCII code and an attribute byte are stored. Writing directly to the buffer to change these values is the way professional word processors often work. We can write characters with attributes that we select using BIOS too, as we'll do now.

Service 9 — Write Attribute/Character at Cursor Position

Set these things:

AH = 9
AL = ASCII code of character to write.
BH = Page Number (usually 0)
BL = Character's attribute
CX = Number of times to write character (restricted to 1 line on screen)

68 ▶ Advanced Assembly Language

This is the way to type out colored characters on the screen. You can even type out multiple copies of the same character if you set CX to a value greater than one.

> **NOTE** When you are typing multiple copies of the same character, however, this service will not type more than one line — it doesn't add carriage return linefeeds.

One problem is that the cursor is not automatically moved to the next space after this call is done. It remains pointing at the just-typed character. If you want to use this service to type both characters and attributes, you will have to take care of the cursor yourself, which we'll do immediately in an example.

> **TIP** To use a BIOS service that will both type characters and advance the cursor, use service 0EH, "teletype write." However, service 0EH will not type attributes.

PRINT_IT.COM Prints All Possible Characters

Let's see an example named PRINT_IT.ASM to bring home the screen handling services we've been seeing. PRINT_IT prints all of the 256 ASCII characters that the PC or PS/2 is capable of displaying, and each one will have an attribute matching its ASCII code (0–255). This way we'll get a look at everything that the PC can type, and in color.

We start with the normal .COM file shell:

```
       .MODEL SMALL
       .CODE
       ORG      100H
ENTRY:
              :
              :
       INT      20H
       END      ENTRY
```

We will use LOOP to loop over all characters and attributes. First, we must set the loop index, CX, to 255. Also, INT 10H service 9, which prints out characters and attributes, requires the ASCII code in AL and the attribute in BL, as we just saw. Let's initialize them both to 0:

```
       .MODEL SMALL
       .CODE
       ORG      100H
```

▶ Screen Handling

```
ENTRY:   MOV    CX,255          ;Loop over all 255 combinations
         MOV    AL,0            ;Start with character 0
         MOV    BL,0            ;And attribute 0
         :
         :
         INT    20H
         END    ENTRY
```

Since this is a BIOS character printing service, we'll have to set the cursor ourselves. That is done with INT 10H service 2, which expects the new cursor row in DH and the column in DL. Let's start off at, say row 4 and column 0. We need to set DH and DL, and then we can enter our character printing loop:

```
            .MODEL SMALL
            .CODE
            ORG    100H
ENTRY:      MOV    CX,255          ;Loop over all 255 combinations
            MOV    AL,0            ;Start with character 0
            MOV    BL,0            ;And attribute 0
            MOV    DL,0            ;Start at column 0
            MOV    DH,4            ;And row 4
COLOR_LOOP:
            PUSH   AX
            MOV    AH,2            ;Set cursor
            INT    10H
            POP    AX
            :
            LOOP   COLOR_LOOP      ;Keep going
            INT    20H
            END    ENTRY
```

We also want to set the cursor position inside our loop since each time through the loop we will have to change it. Notice that, because we can't count on AX being returned from INT 10H safely, we have enclosed our call to INT 10H with PUSH AX and POP AX:

```
            .MODEL SMALL
            .CODE
            ORG    100H
ENTRY:      MOV    CX,255          ;Loop over all 255 combinations
            MOV    AL,0            ;Start with character 0
            MOV    BL,0            ;And attribute 0
            MOV    DL,0            ;Start at column 0
            MOV    DH,4            ;And row 4
COLOR_LOOP:
            PUSH   AX
            MOV    AH,2            ;Set cursor
            INT    10H
            POP    AX
            :
            LOOP   COLOR_LOOP      ;Keep going
            INT    20H
            END    ENTRY
```

70 ▶ Advanced Assembly Language

Now we're ready to print out the character, having set our position on the screen. We can use service 9:

→ AH = 9
  AL = ASCII code of character to write.
  BH = Page number (usually 0)
  BL = Character's attribute
  CX = Number of times to write character (restricted to 1 line on screen)

We've already loaded AL (ASCII code) and BL (attribute), so we just execute INT 10H, service 9. Service 9 also requests a character count in CX, which will be 1 for us. Since we are also using CX as a loop index, we will push it as well as AX before executing INT 10H, and restore it afterwards:

```
            .MODEL  SMALL
            .CODE
            ORG     100H
ENTRY:      MOV     CX,255          ;Loop over all 255 combinations
            MOV     AL,0            ;Start with character 0
            MOV     BL,0            ;And attribute 0
            MOV     DL,0            ;Start at column 0
            MOV     DH,4            ;And row 4
COLOR_LOOP:
            PUSH    AX
            MOV     AH,2            ;Set cursor
            INT     10H
            POP     AX
            MOV     AH,9            ;Now type character/attribute
            PUSH    AX
            PUSH    CX
            MOV     CX,1
            INT     10H
            POP     CX
            POP     AX
            :
            LOOP    COLOR_LOOP      ;Keep going
            INT     20H
            END     ENTRY
```

We've printed out our first character and attribute. Now we have to increment both the ASCII code (in AL) and the attribute (in BL) to prepare us for printing again:

```
            .MODEL  SMALL
            .CODE
            ORG     100H
```

▶ Screen Handling

```
ENTRY:     MOV     CX,255           ;Loop over all 255 combinations
           MOV     AL,0             ;Start with character 0
           MOV     BL,0             ;And attribute 0
           MOV     DL,0             ;Start at column 0
           MOV     DH,4             ;And row 4
COLOR_LOOP:
           PUSH    AX
           MOV     AH,2             ;Set cursor
           INT     10H
           POP     AX
           MOV     AH,9             ;Now type character/attribute
           PUSH    AX
           PUSH    CX
           MOV     CX,1
           INT     10H
           POP     CX
           POP     AX
           INC     AL               ;Select next character
           INC     BL               ;And next attribute
           :
           LOOP    COLOR_LOOP       ;Keep going
           INT     20H
           END     ENTRY
```

Also, of course, we have to prepare DH and DL with the new row and column number to set the cursor to. We just increase the column number. If we are at the end of the screen (compare DL to 79), then we reset the column number to zero (MOV DL,0), and increase the row, moving us down to the next line (INC DH). That completes the loop, and, with it, PRINT_IT.ASM. The complete program is in Listing 3-1. When you run it, you'll notice that, halfway through the display, the blinking bit (bit 7 in the attribute byte) gets set, so the second half of the display blinks.

Listing 3-1. PRINT_IT.COM — Prints All Character Combinations

```
           .MODEL  SMALL
           .CODE
           ORG     100H
ENTRY:     MOV     CX,255           ;Loop over all 255 combinations
           MOV     AL,0             ;Start with character 0
           MOV     BL,0             ;And attribute 0
           MOV     DL,0             ;Start at column 0
           MOV     DH,4             ;And row 4
COLOR_LOOP:
           PUSH    AX
           MOV     AH,2             ;Set cursor
           INT     10H
           POP     AX
           MOV     AH,9             ;Now type character/attribute
           PUSH    AX
           PUSH    CX
           MOV     CX,1
```

Listing 3-1. PRINT_IT.COM — Prints All Character Combinations

```
            INT     10H
            POP     CX
            POP     AX
            INC     AL              ;Select next character
            INC     BL              ;And next attribute
            INC     DL              ;Find new cursor column
            CMP     DL,79           ;Might have to go to next row
            JB      OK_CURSOR
            MOV     DL,0
            INC     DH              ;Go to next row
OK_CURSOR:
            LOOP    COLOR_LOOP      ;Keep going
            INT     20H
            END     ENTRY
```

What if we wanted to print on the screen but didn't want to have to set the attribute as well? For example, when we scroll a line with the scrolling services, we can set the attribute of the whole line. We might want to preserve those attributes when we print in that new line.

In that case, we could use INT 10H, service 0AH. Service 0AH is useful when you're printing on the screen and don't want to disturb the colors already there (which is often).

Service 0AH — Write Character Alone at Cursor Position

Set these things:

AH = 0AH
AL = ASCII code of character to write.
BH = Page number (usually 0).
CX = Number of times to write character (restricted to 1 line on screen).

This is the same as service 9, except that it uses does not change the attribute as it writes. In other words, if the character it is overwriting was red on blue, the new character will be red on blue also. And, like service 9, this service leaves the cursor pointing at the just-typed character instead of advancing it.

We'll get a chance to use this service in our pop-up program chapter, Chapter 7. There is one remaining character-handling service before we head into graphics, and that is service 0EH, the teletype write service. This service is the single BIOS printing service that *does* handle the cursor correctly.

> **TIP** Interrupt 10H services 9 and 0AH have an interesting property: they print out the ASCII characters below ASCII 32 as symbols, while service 0EH and all the DOS services interpret those characters as control characters (for example, ASCII 9 stands for a tab). If you want to use those symbols (including arrows and the card symbols like hearts or spades), use services 9 or 0AH.

Service 0EH — Teletype Write

Set these things:
AH = 0EH
AL = Character to write

This service types character more in the way you'd expect. Services 9 and 0AH type characters but do not advance the cursor past the last character typed.

Service 0EH both advances the cursor and treats carriage returns and line feeds as commands. However, this service will not print out attributes.

That's all the options: printing with attributes, printing without attributes, and printing with cursor advancement. That's also the end of our screen-handling (alphanumeric) work in INT 10H. Now let's turn from alphanumerics to graphics.

Graphics

Despite the rich number of colors now available to us, the actual BIOS programming support for drawing graphics is terrible. The graphics support in BIOS only allows you to write one dot (that is, pixel). This support is minimal, compared certainly to a machine like the Macintosh, which has built-in "Toolbox" routines (like QuickDraw) that can draw circles, lines, boxes, fill shapes, and so on — and quickly. However, we'll work through what's there, and then we'll add some power of our own by seeing how to set pixels in the CGA and EGA video buffer directly.

Before we do anything on the screen, however, we'll have to select what mode (that is, resolution and color options) the screen is running in; and that is done with INT 10H, service 0.

INT 10H Service 0 — Set Video Mode

Set these things:
AH = 0

74 ▶ Advanced Assembly Language

AL = New video mode

This is a big one. Here we will see all the modes possible on all the PS/2 and PC machines — how many colors they support and how many lines they use on the screen. Whenever you want to do graphics, you'll first have to set the mode to the desired resolution. After that has been done, it stays that way until it is set some other way. Setting the mode is usually done quite early in graphics programs.

To set the video mode for your particular screen (CGA, MDA, EGA, or VGA), put 0 in AH, and the new mode in AL. The possible modes are shown below.

The Possible Video Modes

Mode (in AL)	Display lines	Number of colors	Adapters	Maximum pages
0	40 × 25	B&W text	CGA, EGA, VGA	8
1	40 × 25	Color text	CGA, EGA, VGA	8
2	80 × 25	B&W text	CGA, EGA, VGA	4 (CGA) 8 (EGA, VGA)
3	80 × 25	Color text	CGA, EGA, VGA	4 (CGA) 8 (EGA, VGA)
4	320 × 200	4	CGA, EGA, VGA	1
5	320 × 200	B&W	CGA, EGA, VGA	1
6	640 × 200	2 (on or off)	CGA, EGA, VGA	1
7	80 × 25	Monochrome	MDA, EGA, VGA	1 (MDA) 8 (EGA, VGA)
8	160 × 200	16	PCjr	1
9	320 × 200	16	PCjr	1
A	640 × 200	1	PCjr	1
B	Reserved for future use.			
C	Reserved for future use.			
D	320 × 200	16	EGA, VGA	8
E	640 × 200	16	EGA, VGA	4
F	640 × 350	monochrome	EGA, VGA	2
10H	640 × 350	16	EGA, VGA	2
11H	640 × 480	2	VGA	1
12H	640 × 480	16	VGA	1
13H	320 × 200	256	VGA	1

▶ **Screen Handling** 75

Some of these modes are alphanumeric; that is, they are text modes that don't support graphics (modes 0–3, and 7). You can still use text as usual in graphics modes, however.

NOTE   In graphics modes, the cursor will not appear on the screen.

You can see how the modes are partitioned by adapter. Modes 0-6 are used on the CGA (and EGA and VGA, since they're compatible); mode 7 is for the monochrome display adapter, MDA (and EGA and VGA again since they can mimic the MDA); modes 8–0AH are for the PCjr; modes 0DH–10H are for the EGA and VGA (here the VGA is emulating the EGA for compatibility); and modes 11H–13H are just for the VGA (mode 13H is the 256 color one):

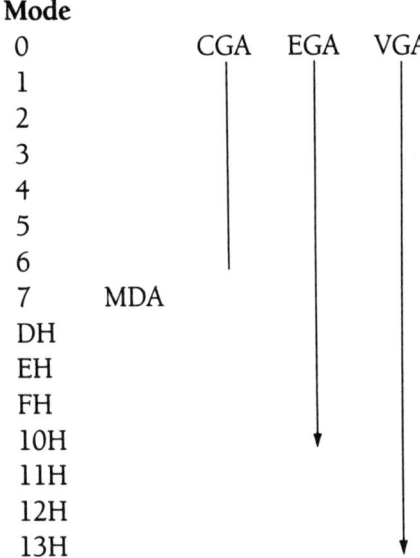

Black and White versus Color

The CGA can work with monitors that have all colors (color monitors) or black and white ones (B&W, often black and green on monitors without color). Its text modes are set up accordingly: modes 0 and 1 are the same, except that mode 0 is B&W, and mode 1 displays in color, modes 2 and 3 are B&W and color, respectively.

Next, come the CGA graphics modes: mode 4 is color, mode 5 is B&W, as indicated in the above list. In addition, in mode 6, pixels can only be on or off. Even though 2 colors are listed, one is black, the other white.

To set the screen the way you want it, just select from the listed modes, and use INT 10H, service 0. That's it. Now that we've set up the screen, let's see if we can't select some colors to use in the CGA modes.

Service 0BH — Set CGA Color Palette (Colors in CGA 320 × 200 mode ONLY)

Set these things:

AH = 0BH
BH = Palette color ID (0 or 1, see below).
BL = Color(s) to set with that Palette color ID (see below).

BH = 0
    BL = Background Color (0–31) From now on, this will be color value 0 to be used in Write and Read Dot. What colors 0–15 actually mean (blue, red, etc) is discussed below. Note that in alphanumeric modes, this background color will determine the screen border color (0–31; 16–31 means high intensity).

BH = 1
    BL = Palette to be used.
        BL = 0 Selects Green/Red/Yellow palette. Color value 1 in Write and Read Dot will be Green; color value 2 will be red, 3 will be yellow.
        BL = 1 Selects this palette and color values: Cyan (color value will be 1)/Magenta (2)/ White (3).

This is another big service. Here you set the four colors the CGA can draw (and the EGA and VGA when operating in the CGA modes) in its 320 × 200 resolution mode (medium resolution). The additional colors that the EGA or VGA can use are set by service 10H — service 0BH is only for the CGA compatibility screen modes.

There are actually three "modes" of resolution in the CGA — low, medium, and high. The number of pixels up and down (in the Y direction) is always the same — 200. The number in the across direction (the X direction) varies from 160 (low resolution), through 320 (medium resolution), to 640 (high resolution).

▶ **Screen Handling** 77

You can only display the maximum number of colors available (16) in low resolution mode. However, there is no support in the PC or PS/2's software, BIOS or DOS, for low resolution. The graphics video controller can be put in low resolution mode, though, so if you want to take the time, you can provide support yourself. As it is, we will concentrate here only on medium- and high-resolution graphics.

Palettes

In medium resolution graphics on the CGA (320 × 200), you can display four colors at any pixel, and in high resolution (640 × 200) only two — black and white (on and off). Here are the CGA's graphics modes:

Mode (in AL)	Display lines	Number of colors	Adapters	Maximum Pages
0	40 × 25	B&W text	CGA, EGA, VGA	8
1	40 × 25	Color text	CGA, EGA, VGA	8
2	80 × 25	B&W text	CGA, EGA, VGA	4 (CGA) 8 (EGA, VGA)
3	80 × 25	Color text	CGA, EGA, VGA	4 (CGA) 8 (EGA, VGA)
→ 4	320 × 200	4	CGA, EGA, VGA	1
→ 5	320 × 200	B&W	CGA, EGA, VGA	1
→ 6	640 × 200	2 (on or off)	CGA, EGA, VGA	1

⋮

Even the four colors of medium resolution are an illusion, however, because you are free to pick only one of the four; the other three (colors 1,2, and 3) can only be chosen by picking one of two *palettes*.

There are two CGA palettes: green, red, and yellow or cyan, magenta, and white. When you turn a pixel on with the write dot service, you also specify a color value (0, 1, 2, or 3) for it. The palette colors make up color values 1, 2, and 3 in order (the background color will make up color value 0).

Let's see this more clearly. To select which palette to use, use service 0BH.

78 ▶ Advanced Assembly Language

Set these things:
AH = 0BH
BH = Palette color ID (0 or 1, see below).
BL = Color(s) to set with that Palette color ID (see below).

BH = 0
  BL = Background Color (0–31). From now on, this will be color value 0 to be used in Write and Read Dot. What colors 0–15 actually mean (blue, red, etc) is discussed below. Note that in alphanumeric modes, this background color will determine the screen border color (0–31; 16–31 means high intensity).

→ BH = 1
  BL = Palette to be used
    BL = 0 Selects Green/Red/Yellow palette. Color value 1 in Write and Read Dot will be Green, color value 2 will be red, 3 will be yellow.
    BL = 1 Selects this palette and color values: Cyan (color value will be 1)/Magenta (2)/ White (3).

Set BH to 1, to indicate that you want to select a three-color palette. Then set BL to either 0 or 1, depending on which palette you want. (Palette 0 = green, red, yellow; palette 1 = cyan, magenta, white).

After you've selected the palette, you've selected colors 1–3 of the colors that will be used by the CGA. Whenever you write a dot on the screen, you can pass a color value that is 0–3 (when in 320 × 200 CGA resolution mode). For example, if you select palette 1, you can write cyan, magenta, or white dots on the screen. The write dot service that we will cover requires a color value for the dot. If you pass it color value 1 with this CGA palette, you will draw a cyan dot.

CGA Background Color

Color values 1–3 come from the palette, and color value 0 is the background color, which you can choose out of 16 choices.

▶ **Screen Handling** 79

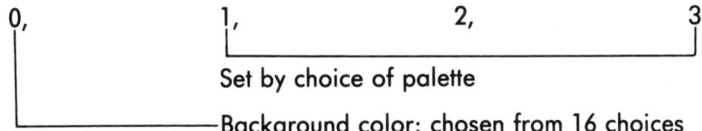

Figure 3-5. *CGA Possible Color Values*

To choose the color that will become color value 0, let's look at our list for this service again:

Set these things:

AH = 0BH
BH = Palette color ID (0 or 1, see below.)
BL = Color(s) to set with that Palette color ID (see below.)

→ BH = 0
BL = Background Color (0–31) From now on, this will be color value 0 to be used in Write and Read Dot. What colors 0–15 actually mean (blue, red, etc) is discussed below. Note that in alphanumeric modes, this background color will determine the screen border color (0–31; 16–31 means high intensity).
BH = 1
BL = Palette to be used
BL = 0 Selects Green/Red/Yellow Palette. Color, value 1 in Write and Read Dot will be Green; color value 2 will be red; 3 will be yellow.
BL = 1 Selects this palette and color values: Cyan (color value will be 1)/Magenta (2)/White (3).

First, set BH to 0 to inform this service that you want to select the CGA background color. Then put the background color number that you want in BL, and execute service 0BH. There are 32 possible colors to choose from — 16 colors and 16 more high intensity versions of the same colors. The colors available to fill BL with (add 16 to make the color high intensity) are shown below.

Colors Available (CGA modes)

Color number	Color
0	Black (off)
1	Blue
2	Green
3	Cyan (Green + Blue)
4	Red
5	Magenta (Red + Blue)
6	Brown
7	White
8	Black
9	Light Blue
10	Light Green
11	Light Cyan
12	Light Red
13	Light Magenta
14	Yellow
15	Light White

NOTE The colors above are also the default first 16 color numbers for the EGA and VGA.

In setting the background color, note that the whole background will no longer be black, but will become the color you've selected.

Let's summarize the CGA medium resolution mode. You select the color values 0–3 by selecting one of two palettes (which will be color values 1–3) and by selecting the background color to select color value 0. When you want to specify a color for a pixel on the screen, this color value (0–3) is what you pass to BIOS.

High-Resolution CGA Mode

In high-resolution CGA mode, 640 × 200 pixels (mode 6), you cannot choose four colors but only two: on or off, 0 or 1. With the amount of memory available to it, the CGA can only save one bit per pixel in this higher resolution mode (i.e., 320 × 200 vs. 640 × 200). Since there are 200 lines down (on graphics monitors characters are 8 scan lines high, and 8 × 25 lines = 200) and 640 lines across, there are 640 × 200 =

128,000 bits needed. This makes 16,000 bytes, rounded up in the CGA's video buffer to 16K.

In medium resolution, 320 × 200, we can specify one of four colors for each pixel, so we need two bits to hold the possible values for each pixel. Since there are only half as many pixels (320 across versus 640 across), we still use the same size video buffer, 16K.

Now we've set the screen mode and selected our colors. It's time to draw on the screen.

Service 0CH — Write Dot

Set these things:

AH = 0CH
DX = Row number (0–199, 0–349, 0–479)
CX = Column number (0–319 or 0–639)
AX = Color value
BH = Page number (0 based) for multi-paged graphics modes.

Here it is: assembly language graphics on the PS/2 and PC. To set a pixel anywhere on any screen (if you've set the mode, service 0, correctly), use Write Dot. Set DX = Row number (0–199, 0–349, 0–479), and CX = Column number (0–319 or 0–639). (0,0) is at the top left of the screen. (See Figure 3-1.)

The big issue in the write dot service is the line AX = Color Value because the color value has three different interpretations under the three different graphics standards: CGA, EGA, and VGA.

The color value can range from 0–3 in CGA modes (but only 0–1 in high CGA resolution, 640 × 200), 0–15 in EGA modes, and 0–255 in the VGA 256 color mode (mode 13H). In CGA modes, these color values are set with service 0BH; in EGA and VGA modes with service 10H. Once the color values are set, you can draw anywhere on the screen with this service. That's what it's designed for. Later on, we'll examine how to do this same thing ourselves by writing directly to the video buffer. Right now let's move on to the EGA services.

The EGA

The EGA has two levels of intensity for each of the three primary colors: red, green, and blue. There are both low intensity (we will refer to those levels as r, g, b) and medium intensity (R, G, B). When they are both on at some pixel location, the result is

82 ▶ Advanced Assembly Language

high intensity (like r + R). When they are both off, the result is nothing. Thus there are four levels of *combined intensity* for each of the three colors. In the case of pure red, the levels would be: off = 0, low = r, medium = R, and high = r + R.

Using both low and medium intensity at the same time, we can fill six bits — rgbRGB — to create a color. With these six bits, we can specify values from 0 to 63 — and this is where the 64 choices of the EGA come from. You can set the 16 palette colors (color values 0 – 15) from among these 64 possibilities in any 16-color mode.

When the PC is turned on, default EGA color values are set in the EGA palette, and they may be good enough for most purposes. The color values (given to the write dot service), colors, and rgbRGB settings for the default colors are shown below.

EGA Colors and rgbRGB Values

Color value	Color	rgbRGB
0	Black	000000
1	Blue	000001
2	Green	000010
3	Cyan	000011
4	Red	000100
5	Magenta	000101
6	Brown	010100
7	White	000111
8	Dark gray	111000
9	Light blue	111001
10	Light green	111010
11	Light cyan	111011
12	Light red	111100
13	Light magenta	111101
14	Yellow	111110
15	Intense white	111111

This means that if you select a color value of 3 and pass that on to the write dot service in a 16-color EGA or VGA mode, a cyan dot will appear (unless you change the defaults).

You can make up your own colors for the EGA by selecting which of the six bits you want on in each palette register. Palette registers go from 0 to 15 — one for each color value. To specify a color to use for a particular color value, you can fill the palette registers with the appropriate rgbRGB number (0–63).

▶ **Screen Handling** 83

Say you load a value of 000011B = 3 (cyan) into palette register 5. From then on, when you ask for color value 5 in 16 color modes, rgbRGB will be set to 000011B, or 3, and you'll get cyan. Let's jump in and see how to set one of the EGA palette registers ourselves.

The Service 10H Functions

All the EGA and VGA services use INT 10H, service 10H to set colors. The way you distinguish between EGA and VGA services is with the setting in AL. In this first service, where we will set an EGA palette register, AL is 0. This is also referred to as INT 10H, service 10H, function 0.

Service 10H Function 0 — Set Individual EGA Palette Register (Set 1 of 16 Colors for 16-Color Mode)

```
              Set these things:
        AH = 10H
        AL = 0
        BL = EGA Palette register to set (0–15)
        BH = rgbRGB value to set it to (0–63)
```

Here's where you set any of the 16 color values in the EGA palette. You can assign a particular rgbRGB setting to any of the EGA palette registers:

```
                        10H → AH
                          0 → AL
         Color value to change (0–15) → BL
    rgbRGB value to change it to (0–63) → BH
```

To do that, select an rgbRGB setting in six bits, and put it into BH. Select a palette register (which is the same as the color value, the number that write dot will see) from 0 to 15, and put it into BL. Then use this function and, congratulations, you've just installed a color for use by your program.

For example, color value 5 is magenta under the default settings. Let's change that to cyan, rgbRGB = 000011B = 3. In other words, we want to change palette register 5 to use an rgbRGB setting of 3:

84 ▶ Advanced Assembly Language

$$10H \rightarrow AH$$
$$0 \rightarrow AL$$
$$\text{Palette register } 5 \rightarrow BL$$
$$\text{New rgbRGB setting } 3 \rightarrow BH$$

In code it looks like this:

```
→ MOV    AH,10H    ;Use INT 10H service 10H
  MOV    AL,0      ;Function 0
  MOV    BL,5      ;Change palette register 5
  MOV    BH,3      ;To rgbRGB = 3, cyan
  INT    10H
```

From now on, when you pass color value 5 to write dot, you'll get cyan instead of magenta. That's it for the EGA palette.

NOTE Every time the mode is reset, the palette colors return to the default setting.

The EGA palette can set the colors used in 16-color modes whether you're using an EGA or VGA. By setting this palette, you can select from 64 choices. If you're really using a VGA, however, you might want to select these 16 colors from among its 256K choices instead. Or you might want to use its 256-color mode (mode 13H). Let's take some time to scrutinize these possibilities.

The VGA

The VGA is different from other displays in that it is an *analog display*. Internally, this means that the VGA has what is called a Digital to Analog Converter (DAC) to help in selecting color.

The DAC has 256 registers, and they can act like the palette registers we've just seen. This is quite an enhancement over the 16 palette registers. Here, color values can go from 0 to 255. In each of the 256 DAC registers there is an 18-bit number, so DAC registers can hold numbers ranging up to 256K. In other words, if you use the DAC registers to set colors, you have a choice of up to 256K colors to work with.

From CGA to EGA to VGA

In CGA modes, you select the background color and choose from one of two palettes for a total of four colors. Color values range from 0 to 3.

▶ **Screen Handling** 85

	Color value
Background color (0–15) →	0
→	1
Choosing 1 of 2 palettes sets all these →	2
→	3

In EGA modes, you can select up to 16 colors using the EGA palette. These numbers (0–15) become the color values you can pass to write dot. Each color can be selected individually as a six-bit rgbRGB setting; to set color value 2 we'd load palette register 2:

	Color value
	0
	1
rgbRGB →	2
	3
	:

In any VGA 16-color mode, you can also set the colors using the EGA palette registers, just as with the EGA. When you set a palette register, you are setting that color value (0–15) from a six-bit selection (rgbRGB), giving you 64 possibilities.

On the other hand, in 16-color modes, the VGA is really using the first 16 DAC registers (since it's a VGA, it always uses the DAC registers). These first 16 DAC registers correspond to the 16 available color values. If you set a color in an EGA palette register while using a VGA, your rgbRGB setting will be translated into an 18-bit setting for the corresponding DAC register. Setting color value 2 looks like this:

	Color value
	0
	1
rgbRGB → 18-bit DAC setting →	2
	3
	:

This means that you can set the 16 colors of a VGA either by changing the EGA palette, where you can select from among 64 rgbRGB possibilities, or by changing a DAC register directly, where you can use 18-bit numbers — giving you a choice of 256K colors.

86 ▶ Advanced Assembly Language

                                Color value
                                    0
                                    1
18-bit DAC setting →   2
                                    3
                                    :

> **NOTE** The default for the VGA is using the first 16 DAC registers as the first 16 color values — you can select which set of DAC registers to use by selecting *color pages,* which we will not do here.

For example, if you wanted to change color value 5 from its default of magenta in the VGA, you could do it by setting palette register 5 to another of the 64 possible colors (we've used cyan before). Your rgbRGB setting would then be translated into an 18-bit number for DAC register 5.

Or you could set this DAC register directly, by putting a new 18-bit number in DAC register 5. With 18 bits to work with, you can specify 256K colors this way. To be able to change a DAC value like that, we've got to be able to decode the 18-bit DAC numbers, which we'll do next.

Using the DAC Registers in the VGA

The way 18 bits are used in a DAC register is as follows: the first six bits give the intensity of the red in this color, the next six bits the intensity of the green, and the last six bits the intensity of the blue. This means that you can always design new DAC colors for yourself.

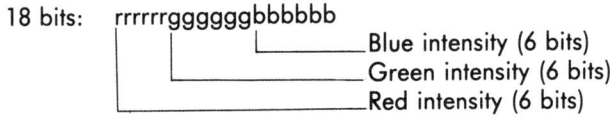

Figure 3-6. *DAC Register*

Let's see how to set one of these DAC registers ourselves. We will use service 10H, with AL = 10H. (That makes this INT 10H, service 10H, function 10H.)

Service 10H Function 10H — Set DAC Register (Set 1 of 255 VGA Colors)

        Set these things:
        AH = 10H

▶ **Screen Handling** 87

    AL = 10H
    BX = register to set (0 – 255)
    CH = Green intensity
    CL = Blue intensity
    DH = Red intensity

Here's where we select 1 of the 16 or 256 colors (depending on the screen mode) that the VGA can display from 256K possible choices. Decide on the relative intensities of the green, blue, and red you want in your color, convert them into six-bit arguments, and place them in their respective registers:

    CH ← Green intensity
    CL ← Blue intensity
    DH ← Red intensity

Then execute this service, and you've set a color for use by the VGA.

The default setting of the first 16 DAC registers give the same colors as the default colors of the EGA (although they use 18 bits and the EGA palette uses six, the DAC values are set to closely match the EGA colors). But we can change that. Let's work through our earlier example and say that we wanted to change DAC register 5 from its default setting (magenta) to an intense green (green value = 00111110B). Here's how we would do that:

```
→ MOV    AH,10H         ;Select service 10H
  MOV    AL,10H         ;Select subservice 10H
  MOV    BX,5           ;Select DAC register to change
  MOV    CH,00111110B   ;Select new green value
  MOV    CL,0           ;Set new red and blue values to 0
  MOV    DH,0
  INT    10H
```

Now, DAC register 5 has become green. When we pass a color value of 5 to the write dot service in a VGA mode, green will appear. Besides 16-color modes, the VGA can handle 256-color modes. Let's look at what makes them different.

VGA 16-color Modes

As we've seen, in 16-color modes on the VGA, you can select colors in two ways. The first way is simply by loading one of the possible EGA colors — rgbRGB (0 – 63) — into the register of the EGA palette. What this really does is to set the corresponding DAC register to that color. In other words, your rgbRGB setting gets translated into an 18-bit DAC register value, and it's stored in the corresponding DAC register.

$$\text{rgbRGB} \rightarrow \text{rrrrrrggggggbbbbbb} \rightarrow \begin{array}{c} \textbf{Color value} \\ 0 \\ 1 \\ 2 \\ 3 \\ \vdots \end{array}$$

The second way is by changing one of the first 16 DAC register contents directly:

$$\text{rrrrrrggggggbbbbbb} \rightarrow \begin{array}{c} \textbf{Color value} \\ 0 \\ 1 \\ 2 \\ 3 \\ \vdots \end{array}$$

NOTE In 16-color modes in the VGA, the first 16 DAC register numbers and the color values are all the same things.

TIP If you have a VGA, it's better to change colors in the VGA palette directly. If you set colors using the EGA palette, you can choose from only 64 choices, while if you change one of the DAC registers (which are what really hold the color settings anyway), you can select from 256K choices.

VGA-only 256-color Mode

In 256-color VGA mode, you can make up colors by selecting red, green, and blue values (six bits each) and putting your values into any of the DAC registers. As usual, the DAC register number is the color value (now 0 – 255) you will pass to write dot. Only the first 64 DAC registers are initalized with default values. In fact, you may even want to stick to the first 16 default color values, which are the same as the EGA ones.

What Monitor Is in Use With the vast number of services available through BIOS INT 10H, it's often hard to know which ones you can use — will my program have to use a CGA, MDA, EGA, or VGA? For this reason, an identification service was

▶ Screen Handling   89

developed, which reports on what advanced video equipment is in use. This is service 1AH of INT 10H.

Service 1AH — Determine Video Equipment

Set these things:

AH = 1AH
AL = 0

Returns:
AL = 1AH → This function is supported.
If supported, BL = Display code (see below).

Display codes

0	No display
1	MDA
2	CGA
4	EGA with standard color
5	EGA with monochrome display
6	PGA (professional Graphics Adapter)
7	VGA with analog monochrome display
8	VGA with analog color display

This service is used to determine what video monitor a PC has attached to it. This is the way IBM itself suggests you determine what monitor will be in use. First, execute an INT 10H Service 1AH with AL = 0 (i.e. service 1AH, function 0). If, when the function returns, AL = 1AH, then this equipment determination service is supported. The *display code* will be in BL (see Figure 3-7, below).

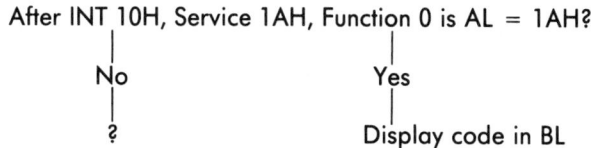

Figure 3-7.

You can determine the type of display below.

Display Codes

0	No display
1	MDA (monochrome display adapter)

90 ▶ Advanced Assembly Language

2	CGA (color graphics display adapter)
4	EGA with standard color
5	EGA with monochrome display
6	PGA (professional Graphics Adapter)
7	VGA with analog monochrome display
8	VGA with analog color display

If AL does not return 1AH, then this service is not supported. In that case, the display options remaining are EGA, CGA, and MDA.

There is a special way to check for an EGA. Execute INT 10H, service 12H, with BL set to 10H. If, on return, BL is not equal to 10H, then an EGA is present. This is the "return EGA information" function of service 12H:

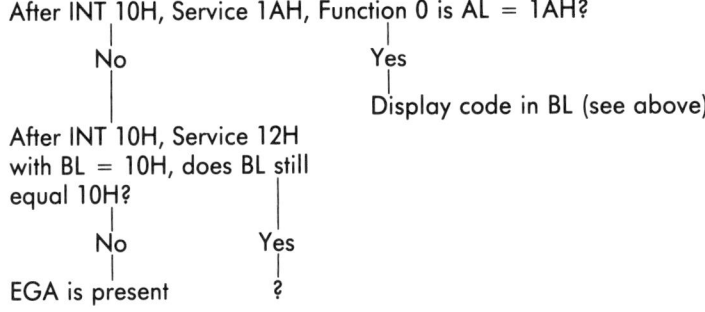

Figure 3-8.

If BL does equal 10H, then there is no EGA. The only two choices you have left are CGA and MDA modes. Let's say that BL equals 10H; that is, an EGA is not present. Then there is one last step to determine which monitor is present. You have to use the Read Mode service, INT 10H service 0FH (video modes 0–6 will be CGA, and video mode 7 will be MDA).

Service 0FH Read Current Video State

Set these things:

AH = 0FH

Returns:

→ AL = Current Mode (see service 00 for a description of modes)
AH = number of character columns on the screen.
BH = current active page (0 based)

▶ Screen Handling 91

If this service returns a mode (in AL) or 0 – 6, you're working with a CGA (if you've already made sure that there's no EGA or VGA). If it returns a mode of 7, you're working with a monochrome display adapter, the MDA:

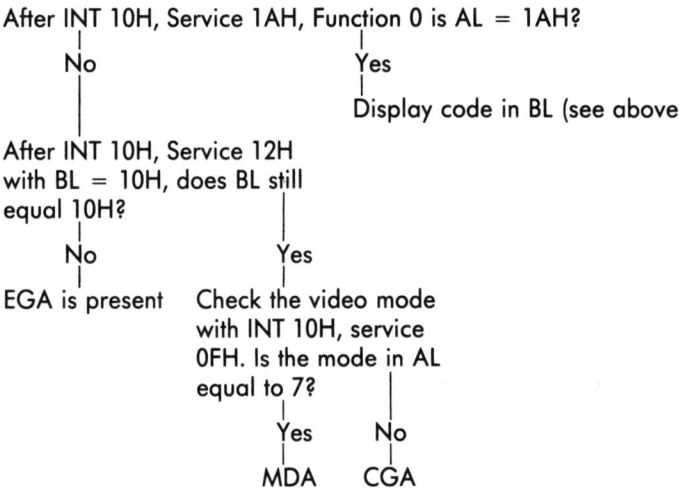

Figure 3-9.

It's a lot of work to make out what display is being used.

Writing Graphics Images Directly in Memory

Now let's put the "advanced" into our assembly language coverage by working with the video buffer directly in graphics mode. We've seen that we can deposit characters in the buffer directly in alphanumeric modes simply by moving them to the right memory location. Now let's do the same for graphics; we'll start off with CGA modes and work up to EGA/VGA modes.

Writing to the Buffer in CGA Modes

In high-resolution CGA mode, 640 × 200 pixels, you can choose only on or off, 0 or 1. The PC only needs to save one bit per pixel in this case. Since there are 200 lines down (on graphics monitors characters are 8 scan lines high, and 8 × 25 lines = 200) and 640 lines across, there are 640 × 200 = 128,000 bits needed. This makes 16,000 bytes, rounded up in the PC's graphics video buffer to 16K.

In medium CGA mode, 320 × 200, we can specify one of four colors for each pixel, so we need two bits to hold the possible values for each pixel. Since there are only half as many pixels (320 across versus 640 across), we still use the same size video buffer, 16K.

In high-resolution CGA mode, it seems natural that if you wanted to turn the pixel on at location (0,0), the top left corner of the screen, you would set the first bit in the video buffer to 1. That is actually how it works. To turn the next pixel in the top row (row 0) on, you would set the next bit to 1 and so forth to the end of the first line on the screen, the first 640 pixels (numbers 0–639).

It also seems natural that if you wanted to turn on the first pixel of the second row (row 1), you would set bit 640 in the video buffer to 1, since the first line goes from 0 to 639. Unfortunately, that is not how it works.

The CGA video buffer is separated into two blocks of 8K each. The first block, starting at location B800:0000, holds the even scan lines on the screen; the second block, starting at B800:2000, holds the odd scan lines. This is done because the video controller scans over all the even lines on the screen first, and then does all the odd ones. To facilitate its operation, we must give it the bits in the order needed. This is an added complication for any program; now it has to split up its image between two blocks in memory as shown in Figure 3-10 (below).

> **NOTE** In practice this is not very hard if you have a subroutine to put pixels on the screen that keeps track of which block they go into, or if you use INT 10H, Service 0CH, Write Dot.

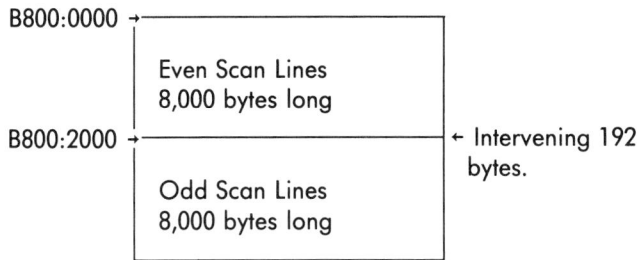

Figure 3-10. CGA Memory Blocks

The scheme in medium resolution is similar, but here there can be four colors, not just two. Four colors demand two bits, so every two bits in the screen buffer can be grouped together into one pixel. Since there are only one-half as many pixels on a line, but twice as many bits per pixel, there are the same number of memory bits corresponding to each screen line, 640. Now let's put this to work.

CGA_PIXEL.COM — Direct CGA Buffer Use

Let's write a small program, CGA_PIXEL, that will turn pixels on in high-resolution CGA mode (640 × 200). CGA_PIXEL will be about three times as fast as the equivalent BIOS service call (Write Dot). CGA_PIXEL's first job is to determine whether the pixel is to be put in an even or odd row. The pixel's coordinates are given to CGA_PIXEL in DX (= row, 0–199) and CX (= column, 0–639). We have to check if DX is odd or even because the first 8K of the screen buffer holds lines 0,2,4,6,8, etc.; the second 8K holds lines 1,3,5,7,9, and so forth. CGA memory block locations are shown below.

CGA Memory Block Locations

Screen row #	1st or 2nd 8K	Line inside 8K Block
0	1	0
1	2	0
2	1	1
3	2	1
4	1	2

For each even screen line, there is a row of 640 bits in the first 8K block, and for each odd line, a row of 640 bits in the second 8K block. To find which line of 640 bits a particular pixel is in, just divide the row number by two and disregard the remainder (see above). This is the same as shifting to the right. Since we have to check the low bit of DX (the block number) anyway, we can shift that bit into the carry bit and do this with JNC:

```
CGA_PIXEL       PROC    NEAR
                ;SUPPLY DX=ROW,CX=COLUMN. ASSUMES ES=B800H
                XOR     BX,BX
      →         SHR     DX,1
      →         JNC     CALC
      →         ADD     BX,8*1024
CALC:           MOV     AX,DX           ;GET 80*DX       →
```

DS:[BX] will be used to point to the byte in the screen buffer we have to change. If the pixel is in an odd row, we just add 8K to BX so it points to the second 8K block.

These commands both check which block the pixel is in and set DX to that pixel's row of 640 bits. To find what offset from the beginning of the 8K block that makes in bytes, we have to multiply the number in DX by 640 bits/8 bits per byte = 80 bytes per row on the screen. Multiplying DX by 80 will give us the byte offset of the pixel's line from the beginning of its block. Here's our multiplication:

94 ▶ Advanced Assembly Language

```
CGA_PIXEL         PROC    NEAR
                  ;SUPPLY DX=ROW,CX=COLUMN. ASSUMES ES=B800H and screen in High
                  ; Resolution mode (Use BIOS INT 10H Service 0).
                  XOR     BX,BX
                  SHR     DX,1
                  JNC     CALC
                  ADD     BX,8*1024
CALC:             MOV     AX,DX           ;GET 80*DX
                  SHL     DX,1
                  SHL     DX,1
                  ADD     DX,AX
                  MOV     AX,CX
                  MOV     CL,4
                  SHL     DX,CL           ;DX NOW MULTIPLIED BY 80 (16*5)
                  ADD     BX,DX           ;ADD TO INDEX
```

> **TIP** The 80×86 has a multiply command, but it is very slow. You should try to avoid using it when speed is important, as it is in graphics. Programmers usually cobble their own multiplication out of left shifts and additions. To multiply by 80 (= 5 × 16), we multiply the value by 4, add the value to it again to make five times, and then multiply by 16. (Multiplying by powers of two, of course, is done by shifting to the left.)

DX now holds the byte offset, inside the 8K block, of the line in which our pixel lies. What we've done so far is find the correct row, as shown in Figure 3-11.

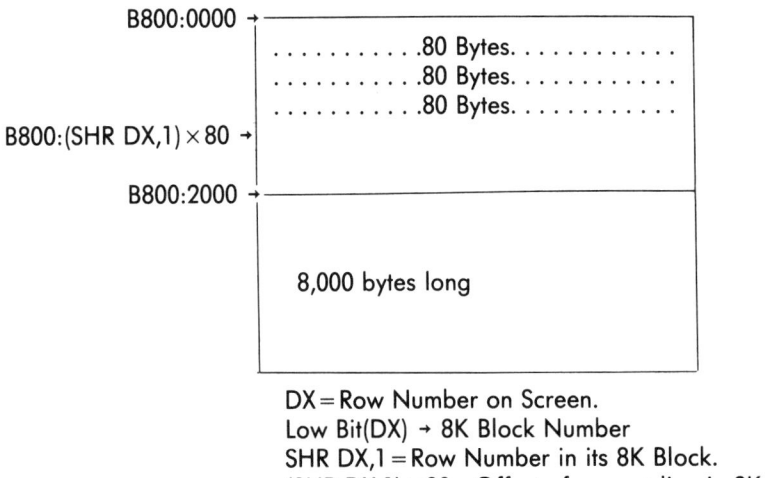

DX = Row Number on Screen.
Low Bit(DX) → 8K Block Number
SHR DX,1 = Row Number in its 8K Block.
(SHR DX,1) × 80 = Offset of correct line in 8K Block.

Figure 3-11. Location of B800:(SHR DX,1) × 80 in the CGA Buffer

To point to the correct line in the buffer that holds the pixel we want to change with [BX], we add (SHR DX,1) × 80 to BX. Once we're in the right row, we still have to find which byte to work on, and that depends on the column required, (0–639). Since each

Screen Handling 95

of these 640 places is a bit, to find the correct byte, we have to divide CX by 8 and add that to BX. This process is shown in Figure 3-12. And here's the code:

```
CGA_PIXEL       PROC    NEAR
        ;SUPPLY DX=ROW,CX=COLUMN. ASSUMES ES=B800H and screen in High
        ; Resolution mode (Use BIOS INT 10H Service 0).
        XOR     BX,BX
        SHR     DX,1
        JNC     CALC
        ADD     BX,8*1024
CALC:   MOV     AX,DX                   ;GET 80*DX
        SHL     DX,1
        SHL     DX,1
        ADD     DX,AX
        MOV     AX,CX
        MOV     CL,4
        SHL     DX,CL                   ;DX NOW MULTIPLIED BY 80 (16*5)
        ADD     BX,DX                   ;ADD TO INDEX
    *   MOV     DX,AX
        AND     DX,7                    ;GET X3 INTO DX
    *   MOV     CL,3
    *   SHR     AX,CL                   ;CX/8
    *   ADD     BX,AX                   ;FIND BYTE ALONG ROW
```

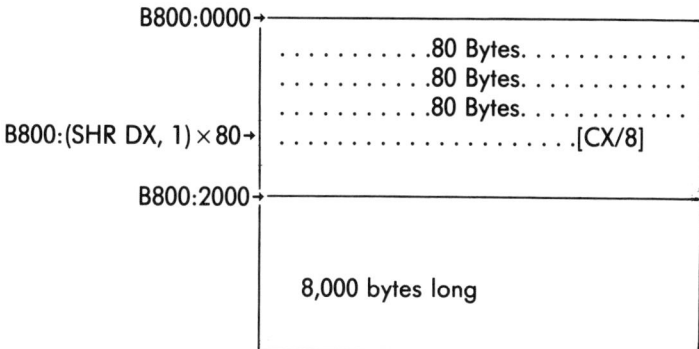

Figure 3-12. *Locating the Pixel in the CGA Buffer*

At the same time, we have to calculate which bit in that byte to turn on. If CX (which can range from 0 to 639) was 0, we would want to turn on the left-most bit of the 0th byte of that line, bit 7. In general, the bit we want to turn on is 7 - (CX Mod 8), where CX Mod 8 is the remainder of dividing CX by 8. CX Mod 8 is just AND CX,7, so we end up with these instructions:

```
CGA_PIXEL       PROC    NEAR
        ;SUPPLY DX=ROW,CX=COLUMN. ASSUMES ES=B800H and screen in High
        ; Resolution mode (Use BIOS INT 10H Service 0).
        XOR     BX,BX
        SHR     DX,1
        JNC     CALC
        ADD     BX,8*1024
```

96 ▶ Advanced Assembly Language

```
CALC:       MOV     AX,DX           ;GET 80*DX
            SHL     DX,1
            SHL     DX,1
            ADD     DX,AX
            MOV     AX,CX
            MOV     CL,4
            SHL     DX,CL           ;DX NOW MULTIPLIED BY 80 (16*5)
            ADD     BX,DX           ;ADD TO INDEX
            MOV     DX,AX
         *  AND     DX,7            ;GET X3 INTO DX
            MOV     CL,3
            SHR     AX,CL           ;CX/8
            ADD     BX,AX           ;FIND BYTE ALONG ROW
         *  NEG     DL
         *  ADD     DL,7
         *  MOV     CL,DL           ;GET BIT TO TURN ON
            MOV     AL,1
            SHL     AL,CL
            :
CGA_PIXEL   ENDP
```

At the end, we put a 1 into AL and shift it DL (= 7 − AND(CL,7)) times, and then we're ready to OR the result with whatever byte is in the screen buffer at location . And that will turn the pixel on. However, if we're dealing with a true CGA, not just an EGA or VGA in CGA mode, there is one more thing to consider.

Screen Flicker   There is one more point to be made concerning screen handling. If you simply put characters into the CGA's screen buffer (B800:0000), screen flicker (or snow) will result. (There is no similar problem on the MDA, EGA, or VGA.) For the purposes of this example program, let's assume we're dealing with a true CGA.

Snow can be avoided easily enough if we do what BIOS does. Before putting a character into the buffer, you must check the status port on the CGA video controller. You should only put characters into the screen buffer when a screen retrace is beginning. This occurs when a particular signal goes low.

The graphics video controller's status port is at I/O address 03DAH, and the monochrome video controller port is at 03BAH. We set up a constant named STATUS_PORT and use it in CGA_PIXEL like this:

```
            STATUS_PORT EQU 03DAH

CGA_PIXEL       PROC    NEAR
            ;SUPPLY DX=ROW,CX=COLUMN. ASSUMES ES=B800H and screen in High
            ; Resolution mode (Use BIOS INT 10H Service 0).
            XOR     BX,BX
            SHR     DX,1
            JNC     CALC
            ADD     BX,8*1024
CALC:       MOV     AX,DX           ;GET 80*DX
```

```
            SHL     DX,1
            SHL     DX,1
            ADD     DX,AX
            MOV     AX,CX
            MOV     CL,4
            SHL     DX,CL           ;DX NOW MULTIPLIED BY 80 (16*5)
            ADD     BX,DX           ;ADD TO INDEX
            MOV     DX,AX
            AND     DX,7            ;GET X3 INTO DX
            MOV     CL,3
            SHR     AX,CL           ;CX/8
            ADD     BX,AX           ;FIND BYTE ALONG ROW
            NEG     DL
            ADD     DL,7
            MOV     CL,DL           ;GET BIT TO TURN ON
            MOV     AL,1
            SHL     AL,CL
            MOV     DX,STATUS_PORT  ;Get ready to read video controller status
P_WAIT_LOW:                         ;Start waiting for a new horizontal scan -
            IN      CL,DX           ;Make sure the video controller scan status
            TEST    CL,1            ;is low
            JNZ     P_WAIT_LOW
P_WAIT_HIGH:                        ;After port has gone low, it must go high
            IN      CL,DX           ;before it is safe to write directly to
            TEST    CL,1            ;the screen buffer in memory
            JZ      P_WAIT_HIGH
            :
            [Put new byte in screen buffer.]
            :
CGA_PIXEL   ENDP
```

The top loop, P_WAIT_LOW, makes sure the signal is low. The next loop, P_WAIT_HIGH, loops while the signal is high. Immediately after becoming low, the falling edge, we put our character into the buffer. The whole program CGA_PIXEL is shown in Listing 3-1.

Listing 3-1. CGA_PIXEL.COM — Turns a CGA Pixel On.

```
            STATUS_PORT EQU 03DAH

CGA_PIXEL   PROC    NEAR
            ;SUPPLY DX=ROW,CX=COLUMN. ASSUMES ES=B800H and screen in High
            ; Resolution mode (Use BIOS INT 10H Service 0).
            XOR     BX,BX
            SHR     DX,1
            JNC     CALC
            ADD     BX,8*1024
CALC:       MOV     AX,DX           ;GET 80*DX
            SHL     DX,1
            SHL     DX,1
            ADD     DX,AX
            MOV     AX,CX
            MOV     CL,4
            SHL     DX,CL           ;DX NOW MULTIPLIED BY 80 (16*5)
            ADD     BX,DX           ;ADD TO INDEX
            MOV     DX,AX
            AND     DX,7            ;GET X3 INTO DX
```

Listing 3-1. CGA_PIXEL.COM — Turns a CGA Pixel On.

```
        MOV     CL,3
        SHR     AX,CL           ;CX/8
        ADD     BX,AX           ;FIND BYTE ALONG ROW
        NEG     DL
        ADD     DL,7
        MOV     CL,DL           ;GET BIT TO TURN ON
        MOV     AL,1
        SHL     AL,CL
        MOV     DX,STATUS_PORT  ;Get ready to read video controller status
P_WAIT_LOW:                     ;Start waiting for a new horizontal scan -
        IN      CL,DX           ;Make sure the video controller scan status
        TEST    CL,1            ;is low
        JNZ     P_WAIT_LOW
P_WAIT_HIGH:                    ;After port has gone low, it must go high
        IN      CL,DX           ;before it is safe to write directly to
        TEST    CL,1            ;the screen buffer in memory
        JZ      P_WAIT_HIGH
→       OR      ES:[BX],AL      ;Move to screen.
→       RET
CGA_PIXEL       ENDP
```

If snow on the screen is ever a problem when you are working with a graphics screen, you can use this simple technique to eliminate it. It will slow down your screen-handling abilities somewhat, but not noticeably unless you are working with the entire screen.

And that's it for CGA_PIXEL. With it, we've seen how to manipulate data in the CGA video buffer directly. Now let's turn to the EGA and VGA.

Writing to the EGA/VGA Buffer

The EGA and VGA work quite differently from the CGA (in non-CGA modes, that is). For example, let's see how to set pixels on the screen in 16-color EGA or VGA modes.

EGA/VGA Bit Planes

Here, color values can range from 0 to 15, which means that the color value is a four-bit number. Each of those bits goes to one of four *bit planes* that make up the EGA/VGA memory in 16-color modes. The first bit plane gets bit 0 of the color value, the second gets bit 1, and so on up to 3.

For example, when you start up an EGA or VGA, the default color scheme means that color value 1 is blue, color 2 is green, and color 4 is red. To make a pixel on the screen blue, we want to give it a color value of 1, which means that we set its bit on plane 0 to

1 and leave the others 0. To make a pixel green, color value 2 (0010B), we set the matching bit on plane 1 to 1 and leave the others 0:

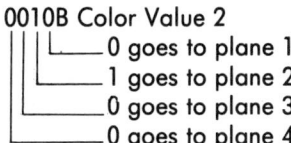

Figure 3-13.

To make a pixel red, color value 4 (0100B), we set its bit on plane 3 and leave the others 0. To make a combination color, such as cyan, color value 3 (0011B), we set that pixel's bit on planes 1 and 2 (since bits 1 and 2 are set in the color value, 0011B):

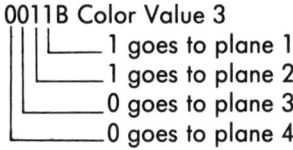

Figure 3-14.

Now let's translate that into code by writing a procedure called EGA_PIXEL, the EGA and VGA 16-color mode equivalent of CGA_PIXEL.

EGA_PIXEL.COM — Direct EGA Buffer Use

Each pixel in EGA and VGA 16-color modes has one bit on each of the four bit planes. These bits make up a linear map of the screen — there are no memory banks as in the CGA. The first pixel on the screen is controlled by the first bit on each of the four bit planes. The tenth pixel on the screen (moving across the top row) is controlled by the tenth bit on each of the four bit planes.

We can pass the row of the pixel to set, as we did in CGA_PIXEL, in DX and the column in CX. We can also pass the color value in BX (note that you can map any of these color values to other colors as we've mentioned earlier. If you want to change color value 1 from its default blue to, say, magenta, just use INT 10H service 10H). To avoid having to set ES each time (and thus wasting time), we'll assume the calling program has set it to A000H, the beginning of the video buffer in EGA and VGA 16-color modes.

Our first task is to determine what byte we want to work on in the video buffer. Since there are 640 pixels in the first row, that makes up the first 640 bits on each bit plane, or 80 bytes. The next row begins with the 81st byte. For this reason, we want to start off, as we did in CGA_PIXEL, by multiplying DX by 80:

100 ▶ Advanced Assembly Language

```
EGA_PIXEL PROC    NEAR
        ;SUPPLY BX=COLOR VALUE, DX=ROW, CX=COLUMN. ASSUMES ES=A000OH

        PUSH    AX
        PUSH    BX
        PUSH    CX
        PUSH    DX
        XOR     DI, DI
        MOV     AX, DX          ;GET 80*DX
        SHL     DX, 1
        SHL     DX, 1
        ADD     DX, AX
        MOV     AX, CX
        MOV     CL, 4
        SHL     DX, CL          ;DX now multiplied by 80 (16*5)
        :
```

In addition, just as in CGA_PIXEL, we have to find the correct byte in this row. That number is just the column number divided by 8. We can place the offset address of the byte we want to work on in DI. We'll also need the column number MOD 7 again to find the bit number in the byte as before:

```
EGA_PIXEL PROC    NEAR
        ;SUPPLY BX=COLOR VALUE, DX=ROW, CX=COLUMN. ASSUMES ES=A000OH

        PUSH    AX
        PUSH    BX
        PUSH    CX
        PUSH    DX
        XOR     DI, DI
        MOV     AX, DX          ;GET 80*DX
        SHL     DX, 1
        SHL     DX, 1
        ADD     DX, AX
        MOV     AX, CX
        MOV     CL, 4
        SHL     DX, CL          ;DX now multiplied by 80 (16*5)
     →  PUSH    DX              ;Put into index.
     :  POP     DI
     :  MOV     DX, AX          ;Get column no.
        AND     DX, 7           ;Find col. no. MOD 7
        MOV     CL, 3
        SHR     AX, CL          ;CX/8
        ADD     DI, AX          ;DI now holds byte addr in video buffer.
        NEG     DL
        ADD     DL, 7
        MOV     CL, DL          ;Get bit to turn on.
        :
```

At this point, ES:DI points to the byte we want to work on, and CL holds the bit number in that byte. Let's make two-bit masks to make the work easier; one mask will have only the bit we're interested in set (so we can OR it to the current byte), and the other mask will have just the reverse — all bits set but it (so we can AND it to the current byte and turn our bit off). Let's put those masks in CH and CL like this:

```
EGA_PIXEL PROC     NEAR
           ;SUPPLY BX=COLOR VALUE, DX=ROW, CX=COLUMN. ASSUMES ES=A0000H

           PUSH    AX
           PUSH    BX
           PUSH    CX
           PUSH    DX
           XOR     DI, DI
           MOV     AX, DX          ;GET 80*DX
           SHL     DX, 1
           SHL     DX, 1
           ADD     DX, AX
           MOV     AX, CX
           MOV     CL, 4
           SHL     DX, CL          ;DX now multiplied by 80 (16*5)
           PUSH    DX              ;Put into index.
           POP     DI
           MOV     DX, AX          ;Get column no.
           AND     DX, 7           ;Find col. no. MOD 7
           MOV     CL, 3
           SHR     AX, CL          ;CX/8
           ADD     DI, AX          ;DI now holds byte addr in video buffer.
           NEG     DL
           ADD     DL, 7
           MOV     CL, DL          ;Get bit to turn on.
         → MOV     AL, 1
         → SHL     AL, CL
         → MOV     CL, AL          ;Bit set in CL is bit to turn on (for ORing).
         → MOV     CH, 0FFH
         → SUB     CH, CL          ;CH has same bit turned off (for ANDing).
           :
```

To turn the bit on, we OR with CL. To turn it off, we AND with CH. Now we'll have to work with each bit plane. For example, if the color value we want to use (as passed in BX) is 0011H, we'll have to set the pixel's bit on plane 1 on, plane 2 on, plane 3 off, and plane 4 off.

To do that, we have to enable the planes one by one with the EGA/VGA plane register, located at address 3C4H on the I/O bus. For example, plane 1 is often called the blue plane (because default color 0001 is blue), and this is how we enable that plane:

```
           PLANE_REG       EQU     3C4H

EGA_PIXEL PROC     NEAR
           ;SUPPLY BX=COLOR VALUE, DX=ROW, CX=COLUMN. ASSUMES ES=A0000H

           PUSH    AX
           PUSH    BX
           PUSH    CX
           PUSH    DX
           XOR     DI, DI
```

102 ▶ Advanced Assembly Language

```
            MOV     AX, DX          ;GET 80*DX
            SHL     DX, 1
            SHL     DX, 1
            ADD     DX, AX
            MOV     AX, CX
            MOV     CL, 4
            SHL     DX, CL          ;DX now multiplied by 80 (16*5)
            PUSH    DX              ;Put into index.
            POP     DI
            MOV     DX, AX          ;Get column no.
            AND     DX, 7           ;Find col. no. MOD 7
            MOV     CL, 3
            SHR     AX, CL          ;CX/8
            ADD     DI, AX          ;DI now holds byte addr in video buffer.
            NEG     DL
            ADD     DL, 7
            MOV     CL, DL          ;Get bit to turn on.
            MOV     AL, 1
            SHL     AL, CL
            MOV     CL, AL          ;Bit set in CL is bit to turn on (for ORing).
            MOV     CH, 0FFH
            SUB     CH, CL          ;CH has same bit turned off (for ANDing).
BLUE:       MOV     DX, PLANE_REG   ;Enable plane 0 (blue)
            MOV     AH, 1           ;Plane 0
            MOV     AL, 2
            OUT     DX, AX
            :
```

Now the first plane is enabled. Next we test the color value that was passed to us in BX. If bit 0 is set, we'll have to turn the pixel's bit on the first plane on. If it's not set, we have to turn it off.

However, we can't just AND or OR our bit masks with what's already there. Instead, we have to load the byte already in the video buffer into what are called *latches*. There is one latch for each bit plane. Only then can we work on them.

To load the byte we're interested in (the one pointed to by ES:DI) into the latch for this bit plane, we only have to read the byte from memory with the CPU. When we read a byte from EGA/VGA video memory, that byte is also read into the bit plane latches (keep in mind that the byte will usually be different on each bit plane). Then we have to tell the EGA or VGA controller what operation we want to perform: either ANDing the byte currently in the latches with our new byte or ORing it. We tell the controller that by using a new register, which we can call the AND/OR register, at location 3CEH on the I/O bus.

For example, let's assume the 0th bit of the color value is set, which means we want to set the pixel's bit on the first plane. We can do that this way:

▶ Screen Handling

```
                AND_OR_REG      EQU   3CEH
                PLANE_REG       EQU   3C4H

    EGA_PIXEL PROC    NEAR
                ;SUPPLY BX=COLOR VALUE, DX=ROW, CX=COLUMN. ASSUMES ES=A0000H

                PUSH    AX
                PUSH    BX
                PUSH    CX
                PUSH    DX
                XOR     DI, DI
                MOV     AX, DX              ;GET 80*DX
                SHL     DX, 1
                SHL     DX, 1
                ADD     DX, AX
                MOV     AX, CX
                MOV     CL, 4
                SHL     DX, CL              ;DX now multiplied by 80 (16*5)
                PUSH    DX                  ;Put into index.
                POP     DI
                MOV     DX, AX              ;Get column no.
                AND     DX, 7               ;Find col. no. MOD 7
                MOV     CL, 3
                SHR     AX, CL              ;CX/8
                ADD     DI, AX              ;DI now holds byte addr in video buffer.
                NEG     DL
                ADD     DL, 7
                MOV     CL, DL              ;Get bit to turn on.
                MOV     AL, 1
                SHL     AL, CL
                MOV     CL, AL              ;Bit set in CL is bit to turn on (for ORing).
                MOV     CH, 0FFH
                SUB     CH, CL              ;CH has same bit turned off (for ANDing).

    BLUE:       MOV     DX, PLANE_REG       ;Enable plane 0 (blue)
                MOV     AH, 1               ;Plane 0
                MOV     AL, 2
                OUT     DX, AX

                TEST    BX, 1
                JZ      BLU_OFF

    BLU_ON:     MOV     DX, AND_OR_REG      ;Select OR function
                MOV     AH, 16
                MOV     AL, 3
                OUT     DX, AX

                OR      BYTE PTR ES:[DI], 0FFH   ;Load latch
                MOV     BYTE PTR ES:[DI], CL     ;Turn bit on.
                JMP     SHORT GREEN
                :
```

Here we test the color value in BX. If we're supposed to set the bit on the blue plane, we inform the AND/OR register that we want to OR a byte with the byte we'll load into a latch by loading AH with 16 and AL with 3, and then sending AX to that register's address. Then we load the latch by ORing the byte in the video buffer with 0FFH (which doesn't affect it). Finally, we turn the bit on by ORing the byte in the latch with CL and replace that byte in the video buffer.

104 ▶ Advanced Assembly Language

On the other hand, if we're supposed to turn the pixel's bit on this plane off, we use the AND function of the AND/OR register by loading AH with 8, sending AX to the AND/OR register, and ANDing CH like this:

```
          AND_OR_REG      EQU     3CEH
          PLANE_REG       EQU     3C4H

EGA_PIXEL PROC    NEAR
          ;SUPPLY BX=COLOR VALUE, DX=ROW, CX=COLUMN. ASSUMES ES=A000OH
          PUSH    AX
          PUSH    BX
          PUSH    CX
          PUSH    DX
          XOR     DI, DI
          MOV     AX, DX              ;GET 80*DX
          SHL     DX, 1
          SHL     DX, 1
          ADD     DX, AX
          MOV     AX, CX
          MOV     CL, 4
          SHL     DX, CL              ;DX now multiplied by 80 (16*5)
          PUSH    DX                  ;Put into index.
          POP     DI
          MOV     DX, AX              ;Get column no.
          AND     DX, 7               ;Find col. no. MOD 7
          MOV     CL, 3
          SHR     AX, CL              ;CX/8
          ADD     DI, AX              ;DI now holds byte addr in video buffer.
          NEG     DL
          ADD     DL, 7
          MOV     CL, DL              ;Get bit to turn on.
          MOV     AL, 1
          SHL     AL, CL
          MOV     CL, AL              ;Bit set in CL is bit to turn on (for ORing).
          MOV     CH, 0FFH
          SUB     CH, CL              ;CH has same bit turned off (for ANDing).

BLUE:     MOV     DX, PLANE_REG       ;Enable plane 0 (blue)
          MOV     AH, 1               ;Plane 0
          MOV     AL, 2
          OUT     DX, AX

          TEST    BX, 1
          JZ      BLU_OFF

BLU_ON:   MOV     DX, AND_OR_REG      ;Select OR function
          MOV     AH, 16
          MOV     AL, 3
          OUT     DX, AX

          OR      BYTE PTR ES:[DI], 0FFH   ;Load latch
          MOV     BYTE PTR ES:[DI], CL     ;Turn bit on.
          JMP     SHORT GREEN

BLU_OFF:  MOV     DX, AND_OR_REG      ;Select AND function
          MOV     AH, 8
          MOV     AL, 3
          OUT     DX, AX
```

```
        OR      BYTE PTR ES:[DI], 0FFH   ;Load latch
        MOV     BYTE PTR ES:[DI], CH     ;Turn bit off.
        :
```

That completes the work we have to do on the first plane. Next comes the other three planes, commonly referred to as the green, red, and intensity planes. The whole program EGA_PIXEL is shown in Listing 3-2.

Listing 3-2. EGA_PIXEL.COM — Turns an EGA Pixel On.

```
        AND_OR_REG      EQU     3CEH
        PLANE_REG       EQU     3C4H

EGA_PIXEL PROC  NEAR
        ;SUPPLY BX=COLOR VALUE, DX=ROW, CX=COLUMN. ASSUMES ES=A000H
        PUSH    AX
        PUSH    BX
        PUSH    CX
        PUSH    DX
        XOR     DI, DI
        MOV     AX, DX              ;GET 80*DX
        SHL     DX, 1
        SHL     DX, 1
        ADD     DX, AX
        MOV     AX, CX
        MOV     CL, 4
        SHL     DX, CL              ;DX now multiplied by 80 (16*5)
        PUSH    DX                  ;Put into index.
        POP     DI
        MOV     DX, AX              ;Get column no.
        AND     DX, 7               ;Find col. no. MOD 7
        MOV     CL, 3
        SHR     AX, CL              ;CX/8
        ADD     DI, AX              ;DI now holds byte addr in video buffer.
        NEG     DL
        ADD     DL, 7
        MOV     CL, DL              ;Get bit to turn on.
        MOV     AL, 1
        SHL     AL, CL
        MOV     CL, AL              ;Bit set in CL is bit to turn on (for ORing).
        MOV     CH, 0FFH
        SUB     CH, CL              ;CH has same bit turned off (for ANDing).
BLUE:   MOV     DX, PLANE_REG       ;Enable plane 0 (blue)
        MOV     AH, 1               ;Plane 0
        MOV     AL, 2
        OUT     DX, AX

        TEST    BX, 1
        JZ      BLU_OFF

BLU_ON: MOV     DX, AND_OR_REG      ;Select OR function
        MOV     AH, 16
        MOV     AL, 3
        OUT     DX, AX
```

Listing 3-2. EGA_PIXEL.COM — Turns an EGA Pixel On.

```
            OR      BYTE PTR ES:[DI], 0FFH   ;Load latch
            MOV     BYTE PTR ES:[DI], CL     ;Turn bit on.
            JMP     SHORT GREEN

BLU_OFF:    MOV     DX, AND_OR_REG           ;Select AND function
            MOV     AH, 8
            MOV     AL, 3
            OUT     DX, AX

            OR      BYTE PTR ES:[DI], 0FFH   ;Load latch
            MOV     BYTE PTR ES:[DI], CH     ;Turn bit off.

GREEN:      MOV     DX, PLANE_REG            ;Enable plane 1 (green)
            MOV     AH, 2                    ;Plane 1
            MOV     AL, 2
            OUT     DX, AX

            TEST    BX, 2
            JZ      GRN_OFF

GRN_ON:     MOV     DX, AND_OR_REG           ;Select OR function
            MOV     AH, 16
            MOV     AL, 3
            OUT     DX, AX

            OR      BYTE PTR ES:[DI], 0FFH   ;Load latch
            MOV     BYTE PTR ES:[DI], CL     ;Turn bit on.
            JMP     SHORT RED

GRN_OFF:    MOV     DX, AND_OR_REG           ;Select AND function
            MOV     AH, 8
            MOV     AL, 3
            OUT     DX, AX

            OR      BYTE PTR ES:[DI], 0FFH   ;Load latch
            MOV     BYTE PTR ES:[DI], CH     ;Turn bit off.

RED:        MOV     DX, PLANE_REG            ;Enable plane 2 (red)
            MOV     AH, 4                    ;Plane 2
            MOV     AL, 2
            OUT     DX, AX

            TEST    BX, 4
            JZ      RED_OFF

RED_ON:     MOV     DX, AND_OR_REG           ;Select OR function
            MOV     AH, 16
            MOV     AL, 3
            OUT     DX, AX

            OR      BYTE PTR ES:[DI], 0FFH   ;Load latch
            MOV     BYTE PTR ES:[DI], CL     ;Turn bit on.
            JMP     SHORT INTENSE

RED_OFF:    MOV     DX, AND_OR_REG           ;Select AND function
            MOV     AH, 8
            MOV     AL, 3
            OUT     DX, AX
```

Listing 3-2. EGA_PIXEL.COM — Turns an EGA Pixel On.

```
            OR      BYTE PTR ES:[DI], 0FFH    ;Load latch
            MOV     BYTE PTR ES:[DI], CH      ;Turn bit off.

INTENSE:    MOV     DX, PLANE_REG             ;Enable plane 3 (intensity)
            MOV     AH, 8                     ;Plane 3
            MOV     AL, 2
            OUT     DX, AX

            TEST    BX, 8
            JZ      INT_OFF

INT_ON:     MOV     DX, AND_OR_REG            ;Select OR function
            MOV     AH, 16
            MOV     AL, 3
            OUT     DX, AX

            OR      BYTE PTR ES:[DI], 0FFH    ;Load latch
            MOV     BYTE PTR ES:[DI], CL      ;Turn bit on.
            JMP     SHORT DONE

INT_OFF:    MOV     DX, AND_OR_REG            ;Select AND function
            MOV     AH, 8
            MOV     AL, 3
            OUT     DX, AX

            OR      BYTE PTR ES:[DI], 0FFH    ;Load latch
            MOV     BYTE PTR ES:[DI], CH      ;Turn bit off.
DONE:       POP     DX
            POP     CX
            POP     BX
            POP     AX
            RET
EGA_PIXEL ENDP
```

And that's it. We've turned the pixel on and set it to the appropriate color. A program that makes use of EGA_PIXEL is shown in Listing 3-3. It draws a red line diagonally part way down the screen, and then, after you press a key, it overwrites the first half of the line in blue.

Listing 3-3. EGA_PIXEL Example.

```
            AND_OR_REG   EQU  3CEH
            PLANE_REG    EQU  3C4H

            .MODEL SMALL
            .CODE
            ORG    100H

START:      MOV    AX, 0A000H       ;Set ES to EGA vid segment
            MOV    ES, AX

            MOV    AX, 0010H        ;Set video mode 10H
            INT    10H
```

Listing 3-3. EGA_PIXEL Example.

```
        MOV     AX, 200
        MOV     BX, 4           ;Color value (red)
        MOV     DX, 0           ;Row
        MOV     CX, 0           ;Column

R_LOOP: CALL    EGA_PIXEL
        INC     CX
        INC     DX
        DEC     AX
        JNZ     R_LOOP

        MOV     AH, 7           ;Wait for a key
        INT     21H

        MOV     AX, 100
        MOV     BX, 1           ;Color value (blue)
        MOV     DX, 0           ;Row
        MOV     CX, 0           ;Column

B_LOOP: CALL    EGA_PIXEL
        INC     CX
        INC     DX
        DEC     AX
        JNZ     B_LOOP

        INT     20H             ;End


EGA_PIXEL PROC  NEAR
        ;SUPPLY BX=COLOR VALUE, DX=ROW, CX=COLUMN. ASSUMES ES=A0000H

        PUSH    AX
        PUSH    BX
        PUSH    CX
        PUSH    DX
        XOR     DI, DI
        MOV     AX, DX          ;GET 80*DX
        SHL     DX, 1
        SHL     DX, 1
        ADD     DX, AX
        MOV     AX, CX
        MOV     CL, 4
        SHL     DX, CL          ;DX now multiplied by 80 (16*5)
        PUSH    DX              ;Put into index.
        POP     DI
        MOV     DX, AX          ;Get column no.
        AND     DX, 7           ;Find col. no. MOD 7
        MOV     CL, 3
        SHR     AX, CL          ;CX/8
        ADD     DI, AX          ;DI now holds byte addr in video buffer.
        NEG     DL
        ADD     DL, 7
        MOV     CL, DL          ;Get bit to turn on.
        MOV     AL, 1
        SHL     AL, CL
        MOV     CL, AL          ;Bit set in CL is bit to turn on (for ORing).
        MOV     CH, 0FFH
```

Listing 3-3. EGA_PIXEL Example.

```
          SUB     CH, CL              ;CH has same bit turned off (for ANDing).

BLUE:     MOV     DX, PLANE_REG       ;Enable plane 0 (blue)
          MOV     AH, 1               ;Plane 0
          MOV     AL, 2
          OUT     DX, AX

          TEST    BX, 1
          JZ      BLU_OFF
BLU_ON:   MOV     DX, AND_OR_REG      ;Select OR function
          MOV     AH, 16
          MOV     AL, 3
          OUT     DX, AX

          OR      BYTE PTR ES:[DI], 0FFH  ;Load latch
          MOV     BYTE PTR ES:[DI], CL    ;Turn bit on.
          JMP     SHORT GREEN
BLU_OFF:  MOV     DX, AND_OR_REG      ;Select AND function
          MOV     AH, 8
          MOV     AL, 3
          OUT     DX, AX

          OR      BYTE PTR ES:[DI], 0FFH  ;Load latch
          MOV     BYTE PTR ES:[DI], CH    ;Turn bit off.

GREEN:    MOV     DX, PLANE_REG       ;Enable plane 1 (green)
          MOV     AH, 2               ;Plane 1
          MOV     AL, 2
          OUT     DX, AX

          TEST    BX, 2
          JZ      GRN_OFF
GRN_ON:   MOV     DX, AND_OR_REG      ;Select OR function
          MOV     AH, 16
          MOV     AL, 3
          OUT     DX, AX

          OR      BYTE PTR ES:[DI], 0FFH  ;Load latch
          MOV     BYTE PTR ES:[DI], CL    ;Turn bit on.
          JMP     SHORT RED
GRN_OFF:  MOV     DX, AND_OR_REG      ;Select AND function
          MOV     AH, 8
          MOV     AL, 3
          OUT     DX, AX

          OR      BYTE PTR ES:[DI], 0FFH  ;Load latch
          MOV     BYTE PTR ES:[DI], CH    ;Turn bit off.

RED:      MOV     DX, PLANE_REG       ;Enable plane 2 (red)
          MOV     AH, 4               ;Plane 2
          MOV     AL, 2
          OUT     DX, AX

          TEST    BX, 4
```

Listing 3-3. EGA_PIXEL Example.

```
            JZ      RED_OFF

RED_ON:     MOV     DX, AND_OR_REG      ;Select OR function
            MOV     AH, 16
            MOV     AL, 3
            OUT     DX, AX

            OR      BYTE PTR ES:[DI], 0FFH   ;Load latch
            MOV     BYTE PTR ES:[DI], CL     ;Turn bit on.
            JMP     SHORT INTENSE

RED_OFF:    MOV     DX, AND_OR_REG      ;Select AND function
            MOV     AH, 8
            MOV     AL, 3
            OUT     DX, AX

            OR      BYTE PTR ES:[DI], 0FFH   ;Load latch
            MOV     BYTE PTR ES:[DI], CH     ;Turn bit off.

INTENSE:    MOV     DX, PLANE_REG       ;Enable plane 3 (intensity)
            MOV     AH, 8               ;Plane 3
            MOV     AL, 2
            OUT     DX, AX

            TEST    BX, 8
            JZ      INT_OFF

INT_ON:     MOV     DX, AND_OR_REG      ;Select OR function
            MOV     AH, 16
            MOV     AL, 3
            OUT     DX, AX

            OR      BYTE PTR ES:[DI], 0FFH   ;Load latch
            MOV     BYTE PTR ES:[DI], CL     ;Turn bit on.
            JMP     SHORT DONE

INT_OFF:    MOV     DX, AND_OR_REG      ;Select AND function
            MOV     AH, 8
            MOV     AL, 3
            OUT     DX, AX

            OR      BYTE PTR ES:[DI], 0FFH   ;Load latch
            MOV     BYTE PTR ES:[DI], CH     ;Turn bit off.

DONE:       POP     DX
            POP     CX
            POP     BX
            POP     AX
            RET
EGA_PIXEL ENDP

            END     START
```

And that's it for screen handling. We've come far, working through both what the system resources have to offer and doing it ourselves. Now, however, it's time to turn to file manipulations.

▶ **Chapter 4**

Getting the Most from Files

▶ Getting the Most from Files

THE REAL GOAL of computing is to produce something useful that can been seen outside the program. Output on the screen is one such method but, without files, computers would be hopelessly lost. Files represent the long-term storage of the PC, and they're still there when you turn your machine off. They can be printed out. They can be arranged to hold data, they can hold letters to the editor, they can be programs. And DOS is equal to the challenge, with its rich set of file-handling services, again in INT 21H.

NOTE The services of INT 21H represent most of the resources that the assembly language programmer uses in DOS. Besides INT 20H (end program), and the interrupts that make files memory-resident, the only other really useful DOS interrupts are the disk reading and writing ones, INT 25H and INT 26H. Meanwhile, the number of services that INT 21H provides just keeps growing. In DOS 4.0, we are up to service 6CH.

File Control Blocks

Before DOS 2.0, DOS used to work with files through what were called file control blocks, or FCBs. FCBs held information about files: their names, the drive they were on, and, although it was in the "reserved" system part, their sizes. However, FCBs restricted file names to 11 characters (8 characters of filename plus 3 of extension, like BASE-BALL.BAT), and this proved to be their fatal flaw.

Beginning with DOS 2.0, IBM introduced directories, and suddenly file names had to include path names as well. But there is just no way to fit C:\PROGRAMS\ASSEM-BLER\MASM.EXE into 11 characters. So *file handles* (which also allow redirection) were introduced.

File Handles

A file handle is a 16-bit word that stands, to DOS, for a file. When you want to use a file, you give DOS a file name, and DOS returns a file handle in a register (usually AX). Whenever you want to do something with that file: rename it, open it, read from it, the INT 21H service will need that 16-bit file handle in some register (usually BX).

A typical sequence for copying a file would run like this: set up the file name as a string in memory, and make the last byte a zero (not as ASCII "0" but a byte whose value is zero). This is referred to as an ASCIIZ string (ASCII Zero), and it tells the INT 21H service that the file name is finished:

```
FILE_36 DB "C:\Novel\Chapter.89",0
```

Next, you open the file and get a file handle for it (execute an INT 21H service 3DH), create a new file (service 3CH), read from the first file (service 3FH), write to the new file (service 40H), and then close them both (service 3EH). Compared to other languages, this is pretty easy.

We are going to work with file handles only, for three reasons. First, FCBs have been out of date for many years; second, handles are much easier to use; and third, the list of things you can do with file handles keeps growing — but not with FCBs.

The DOS File Handle Services

There are so many INT 21H file handle services that one can get lost. To avoid that, we will list all the usual file handle services DOS offers here instead of letting them get strung over the whole chapter. Below, the services we will use are collected into one convenient list that you can refer back to later easily. Looking over it now will indicate what file services are commonly available in DOS.

Common DOS File Services

File handle service	Number	You set	It returns
Create subdirectory	39H	DS:DX to ASCIIZ string	If CY=1, AX has error
Delete subdirectory	3AH	DS:DX to ASCIIZ string	If CY=1, AX has error
Change directory	3BH	DS:DX to ASCIIZ string	If CY=1, AX has error
Create file	3CH	DS:DX to ASCIIZ string CX=attribute	If CY=1, AX has error If CY=0, AX=File Handle
Open file	3DH	DS:DX to ASCIIZ AL=mode	If CY=1, AX has error If CY=0, AX=File Handle
Close file	3EH	BX=File Handle	If CY=1, AX has error

▶ Getting the Most from Files 115

Read from file	3FH	BX = Handle CX = #Bytes wanted DS:DX = Buffer	If CY = 1, AX has error If CY = 0, AX = #Bytes Read
Write to file	40H	BX = Handle CX = #Bytes DS:DX = Buffer	If CY = 1, AX has error If CY = 0, AX = #Bytes actually written
Delete a file	41H	DS:DX to ASCIIZ string	If CY = 1, AX has error

Move read/Write pointer	42H	CX:DX = #Bytes to move
		BX = File Handle
		AL = "method"
			If CY = 1, AX has error
			If CY = 0 DX:AX = new location in file.

Find 1st matching file (use with wildcards)	4EH	DS:DX to ASCIIZ CX = Attribute	If CY = 1, AX has error If CY = 0 then DTA has 21 bytes reserved 1 byte: file's attrib. 1 word: file's time 1 word: file's date 1 Dword: file's size 13 bytes: ASCIIZ name
Find next matching file	4FH	DTA as set by service 4EH	Same as for 4EH
Rename file	56H	DS:DX to ASCIIZ ES:DI to new name (also ASCIIZ)	If CY = 1, AX has error

As you can see, there are plenty of services, including ones that create temporary files, get or set a file's times or dates, and so on. Let's begin to unpack some of this information right now, as we develop a small example program, RUBOUT, whose only purpose is to delete a specified file.

RUBOUT.COM Deletes Files

About the simplest program we could write that works with files is one that deletes them, using service 41H. This service doesn't even require a file handle to delete the file. All that is needed is an ASCII character string, followed by a 0 byte — an ASCIIZ string — holding the file's path name and file name.

We start by reading the file's name into a buffer in memory:

```
            .MODEL SMALL
            .CODE

            ORG 100H
START:      JMP RUBOUT
            THE_BUFFER      DB 50
            BYTES_TYPED     DB 0
            CHARACTERS      DB 50 DUP(0)
RUBOUT      PROC NEAR
            MOV     AH,0AH
            MOV     DX,OFFSET THE_BUFFER
            INT     21H
            :
            :
EXIT:       INT     20H
RUBOUT      ENDP

            END START
```

Here we have made the buffer 50 characters long to accept both path and file names, and made the code into a procedure named RUBOUT. What the program does so far is to fill THE_BUFFER with the ASCII string we type to RUBOUT, which will be the name of the file we want deleted.

> **NOTE** There are easier ways of deleting files than writing RUBOUT, but it is worth noticing that DOS itself — in the DEL command — uses these same services to delete files too.

When the ASCII string is typed in, the last character put into the buffer will be 0DH, which is ASCII for a carriage return. On the other hand, we want our ASCII string to end with 0, to make it ASCIIZ. To do this, we must replace the 0DH, now at location BYTES_TYPED, with 00H like this:

```
            .MODEL SMALL
            .CODE

            ORG 100H
START:      JMP RUBOUT
```

```
                THE_BUFFER      DB 50
                BYTES_TYPED     DB 0
                CHARACTERS      DB 50 DUP(0)
RUBOUT          PROC NEAR
                MOV     AH,0AH
                MOV     DX,OFFSET THE_BUFFER
                INT     21H
                MOV     BH,0
                MOV     BL,BYTES_TYPED
                ADD     BX,OFFSET CHARACTERS
                MOV     BYTE PTR[BX],0              *
                :
                :
EXIT:           INT     20H
RUBOUT          ENDP

                END START
```

To delete a file, we check the entry in our list of common DOS file services:

File handle service	Number	You set	It returns
Delete a File	41H	DS:DX to ASCIIZ string	If CY=1, AX has error

All we have to do is to direct DS:DX to CHARACTERS, where the ASCIIZ string will start, and execute INT 21H, service 41H to delete the file whose name starts at CHARACTERS:

```
                .MODEL SMALL
                .CODE
                ORG 100H
START:          JMP RUBOUT
                THE_BUFFER      DB 50
                BYTES_TYPED     DB 0
                CHARACTERS      DB 50 DUP(0)
RUBOUT          PROC NEAR
                MOV     AH,0AH
                MOV     DX,OFFSET THE_BUFFER
                INT     21H
                MOV     BH,0
                MOV     BL,BYTES_TYPED
                ADD     BX,OFFSET CHARACTERS
                MOV     BYTE PTR[BX],0
                MOV     DX,OFFSET CHARACTERS        *
                MOV     AH,41H                      *
                INT     21H                         *
EXIT:           INT     20H
RUBOUT          ENDP

                END START
```

RUBOUT.ASM is ready to be assembled and run. You will find that it works as written, but when you type RUBOUT at the DOS prompt, the program just silently waits for you to type a file name for it to delete. This is less than user friendly.

We can easily add a prompt to RUBOUT, so that when run, it will prompt: "File to delete?" Service 9 of INT 21H, the string printing service, will work well here. We simply define a string to print (called PROMPT here), and type it out in the beginning, as shown in Listing 4-1.

Listing 4-1. RUBOUT.ASM — Deletes a File.

```
            .MODEL SMALL
            .CODE
            ORG 100H
START:      JMP RUBOUT
            THE_BUFFER      DB 50
            BYTES_TYPED     DB 0
            CHARACTERS      DB 50 DUP(0)
            PROMPT          DB "File to delete? $"
RUBOUT      PROC NEAR
            MOV     DX,OFFSET PROMPT
            MOV     AH,9
            INT     21H
            MOV     AH,0AH
            MOV     DX,OFFSET THE_BUFFER
            INT     21H
            MOV     BH,0
            MOV     BL,BYTES_TYPED
            ADD     BX,OFFSET CHARACTERS
            MOV     BYTE PTR[BX],0
            MOV     DX,OFFSET CHARACTERS
            MOV     AH,41H
            INT     21H
EXIT:       INT     20H
RUBOUT      ENDP

            END START
```

File Error Checking

When we are dealing with files, we encounter something that we have not seen before: the possibility of some error in carrying out an instruction. What if the name of the file was mispelled? What if it can't be found on the specified disk or in the specified subdirectory? RUBOUT should let the user know.

Error checking is a major part of programming when using files. For that reason, we will build (rudimentary) error checking into our example RUBOUT. If you check the list of DOS file services, you will see the line "If CY=1, AX has error" in the entry for service 41H (delete file). The CY stands for one of the internal flags — the carry flag —

and setting the carry flag is DOS' normal way of indicating that there has been an error of some kind.

The carry flag is normally set when a math operation produced a carry while combining two numbers (we'll use it in our fast math chapter). Here, however, if the carry flag is set, then an error code will be returned in the AX register.

DOS Error Codes

There are almost a hundred error codes in DOS now, too many to cover here. However, the more common ones (they are returned in AX) are shown below.

Common DOS Error Codes

Error code	Means
1	Invalid function number
2	File not found
3	Path was not found
4	Too many files open at once
5	Access denied for this operation
6	File handle used is invalid
7	Memory control blocks destroyed
8	Insufficient memory
15	Invalid drive was specified
16	Cannot delete current directory
19	Cannot write on a write-protected diskette
21	Drive not ready
23	Disk data error
25	Disk seek error
27	Sector not found
28	Printer needs paper
29	Write fault
30	Read fault
61	Print queue is full

All these and more information may be found in a volume that IBM sells called the Disk Operating System Technical Reference manual. This book also contains all the INT 21H services and can be quite useful.

> **TIP** There is also a relatively new DOS service 59H — get extended error — which is very useful here. This service returns information on the error that has occurred, where it is, and even suggests what you should do. Information on this advanced service can be found in the DOS Technical Reference manual.

We are not going to get complicated in RUBOUT. We are just going to assume that if there was no error, the file was deleted, and if there was an error, that it was not. We will want, therefore, to check the carry flag, and that can be done with JNC as shown in Listing 4-2.

Listing 4-2. RUBOUT.ASM with Error Checking.

```
              .MODEL SMALL
              .CODE
              ORG 100H
START:        JMP RUBOUT
              THE_BUFFER      DB 50
              BYTES_TYPED     DB 0
              CHARACTERS      DB 50 DUP(0)
              PROMPT          DB "File to delete? $"
              OK_MESSAGE      DB "File deleted $"
              NOT_OK_MESSAGE  DB "File NOT deleted $"
RUBOUT        PROC NEAR
              MOV     DX,OFFSET PROMPT
              MOV     AH,9
              INT     21H
              MOV     AH,0AH
              MOV     DX,OFFSET THE_BUFFER
              INT     21H
              MOV     BH,0
              MOV     BL,BYTES_TYPED
              ADD     BX,OFFSET CHARACTERS
              MOV     BYTE PTR[BX],0
              MOV     DX,OFFSET CHARACTERS
              MOV     AH,41H
              INT     21H
              JNC     ALL_OK
              MOV     DX,OFFSET NOT_OK_MESSAGE
              JMP     PRINT
ALL_OK:       MOV     DX,OFFSET OK_MESSAGE
PRINT:        MOV     AH,9
              INT     21H
EXIT:         INT     20H
RUBOUT        ENDP

              END START
```

That's it for RUBOUT, which has taught us about deleting files, ASCIIZ, the PTR directive, and error handling. To do anything more than delete files, however, we'll need to work with file handles, and our next example does that often enough.

BACK.COM Copies Any File

BACK.ASM is a program that will demonstrate the fluid way that assembly language can work with data. All we'll do in BACK.ASM is make a backup copy of a file you specify, changing the file's extension to ".BAK." For example, if you type: BACK<cr>NOVEL.ONE, then BACK will copy NOVEL.ONE into a new file named NOVEL.BAK.

BACK will be able to backup files of any size. However, we are going to limit BACK to accepting file names with eight letter names and three letter extensions — no path names. This is to avoid having to do string manipulations when we copy the name over and substitute ".BAK" for the extension. You can change this with a little work, but these details of string handling would detract from the main points of file handling.

We'll start out by taking what we need from RUBOUT. Here the program BACK will ask for a file to back up, accept a name, and make an ASCIIZ string out of it:

```
              .MODEL SMALL
              .CODE
              ORG 100H
START:        JMP BACK
              THE_BUFFER      DB 13
              BYTES_TYPED     DB 0
              FILE_ONE        DB 12 DUP(0)
              MAKE_ME_ZERO    DB 0
              FILE_TWO        DB 8 DUP(0), ".BAK",0
              PROMPT          DB "Filename to back up: $"
BACK          PROC NEAR
              MOV     DX,OFFSET PROMPT        ←
              MOV     AH,9                    ←
              INT     21H                     ←
              MOV     AH,0AH                  ←
              MOV     DX,OFFSET THE_BUFFER    ←
              INT     21H                     ←
                :
                :
EXIT:         INT     20H
BACK          ENDP

              END START
```

Note that we've changed the label CHARACTERS to FILE_ONE, since that will be where the first file's name will appear. Also, we've added FILE_TWO, with the extension ".BAK" already. We've set THE_BUFFER to accept 13 characters — 8 bytes of file name, the ".", the 3-byte extension, and 1 last byte for the trailing 0DH that is always returned as the last byte in the buffer by service 0AH (keep in mind that BACK, as written, will *only* work with 12-character file names, so we can always count on the 13th byte being 0DH). To make it easy to write over this byte, we give it a label, MAKE_ME_ZERO:

```
→ THE_BUFFER      DB 13
  BYTES_TYPED     DB 0
→ FILE_ONE        DB 12 DUP(0)
→ MAKE_ME_ZERO    DB 0
→ FILE_TWO        DB 8 DUP(0), ".BAK",0
  PROMPT          DB "Filename to back up: $"
```

First, we set MAKE_ME_ZERO to 0, making the read-in file name an ASCIIZ string, this way:

```
          ORG 100H
START:    JMP BACK
          THE_BUFFER      DB 13
          BYTES_TYPED     DB 0
          FILE_ONE        DB 12 DUP(0)
          MAKE_ME_ZERO    DB 0
          FILE_TWO        DB 8 DUP(0), ".BAK",0
          PROMPT          DB "Filename to back up: $"
BACK      PROC NEAR
          MOV   DX,OFFSET PROMPT
          MOV   AH,9
          INT   21H
          MOV   AH,0AH
          MOV   DX,OFFSET THE_BUFFER
          INT   21H
          MOV   MAKE_ME_ZERO,0  ←
                :
```

If the file's name was BASEBALL.BAT, then THE_BUFFER would look like Figure 4-1 before and after we made MAKE_ME_ZERO zero:

```
                                              MAKE_ME_ZERO ─┐
                                                            ↓
Before
THE_BUFFER 13 12 "B" "A" "S" "E" "B" "A" "L" "L" "." "B" "A" "T" 0DH
After                                                       ↓
THE_BUFFER 13 12 "B" "A" "S" "E" "B" "A" "L" "L" "." "B" "A" "T" 0
```

Figure 4-1.

The Second File Name

Now we need to duplicate the file name with the extension .BAK. Since we've insisted on eight letter names and three letter extensions, all we have to do is move eight letters from FILE_ONE to FILE_TWO using MOVSB:

Getting the Most from Files

```
            ORG     100H
START:      JMP     BACK
            THE_BUFFER      DB 13
            BYTES_TYPED     DB 0
            FILE_ONE        DB 12 DUP(0)
            MAKE_ME_ZERO    DB 0
            FILE_TWO        DB 8 DUP(0), ".BAK",0
            PROMPT          DB "Filename to back up: $"
BACK        PROC NEAR
            MOV     DX,OFFSET PROMPT
            MOV     AH,9
            INT     21H
            MOV     AH,0AH
            MOV     DX,OFFSET THE_BUFFER
            INT     21H
            MOV     MAKE_ME_ZERO,0
            MOV     CX,8
            MOV     SI,OFFSET FILE_ONE
            MOV     DI,OFFSET FILE_TWO
REP         MOVSB
              :
              :
EXIT:       INT     20H
BACK        ENDP
```

The ASCIIZ name of the original file is in FILE_ONE. And now the ASCIIZ name of the new, backup file is in FILE_TWO. We will want to copy from file one to file two. To start, let's open file one.

There are three ways to open a file — for reading only, for writing only, and for reading and writing. Each of these can be selected with the *file access mode* passed in AL to the open file service, service 3DH. Here's what that information looked like in the list of common DOS file services at the beginning of this chapter:

File handle service	Number	You set	It returns
Open File	3DH	DS:DX to ASCIIZ AL = mode	If CY = 1, AX has error If CY = 0, AX = File handle

The access mode, passed in AL, is 0 for reading only, 1 for writing only, and 2 for both:

Access mode for opening files	means
0	Open file for read only
1	Open file for write only
2	Open file for both read and write

124 ▶ Advanced Assembly Language

We will set AL to 0. Here's how we open file one:

```
            ORG  100H
START:      JMP  BACK
            THE_BUFFER      DB  13
            BYTES_TYPED     DB  0
            FILE_ONE        DB  12 DUP(0)
            MAKE_ME_ZERO    DB  0
            FILE_TWO        DB  8 DUP(0), ".BAK",0
            HANDLE_1        DW  0
            HANDLE_2        DW  0
            PROMPT          DB  "Filename to back up: $"
BACK        PROC NEAR
            MOV  DX,OFFSET PROMPT
            MOV  AH,9
            INT  21H
            MOV  AH,0AH
            MOV  DX,OFFSET THE_BUFFER
            INT  21H
            MOV  MAKE_ME_ZERO,0
            MOV  CX,8
            MOV  SI,OFFSET FILE_ONE
            MOV  DI,OFFSET FILE_TWO
    REP     MOVSB
            MOV  DX,OFFSET FILE_ONE     ;Open first file
            MOV  AX,3D00H
            INT  21H
            MOV  HANDLE_1,AX
              :
              :
EXIT:       INT  20H
BACK        ENDP
```

Notice that we have combined loading AH with 3DH and AL with 0 into one instruction, MOV AX,3D00H. The *file handle* for file one is returned by service 3DH in AX. We will store the handle (the way we will reference file one from now on) in HANDLE_1.

> **TIP** If you're using a network, you should know that the top three bits of AL, bits 7,6, and 5, can also be set in service 3DH (in DOS versions after 2.10) to indicate a network sharing mode for the opened file. These modes set bits 7,6, and 5 this way for various "modes": 000 = compatible with all; 001 = deny read/write; 010 = deny write; 011 = deny read; 100 = deny none.

After opening the first file, we have to create the new, backup version of the file. To do this, we will use INT 21H service 3CH. Here is service 3CH from the list at the beginning of the chapter:

▶ Getting the Most from Files 125

File handle service	Number	You set	It returns
Create file	3CH	DS:DX to ASCIIZ string CX = attribute	If CY=1, AX has error If CY=0, AX = File handle

When you create a file you can set its attribute. Here are a list of possible attributes you can set:

File attribute	Means
0	Plain old file
1	Read-only
2	Hidden file (hidden from directory searches)
4	A system file (like IBMDOS.COM)
8	Used for the volume label of a disk
10H	This file name is the name of a subdirectory

To select the attribute, you must load it into CX for service 3CH. We will select an attribute of 0. Service 3CH then returns a file handle for file two in AX, and we will store that in HANDLE_2:

```
        .MODEL SMALL
        .CODE
        ORG 100H
START:  JMP BACK
        THE_BUFFER      DB 13
        BYTES_TYPED     DB 0
        FILE_ONE        DB 12 DUP(0)
        MAKE_ME_ZERO    DB 0
        FILE_TWO        DB 8 DUP(0), ".BAK",0
        HANDLE_1        DW 0
        HANDLE_2        DW 0
        PROMPT          DB "Filename to back up: $"
BACK    PROC NEAR
        MOV     DX,OFFSET PROMPT
        MOV     AH,9
        INT     21H
        MOV     AH,0AH
        MOV     DX,OFFSET THE_BUFFER
        INT     21H
        MOV     MAKE_ME_ZERO,0
        MOV     CX,8
        MOV     SI,OFFSET FILE_ONE
        MOV     DI,OFFSET FILE_TWO
REP     MOVSB
        MOV     DX,OFFSET FILE_ONE      ;Open first file
        MOV     AX,3D00H
        INT     21H
```

126 ▶ Advanced Assembly Language

```
        MOV     HANDLE_1,AX
        MOV     DX,OFFSET FILE_TWO      ←
        MOV     AH,3CH                  ←       ;Create backup file.
        MOV     CX,0                    ←
        INT     21H                     ←
        MOV     HANDLE_2,AX             ←
        :
        :
EXIT:   INT     20H
BACK    ENDP
        END START
```

Now file one is ready to be read from, and file two is ready to be written to. We will have to read the data from the first file into a data area in memory before writing it out to the second file. We can prepare a data area simply by adding a label OUR_DATA at the end of the program but still inside the code segment. This point, immediately after the program, is where data will be read in:

```
        ORG 100H
START:  JMP BACK
        :
BACK    PROC NEAR
        :
        MOV     DX,OFFSET FILE_ONE      ;Open first file
        MOV     AX,3D00H
        INT     21H
        MOV     HANDLE_1,AX
        MOV     DX,OFFSET FILE_TWO
        MOV     AH,3CH                  ;Create backup file.
        MOV     CX,0
        INT     21H
        MOV     HANDLE_2,AX
        :
        :
EXIT:   INT     20H
BACK    ENDP
OUR_DATA:                               ←

        END START
```

Using a label outside our procedure is fine. All this means is that all our data will go immediately after the program in memory. Notice that it was not necessary to reserve space in OUR_DATA with DB. This is because, after our program code is finished, we have the whole rest of the segment (excluding the stack at the high end) to work with. On the other hand, unless we deliberately set aside space in the normal .COM file data area with DB or DW, no space would be reserved. By using the OUR_DATA label at the end of our program, we avoid having to set up a data buffer with DB, which could make our program BACK.COM very large.

▶ Getting the Most from Files 127

Reading from Files We have to read the data in from file one into the data area at the end of the program, and service 3FH reads from an open file. We do not know the file's length, so we do not know how many bytes to read in. However, all we have to do is to ask for the maximum possible, say 60K, and service 3FH will read in as many as it can. It reports the *actual number* of bytes read in AX, and that is all we need. We will tell the writing service, service 40H, to write that many bytes to the second file.

> **TIP** Attempts to read past the end of file do not generate an error with DOS service 3FH. So even if you do not know a file's length, but still want to read the whole thing in, you should just ask DOS to read an enormous number of bytes from it. It will read all that it can and report the result without generating an error. This is a common programming practice.

This is how to use service 3FH, shown in the list of file services:

File handle service	Number	You set	It returns
Read from File	3FH	BX = Handle CX = #Bytes wanted DS:DX = Buffer	If CY = 1, AX has error If CY = 0, AX = #Bytes Read

Service 3FH needs this input: point DS:DX to the buffer used for data (our label OUR_DATA); load BX with the file handle (HANDLE_1); and CX with the number of bytes to read (60K). Here we read the data in from file one:

```
              ORG  100H
START:        JMP  BACK
              THE_BUFFER    DB  13
              BYTES_TYPED   DB  0
              FILE_ONE      DB  12 DUP(0)
              MAKE_ME_ZERO  DB  0
              FILE_TWO      DB  8 DUP(0), ".BAK",0
              HANDLE_1      DW  0
              HANDLE_2      DW  0
              PROMPT        DB  "Filename to back up: $"
BACK          PROC NEAR
              MOV  DX,OFFSET PROMPT
              MOV  AH,9
              INT  21H
              MOV  AH,0AH
              MOV  DX,OFFSET THE_BUFFER
              INT  21H
              MOV  MAKE_ME_ZERO,0
              MOV  CX,8
```

```
                MOV     SI,OFFSET FILE_ONE
                MOV     DI,OFFSET FILE_TWO
        REP     MOVSB
                MOV     DX,OFFSET FILE_ONE              ;Open first file
                MOV     AX,3D00H
                INT     21H
                MOV     HANDLE_1,AX
                MOV     DX,OFFSET FILE_TWO
                MOV     AH,3CH                          ;Create backup file.
                MOV     CX,0
                INT     21H
                MOV     HANDLE_2,AX
                MOV     AH,3FH          ←
                MOV     CX,60*1024      ←
                MOV     DX,OFFSET OUR_DATA  ←
                MOV     BX,HANDLE_1     ←
                INT     21H             ←
                :
                :
        EXIT:   INT     20H
        BACK    ENDP
        OUR_DATA:
```

Writing the Data to File Two

Next we write the data out to file two, the backup file, with service 40H. Here's how to use it:

File handle service	Number	You set	It returns
Write to File	40H	BX = Handle CX = #Bytes DS:DX = Buffer	If CY = 1, AX has error If CY = 0, AX = #Bytes actually written

This service requires DS:DX to point to the data as well (our label OUR_DATA); CX must hold the number of bytes to write (returned from the read operation in AX); and BX must hold the file handle (HANDLE_2). The only trick here is loading CX for service 40H with the number of bytes actually read, returned in AX by service 3FH. All we'll have to do is transfer the value in AX to CX, and then write the bytes in OUR_DATA out:

```
                ORG     100H
        START:  JMP     BACK
                THE_BUFFER      DB 13
                BYTES_TYPED     DB 0
                FILE_ONE        DB 12 DUP(0)
                MAKE_ME_ZERO    DB 0
```

▶ Getting the Most from Files

```
                FILE_TWO        DB 8 DUP(0), ".BAK",0
                HANDLE_1        DW 0
                HANDLE_2        DW 0
                PROMPT          DB "Filename to back up: $"
        BACK    PROC NEAR
                MOV     DX,OFFSET PROMPT
                MOV     AH,9
                INT     21H
                MOV     AH,0AH
                MOV     DX,OFFSET THE_BUFFER
                INT     21H
                MOV     MAKE_ME_ZERO,0
                MOV     CX,8
                MOV     SI,OFFSET FILE_ONE
                MOV     DI,OFFSET FILE_TWO
        REP     MOVSB
                MOV     DX,OFFSET FILE_ONE              ;Open first file
                MOV     AX,3D00H
                INT     21H
                MOV     HANDLE_1,AX
                MOV     DX,OFFSET FILE_TWO
                MOV     AH,3CH                          ;Create backup file.
                MOV     CX,0
                INT     21H
                MOV     HANDLE_2,AX
                MOV     AH,3FH
                MOV     CX,60*1024
                MOV     DX,OFFSET OUR_DATA
                MOV     BX,HANDLE_1
                INT     21H
     →          MOV     CX,AX   ;Set number of bytes to write to number actually read.
     →          MOV     AH,40H
     →          MOV     BX,HANDLE_2
     →          INT     21H
                        :
                        :
        EXIT:   INT     20H
        BACK    ENDP
        OUR_DATA:
```

After this step, we've copied the first section of file one to file two on the disk. Now we should check if there's more data to copy by trying to read again. If the read operation indicates that 0 bytes were read, we can exit. Otherwise, we loop back for more:

```
                .MODEL SMALL
                .CODE
                ORG 100H
        START:  JMP BACK
                THE_BUFFER      DB 13
                BYTES_TYPED     DB 0
                FILE_ONE        DB 12 DUP(0)
                MAKE_ME_ZERO    DB 0
                FILE_TWO        DB 8 DUP(0), ".BAK",0
                HANDLE_1        DW 0
                HANDLE_2        DW 0
                PROMPT          DB "Filename to back up: $"
        BACK    PROC NEAR
```

```
            MOV     DX,OFFSET PROMPT
            MOV     AH,9
            INT     21H
            MOV     AH,0AH
            MOV     DX,OFFSET THE_BUFFER
            INT     21H
            MOV     MAKE_ME_ZERO,0
            MOV     CX,8
            MOV     SI,OFFSET FILE_ONE
            MOV     DI,OFFSET FILE_TWO
REP         MOVSB
            MOV     DX,OFFSET FILE_ONE      ;Open first file
            MOV     AX,3D00H
            INT     21H
            MOV     HANDLE_1,AX
            MOV     DX,OFFSET FILE_TWO
            MOV     AH,3CH                  ;Create backup file.
            MOV     CX,0
            INT     21H
            MOV     HANDLE_2,AX
GET_MOR:    MOV     AH,3FH
            MOV     CX,60*1024
            MOV     DX,OFFSET OUR_DATA
            MOV     BX,HANDLE_1
            INT     21H
            CMP     AX, 0
            JE      FINISH
            MOV     CX,AX   ;Set number of bytes to write to number actually read.
            MOV     AH,40H
            MOV     BX,HANDLE_2
            INT     21H
            JMP     GET_MOR
FINISH:
            :
```

After this loop, it's all done, and all that remains is to close the two files. That is done with service 3EH as seen in our list:

File handle service	Number	You set	It returns
Close File	3EH	BX = File Handle	If CY = 1, AX has error

All this service needs is the file's handle in BX (we'll give it both HANDLE_1 and HANDLE_2). The final program is shown in Listing 4-3.

Listing 4-3. BACK.ASM — Copies Any Size Files.

```
            .MODEL SMALL
            .CODE
            ORG 100H
START:      JMP BACK
            THE_BUFFER      DB 13
            BYTES_TYPED     DB 0
            FILE_ONE        DB 12 DUP(0)
```

Listing 4-3. BACK.ASM — Copies Any Size Files.

```
            MAKE_ME_ZERO    DB 0
            FILE_TWO        DB 8 DUP(0), ".BAK",0
            HANDLE_1        DW 0
            HANDLE_2        DW 0
            PROMPT          DB "Filename to back up: $"
BACK        PROC NEAR
            MOV     DX,OFFSET PROMPT
            MOV     AH,9
            INT     21H
            MOV     AH,0AH
            MOV     DX,OFFSET THE_BUFFER
            INT     21H
            MOV     MAKE_ME_ZERO,0
            MOV     CX,8
            MOV     SI,OFFSET FILE_ONE
            MOV     DI,OFFSET FILE_TWO
REP         MOVSB
            MOV     DX,OFFSET FILE_ONE          ;Open first file
            MOV     AX,3D00H
            INT     21H
            MOV     HANDLE_1,AX
            MOV     DX,OFFSET FILE_TWO
            MOV     AH,3CH                      ;Create backup file.
            MOV     CX,0
            INT     21H
            MOV     HANDLE_2,AX
GET_MOR:    MOV     AH,3FH
            MOV     CX,60*1024
            MOV     DX,OFFSET OUR_DATA
            MOV     BX,HANDLE_1
            INT     21H
            CMP     AX, 0
            JE      FINISH
            MOV     CX,AX   ;Set number of bytes to write to number actually read.
            MOV     AH,40H
            MOV     BX,HANDLE_2
            INT     21H
            JMP     GET_MOR
FINISH:     MOV     AH,3EH
            MOV     BX,HANDLE_1
            INT     21H
            MOV     BX,HANDLE_2
            INT     21H
EXIT:       INT     20H
BACK        ENDP
OUR_DATA:

            END START
```

And that's it. Assemble it and give it a try, but make sure to give it the name of a file with an eight letter name and a three letter extension. For example, like BASEBALL.BAT. BACK.COM will produce and fill BASEBALL.BAK. Our program is capable of copying files: it's not so difficult in assembly language, and it works at high speed as well.

Inside Files

In this chapter, we have seen how to delete files simply by storing their names in memory, pointing to them, and using service 41H of INT 21H. Next we saw how to work with the entire file — all the data at once — by copying the file whole and producing a backup copy. This is also easy to do in contrast to higher level languages that often insist on making distinctions between binary or ASCII files; have rigidly enforced records; or add end-of-file markers. All we had to do was to open the file we wanted to back up, create a new file, copy from file one into file two, and then close them both.

On the other hand, we did very little with the data actually in the file itself. BACK.COM can swallow whole files at once, and write them back again onto the disk, but it knows nothing about what's in them. This is where all the protocol one usually finds in higher level languages was designed to work: by formatting your file into what are known as records.

File Records

A *record* works like this: suppose you wanted to store all your friends' telephone numbers. Each record might then be simply, say, 16 bytes that you set aside for the person's name and another 16 bytes that you set aside for their telephone number. For example, this might be a record, the way we've set it up:

```
       ← 16-Bytes →
       ................   ← The person's name will go here.
       ................   ← The telephone number will go here.
```
Figure 4-2.

> **TIP** One reason to use file handles rather than File Control Blocks is that FCBs insist that you define record sizes and block lengths before using a file. Using file handles (where you simply pass the number of bytes you want to read to DOS) is much easier and quicker.

You could define such a record with DB in memory, like this:

```
NAME     DB 16 DUP(0)
NUMBER   DB 16 DUP(0)
```

This means that each record is 32 bytes long, and begins at label NAME. If you had a name of a friend to store, say "Albert Einstein," and a number, say "299-7980," you could put those bytes into NAME and NUMBER, leaving the leftover bytes at the end untouched.

Both NAME and NUMBER are what is referred to as a *field*. This record has two fields, NAME and NUMBER. You could set NAME and NUMBER up in advance, in this particular case, like this:

```
NAME    DB "Albert Einstein," 0
NUMBER  DB "299-7980," 8 DUP(0)
```

> **TIP** You can also set up records in assembly language with the directive STRUC like this:
>
> ```
> My_Record STRUC
>     NAME    DB 16 DUP (0)
>     NUMBER  DB 16 DUP (0)
> My_Record ENDS
> ```
>
> Then you can declare a variable of type My_Record, initializing it like this: ALBERT My_Record <"Albert Einstein," "299-7980">. Space is put aside for it in memory; now you can refer to the name as ALBERT.NAME and the number as ALBERT.NUMBER.

Notice that in each case, we carefully added zeros at the end of the field to make sure that the field length in memory stayed the same. This way, every record will be the same length in the file when we write it out, and it is critical that they should be so. A fundamental property about records that you want to retrieve from anywhere in a file is that they have the same length to make finding them easier. Each of our records are 32 bytes long, and here is how Albert Einstein's would look:

```
Albert Einstein.   ← The person's name will go here.
299-7980........   ← The telephone number will go here.
```

Figure 4-3.

Making sure records have the same length makes it easy to choose a record at random from anywhere in a file, and this is called *random access*, the only type of file formatting we'll deal with here. The other method allows you to have variable length records, but constrains you to put end-of-record markers into the file to show the boundaries between records. This end-of-record marker is often a carriage return in higher level languages. Since you have to read from the beginning of the file to know the number of the record you are at this way, this is called *sequential access*.

To write this record out to a file, open or create the file, point at NAME, and tell service 40H to write 32 bytes. That's how a record is written in assembly language — as long as you know the record length, you'll always know where you are, or where a given record number is in a file, because the INT 21H services let you specify the number of bytes you want and you can just choose the record length.

You can then make another record with another name and number, say Enrico Fermi, whose number might be 271-8281. This is the way the record would look:

← 16-Bytes →
Enrico Fermi ...
271-8281 ......

Figure 4-4.

Here the dots indicate a zero byte. You can add this information to your data file, which we can call NUMBERS.DAT. To add Enrico Fermi, just write out the 32 bytes of this record. Since we've already written out Albert Einstein, Enrico Fermi will be placed next:

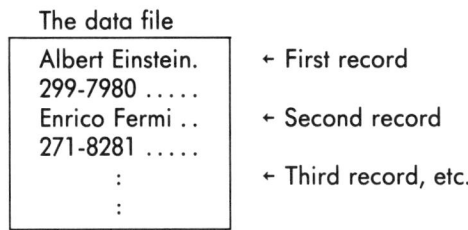

Figure 4-5.

You can continue in this manner until NUMBERS.DAT is as full as you want it. The file itself will always be a multiple of 32 bytes in length. After NUMBERS.DAT is fully stocked, however, there might come a day when you realize that you've forgotten Enrico Fermi's telephone number, and want to look it up. How would you do that?

Retrieving Data from Files

There's not much point in writing data files unless you can use them. And using them isn't so hard as you might think. Here we want to read in a record — the second record of NUMBERS.DAT. You might expect that we can simply open NUMBERS.DAT and request to read 64 bytes in, which encompasses both the first two records, and, of course, we can. But this method demands that we read in two records, and it is clear this method might use up a lot of memory if we wanted record 32,001.

Another method might be to read in the first record, 32 bytes, and then to read in the second record in the same location in memory, so that it will overwrite the first record. Then we'd have record 2 at no additional memory expense. Of course, if we wanted record 32,001, we'd have to wait a long time to reach it. Fortunately, there is a better way.

The Read/Write Pointer

You can simply set the location in the file that you want to start reading bytes from, and that location is called the read/write pointer. In other words, this is how NUMBERS.DAT looks now:

NUMBERS.DAT

Albert Einstein... ─────┐
299-7980 .... ─────┘ Record 1
Enrico Fermi .... ─────┐
271-8281 .... ─────┘ Record 2
Wolfgang Pauli.. ─────┐
314-1592 .... ─────┘ Record 3
:
:
← 16-Bytes →

Figure 4-6.

And to read the second record, we could simply position the Read/Write pointer 32 bytes into the file, that is, at the beginning of record 2:

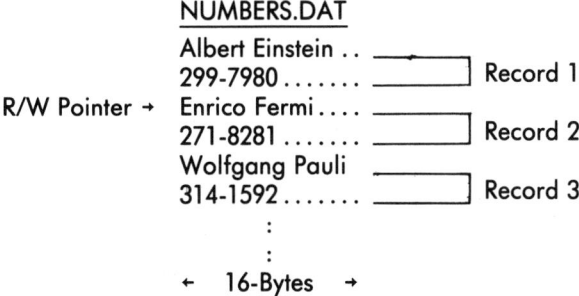

Figure 4-7.

And then read in that record. Ask for 32 bytes to be read in. The location you read from a file or write to it is where the Read/Write pointer is. By setting this pointer yourself, you can

136 ▶ Advanced Assembly Language

position yourself in any file. To position the Read/Write pointer, use service 42H, Move Read/Write Pointer. Here's the entry for service 42H in the list of file services:

File handle service	Number	You set	It returns

Move read/Write pointer	42H	CX:DX = #Bytes to move
		BX = File handle
		AL = "method"
			If CY=1, AX has error
			If CY=0 DX:AX = new location in file.

To use this service, just set CX:DX to the number of bytes that you want to move. The reason two words are specified for this distance is that you may want to move more than 64K bytes, and 64K-1 is the largest number that a word can hold. If the number is larger than that, you'll need more than 16 bits to hold it.

For example, 68K in hex is 11000H. If you wanted to move the Read/Write pointer that many bytes, you'd set the low word — in DX — to 1000H and the high word — in CX — to 0001H. Together, CX and DX as CX:DX would make 0001:1000 = 00011000H. Besides setting up the number of bytes to move, BX must hold the file's handle so service 42H knows which file you mean to use.

In addition, you have to tell service 42H *how* to move the Read/Write pointer. This is called the "method," and can range from 0 to 2. The method is passed to service 42H in AL. The possible methods are shown below.

Methods for INT 21H Service 42H

Method (in AL)	Means
0	Set R/W pointer to CX:DX bytes from the beginning of the file.
1	Mov R/W pointer CX:DX bytes from where we are now.
2	Set R/W pointer to CX:DX bytes from end of file.

NOTE New location of R/W pointer returned in DX:AX. If CY = 1, error code will be in AX.

The standard "method" is to move the Read/Write pointer the specified number of bytes from the beginning of the file. This is method 0. The next method, method 1, moves the Read/Write pointer CX:DX from the Read/Write pointer's current position. For example, if the Read/Write pointer was at byte 32,000 in a file, and you specified method 1, and a distance of one byte, you would end up positioned at 32,001.

The last method, method 2, moves the Read/Write pointer to the end of the file, plus the value stored in CX:DX (that is, past the end of the file).

> **TIP** As a bonus, you can find the length of any file by using method 2 to place the Read/Write pointer at the end of the file (and setting CX:DX to 0000:0000). That is, you simply place the Read/Write pointer at the end of the file. When service 42H returns, it always places the new location of the pointer in DX:AX (DX is the high word, AX the low word), and, in this case, DX:AX will simply hold the length of the file, from beginning to end, in bytes.

Using the Read/Write Pointer

We can get any record we want using the Read/Write pointer. If we know each record is 32 bytes long, and we want the second record, we can use service 42H, method 0, to position the pointer 32 bytes from the beginning of the file, after the first record, and then read in the second record. If we wanted record 32,001, we would position the pointer at byte 32,000*32, and read the record there.

Let's put this knowledge to the test and see how it works in practice with a new example program. We can even use the file we have designed, NUMBERS.DAT. The program, which will look up phone numbers for us, will be called PHONE.COM.

PHONE.ASM — A Database Program

It would be a long, strenuous exercise to write the program that creates NUMBERS.DAT for us, and then a second program, PHONE.ASM to read it in. So we will create NUMBERS.DAT using DEBUG, and not an assembly language program. Since the real point here is data retrieval, we've already written to files. PHONE.ASM will get us started working with the Read/Write pointer.

We want to make NUMBERS.DAT just as a program would write it with 32 bytes (i.e., ASCII characters) for each record. Instead of padding the record fields with 0's to fill them out, let's use the character "$." This will be a shortcut for us in PHONE.ASM since we can then just use the string printing service, INT 21H service 9, to print out both name and phone number. Service 9 stops printing when it reaches a "$," the end of the NAME or NUMBER field.

138 ▶ Advanced Assembly Language

We can use the DEBUG Fill command, F, to fill memory with "$" characters. Let's give NUMBERS.DAT three records, each 32 bytes long, for a total of 3 × 32 = 96 bytes. In other words, our file, NUMBERS.DAT, will be 96 bytes long. DEBUG starts us off at location CS:0100, so we want to fill the 96 bytes (60H) from CS:0100 to CS:015F with "$"s. This is the way to do it:

```
A>DEBUG
-F 100 15F "$"
```

Let's check to make sure, with the "D," or Dump command:

```
A>DEBUG
-F 100 15F "$"
-D100
0EF1:0100  24 24 24 24 24 24 24 24-24 24 24 24 24 24 24 24   $$$$$$$$$$$$$$$$
0EF1:0110  24 24 24 24 24 24 24 24-24 24 24 24 24 24 24 24   $$$$$$$$$$$$$$$$
0EF1:0120  24 24 24 24 24 24 24 24-24 24 24 24 24 24 24 24   $$$$$$$$$$$$$$$$
0EF1:0130  24 24 24 24 24 24 24 24-24 24 24 24 24 24 24 24   $$$$$$$$$$$$$$$$
0EF1:0140  24 24 24 24 24 24 24 24-24 24 24 24 24 24 24 24   $$$$$$$$$$$$$$$$
0EF1:0150  24 24 24 24 24 24 24 24-24 24 24 24 24 24 24 24   $$$$$$$$$$$$$$$$
0EF1:0160  24 FC C3 E8 E2 FF 89 3E-4C F6 CB E8 CA FF 2B CF   .......>L.....+.
0EF1:0170  F2 AE E3 03 EB 16 90 B8-00 00 C8 E8 8A FF 3B 3E   ..............;>
```

Now we have to enter our names and numbers. We have to enter our data with the deposit byte, DB, directive, just as if we were writing a program. Each field will be easy to locate since it is just 16 (that is, 10H) bytes apart. We have to assemble (the A command) at the beginning of each field, and use DB to put the string in. Here's how it looks for the NUMBERS.DAT we've developed:

```
-A100
0EF1:0100 DB "Albert Einstein"
0EF1:010F
-A110
0EF1:0110 DB "299-7980"
0EF1:0118
-A120
0EF1:0120 DB "Enrico Fermi"
0EF1:012C
        :
        :
```

Now that memory should be set up correctly, let's dump it again and check:

Getting the Most from Files 139

```
-D100                   •
OEF1:0100  41 6C 62 65 72 74 20 45-69 6E 73 74 65 69 6E 24   Albert Einstein$
OEF1:0110  32 39 39 2D 37 39 38 30-24 24 24 24 24 24 24 24   299-7980$$$$$$$$
OEF1:0120  45 6E 72 69 63 6F 20 46-65 72 6D 69 24 24 24 24   Enrico Fermi$$$$
OEF1:0130  32 37 31 2D 38 32 38 31-24 24 24 24 24 24 24 24   271-8281$$$$$$$$
OEF1:0140  57 6F 6C 66 67 61 6E 67-20 50 61 75 6C 69 24 24   Wolfgang Pauli$$
OEF1:0150  33 31 34 2D 31 35 39 32-24 24 24 24 24 24 24 24   314-1592$$$$$$$$
OEF1:0160  24 FC C3 E8 E2 FF 89 3E-4C F6 CB E8 CA FF 2B CF   .......>L.....+.
OEF1:0170  F2 AE E3 03 EB 16 90 B8-00 00 CB E8 BA FF 3B 3E   ..............;>
```

We can write NUMBERS.DAT with DEBUG's W command, first filling CX with the number of bytes to fill, 60H, and then naming the file with the N command, as we've seen when we used DEBUG as an assembler:

```
-NNUMBERS.DAT
-RCX
CX 0000
:60
-W
Writing 0060 bytes
-Q
```

Now we're ready for the PHONE program itself. Let's make an ASCIIZ string containing NUMBERS.DAT and open the file here in the beginning of PHONE.ASM, storing the file handle in FILEHANDLE:

```
            .MODEL SMALL
            .CODE
            ORG 100H
START:      JMP PHONE
            FILENAME        DB "NUMBERS.DAT",0
            FILEHANDLE      DW 0
PHONE       PROC NEAR
            MOV     DX,OFFSET FILENAME
            MOV     AL,0        ;Read Only
            MOV     AH,3DH
            INT     21H
            MOV     FILEHANDLE,AX
              :
              :
EXIT:       INT     20H
PHONE       ENDP

            END START
```

Notice that we set the access mode, in AL, to 0 (read only) so that we can only read NUMBERS.DAT. If your program wants to write data as well as read it, use access mode 2 (read and write). We open the file and store the handle, returned in AX, for future use.

In preparation for reading in records, let's set up the two fields that we will need and that we might as well call PERSON_NAME and NUMBER, as we did before:

140 ▶ Advanced Assembly Language

```
            .MODEL SMALL
            .CODE
            ORG 100H
START:      JMP PHONE
            FILENAME        DB "NUMBERS.DAT",0
            FILEHANDLE      DW 0
            PERSON_NAME     DB 16 DUP(0)
            NUMBER          DB 16 DUP(0)
PHONE       PROC NEAR
            MOV     DX,OFFSET FILENAME
            MOV     AL,0     ;Read Only
            MOV     AH,3DH
            INT     21H
            MOV     FILEHANDLE,AX
                :
                :
EXIT:       INT     20H
PHONE       ENDP

            END START
```

Next we'll have to find out what to do from the user: which record — 1, 2, or 3 — should we read in? Or should we quit? Let's type out a prompt that lists the available options:

```
            .MODEL SMALL
            .CODE
            ORG 100H
START:      JMP PHONE
            FILENAME        DB "NUMBERS.DAT",0
            FILEHANDLE      DW 0
            PERSON_NAME     DB 16 DUP(0)
            NUMBER          DB 16 DUP(0)
            PROMPT          DB "Get phone number (1-3) or Quit (Q): $"
PHONE       PROC NEAR
            MOV     DX,OFFSET FILENAME
            MOV     AL,0     ;Read Only
            MOV     AH,3DH
            INT     21H
            MOV     FILEHANDLE,AX
ASK:        MOV     DX,OFFSET PROMPT
            MOV     AH,9
            INT     21H
            MOV     AH,1
            INT     21H
                :
                :
EXIT:       INT     20H
PHONE       ENDP

            END START
```

▶ Getting the Most from Files

Here we can use service 1 to get a one letter response. If that response is "Q," as indicated in the prompt, we should quit. Before we do, however, we must close the files, like this:

```
            .MODEL SMALL
            .CODE
            ORG 100H
START:      JMP PHONE
            FILENAME        DB "NUMBERS.DAT",0
            FILEHANDLE      DW 0
            PERSON_NAME     DB 16 DUP(0)
            NUMBER          DB 16 DUP(0)
            PROMPT          DB "Get phone number (1-3) or Quit (Q): $"
PHONE       PROC NEAR
            MOV     DX,OFFSET FILENAME
            MOV     AL,0            ;Read Only
            MOV     AH,3DH
            INT     21H
            MOV     FILEHANDLE,AX
ASK:        MOV     DX,OFFSET PROMPT
            MOV     AH,9
            INT     21H
            MOV     AH,1
            INT     21H
            CMP     AL,"Q"          ←
            JE      QUIT            ←
              :
              :
QUIT:       MOV     BX,FILEHANDLE   ←      ;Close the files.
            MOV     AH,3EH          ←
            INT     21H             ←
EXIT:       INT     20H
PHONE       ENDP

            END START
```

If the response was not "Q," then we'll assume it was a number, 1–3. To convert the ASCII code now in AL to a record number, we only have to subtract "0" from AL. This converts the ASCII digit to a hex one.

After getting the record number, we have to set the Read/Write pointer. To read in the first record, we want the Read/Write pointer at offset 0; for the second record, at offset 32; and for the third, at 64. In other words, the location of the pointer will be (record number - 1) × 32 bytes from the beginning of the file. Here's how we get the record number and calculate the number of bytes to move the pointer:

```
            .MODEL SMALL
            .CODE
            ORG 100H
START:      JMP PHONE
            FILENAME        DB "NUMBERS.DAT",0
            FILEHANDLE      DW 0
```

```
                PERSON_NAME     DB 16 DUP(0)
                NUMBER          DB 16 DUP(0)
                PROMPT          DB "Get phone number (1-3) or Quit (Q): $"
        PHONE   PROC NEAR
                MOV     DX,OFFSET FILENAME
                MOV     AL,0        ;Read Only
                MOV     AH,3DH
                INT     21H
                MOV     FILEHANDLE,AX
        ASK:    MOV     DX,OFFSET PROMPT
                MOV     AH,9
                INT     21H
                MOV     AH,1
                INT     21H
                CMP     AL,"Q"
                JE      QUIT
                SUB     AL,"0"      *
                MOV     CL,5        *
                DEC     AL          *
                SHL     AL,CL       *
                  :
                  :
        QUIT:   MOV     BX,FILEHANDLE           ;Close the files.
                MOV     AH,3EH
                INT     21H
        EXIT:   INT     20H
        PHONE   ENDP

                END START
```

Here we were lucky enough to be able to use the SHL command, which is an easy way to multiply by factors of two in the PC.

Setting the Read/Write Pointer

To set the Read/Write pointer in PHONE, we must move the number of bytes to move (in AL) into CX:DX. After the byte offset is ready, we will load the file handle (in FILEHANDLE) into BX. Service 42H also demands a method — the position from which to set the pointer — and we are using method 0. Here is how we set the pointer at the asked-for record:

```
                .MODEL SMALL
                .CODE
                ORG 100H
        START:  JMP PHONE
                FILENAME        DB "NUMBERS.DAT",0
                FILEHANDLE      DW 0
                PERSON_NAME     DB 16 DUP(0)
                NUMBER          DB 16 DUP(0)
                PROMPT          DB "Get phone number (1-3) or Quit (Q): $"
        PHONE   PROC NEAR
                MOV     DX,OFFSET FILENAME
                MOV     AL,0        ;Read Only
```

```
            MOV     AH,3DH
            INT     21H
            MOV     FILEHANDLE,AX
ASK:        MOV     DX,OFFSET PROMPT
            MOV     AH,9
            INT     21H
            MOV     AH,1
            INT     21H
            CMP     AL,"Q"
            JE      QUIT
            SUB     AL,"0"
            MOV     CL,5
            DEC     AL
            SHL     AL,CL
→           MOV     CX,0
→           MOV     DH,0
→           MOV     DL,AL
→           MOV     AH,42H
→           MOV     AL,0       ;Set the method.
→           MOV     BX,FILEHANDLE
→           INT     21H
            :
            :
QUIT:       MOV     BX,FILEHANDLE        ;Close the files.
            MOV     AH,3EH
            INT     21H
EXIT:       INT     20H
PHONE       ENDP

            END     START
```

Now we just read in the data, the 32-byte record, into our prepared record area, which starts at the label PERSON_NAME:

```
            .MODEL SMALL
            .CODE
            ORG 100H
START:      JMP PHONE
            FILENAME        DB "NUMBERS.DAT",0
            FILEHANDLE      DW 0
            PERSON_NAME     DB 16 DUP(0)
            NUMBER          DB 16 DUP(0)
            PROMPT          DB "Get phone number (1-3) or Quit (Q): $"
PHONE       PROC NEAR
            MOV     DX,OFFSET FILENAME
            MOV     AL,0       ;Read Only
            MOV     AH,3DH
            INT     21H
            MOV     FILEHANDLE,AX
ASK:        MOV     DX,OFFSET PROMPT
            MOV     AH,9
            INT     21H
            MOV     AH,1
            INT     21H
            CMP     AL,"Q"
            JE      QUIT
            SUB     AL,"0"
            MOV     CL,5
```

```
            DEC     AL
            SHL     AL,CL
            MOV     CX,0
            MOV     DH,0
            MOV     DL,AL
            MOV     AH,42H
            MOV     AL,0        ;Set the method.
            MOV     BX,FILEHANDLE
            INT     21H
    →       MOV     DX,OFFSET PERSON_NAME
    →       MOV     BX,FILEHANDLE
    →       MOV     CX,32
    →       MOV     AH,3FH
    →       INT     21H
            :
            :
    QUIT:   MOV     BX,FILEHANDLE       ;Close the files.
            MOV     AH,3EH
            INT     21H
    EXIT:   INT     20H
    PHONE   ENDP

            END     START
```

And the record is in memory. The person's name is in the field we have labeled PERSON_NAME, and the phone number is in the field we have named NUMBER. We can print out both the name and number using service 9, the string printing service of INT 21H, simply by pointing DS:DX at the correct field to print. After we print out the correct field, let's jump back up to the top of the program again to see if there's another record we should print out (jumping back to the place where we print out the prompt, the label ASK). The final program is in Listing 4-4.

Listing 4-4. PHONE.ASM — A Short Database Program.

```
            .MODEL  SMALL
            .CODE
            ORG     100H
    START:  JMP     PHONE
            FILENAME        DB  "NUMBERS.DAT",0
            FILEHANDLE      DW  0
            PERSON_NAME     DB  16 DUP(0)
            NUMBER          DB  16 DUP(0)
            PROMPT          DB  "Get phone number (1-3) or Quit (Q): $"
    PHONE   PROC NEAR
            MOV     DX,OFFSET FILENAME
            MOV     AL,0        ;Read Only
            MOV     AH,3DH
            INT     21H
            MOV     FILEHANDLE,AX
    ASK:    MOV     DX,OFFSET PROMPT
            MOV     AH,9
            INT     21H
            MOV     AH,1
            INT     21H
            CMP     AL,"Q"
```

Listing 4-4. PHONE.ASM — A Short Database Program.

```
           JE      QUIT
           SUB     AL,"0"
           MOV     CL,5
           DEC     AL
           SHL     AL,CL
           MOV     CX,0
           MOV     DH,0
           MOV     DL,AL
           MOV     AH,42H
           MOV     AL,0      ;Set the method.
           MOV     BX,FILEHANDLE
           INT     21H
           MOV     DX,OFFSET PERSON_NAME
           MOV     BX,FILEHANDLE
           MOV     CX,32
           MOV     AH,3FH
           INT     21H
→          MOV     AH,9
→          MOV     DX,OFFSET PERSON_NAME
→          INT     21H
→          MOV     DX,OFFSET NUMBER
→          INT     21H
→          JMP     ASK
QUIT:      MOV     BX,FILEHANDLE      ;Close the files.
           MOV     AH,3EH
           INT     21H
EXIT:      INT     20H
PHONE      ENDP

           END START
```

PHONE.COM as it stands is not very user friendly. There is no error checking, a serious oversight when working with files, and the prompt is pretty terse. Even so, PHONE gets the point across. You can store data in an efficient manner, easily accessible, just by using files. As you see, retrieving any record that you have stored away is not so difficult using the Read/Write pointer. And that's it for files. Now let's turn to another popular topic, the mouse, next.

Chapter 5

Using the Mouse

Interrupt 33H

In this short chapter, we're going to add support for the mouse. We'll use INT 33H to interface with the mouse. We'll see how to initialize it, read position and button information from it, and work with the mouse cursor. Interrupt 33H represents the entire mouse support available through DOS. So this chapter is going to be an exploration of its services.

> **TIP** In many programs, use of a mouse is optional and depends on whether or not a mouse and mouse driver are installed. You should know that, even if a mouse is optional, you can call and use the mouse services without problem. If there is no mouse, you'll simply see no mouse "events" like cursor movements or button presses. (And you should make sure you don't loop forever, waiting for such events.) In other words, using the mouse services does no harm if there is no mouse.

Getting Started with the Mouse

There are two things you need to know before we start to use the mouse. First, under DOS, you must load the mouse driver software that came with your mouse before trying to use it. You do this by running the .COM file that comes with the mouse (e.g., MOUSE.COM for a Microsoft or a Logitech mouse or MOUSESYS.COM for a Mouse Systems mouse). You must run this driver program before any program can use your mouse. For more information, consult the mouse's documentation. Note that under OS/2 or the DOS mode of OS/2 you do not need to do this — OS/2 sets up the mouse for you.

> **NOTE** The mouse driver program loads the code to handle the mouse interrupt, INT 33H.

Second, you have to initialize the mouse (INT 33H service 0) before using the mouse. Let's start off by doing that.

> **NOTE** Service 0 initializes the mouse driver software that you loaded above.

Initializing the Mouse

Service 0—Set these things:
    AX = 0

   Returns:
    AX = 0 → failure

Using INT 33H service 0 is the necessary first step towards using the mouse. If this service returns a nonzero value, the mouse is initialized. Otherwise, the mouse cannot be used (because it's not installed in the computer or the mouse driver is missing). In that case, and if your program depends on the use of a mouse, you should print out an error message and quit.

Once the mouse is initialized, you're all set until the computer is turned off — you don't have to initialize it again (although doing so does no harm). Note that initializing the mouse does not display the mouse cursor.

A procedure that initalizes the mouse and returns with the carry flag set if there was a problem is shown in Listing 5-1.

Listing 5-1. MOUINIT.ASM—Initialize the Mouse.
```
MOUSE_INITIALIZE PROC
        MOV     AX, 0
        INT     33H
        CLC
        CMP     AX, 0
        JNE     FIN
        STC
FIN:    RET
MOUSE_INTIALIZE ENDP
```

Displaying the Mouse Cursor

Service 1—Set these things:
    AX = 1

Next, we have to display the mouse cursor. We can do that easily with INT 33H service 1. A small procedure that displays the mouse cursor is shown in Listing 5-2.

▶ Using the Mouse 151

Listing 5-2. MOUSHOW.ASM—Display the Mouse Cursor.

```
MOUSE_SHOW_CURSOR PROC
        MOV     AX, 1
        INT     33H
FIN:    RET
MOUSE_SHOW_CURSOR ENDP
```

At this point, the mouse system is active and the cursor has appeared on the screen. We can also make it vanish if we want to. INT 33H service 2 hides the mouse cursor. If the cursor is already off, it stays off. There are times when the mouse cursor can be a distraction on the screen, and this service can fix that.

> **TIP** There is one more little-known — but very important — reason for hiding the mouse cursor. As the mouse cursor moves over the screen, the mouse driver software reads the character at the present position before it displays the mouse cursor. Then, when the mouse cursor moves on, that character is restored, attribute and all. However, this means that if you've changed the screen display behind the mouse cursor (for example, opened a window there), it will still restore the original — and wrong — character, leaving a one-character hole. To avoid this problem, you should always turn the mouse cursor off when displaying a window or overwriting the mouse cursor in any way, and turn it on again immediately afterwards.

We can also read right and left button information from the mouse with INT 33H service 3. Let's look at that process next.

Getting Mouse Information

Service 3—Set these things:
    AX = 3

            Returns:
    BX   Means
    0   No button down
    1   Left button down
    2   Right button down
    3   Both buttons down

    CX = Current mouse cursor column
    DX = Current mouse cursor row

152 ▶ Advanced Assembly Language

This service, service 3, returns information in BX, DX, and CX. BX indicates which button(s) is (are) down:

BX	Means
0	No button down
1	Left button down
2	Right button down
3	Both buttons down

This service also returns the current row and column of the mouse cursor in DX and CX, respectively. These numbers are measured in pixels. For example, in 640 × 200 mode, dx can range from 0 to 199 and CX from 0 to 639.

> **TIP** If you want to convert from pixel to alphanumeric column and rows, just integer divide the pixel ranges by 8 and add 1 to the result.

The most severe limitation here is that this service only provides an instant snapshot of what's going on with the mouse. If you want to use it for mouse input, you have to keep "polling" it, that is, looping over it until something happens.

A better option is to use the later services, such as service 5, in which button action is stored in a "queue," where it waits until you call for it. This way, you don't have to catch a button being pressed exactly as it is being pressed — you can find out about it after it happened.

Reading the Mouse Queue

Service 5—Set these things:
AX = 5
BX = 0 → Get left button information
       1 → Get right button information

Returns:
BX = Number of times button was pressed since last inquiry
CX = Current mouse cursor column
DX = Current mouse cursor row

▶ **Using the Mouse** 153

Service 5 lets you read the number of times the button you specify has been pressed since you last asked. It also gives you the row and column screen position of the mouse cursor the *last* time the button was pressed. Pressing a mouse button is usually more significant than just moving the mouse cursor around the screen. For that reason, you can treat this service as the primary mouse input routine.

The idea here is to call this service when you start accepting input to clear the mouse buffer, and then loop over and call it periodically to see if anything else has happened. If you load BX with 0 and then use this service, you'll get left button press information. If you load it with 1, you'll get right button press information. The number of times the selected button was pressed since you last checked is returned in BX. The row and column of the mouse cursor at the time of the last button press is returned in DX and CX, respectively (pixel ranges).

For example, the program in Listing 5-3 (below) waits until you type a key, and then tells you how many times you've pressed the right mouse button (as long as it's 0–9).

Listing 5-3. MOUPRESS.ASM—Get Mouse Button Information.

```
.MODEL SMALL
.CODE
        ORG     100H
START:  JMP     SHORT TOP
        ANSWER  DB "Number of times right button was pressed: $"
TOP:    MOV     AX, 0       ;Initialize mouse
        INT     33H

        MOV     AX, 1       ;Show cursor
        INT     33H

        MOV     AH, 7       ;Wait for key
        INT     21H

        MOV     BX, 1
        MOV     AX, 5
        INT     33H

        MOV     DX, OFFSET ANSWER
        MOV     AH, 9
        INT     21H

        MOV     DX, BX
        ADD     DL, "0"
        MOV     AH, 2
        INT     21H

        INT     20H

        END     START
```

The limitation here is that this service only returns the location of the *last* time a specific button was pressed and that you still have to poll this periodically to find out what's going on with the mouse (but not as often as with service 3, in which you have to catch the mouse event in the act).

In practice, this means that you should check with service 5 frequently enough to make sure that mouse events don't get a chance to stack up in the mouse queue.

Service 6 is the natural counterpart to service 5:

Service 6—Set these things:
AX = 6
BX = 0 → Get left button information
       1 → Get right button information

Returns:
BX = Number of times button was released since last inquiry
CX = Current mouse cursor column
DX = Current mouse cursor row

This service gives you information about the number of times a particular button was released since you last called it, and it provides the screen row and column of the mouse cursor at the time it was last released.

This service is useful if your program is sensitive to releasing a mouse button as well as pressing it. For example, you might want to "drag" objects around the screen.

As with service 5, set BX to 0 to request left button information and to 1 to request right button information. After the call, we decode the information in exactly the same way as we did for service 5. BX holds the number of times the button was released since we last checked, and the row and column of the mouse cursor at the time of the last release is in DX and CX, respectively.

Handling the Mouse Cursor

Service 4—Set these things:
AX = 4
CX = New mouse cursor column
DX = New mouse cursor row

▶ **Using the Mouse**

Another interrupt 33H service, service 4, gives us control over the mouse cursor. Up to this point, the only way to make the mouse cursor move was to move the mouse (as soon as you show the mouse cursor, it responds to mouse movements). Now, you can pass a row and column number to service 4, and it will position the mouse cursor accordingly.

Just pass the (pixel range) row and column in DX and CX, respectively, and then call this service. For example, the program in Listing 5-4 displays the mouse cursor and then waits for you to press a key. When you do, it moves the mouse cursor back to the origin and waits for another key press.

Listing 5-4. MOUMOVE.ASM — Move Mouse Cursor.

```
.MODEL SMALL
.CODE
          ORG    100H
START:    MOV    AX, 0      ;Initialize mouse
          INT    33H

          MOV    AX, 1      ;Show cursor
          INT    33H

          MOV    AH, 7      ;Wait for key
          INT    21H

          MOV    CX, 0      ;Move to origin
          MOV    DX, 0
          MOV    AX, 4
          INT    33H

          MOV    AH, 7      ;Wait for key
          INT    21H

          INT    20H

          END    START
```

Getting no error back from this service is both a blessing and a curse. On one hand, you're not troubled by error messages; on the other, if you made a genuine error in placing the mouse cursor, you should know about it.

Another service, service 7, restricts the mouse cursor, and therefore mouse events, to a specified range of columns. You just pass the right column number (pixel range) in CX and the left horizontal pixel range in DX and then call this service. That's all there is to it. After restricting the horizontal range, restricting the vertical range makes up the (predictable) next service. Service 8 restricts the mouse cursor to a specified vertical range of screen rows.

> **TIP** Together, mouse services 7 and 8 can restrict mouse operation to a specific window of your choosing, which gives a professional effect to your programs.

You use interrupt 33H service 8 in the same way you use service 7. Here, however, you restrict the mouse cursor not to a specific set of columns but to a specific set of rows. To use service 8, Pass the top row in CX and the bottom row in DX.

The Alphanumeric Mouse Cursor

                Service 0AH — Set these things:
AX = 0AH
BX = 0 → Set software cursor (the default mouse cursor)
       1 → Set hardware cursor
CL = Screen mask character
CH = Screen mask attribute
DL = Cursor mask character
DH = Cursor mask attribute

Service 0AH lets us design the alphanumeric mode cursor (the graphics mode cursor looks like an arrow). This service lets you set the text-mode (only) mouse cursor to whatever ASCII character you want. To use it, you have to define two "masks": the *screen mask* and the *cursor mask*. Each mask consists of both a character and attribute byte, and understanding how to use them takes some time and experimentation.

The screen mask indicates how much of the character at a particular screen position you want to keep when the mouse cursor lands there. This mask is ANDed with that character and the character's attribute. For example, to keep that character intact, use a *screen mask character* of &HFF and a *screen mask attribute* of &HFF. To overwrite it entirely, use a screen mask character and attribute of 0.

The cursor mask then determines what the cursor will look like. The *cursor mask character* and *cursor mask attribute* are XORed with the result of ANDing the present character and attribute with the screen mask.

For example, to use a particular ASCII character as the mouse cursor, overwrite the existing screen character entirely by setting the screen mask character and screen mask attribute to 0. Then load the ASCII code of the character you want as the mouse cursor (such as an up-arrow, ASCII 24) into the cursor mask character and the desired mouse cursor attribute (such as 7 for white on black) into the cursor mask attribute.

▶ Using the Mouse 157

> **TIP**
>
> You can have your mouse cursor *color invert* characters on the screen by setting the screen mask character to FFH, which preserves the ASCII code of the character on the screen, and the screen mask attribute to FFH to preserve its attribute byte. Then set the cursor mask character to 0, to XOR the character with 0 and thus preserve it, and the character mask attribute to 77H to invert its attribute with XOR (use 77H, not FFH, to avoid turning the blinking and intensity bits on). If you just want to invert the character and not the background behind it, set the cursor mask attribute to 7.

For example, the program in Listing 5-5 just changes the mouse cursor to a single dot (i.e., ASCII 250) in the middle of the character position with a normal attribute (i.e., white on black) of 7.

Listing 5-5. MOUCURS.ASM — Make the Mouse Cursor a Single Dot.

```
.MODEL SMALL
.CODE
        ORG     100H
START:  JMP     SHORT TOP
ScreenMaskChar      DB      0       ;← Load masks here
ScreenMaskAttr      DB      0
CursorMaskChar      DB      250
CursorMaskAttr      DB      7
TOP:    MOV     AX, 0   ;Initialize mouse
        INT     33H

        MOV     AX, 1   ;Show cursor
        INT     33H

        MOV     AH, 7   ;Wait for key
        INT     21H

        MOV     BX, 0
        MOV     CH, ScreenMaskAttr
        MOV     CL, ScreenMaskChar
        MOV     DH, CursorMaskAttr
        MOV     DL, CursorMaskChar
        MOV     AX, 0AH
        INT     33H

        MOV     AH, 7   ;Wait for key
        INT     21H

        INT     20H

        END     START
```

You might want to use one of the ASCII characters that look like an arrow instead, in which case you could use one of the ASCII values below.

158 ▶ Advanced Assembly Language

ASCII Characters for Arrow Symbols

ASCII Number	Character
24	Up arrow
25	Down arrow
26	Right arrow
27	Left arrow

And that's it for the specific mouse services, and for our exploration of interrupt 33H. The mouse can be a useful asset in almost any program, and now you can reach it from assembly language. Let's press on with our exploration of the PC now as we turn to disk handling.

Chapter 6

Using the Disks

The Disk Drives in Your Computer

The IBM family uses disks as its primary storage medium. Disks can vary in storage capacity from 160K (single-sided disks under DOS 1.1) to hundreds of megabytes. Even so, their general structure is the same. The four primary parts are the boot record, the File Allocation Table (FAT), the directory, and the data. As you can see below in the list of disk formats, the types and capacities of disks can vary widely:

Disk Formats

Disk	Capacity	FAT	Directory size	Number files	Sectors/cluster	FAT size
SS 8 Sec	160K	FF	4 Sectors	64	1	1 Sector
SS 9 Sec	180K	FC	4	64	1	1
DS 8 Sec	320K	FE	7	112	2	2
DS 9 Sec	360K	FD	7	112	2	2
High Dens.	1.2M	F9	14	224	1	7
3 1/2 SS	720K	F9	7	112	2	3
3 1/2 DS	1.44M	F0	14	224	1	9
XT Disk	10M	F8	32 (Max.)	512 (Max.)	8	8
AT Disk	20M	F8	32 (Max.)	512 (Max.)	4	40
PS/2 60	44M	F8	32 (Max.)	512 (Max.)	4	Varies

Note: The byte in the column labeled FAT indicates the first, identifying byte in the File Allocation Table. Fixed disks have a FAT byte of F8H.

To understand how a disk works, it is necessary to examine all its parts. To do that, we will start with the common denominator of disk storage, which is still the ever popular 360K diskette, and then continue on to the hard disks which, logically, are very much like diskettes.

All disks are broken up into *tracks*. There are 40 tracks on double density 360K diskettes. Hard disks, made up of a number of parallel hard platters, use the concept of *cylinders*, which is really just a convenient idea grouping all the tracks at a certain radius on the platters. Hard disks use cylinders to minimize disk head movement. The idea is to store data with a minimum of head movement by using up all the tracks at a certain radius first.

Tracks are then split up into *sectors*. Sectors are an invariable 512 bytes under any DOS format (so far). Under DOS 1.1, there were 8 sectors per track, but since DOS 2+, there are 9 for 360K diskettes. Under DOS 1.1 and 8 sectors per track, a double-sided five and a quarter inch diskette could hold 40 × 8 × 2 (sides) × 512 = 320K. Since

162 ▶ Advanced Assembly Language

DOS 2.0, a double-sided five and a quarter inch diskette can hold 40 × 9 × 2 (sides) × 512 = 360K.

A Disk Sector by Sector

The way a double-sided 360K diskette is set up is this. The boot record is logical sector 0, the very first sector on the disk. The two pairs of sectors 1-2 and 3-4 each contain a copy of the *File Allocation Table*, two sectors long ever since DOS 2.0. Two copies are made of this table since it's so important, and they may be used to check one another. The directory occupies seven sectors, and fills logical sectors 5-11 on every double-sided, nine-sectored disk.

For those diskettes, which can boot your PC, the file IBMBIO.COM, the disk part of BIOS, starts right after the directory. After IBMBIO.COM comes IBMDOS.COM, also expected to occupy this location on boot disks. After IBMDOS.COM come the actual data, cluster by cluster. This data, your files, are sliced up into clusters and stored carefully.

How the Boot Record Works

The first sector on any diskette is the boot record. Even if you don't have the system files (IBMBIO.COM and IBMDOS.COM) on the diskette — so you can't boot with it — the boot record is still on that disk so it can give you the message: "Nonsystem disk or disk error."

When you boot your PC, the ROM BIOS programs try to read in the boot record of a diskette in drive A: (if it's not there, it might check the hard disk if you have one). If a diskette is present, the boot record is read into memory and control is given to it. It will then try to read in the two programs IBMBIO.COM and IBMDOS.COM. These two programs are always in a specific place on the disk (i.e., right after the directory), which is why you have to put the "system" on the diskette at format time and cannot add it later unless you have specifically left room for it.

Let's take a quick look at a boot record with DEBUG. Using the Load command, we can load the boot record of a 360K diskette into memory at DS:80. We will use drive 0 (A:), sector 0, and load a total of one sector like this:

```
-L 80 0 0 1
```

And then dump it:

▶ Using the Disks

```
-D80
08F7:0080  EB 2C 90 49 42 4D 20 20-32 2E 30 00 02 02 01 00   k,.IBM  4.0.....
08F7:0090  02 70 00 D0 02 7D 02 00-09 00 02 00 00 00 00 00   .p.P.}..........
08F7:00A0  0A DF 02 25 02 09 2A FF-50 F6 0F 02 CD 19 FA 33   ._.%..*.Pv..M.z3
08F7:00B0  C0 8E D0 BC 00 7C 8E D8-A3 7A 00 C7 06 78 00 21   a.P<.|.X#z.G.x.!
08F7:00C0  7C FB CD 13 73 03 E9 95-00 0E 1F A0 10 7C 98 F7   |{M.s.i.... .|.w
08F7:00D0  26 16 7C 03 06 1C 7C 03-06 0E 7C A3 03 7C A3 13   &.|...|...|#.|#.
08F7:00E0  7C B8 20 00 F7 26 11 7C-05 FF 01 BB 00 02 F7 F3   |8 .w&.|...;..ws
08F7:00F0  01 06 13 7C E8 7E 00 72-B3 A1 13 7C A3 7E 7D B8   ...|h~.r3!.|#~}8
```

We can see "IBM 4.0," so we suspect that there is some kind of data here. We can look for a JMP to the real code, normal in a .COM file, with Unassemble:

```
-U80
08F7:0080 EB2C          JMP     00AE     ← Jump to 00AE
08F7:0082 90            NOP
08F7:0083 49            DEC     CX
          :
          :
```

And then Unassemble the code at 00AE:

```
-UAE
08F7:00AE FA            CLI
08F7:00AF 33C0          XOR     AX,AX
08F7:00B1 8ED0          MOV     SS,AX
08F7:00B3 BC007C        MOV     SP,7C00
08F7:00B6 8ED8          MOV     DS,AX
08F7:00B8 A37A00        MOV     [007A],AX
08F7:00BB C7067800217C  MOV     WORD PTR [0078],7C21
08F7:00C1 FB            STI
08F7:00C2 CD13          INT     13
08F7:00C4 7303          JNB     00C9
08F7:00C6 E99500        JMP     015E
08F7:00C9 0E            PUSH    CS
08F7:00CA 1F            POP     DS
08F7:00CB A0107C        MOV     AL,[7C10]
```

You can see that among the very first things the boot record does is to use BIOS INT 13H, the disk interrupt, to start working with the disk. In hard disks, the situation is a little different. There you can *partition* the disk as you want it, even under different operating systems. Before DOS 4.0, disk partitions were limited to 32 MBytes; now that limit is broken, and you can make single partitions out of the entire disk, no matter what the size.

How the File Allocation Table Works

Immediately after the boot record on diskettes comes the *File Allocation Table* (FAT). The way IBM chose to keep track of files on disks is intriguing. The sectors of a disk are grouped into *clusters* (also called allocation units), and it is these clusters that DOS keeps track of individually. This means that the minimum amount of space a file can occupy is a cluster. If you look in the directory listing to find the number of free bytes, you will see that the number is always some multiple of the cluster size.

> **TIP** You can always tell what type of disk you are dealing with by checking the first byte in the FAT; this byte is different for different types of disk configurations (see list of disk formats at the beginning of the chapter). DOS interrupt 21H service 1BH leaves DS:BX pointing at the FAT identification byte in memory.

The number of sectors in a cluster varies from disk format to format. With 360K diskettes, there are two sectors in a cluster. Since each sector is 512 bytes, the free space in a directory listing is always some multiple of 1K. On 1.44M diskettes, a cluster is 512 bytes long, so free space is always a multiple of 512 bytes.

Every cluster on a disk is accounted for. This means that there has to be a table somewhere on the disk with an entry for each cluster. This table is the FAT. For each cluster on the disk, there is one location in the FAT.

Files can be broken up into pieces for disk storage, but the smallest size they can be broken into is one cluster. On a 360K diskette, that's 1,024 bytes. If we had a file that was 1,025 bytes long, it would have to be stored in two clusters, even though the second one would be practically empty. In addition, the file's clusters do not have to come right after one another on the disk.

Let's say your disk's file clusters looked like this:

Cluster	1	2	3	4	5	6	7	8	9	10	11	12	13	14	15
	File 1					File 2		File 3					...		

Figure 6-1.

If File 2 was deleted, they would look like this:

Cluster	1	2	3	4	5	6	7	8	9	10	11	12	13	14	15
	File 1							File 3					...		

Figure 6-2.

▶ **Using the Disks** 165

If we wrote File 4 to the disk now, the optimal use of disk space would be to use what is available. Even if File 4 is long, we could break it up into two pieces as shown here:

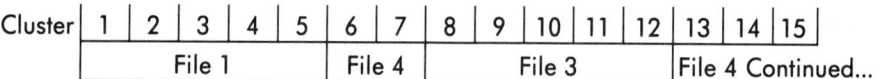

Figure 6-3.

In this way, the clusters that a file is stored in may be scattered all over the disk, matching what space is available. The FAT keeps track of them by the method of *chaining*.

We can get a file's first cluster number from its directory entry (as we'll see below). After we read that cluster from the disk, we have to find the next cluster the file occupies. For that, we have to turn to the FAT. The number stored in the cluster's FAT entry is the FAT entry of the file's next cluster on the disk. Stored in that location is the number of the next cluster used, and so on throughout the disk.

Let's examine how this works by assuming that we want to put a file that is 3,073 bytes long on the disk. If the FAT looks like Figure 4-4 (below) (starting with the first allowed entry number, that for cluster #2), then when DOS enters, it will scan up this line.

```
FAT
Entry #  2   3   4   5     6   7   8     9  10  11  12  13
         3   4   5  FFFF   0   0  FFF7   0   0   0   0   0
```

Figure 6-4.

It finds a 0 recorded for cluster 6, which means that this cluster is available. It continues up the FAT, finding another 0 in entry 7. DOS allocates the first 1,024 bytes of the file to cluster 6 and indicates where the next cluster is to be found by placing a 7 in entry 6:

```
                              ↓
         Entry #  2   3   4   5   6   7   8     9  10  11  12  13
                  3   4   5  FFFF  0   0  FFF7  0   0   0   0   0
```

Figure 6-5.

A 6 is recorded also in the file's directory entry as the file's first cluster number. To read the file you read in cluster 6 first, and, seeing FAT entry 6 holds a 7, you read in cluster 7 next. DOS can allocate the first 3 K (3,072) bytes of the file by chaining it together (FFF7 marks a bad cluster):

166 ▶ Advanced Assembly Language

```
                        ↓   ↓       ↓
Entry #   2   3   4   5   6   7   8   9   10  11  12  13
          3   4   5  FFFF  7   9  FFF7 10   0   0   0   0
```

Figure 6-6.

Since the file is 3,073 bytes long, though, there is still one awkward byte to keep track of, and DOS must allocate an entire cluster (1,024 bytes on a 360K diskette) for it. DOS reserves this last cluster by placing an end of file marker, 0FFFFH, in the FAT, telling any program chaining through the file that the chain is finished. This 0FFFFH looks like this:

```
                                          ↓
Entry #   2   3   4   5   6   7   8   9   10  11  12  13
          3   4   5  FFFF  7   9  FFF7 10 FFFF  0   0   0
```

Figure 6-7.

You might also notice that DOS has skipped over the bad cluster, marked with an 0FFF7H, in cluster 8's entry. The process looks simple, and it is conceptually simple, but the real FAT on disk is hardly as smooth as this abbreviated example might indicate. In particular, there are two types of FATs — 12-bit and 16-bit entry FATs. The 12-bit type is only used when the total storage is less than or equal to 4,078 clusters.

Twelve bits seems like an unusual choice, but it is actually very economical. There are more than 300 clusters on a double-sided diskette, so DOS couldn't point to them all with an 8-bit entry for each (since the largest number you can fit into 8 bits is 255). With single-sided diskettes, IBM wanted to keep the FAT to a minimum of space (i.e., one sector on the disk), but, since there are only 256 words in a sector, not each cluster could have its own word. Compromise gave each cluster 12 bits; that is, 1.5 bytes. This means each 12-bit FAT entry must be expressed as a three-digit hex number such as CCCH or FFFH.

However, the 80×86's method of storing words by reversing the bytes, and the fact that each FAT entry is only 12 bits long here makes the FAT quite a tangle. Here is the method of finding what's in the 12-bit FAT for a given entry number:

1. If you have some cluster's number and want to read its FAT entry, multiply it by 1.5 (the number of bytes in each entry) and keep only the whole part of the result (in other words, find INT(3 × cluster number/2)).

▶ **Using the Disks** 167

2. The resulting number is your index into the FAT. Using the MOV instruction, move the word at that location in the FAT into a register (something like this: MOV AX,[BX]).

3. If your original cluster number was even, keep the low order 12 bits of the result, if it was odd, keep the higher 12 bits.

These 12 bits are the entry in the FAT for that cluster number.

Let's take a look at an example of a 12-bit FAT for experience. For instance, if the entries for clusters 4 and 5 are 123H and 456H, they would appear in a 12-bit FAT as shown in Figure 6-8.

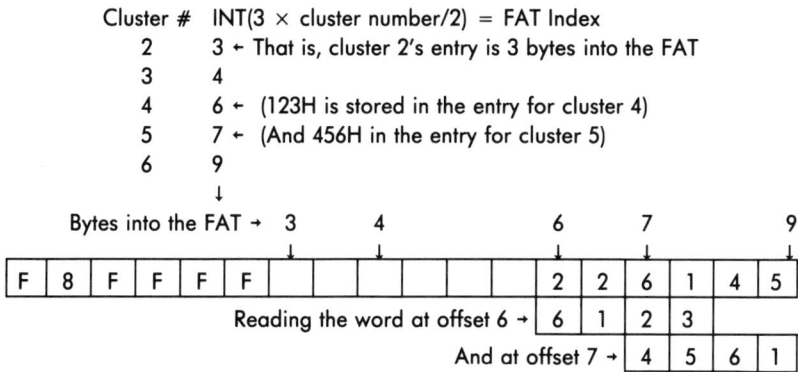

Figure 6-8. *A 12-bit FAT Example*

If our numbers 123H and 456H are the entries for clusters 4 and 5, then, to find them, we have to read the words at locations 6 and 7 in the FAT. These two words, read into a register, are 6123H and 4561H. Using the rule above covering odd and even cluster numbers, we regain our original 123H and 456H. 123H and 456H were translated in the FAT into the almost unrecognizable bytes 23 61 45, mixing them thoroughly.

The 16-bit FAT is much easier to work with. To find the entry for a cluster in a 16-bit FAT, just multiply the cluster number by 2 and look at that offset in the FAT. And that's all there is to it.

> **TIP** If you're working through the FAT, you might notice some odd values. Here's how to decode them: 0 indicates an unused cluster; 0FFF0H – 0FFF6H indicates a reserved cluster; 0FFF7H indicates a bad cluster (i.e., a bad section of disk); and 0FFF8H – 0FFFFH indicates an end of the file mark.

168 ▶ Advanced Assembly Language

The Directory on a Disk

Right after the two copies of the FAT comes the disk directory. On a 360K diskette, for example, the directory fills logical sectors 5–11. Here's a copy of the directory entry for a file named BASEBALL.BAT. All directory entries are 32 bytes long. The first 8 bytes are given to the file's name, in our case, BASEBALL. The next three bytes, 8–10, are given to the file's extension, BAT, as in Figure 6-9.

Byte #	0	1	2	3	4	5	6	7
0	B	A	S	E	B	A	L	L
8	B	A	T	File Attrib.	Reserved			
16	Also Reserved						Time file made or updated	
24	Date file made or updated		The starting cluster		File Size in Bytes — Low Order, High Order			

Figure 6-9. Directory Entry for BASEBALL.BAT

Byte 11 carries the file's attribute. Bytes 12–21 are reserved for use by DOS and are available for future expansion. The file's creation time, or the time it was last written to, is densely packed into bytes 22–25. The two bytes 22 and 23 store the creation time of day in a word formed like this:

$$\text{Time} = (\text{seconds}/2) + 2^5 \times (\text{minutes}) + 2^{11} \times (\text{hours})$$

The date is stored in bytes 24–25 like this:

$$\text{Date} = (\text{days}) + 2^5 \times (\text{months}) + 2^9 \times (\text{year} - 1980)$$

Both of these words are stored, as usual, with the low byte first. Subtracting 1,980 from the year is an economical thing to do since you can pack more bits into the space you have left.

Bytes 26–27 contain the starting cluster number of the file on the disk and the next four contain the file size. These bytes give you the number of the cluster where the very first section of your file is stored.

The last four bytes, 28–31, are the file size in bytes. This is the only place DOS keeps accurate track of the file's size. As usual, these are stored low word, high word, and in each word the low byte comes first.

> **TIP** Bytes 26–31 make it possible to undelete a file! When a file is deleted, the *only* changes made are to overwrite the first byte in the directory entry with a special character, ASCII 229, and to zero all locations it had in the FAT.

▶ Using the Disks

However, if you work with the rest of the data in the directory entry — particularly the location of the first cluster in the FAT and the length of the file (i.e., the number of clusters you'll need), you can rebuild the FAT entries and restore the file.

Using DEBUG, we can take a direct look at a file's directory entry. On a 360K diskette, there are seven sectors of directory, so there are 7 × 512/32 = 112 directory entries possible. Let's load such a directory into DEBUG and take a look:

```
-L100 0 5 1
-D100
08F7:0100  49 42 4D 42 49 4F 20 20-43 4F 4D 27 00 00 00 00   IBMBIO  COM'....
08F7:0110  00 00 00 00 00 00 00 60-54 07 02 00 80 12 00 00   .......`T.......
08F7:0120  49 42 4D 44 4F 53 20 20-43 4F 4D 27 00 00 00 00   IBMDOS  COM'....
08F7:0130  00 00 00 00 00 00 00 60-54 07 07 00 80 42 00 00   .......`T....B..
08F7:0140  43 4F 4D 4D 41 4E 44 20-43 4F 4D 20 00 00 00 00   COMMAND COM ....
08F7:0150  00 00 00 00 00 00 00 60-54 07 18 00 80 45 00 00   .......`T....E..
08F7:0160  44 4F 53 20 32 2D 31 30-20 20 20 08 00 00 00 00   DOS 2-10   .....
08F7:0170  00 00 00 00 00 00 47 72-4B 08 00 00 00 00 00 00   ......GrK.......
-Q
```

You can see that each directory entry takes up 32 bytes here. First comes the name, such as "IBMBIO   COM" and then the attribute, 27 (Read-Only, Hidden, System, and the Archive Bit are all set at once). The last four bytes of IBMBIO.COM's entry are 80 12 00 00, and from that we get the size 0000 1280, or 4,736 bytes.

Let's see how we can use DOS and BIOS (as opposed to DEBUG) to read individual sectors from a disk. BIOS and DOS have different conventions for naming sectors. We will see that this comes in handy for hard disks — the DOS services will treat the first available sector on the disk as the first one in the DOS partition, and the BIOS services will treat it as the actual, physical first sector on the disk.

Logical Sectors and Tracks

BIOS INT 13H (the low-level BIOS disk interface) requires you to specify a sector by giving the track number, and then the sector number in that track. For example, track 0, sector 1 on a diskette holds the boot record — the very first sector in a track under BIOS is number 1, not 0. On the other hand, DOS interrupts 25H and 26H (the low-level DOS disk interface) require the use of *logical* sectors.

Logical sectors start from 0. On a 360K diskette, they run up to 2(sides) × 40(tracks) × 9(sectors) − 1 = 719. Logical sector 0 is Track 0, Head 0, Sector 1 in BIOS' terms (not Track 0, Head 0, Sector 0). Logical sector 1 is Track 0, Head 0, Sector 2. This continues until all the sectors in the current track and current head (that is, side) are used.

On a 360K diskette, logical sector 8 is Track 0, Head 0, Sector 9. Logical Sector 9 is Track 0, Head 1, Sector 1 — the head value changes before the track does on a double-sided diskette. After we reach the end of track 0, head 1, we move on to track 1, head 0.

Hard Disks and Partitions

If you are going to work directly with FATs and directories, you still need to know one important item. A fixed disk can be divided up into multiple paritions and can carry up to four completely different operating systems. How are you to know where to find just where something is in an absolute sense?

If you want to look at the directory sectors themselves, you must find the correct sectors at the beginning of the partition and read them in using DOS interrupt 25H (which we'll review later). In a DOS partition, everything is set up the same way as on a diskette: the single-sector boot record comes first, then the FAT, then the directory, and so on. To DOS interrupts 25H and 26H, the first logical sector is the first sector in the current DOS partition, not the first sector on the disk itself.

Let's take a look at the boot record of a partition on a fixed disk formatted under DOS 4.0 with DEBUG. The boot record on a fixed disk is logical sector 0, so we read that in with DEBUG (which uses logical sectors, just as the DOS interrupts do):

```
F:\>DEBUG
-L 100 2 0 1
-D100
1CE4:0100  EB 3C 90 49 42 4D 20 20-34 2E 30 00 02 04 01 00   .<.IBM  4.0.....
1CE4:0110  02 00 02 5B EF F8 3C 00-19 00 04 00 19 00 00 00   ...[..<.........
1CE4:0120  00 00 00 00 80 00 29 5C-4A 44 16 53 54 45 56 45   ......)\JD.STEVE
1CE4:0130  53 20 44 49 53 4B 46 41-54 31 36 20 20 20 FA 33   S DISKFAT16   .3
1CE4:0140  C0 8E D0 BC 00 7C 16 07-BB 78 00 36 C5 37 1E 56   .....|...x.6.7.V
1CE4:0150  16 53 BF 3E 7C B9 0B 00-FC F3 A4 06 1F C6 45 FE   .S.>|.........E.
1CE4:0160  0F 8B 0E 18 7C 88 4D F9-89 47 02 C7 07 3E 7C FB   ....|.M..G...>|.
1CE4:0170  CD 13 72 7C 33 C0 39 06-13 7C 74 08 8B 0E 13 7C   ..r|3.9..|t....|
-Q
```

Here we see that the disk was formatted under IBM 4.0, and we can also see the physical drive number, 80H (which indicates that you can boot from this partition), at offset 124H.

On the other hand, there are times when the real structure (as opposed to the partition structure) of the disk becomes important. In those cases, we can use INT 13H, the BIOS disk interrupt, which doesn't pay attention to the partitions. With this interrupt, you can specify cylinder number and head number at the most basic level.

▶ **Using the Disks** 171

Every hard disk starts (on the first sector of the disk, BIOS cylinder 0, head 0, sector 1) with the boot record and *Partition Table*. This boot record is not the same one you will find at the beginning of the DOS partition, since its primary task is to read in the correct boot record (the one in the "bootable" partition) and give it control. Only one partition can be bootable on the disk.

This master boot record ends with the characteristic signature 55AAH. The partition table is kept just before that signature, at offset 1BEH to 1FDH in the boot record. The partition table carries this information for each partition: whether it is a DOS partition or not, whether it is the one to boot from, where it starts (head, sector, and cylinder numbers), where it ends, and how many sectors come before it on the disk (that is, how far it is from the beginning in sectors). The way the partition table is set up (the offsets are from the beginning of the 512-byte boot record, the very first sector on the disk) is shown below in Figure 6-10.

Offset	Field		Head	Sector	Cylinder
000	Beginning of Boot Record				
1BE	Partition 1 starts at	Boot			
1C2	Partition 1 ends at	SYS			
1C6	Partition 1 sect. start				
1CA	Partition 1 No. Sectors				
:	Partition 2 starts at	Boot			
:	Partition 2 ends at	SYS			
	Partition 2 sect. start				
	Partition 2 No. Sectors				
	Partition 3 starts at	Boot			
	Partition 3 ends at	SYS			
	Partition 3 sect. start				
	Partition 3 No. Sectors				
	Partition 4 starts at	Boot			
:	Partition 4 ends at	SYS			
:	Partition 4 sect. start				
1FA	Partition 4 No. Sectors				
1FE	Boot Signature	55	AA		

Figure 6-10. Hard Disk Partition Table

Each partition is given 16 bytes. The boot field, always the first field in any partition's record, is 80H if you can boot from that partition, and 00 otherwise. Only one partition

172 ▶ Advanced Assembly Language

can have 80H as the first byte. The field labeled SYS above is a system label — 1 if the operating system of that partition is DOS with a 12-bit FAT, and 4 for a 16-bit FAT. For example, the master boot record for the hard disk we looked at above has this partition table in it (from the boot record in the very first sector on the disk):

```
25B0:02C0    80 01 01 00 04 03 99-64 19 00 00 00 5B EF 00    .......d....[..
25B0:02D0    00 00 00 00 00 00 00 00-00 00 00 00 00 00 00 00    ................
25B0:02E0    00 00 00 00 00 00 00 00-00 00 00 00 00 00 00 00    ................
25B0:02F0    00 00 00 00 00 00 00 00-00 00 00 00 00 00 00 00    ................
25B0:0300    00 55 AA                                           .U.
```

You can see that the first partition has a boot field of 80H, so we can boot from it, and the SYS byte is 4, indicating a 16-bit DOS FAT. Let's put this together into a small program that we can run on disks to see whether or not they're DOS-bootable.

DOSCHECK.COM Checks for DOS Booting

In this program, we'll just read in the first physical sector on the disk, check for a bootable partition, and make sure that the operating system is DOS. Then we can print out the correct response: "DOS Bootable" or "Not DOS Bootable." We start by defining our message and reading in head 0, cylinder 0, sector 1 with interrupt 13H (we'll see how to pass values to this interrupt later):

```
            .MODEL SMALL
            .CODE
            ORG     100H
ENTRY:      JMP     GO

            NOT_MSG DB  'Not '
            MSG     DB  'DOS Bootable$'

GO:         MOV     DL,80H          ;First hard disk (drive C:)
            MOV     DH,0            ;Head 0
            MOV     CH,0            ;Cylinder 0
            MOV     CL,1            ;Sector 1
            MOV     AL,1            ;Read 1 sector
            MOV     AH,2            ;Select service 2
            MOV     BX,200H         ;Read in at location CS:200H
            INT     13H             ;Read disk
            :
```

We know that the partition table begins at offset 1BEH in the master boot record (see the above diagram), and we've loaded that record at address 200H. Each partition gets 16 bytes, so we check for a boot field of 80H like this:

```
                .MODEL SMALL
                .CODE
                ORG     100H
ENTRY:          JMP     GO

                NOT_MSG DB 'Not '
                MSG     DB 'DOS Bootable$'

GO:             MOV     DL,80H              ;First hard disk (drive C:)
                MOV     DH,0                ;Head 0
                MOV     CH,0                ;Cylinder 0
                MOV     CL,1                ;Sector 1
                MOV     AL,1                ;Read 1 sector
                MOV     AH,2                ;Select service 2
                MOV     BX,200H             ;Read in at location CS:200H
                INT     13H                 ;Read disk
                MOV     BX,200H+1BEH        ;Beginning of partition table
                MOV     CX,4                ;Check up to 4 partitions
                LEA     DX,NOT_MSG          ;Default = not DOS bootable
LOOPER:         CMP     BYTE PTR [BX],80H   ;Boot partition?
                JE      CHKDOS              ;If yes, check for DOS
                ADD     BX,16               ;No, check next one.
                LOOP    LOOPER
                :
```

If we find a bootable partition, we have to check the SYS byte. If it's 1 we have a DOS bootable disk with a 12-bit FAT. If it's 4, the disk is also DOS bootable, but with a 16-bit FAT. The rest of the program, putting all this to work, is in Listing 6-1.

Listing 6-1. DOSCHECK.ASM — Checks Whether or Not a Disk Boots with DOS.

```
                .MODEL SMALL
                .CODE
                ORG     100H
ENTRY:          JMP     GO

NOT_MSG DB 'Not '
MSG     DB 'DOS Bootable$'

GO:             MOV     DL,80H              ;First hard disk (drive C:)
                MOV     DH,0                ;Head 0
                MOV     CH,0                ;Cylinder 0
                MOV     CL,1                ;Sector 1
                MOV     AL,1                ;Read 1 sector
                MOV     AH,2                ;Select service 2
                MOV     BX,200H             ;Read in at location CS:200H
                INT     13H                 ;Read disk
                MOV     BX,200H+1BEH        ;Beginning of partition table
                MOV     CX,4                ;Check up to 4 partitions
                LEA     DX,NOT_MSG          ;Default = not DOS bootable
LOOPER:         CMP     BYTE PTR [BX],80H   ;Boot partition?
                JE      CHKDOS              ;If yes, check for DOS
                ADD     BX,16               ;No, check next one.
```

Listing 6-1. DOSCHECK.ASM — Checks Whether or Not a Disk Boots with DOS.

```
            LOOP    LOOPER
            JMP     PRINT           ;Exit with default message
CHKDOS:     CMP     BYTE PTR [BX+4],1   ;12-bit DOS FAT?
            JNE     CHK16           ;No, check for 16-bit DOS FAT
            LEA     DX,MSG          ;Yes, print bootable message
            JMP     SHORT PRINT
CHK16:      CMP     BYTE PTR [BX+4],4   ;16-bit DOS FAT?
            JNE     PRINT           ;No, not DOS bootable
            LEA     DX,MSG          ;Yes, print bootable message
PRINT:      MOV     AH,9            ;Print out message here
            INT     21H
            INT     20H             ;End
            END     ENTRY
```

Now we have a good handle on disk structure. The very first sector is the master boot record, which tells us how the rest of the disk is set up into partitions; the first sector of the partition is that partition's boot record, followed by the FAT, the directory, and so on. But there is one more significant innovation here that we haven't worked through yet — subdirectories. A subdirectory is just a file itself, except that it holds directory information about other files. Since we're working our way through that kind of information, let's take a little time to see how subdirectories work.

How Subdirectories Work

Subdirectories on the PC were a great innovation — in fact, it would be very difficult to use a hard disk without them. Here we're going to actually dissect a subdirectory and see how it works. For this purpose, let's say we had a subdirectory named A:\TEST, which contained two files, BASICA.COM and PRINT.COM. Let's try to take A:\TEST apart.

To get a look at TEST's directory entry, we first load in the directory sectors from the A disk. On a 360K diskette, the directory is seven sectors long, beginning at sector five. We can therefore load in the directory this way in DEBUG:

```
F:\>DEBUG
-L 100 0 5 7
```

As it happens, the file corresponding to the subdirectory named TEST is very near the beginning of the directory, as we can see with a quick dump of memory starting at CS:100:

▶ Using the Disks 175

```
-D100
08F7:0100  44 45 42 55 47 20 20 20-43 4F 4D 20 00 00 00 00   DEBUG   COM ....
08F7:0110  00 00 00 00 00 00 00 00-60-54 07 02 00 80 2E 00 00   .......'T......
08F7:0120  45 44 4C 49 4E 20 20 20-43 4F 4D 20 00 00 00 00   EDLIN   COM ....
08F7:0130  00 00 00 00 00 00 00 00-60-54 07 0E 00 00 12 00 00   .......'T......
08F7:0140  4D 4F 52 45 20 20 20 20-43 4F 4D 20 00 00 00 00   MORE    COM ....
08F7:0150  00 00 00 00 00 00 00 00-60-54 07 13 00 80 01 00 00   .......'T......
08F7:0160  54 45 53 54 20 20 20 20-20 20 10 00 00 00 00 00   TEST        ....
08F7:0170  00 00 00 00 00 00 EA A5-74 0C 14 00 00 00 00 00   ......j%t......
```

Directly after the spaces (ASCII 20H) that fill out the file name is the file's attribute, 10H, which makes TEST a subdirectory. Before we can read in the file TEST to examine its contents, we have to give it a nonzero length (the length is stored in the last four bytes of the directory entry). To do that, we first turn it into a normal file (attribute 0).

We can change the attribute to 0 with an edit command. By counting spaces, you can see that the byte we want to edit is byte 11 (the twelfth byte) in the line beginning 08F7:0160. So we edit 08F7:016B, changing the attribute to 0:

```
-D100
08F7:0100  44 45 42 55 47 20 20 20-43 4F 4D 20 00 00 00 00   DEBUG   COM ....
08F7:0110  00 00 00 00 00 00 00 00-60-54 07 02 00 80 2E 00 00   .......'T......
08F7:0120  45 44 4C 49 4E 20 20 20-43 4F 4D 20 00 00 00 00   EDLIN   COM ....
08F7:0130  00 00 00 00 00 00 00 00-60-54 07 0E 00 00 12 00 00   .......'T......
08F7:0140  4D 4F 52 45 20 20 20 20-43 4F 4D 20 00 00 00 00   MORE    COM ....
08F7:0150  00 00 00 00 00 00 00 00-60-54 07 13 00 80 01 00 00   .......'T......
08F7:0160  54 45 53 54 20 20 20 20-20 20 10 00 00 00 00 00   TEST        ....
08F7:0170  00 00 00 00 00 00 EA A5-74 0C 14 00 00 00 00 00   ......j%t......
-E16B
08F7:016B  10.00
```

Now we have to give our new file a length. We know that each directory entry uses 32 (20H) bytes and that there are two files in this subdirectory — BASICA.COM and PRINT.COM. We also know that there are two other entries in any subdirectory, seen as the "." and ".." entries when you type "DIR." That makes, we expect, four directory entries, so we will give the file TEST a length of 4 × 20H, or 80H. The file's length is kept in the last four bytes as low word, high word, so we choose the first of the four bytes to edit, 08F7:017C:

```
-D100
08F7:0100  44 45 42 55 47 20 20 20-43 4F 4D 20 00 00 00 00   DEBUG   COM ....
08F7:0110  00 00 00 00 00 00 00 00-60-54 07 02 00 80 2E 00 00   .......'T......
08F7:0120  45 44 4C 49 4E 20 20 20-43 4F 4D 20 00 00 00 00   EDLIN   COM ....
08F7:0130  00 00 00 00 00 00 00 00-60-54 07 0E 00 00 12 00 00   .......'T......
08F7:0140  4D 4F 52 45 20 20 20 20-43 4F 4D 20 00 00 00 00   MORE    COM ....
08F7:0150  00 00 00 00 00 00 00 00-60-54 07 13 00 80 01 00 00   .......'T......
08F7:0160  54 45 53 54 20 20 20 20-20 20 10 00 00 00 00 00   TEST        ....
08F7:0170  00 00 00 00 00 00 EA A5-74 0C 14 00 00 00 00 00   ......j%t......
-E16B
```

```
08F7:016B  10.00
-E17D       .
08F7:017C  00.80
```

Let's take a final look before writing out this modified directory to the diskette:

```
-D100
08F7:0100  44 45 42 55 47 20 20 20-43 4F 4D 20 00 00 00 00   DEBUG   COM ....
08F7:0110  00 00 00 00 00 00 00 60-54 07 02 00 80 2E 00 00   .......'T.......
08F7:0120  45 44 4C 49 4E 20 20 20-43 4F 4D 20 00 00 00 00   EDLIN   COM ....
08F7:0130  00 00 00 00 00 00 00 60-54 07 0E 00 00 12 00 0C   .......'T.......
08F7:0140  4D 4F 52 45 20 20 20 20-43 4F 4D 20 00 00 00 00   MORE    COM ....
08F7:0150  00 00 00 00 00 00 00 60-54 07 13 00 80 01 00 00   .......'T.......
08F7:0160  54 45 53 54 20 20 20 20-20 20 20 00 00 00 00 00   TEST       .....
08F7:0170  00 00 00 00 00 00 00 EA A5-74 0C 14 00 80 00 00 00   ......j%t......
```

We have to make sure we write it in the correct sectors on the diskette. Since the Write command is the opposite of the Load command, we can use practically the same syntax to write:

```
-W 100 0 5 7
```

Now TEST is just a file like any other file and we can load it into DEBUG with the Load command. First we set the name of the file we will be working on with the N or Name command, and then load TEST in:

```
-NTEST
-L
-D
08F7:0100  2E 20 20 20 20 20 20 20-20 20 20 10 00 00 00 00   .          .....
08F7:0110  00 00 00 00 00 00 EA A5-74 0C 14 00 00 00 00 00   ......j%t.......
08F7:0120  2E 2E 20 20 20 20 20 20-20 20 20 10 00 00 00 00   ..         .....
08F7:0130  00 00 00 00 00 00 EA A5-74 0C 00 00 00 00 00 00   ......j%t.......
08F7:0140  42 41 53 49 43 41 20 20-43 4F 4D 20 00 00 00 00   BASICA  COM ....
08F7:0150  00 00 00 00 00 00 00 60-54 07 15 00 00 66 00 00   .......'T....f..
08F7:0160  50 52 49 4E 54 20 20 20-43 4F 4D 20 00 00 00 00   PRINT   COM ....
08F7:0170  00 00 00 00 00 00 00 60-54 07 2F 00 00 12 00 00   .......'T./.....
```

Here is the inner workings of the subdirectory TEST. Most important is the starting cluster in the FAT. Since the FAT has an entry for all clusters on the disk, there is only one FAT on a diskette. There is no separate FAT for this subdirectory. The file TEST reserves space in the FAT for the files it contains. The starting cluster numbers for the various files of the subdirectory TEST are shown below.

Using the Disks

Starting Cluster for the TEST Subdirectory

Filename	Starting cluster
.	14H
..	00
BASICA.COM	15H
PRINT.COM	2FH

The entry marked ".." tells DOS what TEST's parent directory is. In this case the parent directory is the main directory, so it "begins" at 00 in the FAT. The entry marked "." is the space in the FAT for the file TEST itself, the one that holds the directory entries. Here we see that TEST begins at cluster 14H on the disk. If you look back to the original directory, you will see that the file preceeding TEST in the directory is MORE.COM, a 384-byte file (180H). MORE.COM takes up only one cluster, and, by looking at its directory entry, you can see that one cluster is cluster 13H.

TEST starts at cluster 14H, and that one cluster is enough to hold the four directory entries it contains. The first file in A:\TEST, BASICA.COM, is free to start right after TEST on the disk, so it starts at cluster 15H. BASICA.COM is about 26K long, or 26 (1AH) clusters, so the next file (PRINT.COM) can be stored starting 26K further down at cluster 2FH.

That's how subdirectories work. Unless you really need to do all the work yourself (as is the case in undeleting files), it is better to use the DOS subdirectory services if you can.

Now that we've examined disk structure in some detail, we're able to take a look at what system services are offered. We will examine all that INT 13H has to offer us, since we now have the background to be able to use it. There is, after all, no reason to do all the work yourself if the system services will do it for you.

The BIOS Disk Support

BIOS is the fundamental channel to the disks in the IBM PC. It offers the large disk I/O interrupt, INT 13H. Mostly, for our purposes, this interrupt is worthwhile because it will read and write sectors. But it will also format tracks, run diagnostics, or recalibrate a drive. We'll look at the major interrupt 13H services here.

INT 13H works for both hard disks and diskette drives. To distinguish between the two, different drive numbers are used. For diskette-disk drives, the numbers 0–3 are allowed and, for hard disks, 80H–87H (drive C corresponds to 80H).

INT 13H Service 1 Read Status of Last Operation

Input	Output
AH = 1	Disk error codes:
DL = Drive (e.g. A = 0)	
Fixed disks:	AL = 00 No error.
	AL = 01 Bad command passed to controller.
set bit 7	AL = 02 Address mark not found.
(e.g. C = 80H)	AL = 03 Diskette is write protected.
	AL = 04 Sector not found.
	AL = 05 Reset failed.
	AL = 07 Drive parameters wrong.
	AL = 09 DMA across segment end.
	AL = 0BH Bad track flag seen.
	AL = 10H Bad error check seen.
	AL = 11H Data is error corrected.
	AL = 20H Controller failure.
	AL = 40H Seek operation has failed.
	AL = 80H No response from disk.
	AL = 0BBH Undefined error.
	AL = 0FFH Sense operation failed.

NOTE   Hard disk systems: DL < 80H use diskette(s)
               DL > = 80H use hard disk.

This service is valid for diskettes and hard disks, and it checks status of the last disk operation done. If you have a hard disk in the system, you must select whether you want a report from the diskette controller or the hard disk controller by setting DL above or below 80H (e.g., while DL is 0 for drive A:, it is 80H for drive C:). The return value comes in AL and is set according to the list of disk error codes above. As you can see, the number of things that can go wrong with a system as complex as disks is large. The disks, after all, are the subsystem of the PC with the most moving parts.

INT 13H Service 2 Read Sectors into Memory

Input	Output
AH = 2	No Carry → AH = 0, Success.
DL = Drive number	Carry → AH = Disk error code. (See Service 1)

▶ Using the Disks

DH = Head number
CH = Cylinder or track (diskette) number
CL = Sector number
AL = Number of sectors to read (diskettes 1–8
              hard disks 1–80H)
ES:BX = Address of buffer for reads and writes.

NOTE For hard disks, the drive number in DL can range from 80H to 87H. See note below on packing cylinder numbers greater than 255.

Here's the way DOS or BIOS reads from the disk. You must supply the drive number, head number, cylinder number, and sector number. If you want to find the number of heads and tracks on a disk that you are working on, use INT 13H service 8, which returns that information.

If we wanted to read from an XT hard disk, for example, there are two platters or four heads. There are 17 sectors per track. As mentioned, a cylinder is made up of all the tracks that can be reached with the heads in one position. A 10M hard disk has 306 tracks per surface, so there are 306 cylinders, for a total of 306 × 4 (heads) = 1,224 tracks. As always, there are 512 bytes per sector.

Only the CH register is available to hold the cylinder number, but, in hard disks, the cylinder number can be greater than 255. BIOS allows values up to 1,023 in an attempt to leave options open for the future. The problem that remains is packing 10 bits into 8, and that is done is by storing only the bottom 8 bits of the cylinder number in CH. The top two bits of the cylinder number go into the top two bits of CL (in addition to the sector number already there).

For example, to read Sector 16 (10H) of Cylinder 304 (130H), put the bottom eight bits of the cylinder number (30H) into CH. Then multiply the high byte of the cylinder number (01H) by 40H, and add it to the sector number in CL, 16 (10H). This leaves 30H in CH, and 40H + 10H = 50H in CL.

TIP If you don't have time or the motivation to figure out the track, head, and sector numbers required by the BIOS interrupts, you are usually better off with DOS interrupts 25H and 26H.

After you set the track/cylinder number, the sector number (starting with 1 on every track), and the head number, you can read in the sector(s) you want. With diskettes you can read in up to 8 sectors at once. With hard disks, up to 80H sectors.

INT 13H Service 3 Write Sectors to Disk

Input	Output
AH = 3	No Carry→AH = 0, Success.
DL = Drive number	Carry→AH = Disk error code. (See Service 1)
DH = Head number	
CH = Cylinder or track (diskette) number	
CL = Sector number	
AL = Number of sectors to write (diskettes 1–8 hard disks 1–80H)	
ES:BX = Address of buffer for reads and writes.	

NOTE For hard disks, the drive number in DL can range from 80H to 87H. See the note in service 2 about packing cylinder numbers.

This service has practically the same inputs and outputs as the last service, except this one writes to the disk. This interrupt, in the wrong hands, can do damage. It will write directly to the disk sector by sector (or even write multiple sectors), so there is a risk that you may overwrite sensitive data. With this service you can write a new directory onto any disk or a new FAT. Sector-by-sector writing is very powerful. With this and the preceding service, you can custom-tailor disks.

If there was an error, the carry flag will be set and AH will hold the error code. (See Disk Error Codes in service 1.)

INT 13H Service 8 Return Drive Parameters

Input	Output
AH = 8	DL = Number of drives attached to controller.
DL = drive number (0-based. 80H and up for hard disks.)	DH = Maximum value for head number.
	CH = Maximum cylinder value.
	CL = Maximum value for sector number and high bits of cylinder number (See below).
	BL = 1 → 360K drive
	2 → 1.2M drive
	3 → 720K drive
	4 → 1.44M drive

> **Using the Disks** 181

NOTE This service does not work for the diskette system of the PCjr, the PC, the PC XT, or for AT BIOS dated 1/10/84. The value in BL is set for diskette systems only.

This is an exceptionally handy tool to have if you want to work on hard disks. For example, let's say you want to undelete a file (recover an erased file). You have to know what type of disk you're working with, and what values it may have for various parameters.

The values in CX and DX are returned in the standard INT 13H manner. DH returns the maximum value for head number. CH returns the maximum possible cylinder value. CL returns the maximum possible sector value, and the top two bits of the cylinder number are again packed into CL. In addition, DL returns the number of drives attached to the hard disk controller.

INT 13H Service 16H Diskette Change Line Status

Input	Output
AH = 16H (RAM Diagnostic)	AH = 0 → Diskette change signal not active.
DL = Drive (A=0, B=1, etc)	1 → Invalid diskette parameter.
	6 → Diskette change signal active.
	80H → Diskette drive not ready.

This is the last of the INT 13H services that we'll look at, and it's only valid for the AT, XT with BIOS after 1/10/86, XT 286, PC Convertible, and PS/2s. This service lets you check whether the diskette drive door was opened by letting you examine a signal called the diskette change signal. If AH equals 6 on return, the diskette drive door has been opened since you last checked.

The DOS Services

DOS also provides disk services. In particular, DOS provides INTs 25H and 26H, Absolute Disk Read and Write, and a number of INT 21H services. We will cover the two interrupts 25H and 26H before finishing up with the INT 21H services.

INTs 25H/26H Disk Read/Write

Input media < 32M	Output
AL = Drive number (0=A, 1=B, etc).	No Carry → Success.

182 ▶ Advanced Assembly Language

CX = Number of sectors.
DX = First logical sector.
DS:BX = Buffer address.

Carry→AH = 80H Disk didn't respond.
AH = 40H Seek failed.
AH = 20H Controller failure.
AH = 10H Bad CRC error check.
AH = 08 DMA overrun.
AH = 04 Sector not found.
AH = 03 Write protect error.
AH = 02 Address mark missing.
AH = 00 Error unknown.
AX = 207H Attempt to access media > 32M.

Input Media > 32M (DOS 4+)
AL = Drive number (0 = A, 1 = B, etc).
DS:BX = Address of packet.
CX = 0FFFFH (indicates > 32M media)

Output
No Carry→ Success.
Carry→AH = 80H Disk didn't respond.
AH = 40H Seek failed.
AH = 20H Controller failure.
AH = 10H Bad CRC error check.
AH = 08 DMA overrun.
AH = 04 Sector not found.
AH = 03 Write protect error.
AH = 02 Address mark missing.
AH = 00 Error unknown.

Packet LABEL BYTE
    DD   Beginning sector (0 origin).
    DW   Number of sectors to read or write.
    DD   Address of data buffer.

> **Using the Disks** 183

> **NOTE** The flags are left on the stack after this INT call because information is returned in the current flags. After you check the flags that were returned, make sure you do a POPF. Also, this INT destroys the contents of all registers.

DOS INT 25H reads from the disk and DOS INT 26H writes to the disk. The registers are set in the same fashion for each interrupt; the only difference is that in one case you are reading from the disk and in the other you are writing to it.

The only real difference here between the DOS disk handling and the BIOS disk handling is that BIOS requires track or cylinder number, head number, and so on, while the DOS Interrupts require that you use the logical sector number (as discussed earlier). All DOS really does is to calculate the head number, cylinder number, and so forth, and pass control directly to BIOS.

Even so, DOS INTs 25H and 26H do not even save the registers they use. You must assume that all registers have been changed. In addition, information is returned in the carry flag (that is, if there was an error, it will be set), so the flags that were originally set when the INT 25H call was made are left on the stack. After you check whether the carry flag has been set, pop the flags (POPF) to make sure the stack doesn't grow and grow. This can be catastrophic in an .EXE file as you outgrow the space allocated in the STACK segment or in a .COM file when the stack grows back from the end of the segment and overwrites code or data.

> **TIP** The DOS disk interrupts are the interrupts to monitor (with a TSR program — see Chapter 7) if you want to keep an eye on the health of your disk drives. When DOS receives an error code from a disk operation, it retries the operation (up to five times) to eliminate the error. Since the retries cover up problems, you often do not get any advance warning that errors have been occurring on one of your drives until it crashes. If you watch the errors yourself, you can get some advance warning.

Note that INTs 25H and 26H were changed to handle disks with partitions greater than 32M (i.e., DOS 4+). In such cases, you have to supply the address of a *control packet*, which includes the first sector to read, the number of sectors to read, and the address at which to place the data. If you try to read from or write to media greater than 32M without using a control packet, the error code returned in AX will be 207H.

184 ▶ Advanced Assembly Language

INT 21H Services 1BH/1CH FAT Information

Input	Output
AH = 1BH (Use default drive)	DS:BX points to the "FAT Byte."
= 1CH (Use drive specified in DL 0 = Default, 1 = A...).	DX = Number of clusters.
	AL = Number of sectors/cluster.
	CX = Size of a sector (512).

These services are often useful. In the earliest version of DOS, the entire FAT was kept in memory, and DS:BX would return pointing to the FAT. Starting with DOS 2.0, however, this was no longer the case. Only the "FAT Byte," the disk identification byte is pointed to by DS:BX. Once you know what this byte is, you know exactly what disk format you are expected to work with.

In addition, the number of clusters on the disk is returned in DX, the number of sectors per cluster in AL, and the size of sectors in CX (so far, always 512). This information often comes in handy.

To get this information for the default drive, use service 1BH. To specify the drive you want, use service 1CH. We can take a quick look at service 1CH with DEBUG. Here there is a 360K diskette in the B drive:

```
-A100
08F7:0100 MOV     AH,1C    ;Select Service 1CH
08F7:0102 MOV     DL,2     ;And Look at Drive B:
08F7:0104 INT     21
08F7:0106 INT     20
08F7:0108
-G106

AX=1C02  BX=420E  CX=0200  DX=0162  SP=FFEE  BP=0000  SI=0000  DI=0000
DS=00E3  ES=08F7  SS=08F7  CS=08F7  IP=0106   NV UP DI PL NZ NA PO NC
08F7:0106 CD20              INT     20
```

DX holds the number of usable clusters (162H = 354). If we add to this 1 sector for the boot record, 4 sectors of FAT (since there are two copies), and 7 sectors of directory, that is an additional 12 sectors or 6 clusters. This adds up to the total space on the disk — 2 sides × 40 tracks × 9 sectors per track / 2 sectors per cluster = 360K.

AL holds the number of sectors/cluster, two, and CX holds the size of a physical sector, 200H = 512. DS:BX, the location of the FAT byte, is 00E3:420E. If we dump that address, we find:

▶ **Using the Disks** 185

```
-D00E3:420E
00E3:420E  FD 00                                                  }.
00E3:4210  56 42 E3 00 00 00 F6 F6-F6 F6 F6 F6 F6 F6 F6 F6         VBc...vvvvvvvvvv
00E3:4220  F6 F6 F6 F6 F6 F6 F6 F6-F6 F6 F6 F6 F6 F6 F6 F6         vvvvvvvvvvvvvvvv
00E3:4230  F6 F6 F6 F6 F6 F6 F6 F6-F6 F6 F6 F6 F6 F6 F6 F6         vvvvvvvvvvvvvvvv
00E3:4240  F6 F6 F6 F6 F6 F6 F6 F6-F6 F6 F6 F6 F6 F6 F6 F6         vvvvvvvvvvvvvvvv
00E3:4250  F6 F6 F6 F6 F6 F6 02 02-00 02 01 01 01 00 02 70         vvvvvv.........p
00E3:4260  00 0C 00 63 01 02 05 00-CC 03 70 00 FD FF FF FF         ...c....L.p.l...
00E3:4270  FF FF 00 00 F6 F6 F6 F6-F6 F6 F6 F6 F6 F6 F6 F6         ....vvvvvvvvvvvv
00E3:4280  F6 F6 F6 F6 F6 F6 F6 F6-F6 F6 F6 F6                     vvvvvvvvvvvv
-q
```

As expected, the first byte is 0FDH, the code for a double-sided, nine-sectored diskette.

INT 21H Service 36H Get Free Disk Space

Input	Output
AH = 36H	AX = 0FFFH → Drive number invalid.
DL = Drive number (0 = Default	AX = Number of sectors/cluster.
1 = A...)	BX = Number of available clusters.
	CX = Size of a sector (512).
	DX = Number of clusters.

This service returns just the same output as the last service, 1CH, except that instead of pointing at the FAT byte, BX holds the number of free clusters. Let's take a look at the same diskette we used in the last example with this service to find out how much space is available on it.

```
-A100
08F7:0100 MOV    AH,36    ;Select Service 36H
08F7:0102 MOV    DL,2     ;And look at Drive B: again.
08F7:0104 INT    21
08F7:0106 INT    20
08F7:0108
-G106

AX=0002  BX=00C0  CX=0200  DX=0162  SP=FFEE  BP=0000  SI=0000  DI=0000
DS=08F7  ES=08F7  SS=08F7  CS=08F7  IP=0106   NV UP DI PL NZ NA PO NC
08F7:0106 CD20           INT    20
-q
```

This time, the registers come back with the same information as before, except for BX, which holds the number of free clusters. In this case, that is 0C0H. This means that there are 2 × 512 × 0C0H (192) = 196,608 free bytes on the disk or 192K.

This is the service DOS uses when looking at a directory to tell you how many free bytes there are available. Since the smallest piece of the disk that is kept track of is the cluster, 1,024 bytes on this kind of diskette, the amount of disk space available will always be exactly some multiple of 1,024.

If you are writing large amounts of data to a disk, it might be prudent to check how much space is left from time to time.

That's it for our survey of the PC's disks. There is more to the story than we've been able to cover. If you need more information, you should turn to the DOS Technical Reference Manual, or the BIOS Interface Technical Reference Manual, both available from IBM.

▶ Chapter 7

Writing Your Own Pop-up Programs

▶ Writing Your Own Pop-up Programs

ONE OF THE MAIN reasons assembly language is popular is its ability to run behind the scenes, so to speak, and support pop-up, terminate-and-stay-resident (TSR) programs. They have become so prevalent that they can hardly be left out of a book on advanced assembly language programming, and it is not difficult to write them.

Popular examples of memory-resident programs include calculators that can "pop up" onto the screen even when you're running another program; screen clocks that are always there; notepads; and utilities that can dial phone numbers, report on the printer, catch disk errors, let you run DOS commands, and so forth.

Memory-resident programs are just that: they stay in memory, even when you start to run other programs. Usually, the program loader in COMMAND.COM loads programs in memory right after the space used by DOS, runs your program, and then exits, marking that space as free once again. With a memory-resident program, that final step does not occur. Instead, the space that is marked as belonging to DOS is increased, until the code you've written is protected from being written over by the next program to be run. In this way, it becomes part of DOS. Only .COM files with their compact format can be made memory-resident unless you take special precautions.

> **TIP** What memory-resident programs can appear to do — let two programs run at once, for example, when you pop up a calculator — OS/2 does for real. With a pop-up, you have to explicitly select it to run it. Under OS/2, the machine itself can automatically give time to many different programs.

Writing Memory-Resident Code

Even though it may sound difficult, making programs memory-resident is really simple. The real problem to be solved is this: even if you add a section of code to DOS, it will do nothing by itself until called. Just making it memory-resident doesn't mean it will run — it will lie fallow until you can enter it again. For example, we could add the instructions:

```
MOV   AX,5
MOV   DX,32001
INC   DI
```

to the end of DOS rather easily with either of the two DOS interrupts (INT 27H or INT 2H, service 31H) designed to make code memory-resident. This would work simply by setting a few registers and ending the program with one of those interrupts, and not INT 20H as we have usually done. Now that those instructions are there, however, they are just bytes in memory. There is no reason they will run until CS:IP is set to them. In the same way, the code in DOS and BIOS doesn't all run at once everywhere. It waits until it is called.

> **NOTE** In the language of OS/2, we say DOS only has one *thread*. OS/2 can have multiple threads, which means many programs can be active at once.

There is really only one way to run memory-resident code like this and that is with software or hardware interrupts. Software interrupts we know about already. Hardware interrupts are not generated by a program, but instead they occur when something happens in the PC's peripherals. For example, if you touch a key on the keyboard, an interrupt, interrupt 9, is generated. The disk can generate other hardware interrupts if some operation takes place there, as can an internal clock inside the PC (the clock interrupt is in fact made 18.2 times a second).

A hardware interrupt causes the PC to temporarily stop — interrupt — the program it is running and attend instead to the hardware interrupt. Hardware interrupts can be "turned off" (except for some low-level ones) by programs with the CLI instruction, Clear Interrupt flag. This internal flag is there simply to do this: indicate whether hardware interrupts will be recognized or ignored by the microprocessor. If your program executes a CLI instruction, no typed keys will be recognized or recorded, for example. You can reset this flag with STI, Set Interrupt flag, which allows hardware interrupts to be recognized again.

Typically, memory-resident programs are popped onto the screen with a *hot key*, a key that, when pressed, will pop the calculator or whatever onto your screen. This is because they make use of the keyboard interrupt. Hardware interrupts are much like software interrupts in that every time they occur, some program can be run. In this case, the program that will be run is our memory-resident one. For memory resident code in pop-up programs, we use hardware interrupts, and not software ones. This is because the software interrupts would have to executed by the program then running, while you could interrupt that program with a hot key hardware interrupt at any time, and that is what we are aiming for.

Hardware and software interrupts do share one thing, however, and that is the way the microprocessor finds the address of the program to run when they occur. If your program executes an INT 10H instruction, for example, the microprocessor searches for the program that is to be run to handle it in the same way that it does if you pressed a key on the keyboard and generated an INT 9.

Since it is our intention to get our program run when a hardware interrupt is generated, we'll have to understand what this process is.

How Interrupts Work

What actually occurs when an interrupt (hardware or software) is executed is this: the microprocessor loads the address of the program for that interrupt from a specially designed table in low memory, called the *interrupt vector table*. This table is given the very first position in memory, starting at 0000:0000. For each interrupt, two words are stored: the segment address and the offset address of the program that is to be run when that interrupt occurs. As shown in Figure 7-1, the first two words in memory correspond to interrupt 0, the next two correspond to interrupt 1, and so on.

0000:000E	CS	Address of Interrupt 3
0000:000C	IP	
0000:000A	CS	Address of Interrupt 2
0000:0008	IP	
0000:0006	CS	Address of Interrupt 1
0000:0004	IP	
0000:0002	CS	Address of Interrupt 0
Bottom of memory →0000:0000	IP	

Figure 7-1. The Interrupt Vector Table

To find the address of the interrupt handling routine, the microprocessor turns to the interrupt vector table. It multiplies the interrupt number by 4 (actually, it shifts it left twice), and produces the address at which the interrupt's vector (that is, the full address of the interrupt's routine) is stored. Each interrupt vector takes up 4 bytes.

Next, the microprocessor pushes three words onto the stack to preserve them for later use: the current value of all the flags (these are stored as bits in one 16-bit word, the flags register), the current value of IP, and the current value of CS. Then, it heads off to handle the interrupt. After the interrupt is done, the microprocessor can pop these values from the stack, restoring them, and continue with the program that was in progress when the interrupt occurred (even down to the flags). This is done for either software or hardware interrupts.

If you write a procedure for an interrupt, it must end with IRET, not RET. IRET pops all three words off the stack and restores them. Then the interrupted program can continue.

For example, in a notepad program, let's say we press a key. An INT 9 is generated, and a code will have been added that checks every INT 9 to see if the hot key has been pressed. If not, a normal INT 9, ending with IRET, is executed (the microprocessor finds the address from 4 × 9 = 36 = 24H, or 0000:0024). If the hot key has been pressed,

192 ▶ Advanced Assembly Language

the notepad becomes active. It may have its own program, also ending with IRET, that will handle typed-in keys from then on.

Intercepting Interrupt Vectors

A clever program will set itself up in memory by changing the interrupt vector stored for a particular interrupt so that when that interrupt occurs, the microprocessor will come to the program and not to the interrupt routine. This is how memory-resident programs get run.

For example, a notepad program would change the address stored at 0000:0024, the INT 9 vector, to point to itself instead. It might store the original address of INT 9 to let it handle what the notepad doesn't want. Here's the way the interrupt vector might start out in the interrupt vector table.

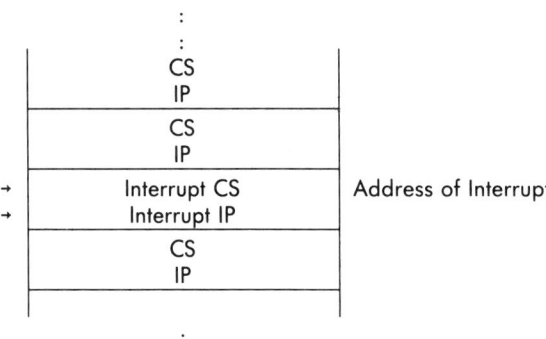

Figure 7-2.

And our program might be at some high point in memory at a specific value of CS:IP.

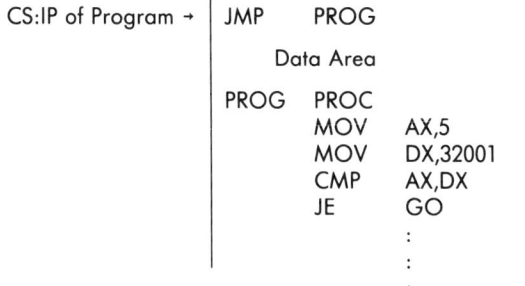

Figure 7-3.

What we want to do is to supplant the routine that services the interrupt with our own program, PROG. In other words, we want the two words in the interrupt vector

▶ Writing Your Own Pop-up Programs 193

table called Interrupt CS and Interrupt IP to be changed to the corresponding values of our program's beginning location, Program CS and Program IP.

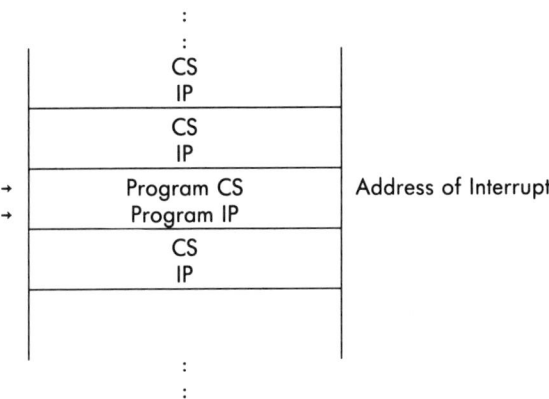

Figure 7-4.

Usually, a program that intercepts an interrupt doesn't handle all the functions of that interrupt, but occasionally passes on those things it doesn't want to do to the old interrupt routine. For this reason, Interrupt CS and Interrupt IP are stored in the data area of the program.

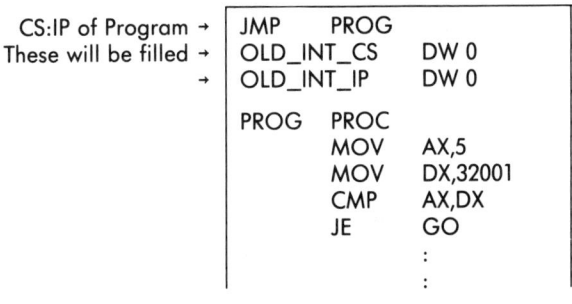

Figure 7-5.

That's all there is to it. When that interrupt occurs, control will come to us, not to the old interrupt routine. Our program PROG was loaded by COMMAND.COM into the beginning of available memory. When we make it memory-resident, PROG will stay where it is (that is, Program CS and Program IP will not change), and the address where programs get loaded will be moved to the end of PROG.

At this point we have to investigate how to fill the interrupt vector of a selected interrupt with the addresses CS and IP of our own program. The interrupt vectors are at the very bottom of memory. How do we reach them?

The Get and Set Interrupt Vector Services of INT 21H

There is a DOS interrupt 21H service to get an interrupt's current vector, service 35H. And there is also one to set the interrupt's vector to a new address, service 25H.

Since we will usually want to use the old interrupt routine for some things (for example, we will let the keyboard routine read the keyboard port and interpret the key that was typed for us), we want to retain its address before setting the vector to point to us. We can do that by storing the original interrupt vector in the data area of our own program. There we will set up two memory words in our program's data area, beginning at our label OLD_INTERRUPT like this:

```
            .MODEL SMALL
            .CODE
            ORG       100H          ;ORG = 100H to make this into a .COM file
    FIRST:  JMP       LOAD_PROG     ;First time through jump to initialize routine
              :
 →          OLD_INTERRUPT  DW 2 DUP(0)
              :
    PROG    PROC                    ;The keyboard interrupt will now come here.
```

Now we can copy the old interrupt vector into these two words at OLD_INTERRUPT in our program's data area. To get this old vector, we use INT 21H, service 35H, Get Vector:

INT 21H Service 35H Get Vector
Input: AH = 35H
        AL = Interrupt number.
Output: ES:BX = Interrupt's vector.

Getting the Old Interrupt Vector

To get the old interrupt vector, we'll put service 35H to work. Let's say that we want to intercept the keyboard interrupt, interrupt 9. In that case, we could set a constant named INTERRUPT_NUMBER to 9, and then we get the old interrupt vector like this:

```
        INTERRUPT_NUMBER     EQU 9
          :
          :
 →      MOV       AH,35H              ;Get old vector into ES:BX
 →      MOV       AL,INTERRUPT_NUMBER ;See EQU at beginning
 →      INT       21H
          :
```

Writing Your Own Pop-up Programs 195

Service 35H returns the interrupt's vector in ES:BX, and we want to store this address in the space we have set aside in the data area using the two words named OLD_INTERRUPT:

```
            .MODEL SMALL
            .CODE
            ORG     100H            ;ORG = 100H to make this into a .COM file
FIRST:      JMP     LOAD_PROG       ;First time through jump to initialize routine
            :
→           OLD_INTERRUPT  DW 2 DUP(0)
            :
PROG        PROC                    ;The keyboard interrupt will now come here.
```

Later, we are going to treat these two words as a single, double-word quantity. You may recall that the 80×86 has an odd way of storing objects larger than bytes in memory. It stores double words with the low word first. For example, 01020304H would be stored like this: 04 03 02 01 (remember that the 80×86 also exchanges the bytes in a word). This means that the offset address of the old interrupt's vector (in BX) goes into the first word of our storage, and the segment address (in ES) goes into the second word:

```
        INTERRUPT_NUMBER    EQU 9
        :
        :
        MOV     AH,35H              ;Get old vector into ES:BX
        MOV     AL,INTERRUPT_NUMBER ;See EQU at beginning
        INT     21H
→       MOV     OLD_INTERRUPT,BX    ;Store old interrupt vector
→       MOV     OLD_INTERUPT[2],ES
        :
```

Resetting the Interrupt Vector

Now it's time to move ourselves into the interrupt vector table. We want to be able to change the vector to point to us not to the old interrupt routine. That is, we want to load our program's IP and Program CS into the interrupt's vector. To do this, we can use INT 21H, service 25H, Set Vector:

       INT 21H Service 25H Set Vector
Input: AH = 25H
       AL = Interrupt number
       DS:DX = New interrupt handler address
Output:(None)

We have to give service 25H the new address — the address of our program — in DS:DX. Since we haven't changed DS in our .COM file, we can leave that alone, but we do have to get the offset of our program — let's call it PROG — into DX. We can do that with LEA:

```
        INTERRUPT_NUMBER    EQU 9
        :
        :
        MOV     AH,35H              ;Get old vector into ES:BX
        MOV     AL,INTERRUPT_NUMBER ;See EQU at beginning
        INT     21H
        MOV     OLD_INTERRUPT,BX    ;Store old interrupt vector
        MOV     OLD_INTERUPT[2],ES
→       MOV     AH,25H              ;Set new interrupt vector
→       LEA     DX,PROG
→       INT     21H
        :
```

At this point, we have changed the interrupt's interrupt vector so that it points to our program. Every time that interrupt is executed, we will get control.

Making Code Memory-Resident

Our code is now able to reset the interrupt so that it will come to us instead of the old interrupt handling routine. But how do we make sure that our program will stay in memory? There are two ways to do this, using either DOS INT 27H and INT 21H service 31H. To use INT 27H, simply set DS:DX to the last address you want to keep in memory, and execute INT 27H. That's it.

INT 21H service 31H can give a *return code*, which can be examined by either the ERRORLEVEL batch command or INT 21H service 4DH. Since we are not going to use return codes in this book, we will use INT 27H. Nonetheless, to use INT 21H service 31H, set the number of *paragraphs* that you want to keep in memory into DX. A paragraph is 16 bytes. Move the number you want to use as the return code into AL, set AH to 31H and execute INT 21H.

Here's how we will use INT 27H. As most programs that install themselves in memory do, we will set up a small initialization part of the program at the very end of the code. This part is only to install the program in memory, and it will be jettisoned when the program is installed. For this reason, it is occasionally called the *transient* part of the program. Our program is called PROG. Let's call the transient part LOAD_PROG. LOAD_PROG will come after PROG in the .ASM file.

Writing Your Own Pop-up Programs 197

When we first run the .COM file that will attach itself in memory, we start at ORG 100H. At this location, we have been used to seeing the instruction JMP PROG. In this case, that will change to JMP LOAD_PROG. What LOAD_PROG will do, the first time that the .COM file is run, is to reset the appropriate interrupt vectors so that they point to PROG. We do not want to run PROG when we run the .COM file (so we didn't say JMP PROG at ORG 100H). We only want PROG to run when the interrupts it is intercepting are executed.

Instead, this first time, LOAD_PROG is run. After resetting the correct interrupt vectors to PROG, LOAD_PROG will point DS:DX at the beginning of itself and execute an INT 27H. This means that INT 27H will retain in memory all our program up to the point where LOAD_PROG starts. The next program that is loaded will therefore preserve PROG but write over LOAD_PROG. See Figure 7-6 for an idea of how it looks (PROG will become memory-resident, and LOAD_PROG will be jettisoned after the INT 27H).

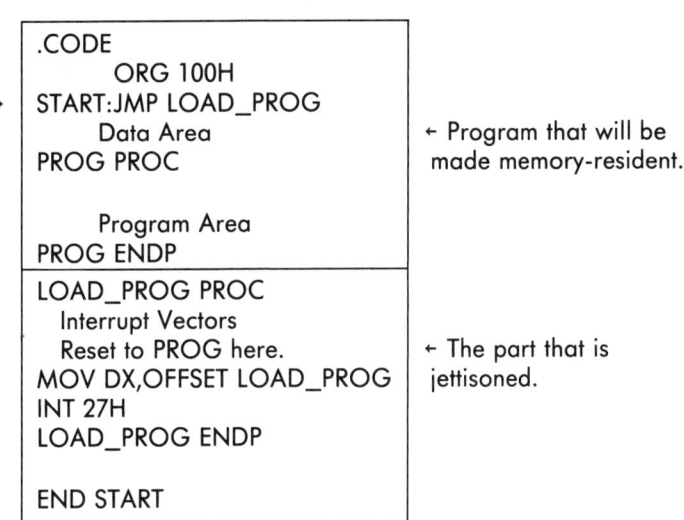

Figure 7-6. Making PROG Memory-Resident

We have already written the transient part that resets the interrupt vector. All we have to add is the part that secures PROG in memory. That looks like this:

```
              :
              :
              :
PROG     ENDP

LOAD_PROG     PROC              ;This procedure intializes everything

         MOV  AH,35H             ;Get old vector into ES:BX
         MOV  AL,INTERRUPT_NUMBER    ;See EQU at beginning
         INT  21H
         MOV  OLD_KEY_INT,BX     ;Store old interrupt vector
```

198 ▶ Advanced Assembly Language

```
            MOV     OLD_KEY_INT[2],ES

            MOV     AH,25H          ;Set new interrupt vector
            LEA     DX,PROG
            INT     21H

EXIT2:      MOV     DX,OFFSET LOAD_PROG
            INT     27H
LOAD_PROG   ENDP
```

Now PROG is safely installed in memory. This is the entire LOAD_PROG procedure, the whole transient part of our program. Soon we will bring all this together into a .COM file shell that can be made memory-resident, but first we have to make sure that PROG can handle interrupts.

Writing a Program That Can Handle Interrupts

We've finished designing the transient part of our program. Now we come to more familiar territory, that of the program itself, which simply handles whatever it is we want to do when the interrupt is executed. Let's look at that part in some detail.

In outline, the program, which we'll call PROG for this example, will fit in as shown in Figure 7-7.

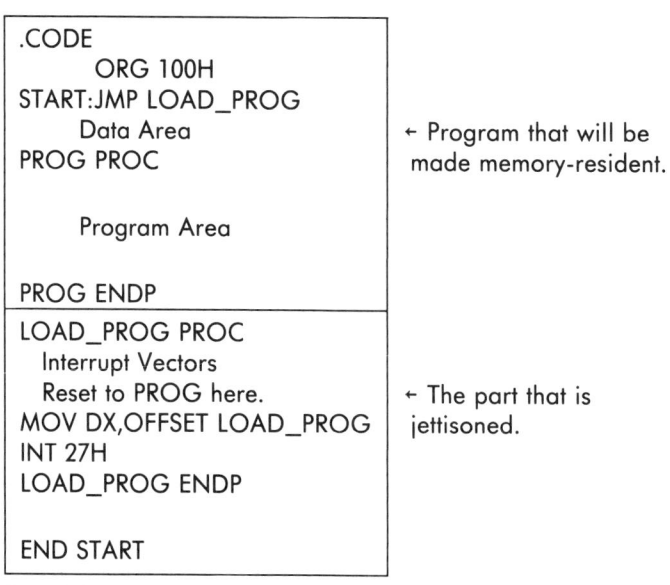

Figure 7-7. *Development of PROG*

And after the transient part has installed the program, all we'll be left with is this:

▶ Writing Your Own Pop-up Programs 199

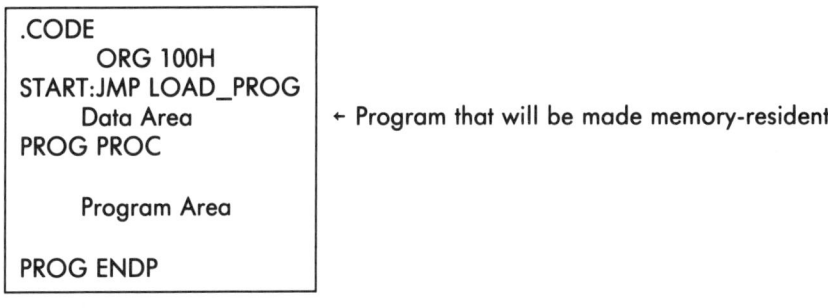

← Program that will be made memory-resident.

Figure 7-8.

This program has the normal data area and code areas that we're used to. In essence, it will be like any other program we've written, with one or two changes.

Those changes are these: we will usually include a call to the original interrupt routine to let it handle some things (like reading keys from the keyboard port, and then we'll read the key from memory). Also, we'll be very careful in the beginning and end of the program to save and then restore all registers.

The reason we save and then restore all registers is a common sense one: imagine that you had just pressed a hot key for your pop-up calculator program. When you're done, you press it again, and the program you had been running takes up where it left off.

You can see how things would be if all the registers had been changed. It's like changing all the variables in midprogram, which will most likely cause the program to crash. To avoid this, we'll push all registers and pop them before exiting. Here is PROG in outline:

```
        .MODEL SMALL
        .CODE
        ORG     100H            ;ORG = 100H to make this into a .COM file
FIRST:  JMP     LOAD_PROG       ;First time through jump to initialize routine
        :
        Data Area
        :
PROG    PROC                    ;The keyboard interrupt will now come here.
  →     PUSH    AX              ;Save the used registers for good form
  →     PUSH    BX
  →     PUSH    CX
  →     PUSH    DX
  →     PUSH    DI
  →     PUSH    SI
  →     PUSH    DS
  →     PUSH    ES

        ;Prog goes here.
EXIT:→  POP     ES              ;Having done Pushes, here are the Pops
  →     POP     DS
  →     POP     SI
  →     POP     DI
  →     POP     DX
  →     POP     CX
  →     POP     BX
```

```
         POP     AX
         IRET                    ;An interrupt needs an IRET
PROG     ENDP
```

Also, we have ended our program PROG with IRET, the proper end for an interrupt routine. At the end of every executed INT instruction, there is an IRET or something equivalent. IRET is a normal FAR return (that is, both CS and IP are retrieved from the stack) with the flags added on. We can push all the microprocessor's flags with the instruction PUSHF and pop them again, restoring all flags, with POPF.

It is important to realize that we can no longer rely on DS and ES being set to our code segment: if we interrupt another program, then the segment registers will naturally be set to the ones it was using at the time we take over control. This means that we will often fill those registers from the CS value, giving us the environment we are used to and using only one segment. As we've seen, if you want to load DS from CS, you do it this way:

```
ASSUME  DS:@CODE
MOV     AX,CS
MOV     DS,AX
```

The @CODE keyword is translated into same segment name as the .CODE directive. (If you use another segment directive, such as .DATA, you can use @DATA.)

Calling the Old Interrupt

Usually, we will want the old interrupt to do work for us. As mentioned in Chapter 2, the keyboard interrupt reads keys that were struck directly from the keyboard, port 60H on the I/O bus. This information would be practically meaningless to us. The keyboard interrupt does a lot of processing to convert that key into an ASCII code (it has to look the bytes it receives up in an internal table, for example), which is work that we don't want to duplicate.

However, when the key is interpreted, it is placed in memory in the keyboard buffer, and it is a simple matter to read the keyboard buffer, to see what was typed, and whether or not the key was our hot key. For this reason, we'll want to call the keyboard interrupt to read the struck key and interpret it for us. Before we return to the program that was interrupted by the keystroke, we will be able to examine the key that was struck in the keyboard buffer.

▶ Writing Your Own Pop-up Programs 201

> **TIP** Even if you do not want to use the old interrupt routine for anything, it is often a good thing to call it anyway, in case another memory-resident program has already been installed that intercepts this interrupt. Unless you called the old interrupt, this earlier memory-resident program would never be run.

We've already stored the old interrupt routine's address in the data area of PROG (LOAD_PROG did that). Now all we have to do is call it.

Indirect Calls and the DD and LABEL Directives

There is a simple way of calling such addresses. Up until now, we've had to name our procedures and call them by name, like this:

```
        ORG     100H
        FIRST:  JMP PROG_A
                :
                Data Area
                :
        PROG_A  PROC
                :
→               CALL    PROG_B
                :
        PROG_A  ENDP
        PROG_B  PROC
                :
                RET
        PROG_B  ENDP
```

On the other hand, we could have said this:

```
        ORG     100H
        FIRST:  JMP PROG_A
→   PROG_B_ADDR     DW 0
        PROG_A  PROC
                :
→               MOV     PROG_B_ADDR,OFFSET PROG_B
→               CALL    PROG_B_ADDR
                :
        PROG_A  ENDP

        PROG_B  PROC
                :
                RET
        PROG_B  ENDP
```

All that we've done is to store the offset address of the label PROG_B in a memory word, PROG_B_ADDR. Then, the microprocessor allows us to execute an instruction like this: CALL PROG_B_ADDR, which is the same thing as CALL PROG_B. This is helpful to us here, since we do not know in advance where the old interrupt routine will be in memory and, therefore, cannot give it a name like PROG_B.

In our case, however, we cannot assume that only the offset address is needed; the old interrupt routine is almost certainly not in our current segment. Instead, we will have to use both words of the address, offset and segment addresses. To do this, We will define OLD_INTERRUPT_ADDR with DD this way in the data area of our program:

```
            .MODEL SMALL
            .CODE
            ORG     100H            ;ORG = 100H to make this into a .COM file
FIRST:      JMP     LOAD_PROG       ;First time through jump to initialize routine
→           OLD_INTERRUPT_ADDR  DD  ?           ;Location of old interrupt

PROG        PROC                    ;The interrupt will now come here.
            PUSH    AX              ;Save the used registers for good form
            PUSH    BX
            PUSH    CX
            PUSH    DX
            PUSH    DI
            PUSH    SI
            PUSH    DS
            PUSH    ES
            PUSHF                   ;First, call old interrupt
            CALL    OLD_INTERRUPT_ADDR

            ;Prog goes here.

EXIT:       POP     ES              ;Having done Pushes, here are the Pops
            POP     DS
            POP     SI
            POP     DI
            POP     DX
            POP     CX
            POP     BX
            POP     AX
            IRET                    ;An interrupt needs an IRET
PROG        ENDP
```

so that we can CALL OLD_INTERRUPT_ADDR. And then we will label the first word as OLD_INTERRUPT like this:

```
            .MODEL SMALL
            .CODE
            ORG     100H            ;ORG = 100H to make this into a .COM file
FIRST:      JMP     LOAD_PROG       ;First time through jump to initialize routine
→           OLD_INTERRUPT    LABEL   WORD
            OLD_INTERRUPT_ADDR  DD  ?           ;Location of old interrupt
```

▶ Writing Your Own Pop-up Programs

```
PROG      PROC                    ;The interrupt will now come here.
          PUSH    AX              ;Save the used registers for good form
          PUSH    BX
          PUSH    CX
          PUSH    DX
          PUSH    DI
          PUSH    SI
          PUSH    DS
          PUSH    ES
          PUSHF                   ;First, call old interrupt
          CALL    OLD_INTERRUPT_ADDR

          ;Prog goes here.

EXIT:     POP     ES              ;Having done Pushes, here are the Pops
          POP     DS
          POP     SI
          POP     DI
          POP     DX
          POP     CX
          POP     BX
          POP     AX
          IRET                    ;An interrupt needs an IRET
PROG      ENDP
```

LABEL is useful when you have to refer to a particular memory location in two ways, as if, for example, it was defined with DW and DD. LOAD_PROG is satisfied, since it will be able to load individual words into OLD_INTERRUPT, and PROG itself is satisfied, because it will be able to CALL OLD_INTERRUPT_ADDR as a double word.

Waiting at the end of the old interrupt routine that we are about to call, however, is not a normal return, but an IRET, and IRET pops the flags off the stack (this is the final word it pops before returning to the calling program). To take care of this, we will not simply call OLD_INTERRUPT_ADDR this way:

```
CALL    OLD_INTERRUPT_ADDR
```

but instead will add the flags to the stack first with PUSHF:

```
PUSHF                   ;First, call old interrupt
CALL    OLD_INTERRUPT_ADDR
```

And now we are all set to call the old interrupt without trouble.

Use This TSR Shell

Our entire terminate-and-stay-resident (TSR) .COM file shell can be seen in Listing 7-1. Now that it's built, we can simply use this shell, instead of building it from scratch each time. As it stands, this shell is a little barren. We will add some code to it specifically so that it can intercept the keyboard interrupt (the most widely intercepted interrupt) and report the character that was typed in DX a little later. Before we do that, we will develop an example, using the shell as it stands.

Listing 7-1. Terminate and Stay Resident .COM File Shell.   1 of 2

```
            .MODEL SMALL
INTERRUPT_NUMBER        EQU     9 ← Put the INT number here

            .CODE
            ORG     100H            ;ORG = 100H to make this into a .COM file
FIRST:      JMP     LOAD_PROG       ;First time through jump to initialize routine
            OLD_INTERRUPT   LABEL   WORD
            OLD_INTERRUPT_ADDR      DD      ?       ;Location of old interrupt

PROG        PROC                    ;The interrupt will now come here.
            PUSH    AX              ;Save the used registers for good form
            PUSH    BX
            PUSH    CX
            PUSH    DX
            PUSH    DI
            PUSH    SI
            PUSH    DS
            PUSH    ES
            PUSHF                   ;First, call old interrupt
            CALL    OLD_INTERRUPT_ADDR

            ;Prog goes here.

EXIT:       POP     ES              ;Having done Pushes, here are the Pops
            POP     DS
            POP     SI
            POP     DI
            POP     DX
            POP     CX
            POP     BX
            POP     AX
            IRET                    ;An interrupt needs an IRET
PROG        ENDP

LOAD_PROG   PROC                    ;This procedure intializes everything

            MOV     AH,35H          ;Get old vector into ES:BX
            MOV     AL,INTERRUPT_NUMBER     ;See EQU at beginning
            INT     21H

            MOV     OLD_INTERRUPT,BX        ;Store old interrupt vector
            MOV     OLD_INTERRUPT[2],ES

            MOV     AH,25H          ;Set new interrupt vector
            LEA     DX,PROG
```

Listing 7-1. Terminate and Stay Resident .COM File Shell.

```
            INT     21H
EXIT2:      MOV     DX,OFFSET LOAD_PROG     ;Set up everything but LOAD_PROG to
            INT     27H                     ;stay and attach itself to DOS
LOAD_PROG   ENDP

            END     FIRST   ;END "FIRST" so 80x86 will go to FIRST first.
```

Some Things You Can't Do

It would be great if we could do anything from a TSR program; however, you cannot. We cannot, for example, use any DOS interrupts (including DOS INT 21H). The reason is that the DOS interrupts are comparatively fragile. If our main program is executing something in INT 21H, then we take over with a memory-resident program and try to run the same code, we'll destroy the memory variables that were already set for the first program. When we finish and go back to the first program, everything will be in a shambles.

> **NOTE** In computer language, DOS is not *reentrant* (OS/2 is reentrant). The DOS interrupts actually can be used, if you add a large amount of overhead programming, but we're not going to do that here.

> **TIP** You can, however, use the BIOS interrupts without problem in a TSR! They are considerably more sturdy than the DOS interrupts here. The BIOS interrupts make up the interrupts up to 1FH. Later, we are going to use INT 10H, the BIOS video interrupt, to print on the screen from a TSR.

Some Things You Can Do

One thing we can do is to write an example program right now. After having developed all the technology of memory-resident programs, let's put it into practice.

Example program: There is no cursor on the screen in graphics modes, but we can make a program that will add one. There is a certain hardware interrupt that is very useful to memory-resident programs, the timer interrupt, INT 8. This interrupt is made 18.2 times a second all the time. The PC or PS/2 stops work 18.2 times a second to check on the timer (unless we turn off hardware interrupts).

We'll intercept that interrupt and use it, 18.2 times a second, to print out an underscore ("_") as a cursor at the current cursor position with INT 10H service 0AH (recall

206 ▶ Advanced Assembly Language

that although INT services 9 and 0AH write out characters, they do not advance the cursor). Our program, PROG, will be very easy. All we really have to do is make sure we set INTERRUPT_NUMBER to 8 and then print out "_". Here's the program:

```
INTERRUPT_NUMBER        EQU     8
        .MODEL SMALL
        .CODE
        ORG     100H            ;ORG = 100H to make this into a .COM file
FIRST:  JMP     LOAD_PROG       ;First time through jump to initialize routine
        OLD_INTERRUPT   LABEL   WORD
        OLD_INTERRUPT_ADDR      DD      ?       ;Location of old interrupt

PROG    PROC                    ;The interrupt will now come here.
        PUSH    AX              ;Save the used registers for good form
        PUSH    BX
        PUSH    CX
        PUSH    DX
        PUSH    DI
        PUSH    SI
        PUSH    DS
        PUSH    ES
        PUSHF                   ;First, call old interrupt
        CALL    OLD_INTERRUPT_ADDR
→       MOV     AH,0AH
→       MOV     CX,1
→       MOV     BH,0
→       MOV     AL,"_"
→       INT     10H
        POP     ES      ;Having done Pushes, here are the Pops
        POP     DS
        POP     SI
        POP     DI
        POP     DX
        POP     CX
        POP     BX
        POP     AX
        IRET                    ;An interrupt needs an IRET
PROG    ENDP

LOAD_PROG       PROC            ;This procedure intializes everything

        MOV     AH,35H          ;Get old vector into ES:BX
        MOV     AL,INTERRUPT_NUMBER     ;See EQU at beginning
        INT     21H
        MOV     OLD_INTERRUPT,BX        ;Store old interrupt vector
        MOV     OLD_INTERRUPT[2],ES

        MOV     AH,25H          ;Set new interrupt vector
        LEA     DX,PROG
        INT     21H
EXIT:   MOV     DX,OFFSET LOAD_PROG     ;Set up everything but LOAD_PROG to
        INT     27H                     ;stay and attach itself to DOS
LOAD_PROG       ENDP

        END     FIRST   ;END "FIRST" so 80x86 will go to FIRST first.
```

Writing Your Own Pop-up Programs

The body of PROG just types out this cursor, "_". We select graphics page 0 (the usual page) with MOV BH,0; set the count of characters to write to 1 with MOV CX,1; select service 0AH with MOV AH,0AH; and type a "_" by placing that character in AL:

```
→ MOV     AH,0AH
→ MOV     CX,1
→ MOV     BH,0
→ MOV     AL,"_"
→ INT     10H
```

This is our first TSR program. To use it, just type it in, assemble it, link it, and run it through EXE2BIN. Then put yourself in a graphics mode on the screen, as discussed in Chapter 3 (note that there is no cursor), and run CURSOR.COM.

A cursor will appear: just as an unblinking underscore, but the underscore will stay there wherever the cursor is. Unfortunately, sometimes the cursor is moved around on the screen discontinuously; that is, no character is typed to overwrite the "_" before the cursor moves on. Most of the time this is not the case, but sometimes you will see underscores in odd places on the page.

> **TIP** You can easily make the cursor blink by counting the number of times the timer interrupt has been called and by typing either a "_" or a blank space " ". You can also fix the problem of left-behind cursors (when the cursor is moved discontinuously), if you really want to, but you will have to intercept INT 10H also, and check when the move cursor service, service 2, is called.

Intercepting the Keyboard Interrupt

This is the big one, the interrupt that most pop-up type programs really use, the keyboard interrupt. As mentioned before, whenever a key is struck, an INT 9 is generated. The PC stops work to go off to the keyboard interrupt routine (whose vector is at 4 × 9 = 36 = 24H; 0000:0024); this routine reads in the key codes, and places the key's ASCII code into the keyboard buffer, along with its scan code.

We can set up labels for all the parts of the keyboard buffer by defining a segment with the AT directive. For example, here's how we can set up our ROM_BIOS_DATA segment:

```
ROM_BIOS_DATA    SEGMENT AT 40H   ;BIOS statuses held here, also keyboard buffer
         ORG     1AH
         HEAD DW     ?                ;Unread chars go from Head to Tail
         TAIL DW     ?
```

208 ▶ Advanced Assembly Language

```
                BUFFER          DW      16 DUP (?)      ;The buffer itself
                BUFFER_END      DW ?

        ROM_BIOS_DATA   ENDS
```

To read a key from the keyboard buffer, we'll have to set DS to the ROM_BIOS_ DATA segment (after the appropriate ASSUME), and check where the tail is in the keyboard buffer (the location where the next key will be placed). The key just before that in the keyboard buffer is the new one. We'll read it from the buffer and place its scan code in DH, and its ASCII code in DL. Your program can then take over and see if it's the hot key expected. If not, you should just exit; that is, jump to the label EXIT.

If the key is the one you were expecting, your program might want to spring into action and start intercepting all keys as input. This means that your program will have to remove keys from the keyboard buffer as soon as they are typed (and place them into a notepad, for example).

To remove a key from the keyboard buffer, all you need to do is to move the tail of the buffer to overwrite the key. At the point your program takes over (made clear in the keyboard-intercepting .COM file shell to follow), BX will hold the offset address of the current key in the buffer. To remove this key, just use the instruction MOV TAIL,BX.

```
At the point your program takes over:
        [Check scan code (in DH) and ASCII code (in DL)]
            [Is it a key you want to accept as input?]
                 |                              |
                Yes                             No
                 |                              |
        [Remove this key                [JMP to EXIT, leaving this
         from the keyboard               key to be used by other
         buffer with MOV TAIL,BX]        programs.]
        [Do work]
        [JMP to EXIT]
```

For example, if your program wanted to remove all typed ^N's (so they never appeared on the screen or got read by any program), it would check for the correct scan code in DH (31H) and the correct ASCII code in DL (0EH). If it found what it was looking for, it would remove the key. If not, it wouldn't interfere. To do this, all you would need are these instructions in the .COM file shell where you take over:

```
        CMP     DX,310EH        ;Is this a ^N?
        JNE     EXIT            ;No, just exit
        MOV     TAIL,BX         ;Yes, remove it
        JMP     EXIT            ;And leave
```

We'll develop an example after introducing our key-intercepting .COM file shell to make this clear.

The Key-intercepting .COM File Shell

The key-intercepting TSR .COM file shell is shown in Listing 7-2, complete with instructions on what to do when your program takes over, and how to accept a typed key as input by removing it from the keyboard buffer (notice the ASSUME — if you want to change DS back to the value in CS, you must use another ASSUME just before you do).

Listing 7-2. TSR_KEY.ASM — A Key-intercepting TSR .COM File Shell.

```
INTERRUPT_NUMBER     EQU     9

        .MODEL SMALL
ROM_BIOS_DATA   SEGMENT AT 40H  ;BIOS statuses held here, also keyboard buffer

        ORG     1AH
        HEAD DW     ?                        ;Unread chars go from Head to Tail
        TAIL DW     ?
        BUFFER      DW      16 DUP (?)       ;The buffer itself
        BUFFER_END  LABEL   WORD

ROM_BIOS_DATA   ENDS

        .CODE
        ORG     100H                ;ORG = 100H to make this into a .COM file
FIRST:  JMP     LOAD_PROG           ;First time through jump to initialize routine

        OLD_KEY_INT     LABEL   WORD
        OLD_KEYBOARD_INT        DD      ?       ;Location of old kbd interrupt

PROG    PROC                        ;The keyboard interrupt will now come here.
        PUSH    AX                  ;Save the used registers for good form
        PUSH    BX
        PUSH    CX
        PUSH    DX
        PUSH    DI
        PUSH    SI
        PUSH    DS
        PUSH    ES
        PUSHF                       ;First, call old keyboard interrupt
        CALL    OLD_KEYBOARD_INT

→       ASSUME  DS:ROM_BIOS_DATA    ;Examine the char just put in
→       MOV     BX,ROM_BIOS_DATA
→       MOV     DS,BX

→       MOV     BX,TAIL             ;Point to current tail
→       CMP     BX,HEAD             ;If at head, kbd int has deleted char
→       JE      IN                  ;So leave
→       SUB     BX,2                ;Point to just read in character
```

Listing 7-2. TSR_KEY.ASM — A Key-intercepting TSR .COM File Shell.

```
          CMP     BX,OFFSET BUFFER         ;Did we undershoot buffer?
          JAE     NO_WRAP                  ;Nope
          MOV     BX,OFFSET BUFFER_END     ;Yes -- move to buffer top
          SUB     BX,2                     ;Point to just read in character
NO_WRAP:  MOV     DX,[BX]                  ;Char in DX now
```

> **NOTE** Your program takes over here (keep in mind that DS is still at ROM_BIOS_DATA segment). The just-struck key's scan code is in DH and its ASCII code in DL at this point. If you want to remove this key from the keyboard buffer (i.e., accept it as input), use the instruction MOV TAIL,BX here. Otherwise, you may exit by jumping to the label EXIT.

```
          ;MOV     TAIL,BX         ;-Optional removal of key from buffer.
               :
          [Your code here.]
               :
EXIT:     POP     ES              ;Having done Pushes, here are the Pops
          POP     DS
          POP     SI
          POP     DI
          POP     DX
          POP     CX
          POP     BX
          POP     AX
          IRET                    ;An interrupt needs an IRET
PROG      ENDP

LOAD_PROG PROC                    ;This procedure intializes everything

          MOV     AH,35H          ;Get old vector into ES:BX
          MOV     AL,INTERRUPT_NUMBER    ;See EQU at beginning
          INT     21H

          MOV     OLD_KEY_INT,BX         ;Store old interrupt vector
          MOV     OLD_KEY_INT[2],ES

          MOV     AH,25H          ;Set new interrupt vector
          LEA     DX,PROG
          INT     21H

          MOV     DX,OFFSET LOAD_PROG    ;Set up everything but LOAD_PROG to
          INT     27H                    ;stay and attach itself to DOS
LOAD_PROG ENDP

END       FIRST          ;END "FIRST" so 80x86 will go to FIRST first.
```

Let's put together an example.

SWITCH.ASM: A Memory-Resident Hot Key Program

Here we'll put our keyboard interceptor to work and see how everything fits together. We'll write a program named SWITCH.ASM that lets you switch between two screens, the MDA and CGA, if you have both installed. The hot key will be Alt-S. In other words, when you are using one screen and type Alt-S, you will switch to the other screen, no matter what program is running.

To switch screens, it is not enough to simply switch video modes. If you are using the same screen, switching video modes is fine, but it will not automatically change the monitor you are using if your current monitor does not support the mode you select.

You also must change one of the words in the BIOS data area, the equipment word (also called, inaccurately, the equipment flag). In this case, you load this word from 40:0010 into some register — for example, CX. The instruction AND CX,11101111B will reset the appropriate bit to switch to the graphics screen. OR CX,00010000B will set you up for monochrome (then, of course, you must return the contents of CX to memory location 40:0010).

By checking a particular bit in the equipment word, we can tell whether or not a monochrome screen or a CGA screen is in use, and then toggle to the other option. The hot key here is ALT-S, which means the scan code we are looking for is 1FH and the ASCII code is 0. DX will hold 1F00H if Alt-S has been typed when our program takes over from the keyboard intercepting shell, and we will spring into action.

If Alt-S *has* been typed, we remove it from the keyboard buffer. In that way, the Alt-S will not be left over after we've finished changing screens. To erase the key, we'll use MOV TAIL,BX. Here is the part of the program that both detects whether or not the hot key was typed, and if it was, erases it from the buffer (and, if it was not, exits):

```
         MOV     BX,TAIL              ;Point to current tail
         CMP     BX,HEAD              ;If at head, kbd int has deleted char
         JE      OUT                  ;So leave
         SUB     BX,2                 ;Point to just read in character
         CMP     BX,OFFSET BUFFER     ;Did we undershoot buffer?
         JAE     NO_WRAP              ;Nope
         MOV     BX,OFFSET BUFFER_END ;Yes -- move to buffer top
         SUB     BX,2                 ;Point to just read in character
NO_WRAP: MOV     DX,[BX]              ;Char in DX now
         CMP     DX,1F00H             ;Is the char an ALT-S?
         JNE     EXIT                 ;No
         MOV     TAIL,BX              ;Yes -- delete it from buffer
```

The whole program SWITCH, which just switches us back and forth between the MDA and CGA, can be seen in Listing 7-3.

Listing 7-3. SWITCH.ASM — Switches between MDA and CGA Screens.

```
                ;Uses ALT-S to toggle between screens (Graphics <--> Monochrome)
INTERRUPT_NUMBER        EQU     9
        .MODEL SMALL
ROM_BIOS_DATA   SEGMENT AT 40H  ;BIOS statuses held here, also keyboard buffer

        ORG     1AH
        HEAD DW         ?                       ;Unread chars go from Head to Tail
        TAIL DW         ?
        BUFFER          DW      16 DUP (?)      ;The buffer itself
        BUFFER_END      LABEL   WORD

ROM_BIOS_DATA   ENDS

        .CODE
        ORG     100H                    ;ORG = 100H to make this into a .COM file
FIRST:  JMP     LOAD_PROG               ;First time through jump to initialize routine

        OLD_KEY_INT     LABEL   WORD
        OLD_KEYBOARD_INT        DD      ?       ;Location of old kbd interrupt

PROG    PROC                    ;The keyboard interrupt will now come here.
        PUSH    AX              ;Save the used registers for good form
        PUSH    BX
        PUSH    CX
        PUSH    DX
        PUSH    DI
        PUSH    SI
        PUSH    DS
        PUSH    ES
        PUSHF                   ;First, call old keyboard interrupt
        CALL    OLD_KEYBOARD_INT

        ASSUME  DS:ROM_BIOS_DATA        ;Examine the char just put in
        MOV     BX,ROM_BIOS_DATA
        MOV     DS,BX

        MOV     BX,TAIL                 ;Point to current tail
        CMP     BX,HEAD                 ;If at head, kbd int has deleted char
        JE      EXIT                    ;So leave
        SUB     BX,2                    ;Point to just read in character
        CMP     BX,OFFSET BUFFER        ;Did we undershoot buffer?
        JAE     NO_WRAP                 ;Nope
        MOV     BX,OFFSET BUFFER_END    ;Yes -- move to buffer top
        SUB     BX,2                    ;Point to just read in character
NO_WRAP:MOV     DX,[BX]                 ;Char in DX now
→       CMP     DX,1F00H                ;Is the char an ALT-S?
→       JNE     EXIT                    ;No
→       MOV     TAIL,BX                 ;Yes -- delete it from buffer
→
→       MOV     BX,10H                  ;Get equipment flag
→       MOV     AX,[BX]
→       MOV     CX,AX                   ;Put a copy in CX
→       AND     AX,00010000B            ;Is CGA in use?
→       CMP     AX,0
→       JE      TO_MONOCHROME           ;Yes
TO_GRAPHICS: ←                          ;No, switch to CGA
→       AND     CX,11101111B            ;Set up equipment byte
```

Listing 7-3. SWITCH.ASM — Switches between MDA and CGA Screens.

```
                MOV     [BX],CX                 ;And reinstall it
                MOV     AX,0002                 ;Set up a CGA screen mode
                INT     10H
                JMP     EXIT                    ;And leave
TO_MONOCHROME:                                  ;Turn on monochrome here
                OR      CX,00010000B            ;Set up equipment byte
                MOV     [BX],CX                 ;And reinstall it
                MOV     AX,0007                 ;Set up monochrome video mode
                INT     10H

EXIT:           POP     ES                      ;Having done Pushes, here are the Pops
                POP     DS
                POP     SI
                POP     DI
                POP     DX
                POP     CX
                POP     BX
                POP     AX
                IRET                            ;An interrupt needs an IRET
PROG            ENDP

LOAD_PROG       PROC                            ;This procedure intializes everything

                MOV     AH,35H                  ;Get old vector into ES:BX
                MOV     AL,INTERRUPT_NUMBER     ;See EQU at beginning
                INT     21H
                MOV     OLD_KEY_INT,BX          ;Store old interrupt vector
                MOV     OLD_KEY_INT[2],ES

                MOV     AH,25H                  ;Set new interrupt vector
                LEA     DX,PROG
                INT     21H

                MOV     DX,OFFSET LOAD_PROG     ;Set up everything but LOAD_PROG to
                INT     27H                     ;stay and attach itself to DOS
LOAD_PROG       ENDP
                END     FIRST
```

There's not much to this program: we just check to see if the CGA is in use, and, if it is, turn on monochrome instead by setting the equipment byte and changing to the monochrome video mode. If the CGA was not in use, we turn it on by setting up the equipment byte and changing to a CGA video mode. Of course, we restore all registers to the way they were before returning to the program then running (including segment registers).

> **TIP** If you want to write a pop-up notepad, you can use BIOS INT 10H, service 9 or 0AH, to write out the notepad on the screen. Then, while the pad was active, you can remove typed keys from the keyboard buffer (MOV BX,TAIL) and put them into the notepad area of memory. When the hot key

214 ▶ Advanced Assembly Language

> was typed again, you just stop intercepting typed characters, and take the notepad off the screen.

That is the end of our discussion of TSR programs. Their uses vary from programs that will take snaphots of the screen; that will log screen output; that will remember what's gone on the screen many screen-fuls ago (and let you scroll through it); that will pop-up utilities of all descriptions; that will put in disk caches to let disks go faster; and the list goes on. Let's press on now with our exploration of assembly language by looking at some fast math.

Chapter 8

Truly Fast Math

▶ **Truly Fast Math** 217

COMPUTERS WERE MADE to do at least one thing well: work with numbers. A large part of the 80×86 instruction set is set up exclusively to handle numbers, and some of these are not usually covered in introductory books. We will meet in some of these instructions in this chapter like IMUL, IADD, ADC, SHR, NOT, NEG, SBB, ROR, and others. In fact, we will discover that there is a whole new way of looking at numbers in the PC. We can look at them as signed numbers, and we will use conditional jumps like JG and JL, rather than JA and JB. Our picture of what the computer can do in handling numbers will be made complete in this chapter. Let's begin by covering just how signed numbers can be used in the PC.

How Signed Numbers Work

The 80×86 instructions only work with integer arithmetic — no floating point calculations. The math coprocessors, the 80×87 chips, are designed to work with huge floating point numbers.

> **TIP** If you have a Microsoft high-level language, you can use some 80×87 emulation routines, even if you do not have an 80×87. See the "/E" option for assembling programs. After assembling, you can link with the high-level language's modules, and the 80×87 emulation code will be linked in. Of course, emulating the real thing is slower than actually using it.

Up to this point, all the numbers we've been using have been unsigned whole numbers. Previously, a number could range from 0000H to FFFFH and that was it. Unsigned means, really, positive, and positive numbers are only half the story. Temperatures run negative as well as positive, as do budgets or voltages or any number of categories. To keep track of these, any modern computer has to be able to use signed numbers.

The Sign Bit

The highest bit — the leftmost bit — in a byte or word is used as the sign bit. What makes a number a signed number is whether or not you pay attention to this bit. In unsigned bytes or words, this bit was always there, certainly, but it was only the highest bit and had no other significance. To make a number signed you just have to treat it as signed, which means starting to pay attention to the sign bit.

To let us treat this bit specially, there are a whole new set of instructions that we will examine here. For example, conditional jumps like JA change to their signed equivalent

JG (jump if greater). What's important to realize is that the byte or word looks the same as before. It is the significance that we give to the highest bit that determines whether we are treating it as signed or not. A 1 in the highest bit will mean that the number, if regarded as signed, is negative (see Figure 8-1).

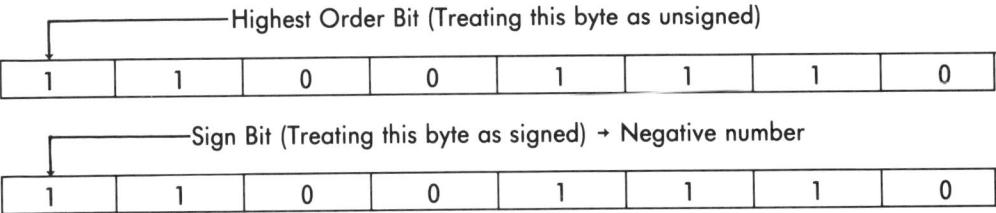

Figure 8-1. *High Order Bits and Sign Bits*

Creating Your Own Signed Numbers

The whole scheme of signed numbers in the 80×86 comes from the simple fact that 1 + (-1) = 0. We realize that if we want to do any calculation with negative numbers in the PC, the number we choose to be -1, when added to 1, has to give 0. Yet this seems impossible. Can you think of an 8-bit number which, when added to 1, will give a result of 0? It seems as though the result must always be 1 or greater. In fact, if we limit ourselves to the 8 bits of the byte, there is an answer. If we add 255 (= 11111111B) and 1,

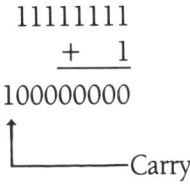

it yields 100000000B. That is, the 8-bit register is left holding 00000000, or 0, and there is a carry, since the 1 is in the 2^8 place (256), more than the register's capacity to hold. This carry means that the *carry flag* will be set. If we ignore this carry, and only look at the eight bits that fit into the byte, we are left with 00000000B. In other words, FFH + 1 = 0.

This is exactly what happens when we are working with negative numbers: we ignore the carry flag. The only way it is used is if we explicitly check it (with, for example, JC), and, with signed calculations, we ignore the way it is set. Therefore, to us, 11111111B + 1 = 0, when dealing with signed numbers.

Two's Complement Numbers

It might seem very odd that a number like FFFFH is equal to -1, even if we understand the reasoning. The positive numbers in a byte can range from 00000000B to 01111111B (=127), and there seems to be no problem with that: we can have positive numbers all the up to the point where the sign bit is set.

But the negative numbers reach from 11111111B = -1 to 10000000B = -128. This seems very odd. On one hand, we can see that it is true, since 10000000B (-128) + 01111111B (127) = 11111111B (-1), but understanding that the more ones you have in a negative number, the *less* negative it is (-1 is less negative than -128) is difficult.

> **NOTE** Note that the most negative number you can have for a byte is 80H = -128. Similarly, 8000H is the most negative number you can have in a word, -32,768.

Finding a Two's Complement As a practical matter, how are these negative numbers found? For instance, if we wanted to know what -109 was, how could we find it?

To find -109, we would start with 109 and find what is called its *two's complement*. Two's complement math is the math used in computers for dealing with negative numbers. We already know one two's complement: the two's complement of 1 is FFFFH.

We can find any number's two's complement easily. We begin by noting that if you take a number like 5, which is 00000101B in binary, then flip all its bits, 11111010B (= FAH), and add the two together, you get all 1s:

```
  00000101   ← 5
+ 11111010   ← 5 with bits flipped [ FAH ]
  11111111   = FF
```

That is, 5 + FAH = 11111111B. This is close to what we want, adding 1 to this sum gives us 0 with a carry. If we ignore the carry, we can see that 5 + FAH + 1 = 0. In other words, adding 5 to (FAH + 1) gives 0 with the (ignored) carry.

This means that -5 must equal (FAH + 1), which is FBH. This is how negative numbers are found. The rule is simple: to find any number's two's complement (and thus to change its sign), just flip the bits and add 1. Thus we see that -1 = Flip(1) + 1 = 11111110B + 1 = 11111111B = FFH (in byte form).

The number of positive numbers you can hold in a word or byte is one less than the number of negative numbers, since 00000000 — 0 — is treated as part of the positive range.

220 ▶ Advanced Assembly Language

An unsigned byte can hold numbers from 0 to 255. A signed byte can hold numbers from -128 (10000000B = 80H) to 127 (01111111 = 7FH).

For words, the unsigned range goes from 0 to 65,535. If we treat the word as signed, the range is from -32,768 (= 8000H) to 32767 (= 7FFFF).

The NOT and NEG Instructions

To flip the bits in a word or byte, you can use the NOT instruction. For example, if AX was equal to 00000000, then NOT AX would make AX equal to 11111111. If BX was equal to 01010101, then NOT BX would make it 10101010. If you NOT a word or byte, and then add 1 to the result, you will have that word or byte's two's complement.

There is a special 80×86 instruction that does just this: NEG. NEG is the same as NOT, except that it adds 1 at the end to make a two's complement of the number. If AX held 1, then NEG AX would give it 1111111111111111 or FFFF.

> **NOTE** Note that NEG flips signs; it does not always make signs negative. For example, NEG -1 = 1.

New Jumps, Not New Numbers When we decide to use signed numbers, the registers in our machine do not change, they are still the same. The way that we know that we are using signed numbers is by paying special attention to the sign bit, and ignoring the carry flag.

Besides this, the way we make comparisons will have to change. The way we used to compare two numbers, say FFH (= 11111111B) and 7FH (=01111111B) was with conditional jumps like JA or JB. For example:

```
MOV     AX,11111111B    [FF]
CMP     AX,01111111B    [7F]
JA      AX_BIG
```

If this jump is made, then we'd say that the value in AX, 11111111B, is bigger than the value it's being compared to, 01111111B. That is completely true if we are using unsigned numbers — FFH is bigger than 7FH. On the other hand, if we want to use signed numbers, we use a new set of conditional jumps that pay attention to the sign. Here, we use JG, or jump if greater:

```
     MOV     AX,11111111B    [ -1  ]
     CMP     AX,01111111B    [ 127 ]
 →   JG      AX_BIG
```

The JG instruction sees that 127 is greater than -1. The jump to AX_BIG is NOT made. In this way, we will be able to work with negative as well as positive numbers.

For all the comparison jumps, there is both an unsigned and a signed version. "Above" becomes "greater" and "below" becomes "less." You can see these jumps below.

Signed and Unsigned Jumps

Jumps	Unsigned	Jumps	Signed
JA	Jump if Above	JG	Jump if Greater
JNA	Jump if Not Above	JNG	Jump if Not Greater
JB	Jump if Below	JL	Jump if Less
JNB	Jump if Not Below	JNL	Jump if Not Less
JAE	Jump if Above or Equal	JGE	Jump if Greater or Equal
JNAE	Jump if Not Above or Equal	JNGE	Jump if Not Greater or Equal
JBE	Jump if Below or Equal	JGE	Jump if Greater or Equal
JNBE	Jump if Not Below or Equal	JNLE	Jump if Not Less or Equal

Note in the "N" jumps, like JNA and JNB, the "N" means "not." JNA means Jump if Not Above (an unsigned comparison), and JNB means Jump if Not Below (also an unsigned comparison).

Now we've got a pretty good idea how negative numbers work in the PC. Here's an example: let's say we want a program to take the number stored at the memory location NUMBER and put its absolute value at ABS_VAL. We start with a normal .COM file shell:

```
            .MODEL  SMALL
            .CODE
            ORG     100H
ENTRY:      JMP     PROG
            NUMBER  DW   -10
            ABS_VAL DW   ?
PROG        PROC    NEAR

            INT     20H
PROG        ENDP
            END     ENTRY
```

> **TIP** As you can see, we can use DW to store negative as well as positive numbers. Here, the correct two's complement is automatically generated by the assembler. This gets rid of the need to figure out two's complements by yourself.

Our first step is to load NUMBER into AX. Then we test it: if it is less than zero, we use NEG. Otherwise, we just store it at ABS_VAL as shown in Listing 8-1.

Listing 8-1. ABS_VAL.ASM — Finds an Absolute Value.

```
        .MODEL  SMALL
        .CODE
        ORG     100H
ENTRY:  JMP     PROG
        NUMBER  DW  -10
        ABS_VAL DW  ?
PROG    PROC    NEAR
        MOV     AX,NUMBER       *
        CMP     AX,0            *
        JG      LOAD_ABS_VAL    *
        NEG     AX              *
LOAD_ABS_VAL:                   *
        MOV     ABS_VAL,AX      *
        INT     20H
PROG    ENDP
        END     ENTRY
```

This program will leave 10 in ABS_VAL. We can see that in cases like these, we have to use the signed conditional jump JG, and not the unsigned version JA. (Remember that JA treats a number like FFFFH as bigger than a number like 0003H.)

The Overflow Flag There is still a problem with this scheme. Having done away with the carry flag, we've left ourselves without a means of checking on possible overflows. For instance, if we were to add -1 and -128,

```
      11111111
   +  10000000
     101111111
```

the result is -129. Now, -129 is a more negative number than the most negative a number can be and still be in one byte (-128). The byte is left holding 01111111B, which looks like a positive number, not -129 at all. There is a special, new flag, which is set when a number's sign is inadvertantly changed, that is, when the result of some math operation gave a result that could not be held in the byte or word's two's complement capacity.

This flag is the *overflow flag*. Before, when we were concerned about the possible size of a result, we could use the carry flag:

```
        ADD     AX,BX
   *    JC      TOO_BIG
```

▶ Truly Fast Math   223

If adding AX and BX gave an unsigned number greater than FFFFH, the carry flag would be set, and, checking it, we could make the appropriate corrections. When dealing with signed numbers, the overflow flag is used in the same way, with JO (Jump if Overflow) and JNO (Jump if No Overflow):

```
ADD     AX,BX
JO      SIGN_CHANGED
```

If we are worried that the result of a calculation exceeded the size that was legal, we can check with the overflow flag this way.

That completes our introduction to negative numbers in the PC, although we'll have more to say about them later in this chapter. Let's take a look at some of the 80×86 instructions that were designed for signed numbers.

Signed Multiplication — IMUL

The 80×86 has the abitility to do multiplication and division that will keep track of the correct sign. These two commands are IMUL and IDIV.

> **TIP** For accuracy, you might sometimes want to use all bits in a word, even the sign bit. In that case, you should use unsigned numbers, but keep track of the sign yourself, adjusting it correctly at the end of the calculation.

IMUL is the integer multiply instruction. Fundamentally, it is just like MUL, but it works with signed numbers. If you say,

```
IMUL    CL
```

then the microprocessor will multiply AL × CL (including signs) and put the result in (the full 16 bits of) AX. If you say,

```
IMUL    CX
```

then the microprocessor will multiply AX × CX (including signs, of course), and put the result into DX:AX. Let's give this a try by multiplying 5 by -1. We already know that -5 = FBH, so we expect that as an answer. In byte multiplication, you end with a full word answer, so we expect a result of FFFBH.

224 ▶ Advanced Assembly Language

In DEBUG, we load the registers — let's use BL — assemble an IMUL BL, and then trace through it:

```
A>DEBUG

-RAX              ← Load AL with 5
AX 0000
:5
-RBX              ← Load BL with -1
BX 0000
:FF
-A100
0EF1:0100 IMUL    BL    ← Get our IMUL instruction ready
0EF1:0102
-R
AX=0005  BX=00FF  CX=0000  DX=0000  SP=FFEE  BP=0000  SI=0000  DI=0000
DS=0EF1  ES=0EF1  SS=0EF1  CS=0EF1  IP=0100   NV UP EI PL NZ NA PO NC
0EF1:0100 F6EB          IMUL    BL
-
```

And we're all ready to trace through IMUL and multiply 5 by -1. Here's the result:

```
-R
AX=0005  BX=00FF  CX=0000  DX=0000  SP=FFEE  BP=0000  SI=0000  DI=0000
DS=0EF1  ES=0EF1  SS=0EF1  CS=0EF1  IP=0100   NV UP EI PL NZ NA PO NC
0EF1:0100 F6EB          IMUL    BL
-T                ← Trace through IMUL

AX=FFFB  BX=00FF  CX=0000  DX=0000  SP=FFEE  BP=0000  SI=0000  DI=0000
DS=0EF1  ES=0EF1  SS=0EF1  CS=0EF1  IP=0102   NV UP EI PL ZR AC PE NC
0EF1:0102 0402          ADD     AL,02
-Q
```

The result, as expected, is FFFBH, the word representation of -5.

> **NOTE** Note that the byte representation of -5 is FBH, the word representation is FFFBH, and the double word representation is FFFF:FFFBH.

Just to see what happens, let's multiply the two bytes FFH (-1) by FFH (-1). We expect an answer of 1 to show up in AX:

```
A>DEBUG

-RAX              ← Load AL with -1
AX 0000
:FF
-RBX              ← Load BL with -1
BX 0000
```

```
:FF
-A100
0EF1:0100 IMUL     BL        ← Get ready to IMUL them.
0EF1:0102
-R
AX=00FF  BX=00FF  CX=0000  DX=0000  SP=FFEE  BP=0000  SI=0000  DI=0000
DS=0EF1  ES=0EF1  SS=0EF1  CS=0EF1  IP=0100  NV UP EI PL NZ NA PO NC
0EF1:0100 F6EB          IMUL    BL             ← All set. Let's Trace.
-T

AX=0001  BX=00FF  CX=0000  DX=0000  SP=FFEE  BP=0000  SI=0000  DI=0000
DS=0EF1  ES=0EF1  SS=0EF1  CS=0EF1  IP=0102  NV UP EI PL ZR NA PE NC
0EF1:0102 0402          ADD     AL,02
-Q
```

And we find that IMUL handled the sign correctly: -1 × -1 = 1.

The IDIV Instruction IDIV is the corresponding signed division instruction. Again, you use it just like DIV, but the signs are kept track of automatically.

If you say,

```
IDIV    CL
```

then AX/CL is calculated and the result goes into AL and the remainder into AH. If you say,

```
IDIV    CX
```

then, as before, DX:AX/CX is calculated. The result goes into AX and the remainder into DX.

NOTE What's wrong with an instruction like IDIV DX?

Using IMUL and IDIV can be important if you want to keep track of signs. Keep in mind that, once you choose, you must stick with using IMUL and IDIV throughout your program. FFFFH looks like -1 to IMUL and IDIV, but it looks like a big number to MUL and DIV. If you mix these instructions, you'll get mixed results.

Adding with Carries

One word isn't really very long. At best, values up to 65,535 can be stored. Can you imagine a calculator that could only work with numbers up to 65,535? That's only four places of accuracy. If you wanted to enter a number like 90,017, you'd be beyond the calculator's range.

That is just what happens in the 80×86. If you are restricted to one-word numbers, then our accuracy is very poor (unless you have a math coprocessor inside your machine). In an effort to help rectify this, INTEL added some instructions that let you chain a number of addition or subtraction instructions together by keeping track of the carry bit. ADC is the instruction for adding when the carry bit is involved. ADC means Add with Carry.

ADC is an add instruction you use after ADD. If you wanted to use double word numbers (and couldn't take advantage of the 80×86's 32-bit registers) like DX:AX and BX:CX, you can still add them together using ADD followed by ADC. What we want is this:

$$\begin{array}{r} DX:AX \\ + \underline{BX:CX} \end{array}$$

And this can be broken down into adding AX and CX first — this might produce a carry — and then adding the possible carry with DX and BX.

In assembly language, this is the way you'd do it:

```
ADD     AX,CX
ADC     BX,CX
```

First, we add AX and CX in the usual way. If there was a carry, then the carry flag was set. The ADC BX,CX instruction adds the carry flag (1=set, 0= not set) in with the two registers, BX and CX.

NOTE Keep in mind that carries in the binary addition of two numbers can only be 0s or 1s. You cannot have a carry of 3, for example. Thus, the carry flag is adequate to hold the carry bit.

In this way, the carry from the first addition is correctly treated. Keep in mind that the second addition (ADC BX,CX) could have produced a carry as well, and, to be sure, you should check for it.

Here's an example that preserves 48-bit accuracy. If we have a program with six memory word locations (A1 - A3 and B1 - B3), and we wanted to add them like this:

$$\begin{array}{r} B3:B2:B1 \\ + \underline{A3:A2:A1} \end{array}$$

▶ **Truly Fast Math** 227

Then our program might look something like the one in Listing 8-2 below.

Listing 8-2. BIGADD.ASM — Adds Two Large Numbers.

```
            .MODEL  SMALL
            .CODE
            ORG     100H
ENTRY:      JMP     PROG
            A3      DW      ?       ← Define A1 - A3
            A2      DW      ?
            A1      DW      ?
            B3      DW      ?       ← Define B1 - B3
            B2      DW      ?
            B1      DW      ?
            CARRY   DW      0       ← Possible carry from whole addition
PROG        PROC    NEAR
            MOV     AX,A1           ← Put A1, A2, A3 into AX, BX, CX
            MOV     BX,A2
            MOV     CX,A3
            MOV     DX,0            ← Clear DX
            ADD     AX,B1           ← First ADD
            ADC     BX,B2           ← Then ADC
            ADC     CX,B3
            ADC     CARRY,DX        ← Put carry into CARRY.
            INT     20H
PROG        ENDP

            END     ENTRY
```

What happens here is that first we load the memory words A1 -A3 into the registers AX, BX, and CX for easy handling. This is because we cannot ADD A1 to B1 directly. You cannot use two memory locations in the same instruction. We have to add a memory location to a register instead. Then we simply use ADD followed by ADC:

```
ADD     AX,B1           ← First ADD
ADC     BX,B2           ← Then ADC
ADC     CX,B3
```

At the very end, we include this line, having previously set DX to zero:

```
ADC     CARRY,DX        ← Put carry into CARRY.
```

All this does is to keep track of the possible carry from the whole addition A3:A2:A1 + B3:B2:B1. If there is a carry, CARRY will end up being 1. If there was no carry, CARRY will be zero.

The carry from the whole calculation could be treated as an error, if you wanted to. If we wanted to add the number held in DX:AX to the number held in BX:CX, and if both were unsigned (or could be made so by finding their two's complements), we might use these instructions:

```
ADD     AX,CX           [Add DX:AX + BX:CX]
ADC     DX,BX
JC      ERROR
```

We first add the lower 16 bits of both numbers, held respectively in AX and CX. The result is stored in AX. If this answer is too large to hold in 16 bits, there will be a carry and the carry flag will be set. To include that carry in the subsequent addition of the top 16 bits, we use ADC:

```
    ADD     AX,CX           [Add DX:AX + BX:CX]
→   ADC     DX,BX
    JC      ERROR
```

ADC includes the carry, if there was one, in this addition. The final result is stored in DX:AX. In this calculation we are not prepared for answers longer than 32 bits (although that can be handled with an additional ADC to as many stages as you desire). So if there was a carry after the second addition, we jump to a location marked Error.

The SBB Instruction

There is a counterpart for subtraction, SBB. SBB means Subtract with Borrow. After subtracting the two operands, it subtracts the carry flag from the result.

If we subtract a big number from a small one, we have to borrow from higher order places. The 80×86's designers included the SBB, subtract with borrow, command for expressly this use:

```
    SUB     AX,CX           [Sub DX:AX - BX:CX]
→   SBB     DX,BX
    JC      ERROR
```

Here we can figure out what DX:AX - BX:CX is:

    DX:AX
- BX:CX

▶ **Truly Fast Math** 229

First, we subtract CX from AX (with SUB AX,CX). If this left the carry flag set, a "borrow" from a higher place was required. This is taken into account when we use SBB for the second instruction (with SBB DX,BX). The result will be left in DX:AX.

Again, if there is a net carry, we consider it an error and jump to ERROR, although you could handle it another way if you wished.

Big Time Multiplying

What if we did not want to limit ourselves to multiplication results that were only two words long? What if what we were doing required more accuracy? We've just seen how to extend addition and subtraction calculations to arbitrary lengths (by the use of ADD, followed by successive ADCs, or SUB followed by SBBs). Can we do the same for MUL and DIV?

The MUL instruction insists that you start out with the AX register. If you say MUL BX, then the 80×86 multiplies AX by BX and leaves the 32-bit result in DX:AX. If we wanted to multiply AX:DX by BX:CX, we must be prepared for a 64-bit result, using up all our registers.

More common when we deal with multiplication of larger numbers is the use of memory locations. We could, for instance, multiply the number Y1:Y0, held in 16-bit words we've named Y1 and Y0, by the number Z1:Z0, locations Z1 and Z0. We would have to be prepared to store our result in four memory words as the number, say, A:B:C:D.

In other words, this is what we want to do:

$$\begin{array}{r} Y1 : Y0 \\ \times\ Z1 : Z0 \\ \hline Z0 \times Y0 \\ +\ \ Z0 \times Y1 \\ +\ \ Z1 \times Y0 \\ +\ Z1 \times Y1 \\ \hline 2^{32}\ Z1\times Y1\ +\ 2^{16}\ Z0\times Y1\ +\ 2^{16}\ Z1\times Y0\ +Z0\times Y0 \end{array}$$

We supply Y1:Y0 and Z1:Z0. What we want to get out is A:B:C:D, and this number is equal to the final line above:

$$A:B:C:D\ =\ 2^{32}\ Z1\times Y1\ +\ 2^{16}\ Z0\times Y1\ +\ 2^{16}\ Z1\times Y0\ +\ Z0\times Y0$$

Let's write a program to do this, giving us four-word multiplication accuracy. We're not going to go through this program step by step because it would be too tedious. All we are doing is mirroring the normal multiplication process anyway. The program appears in Listing 8-3. To use it, load Z1:Z0 and Y1:Y0 in the data area. The result will be left in A:B:C:D.

Listing 8-3. BIGMUL.ASM — Multiplies Two Large Numbers.

```
        .MODEL SMALL
        .CODE
        ORG     100H
ENTRY:  JMP     MULTI
        Y0      DW      0
        Y1      DW      0
        Z0      DW      0
        Z1      DW      0
        A       DW      0
        B       DW      0
        C       DW      0
        D       DW      0
MULTI:  MOV     B,0             ;Multiplies Y1:Y0 by Z1:Z0 to get A:B:C:D
        MOV     A,0
        MOV     AX,Z0
        MUL     Y0
        MOV     D,AX
        MOV     C,DX
        MOV     AX,Z0
        MUL     Y1
        ADD     C,AX
        ADC     B,DX
        ADC     A,0
        MOV     AX,Z1
        MUL     Y0
        ADD     C,AX
        ADC     B,DX
        ADC     A,0
        MOV     AX,Z1
        MUL     Y1
        ADD     B,AX
        ADC     A,DX
        INT     20H
        END     ENTRY
```

By breaking up the result into partial results, we were able to multiply Y1:Y0 by Z1:Z0 to get A:B:C:D. This result is 64 bits long, not bad as far as accuracy is concerned (although the math coprocessor's registers are 80 bits long).

Big Time Division

In division our path is less smooth. In all three of the previous cases we were able to divide our calculations into subparts and then join the results together from those parts. Unfortunately, division cannot be dissected that way. We are reduced to dividing on a bit-by-bit level if we want 32-bit accuracy. Here we will use an actual hardware divide algorithm. This algorithm, usually expressed in cryptic computer design language, is not the fastest available, but it is at least intelligible using the model of long division and expresses a wonderful economy in the use of registers that is something of an art in itself.

As we have seen, the 80×86 has an internal DIV command that will divide 32 bits (held in the two registers DX:AX) by a 16-bit number (like this: DIV BX, which divides DX:AX by BX) to return a 16-bit result and a 16-bit remainder. However, we want to maintain our 32-bit accuracy, so here we will develop a bit-by-bit divide algorithm that divides a 64-bit number by a 32-bit number, giving powerful 32-bit results and remainders.

To refresh our memories concerning long division, especially in binary, let's work through a short example. Here we will divide 14 by 6. Our answer will, as all division in the PC does, come out in whole numbers as an answer and a remainder. 14/6 will yield an answer of 2 and a remainder of 2. We start here:

$$A \overline{)B} \rightarrow 6 \overline{)14} \rightarrow 0110 \overline{)1110}$$

To keep the example short, we'll only use four bits and leave using 64 up to the imagination. Our first move is to compare 0110 against progressively more of the number being divided (B, above):

$$0110 \overline{)1_\wedge 110}$$

Since 0110 is bigger than 1, we place a 0 above it and subtract 0 from it:

$$\begin{array}{r} 0 \leftarrow \\ 0110 \overline{)1110} \\ -\underline{0} \\ 1 \end{array}$$

And we bring down the next digit of B:

$$\begin{array}{r} 0 \\ 0110 \overline{)1110} \\ -\underline{0\downarrow} \\ 11 \end{array}$$

We're now comparing A, 0110, against the first two digits of B, 11. Since 0110 is also bigger than 11, we put in another 0 up on top, subtract 0 from 11 and bring down another digit, a 1:

232 ▶ Advanced Assembly Language

```
        00  ←
0110 ) 1110
       - 0
       ___
        11
      - 00 ↓
      ____
        111
```

Now we are comparing A to the first three digits of B, 111, and 0110 goes smoothly into 111 once, so we put a 1 on top, subtract 0110 from 111 and bring down another digit:

```
        001  ←
0110 ) 1110
       - 0
       ___
        11
      - 00
      ____
        111
      - 110 ↓
      _____
        0010
```

Now we have to compare 0110 to what is left on the bottom, 0010. Since 0110 is greater than 0010, another 0 goes on top:

```
        0010   Answer
0110 ) 1110
       - 0
       ___
        11
      - 00
      ____
        111
      - 110
      _____
        0010
      - 0000
      _____
        0010   Remainder
```

which leaves us with a 4-bit answer, 0010 (2) and a 4-bit remainder, 0010 (also 2). To make an algorithm out of this, we have to decide just what it was that we did at each stage. If the problem looked like this

$$A \overline{)B}$$

then we compared A to progressively more and more of B, the number being divided. If A was bigger than B, we entered a 0 in the answer, but if A was smaller than B, we entered a 1 and subtracted A. We kept going until we had done this four times, once for every bit in B.

Computerizing Our Dividing Example

Since we compare registers easily in the PC, or in computers in general, we can make a leap and say that to compare A to progressively more of B, we can just compare two registers using CMP. All we have to do is to use CMP AX,BX where AX holds A and BX holds B.

To get more and more of B into BX, we can simply shift B into it one bit at a time. Progressively, then, we can compare A to more and more of B as more and more of B appears in BX. If A is bigger than what we have of B, we put 0 in the answer. If A is smaller, then we subtract B - A and put a 1 into the answer.

In other words, if we start off with AX, BX, and CX loaded like this for 14/6 (treating them as only 4-bit registers):

AX = 6	BX	CX = 14
0110	0000	1110

Then we start by shifting the first digit into BX this way:

AX = 6	BX		CX = 14
0110	0001	←	110

Since we've got a new BX, we compare AX to it and see immediately that AX > BX. This means that the first bit of the answer is 0.

This algorithm does not waste any space whatsoever. It immediately slips this first bit into the newly vacated rightmost bit of CX. When we are all done, the answer will be fully in CX:

AX = 6	BX		CX = 14
0110	0001		110˄0 ←

With the first bit of the answer secure, we shift CX again to the left

AX = 6	BX		CX = 14
0110	0011	←	10˄0

234 ▶ Advanced Assembly Language

and again compare AX to the new part of B we have in BX. Since again AX > BX, another 0 goes into the answer in CX:

AX = 6	BX	CX = 14
0110	0011	10ˬ00 ←

Now we have to get a new value in BX, and so shift CX left again:

AX = 6	BX		CX = 14
0110	0111	←	0ˬ00

Now when we compare AX to BX, we have enough bits in BX to make AX < BX. Just as in our long division example, this means that we subtract A (in AX) from what we have of B (in BX) and put a 1 into the answer this way:

AX = 6	BX	CX = 14
0110	0111	0ˬ001 ←
	-0110	
	0001	

This leaves a 1 in BX:

AX = 6	BX	CX = 14
0110	0001	0ˬ001

So we shift the final 0 from CX into BX;

AX = 6	BX		CX = 14
0110	0001	←	ˬ001

Since 0110 > 10, we have to finish by putting a 0 into CX:

AX = 6	BX	CX = 14
0110	0010	0010
	Remainder	Answer

We've now done our comparison four times so we're done. The leftover bits of B that A didn't divide evenly are the remainder, left in BX, and the final answer that we built bit by bit is in CX. In a direct — although maybe not self-evident — way, this algorithm has provided a clever translation of long division into the language of registers and left shifts.

How Does Division Look in Code?

To get this into code that you can use, let us suppose that we want to divide A:B:C:D by Z1:Z0, 64 bits by 32. The quotient will be left in A:B:C:D. The actual divison code is relatively small, and you will find it in Listing 8-4.

Listing 8-4.   BIGDIV.ASM — 64 Bit By 32 Bit Division.

```
        ;Divides memory locations A:B:C:D by Z1:Z0
        MOV     COUNT,64
        XOR     AX,AX           ;Going to divide A:B:C:D by BX:CX
        XOR     DX,DX           ; End up with quotient in A:B:C:D
        MOV     BX,Z1
        MOV     CX,Z0
SHIF:
        CALL    SHLA            ;SHL DX:AX:A:B:C:D by 1 place (96 bits !)
        CMP     DX,BX
        JB      NOT_YET
        JA      HIT
        CMP     AX,CX           ;DX = BX, Check AX,CX
        JB      NOT_YET
HIT:    SUB     AX,CX
        SBB     DX,BX
        ADD     D,1             ;Put in a 1 since divisor went into dividend once
NOT_YET:
        DEC     COUNT
        CMP     COUNT,0
        JNE     SHIF            ;Keep going all 64 times
```

The variable COUNT will serve as a loop index. We begin by clearing the registers AX and DX and loading BX:CX with Z1:Z0:

```
        MOV     COUNT,64
        XOR     AX,AX           ;Going to divide A:B:C:D by BX:CX
        XOR     DX,DX           ; End up with quotient in A:B:C:D
        MOV     BX,Z1
        MOV     CX,Z0
```

XOR AX,AX is a method used by professional programmers to clear the AX register, and you can often find it in the BIOS listing. No matter what was in AX before, XOR AX,AX will leave it 0. When you XOR a number with itself, all ones are sure to meet ones and all zeros sure to meet zeros, so the result is zero. XOR AX,AX is sure to make the contents of AX zero.

We will gradually shift more and more of A:B:C:D into DX:AX and compare it to BX:CX. As we shift A:B:C:D into DX:AX we gradually leave zeroes behind us in D. Every time that DX:AX is greater than BX:CX, however, we will put a 1 in instead.

236 ▶ Advanced Assembly Language

The whole process begins by shifting a bit from A:B:C:D into DX:AX. In other words, we'd like to execute a command like: SHL DX:AX:A:B:C:D,1. In the absence of such a handy command, though, we have to make one for ourselves. Ours will be called SHLA, and can be found in Listing 8-5.

Listing 8-5. SHLA — A Subroutine to Shift 96 Bits at Once.

```
SHLA    PROC    NEAR
        ;Shifts 96 (!!) bits of DX:AX:A:B:C:D left by 1
        PUSH    BX
        PUSH    CX
        MOV     BX,0
        MOV     CX,0
        SHL     D,1             ;Start with rightmost
        ADC     BX,0            ;Overflow in BX
        SHL     C,1
        ADC     CX,0            ;New overflow in CX, old in BX
        ADD     C,BX
        MOV     BX,0
        SHL     B,1
        ADC     BX,0            ;BX has new overflow, old in CX
        ADD     B,CX
        MOV     CX,0
        SHL     A,1
        ADC     CX,0            ;CX has new overflow, old in BX
        ADD     A,BX
        MOV     BX,0
        SHL     AX,1
        ADC     BX,0            ;BX has new overflow, old in CX
        ADD     AX,CX
        SHL     DX,1            ;Disregard overflow here
        ADD     DX,BX
        POP     CX
        POP     BX
        RET
SHLA    ENDP
```

When we shift a 16-bit word to the left one place and end up shifting a 1 out to the left, the carry bit gets set. SHLA follows all those carries up the line with ADC, Add with Carry, into successive words, and that accounts for the majority of its length.

Comparing DX:AX and BX:CX

After we've shifted the first part of A:B:C:D into DX:AX, we have to compare it to the number we're dividing by, BX:CX. We could use a CMP DX:AX,BX:CX command here. Instead, we'll have to do the same thing 16 bits at a time, starting with the highest bits.

DX > BX: If DX is greater than BX, then DX:AX is definitely greater than BX:CX and we have a "hit," so we move 1 into A:B:C:D.

▶ Truly Fast Math

DX < BX: If DX is less than BX, then DX:AX is less than BX:CX, and we will leave the 0 that was shifted into the end.

DX = BX: If, though, DX = BX, then we must check AX and CX. The entire process goes this way:

```
SHIF:      CALL    SHLA      ;SHL DX:AX:A:B:C:D by 1 place (96 bits !)
      →    CMP     DX,BX
           JB      NOT_YET
           JA      HIT
      →    CMP     AX,CX                ;DX = BX, Check AX,CX
           JB      NOT_YET
HIT:       SUB     AX,CX
           SBB     DX,BX
           ADD     D,1       ;Put in a 1 since divisor went into dividend once
NOT_YET: [Shift more of A:B:C:D into DX:AX]
```

Notice the use of two conditional jumps, one right after the other. Since conditional jumps do not affect the flags that are set, this will work (check your assembler's documentation to learn which commands affect which flags).

If the part we have of A:B:C:D is bigger than what we're dividing by, we want to subtract it by subtracting DX:AX from BX:CX. This is done at the label HIT:

```
HIT:       SUB     AX,CX
           SBB     DX,BX
           ADD     D,1       ;Put in a 1 since divisor went into dividend once
```

And we also put a 1 into the end of A:B:C:D. After we've either let the shifted-in 0 stand or put in a 1, we have to go back and shift more of the number we're dividing into DX:AX and decrease the count.

```
SHIF:
           [Shift to the left and compare]
                :
                :
           DEC     COUNT
           CMP     COUNT,0
           JNE     SHIF      ;Keep going all 64 times
```

When you use this algorithm, load the 64-bit number to divide into A:B:C:D, load the number to divide it by into Z1:Z0, and execute the algorithm. The quotient will be left in A:B:C:D, and the remainder in Z1:Z0.

Bit-by-Bit Manipulations

It is frequently important in assembly language to work with individual bits in a word or byte. As we have seen, the operating system stores information in the bits of specific bytes in its data areas.

There are a number of assembly language instructions that we can use here. The first are our old friends, SHL and SHR.

> **TIP** The 80386 has a series of *bit test* instructions, BT, BTC, BTR, and BTS. These let you work on individual bits with great speed, and without the need for bit masks.

SHR and SHL

These two, SHR and SHL, shift quantities to the right and left, respectively. You can shift a number of times to the right or left. On the 8088 and 8086, if the number of places to shift is greater than one, place it into CL (then use SHR AX,CL). Otherwise, you can say SHR BX,1 or SHL CX,1. On the 80186 - 80486, you can use an immediate number, and do not need to use CL.

With SHR and SHL, the bit that is "opened" up is set to zero. For example, if we shift AL to the right one:

```
       AL:   10101010
              :
          Shift to the right by 1 using
       SHR
              :
             01010101
              →
```

Figure 8-2.

In addition, the bit that was shifted "out" by SHR or SHL — here a 0 was shifted off the right hand side — goes into the carry flag. You can test what this bit was with JC or JNC. In fact, this is a common way of checking bit values.

```
                Shifting Right   AL:  10101010
                                       ⋮
                                      SHR AL,1
                                       ⋮
                                      01010101  → 0 → Carry Flag
                                           →
                Shifting Left    AL:  10101010
                                       ⋮
                                      SHL AL,1
                                       ⋮
                Carry Flag ← 1 ←      01010100
                                           ←
```

Figure 8-3.

SHL may be used for multiplication, as well. Every time you shift one place to the left, it is the same as mutliplying by two. For example, you could multiply AX by 5 (5 = 2 × 2 + 1) this way:

```
MOV    BX,AX    ← Make a copy of AX
SHL    AX,1     ← Multiply it by 2
SHL    AX,1     ← And 2 again to make 4
ADD    AX,BX    ← Add the copy in BX to make 5
```

> **TIP** Since SHL and ADD combinations are *much* faster than ordinary MUL instructions, use them whenever you can. Graphics routines, where time is crucial, usually try to break up math this way.

In the same way, SHR can be used as a crude version of DIV, since shifting to the right once is equivalent to dividing by 2. The "remainder" of this division will be put into the carry flag.

SAR and SAL

These two instructions, SAR and SAL stand for Arithmetic Shift Right and Arithmetic Shift Left. These are what you can use on signed numbers.

If you shift a number like 01010101B to the left by 1 with SAL, the sign bit will change (since the new number is 10101010B). On the other hand, SAL will set the overflow flag in this case, and you can check it to see if the sign did change. (For some reason, the overflow flag is only set correctly if you shift to the left once—more than that means that the overflow flag will be undefined.)

240 ▶ Advanced Assembly Language

The SAR instruction preserves the sign of the operand it is shifting to the right. Let's look at the number 10101010B. This can be regarded as a negative number. SAR would have preserved its sign, whereas SHR would not (remember that SHR always sets the newly opened bit to 0). SAR will place a 1 in the top bit to preserve the sign bit in this case:

AL: 10101010
:
Shift to the right by 1 using SHR
:
11010101
→

Figure 8-4.

Again, the bit that is pushed off either end will go into the carry flag.

Arithmentic Shifting Right   AL: 10101010
:
SAR AL,1
:
11010101   → 0 → Carry Flag
→

Arithmetic Shifting Left   AL: 10101010
:
SAL AL,1
:
Carry Flag ← 1 ←   01010100
←

Figure 8-5.

The Rotate Instructions: RCL, RCR, ROL, and ROR

Here are four more instructions that work on a bit-by-bit level on either bytes or words. These instructions *rotate* words or bytes.

For example, let's examine ROL, rotate left. When ROL is used, the top-most bit, that is, the leftmost bit, is taken out, and all the other bits are shifted to the left by 1. Then the original leftmost bit goes into the rightmost location. See Figure 8-6 to see what it looks like if we were to ROL AX,1.

ROL AX,1

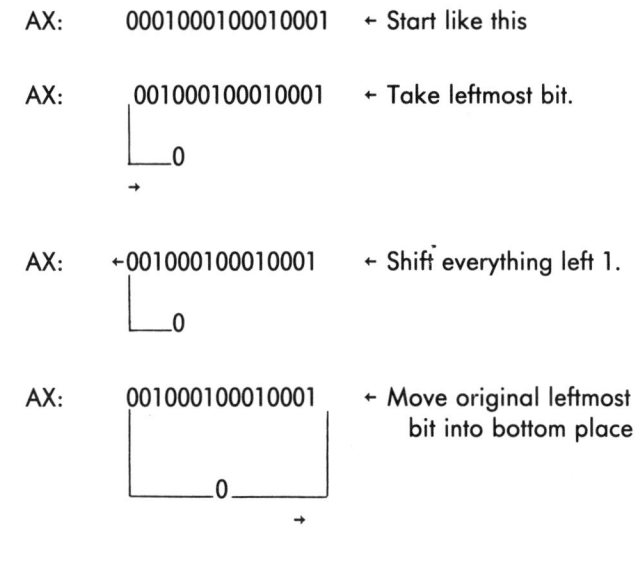

Figure 8-6. *Rotating AX Left by One Place*

We can see that 0001000100010001B rotated once to the left becomes 0010001000100010B. Let's do this exact example in DEBUG. We start off with AX = 0001000100010001B = 1111H (since there are four binary digits per hex digit), and we'll ROL a few times by assembling ROL AX,1 starting at 100H:

```
C>DEBUG
-A100
0EF1:0100 ROL      AX,1         ← Set up our ROLs.
0EF1:0102 ROL      AX,1
0EF1:0104 ROL      AX,1
0EF1:0106 ROL      AX,1
0EF1:0108
-RAX                             ← Set up AX to 1111H.
AX 0000
:1111
-R
AX=1111  BX=0000  CX=0000  DX=0000  SP=FFEE  BP=0000  SI=0000  DI=0000
DS=0EF1  ES=0EF1  SS=0EF1  CS=0EF1  IP=0100   NV UP EI PL NZ NA PO NC
0EF1:0100 D1C0              ROL     AX,1      ← Ready to rotate.
-T
```

We can trace through the first ROL AX,1. As we saw, this changed 0001000100010001B to 0010001000100010B. Here's what happens:

```
-R
AX=1111  BX=0000  CX=0000  DX=0000  SP=FFEE  BP=0000  SI=0000  DI=0000
DS=0EF1  ES=0EF1  SS=0EF1  CS=0EF1  IP=0100   NV UP EI PL NZ NA PO NC
0EF1:0100 D1C0          ROL     AX,1    ← Ready to rotate.
-T              ← Rotate AX to the left once.

AX=2222  BX=0000  CX=0000  DX=0000  SP=FFEE  BP=0000  SI=0000  DI=0000
DS=0EF1  ES=0EF1  SS=0EF1  CS=0EF1  IP=0102   NV UP EI PL NZ NA PO NC
0EF1:0102 D1C0          ROL     AX,1
```

The result is 2222H, as it should be: 0010001000100010B = 2222H. We can rotate again to get 4444H, and then 8888H. Then a final rotation (the fourth) will move the original 1s back into place, one hex digit higher. Here it is:

```
-R
AX=1111  BX=0000  CX=0000  DX=0000  SP=FFEE  BP=0000  SI=0000  DI=0000
DS=0EF1  ES=0EF1  SS=0EF1  CS=0EF1  IP=0100   NV UP EI PL NZ NA PO NC
0EF1:0100 D1C0          ROL     AX,1    ← Ready to rotate.
-T              ← Rotate AX to the left once.

AX=2222  BX=0000  CX=0000  DX=0000  SP=FFEE  BP=0000  SI=0000  DI=0000
DS=0EF1  ES=0EF1  SS=0EF1  CS=0EF1  IP=0102   NV UP EI PL NZ NA PO NC
0EF1:0102 D1C0          ROL     AX,1
-T

AX=4444  BX=0000  CX=0000  DX=0000  SP=FFEE  BP=0000  SI=0000  DI=0000
DS=0EF1  ES=0EF1  SS=0EF1  CS=0EF1  IP=0104   NV UP EI PL NZ NA PO NC
0EF1:0104 D1C0          ROL     AX,1
-T

AX=8888  BX=0000  CX=0000  DX=0000  SP=FFEE  BP=0000  SI=0000  DI=0000
DS=0EF1  ES=0EF1  SS=0EF1  CS=0EF1  IP=0106   OV UP EI PL NZ NA PO NC
0EF1:0106 D1C0          ROL     AX,1
-T

AX=1111  BX=0000  CX=0000  DX=0000  SP=FFEE  BP=0000  SI=0000  DI=0000
DS=0EF1  ES=0EF1  SS=0EF1  CS=0EF1  IP=0108   OV UP EI PL NZ NA PO CY
0EF1:0108 CB            RETF
-Q
```

That's how ROL works. ROR works the same way, except that bits are rotated to the "right" instead. For example, if we rotated 1111H to the right once, we'd end up with 8888H, as you can see in Figure 8-7.

Truly Fast Math

ROR AX,1

```
AX:    0001000100010001    ← Start like this
AX:    0001000100010000    ← Take rightmost bit.
               1_|
                ←
AX:    0001000100001000    → Shift everything right 1.
               1_|
AX:    000100010001000     ← Move original rightmost
       |_____|    bit into the top place
                |_1_|
                 ←
AX:    1000100010001000    ← Yielding this.
```

Figure 8-7. Rotating AX Right by One Place

Rotating through the Carry

RCL and RCR are somewhat different. They include the carry flag in their rotations: the bit that is rotated "out" becomes the new carry flag, and the carry flag is rotated in to take its place. In other words, these instructions rotate through the carry flag.

Let's look at RCL. If we had 1111H in AX, and 1 in the carry flag (CY), then Figure 8-8 shows what would happen when we used RCL AX,1.

RCL AX,1

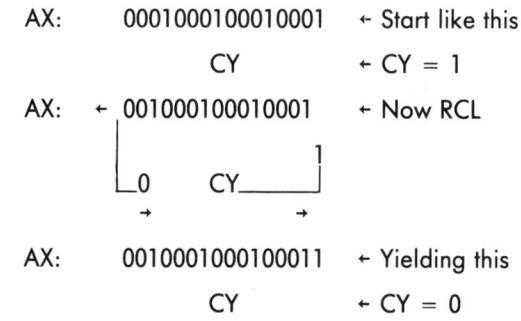

Figure 8-8. Rotating AX Left through the Carry Bit

In this case, we would have gotten 2223H, since the carry flag was rotated in to make the last digit 3, not 2 (and CY became 0).

244 ▶ Advanced Assembly Language

If you think of the carry flag as the 9th bit of a byte, or the 17th bit of a word, then RCL and RCR rotate these 9-bit bytes or 17-bit words. If you want to examine the carry bit, or want to move a bit into the carry bit, this is good way of doing it.

RCR also rotates through the carry flag, but to the right. If we had 0 in the carry flag (CY) and 1111H in AX, Figure 8-9 shows what RCR AX,1 would look like.

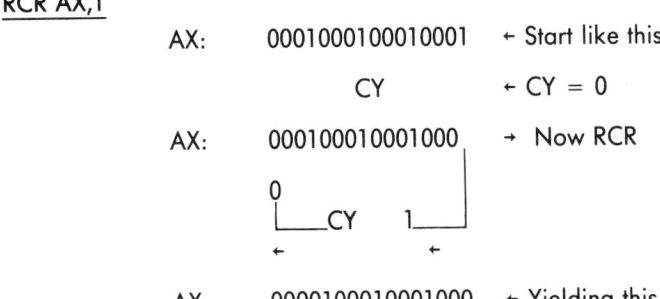

Figure 8-9. Rotating AX Right through the Carry Bit

In this case, RCR AX,1 yields 0888H (and CY = 1). Again, with ROL, ROR, RCL, and RCR, you have to specify the number of times to rotate in CL — if that number is greater than 1 — on the 8088 and 8086. With the 80186–80486, you can give immediate values.

That's it for new instructions in this chapter. Let's finish up our discussion of math with a popular topic: converting between bases.

Converting between Bases

In this example, we'll convert the number in AX into an ASCII string representing a decimal number. This is always a popular program, since it lets you print your numerical results out. Let's say that we had a number like 503, in decimal already. In that case, we could peel off successive digits by dividing it by 10 and checking the remainder: 503/10 = 50 with a remainder of 3. This remainder, 3, is the rightmost digit in the number. This is where remainders come in handy.

If we kept going, 50/10 = 5 with a remainder of 0, and 5/10 = 0 with a remainder of 5, and we see that, each time we divide by 10, the remainder gives us successive digits (in the backwards order: 3, 0, 5).

▶ Truly Fast Math

This will work if we divide hex numbers too. If we take the hex number 10H (= 16 decimal) and divide it by 10 (decimal), then the result would be 1 with a remainder of 6. That is, if we had 10H in the AX register and divided it by 10D (10D = 10 decimal), then we would get a result of 1 and a remainder of 6. In this way, we can keep dividing numbers by 10, and storing the remainders, until there is nothing left. Each time we divide by 10D, we peel off another decimal digit.

In our example, we want to convert the number in AX to decimal and leave that number as an ASCII string in memory. We can start off this way:

```
           .MODEL  SMALL
           .CODE
           ORG     100H
ENTRY:     JMP     CONVERT
           ASCII_STRING    DB 7 DUP("$")
CONVERT    PROC    NEAR
           :
```

Next, we have to make sure that the value in AX is positive. If not, we have to make a minus sign "-", the first character in ASCII_STRING. In addition, we will load BX with 10 to prepare for the division. We are going to take the number in DX:AX (DX will hold 0), and divide it by one word, BX, which will always hold 10:

```
           .MODEL  SMALL
           .CODE
           ORG     100H
ENTRY:     JMP     CONVERT
           ASCII_STRING    DB 7 DUP("$")
CONVERT    PROC    NEAR
           LEA     SI,ASCII_STRING
           CMP     AX,0
           JGE     POSITIVE
           NEG     AX
           MOV     BYTE PTR [SI],"-"
           INC     SI
POSITIVE:
           MOV     BX,10    ◀
           :
           INT     20H
CONVERT    ENDP

           END     ENTRY
```

Using a word register, BX, with DIV means that we will be dividing DX:AX by BX. Since we only want to divide the number in AX by BX, we will make sure that DX is always 0 before the division. We will need the loop that peels decimal digits off the value in AX next. In this loop, we will keep dividing the number in AX by 10 until there is nothing left. And we will keep track of the number of times we have looped in CX. This will be the number of digits in the result:

```
        .CODE
        ORG     100H
ENTRY:  JMP     CONVERT
        ASCII_STRING    DB 7 DUP("$")
CONVERT PROC    NEAR
        LEA     SI,ASCII_STRING
        CMP     AX,0
        JGE     POSITIVE
        NEG     AX
        MOV     BYTE PTR [SI],"-"
        INC     SI
POSITIVE:
        MOV     BX,10
        MOV     CX,0
THELOOP:
        MOV     DX,0            ← Set up DX:AX
        [Divide by 10.]
        [Store the remainder.]
        [Increment CX = Number of digits.]
        [Check whether the result is zero yet.]
        JNE     THELOOP
        INT     20H
CONVERT ENDP

        END     ENTRY
```

Here is what our loop looks like in pseudo-programming language:

```
THELOOP:
        MOV     DX,0    ← Set up DX for the division DX:AX/BX
        [Divide AX by 10.]
        [Store the remainder.]
        [Increment CX = Number of digits.]
        [Check whether the result is zero yet.]
        JNE     THELOOP
```

Dividing by 10 is easy. All we have to do is to say DIV BX (since BX will always hold 10). This will leave the result in AX and the remainder in DX. We want to save the remainder and keep the result for the next time when we divide by 10 again.

Notice that as we divide successively by 10, we will be shaving decimal digits off in reverse order. 503 will come apart like this: 3, 0, 5. There is a perfect way of storing these numbers and then retrieving them in the reverse order that we want — the stack. This is the usual thing to do when converting numbers to base 10. As base 10 digits are peeled off, we could push them onto the stack (3, 0, 5). Later, when we pop them, they'll be in the right order (5, 0, 3). This means that storing the remainder is easy. We just have to push the register it's in, DX:

```
            .CODE
            ORG     100H
ENTRY:      JMP     CONVERT
            ASCII_STRING    DB 7 DUP("$")
CONVERT PROC        NEAR
            LEA     SI,ASCII_STRING
            CMP     AX,0
            JGE     POSITIVE
            NEG     AX
            MOV     BYTE PTR [SI],"-"
            INC     SI
POSITIVE:
            MOV     BX,10
            MOV     CX,0
THELOOP:
            MOV     DX,0
            DIV     BX
            PUSH    DX
            INC     CX
            [Check whether the result is zero yet.]
            JNE     THELOOP
            INT     20H
CONVERT ENDP

            END     ENTRY
```

Now we have to prepare for the next time we divide DX:AX by 10. At the top of the loop, we set DX to zero, so DX:AX will really be 0000:AX, as it should be. AX holds the result of the last division, as it should because this is the result that we want to divide by 10 again the next time around.

Before we do that, however, we have to check and see whether or not AX — the result — is zero. If it is, there are no more digits to get, and, if there are no more digits to get, then we want to finish with this loop. We can check this with the last two lines in the loop:

```
            .CODE
            ORG     100H
ENTRY:      JMP     CONVERT
            ASCII_STRING    DB 7 DUP("$")
CONVERT PROC        NEAR
            LEA     SI,ASCII_STRING
            CMP     AX,0
            JGE     POSITIVE
            NEG     AX
            MOV     BYTE PTR [SI],"-"
            INC     SI
POSITIVE:
            MOV     BX,10
            MOV     CX,0
THELOOP:
            MOV     DX,0
            DIV     BX
            PUSH    DX
            INC     CX
```

248 ▶ Advanced Assembly Language

```
            CMP     AX,0
            JNE     THELOOP
            :
            INT     20H
CONVERT ENDP

            END     ENTRY
```

If AX is not zero, we will keep looping until it is, and all the digits have been peeled off onto the stack.

After the loop is done, we have to get the digits off the stack and into ASCII_STRING. We kept track of how many digits there were in CX. That means that we can simply pop CX times — using CX as a loop index — and put the digit popped each time into ASCII_STRING. Our location in ASCII_STRING is [SI], which we will have to increase each time we put a character into it. Here's how the POP loop looks:

```
            .CODE
            ORG     100H
ENTRY:      JMP     CONVERT
            ASCII_STRING    DB 7 DUP("$")
CONVERT PROC NEAR
            LEA     SI,ASCII_STRING
            CMP     AX,0
            JGE     POSITIVE
            NEG     AX
            MOV     BYTE PTR [SI],"-"
            INC     SI
POSITIVE:
            MOV     BX,10
            MOV     CX,0
THELOOP:
            MOV     DX,0
            DIV     BX
            PUSH    DX
            INC     CX
            CMP     AX,0
            JNE     THELOOP
POPLOOP:    POP     AX
            :
            :
            LOOP    POPLOOP
            INT     20H
CONVERT ENDP

            END     ENTRY
```

Every time we pop a value into AX, the digit we want will be in AL. To make it an ASCII value, we will have to add "0" to it. Then we can store it in ASCII_STRING at location [SI], increase SI for the next digit, and we can loop again to pop the next digit. That's it for the program CONVERT.ASM; you can find the whole thing in Listing 8-10.

Listing 8-10. CONVERT.ASM — Converts Hex Number to Decimal.

```
        .CODE
        ORG     100H
ENTRY:  JMP     CONVERT
        ASCII_STRING    DB 7 DUP("$")
CONVERT PROC    NEAR
        LEA     SI,ASCII_STRING
        CMP     AX,0
        JGE     POSITIVE
        NEG     AX
        MOV     BYTE PTR [SI],"-"
        INC     SI
POSITIVE:
        MOV     BX,10
        MOV     CX,0
THELOOP:
        MOV     DX,0
        DIV     BX
        PUSH    DX
        INC     CX
        CMP     AX,0
        JNE     THELOOP
POPLOOP:POP     AX
        ADD     AL,"0"
        MOV     [SI],AL
        INC     SI
        LOOP    POPLOOP
        INT     20H
CONVERT ENDP

        END     ENTRY
```

Give CONVERTS a try, or use it in your own programs. Just pass a number in AX, and the corresponding base 10 number will appear in ASCII in ASCII_STRING. A little program like this has many uses since it converts from machine arithmetic to human arithmetic. For example, if you are debugging and want to know the contents of one of the registers, you can have CONVERT make up an ASCII string and have it printed out at run time.

And that's it for our chapter on fast math. Let's turn now to macros and advanced directives in Chapter 9.

Chapter 9

Using Macros and Advanced Directives

Using Macros and Advanced Directives

UNTIL NOW, we have been working with *what* you have been programming rather than *how*. If you have mastered the concepts up to this point, you understand much of what assembly language is all about on the PC, and you can do many of the things it is capable of doing.

On the other hand, when it comes time to develop major applications, the style we have developed is a little clumsy. In practice it is often difficult to confine a large program to a single .ASM file. For example, it is much better to divide the code between several such files. When you change the code in one, you won't have to assemble and link the entire program at once, but you can link in already assembled sections without changing them. And what we learn about linking in this chapter will help us in Chapter 10 when we link into high-level languages.

Much of what we will examine in this chapter is what people think of when they think of advanced assembly language — macros, libraries, and so on. The advanced use of assembly language is whatever helps you program more effectively, and macros are as much a part of that as is knowledge about the disk system.

Printing Out a Trial Message

In the coming pages, we will examine the various ways of performing a very mundane task: printing out the message, "This is a test. This is ONLY a test." The number of ways this is possible are practically endless, but we will limit ourselves to the main variations.

Printing the Trial Message Directly

The first, simplest way to print out our trial message is simply to print it from the main body of the program, using INT 21H, Service 9. This is all we have to do:

```
            .MODEL SMALL
            .CODE
            ORG     100H
ENTRY:      JMP     TEST

            MSG     DB 'This is a test. This is ONLY a test.$'

TEST:       LEA     DX,MSG
        →   MOV     AH,9
        →   INT     21H
            INT     20H
            END     ENTRY
```

This is the shortest way. All we've done is to make a .COM file (all our examples will be .COM files in this chapter) that has an entry point at 100H and skips over the data area with JMP TEST. We don't even need a PROC or ENDP directive, we can use labels instead. We could have used TEST PROC NEAR and TEST ENDP, but the final .COM file would have been identical because PROC NEAR just serves to label a location, as TEST: does.

Labels can be either NEAR or FAR. A NEAR label is reached from inside the same segment, and a FAR label can be reached from outside (in other words, NEAR labels only use offsets and FAR labels use both segment and offset values). A NEAR label can be defined these ways:

```
TEST:
TEST    EQU     $
EXTRN   TEST:NEAR
TEST    LABEL   NEAR
TEST    PROC    NEAR
```

All of these are equivalent. TEST EQU $ takes a little explaining. The "$" character in an assembly language file stands for the current position of assembly in the file (in bytes). It is very much like the value IP, the instruction pointer, would have if the file were running. TEST EQU $ sets the name TEST to the current address in the file.

The statement EXTRN TEST:NEAR will be covered later. It tells the assembler that it won't find TEST defined in the current .ASM file, but that the label TEST is to be found in a file that will be linked together with this one. In the meantime, the assembler is directed to treat the label as a NEAR label and to leave space for its address in assembled instructions. The linker will fill this address space in.

FAR labels can be defined this way:

```
EXTRN   TEST:FAR
TEST    LABEL   FAR
TEST    PROC    FAR
TEST    EQU FAR PTR $
```

These labels can all be JMPed to from another segment. The only one that takes a little explaining is TEST EQU FAR PTR $. All that we're doing there is overriding the usual offset-only value of $ with a PTR operator. To make our example above into a working .COM file, all you have to do is assemble it, LINK it, and then run it through EXE2BIN.

Subroutines

The next level is just to use a subroutine. In this case, we don't have the code to print out the message in the main part of the program. Instead we wrap it up into a subroutine, PRINT_MSG. To send our message, we only need to call PRINT_MSG as shown in Listing 9-1.

Listing 9-1. PRINT_MSG Procedure.

```
        .MODEL  SMALL
        .CODE
        ORG     100H
ENTRY:  JMP     TEST

MSG     DB 'This is a test. This is ONLY a test.$'

TEST    PROC    NEAR
        CALL    PRINT_MSG
        INT     20H
TEST    ENDP

PRINT_MSG       PROC    NEAR
        LEA     DX,MSG
        MOV     AH,9
        INT     21H
        RET
PRINT_MSG       ENDP

        END     ENTRY
```

When you call a NEAR subroutine, the instruction pointer IP is pushed onto the stack and then filled with the address stored in the CALL instruction. When you call a FAR subroutine, first CS and then IP are pushed onto the stack, and then they are filled with the values stored in the CALL instruction. The RET always found at the end of subroutines will pop either one word (NEAR) or two words (FAR), depending on how the PROC is defined. Usually, we'll let the memory model define the size of the code section for us (i.e., if the code can be many segments long, all calls are made into FAR calls), but, if you have explicitly written TEST PROC FAR, two words get popped. You can also, as we have done, call an address that is stored in memory. For instance, a NEAR call may look like:

```
CALL WORD PTR [BX]
```

A FAR call like this:

```
CALL DWORD PTR [BX]
```

This kind of programming is often useful if you have a central "dispatching" section of the program, as DOS INT 21H does, that has to send control to various places depending on what is required. All it has to do is store a table of addresses and send control to them by calling them.

Linking

The next way of printing out our message is to divide the work between two files and to link them together in the end. The two files we can use as an example are shown in Listing 9-2.

Listing 9-2. Files 1 and 2 for Linking.

```
        File 1. -------------------------------------------------

        .MODEL  SMALL
        .CODE
        EXTRN   MSG:NEAR
        ORG     100H

TEST    PROC    NEAR
        LEA     DX,MSG
        MOV     AH,9
        INT     21H
        INT     20H
TEST    ENDP


        END     TEST


        File 2. -------------------------------------------------

        .MODEL  SMALL
        .CODE
        PUBLIC  MSG

        MSG     DB 'This is a test. This is ONLY a test.$'

        END
```

We are putting the main part of our code in File 1, and the message itself into File 2. When the assembler assembles File 1, it will find the line LEA DX, MSG:

▶ Using Macros and Advanced Directives   257

```
        .MODEL  SMALL
        .CODE
        EXTRN   MSG:NEAR
        ORG     100H

TEST    PROC    NEAR
    →   LEA     DX,MSG
        MOV     AH,9
        INT     21H
        INT     20H
TEST    ENDP
```

On the other hand, there is no MSG in File 1. This would generate an error unless we let the assembler know that it shouldn't expect to find MSG in this file with the EXTRN directive:

```
        .MODEL  SMALL
        .CODE
    →   EXTRN   MSG:NEAR
        ORG     100H

TEST    PROC    NEAR
    →   LEA     DX,MSG
        MOV     AH,9
        INT     21H
        INT     20H
TEST    ENDP
```

This EXTRN directive says that MSG will be found only at link time, and it will be a NEAR label. The assembler then assembles LEA DX,MSG, leaving a blank space in the command for the offset of MSG. If LINK does not subsequently find a label MSG in some other file, you will get an error message: UNRESOLVED EXTERNALS: MSG.

You must match all your EXTRNs with PUBLICs in other files. FILE2 looks like this:

```
        .MODEL  SMALL
        .CODE
    →   PUBLIC  MSG

MSG     DB 'This is a test. This is ONLY a test.$'

        END
```

Notice in particular the line PUBLIC MSG. This line is to match the corresponding EXTRN MSG:NEAR in FILE1. Every time you have an EXTRN in one file, it must be matched by a PUBLIC directive in another file. In this case, we are requesting the assembler to notice that MSG will be required by some other file. Any label can be made PUBLIC: labels in the code like TEST:, or procedures like TEST PROC FAR.

Unless you have a PUBLIC for each EXTRN, the linker will give you error messages for unresolved externals. Only if you declare a label PUBLIC will the label itself be retained so it can be matched to EXTRNs in other files. Otherwise, the label is lost and replaced by a number.

As in a normal .COM file, control will enter at 100H, so we have to make some provision for it. This can be done with the ORG 100H statement in File 1. Even though other parts of the final .COM file will come later, we are requiring that this part go at 100H.

In File 2 we don't need to supply any ORG statements, although we could have done so if we wished. For example, we could say ORG 200H and everything would have worked well since the code generated by File 1 at ORG 100H ends long before 200H, where FILE2 would be loaded.

In addition, the assembler has certain rules about this process. For example, whenever the assembler assembles an .ASM file, it orders the segments alphabetically. In other words, DATA_SEG is put after CODE_SEG. This default setting of the assembler can be overridden by the /S switch, which directs the assembler not to sort the segments, but to leave them in the order encountered. In our example here, we only have one segment in both files, the code segment.

Another point to be made here is that each .COM or .EXE file can have only one entry point. The address control is transferred to when the program is started. Here, though, we are linking multiple files together, so you must select the entry point yourself. In this case, we want to enter at 100H in FILE1 since FILE1 is the main program. For this reason, we put the statement END TEST, below, at the end of FILE1.

```
            .MODEL  SMALL
            .CODE
            EXTRN   MSG:NEAR
            ORG     100H

TEST        PROC    NEAR
            LEA     DX,MSG
            MOV     AH,9
            INT     21H
            INT     20H
TEST        ENDP

            END     TEST  ←
```

This defines an entry point that is stored in the .EXE file's header. At the end of FILE2, by contrast, there is no specified entry point:

▶ Using Macros and Advanced Directives

```
.MODEL SMALL
.CODE
PUBLIC  MSG

MSG     DB 'This is a test. This is ONLY a test.$'

END  -
```

And this is the way it should be for all subsequent files linked in. To LINK these two files together, this is the command we use:

```
LINK FILE1+FILE2
```

The LINK command works like this:

```
F:\>LINK FILE1+FILE2
Microsoft (R) Overlay Linker  Version 3.69
Copyright (C) Microsoft Corp 1983-1988.  All rights reserved.

Run File [FILE1.EXE]: TEST.EXE
List File [NUL.MAP]:
Libraries [.LIB]:
```

We get the chance to specify the name of the .EXE file. Here we call it TEST.EXE (the default would have been FILE1.EXE, since FILE1 was the first file linked). In addition, we can specify the names of libraries to search. (We will see later in this chapter how to create our own libraries with the LIB.EXE program.) Now that TEST.EXE has been created, it can be run through EXE2BIN to produce TEST.COM. Once we run TEST.COM, MSG will be printed on the screen.

Linked Subroutines

All we've done so far is to link in MSG — that is, data — after the end of the code in FILE1. The next step is to link in an entire subroutine. For example, let's say we had a main procedure, named MAIN, which called a subroutine named SUB in another file. SUB, in turn, calls SUB_1, back in the first file, and SUB_1 prints the message. How the two files, FILE1 and FILE2, would look is shown in Listing 9-3.

260 ▶ Advanced Assembly Language

Listing 9-3. Files 1 and 2 with Procedures for Linking.

```
        File 1. -------------------------------------------------

            .MODEL SMALL
            .CODE
            PUBLIC  SUB_1
            EXTRN SUB:NEAR
            ORG     100H
ENTRY:  JMP     MAIN
MSG     DB      'This is a test. This is ONLY a test.$'

MAIN    PROC    NEAR
        CALL    SUB
        INT     20H
MAIN    ENDP

SUB_1   PROC NEAR
        LEA     DX,MSG
        MOV     AH,9
        INT     21H
        RET
SUB_1   ENDP

        END ENTRY

        File 2. -------------------------------------------------

            .MODEL SMALL
            .CODE
            EXTRN   SUB_1:NEAR
            PUBLIC  SUB

SUB     PROC    NEAR
        CALL    SUB_1
        RET
SUB     ENDP

        END
```

Notice that in FILE1, SUB, a label like any other, is proclaimed EXTRN, and SUB_1, which is called from the other file, is proclaimed PUBLIC:

```
.MODEL SMALL
.CODE
PUBLIC  SUB_1
EXTRN SUB:NEAR
ASSUME CS:CSEG,DS:CSEG
```

In FILE2 we declare SUB_1 EXTRN and SUB PUBLIC (since MAIN will call it). When LINK encounters FILE2, it realizes that the segment there has the same name as the segment in FILE1, so the code in FILE2 goes right after the code in FILE1.

When the program is entered at 100H, control will jump to MAIN. MAIN calls SUB, now linked at the end of the program. SUB calls SUB_1, and SUB_1 does all the work. To make one .COM file out of these two, we first MASM them independently:

Using Macros and Advanced Directives

```
MASM FILE1;
MASM FILE2;
```

then link:

```
LINK FILE1+FILE2;
```

and finally convert to a .COM file with EXE2BIN. The final result can be run and print out MSG.

Using Data in FILE2

Note that although we were able to link in SUB from FILE2 this way, the MSG that is actually printed out is in FILE1. This is because if we had included the statement LEA DX,MSG in FILE2, we would have had trouble. If we include MSG in FILE2, we would have the result shown in Figure 9-1.

```
              FILE1
        ORG     100H

        CALL    SUB
                :

              FILE2
        MSG     'This is a test.$'

        SUB     PROC    NEAR
                :
        LEA     DX,MSG
                :
```

Figure 9-1. Files 1 and 2 after Linking

When the assembler assembled FILE2, it would have seen LEA DX,MSG and stored the offset of MSG in the assembled command. Yet the offset it found was from the beginning of FILE2, not FILE1. (If MSG was in a different file, as in our example earlier, you could declare it EXTRN, and there would be no problem.) When the files are linked, FILE2 comes after FILE1, so the offset from the beginning of the segment will be wrong.

In other words, to use a command like LEA DX,MSG, or to reference any data in FILE2 with commands in FILE2, we need to know how far from the beginning of the program FILE2 will be. For this reason, *groups* were invented.

How to Use Groups

We've been able to link in subroutines if they only contain code, but we can ask ourselves what would happen if we wanted to link a subroutine with data in like this into the main program:

```
MSG         DB      'This is a test. This is ONLY a test.$'
SEND_MSG    PROC    NEAR
            LEA     DX,MSG
            MOV     AH,9
            INT     21H
            RET
SEND_MSG    ENDP
```

In this case, MSG is stored in the same file that types it out. As we have mentioned, the statement LEA DX,MSG will give us problems since it will be assembled to include the offset of MSG from the beginning of the file it is in, not the main file. To correct this problem, the assembler introduces groups. All the GROUP directive does is to collect a number of segments, even segments with different names, into one 64K or less area. When the files are linked together, the segments that belong to a particular group are all put inside that group in the order they were encountered by LINK.

The important thing about groups is that all the segments added together share a common segment address. We'll use our own segment names here so that we can combine them into a single group. You can load the segment registers in your program with this value instead of the value of the local segment. At link time, the linker sets all the offsets correctly. You can see how it looks in Listing 9-4.

Listing 9-4. Files 1 and 2 with Groups.

```
        File 1. ----------------------------------------------

CODE_GROUP      GROUP   CODE_SEG
        EXTRN   SEND_MSG:NEAR
CODE_SEG SEGMENT
        ASSUME  CS:CODE_GROUP,DS:CODE_GROUP
        ORG     100H

TEST    PROC    NEAR
        CALL    SEND_MSG
        INT     20H
TEST    ENDP

CODE_SEG ENDS
        END     TEST

        File 2. ----------------------------------------------

CODE_GROUP      GROUP   CSEG
```

Listing 9-4. Files 1 and 2 with Groups. 2 of 2

```
CSEG      SEGMENT
          ASSUME   CS:CODE_GROUP,DS:CODE_GROUP
          PUBLIC   SEND_MSG

MSG       DB  'This is a test. This is ONLY a test.$'

SEND_MSG PROC    NEAR
          LEA     DX,MSG
          MOV     AH,9
          INT     21H
          RET
SEND_MSG          ENDP

CSEG      ENDS
          END
```

Note that we had to add the ASSUME directive explicitly (it's normally part of the .CODE directive). The new parts (but don't forget about the PUBLICs and EXTRNs) are the statements:

```
CODE_GROUP       GROUP CODE_SEG
CODE_SEG SEGMENT
         ASSUME CS:CODE_GROUP,DS:CODE_GROUP
```

All we've done is to let the assembler know that the segment CODE_SEG (or CSEG in file 2) will go into CODE_GROUP, and then we've defined CODE_SEG with the SEGMENT directive rather than using .CODE. The ASSUMEs let the assembler know how the segment registers CS and DS will be set when the program is run. Now we are free to use CS and DS as if we were putting everything together in the same .ASM file. You can reference the CODE_GROUP group with statements just as you had used for segments:

```
MOV    AX,@CODE    →    MOV    AX,CODE_GROUP
```

You can also use group names as segment overrides, like this:

```
MOV    AX,OFFSET CS:SEND_MSG    →    MOV    AX,OFFSET CODE_GROUP:SEND_MSG
```

When we use groups, we can reference data safely, as in this use in File 2 (where DS will be set to CODE_GROUP, so no segment override is needed):

```
        File 2.
CODE_GROUP      GROUP CSEG
CSEG    SEGMENT
        ASSUME  CS:CODE_GROUP,DS:CODE_GROUP
        PUBLIC  SEND_MSG

MSG     DB 'This is a test. This is ONLY a test.$'

SEND_MSG PROC   NEAR
        LEA     DX,MSG
        MOV     AH,9
        INT     21H
        RET
SEND_MSG        ENDP

CSEG    ENDS
        END
```

We can even change these files so that we can reference MSG even if it is in File 1:

```
        File 1. ----------------------------------------------
CODE_GROUP      GROUP CODE_SEG
        EXTRN   SEND_MSG:NEAR
        PUBLIC  MSG
CODE_SEG SEGMENT
        ASSUME CS:CODE_GROUP,DS:CODE_GROUP
        ORG     100H
ENTRY:  JMP     TEST
MSG     DB 'This is a test. This is ONLY a test.$'

TEST    PROC    NEAR
        CALL    SEND_MSG
        INT     20H
TEST    ENDP

CODE_SEG ENDS
        END     ENTRY

        File 2. ----------------------------------------------
CODE_GROUP      GROUP CSEG
CSEG    SEGMENT
        ASSUME  CS:CODE_GROUP,DS:CODE_GROUP
        EXTRN   MSG:NEAR
        PUBLIC  SEND_MSG

SEND_MSG PROC   NEAR
        LEA     DX,MSG
        MOV     AH,9
        INT     21H
        RET
SEND_MSG        ENDP

CSEG    ENDS
        END
```

Using Macros and Advanced Directives 265

Keep in mind that an entry point is always needed in one (and only one) module, so we have an instruction END ENTRY at the end of File 1. At the end of File 2, there is no entry point instruction.

GROUPs and Different Segments

Groups can also collect different segments together. For example, see the code in Listing 9-5.

Listing 9-5. Groups Collecting Different Segments Together.

```
File 1. --------------------------------------------------

CODE_GROUP      GROUP    SEG1,SEG2
SEG1    SEGMENT
        :
SEG1    ENDS
SEG2    SEGMENT
        :
SEG2    ENDS


File 2. --------------------------------------------------

CODE_GROUP      GROUP    SEG3
SEG3    SEGMENT
        :
SEG3    ENDS
```

When these files are linked together,

```
LINK FILE1+FILE2;
```

the segments will appear in the final code like this: SEG1,SEG2,SEG3. The group CODE_GROUP will let you keep your label offsets straight automatically. Using groups lets you freely use memory storage such as MOV NUMBER,5, in any module.

The only tricky part is making sure you always use the same group name, especially if you link your object modules into libraries. Also, keep in mind that even though groups will take care of the offsets for you at link time, you still have to declare labels EXTRN and PUBLIC if they are needed in another object module, since otherwise the assembler will give you errors.

Libraries

After a time, you may find yourself with quite a collection of suroutines that you link together, and it may become difficult trying to remember just which subroutines are in which .OBJ files. At that point, it is advisable to make your own *library* which can contain a number of assembled modules.

As you may recall, when you link files together, you can specify the names of libraries. The linker looks in these libraries only to find unresolved external references. If it finds the external symbol it is looking for in one of the libraries, the linker can link it in. Let's try this out by making a library out of FILE.ASM, which looks like this:

```
                .MODEL  SMALL
                .CODE
                PUBLIC  SUB

        SUB     PROC    NEAR
                :
                [Do work.]
                :
                RET
        SUB     ENDP

                END
```

To make this into a true library and not just another .OBJ file, let's add a dummy module made from DUMMY.ASM so that the final library will have two modules in it:

```
                .MODEL  SMALL
                .CODE
                PUBLIC  DUMMY

        DUMMY   PROC    NEAR
                RET
        DUMMY   ENDP

                END
```

First, we assemble the files:

```
F:\>MASM FILE;
F:\>MASM DUMMY;
```

And then create our library, TEST.LIB. To make TEST.LIB, we will add FILE.OBJ to DUMMY.OBJ like this:

▶ Using Macros and Advanced Directives 267

```
F:\>LIB TEST.LIB FILE+DUMMY;

IBM Personal Computer Library Manager
Version 1.00
(C)Copyright IBM Corp 1984
(C)Copyright Microsoft Corp 1984
```

This procedure produces our own library, TEST.LIB. To create a working .COM file, we need a program that references the SUB procedure in TEST.LIB. If that program is in USES_SUB.ASM, then we can create an executable module like this:

```
F:\>LINK
Microsoft (R) Overlay Linker  Version 3.69
Copyright (C) Microsoft Corp 1983-1988.  All rights reserved.

Object Modules [.OBJ]: USES_SUB +
Run File [FILE1.EXE]:
List File [NUL.MAP]:
Libraries [.LIB]: TEST
Warning: No STACK segment

There was 1 error detected.
```

We get the usual STACK segment error since we are making a .COM file. All that remains is to run USES_SUB.EXE file through EXE2BIN and to run USES_SUB.COM. In this way, you can create libraries of all your most useful subroutines.

Library Commands

There are other ways of manipulating libraries. For example, the advanced user can add modules to a library, delete them, extract .OBJ files from them, or replace a module inside them with something newer. Although we won't go into detail here, here are the symbols that LIB expects you to use for the various operations:

Add	Delete	Extract	Replace	Del&Extract
+	-	*	-+	-*

For example, let's say we have a large library named CONGRESS.LIB. To add a new .OBJ file, NEW.OBJ, to it, you could type:

```
F:\>LIB CONGRESS.LIB +NEW.OBJ;
```

To extract the module CHECK from CONGRESS.LIB and put it into CHECK.OBJ, we would type:

```
F:\>LIB CONGRESS.LIB *CHECK;
```

If OLD.OBJ was originally put into CONGRESS.LIB, we could delete it from CONGRESS.LIB this way:

```
F:\>LIB CONGRESS.LIB -OLD;
```

> **TIP** Keep in mind that if a subroutine in one of your .LIB files calls a subroutine in some other .LIB file, you should link the one with the call first. LINK won't know that it is supposed to include a particular module unless it is called. If it has already searched the correct library before you make the call, it won't be able to find the subroutine when you finally do call it.

How Macros Work

The methods we've covered so far have to do with linking. We have to turn now to a different subject that doesn't have to do with linking of files, but can get MSG printed out nonetheless. That subject is macros.

Macros seem to be an esoteric subject to many people, but in fact they are not complex at all. Macros can be short, and all they need are two directives, MACRO and ENDM. A macro is simply some lines of code, like this one:

```
PRINTOUT MACRO
         MOV    AH,9
         LEA    DX,MSG
         INT    21H
         ENDM
```

Whenever you use PRINTOUT as a command in your program, these three lines, below, will be put into code.

```
MOV    AH,9
LEA    DX,MSG
INT    21H
```

▶ Using Macros and Advanced Directives 269

In other words, the assembler expands (notice the macro definition comes before we use PRINTOUT)

```
PRINTOUT MACRO
         MOV     AH,9
         LEA     DX,MSG
         INT     21H
         ENDM

         .MODEL SMALL
         .CODE
         ORG     100H
ENTRY:   PRINTOUT +
         PRINTOUT +

         INT     20H
         END     ENTRY
```

into this:

```
         .MODEL SMALL
         .CODE
         ORG     100H
ENTRY:   MOV     AH,9
         LEA     DX,MSG
         INT     21H

         MOV     AH,9
         LEA     DX,MSG
         INT     21H

         INT     20H
         END     ENTRY
```

That means that we could print out the message with the code shown in Listing 9-6.

Listing 9-6. Macro to Print Out the Message.

```
PRINTOUT MACRO
         MOV     AH,9
         LEA     DX,MSG
         INT     21H
         ENDM

         .MODEL SMALL
         .CODE
         ORG     100H
ENTRY:   JMP     TEST

         MSG     DB 'This is a test. This is ONLY a test.$'
TEST:    PRINTOUT
         INT     20H
         END     ENTRY
```

After we assemble this and run it through LINK and EXE2BIN, we can DEBUG it. We expect to see the JMP at 100H, followed by the message 'This is a test. This is ONLY a test.$', and then the code MOV AH,9; LEA DX,[Address of MSG]; INT 21H; INT 20H. Here's what we find:

```
F:\>DEBUG TEST.COM
-R
AX=0000  BX=0000  CX=0032  DX=0000  SP=FFFE  BP=0000  SI=0000  DI=0000
DS=0905  ES=0905  SS=0905  CS=0905  IP=0100   NV UP DI PL NZ NA PO NC
0905:0100 EB26          JMP      0128   <- Here's the JMP over MSG.
-T

AX=0000  BX=0000  CX=0032  DX=0000  SP=FFFE  BP=0000  SI=0000  DI=0000
DS=0905  ES=0905  SS=0905  CS=0905  IP=0128   NV UP DI PL NZ NA PO NC
0905:0128 B409          MOV      AH,09  <- Here's the beginning of our program.
-U128 130
0905:0128 B409          MOV      AH,09
0905:012A 8D160301      LEA      DX,[0103]
0905:012E CD21          INT      21
0905:0130 CD20          INT      20
-Q
```

The assembler, as expected, expanded our macro into its component instructions. This use of a macro was simple. It might seem inefficient to include the full code for some task every time you want to do that task. After all, that is what subroutines are for. On the other hand, there are a number of times when you would have to duplicate instructions anyway. For example, if you have many subroutines, you might do a lot of PUSHing registers upon entry and POPping when you leave. You could define a macro PUSHA, named after the 80×86 (where x is 2 or greater) instruction that it emulates:

```
PUSHA   MACRO
        PUSH    AX
        PUSH    CX
        PUSH    DX
        PUSH    BX
        PUSH    SP
        PUSH    BP
        PUSH    SI
        PUSH    DI
        ENDM
```

Followed at the end of each subroutine with POPA:

```
POPA    MACRO
        POP     DI
        POP     SI
        POP     BP
        POP     SP
        POP     BX
        POP     DX
        POP     CX
        POP     AX
        ENDM
```

We could, for no particular reason, include PUSHA and POPA in the above example as shown in Listing 9-7.

Listing 9-7. Macro to Print Out the Message — With Added Pushes.

```
PRINTOUT MACRO
         MOV     AH,9
         LEA     DX,MSG
         INT     21H
         ENDM
PUSHA    MACRO
         PUSH    AX
         PUSH    CX
         PUSH    DX
         PUSH    BX
         PUSH    SP
         PUSH    BP
         PUSH    SI
         PUSH    DI
         ENDM

POPA     MACRO
         POP     DI
         POP     SI
         POP     BP
         POP     SP
         POP     BX
         POP     DX
         POP     CX
         POP     AX
         ENDM

         .MODEL  SMALL
         .CODE
         ORG     100H
ENTRY:   JMP     TEST

         MSG     DB 'This is a test. This is ONLY a test.$'

TEST:    PUSHA
         PRINTOUT
         POPA
         INT     20H
         END     ENTRY
```

Another such macro would be one that sets you up for INT 25H or 26H. Macros are also useful at assembly time. Here's a macro that will locate you the next multiple of 1K from the beginning of the code segment when you assemble. It also introduces us to the use of IF and ENDIF:

```
QUADPAGE  MACRO
          IF $ MOD 1024
          ORG $+1024-($ MOD 1024)
          ENDIF
          ENDM
```

Here the assembler evaluates $ MOD 1024 (keep in mind that $ is just like the current value of IP — it stands for the current offest in the code from the beginning of the code segment). If it is not zero, it performs the following commands until it sees ENDIF. If $ MOD 1024 is 0, those commands are not performed.

If $ MOD 1024 is not zero, then ORG $+1024-($ MOD 1024) is put in the program as a command, and this sets the new origin to be some multiple of 1K into the code segment. In general, the use of IF allows you to select what code goes into the final program. Some code will be selected if the IF condition is true, for example, and some other code if the condition is false.

The conditions you can select include whether or not a symbol has been defined as EXTRN, whether or not some expression is 0 (such as $ MOD 1024), and what *pass* the assembler is in. This last concept is not one we will work with much in this book, but it is worth knowing that MASM (or TASM) is a two-pass assembler. That is, code is always read twice.

The first time through, the assembler calculates the relative offsets of labels from each other and stores them in a symbol table. The second time through, the actual code is generated. There are times when you want to do something in Pass 1, but not in Pass 2. If, however, you manipulate the code too much between passes, you will generate what is called a *phase error*, which means the assembler found different offsets for some label in the two different passes.

The possible Macro IFs and their conditions are shown below.

Type of IF	Condition
IF X	True if X is NOT 0.
IFE X	True if X is 0.
IF1	True if the assembler is in Pass 1.
IF2	True if the assembler is in Pass 2.
IFDEF SYM	True if SYM has been defined.

▶ Using Macros and Advanced Directives

IFNDEF SYM	True if SYM is undefined.
IFB <XXX>	True if XXX is blank — see below.
IFNB <XXX>	True if XXX is not blank — see below.
IFIDN <XXX>,<YYY>	True if string XXX is the same as string YYY.
IFDIF <XXX>,<YYY>	True if string XXX is different from string YYY.
ENDIF	EVERY IF must end with an ENDIF.
ELSE	An option to make IFs into Either-Or blocks.

The simplest type of IF works like the one we've already seen:

```
QUADPAGE  MACRO
     IF $ MOD 1024
     ORG $+1024-($ MOD 1024)
     ENDIF
     ENDM
```

If the expression $ MOD 1024 is 0, then the following line(s) are executed. Notice the use of ENDIF at the end. ENDIF must follow all IF statements.

As you can see, there are many types of IFs. A number of these IFs are extremely useful when using macros. Since a macro is a set of commands that can be modified each time it is invoked by specifying parameters, it is sometimes desirable to know whether parameters have indeed been specified or whether they were left blank. For example, consider this macro in a file TEST.ASM, which uses the parameter OVERRIDE:

```
       DEFAULT MACRO    OVERRIDE
       IFNB <OVERRIDE>
       NUMBER DB OVERRIDE
       ELSE
       NUMBER  DB 255
       ENDIF
       ENDM

       .MODEL SMALL
       .CODE
       ORG     100H
ENTER: JMP     SHORT TEST
       DEFAULT          ;Data Area - Macro being used.
TEST:  INT     20H
       END     ENTER
```

This is one way of including a default in your macros. Here DEFAULT is used in the data area of TEST.ASM to define a memory location NUMBER and initialize it. If we simply specify the macro's name, DEFAULT, the dummy OVERRIDE will be blank.

274 ▶ Advanced Assembly Language

Looking at our macro, this means that the IFNB will not be fufilled, so the ELSE condition will come into effect. Here the ELSE condition is NUMBER DB 255.

In other words, unless we specify some number when invoking DEFAULT, we will get NUMBER DB 255 in the code. You can examine the results of invoking a macro by looking at the listing file (optionally) generated when you use the assembler. Let's assemble TEST.ASM, the previous file, and look at what the use of DEFAULT in the data area has done. In this case, we ask for a .LST file, TEST.LST:

```
F:\>MASM TEST

Object filename [TEST.OBJ]:
Source listing [NUL.LST]: TEST.LST
Cross reference [NUL.CRF]:
49980 Bytes free

Warning Severe
Errors  Errors
0       0
```

The file TEST.LST looks like the listing in Listing 9-8.

Listing 9-8. List File of the Macro Example.

```
IBM Personal Computer MACRO Assembler            Page    1-1

                             DEFAULT MACRO    OVERRIDE
                             IFNB <OVERRIDE>
                             NUMBER DB OVERRIDE
                             ELSE
                             NUMBER  DB 255
                             ENDIF
                             ENDM
0000                         .CODE
0100                         ORG     100H
0100 EB 01          ENTER:   JMP     SHORT TEST
                             DEFAULT
0102 FF             +                NUMBER  DB 255
0103 CD 20          TEST:    INT     20H
                             END     ENTER
```

The expansion of every line of a macro in .LST files is always preceeded by the + character you can see above. We can see that the macro DEFAULT has assembled into NUMBER DB 255. If, by contrast, we have used DEFAULT 0 instead of just DEFAULT, we would have ended up with NUMBER DB 0 in the code. The utility of a statement like IFNB or IFB is evident.

Passing Parameters to a Macro

The situation can be more complex. What if we had wanted to use DEFAULT, but we didn't have an immediate value (like 255 or 0) ready? In other words, what if we were using some counter, like VALUE in the example below, whose value was different at different points in the program? This is actually simple enough: we want to end up with a statement like NUMBER DB VALUE, and we can do it as shown in Listing 9-9.

Listing 9-9. Macro Example with a Counter.

```
        DEFAULT MACRO   OVERRIDE
        IFNB <OVERRIDE>
        NUMBER DB OVERRIDE
        ELSE
        NUMBER  DB 255
        ENDIF
        ENDM

        VALUE   = 1
        VALUE   = VALUE + 1

        .MODEL SMALL
        .CODE
        ORG     100H
ENTER:  JMP     SHORT TEST
        DEFAULT VALUE   ;Data Area <-- Macro being used.
TEST:   INT     20H
        END     ENTER
```

TIP This same example could not have been done with EQU. If we had said VALUE EQU 1, then VALUE would have been 1 forever. Its value cannot be changed. On the other hand, the importance of the = directive is that it allows reassignment, so the value of VALUE can be changed at different points throughout the program. In this way, = is much more flexible than EQU.

The example in Listing 9-9 assembles into the final command NUMBER DB VALUE. Since VALUE equals two, this becomes NUMBER DB 2. We could only use this DEFAULT macro once in the program. Using more than once would lead to multiple definitions of the label NUMBER, and consequently to errors.

Using % and & in Macros

What if the first time we wanted to define NUMBER1; the second time NUMBER2; and so forth? If we do things this way, we can use DEFAULT as often as we wish. This can be done with two new macro operators, % and &. An example, showing how this is accomplished, can be seen in Listing 9-10.

Listing 9-10. Example Defining NUMBER1, NUMBER2, etc.

```
        DEFAULT MACRO   OVERRIDE
COUNTER=COUNTER+1
        IFNB    <OVERRIDE>
        DEFINE  %COUNTER,OVERRIDE
        ELSE
        DEFINE  %COUNTER,255
        ENDIF
        ENDM


        DEFINE  MACRO   NUM,VAL
NUMBER&NUM      DB VAL
        ENDM


        COUNTER = 0     ;+ Initialize COUNTER to start with NUMBER1.

        .MODEL SMALL
        .CODE
        ORG     100H
ENTER:  JMP     SHORT TEST
        DEFAULT 0       ;Data Area + Macro being used.
        DEFAULT         ;Data Area + Macro being used.
TEST:   INT     20H
        END     ENTER
```

The special operator % makes sure that instead of the parameter name itself (such as COUNTER above) the value that COUNTER represents is used. What & does is join a passed parameter together with text already in the macro. For example, look at the macro DEFINE:

```
DEFINE   MACRO    NUM,VAL
NUMBER&NUM       DB VAL
ENDM
```

We want to generate NUMBER1 as the label the first time this macro is used, NUMBER2 the next time, and so on. If we had made DEFINE this way instead,

```
DEFINE   MACRO    NUM,VAL
NUMBERNUM        DB VAL
ENDM
```

▶ Using Macros and Advanced Directives 277

the assembler would not see NUM at the tail end of "NUMBERNUM" at all, assuming it was merely one word. The correct way to merge NUMBER and the value represented by NUM is with &:

```
NUMBER&NUM      DB VAL
```

The assembler then fills in the parameter NUM as required.

On the other hand, when we call DEFINE from our first macro, DEFAULT, we want to pass the current value of COUNTER, which is increased each time DEFAULT is used. We cannot, however, issue a directive like

```
DEFAULT COUNTER,255
```

since that will result in "COUNTER" being passed as a parameter, giving us:

```
NUMBERCOUNTER   DB 255
```

The correct thing is to pass COUNTER's *value*, not its name, and that is done with the % character:

```
DEFINE  %COUNTER,OVERRIDE
```

Take a moment to study this example since it is typical of the macros you might run into. Note also that we initialized COUNTER (with COUNTER = 0) before increasing it in DEFAULT. In this example, we are free to use DEFAULT more than once:

```
CODE_SEG SEGMENT
        ASSUME  CS:CODE_SEG,DS:CODE_SEG
        ORG     100H
ENTER:  JMP     SHORT TEST
        DEFAULT 0           ;Data Area - Macro being used.
        DEFAULT             ;Data Area - Macro being used.
TEST:   INT     20H
CODE_SEG        ENDS
        END     ENTER
```

The first use will result in NUMBER1 DB 0, and the second use will result in NUMBER2 DB 255. If you wish, you can practically define your own language simply using macros.

The LOCAL Directive in Macros

There is another, and easier, way of making sure that you do not have multiple definition problems when defining labels in macros, and that is the use of the LOCAL directive. Whenever you use LOCAL, it *must* be the line immediately after the macro definition, as shown below in Listing 9-11.

```
Listing 9-11. The LOCAL Directive at Work.

CODE_GROUP       GROUP    CODE_SEG,DATA_SEG

PRINTOUT MACRO   MESSAGE
         LOCAL   MSG
DATA_SEG         SEGMENT BYTE PUBLIC 'DATA'
         MSG     DB MESSAGE,'$'
DATA_SEG ENDS
         MOV     AH,9
         LEA     DX,MSG
         INT     21H
         ENDM

CODE_SEG SEGMENT BYTE PUBLIC 'CODE'
         ASSUME CS:CODE_GROUP,DS:CODE_GROUP
         ORG     100H
ENTRY:   PRINTOUT 'This is a test. This is ONLY a test.'
         INT     20H
CODE_SEG ENDS
         END     ENTRY
```

In this case, we are defining MSG as LOCAL in the macro PRINTOUT. This means that, whenever PRINTOUT is invoked, it will use a unique name for MSG so we will not be redefining the label. LOCAL is almost always used when the macro needs internal labels, but not when these labels are to be referenced externally (such as NUMBER1 and NUMBER2 above).

Macro Libraries

Another fancy option is to include your macros in a *macro library*. This library, usually named with the extension .MAC, is read in at assembly time. We can convert our last macro example to use a macro library named TEST.MAC. Here is the file TEST.MAC:

▶ Using Macros and Advanced Directives   279

```
PRINTOUT MACRO   MESSAGE
         LOCAL   MSG
DATA_SEG         SEGMENT BYTE PUBLIC 'DATA'
         MSG     DB MESSAGE,'$'
DATA_SEG ENDS
         MOV     AH,9
         LEA     DX,MSG
         INT     21H
         ENDM
```

And this is what is in the .ASM file:

```
CODE_GROUP       GROUP   CODE_SEG,DATA_SEG

INCLUDE TEST.MAC

CODE_SEG SEGMENT BYTE PUBLIC 'CODE'
         ASSUME CS:CODE_GROUP,DS:CODE_GROUP
         ORG    100H
ENTRY:   PRINTOUT 'This is a test. This is ONLY a test.'
         PRINTOUT 'This is a test. This is ONLY a test.'
         INT    20H
CODE_SEG ENDS
         END    ENTRY
```

This assembly is done as usual. The macro(s) in TEST.MAC are simply put into the code at the position of the INCLUDE TEST.MAC statement. You can even include drive and path names with the INCLUDE command.

The other macro directives available are these: EXITM, IRP, IRPC, PURGE, and REPT, and they each deserve some attention.

The EXITM Directive

The EXITM command can get you out of any macro. All it does is to place you after the ENDM command.

> **TIP** The EXITM directive is useful when you have loops in your macro (such as REPT allows: see below) and want to exit on some condition. You can, for example, keep looping until an IF statement becomes true, and then execute an EXITM, as we'll see in an example later.

IRP and IRPC

The IRP and IRPC directives can be very useful under some circumstances. IRP lets you repeat an operation a number of times, taking arguments from a list. For example, here's how you could use IRP:

```
IRP     NAME,<"This","is a","test.$">
DB      NAME
```

The angle brackets around the strings are required, but no angle brackets are required when defining the dummy (NAME in this case,) that will be replaced with values. This example will be expanded into:

```
DB      "This"
DB      "is a"
DB      "test.$"
```

This in itself might not seem useful, but consider that you can do the same for lists of numbers or even individual characters. IRPC is set up to take character by character from a string, and repeat a particular operation until the string is exhausted:

```
IRPC    VALUE,56789
DB      VALUE-3
```

This example generates:

```
DB      2
DB      3
DB      4
DB      5
DB      6
```

If we had enclosed 56789 in quotation marks, however, the entire string would have been treated as one argument, as in the previous example.

REPT

REPT is the directive that loops in macros. You can give REPT a number and the loop will be performed that many times, unless you include an EXITM directive as an exiting condition. You can use REPT to pad spaces in between parts of code so it ends on 256-

▶ Using Macros and Advanced Directives 281

byte boundaries, execute another macro a number of times, or even compare lists of parameters until a match is found.

Every REPT must end with an ENDM. If you are including REPT inside a macro (it need not be inside a macro, however), include an extra ENDM for the REPT part, as in the example below.

An Example Using Macro Directives

Let's put together an example using REPT, EXITM, and IF. This macro will pad space in your program with as many zeros as you want, up to a maximum of 16. Once it reaches that limit, it will quit. The code itself is in Listing 9-12.

Listing 9-12. Example with REPT, EXITM, and IF.

```
        PAD       MACRO    NUMBER
        COUNTER = 0        ;← Initialize COUNTER to start.
        REPT      NUMBER
        IF        COUNTER-16
        DB        0
        ELSE
        EXITM
        ENDIF
        COUNTER=COUNTER+1
        ENDM               ;← Note: TWO ENDMs; one for REPT
        ENDM               ;← and one for MACRO.

        .MODEL SMALL
        .CODE
        ORG       100H
ENTRY:  JMP       SHORT TEST
        PAD       20
TEST:   INT       20H
        END       ENTRY
```

We can look at the .LST file in Listing 9-13 to see what happened. As we expected, there are 16 zeros, even though we invoked the macro with PAD 20.

Listing 9-13. Listing File of Macro Example.

```
IBM Personal Computer MACRO Assembler                Page   1-1

                       PAD     MACRO   NUMBER
                       COUNTER = 0       ;* Initialize COUNTER to start.
                       REPT    NUMBER
                       IF      COUNTER-16
                       DB      0
                       ELSE
                       EXITM
                       ENDIF
                       COUNTER=COUNTER+1
                       ENDM
                       ENDM

0000                           .CODE
0100                           ORG     100H
0100 EB 10             ENTRY:  JMP     SHORT TEST
                               PAD     20
0102 00                        +       DB      0
0103 00                        +       DB      0
0104 00                        +       DB      0
0105 00                        +       DB      0
0106 00                        +       DB      0
0107 00                        +       DB      0
0108 00                        +       DB      0
0109 00                        +       DB      0
010A 00                        +       DB      0
010B 00                        +       DB      0
010C 00                        +       DB      0
010D 00                        +       DB      0
010E 00                        +       DB      0
010F 00                        +       DB      0
0110 00                        +       DB      0
0111 00                        +       DB      0
0112 CD 20             TEST:   INT     20H
                               END     ENTRY
```

PURGE

The last of the macro directives is PURGE. PURGE is very simple. Its use eliminates a specified macro. For example, we could have said PURGE PAD above, and removed the definition of PAD from memory, allowing that space to be used for another macro definition. If you merely want to change the definition of a particular macro, however, you need not PURGE it first. Just redefining the macro will overwrite its definition. This brings us to our last macro topic: self-redefining macros.

Using Self-Redefining Macros

Despite an exotic sounding name, self-redefining macros are actually easy to use, and they are quite common. You may have noticed that a major drawback with macros is that, whenever invoked, they are expanded to their full length right there in the code. If you have a number of instructions that are more conveniently put into a subroutine, you probably wouldn't want to repeat them every time you wanted to use them. You would simply call the subroutine. With a normal macro, of course, you would get the full length (all the instructions) right there in your program.

If, however, a macro itself contains a macro definition, the second macro is not defined until the first one — the one enclosing it — is run. That enclosed macro can have the same name, in fact. When that happens, the macro is redefined — the old definition is simply written over. Let's develop an example named OUTPUT. The first time this macro is run, it defines the procedure PRINT and calls it. It also redefines itself so that from then on, OUTPUT just expands into CALL PRINT. You can see the code in Listing 9-14.

Listing 9-14. Self-Redefining Macro Example.

```
        OUTPUT  MACRO
        JMP     SHORT OVER
MSG     DB      'This is a test. This is ONLY a test.$'
        PRINT   PROC    NEAR
        LEA     DX,MSG
        MOV     AH,9
        INT     21H
        RET
        PRINT   ENDP
OVER:   CALL    PRINT
        OUTPUT  MACRO           ;- Macro being redefined.
        CALL    PRINT           ;- Macro being redefined.
        ENDM                    ;- Macro being redefined.
        ENDM

        .MODEL  SMALL
        .CODE
        ORG     100H
ENTRY:  OUTPUT
        OUTPUT
TEST:   INT     20H
        END     ENTRY
```

Notice that we have a full macro definition inside OUTPUT, and that definition redefines OUTPUT:

```
OUTPUT  MACRO           ;- Macro being redefined.
CALL    PRINT           ;- Macro being redefined.
ENDM                    ;- Macro being redefined.
```

It is also worth noticing that, although we use labels in this macro (MSG and PRINT), we don't have to use LOCALs, since the macro that defines them is only used once. In the example, OUTPUT is called twice. We can take a look at the resulting .LST file that this example produces in Listing 9-15.

Listing 9-15. List File of Self-Redefining Macro Example.

```
IBM Personal Computer MACRO Assembler                Page    1-1

                        OUTPUT  MACRO
                        JMP     SHORT OVER
                MSG     DB      'This is a test. This is ONLY a test.$'
                        PRINT   PROC    NEAR
                        LEA     DX,MSG
                        MOV     AH,9
                        INT     21H
                        RET
                        PRINT   ENDP
                OVER:   CALL    PRINT
                        OUTPUT  MACRO   ;- Macro being redefined.
                        CALL    PRINT   ;- Macro being redefined.
                        ENDM
                        ENDM

0000                    .CODE
0100                    ORG     100H
0100            ENTRY:  OUTPUT
0100  EB 2E         +           JMP     SHORT OVER
0102  54 68 69 73 20 69 +       MSG DB 'This is a test. This is ONLY a test.$'
0127              +             PRINT   PROC    NEAR
0127  8D 16 0102 R    +         LEA     DX,MSG
012B  B4 09           +         MOV     AH,9
012D  CD 21           +         INT     21H
012F  C3              +         RET
0130              +             PRINT   ENDP
0130  E8 0127 R       +    OVER: CALL   PRINT
                        OUTPUT
0133  E8 0127 R       +         CALL    PRINT    ;Redefined.
0136  CD 20        TEST: INT    20H
                        END     ENTRY
```

As we can see from the second invocation of OUTPUT, it has been redefined to a simple CALL PRINT. This is as fancy as we'll get with macros. If you become proficient with them, you can practically make up your own language, but there is almost always a trade-off between speed and size. Still, if you are involved in long projects, macros help standardize code and make programming that much faster.

And that's it for advanced directives. No single example program can encompass the number of methods we have covered in this chapter. Instead, it is recommended that you type in a few of the examples and try something such as macro libraries or groups for yourself. Give it a try. They can be very useful.

In the meantime, however, we'll move on to another very useful topic, linking to high-level languages in Chapter 10.

Chapter 10

Linking to BASIC, FORTRAN, C, and Pascal

▶ **Linking to BASIC, FORTRAN, C, and Pascal 287**

LINKING ASSEMBLY LANGUAGE routines into your high-level programs is often a good idea where speed or system resources (which otherwise might not be available) are concerned. Not all languages let you link assembly language routines in with your program, but most do. And when you can link in assembly language routines to high-level language programs, you can add some zest to them.

> **TIP** One reason to link to high-level languages is to take advantage of their specialities. For example, you can use FORTRAN's number-crunching abilities, Pascal's I/O, or the large library of C graphics functions by interfacing to those languages. In addition, all the library functions in those languages become available to you this way.

As surprising as it may seem in the frenetic world of microcomputing, there are certain conventions that are set for such interfaces that almost all high-level languages conform to. This means that what we develop here for, say, Pascal, can be used with almost any Pascal package because of the *Pascal calling convention*. This is a convention that sets the order in which parameters passed in a call are pushed onto the stack. There are calling conventions for BASIC, FORTRAN, Pascal, and C.

How Calling Conventions Work

A calling convention indicates the way a higher level language passes parameters to routines that it calls. It specifies these things: the order parameters are pushed in; how they are pushed (as addresses or immediate values); and how to reset the stack when we're done. If we are going to successfully link to the high-level language, we are going to have to mimic what it might expect from its own library of routines.

Some languages push parameters in the order you see them, and some in reverse order. Some languages (like FORTRAN) don't push the values 3 and 2 at all, but rather, their addresses. Also, at the end of the call, when we are about to return, we will have to make sure that the stack is reset in the proper way. This usually (BASIC, FORTRAN, and Pascal) means that after returning to the high-level language, the stack should be just the way it was before the parameters were pushed for the call. In other words, we should pop the pushed parameters off before we return (or let the assembler take care of this for us, as we'll see).

This information all comes together in the calling convention table (as you can see below, no one calling convention matches any other).

Calling Convention Table

Language	Parameters pushed	Parameters passed	Return type
BASIC	In order	As offset addresses	RET #
FORTRAN	In order	As FAR addresses	RET #
C	In REVERSE order	As values	RET
Pascal	In order	As values	RET #

NOTE Pushing parameters in order means that SUMMER(3,2) would go like this: PUSH 3, PUSH 2, CALL SUMMER. Parameters are passed as immediate values or as addresses. Where RET # is used, # = the total size in bytes of all pushed parameters.

High-level languages pass parameters to subroutines and functions on the stack. There's some information that we will explore later that indicates how parameter passing works (whether parameters are passed by address or by their actual value) in the list below:

Passing by Reference or Value

Language	Near references	Far references	By value
BASIC	Everything		
FORTRAN		Everything	
C	Near arrays	Far arrays	Everything else
Pascal	VAR, CONST	VARS, CONSTS	Everything else

The latest versions of the assembler (MASM 5.1 or later, TASM 1.0 or later) will actually be able to handle many of the details of linking to a high-level language for us. On the other hand, we'll spend some time working through the details of stack manipulation ourselves — doing it the hard way — because sometimes the assembler shortcuts are inadequate (as we'll see when we deal with Microsoft Windows and the OS/2 Presentation Manager), and advanced programmers should be able to handle those cases.

Since this book is example-oriented, let's begin with an example right away. Linking to Pascal is relatively easy, so let's say that we had a function defined in Pascal named SUMMER, which just sums two numbers (SUMMER(3,2) would return 5, for example), then Pascal will place the parameters, 3 and 2, onto the stack before calling the address it has for SUMMER. Let's see how that works by working with the stack ourselves.

Linking to a Pascal Example

When our assembly language code is called, our strategy will be the same one that library routines normally use. Instead of actually popping parameters off the stack, we will make a copy of the stack pointer, SP, in the BP register. The SP register points to the top of the stack, and the SS register holds the segment address of the stack. In addition, BP can be used as a base pointer, which means using indirect addressing like this: MOV AX,SS:[BP], while SP cannot.

In fact, not only can we have instructions like this:

```
MOV        AX,SS:[BP]
```

but we can also have instructions like this:

```
MOV        AX,SS:[BP+8]
```

where we can use the (unchanged) BP pointer as a base, and simply pick off words from the stack at will by adding immediate values to BP.

> **TIP** This method of adding immediate values will work with *any* form of indirect addressing, [BX] included. Expressions like [BX+8] are valid. Using BP this way will make it easy to retrieve parameters from the stack without a confusing number of pops and pushes.

For example, let's consider our Pascal function SUMMER. If we had this line in a Pascal program:

```
program add1(input, output);
function summer(a,b:integer):integer; extern;
var
        a:integer;
        b:integer;
begin
        a := 3;
        b := 2;
        writeln('3 + 2 = ',summer(a,b));
end.
```

Then Pascal would print out the character string "3 + 2 = ," followed by the value of the function call, SUMMER(3,2). To reach SUMMER, Pascal will first push the parameters on the stack and then call SUMMER, like this:

```
PUSH   3
PUSH   2
CALL   SUMMER
```

When we arrive at the procedure SUMMER, which we're going to write in assembly language, this is what the stack would look like (here, we are assuming Pascal integer format for the parameters 3 and 2, which means that they are each stored as one word):

```
|    3    |  ← SP+6
|    2    |  ← SP+4
| Return  |  ← SP+2
| Address |  ← SP
```

Figure 10-1.

Keep in mind that the stack "grows" downwards in memory. That is, SP is decreased by 2 every time you push something onto the stack. This means that 3 is pushed first and then 2:

```
|    3    |  ← SP

|    3    |  ← SP+2
|    2    |  ← SP
```

Figure 10-2.

And then the call is made. Whenever a CALL is executed, the return address is pushed onto the stack: a one word (offset) address is pushed if the call is NEAR, and a two-word (4-byte) address if the call is FAR.

As we will see, we will always be receiving FAR calls, except for C programs that have been declared to be of a certain size beforehand (with the .MODEL directive, as below). A FAR return address will take up two words, so, when we arrive at SUMMER, this is what we will see:

▶ **Linking to BASIC, FORTRAN, C, and Pascal** 291

```
          ┌──────────┐
          │    3     │ ← SP+6
          ├──────────┤
          │    2     │ ← SP+4
          ├──────────┤
          │  Return  │ ← SP+2
          │  Address │ ← SP
          └──────────┘
```

Figure 10-3.

Using BP and Stack Frames

In our procedures, however, we will first make a backup copy of BP by pushing it onto the stack, and then loading it with the current value of SP. That is, the first two lines of SUMMER.ASM will look like this:

```
SUMMER  PROC    FAR
        PUSH    BP
        MOV     BP,SP
```

Doing this is standard. It provides us with a copy of SP in BP, which can now be used to pick parameters off the stack. On the other hand, it also means that the stack that we will have to deal with will really look like Figure 10-4.

```
          ┌──────────┐
          │    3     │ ← BP+8
          ├──────────┤
          │    2     │ ← BP+6
          ├──────────┤
          │  Return  │ ← BP+4
          │  Address │ ← BP+2
          ├──────────┤
          │  Old BP  │ ← BP
          └──────────┘
```

Figure 10-4.

Now if we wanted to, we could just pick the parameters off the stack. In our procedure SUMMER, we could place the first parameter (3) into AX and the second parameter (2) into BX like this:

```
SUMMER  PROC    FAR
        PUSH    BP
        MOV     BP,SP
        MOV     AX,[BP+8]
        MOV     BX,[BP+6]
```

292 ▶ Advanced Assembly Language

It's easy enough. The only real trouble is keeping track of the number to add to BP, and the examples we'll develop later for each language will make that clear. In addition, we'll usually be able to let the assembler handle that process for us.

The high-level language usually assumes that some of the registers passed to you with the call will be preserved. At a minimum, you should preserve DI, SI, SS, and DS. Here is what SUMMER may look like with those pushes added:

```
SUMMER   PROC    FAR
         PUSH    BP
         MOV     BP,SP

         PUSH    SI      ←
         PUSH    DI      ←
         PUSH    DS      ←
         PUSH    SS      ←

         MOV     AX,[BP+8]
         MOV     BX,[BP+6]
         :
```

And in the end, before leaving the program, we'll want to restore the saved registers:

```
SUMMER   PROC    FAR
         PUSH    BP
         MOV     BP,SP

         PUSH    SI
         PUSH    DI
         PUSH    DS
         PUSH    SS

         MOV     AX,[BP+8]
         MOV     BX,[BP+6]
         :

         POP     SS      ←
         POP     DS      ←
         POP     DI      ←
         POP     SI      ←
```

Notice that even though we used the stack here (to save registers with), we did not change the numbers added to BP (e.g., MOV AX,[BP+8] did not change). This is because the value stored in BP has not changed. Although SS:SP is changing, the location pointed to by SS:BP does not. If we do not change BP throughout our program, we are free to use the stack as we wish and still use the offsets developed in the examples coming up.

All about Functions and Subroutines

High-level languages make the distinction between subroutines and functions, assembly language does not (it's all procedures).

```
A = FUNC(12,1)    - A function returns a value.
CALL SUBROUT(A)   - A subroutine does not.
```

To satisfy your high-level language, you might have to declare the assembly language routine as a function or a subroutine. If you don't want to return a value, declare it an external subroutine in the higher level language. If you do want to return a value, declare it as an external function (examples are coming later). How the high-level languages work is shown below:

High-Level Language Functions and Subroutines

Language	Returns a value	Returns no value
BASIC	Function	Subprogram
FORTRAN	Function	Suroutine
C	Function	Void function
Pascal	Function	Procedure

NOTE Although a subroutine might change the values of the variables passed to it if given their addresses, it doesn't return an immediate value in the way that a function does.

How to Return Values from Functions

If you *do* want to return a value, you will be writing an external function for your language. Returning values in this way is a very important part of interfacing to high-level languages, so let's work through it. The convention is to use the registers shown below to return values from functions.

Registers to Use to Return Values from Functions

Returning	Use
Byte Value	AL
Word Value	AX
Doubleword Value	DX:AX
Addresses	DX:AX = Address
>4 Bytes	DX:AX = Address of data

Byte values are simply returned in AL. Word values (like short integers) in AX. Doubleword values in DX:AX (DX = high word, AX = low word). In our examples, we will be dealing with functions that return word values (in AX), or doubleword values (in DX:AX).

If you want to return a value (or values, such as an array) longer than four bytes, you must follow a special procedure. First, of course, you must know the format of the data type you are going to work with (array, character string, floating point number, etc). For these details, see the manual of your individual language. Then your assembly language procedure must pass back the address at which the returned data will be.

Returning Big Values in C

In C, this is easy. You only need to set DX:AX to the address of the data that you want to return (>4 bytes long) and return. If your data is at DS:BX, just set DX to DS and AX to BX, and return. That's it. As long as the data is in the right format, you'll be fine.

Unfortunately, the other three languages that we are dealing with, BASIC, Pascal, and FORTRAN, are more particular. They actually pass you the address at which they expect the data to be returned.

Returning Big Values in BASIC, FORTRAN, and Pascal

When BASIC, Pascal or FORTRAN uses a function that returns a value larger than four bytes, it will automatically push one extra word onto the stack. Normally, the stack would look as shown in Figure 10-5.

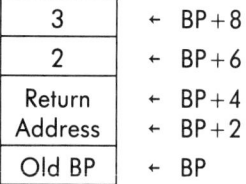

Figure 10-5.

Now, there is one more data item (a word) that is passed to you when a big value (>4 bytes) is expected to be returned by a function. This word is the *offset address* at which the data is to be placed, and will appear on the stack as shown in Figure 10-5.

Linking to BASIC, FORTRAN, C, and Pascal

```
       3      ← BP+10
       2      ← BP+8
    Offset    ← BP+6
    Return    ← BP+4
   Address    ← BP+2
    Old BP    ← BP
```

Figure 10-6.

The segment address at which you are to return data will be in SS. So, upon return, you will have to take the value at BP+6, the return offset, and place the data you want to return at SS:(return offset). Then, since the language expects the address of the returned data in DX:AX, you must also fill DX with the value currently in SS, and fill AX with offset (from BP+6).

Note that this adds 2 to each of the parameter locations. When preparing the stack to return to the calling program, keep in mind that you will have to pop off this extra parameter, the return offset (i.e., in a RET # statement, as we'll use shortly, add 2 to # to take care of the return offset parameter). Also, since a function only returns one value, a maximum of one address will be pushed this way.

In general, it is not difficult to return values longer than four bytes, but you have to be prepared to use the address that will be pushed in this case.

Returning Data in Our Example

In our program SUMMER, we want to return a Pascal integer value, so we will use AX. When we left SUMMER, we had loaded the first parameter (that is, a value of 3) into AX and the second parameter (2) into BX. We can just ADD AX,BX like this:

```
SUMMER  PROC    FAR
        PUSH    BP
        MOV     BP,SP

        PUSH    SI
        PUSH    DI
        PUSH    DS
        PUSH    SS

        MOV     AX,[BP+8]
        MOV     BX,[BP+6]

        ADD     AX,BX    ←

        POP     SS
        POP     DS
        POP     DI
        POP     SI
```

296 ▶ Advanced Assembly Language

Pascal is one of those languages in which we have to make sure that we pop the parameters off the stack (C takes care of this for us). This means that we will have to end SUMMER with a RET # instruction, where # is the number of bytes that we pushed onto the stack before the call to SUMMER was made (in C, we'd just use RET).

In other words, when control returns to the calling program, there should be nothing extra on the stack. Here's how the stack looks when we're ready to return in SUMMER (this is after we've restored SS, DS, DI, and SI):

3	← BP+8
2	← BP+6
Return	← BP+4
Address	← BP+2
Old BP	← BP

Figure 10-7.

(The first value that would be popped off is at the bottom, Old BP). A normal FAR RET will pop the two words of return address, but we still have four bytes of parameters to release. So, we will do this: first, restore BP with POP BP, then issue a RET 4 instruction.

RET 4 not only returns us to the calling program, but also pops four additional bytes (2 words) off the stack. These words go nowhere, and they will not be stored in a register. So that is how we can end SUMMER, shown in Listing 10-1.

Listing 10-1. SUMMER.ASM — Pascal Function in Assembly Language.

```
SUMMER   PROC    FAR
         PUSH    BP
         MOV     BP,SP

         PUSH    SI
         PUSH    DI
         PUSH    DS
         PUSH    SS

         MOV     AX,[BP+8]
         MOV     BX,[BP+6]

         ADD     AX,BX

         POP     SS
         POP     DS
         POP     DI
         POP     SI
         POP     BP
         RET     4
SUMMER   ENDP
```

This is the whole procedure, and it emulates a Pascal function. A Pascal program that calls this procedure wouldn't know it from a Pascal library function. We'll see how to link it into a Pascal program shortly. Now that we've seen the basics, let's look at each of the high-level language interfaces.

The BASIC–Assembly Interface

Procedures called from BASIC should be declared as FAR. Since we are using the .MODEL directive, that is taken care of for us (we don't need to declare procedures NEAR or FAR, and whether the return at the end is near or far will also be adjusted automatically). BASIC usually uses the medium memory model, so we will include the line .MODEL MEDIUM in our program.

> **NOTE** If you're unsure of the memory model used by your language, check your manual.

Let's say we wanted a BASIC function that would just return the value 5. All a function like that would have to do is to move 5 into AX. We might set up a BASIC program like this:

```
10      DEFINT A-Z
20      DECLARE FUNCTION MOVAX05
30      PRINT "The result is: ";
40      PRINT MOVAX05
50      END
```

If we had not wanted to return a value, we could have used a subroutine (use CALL) instead of a function. Here what happens is this: there are no parameters to push so when our program starts (after the BP push), this is what the stack looks like Figure 10-8 below:

```
         ┌─────────┐
         │ Return  │ ← BP+4
         │ Address │ ← BP+2
         ├─────────┤
         │ Old BP  │ ← BP
         └─────────┘
```

Figure 10-8.

There are no parameters on it. The program will return the value 5 as a small integer in BASIC (one word), so it will use AX. Our assembly language program looks like the one shown in Listing 10-2.

Listing 10-2. ADD5.ASM — BASIC Function Example.

```
        .MODEL  MEDIUM
        .CODE
                PUBLIC  MOVAX05         ;For BASIC Interface
        MOVAX05 PROC
                PUSH    BP
                MOV     BP,SP
                PUSH    SI
                PUSH    DI
                PUSH    DS
                PUSH    SS

                MOV     AX,5


                POP     SS
                POP     DS
                POP     DI
                POP     SI


                POP     BP
                RET
        MOVAX05 ENDP
                END
```

That's all there is to it: since there were no parameters on the stack, we could simply end the program with a RET. Notice that we had to declare MOVAX05 PUBLIC. Usually, the assembler removes all labels when it assembles a program: the PUBLIC directive instructs it to retain the following label so another program can find it at link time. Also, we simply ended with END, not END MOVAX05 (MOVAX05 is not the entry point; it is just being linked in).

If your assembly language routine needed to use data, you can just declare a .DATA segment as we have been doing, and then refer to the data as normally. When the whole program is linked together (into the final .EXE file), your data will automatically be linked into the common data segment or group.

To use this assembly language routine, just compile the BASIC program, assemble the assembly language one, and link the two .OBJ files together. The linker will find the definition it needs (MOVAX05) in the MOVAX05.OBJ module, and set things up correctly. Linking to BASIC is that easy.

Passing Parameters in BASIC

If we had parameters to push, it would be a different story. Let's say we wanted to call SUMMER from BASIC. Here is what the BASIC program would look like:

```
10      DEFINT A-Z
20      DECLARE FUNCTION SUMMER(A%,B%)
30      PRINT "3 + 2 = ";
40      PRINT SUMMER(3,2)
50      END
```

BASIC conforms to the BASIC calling convention (from the list at the beginning of the chapter):

Language	Parameters pushed	Parameters passed	Return type
→ BASIC	In order	As offset addresses	RET #
FORTRAN	In order	As FAR addresses	RET #
C	In REVERSE order	As values	RET
Pascal	In order	As values	RET #

Parameters must be popped off the stack upon return, and the parameters are pushed in the order they appear (here it would be PUSH 3, PUSH 2). Also, in BASIC, parameters are passed as offset addresses (so a subroutine could change them). Here is what the stack looks like when we start using it in SUMMER:

Off of 1	← BP+8
Off of 2	← BP+6
Return Address	← BP+4
	← BP+2
Old BP	← BP

Figure 10-9.

The return address for BASIC is always four bytes, no matter what model, since BASIC calls external functions as FAR. Here, "Off of 1" is the offset address of the value 3 in memory; "Off of 2" is the address of the value 2; and so on. Since data can take up at most one segment in BASIC, addresses are always passed as only two bytes.

300 ▶ Advanced Assembly Language

The only unusual thing here is that data is passed as an offset address, and not as an immediate value. This means that we will have to load the data from the passed addresses, and then add them (leaving the result in AX) and return, as shown in Listing 10-3.

Listing 10-3. BASIC Example with Parameters.

```
        .MODEL  MEDIUM
        .CODE
                PUBLIC  SUMMER  ;For BASIC Interface
        SUMMER  PROC
                PUSH    BP
                MOV     BP,SP

                PUSH    SI
                PUSH    DI
                PUSH    DS
                PUSH    SS
→               MOV     BX,[BP+8]
→               MOV     AX,[BX]
→               MOV     BX,[BP+6]
→               MOV     BX,[BX]

→               ADD     AX,BX

                POP     SS
                POP     DS
                POP     DI
                POP     SI

                POP     BP
                RET     4
        SUMMER  ENDP
                END
```

Notice that we used .MODEL MEDIUM here too, and that at the end that we had to pop off the four bytes of passed parameters (two offset addresses at two bytes each) with a RET 4 instruction, which returns and pops 4 extra bytes off. We return our one-word result, a simple integer, in AX.

Shortcut Parameter Passing in BASIC

In recent versions of the MicroSoft Assembler (Version 5.1) or the Turbo Assembler (Version 1.0), passing parameters has been made even easier. The .MODEL and PROC directives have been extended. We begin by specifying not only the model but also the language:

▶ **Linking to BASIC, FORTRAN, C, and Pascal** 301

```
→ .MODEL  MEDIUM, BASIC
              :
              :
```

Now the assembler knows how parameters will be pushed on the stack when we reach this function. Next, we use a modified PROC statement:

```
  .MODEL  MEDIUM, BASIC

  .CODE
          PUBLIC  SUMMER          ;For BASIC Interface
→ SUMMER PROC FAR USES DI SI, VALUE1:WORD, VALUE2:WORD
              :
              :
```

This is going to make everything much easier. Here we instruct the assembler to push DI and SI at the beginning of our code (it will add the push instructions) and to pop them at the end. With the USES directive we can save and restore registers easily inside a procedure. Following the register list (note that there is no comma between them), we specify what will be passed to this procedure.

We give the name VALUE1 to the first parameter and VALUE2 to the second parameter, specifying that they are both words. Other keywords you can use include BYTE and DWORD here. Now that the assembler knows how long the parameters will be on the stack, it can actually generate the [BP+n] addresses for you, as long as we refer to the parameters by the names VALUE1 and VALUE2 throughout the program, like this:

```
  .MODEL  MEDIUM, BASIC
  .CODE
          PUBLIC  SUMMER          ;For BASIC Interface
  SUMMER PROC FAR USES DI SI, VALUE1:WORD, VALUE2:WORD

→         MOV     BX,VALUE1
→         MOV     AX,[BX]
→         MOV     BX,VALUE2
→         ADD     AX,[BX]

          RET
  SUMMER ENDP
          END
```

When the program is assembled, VALUE1 and VALUE2 will be replaced automatically with the [BP+n] addresses required. (Note that it is important to specify the language in the .MODEL directive so the assembler knows how long the parameters will be on the stack, and in what order they will be pushed.) In addition, you should note that we can end the program with a simple RET instruction. The assembler handles all the details for us (here turning RET into RET 4).

Now that we are able to pass parameters to our BASIC functions, let's turn to FORTRAN.

The FORTRAN–Assembly Interface

Fortran is a venerable language, going back many years. Usually, FORTRAN (because of its reputation as a number-cruncher) is compiled as LARGE (if in doubt, check your compiler manual). In Microsoft FORTRAN versions before FORTRAN 4.0, the model used was always LARGE. Starting with version 4.0, Microsoft FORTRAN supports the HUGE and MEDIUM models as well. We will use LARGE.

Let's say that we wanted to link our procedure that returned 5 into a FORTRAN program. We have to set up what is called an *interface* to MOVAX05. Our program might look like this:

```
      INTERFACE TO INTEGER FUNCTION IMOV(A)
      INTEGER*2 A
      END
C
      INTEGER*2 A
      A=0
      WRITE (*,*) 'The result is ',IMOV(A)
      END
```

Here our interface looks like this:

```
      INTERFACE TO INTEGER FUNCTION IMOV(A)
      INTEGER*2 A
      END
```

This indicates to FORTRAN that we are interfacing to a function that will return a value. We have to tell FORTRAN what type of value will be returned, which is why we specify INTEGER (a 4-byte integer, the normal INTEGER type in FORTRAN).

In this example, we are beginning our function name — "IMOV" (not MOVAX05) — with "I" in deference to FORTRAN's default integer definitions, and passing a parameter to it, even though IMOV does not need any parameters. This is because, in FORTRAN, you have to pass at least one parameter to a function to have it called. We will use a dummy parameter named A (defined as a 2-byte integer, INTEGER*2, in the INTERFACE statement). We will simply make A zero and pass it to satisfy FORTRAN:

► Linking to BASIC, FORTRAN, C, and Pascal

```
        INTERFACE TO INTEGER FUNCTION IMOV(A)
        INTEGER*2 A
        END
C
        INTEGER*2 A
        A=0
        WRITE (*,*) 'The result is ',IMOV(A)
        END
```

Again, if we were interfacing to a routine that did not return a value, we would call it a subroutine. For example, if we had a subroutine named SORT, the interface could be this:

```
INTERFACE TO SUBROUTINE SORT(A,B)
INTEGER*2 A,B
END
```

Notice that we did not have to indicate the returned data type (like INTEGER) since a subroutine returns no value. All we have to do in IMOV is to put 5 into AX and return. Our FORTRAN MOVAX05 is shown in Listing 10-4.

Listing 10-4. Fortran Example.

```
        .MODEL  LARGE
        .CODE
                PUBLIC  IMOV        ;for FORTRAN Interface
        IMOV PROC
                PUSH    BP
                MOV     BP,SP

                PUSH    SI
                PUSH    DI
                PUSH    DS
                PUSH    SS

                MOV     AX,5

                POP     SS
                POP     DS
                POP     DI
                POP     SI

                POP     BP
                RET     4
        IMOV ENDP
                END
```

IMOV is all ready to link into a FORTRAN program. You may have noticed that we ended the program with RET 4. This is to take care of the dummy parameter, A, that was passed to IMOV. Let's look next at why we have to pop 4 bytes for just one passed parameter.

Passing Parameters in FORTRAN

The way parameters are passed depends on the memory model used. For LARGE and HUGE models, parameters are passed as two-word addresses (segment and offsets); for MEDIUM models, as one-word addresses (offsets alone). Since the FORTRAN program is using the LARGE memory model here, values would be passed as two-word addresses.

The FORTRAN convention (see calling conventions listed earlier) specifies that we will have to clear the stack of any parameters upon return. Let's use our example procedure SUMMER, and call it ISUM here. ISUM will use two passed values. The new FORTRAN code will look like this (including the new INTERFACE declaration):

```
      INTERFACE TO INTEGER FUNCTION ISUM(A,B)
      INTEGER*2 A,B
      END
C
      INTEGER*2 A,B
      A = 3
      B = 2
      I = ISUM(A,B)
      WRITE (*,*) '3 + 2 = ',I
      END
```

Our new interface looks like this:

```
      INTERFACE TO FUNCTION INTEGER ISUM(A,B)
      INTEGER*2 A,B
      END
```

Here we informed FORTRAN that ISUM will return a 4-byte INTEGER value, but that it takes two 2-byte integers (INTEGER*2) named A and B as parameters. This is just for convenience in our example program: we can load the 2-byte parameters into one register each and add them more easily than the 4-byte standard FORTRAN integers.

When we start working our procedure ISUM, FORTRAN will have loaded the stack in compliance with the FORTRAN calling convention (see below):

▶ Linking to BASIC, FORTRAN, C, and Pascal

Language	Parameters pushed	Parameters passed	Return type
BASIC	In order	As offset addresses	RET #
→ FORTRAN	In order	As FAR addresses	RET #
C	In REVERSE order	As values	RET
Pascal	In order	As values	RET #

In the LARGE model, FORTRAN passes parameters as two word addresses, which we'll have to pick off the stack. The stack will look like Figure 10-10:

Seg of 2	← BP+12
Off of 2	← BP+10
Seg of 1	← BP+8
Off of 1	← BP+6
Return	← BP+4
Address	← BP+2
Old BP	← BP

Figure 10-10.

Where "Seg of 2" is shorthand for the segment that contains parameter 2, "Off of 2" is shorthand for parameter 2's offset, and so on. In order to pass these two values, 8 bytes had to be pushed onto the stack, so we'll have to end with RET 8. To get the values of these parameters for ourselves, we'll have to get their segment and offset addresses off the stack. The assembly language code, ready to be linked in, is in Listing 10-5. Notice the model declaration is LARGE, and the number of instructions needed to actually get the values that FORTRAN is passing.

Listing 10-5. FORTRAN Example with Parameters.

```
        .MODEL  LARGE
        .CODE
        PUBLIC  ISUM            ;For FORTRAN Interface
ISUM    PROC
        PUSH    BP
        MOV     BP,SP

        PUSH    SI
        PUSH    DI
        PUSH    DS
        PUSH    SS

→       MOV     DX,[BP+12]      ;Get segment address
→       MOV     ES,DX
→       MOV     BX,[BP+10]      ;Get offset address
→       MOV     AX,ES:[BX]
→       MOV     DX,[BP+8]
```

Listing 10-5. FORTRAN Example with Parameters.

```
        →       MOV     ES,DX
        →       MOV     BX,[BP+6]
        →       MOV     BX,ES:[BX]

        →       ADD     AX,BX
        →       MOV     DX,0

                POP     SS
                POP     DS
                POP     DI
                POP     SI

                POP     BP
                RET     8
        ISUM    ENDP
                END
```

And that's it: ISUM is ready to be used with FORTRAN. Notice that since we said that ISUM would return a 4-byte value, FORTRAN will read DX:AX after the call. Since the result will fit into AX alone (unless you want to make some provision for overflow into a higher word), we zero DX before returning.

Shortcut Parameter Passing in FORTRAN

Sometimes, you won't need to do stack manipulations: all you'll want to do is to use the parameters pushed onto the stack. In that case, we can use the shortcut method of reading parameters with the extended PROC and .MODEL directives. We first specify the language:

```
.MODEL  LARGE, FORTRAN
        :
        :
```

Next, we specify what registers to push with USES. The assembler will automatically add the pushes to store the registers at the beginning of the procedure and to pop them at the end. Because FORTRAN passes FAR addresses, we can take the segment and offset values off the stack by specifying the names of 4 words, like this:

```
                .MODEL  LARGE, FORTRAN
        .CODE
                PUBLIC  ISUM                    ;For FORTRAN Interface
        → ISUM  PROC USES DI SI, V1:WORD, V2:WORD, V3:WORD, V4:WORD
                :
                :
```

Now that we have the words from the stack, we can use them as before:

```
            .MODEL   LARGE, FORTRAN
    .CODE
            PUBLIC   ISUM                ;For FORTRAN Interface
    ISUM    PROC USES DI SI, V1:WORD, V2:WORD, V3:WORD, V4:WORD

            MOV      DX,V1
            MOV      ES,DX
            MOV      BX,V2
            MOV      AX,ES:[BX]
            MOV      DX,V3
            MOV      ES,DX
            MOV      BX,V4
            MOV      BX,ES:[BX]

            ADD      AX,BX
            MOV      DX,0

            RET
    ISUM    ENDP
            END
```

Notice again that we were able to end simply with RET, and did not need to use RET 8. The assembler will convert the instruction as needed automatically.

The C–Assembly Interface

This convention differs from those used in BASIC, FORTRAN, and Pascal in that the language itself removes passed parameters from the stack after the function call. We will only have to end our programs with RET, as opposed to, say, RET 4, (see calling conventions below):

	Language	Parameters pushed	Parameters passed	Return type
	BASIC	In order	As offset addresses	RET #
	FORTRAN	In order	As FAR addresses	RET #
→	C	In REVERSE order	As values	RET
	Pascal	In order	As values	RET #

C parameters are always passed by value (not as addresses as is the case with FORTRAN or BASIC), except for arrays, which are passed by reference. This reference will be the address of the first element of the array, and will be either 2 or 4 bytes long. For NEAR arrays, it will be 2 bytes. For FAR arrays it will be 4 bytes.

As usual, we will let the NEAR or FAR declarations of our procedures be made for us automatically by MASM (which knows what to do depending on the memory model specified).

The C calling convention also differs in that it pushes the values to pass in reverse order. We will see this more clearly when we discuss the stack upon entering our assembly language procedures.

Here is the C code that we might use with function MOVAX05:

```
extern int movax05();
main()
{
        printf("The result is: %d\n", movax05());
}
```

Again, we declared MOVAX05 as external with the line "extern int movax05;" that is, movax05 will return an integer value (one word in C). We will pass no parameters to MOVAX05.

Let's assume that the C program was compiled under the SMALL or COMPACT model (and therefore the call to MOVAX05 will be a near call). Here's the way the stack would look when we get into MOVAX05 (after the initial PUSH BP):

Return	← BP+2
Old BP	← BP

Figure 10-11.

Since this is a near call, there is only one word (the return offset address) pushed onto the stack by the C call instruction.

C differs once again in the naming of our procedure MOVAX05. Instead of defining a procedure "MOVAX05," the C naming convention is to use an underscore before the name of the procedure to be linked in like this: "_MOVAX05" (and to also declare it as PUBLIC in the assembly language program, of course). MOVAX05 will return its value in AX, and the way the assembly language program might look (keep in mind that we have to use "_MOVAX05" and not "MOVAX05") is shown in Listing 10-6.

Listing 10-6. C Example.

```
.MODEL  SMALL
.CODE
        PUBLIC  _MOVAX05        ;For C Interface
_MOVAX05        PROC
        PUSH    BP
        MOV     BP,SP

        PUSH    SI
        PUSH    DI
        PUSH    DS
        PUSH    SS

        MOV     AX,5

        POP     SS
        POP     DS
        POP     DI
        POP     SI

        POP     BP
        RET
_MOVAX05        ENDP
        END
```

There is nothing special here. The only unusual concerns will appear when we try to pass parameters to a linked function or subroutine.

Passing Parameters to C

As mentioned, C passes parameters as immediate values, except for arrays, and pushes them in reverse order. If we wanted to use our function SUMMER in C, this is the way it might look:

```
extern int SUMMER(int,int);
main()
{
        printf("3 + 2 = %d\n",SUMMER(3,2));
}
```

In the other three languages, the 3 would be pushed (or its address), followed by the 2. However, C pushes parameters in reverse order, so the 2 will be pushed first, followed by the 3. Here is what the stack will look like when we start to use it in SUMMER (note that since we're assuming that the C program was compiled as SMALL or COMPACT, the return address is only one word long):

310 ▶ Advanced Assembly Language

```
       ┌────────┐
       │   2    │  ← BP+6
       ├────────┤
       │   3    │  ← BP+4
       ├────────┤
       │ Return │  ← BP+2
       ├────────┤
       │ Old BP │  ← BP
       └────────┘
```

Figure 10-12.

In the case of LARGE, MEDIUM, or HUGE memory models, the return address will be 4 bytes long, which means that the locations of all parameters will be shifted up by 2 bytes:

```
       ┌────────┐
       │   2    │  ← BP+8
       ├────────┤
       │   3    │  ← BP+6
       ├────────┤
       │ Return │  ← BP+4
       │  Addr  │  ← BP+2
       ├────────┤
       │ Old BP │  ← BP
       └────────┘
```

Figure 10-13.

Let's assume the SMALL model for our example. To pick the parameters off the stack, we have to know the order in which they are pushed. Sometimes, of course (as with SUMMER), the order of the parameters will not matter. What SUMMER.ASM would look like is shown in Listing 10-7.

Listing 10-7. C Example with Parameters.

```
       .MODEL   SMALL
       .CODE
                PUBLIC   _SUMMER          ;For C Interface
       _SUMMER  PROC
                PUSH     BP
                MOV      BP,SP

                PUSH     SI
                PUSH     DI
                PUSH     DS
                PUSH     SS

  →             MOV      AX,[BP+4]
  →             MOV      BX,[BP+6]

  →             ADD      AX,BX

                POP      SS
                POP      DS
                POP      DI
                POP      SI

                POP      BP
                RET
       _SUMMER  ENDP
                END
```

▶ Linking to BASIC, FORTRAN, C, and Pascal   311

Notice that we started the procedure name with an underscore (_SUMMER), and that we ended with a simple RET, since C will handle the parameters itself. SUMMER is now ready to use with C.

> **TIP** The fact that the calling function is supposed to take care of the stack for you on return (as opposed to Pascal, BASIC, or FORTRAN, where you have to clear the stack before returning) is sometimes considered a weakness because the calling function might hide programming errors by recovering the stack itself. For that reason, even though most Windows and OS/2 programming is done in C, the Pascal calling convention is used because that calling convention is considered more "robust."

Shortcut Parameter Passing in C

We can use the extended .MODEL and PROC directives here also. We begin by specifying that we are using C (so the assembler knows how the parameters were pushed):

```
→    .MODEL  SMALL, C
            :
            :
```

Next, we can refer to the parameters directly like this:

```
    .MODEL  SMALL, C
    .CODE
            PUBLIC  SUMMER          ;For C Interface
→   SUMMER PROC NEAR USES DI SI, VALUE1:WORD, VALUE2:WORD
            :
            :
```

The rest of the program is easy:

312 ▶ Advanced Assembly Language

```
        .MODEL  SMALL, C

        .CODE
        PUBLIC  SUMMER          ;For C Interface
SUMMER  PROC NEAR USES DI SI, VALUE1:WORD, VALUE2:WORD

        MOV     AX,VALUE1
        ADD     AX,VALUE2

        RET
SUMMER  ENDP
        END
```

And that's all there is to C if you don't want to manipulate the stack yourself but only want to read passed parameters from it.

The last language that we will cover is Pascal, with which we already have some experience. Pascal may be the easiest interface to work with that we've come across.

The Pascal–Assembly Interface

Use the memory model LARGE (i.e., .MODEL LARGE) in Pascal. Here, parameters are passed by value, and we have to clear the stack at the end. In addition, parameters are pushed in the order in which they appear. Calling SUMMER(3,2) would result in 3 being pushed first, followed by 2. The Pascal calling convention is used (see list of calling conventions):

	Language	Parameters pushed	Parameters passed	Return type
	BASIC	In order	As offset addresses	RET #
	FORTRAN	In order	As FAR addresses	RET #
	C	In REVERSE order	As values	RET
→	Pascal	In order	As values	RET #

Here's the Pascal code that might call MOVAX05:

```
program screener(input, output);
function movax05(a:integer):integer; extern;
begin
      writeln('The result is: ',movax05(0));
end.
```

Again, we have to pass a dummy parameter to MOVAX05, as we did in FORTRAN. We will just set this value to zero and ignore it. MOVAX05.ASM might look like the code in Listing 10-8.

Listing 10-8. Pascal Example.

```
.MODEL   LARGE
.CODE
         PUBLIC   MOVAX05           ;for Pascal Interface
MOVAX05 PROC
         PUSH     BP
         MOV      BP,SP

         PUSH     SI
         PUSH     DI
         PUSH     DS
         PUSH     SS

         MOV      AX,5

         POP      SS
         POP      DS
         POP      DI
         POP      SI

         POP      BP
         RET      2
MOVAX05 ENDP
         END
```

Notice that we had to end with RET 2. This takes care of the 2 bytes that we pushed to pass our dummy parameter.

Passing Parameters to Pascal

We used the Pascal version of SUMMER as our first example in this chapter, so we know what SUMMER.ASM will look like already. The corresponding Pascal program might look like this:

```
program add1(input, output);
function summer(a,b:integer):integer; extern;
var
        a:integer;
        b:integer;

begin
        a := 3;
        b := 2;
        writeln('3 + 2 = ',summer(a,b));
end.
```

The stack as we will work with it will look like Figure 10-13:

314 ▶ Advanced Assembly Language

```
     3       ← BP+8
     2       ← BP+6
  Return     ← BP+4
  Address    ← BP+2
  Old BP     ← BP
```

Figure 10-13.

And SUMMER.ASM will appear as shown in Listing 10-9 (note the addition to our earlier Pascal-compatible SUMMER.ASM of .MODEL LARGE and .CODE).

Listing 10-9. Pascal Example with Parameters.

```
        .MODEL  LARGE
        .CODE
                PUBLIC  SUMMER      ;For Pascal Interface
SUMMER  PROC
                PUSH    BP
                MOV     BP,SP

                PUSH    SI
                PUSH    DI
                PUSH    DS
                PUSH    SS

→               MOV     AX,[BP+8]
→               MOV     BX,[BP+6]

→               ADD     AX,BX

                POP     SS
                POP     DS
                POP     DI
                POP     SI

                POP     BP
                RET     4
SUMMER  ENDP
        END
```

The parameters have been pushed as immediate values, and we know their order from the Pascal calling convention. To reset the stack for return to Pascal, we have to end with RET 4, stripping off the 4 bytes of parameters that had been pushed.

Shortcut Parameter Passing in Pascal

We can use the shortcut extended PROC and .MODEL directives here too. We begin by indicating that we are using Pascal:

```
    .MODEL  LARGE, PASCAL
            :
            :
```

Then we specify that we want the DI and SI registers pushed, and that two word values, which we will call VALUE1 and VALUE2, will be pushed before the procedure is called:

```
.MODEL  LARGE, PASCAL

.CODE
        PUBLIC  SUMMER          ;For Pascal Interface
SUMMER PROC FAR USES DI SI, VALUE1:WORD, VALUE2:WORD
        :
        :
```

The whole program is then reduced to this:

```
.MODEL  LARGE, PASCAL

.CODE
        PUBLIC  SUMMER          ;For Pascal Interface
SUMMER PROC FAR USES DI SI, VALUE1:WORD, VALUE2:WORD

        MOV     AX,VALUE1
        ADD     AX,VALUE2

        RET
SUMMER  ENDP
        END
```

That's all for Pascal. Linking our procedures in is no problem. In fact, since we are dealing with immediate values, it's even easier than most.

High-Level Languages in General

It often pays to abandon high-level languages for assembly language, especially where speed is an asset. If you find yourself frequently using assembly language routines in your high-level programs, you might want to start putting together a library. Some languages, like FORTRAN, will even list assembly language instructions for its various functions so that you may modify and streamline them. Besides speed for such things as indexing, sorting, or math manipulations, assembly language can be used to do things that high-level languages simply cannot do or are not good at. Now, however, we're ready to see the math coprocessor in action.

Chapter 11

Using the 80×87

▶ Using the 80×87

OVER THE YEARS, the math coprocessor chips, the 80×87s, have caught on. This chapter introduces us to the assembly language instructions that they use.

Starting with MASM release 2.0 (and of course also included in TASM 1.0), the macro assembler can assemble about 80 80×87 commands. This is an immense improvement over the old days, when you had to include 80×87 machine language in your program explicitly.

The 80×87 is the math coprocessor designed and built to function with the 80×86 that is already inside the PC. As we know, the 80×86 itself has only some math capability. Without further programming, it can multiply up to results not larger than 32 bits, and divide numbers of up to only 32 bits by 16 bits, generating a 16-bit quotient and a 16-bit remainder. This type of division means that, unless we do a lot of work, we cannot count on more than 16 bits of accuracy in the result (four decimal places).

Furthermore, the 80×86 can only handle integer arithmetic. If we want to work with floating point numbers, we have to write our own algorithms and implement them. In general, this is pretty difficult. Floating point simulations are usually very slow. And that's just the start. We might want to do more, such as calculate sines and cosines, logs and natural logs, square roots and powers. It is for such a purpose that the 80×87 was designed. The 80×87 can be counted on to make math calculations go hundreds of times faster. And the 80×87 is more accurate.

The internal accuracy of the 80×87 is considerable. There are eight stack registers (it is a stack-oriented chip), and each one is 80 bits long (10 bytes). For integers, this means an accuracy up to 18 digits and, for floating point numbers, an accuracy up to 16 digits. If your PC has an 80×87 in it, you too can enjoy this type of accuracy.

Getting Started with the Math Coprocessor

The assembler does not recognize 80×87 commands immediately. Instead, you must include a special directive in your .ASM files like this:

```
→   .8087
    .MODEL SMALL
    .CODE
    ORG    100H
        :
```

Here we are enabling the assembly of 8087 instructions (other directives include .287 and .387). The assembler not only assembles 80×87 commands, it also includes a WAIT command to the 80×86 for each one (with the exception of one or two special no-wait commands detailed later). This means that the 80×86 will wait until the

80×87 is done processing before proceeding. Control is coordinated automatically between the two chips this way. We won't have to do anything special besides simply placing 80×87 instructions in our programs. When we use DEBUG later on, we will see these WAITs.

Adding Integers with the 80×87

Let's begin immediately with one of the simplest of examples: adding two integers. In this example, we will add 3 and 1. Here's the code (we'll use the 8087 as the common denominator among coprocessors in this chapter, rather than expecting everyone to have an 80287 or an 80387):

```
             .8087
             .MODEL  SMALL
             .CODE
             ORG     100H
ENTRY:       JMP     PROG
             OPERAND1 DW    3
             OPERAND2 DW    1
             RESULT   DW    0
PROG:        FILD    OPERAND1
             FIADD   OPERAND2
             FISTP   RESULT
             INT     20H
             END     ENTRY
```

Everything looks the same as usual until we get to the body of the program where the 80×87 instructions are. The first instruction tells the 80×87 to load the integer number at OPERAND1 in memory onto the top of its stack:

```
PROG:        FILD    OPERAND1
             FIADD   OPERAND2
             FISTP   RESULT
```

> **TIP** There's an easy way to tell 80×86 and 80×87 instructions apart. Every 80×87 instruction begins with an F, and no 80×86 instructions do.

FILD is the integer load instruction (as opposed to the floating point load, FLD). The next instruction is the instruction for integer addition:

▶ Using the 80×87

```
PROG:   FILD    OPERAND1
        FIADD   OPERAND2
        FISTP   RESULT
```

Floating point addition, which we'll cover later, uses FADD. Here, OPERAND2 is added to the value in the top of the 80×87's stack. This is the result we want, so we store this number in memory, at the location RESULT:

```
PROG:   FILD    OPERAND1
        FIADD   OPERAND2
        FISTP   RESULT
```

This instruction is an integer store (as opposed to FST, the floating point store) and pop instruction. The number on the top of the stack is stored in memory and then the stack is popped, leaving it free for further operations.

> **TIP** If you're having problems with 80×87 programs, one thing to check is the stack. Popping the stack is an important part of any program. If you do not pop it, the stack will fill, and your program will stop.

We have stored the result in memory, and we can take a look at it with DEBUG. For this example we will use the shortest integer format available, one word integers. These are defined with DW:

```
OPERAND1 DW     3
OPERAND2 DW     1
RESULT   DW     0
```

This is only one of the six different available formats, and we'll look at some others soon. We can assemble this program since we've included the .8087 directive:

```
        .8087
        .MODEL SMALL
        .CODE
        ORG     100H
ENTRY:  JMP     PROG
        OPERAND1 DW     3
                :
                :
```

Under MASM, for example, all we need to do is to type MASM TEST;, link it with LINK TEST, and create TEST.COM with EXE2BIN TEST TEST.COM (and make sure our PC has an 80×87 in it).

322 ▶ Advanced Assembly Language

The .COM file can be debugged this way:

```
C:\>DEBUG TEST.COM
-R
AX=0000  BX=0000  CX=001A  DX=0000  SP=FFFE  BP=0000  SI=0000  DI=0000
DS=090B  ES=090B  SS=090B  CS=090B  IP=0100   NV UP DI PL NZ NA PO NC
090B:0100 EB07          JMP     0109     ← Here's our first jump.
-T

AX=0000  BX=0000  CX=001A  DX=0000  SP=FFFE  BP=0000  SI=0000  DI=0000
DS=090B  ES=090B  SS=090B  CS=090B  IP=0109   NV UP DI PL NZ NA PO NC
090B:0109 9B            WAIT
```

Let's take a look at the rest of the program by unassembling it:

```
-U
090B:0109 9B            WAIT
090B:010A DF060301      FILD    WORD PTR [0103]
090B:010E 9B            WAIT
090B:010F DE060501      FIADD   WORD PTR [0105]
090B:0113 9B            WAIT
090B:0114 DF1E0701      FISTP   WORD PTR [0107]
090B:0118 CD20          INT     20
090B:011A 36            SS:
090B:011B 9C            PUSHF
090B:011C F6FF          IDIV    BH
090B:011E 76C2          JBE     00E2
090B:0120 9A9A003F0B    CALL    0B3F:009A
090B:0125 FF76C2        PUSH    [BP-3E]
090B:0128 E85ADE        CALL    DF85
```

As you can see, the assembler has added the required wait states for the 80×86 while it waits for the 80×87 to finish processing. From the above addresses, we see that OPERAND1 is at [103], OPERAND2 at [105], and RESULT at [107]. Let's take a look at them by dumping them:

```
-D103
090B:0103          03 00 01 00 00-00 9B DF 06 03 01 9B DE   ......._....^
090B:0110 06 05 01 9B DF 1E 07 01-CD 20 36 9C F6 FF 76 C2   ....._...M 6.v.vB
090B:0120 9A 9A 00 3F 0B FF 76 C2-E8 5A DE E8 CF E5 E9 CB   ...?..vBhZ^h0eiK
090B:0130 00 A1 9A F6 2B 06 98 F6-89 46 C2 A1 4E F6 3B 06   .!.v+..v.FB!Nv;.
090B:0140 98 F6 B9 00 00 72 01 41-3B 06 9A F6 BA 00 00 73   .v9..r.A;..v:..s
090B:0150 01 42 22 CA D1 E9 73 16-BF CA F6 BE C6 FE B9 11   .B"JQis.?Jv>F-9.
090B:0160 00 1E 07 FC F3 A5 9A 79-01 FE 09 E9 89 00 E8 1F   ...!sX.y.~.i..h.
090B:0170 E1 D1 E8 72 03 E9 7F 00-A1 4E F6 3B 06 98 F6 73   aQhr.i..!Nv;..vs
090B:0180 18 89 46                                          ..F
```

The 3 and 1 in OPERAND1 and OPERAND2 are seen immediately. (Recall that the 80×86 stores the low byte at a lower address so they appear as 03 00 01 00 instead of

▶ **Using the 80×87** 323

00 03 00 01.) RESULT holds 0. If we execute the entire program with a Go command, we'll load OPERAND1, add OPERAND2 to it, and then store the result in RESULT. Let's execute the program and dump the results:

```
-G118              ← Execute to the INT 20H instruction.
AX=0000  BX=0000  CX=001A  DX=0000  SP=FFFE  BP=0000  SI=0000  DI=0000
DS=090B  ES=090B  SS=090B  CS=090B  IP=0118   NV UP DI PL NZ NA PO NC
090B:0118 CD20            INT     20

-D103              ← And take a look at RESULT
                    ↓
090B:0103  03 00 01 00 04-00 9B DF 06 03 01 9B DE    ......._....^
090B:0110  06 05 01 9B DF 1E 07 01-CD 20 36 9C F6 FF 76 C2  .........M 6.v.vB
090B:0120  9A 9A 00 3F 0B FF 76 C2-E8 5A DE E8 CF E5 E9 CB  ...?..vBhZ^hOeiK
090B:0130  00 A1 9A F6 2B 06 98 F6-89 46 C2 A1 4E F6 3B 06  .!.v+...v.FB!Nv;.
090B:0140  98 F6 B9 00 00 72 01 41-3B 06 9A F6 8A 00 00 73  .v9..r.A;..v;..s
090B:0150  01 42 22 CA 01 E9 73 16-BF CA F6 BE C6 FE B9 11  .B"JQis.?Jv>F-9.
090B:0160  00 1E 07 FC F3 A5 9A 79-01 FE 09 E9 89 00 E8 1F  .....isX.y.~.i..h.
090B:0170  E1 D1 E8 72 03 E9 7F 00-A1 4E F6 3B 06 98 F6 73  aQhr.i..!Nv;...vs
090B:0180  18 89 46                                         ..F
-Q
```

Now the location RESULT holds 4, as it should. Since the format of word integers is so simple, this is just about the easiest example we could choose. The next easiest example, of course, is subtraction.

Subtracting Integers with the 80×87

All we have to do here is to replace FIADD with the logical counterpart, FISUB:

```
        .8087
        .MODEL SMALL
        .CODE
        ORG     100H
ENTRY:  JMP     PROG
        OPERAND1 DW     3
        OPERAND2 DW     1
        RESULT   DW     0
PROG:   FILD    OPERAND1
        FISUB   OPERAND2        ←
        FISTP   RESULT
        INT     20H
        END     ENTRY
```

From this we can make a .COM file and use DEBUG as before:

324 ▶ Advanced Assembly Language

```
-R
AX=0000  BX=0000  CX=001A  DX=0000  SP=FFFE  BP=0000  SI=0000  DI=0000
DS=090B  ES=090B  SS=090B  CS=090B  IP=0100   NV UP DI PL NZ NA PO NC
090B:0100 EB07           JMP      0109
-T

AX=0000  BX=0000  CX=001A  DX=0000  SP=FFFE  BP=0000  SI=0000  DI=0000
DS=090B  ES=090B  SS=090B  CS=090B  IP=0109   NV UP DI PL NZ NA PO NC
090B:0109 9B             WAIT
-U
090B:0109 9B             WAIT
090B:010A DF060301       FILD     WORD PTR [0103]
090B:010E 9B             WAIT
090B:010F DE260501       FISUB    WORD PTR [0105]
090B:0113 9B             WAIT
090B:0114 DF1E0701       FISTP    WORD PTR [0107]
090B:0118 CD20           INT      20
090B:011A 6F             DB       6F
090B:011B 8B4606         MOV      AX,[BP+06]
090B:011E 257F00         AND      AX,007F
090B:0121 8B5E0A         MOV      BX,[BP+0A]
090B:0124 89470E         MOV      [BX+0E],AX
090B:0127 81660680FF     AND      WORD PTR [BP+06],FF80
```

Here's how the data area looks before we run the program (note the 0 at [107]):

```
-D103
090B:0103    03 00 01 00 00-00 9B DF 06 03 01 9B DE    ......._....^
090B:0110 26 05 01 9B DF 1E 07 01-CD 20 6F 8B 46 06 25 7F   &..._...M o.F.%.
090B:0120 00 8B 5E 0A 89 47 0E 81-66 06 80 FF 8B 46 06 89   ..^..G..f....F..
090B:0130 47 0A 8B 46 08 89 47 0C-53 C4 46 06 06 50 B8 00   G..F..G.SDF..P8.
090B:0140 00 50 9A EB 03 C1 0C 89-5E 06 8C 46 08 8B 5E 0A   .P.k.A..^..F..^.
090B:0150 8B 47 02 89 46 F6 53 50-9A 06 00 43 09 06 53 8B   .G..FvSP...C..S.
090B:0160 5E F4 FF 77 04 9A 50 03-C1 0C 8B 5E 0A 89 47 06   ^t.w..P.A..^..G.
090B:0170 8B 76 0A 8B 7C 06 8B 4C-04 2B CF 8B 5E F6 8D 39   .v..|..L.+.^v.9
090B:0180 B0 00 1E                                         0..
```

If we run the program we can find that 3 - 1 is indeed 2:

```
-G118

AX=0000  BX=0000  CX=001A  DX=0000  SP=FFFE  BP=0000  SI=0000  DI=0000
DS=090B  ES=090B  SS=090B  CS=090B  IP=0118   NV UP DI PL NZ NA PO NC
090B:0118 CD20           INT      20

-D103                        ↓
090B:0103    03 00 01 00 02-00 9B DF 06 03 01 9B DE    ......._....^
090B:0110 26 05 01 9B DF 1E 07 01-CD 20 6F 8B 46 06 25 7F   &..._...M o.F.%.
090B:0120 00 8B 5E 0A 89 47 0E 81-66 06 80 FF 8B 46 06 89   ..^..G..f....F..
090B:0130 47 0A 8B 46 08 89 47 0C-53 C4 46 06 06 50 B8 00   G..F..G.SDF..P8.
090B:0140 00 50 9A EB 03 C1 0C 89-5E 06 8C 46 08 8B 5E 0A   .P.k.A..^..F..^.
090B:0150 8B 47 02 89 46 F6 53 50-9A 06 00 43 09 06 53 8B   .G..FvSP...C..S.
090B:0160 5E F4 FF 77 04 9A 50 03-C1 0C 8B 5E 0A 89 47 06   ^t.w..P.A..^..G.
090B:0170 8B 76 0A 8B 7C 06 8B 4C-04 2B CF 8B 5E F6 8D 39   .v..|..L.+.^v.9
090B:0180 B0 00 1E                                         0..
-Q
```

▶ Using the 80×87

The last two easy examples here are multiplication and division.

Multiplying and Dividing Integers with the 80×87

As might be expected from our previous programs, there are two matching instructions for integer multiplication and division, FIMUL and FIDIV. We can multiply 3 by 2, for example, with this program:

```
            .8087
            .MODEL SMALL
            .CODE
            ORG     100H
ENTRY:      JMP     PROG
            OPERAND1 DW    3
            OPERAND2 DW    2
            RESULT  DW     0
PROG:       FILD    OPERAND1
            FIMUL   OPERAND2        ←
            FISTP   RESULT
            INT     20H
            END     ENTRY
```

We will find 6 deposited in RESULT. What happens, though, when we try dividing 3 by 2 in integer arithmetic? For example, what if we did this:

```
            .MODEL SMALL
            .CODE
            .8087
            ORG     100H
ENTRY:      JMP     PROG
            OPERAND1 DW    3
            OPERAND2 DW    2
            RESULT  DW     0
PROG:       FILD    OPERAND1
            FIDIV   OPERAND2        ←
            FISTP   RESULT
            INT     20H
            END     ENTRY
```

We can create a .COM file from the above program, called FIDIV.COM, and DEBUG it:

```
-R
AX=0000  BX=0000  CX=001A  DX=0000  SP=FFFE  BP=0000  SI=0000  DI=0000
DS=090B  ES=090B  SS=090B  CS=090B  IP=0100  NV UP DI PL NZ NA PO NC
090B:0100 EB07           JMP     0109       ← Jump over the data.
-T

AX=0000  BX=0000  CX=001A  DX=0000  SP=FFFE  BP=0000  SI=0000  DI=0000
DS=090B  ES=090B  SS=090B  CS=090B  IP=0109  NV UP DI PL NZ NA PO NC
```

326 ▶ Advanced Assembly Language

```
090B:0109 9B            WAIT
-U
090B:0109 9B            WAIT
090B:010A DF060301      FILD    WORD PTR [0103]
090B:010E 9B            WAIT
090B:010F DE360501      FIDIV   WORD PTR [0105]        ← Our division.
090B:0113 9B            WAIT
090B:0114 DF1E0701      FISTP   WORD PTR [0107]
090B:0118 CD20          INT     20
090B:011A 6F            DB      6F
090B:011B 8B4606        MOV     AX,[BP+06]
090B:011E 257F00        AND     AX,007F
090B:0121 8B5E0A        MOV     BX,[BP+0A]
090B:0124 89470E        MOV     [BX+0E],AX
090B:0127 81660680FF    AND     WORD PTR [BP+06],FF80
```

Once again, we check to make sure RESULT at [107] is zero before starting:

```
-D103
090B:0103   03 00 02 00 00-00 9B DF 06 03 01 9B DE        ......._....^
090B:0110   36 05 01 9B DF 1E 07 01-CD 20 6F 8B 46 06 25 7F   6..._...M o.F.%.
090B:0120   00 8B 5E 0A 89 47 0E 81-66 06 80 FF 8B 46 06 89   ..^..G..f....F..
090B:0130   47 0A 8B 46 08 89 47 0C-53 C4 46 06 06 50 B8 00   G..F..G.SDF..P8.
090B:0140   00 50 9A EB 03 C1 0C 89-5E 06 8C 46 08 8B 5E 0A   .P.k.A..^..F..^.
090B:0150   8B 47 02 89 46 F6 53 50-9A 06 00 43 09 06 53 8B   .G..FvSP...C..S.
090B:0160   5E F4 FF 77 04 9A 50 03-C1 0C 8B 5E 0A 89 47 06   ^t.w..P.A..^..G.
090B:0170   8B 76 0A 8B 7C 06 8B 4C-04 2B CF 8B 5E F6 8D 39   .v..|..L.+0.^v.9
090B:0180   80 00 1E                                          0..
```

Then we run the program to check RESULT:

```
-G118
AX=0000  BX=0000  CX=001A  DX=0000  SP=FFFE  BP=0000  SI=0000  DI=0000
DS=090B  ES=090B  SS=090B  CS=090B  IP=0118   NV UP DI PL NZ NA PO NC
090B:0118 CD20          INT     20
-D103
090B:0103   03 00 02 00 02-00 9B DF 06 03 01 9B DE        ......._....^
090B:0110   36 05 01 9B DF 1E 07 01-CD 20 6F 8B 46 06 25 7F   6..._...M o.F.%.
090B:0120   00 8B 5E 0A 89 47 0E 81-66 06 80 FF 8B 46 06 89   ..^..G..f....F..
090B:0130   47 0A 8B 46 08 89 47 0C-53 C4 46 06 06 50 B8 00   G..F..G.SDF..P8.
090B:0140   00 50 9A EB 03 C1 0C 89-5E 06 8C 46 08 8B 5E 0A   .P.k.A..^..F..^.
090B:0150   8B 47 02 89 46 F6 53 50-9A 06 00 43 09 06 53 8B   .G..FvSP...C..S.
090B:0160   5E F4 FF 77 04 9A 50 03-C1 0C 8B 5E 0A 89 47 06   ^t.w..P.A..^..G.
090B:0170   8B 76 0A 8B 7C 06 8B 4C-04 2B CF 8B 5E F6 8D 39   .v..|..L.+0.^v.9
090B:0180   80 00 1E                                          0..
-Q
```

Apparently, 3 divided by 2 is 2. The cause for this is easy to spot, however. In integer arithmetic, numbers are rounded off. When we load 3 with FILD, it is stored in the 80×87 stack in *temporary real format*, a format that uses the full 80 bits the 80×87 is capable of.

▶ Using the 80×87

When we divided by 2, we got a result of 1.5, but FIDIV rounds up any fractional answers by adding .5 to the result and then discarding the fractional part. This process is what gave us the 2 we finally see. Even if we had used FDIV, which would have given an answer of 1.5, FISTP rounds numbers off in just the same way before storing them, by adding .5 to the number in the stack top and then discarding the fractional part.

This raises the issue of how the 80×87 stores numbers. In itself, this subject takes a little study.

80×87 Integer Formats

We already know one format used by the 80×87: word integers, defined with DW (see Figure 11-1 below):

```
Bit #   15   14        0
        [              ]  ← One Word
```

Figure 11-1.

These integers are stored in 16 bits, and they correspond to the integer type in languages like BASIC and Pascal. The leftmost bit is used to store the integer's sign, so what is left to hold the number itself are the remaining 15 bits, giving a range of -32,768–32,767 (the range is unsymmetric because zero is counted as a positive number). These numbers are stored in just the same way as are the normal numbers the PC operates on. They are stored in two's complement notation, which we have seen in Chapter 8.

The next size integer is the so-called *short integer*, which is 32 bits long, and is defined with DD, define doubleword:

```
SHORT_INT   DD   12345678
```

These integers can range from -2×10^9 to 2×10^9. Here's how their bits are stored:

```
Bit #   31   30        0
        [              ]  ← Double Word
```

Figure 11-2.

The 80×87 short integer is really the same as most high-level language's *long integer*. The sign bit is held in bit 31, the leftmost bit, as usual. Finally, if you need really big integers, there is the *long integer format*. This format is 64 bits, and can hold integers from -9×10^{18} to 9×10^{18}. If you need numbers larger than this, you must go to floating point notation. As it is, the 80×87 can preserve 18 decimal places of accuacary with long integers. Long integers are defined with DQ, Define Quadword, since four words make up 64 bits:

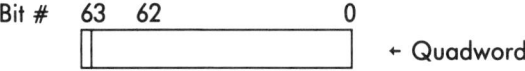

The bit pattern of Long Integers is as expected, with 63 bits (bits 0–62) of integer and one sign bit (bit 63):

Figure 11-3.

We are already familiar with two's complement notation, so we know how to set these numbers up.

80 × 87 Floating Point Formats

Floating point calculations make up most of the work for the 80×87. The format for such numbers, however, takes a little getting used to. If we have a number like 32.1, we know that we have 3×10^1 plus 2×10^0 and 1×10^{-1}. On the other hand, the computer is a binary machine, so a number like 10.5 must be stored as 1×2^3 plus 1×2^1 plus 1×2^{-1} or 1010.1, where the point is a binary point. It is possible to store any number in binary that can be stored in decimal, it just takes more places. For instance, 0.75 can be broken down into $1/2 + 1/4$, or $2^{-1} + 2^{-2}$, so .75 = .11B.

Normalized 80 × 87 Format

The numbers stored in the 80×87 are all "normalized," which means they appear with the binary point near the beginning, so 1,010.1 would appear like this: 1.0101×2^3. To expand this, just move the binary point three places to the right, giving us 1,010.1 again. You can see that the first digit in any normalized binary number is always one. INTEL took advantage of that to make the leading 1 *implicit*. In other words, all that is stored of the *significand* is 0101. The exponent is still three, but, to make matters even more complex, all exponents are stored after being added to some offset or bias.

For a short real, this bias is 7FH, or 127. For long reals, this number is 3FFH or 1,023. If our number is going to be stored as a short real, the exponent will be 3 + 127 = 130 = 82H. Finally, the first bit of any number is going to be the sign bit. Real numbers, like BCD numbers, are NOT stored in two's complement notation. If the sign bit is 1, the number is negative; if it is 0, the number is positive. That's the only distinction. The short real format looks like Figure 11-4:

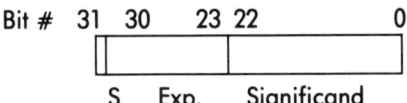

Figure 11-4.

So 10.5 = 1010.1B will look like this:

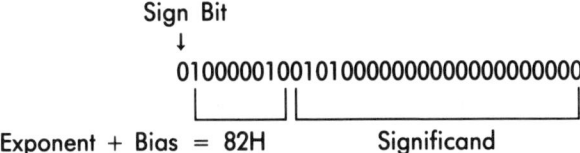

Figure 11-5.

This can be made into Hex by grouping every four binary digits together:

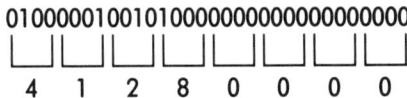

Figure 11-6.

So 10.5 is stored as 41280000H. In fact, due to the the 80 × 86's method of storing low bytes first inside a word and then low words first, 10.5 actually shows up in memory as 00 00 28 41.

The format for long reals is this:

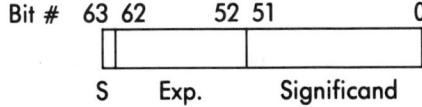

Figure 11-7.

330 ▶ Advanced Assembly Language

Short reals have 1 sign bit, 8 exponent bits, and 23 significand bits, for a total of 32 (define short reals with DD). Long reals have a sign bit, 11 bits of exponent (with a bias of 1023 (3FFH)) and 52 bits of significand, for a total of 64 bits (define long reals with DQ, Define Quadword). The values that each of the formats can hold are shown below:

Ranges for the 80×87 Formats

Format	Bits	Range
Word integer	16	-32,768 to 32,767
Short integer	32	-2×10^9 to 2×10^9
Long integer	64	-9×10^{18} to 9×10^{18}
BCD	80	-9...9 to 9...9 (18 9s)
Short real	32	8.43×10^{-37} to 3.37×10^{38}
Long real	64	$3.4 \times 10^{-4,932}$ to $1.2 \times 10^{4,932}$

TIP To use floating point format, we can do one of four things: we can let a high-level language do the dirty work of manipulating the number; we can let the assembler do it by including constants in our .ASM file:

```
LONG_VAL DQ 3.14159
```

we can do the dirty work ourselves; or we can let the 80×87 store the number in an easier (integer) format.

Binary Coded Decimal One more way of storing numbers in a format recognizable to the 80×87 is in binary coded decimal or BCD. BCD is particularly easy to work with for most people since it looks just like base 10 numbers. BCD numbers are 10 bytes long (defined with DT, Define Tenbytes) and the largest allowable digit is 9. Again, however, the leftmost bit, bit 79, is used for the sign. Unlike two's complement math, the only thing different about two numbers like 4 and -4 is the sign bit. If a BCD number is negative, the first byte is 80H. If positive, it is 0:

```
NUMBER DT 00123456789999999999H
```

The only difference with BCD numbers is that you have to load them with FBLD instead of FILD and store them in memory with FBSTP (store and pop) instead of FISTP. Here is a program that will give a result, in RESULT, of zero:

```
                .MODEL SMALL
                .CODE
                .8087
                ORG     100H
ENTRY:          JMP     PROG
        OPERAND1 DT     00123456789999999999H
        OPERAND2 DT     80123456789999999999H   ;<- Note this is -1xOPERAND1.
        RESULT   DW     0
PROG:   FBLD    OPERAND1                ;<- Load the two BCD numbers.
        FBLD    OPERAND2
        FADD                            ;Add Stack top plus number below it.
        FISTP   RESULT                  ;Store RESULT as an integer.
        INT     20H
        END     ENTRY
```

Here we add the BCD number 00123456789999999999H to the BCD number 80123456789999999999H, which is the same thing, except that the leading bit has been made 1. The result of this addition is 0. Note the use of FBLD in the above program to load the BCD numbers into the coprocessor.

> **TIP** The most common use for binary coded decimal is in financial transactions. Using base 10 numbers can elimate round-off errors that appear during conversions to and from decimal.

The 80×87 Instructions

There are plenty of coprocessor instructions, but an introductory chapter is not the place to see them all in action. Instead, and for reference, we will list and discuss the most frequently used 80×87 instructions below.

> **NOTE** Immediately after the name of the instruction, we see what the instruction does with a line like: $2^{ST} - 1 \rightarrow ST$. This means that the stack (ST) is replaced by the value $2^{ST} - 1$.

F2XM1 — 2^X Minus 1

Logic: $ST \leftarrow 2^{ST} - 1$

Many 80×87 instructions have hard to remember mnemonics — this one certainly does: F2XM1 stands for 2 to the X minus 1. This instruction sounds exceptionally useful until you find out that the power you raise two to must be in the interval of 0. to .5.

($-1.0 <$ ST < 1.0 on the 80×87). Nevertheless, if you are willing to work with square roots and multiplications, you can fabricate any power of two this way.

The abbreviation ST always stands for the stack top, ST(1) as the value on the stack below it, all the way down to ST(7). Don't forget that it is your responsibilty to keep the stack from getting completely filled.

This instruction takes no arguments, and it uses only the stack top. Some formulas you might want to keep in mind while using this instruction include:

$$10^{ST} = 2^{ST} \times LOG_2 10$$
$$e^{ST} = 2^{ST} \times LOG_2 e$$
$$Y^{ST} = 2^{ST} \times LOG_2 Y$$

With these formulas, you can find 10ST, e^{ST}, and Y^{ST} from 2ST. There are special instructions to load $LOG_2 e$ (FLDL2E) and to load $LOG_2 10$ (FLDL2T). These instructions simply load their respective values into ST.

FABS Absolute Value

Logic: ST ← ABS(ST)

FABS changes the top of the stack to its own absolute value. This instruction provides a fast way of making sure a value is greater than or equal to 0.

FADD Addition

Logic: ST(1) ← ST(1) + ST, pop stack   (no operands)
ST ← ST + memory   (source only)
ST ← ST + ST(i)   (destination, source)

We have already seen this instruction at work. It simply adds two floating point numbers. If there are no arguments, the 80×87 adds ST and ST(1) together, loads this new number into ST(1), and then pops the 80×87 stack, leaving the result in ST.

If you use an argument like the one below,

```
FADD    LONG_REAL
```

then LONG_REAL is added to ST, and the answer is left in ST. On the other hand, you can use instructions like:

```
FADD ST,ST(3)
```

in which case ST(3) will be added to ST, and the result will be left in ST. Similarly, the instruction:

```
FADD ST(3),ST
```

will add ST to ST(3), and will leave the result in ST(3) — not ST.

The integer version of this instruction is FIADD.

NOTE Note that the stack is popped in the no-operands form only.

FBLD Load BCD Number

Logic: push stack
ST ← memory operand

FBLD converts a memory operand from BCD (packed decimal) format to temporary real and loads it into ST. The sign of the memory operand is preserved. FBLD is for loading BCD numbers, and we have already seen this instruction in action. Its use is quite simple, provided you have stored the BCD number correctly (with DT, Define Tenbytes):

```
FBLD    BCD_NUMBER
```

The counterpart of this instruction is the one that follows, FBSTP.

FBSTP Store BCD Number

Logic: [memory location] ← ST
pop stack

This accomplishes the reverse of FBLD and also pops the stack. FBSTP stores a number in BCD format. If you wanted to convert from, say, integer to BCD, you could load the integer with FILD and store it with FBSTP. This instruction also keeps the stack trim by popping it.

FCHS Change Sign

        Logic: ST ← -1 * ST

FCHS simply changes the sign of the value in ST. It is quicker than multiplying by -1.0.

FCLEX Clear Exceptions

        Logic: clear exception flags

The 80×87 has a set of flags like the 80×86, and those flags will be covered in the following section on errors. The flags are stored in the 80×87's status word. To check them, you have to store the status word in memory. The important part for PC users is that these flags are not automatically reset. They stay set so that they can propagate through a whole calculation, and we can check any accumulated errors at the end if we wish. FCLEX clears these flags and sets them back to zero. If we intend to use error checking, we should start off any calculation with FCLEX.

FCOM Comparison

        Logic: cmp ST, source
                    sets condition codes in the status word:

C3	C2	C1	C0	Means
0	0	?	0	ST > source
0	0	?	1	ST < source
1	0	?	0	ST = source
1	1	?	1	ST not comparable to source

FCOM compares a real number to ST and leaves the result encoded in the 80×87 *status word* as shown above. If no source is specified, ST(1) is compared to ST. Otherwise, source is compared to ST.

This is the first of the 80×87's comparison instructions. FCOM is used with real numbers, short or long reals. To use it (the comparison to ST is implicit), just issue a instruction like:

```
FCOM    LONG_REAL_NUMBER
```

Using the 80×87

The results of this comparison are stored in the 80 × 87's status word. The condition bits in the status word are of interest here. We can store the status word in memory with the instruction FSTSW (see below) and examine it. The bits C3 - C0 will be returned this way after the comparison:

C3	C2	C1	C0	Means
0	0	?	0	ST > source
0	0	?	1	ST < source
1	0	?	0	ST = source
1	1	?	1	ST not comparable to source

C0 is bit 8 of the status word, and C3 is bit 14. We can use this information immediately in a little test program to check the relative sizes of two memory values, A and B.

The RECORD and MASK Directives

There is an easy way of working with individual bits in the status word. We will use the new directive RECORD to split our status word up into bit-by-bit fields. That way, we can use the MASK directive later to generate masks to specify individual bits. We use record to give a name to all the bits in a word this way: M RECORD BY:1,C3:1,TOP:3,C2:1,C1:1,C0:1,IT:1,X:1,P:1,U:1,O:1,Z:1,D:1,I:1. Here we define a dummy record, named M, just so we can give names to all the bits in it. The first bit is named BY (which stands for "busy"), the next bit C3, the following three bits TOP, and so on.

The reason the bit names are so short is that a RECORD must be completely defined on one line (that is, in 132 characters or less). Notice also that the field TOP, which tells you which of the eight 80 × 87 registers is the stack top currently, is 3 bits long, because it must be able to hold numbers up to 8.

Now that we've defined the name C3 as part of a word, we can use the MASK directive. When we then use the instruction TEST ST8087,MASK C3, the assembler will substitute the correct hex number for MASK C3. C3 is bit 14, and the assembler will generate a *mask* which has bit 14 set. The program is in Listing 11-1.

Listing 11-1. 80×87 Comparison between Values A and B.

```
            .MODEL  SMALL
            .CODE
            .8087
            ORG     100H
ENTRY:      JMP     PROG
        A           DQ 10.0
        B           DQ 5.0
            ST8087  DW  0
→       M RECORD BY:1,C3:1,TOP:3,C2:1,C1:1,C0:1,IT:1,X:1,P:1,U:1,O:1,Z:1,D:1,I:1
PROG:       FINIT
            FLD     A
            FCOMP   B
            FSTSW   ST8087
            MOV     DL,'A'
            MOV     AH,2
            INT     21H
            ;C3=0   C0=0 → A>B
            ;C3=0   C0=1 → A<B
            ;C3=1   C0=0 → A=B
→           TEST    ST8087,MASK C3
            JZ      NOTEQ
            MOV     DL,'='
            JMP     SHORT PRINT
NOTEQ:      TEST    ST8087,MASK C0
            JNZ     LESS
            MOV     DL,'>'
            JMP     SHORT PRINT
LESS:       MOV     DL,'<'
PRINT:      MOV     AH,2
            INT     21H
            MOV     DL,'B'
            INT     21H
            FCLEX
            INT     20H
            END     ENTRY
```

We start off with a data area, as usual. Here we make A and B into single precision size by using DQ, and store the status word in the word we have labeled ST8087:

```
            .MODEL  SMALL
            .CODE
            .8087
            ORG     100H
ENTRY:      JMP     PROG
→       A           DQ 10.0
→       B           DQ 5.0
→           ST8087  DW  0
        M RECORD BY:1,C3:1,TOP:3,C2:1,C1:1,C0:1,IT:1,X:1,P:1,U:1,O:1,Z:1,D:1,I:1
PROG:       FINIT
            :
            :
```

The first instruction used here is the useful instruction FINIT, which initializes the 80×87 and clears the stack. We then load A and compare it to B with FCOMP, the version of FCOM that also pops the stack. Immediately afterward, we store the status

► Using the 80×87 337

word in ST8087. In preparing to type out the answer (either A>B, A<B, or A=B), we first type out "A" this way:

```
        .MODEL  SMALL
        .CODE
        .8087
        ORG     100H
ENTRY:  JMP     PROG
        A       DQ  10.0
        B       DQ  5.0
        ST8087  DW  0
        M RECORD BY:1,C3:1,TOP:3,C2:1,C1:1,C0:1,IT:1,X:1,P:1,U:1,O:1,Z:1,D:1,I:1
PROG:   FINIT
   →    FLD     A                       ;Load A
   →    FCOMP   B                       ;Compare to B
   →    FSTSW   ST8087                  ;Store the status word in memory.
   →    MOV     DL,'A'                  ;Print out "A"
   →    MOV     AH,2
   →    INT     21H
        :
        :
```

Next we check C3 and C0 after the comparison. If C3=1, then A=B. If C0=1, then A<B. Here's the way the program types out either "=", "<", or ">", followed by "B":

```
        .MODEL  SMALL
        .CODE
        .8087
        ORG     100H
ENTRY:  JMP     PROG
        A       DQ  10.0
        B       DQ  5.0
        ST8087  DW  0
        M RECORD BY:1,C3:1,TOP:3,C2:1,C1:1,C0:1,IT:1,X:1,P:1,U:1,O:1,Z:1,D:1,I:1
PROG:   FINIT
        FLD     A
        FCOMP   B
        FSTSW   ST8087
        MOV     DL,'A'
        MOV     AH,2
        INT     21H
        ;C3=0   C0=0 → A>B
        ;C3=0   C0=1 → A<B
        ;C3=1   C0=0 → A=B
   →    TEST    ST8087,MASK C3
        JZ      NOTEQ                   ;C3 NOT set → jump.
   →    MOV     DL,'='
        JMP     SHORT PRINT
NOTEQ:  TEST    ST8087,MASK C0
        JNZ     LESS                    ;C0 set → jump.
   →    MOV     DL,'>'
        JMP     SHORT PRINT
LESS:   MOV     DL,'<'
PRINT:  MOV     AH,2
        INT     21H
        MOV     DL,'B'
        INT     21H
        FCLEX
        INT     20H
        END     ENTRY
```

We can see not only how to use the status word this way, but also the RECORD and MASK directives.

FDIV Division

Logic: ST(1) ← ST(1)/ST, pop stack   (no operands)
          ST ← ST/memory location   (source only)
          ST ← ST/ST(i)   (destination, source)

We have seen FDIV before. This is the floating point divide instruction. If you use it without labels:

```
FDIV
```

it will divide ST(1) by ST, store the result in ST, and pop the stack. If you use a real memory operand:

```
FDIV Long_Real
```

then ST will be divided by the real number and the result is left in ST. Finally, if you use it with both ST and ST(n), then ST will be loaded with ST/ST(n):

```
FDIV ST,ST(n)
```

The integer version of FDIV is FIDIV.

NOTE Note that the stack is popped only in the no operands form.

FIADD Integer Add

Logic: ST ← ST + memory operand

▶ **Using the 80×87** 339

FIADD adds two integers and leaves the result in the stack top. The source must be a memory word or short integer. The destination implied in the instruction is always ST.

FICOM Integer Compare

Logic: cmp source, ST
sets condition codes in the status word.

C3	C2	C1	C0	Means
0	0	?	0	ST > source
0	0	?	1	ST < source
1	0	?	0	ST = source
1	1	?	1	ST not comparable to source

FICOM compares two integers and leaves the result encoded in the status word as shown above. The source operand can be either a memory short integer or a memory word integer, and the implied destination is ST.

FIDIV Integer Divide

Logic: ST ← ST/memory operand

FIDIV is an integer division instruction. It divides the destination, which is always ST, by the specified memory operand and stores the result in ST. The memory operand can be either a word integer or a short integer.

FILD Load Integer

Logic: ST ← memory operand

FILD is the way you load integers into ST.

> **TIP** Since the only format that the 80×86 and the 80×87 have in common is the word integer format (16 bits and two's complement signed), this instruction is quite popular. The corresponding instruction to store integers is FIST. In particular, if you have done calculations with the 80×87 and wish to manipulate the results by transferring them back to the 80×86, FIST is very useful.

FIMUL Integer Multiply

Logic: ST ← ST * memory operand

FIMUL performs an integer multiplication of the memory operand and ST and leaves the result in ST. The memory operand can be either a short integer or a word integer.

FINIT Initialize 80×87

Logic: initialize 80×87

This instruction is especially useful. It initializes and resets the 80×87. If the stack has become full or if (for any other reason) you want to start from scratch, you can use FINIT. The timing between the 80×87 and the 80×86 is preserved. If, on the other hand, you suspect that the 80×86 and 80×87 are no longer communicating well (i.e., each is waiting for the other to finish), you might use FNINIT, which executes an immediate FINIT, instead of first waiting until the 80×87 signals that it is free.

FIST Store Integer

Logic: [memory location] ← ST

FIST, as mentioned, provides a way of downloading 80×87 results in a manner readable by the 80×86. We can do whatever we want with floating point numbers and then, finally, load the final answer into memory with FIST, where it can be examined by the 80×86.

FISTP Store Integer and Pop Stack

Logic: [memory location] ← ST, pop stack

FISTP has all the advantages of FIST, and two more. FISTP also pops the stack and keeps it from growing too large. It can also store numbers in the Long_Integer format (64 bits — use DQ), while FIST cannot. As with FIST, you can do all your floating point calculations first and then store them in integer format so they can be read by the 80×86 CPU.

FISUB Integer Subtract

      Logic: ST ← ST - memory operand

FISUB subtracts two integers (ST - memory operand) and leaves the result in the stack top. You use it like this: FISUB MEM_INT. The memory operand must be a word or short integer. The destination implied in the instruction is always ST.

FLD Load Real

      Logic: ST(1) ← ST(1) + ST   (no operands)
                  ST ← ST + memory operand   (source only)
                  ST ← ST + ST(i)   (destination, source)

FLD is the usual way of loading floating point numbers into ST. With it, you can load short or long reals, as well as the temporary real format (80 bits) used internally in the 80x87. The format is simply this:

```
FLD SHORT_REAL
```

as we have already seen. This is the way that the 80×87 operates. We have to load its stack before we can use it. Of course, all numbers that are loaded this way must be stored in the correct floating point format. Keep track of the number of FLDs you have executed to make sure the stack does not grow uncontrollably.

FMUL Multiply

      Logic: ST(1) ← ST(1) * ST, pop stack   (no operands)
                  ST ← ST * memory location   (source only)
                  ST ← ST * ST(i)   (destination, source)

FMUL is the 80×87's all-purpose real number multiplication instruction. With it you can multiply ST(1) and ST, pop the stack, and move the result from ST(1) into ST:

```
FMUL
```

or you can load a real number into ST with FLD and multiply it by some real number stored in memory:

```
FMUL SHORT_INTEGER
FMUL LONG_INTEGER
```

FMUL can also multiply different stack elements. For example:

```
FMUL ST, ST(7)
```

multiplies ST by ST(7) and leaves the result in ST. The other way around:

```
FMUL ST(7),ST
```

multiplies ST(7) by ST and leaves the results in ST(7).

The integer version of FMUL is FIMUL.

NOTE Note that the stack is popped only in the no-operands form.

FNCLEX Clear Exceptions — No Wait

Logic: clear exceptions without waiting

This is the version of FCLEX that does not wait until the 80×87 signals that it is free. Usually, there is no advantage to using FNCLEX instead of FCLEX. If, however, you write what is called an exception handler, analogous to interrupt handlers in the PC, then you have to issue this instruction before returning to the interrupted calculation. (We will not deal with exception handlers in this book.)

FNOP No Operation

Logic: ST ← ST

FNOP performs no operation. It can be used to replace a deleted instruction in an assembly language program while preserving the effective offsets of the remaining instructions. Unfortunately, this instruction is 3 bytes long (instead of the corresponding 80×86 instruction NOP, which is 1 byte long), which makes it difficult to replace instructions that are, say, 2 or 5 bytes long.

FNSTSW Store Status — No Wait

    Logic: store status word without waiting

This is another instruction that does not wait until the 80×87 signals it is free before operating. This instruction is usually used to examine the busy bit (bit 15) of the status word to determine when the 80×87 is no longer busy. Typically, loops are put into 80×86 code which checks this bit until it becomes 0, at which time the 80×87 is free. This instruction is used like this:

```
FNSTSW  WORD_LENGTH_OP
```

FPATAN Arc Tangent

    Logic: T1 ← ARCTAN(ST(1)/ST)
               pop stack
               ST ← T1

FPATAN is the instruction for partial arc tangent. This instruction takes no arguments. All we must do is supply it with the ratio Y/X, where X = ST, and Y is ST(1). To load Y, we can use FLD. Another FLD for X will push Y into ST(1) and put X into ST. The resulting angle is left in ST and can be stored in memory with FSTP. For the 8087 and 80287, ST must be greater than ST(1), and both must be positive. There is no restriction on ST or ST(1) in the 80387.

FPREM Partial Remainder

    Logic: ST ← repeat (ST - ST(1)) until ST ≤ ST(1)
               If ST > ST(1) then C2 = 1, PREM = ST
               If ST = ST(1) then C2 = 0, REM = 0
               If ST < ST(1) then C2 = 0, REM = ST

FPREM calculates ST mod (ST(1)). It leaves the remainder of the division ST/ST(1) in ST. The sign of the remainder is the same as the sign of the original dividend. This instruction also indicates the least significant 3 bits of the quotient generated by FPREM in C3 C1 and C0 as shown below.

FPREM Results

C3	C2	C1	C0	Meaning
?	1	?	?	Incomplete reduction
0	0	0	0	quotient MOD 8 = 0
0	0	0	1	quotient MOD 8 = 4
0	0	1	0	quotient MOD 8 = 1
0	0	1	1	quotient MOD 8 = 5
1	0	0	0	quotient MOD 8 = 2
1	0	0	1	quotient MOD 8 = 6
1	0	1	0	quotient MOD 8 = 3
1	0	1	1	quotient MOD 8 = 7

FPTAN Tangent

Logic: Y/X ← TAN(ST)
ST ← Y
push stack
ST ← X

FPTAN is the 80×87's partial tangent instruction. With this instruction, you can also calculate sines and cosines, given the right trigonometric identities. The value of ST must be 0 < ST < Pi/4. Instead of simply delivering a floating point answer, FPTAN gives us a ratio Y/X (Y in ST(1) and X in ST). This makes it easier to calculate other trigonometric values.

If we want one number, we would divide Y by X with FDIV. The 80387 also lets you calcluate sines and cosines directly (with its FCOS and FSINE instructions).

FSQRT Square Root

Logic: sqrt(ST) → ST

This instruction just gives us the square root of ST. In order not to give an undefined answer, ST must be positive. Finding square roots with the 80×87 is actually a fast process, taking about the same time as division. Needless to say, emulating this instruction with the 80×86 is a time consuming and frustrating process.

FST Store Real

        Logic: destination ← ST

FST copies the value in ST to the destination. The destination can be a short or long real memory operand, or a coprocessor register, ST(i).

FSTSW Store Status

        Logic: status word → memory operand

This is a very common instruction used when you are doing error checking. The Status Word, as you'll see in the next section, defines the current state of the 80×87 and includes the error flags. This instruction is preferred over the No-Wait version of the same thing, FNSTSW. FNSTSW is used almost exclusively in tight loops that check when the 80×87 is not busy by checking the busy bit in the Status Word. We will make more use of the status word later.

FSUB Subtraction

        Logic: ST(1) ← ST(1) - ST, pop stack   (no operands)
                  ST ← ST - memory operand   (source only)
                  ST ← ST - ST(i)   (destination, source)

FSUB is the 80×87's real subtraction instruction. It is advisable after any FSUB to check the status word for errors. FSUB can take these forms:

Instruction	Result
FSUB	(ST(1)-ST → ST(1)), pop stack
FSUB SHORT_REAL	ST-Short_Real → ST
FSUB LONG_REAL	(ST-Long_Real → ST)
FSUB ST,ST(3)	(ST-ST(3) → ST)
FSUB ST(7),ST	(ST(7)-ST → ST(7))

The integer version of this instruction is FISUB.

NOTE Note that the stack is popped in the no operands form only.

FTST Test for Zero

Logic: ST ← ST - 0.0

FTST compares ST to 0.0. The result of the floating-point comparison is left in the condition codes of the status word:

C3	C0	Means
0	0	ST > 0
0	1	ST < 0
1	0	ST = +0 or -0
1	1	ST is not comparable

FWAIT Wait

Logic: 80×86 wait

FWAIT causes the 80×86 microprocessor to wait until the current 80×87 instruction is completed. It is used to synchronize the 80×86 and 80×87.

FWAIT is the same instruction as the 80×86 WAIT instruction. However, you should use the FWAIT instruction since WAIT may cause an infinite wait under some circumstances.

NOTE   You should note that if an FWAIT instruction is necessary, the assembler will usually put one in.

FXAM Examine

Logic: sets condition codes according to the value in ST

FXAM causes the coprocessor to examine the value currently in ST. The condition codes are set as shown below in the list of FXAM results.

FXAM Results

C3	C2	C1	C0	Means
0	0	0	0	+Unnormal
0	0	0	1	+NAN
0	0	1	0	-Unnormal

▶ **Using the 80×87** 347

0	0	1	1	-Unnormal
0	1	0	0	+Normal
0	1	0	1	+Infinity
0	1	1	0	-Normal
0	1	1	1	-Infinity
1	0	0	0	+0
1	0	0	1	Empty
1	0	1	0	-0
1	0	1	1	Empty
1	1	0	0	+Denormal
1	1	0	1	Empty
1	1	1	0	-Denormal
1	1	1	1	Empty

FXCH Exchange Registers

Logic: T1 ← ST(i)
        ST(i) ← ST
        ST ← T1

FXCH exchanges the contents of ST with the contents of the destination register. If no destination is specified, ST is exchanged with ST(1). This instruction is very useful on a stack-based processor like the 80×87.

FXTRACT Extract Exponent and Significand

Logic: T1 ← exponent(ST)
        T2 ← significand(ST)
        ST ← T1
        push stack
        ST ← T2

FXTRACT extracts the exponents and significand of the value in ST. It leaves the exponent in ST(1) and the significand in ST.

FYL2X Y—Log$_2$X

Logic: T1 ← ST(1) * Log2(ST)

pop stack
ST ← T1

FYL2X is one of the two instructions in the 80×87 that can calculate Log_2 values (the other is FYL2XP1). Nowhere do the 80×87 mnemonics make less apparent sense. What FYL2X means is $Y \times \text{Log}_2 X$. This immediate multiplication is useful, since you can find logs in other bases with the identity:

$$\text{Log}_n X = [1/\text{Log}_2 n] \times \text{Log}_2 X$$

TIP This is the 80×87's method of raising numbers to powers. You must take the number's log first, multiply by the appropriate power, and then take the anti-log by exponentiating (using F2XM1).

80×87 Errors and Error Checking

No math-related computer discussion would be complete without a discussion of errors. Just as we can check the carry flag in the 80×86, so there are provisions in the 80×87 for error checking. Unless you know beforehand just what your input will be, you should check for errors.

The register that holds the 80×87's error flags and status flags is called the Status Word. This word can be stored in memory with FSTSW like this: FSTSW MEM_WORD.

The status word is divided into status bits and exception flags (error flags). The top byte looks like this:

Bit #	15	14	13	12	11	10	9	8
	B	C3	\multicolumn{3}{c}{Top of Stack Register #}	C2	C1	C0

Figure 11-8.

The topmost bit, bit 15, is the busy bit. If this bit is 1, the 80×87 is busy executing some instruction. If this bit is 0, the 80×87 is idle. If you use FSTSW, this bit should always be 0 since this instruction waits until the 80×87 is free before executing. On the other hand, the no-wait form of this instruction, FNSTSW, does not wait until the 80×87 is free, and you can check on the 80×87 at any time with it.

The four *condition codes*, C3-C0, are used to hold the results of comparisons, as we saw with FCOM. If we used the instruction FCOM MEM_OP, this is the way the condition codes C3-C0 would be set (C1 is not set for compare instructions):

▶ **Using the 80×87** 349

C3	C2	C1	C0	Means
0	0	-	0	ST > MEM_OP
0	0	-	1	ST < MEM_OP
1	0	-	0	ST = MEM_OP

The 80×87 also has an examine instruction, FXAM, which will set C3-C0 depending on the contents of ST. This instruction is often very useful. (See the list of the results of FXAM.)

A normalized number is one that fits into the normal format of 80×87 reals — biased exponent and implicit leading one. If, though, a number is very small, it would have leading zeros (not ones) once the smallest exponent for that format has been used. In that case, the number is no longer normalized, but the 80×87 can still operate on it.

The 3 bits labeled Top of Stack Register # hold the number (0–7) of the register that is the current top of stack (ST). You can watch this number to make sure you know where you are in the stack and that it does not overflow.

The bottom 8 bits of the status word look like Figure 11–9 below:

Bit #	7	6	5	4	3	2	1	0
	IR		P	U	O	Z	D	I

Figure 11–9.

The IR bit indicates whether or not an Interrupt Request is pending from the 80×87 to the 80×86.

The six flags — P, U, O, Z, D, and I — indicate exceptions and can be checked after every math operation. Until these flags are cleared with FCLEX or FINIT, however, they stay set once they are set. As mentioned, this means that error flags can propagate through an entire calculation, even an involved one, and can be checked at the end.

If the exception occurred, the corresponding bit is one. Otherwise, the bit is 0. The exception flags are shown below.

80×87 Exception Flags

Flag	Means
P	Precision. Some precision has been lost in working with the current operand.
U	Underflow. The number's exponent is too small to be represented in the requested format. In other words, the result is nonzero but too small to fit in the format asked for.

O   Overflow. The other extreme: The number is too large to fit into the requested format.

Z   A divide by zero occurred.

D   Denormalization. At least one of the operands used was denormalized, e.g., it has the smallest possible exponent but a nonzero significand.

I   Invalid operation. Some invalid operations include stack over- and under-flow, dividing zero by zero, taking the negative square root of a number.

Putting Error Checking to Work

We can put this knowledge to work at once. In this example, we will perform two divisions, one a valid division and one a division by zero. Each time we will check the status word to examine the exception flags. The program may be seen in Listing 11-2.

Listing 11-2. 7ERROR.ASM — 80x87 Error Checking Example.

```
            .MODEL  SMALL
            .CODE
            .8087
            ORG     100H
ENTRY:      JMP     PROG
OP1         DQ      10.0
OP2         DQ      5.0
OP3         DQ      0.0
NOPROB      DB      'No '
PROB        DB      'Divide by Zero',13,10,'$'
ST8087      DW      0
SW          RECORD  B:1,C3:1,TOP:3,C2:1,C1:1,C0:1,IT:1,X:1,P:1,U:1,O:1,Z:1,D:1,I:1
PROG:       FINIT
            FLD     OP1
            FDIV    OP2
            MOV     AH,9
            LEA     DX,NOPROB
            FSTSW   ST8087
            TEST    ST8087,MASK Z
            JZ      OK1
            LEA     DX,PROB
OK1:        INT     21H
            FCLEX
            FINIT
            FLD     OP1
            FDIV    OP3
            MOV     AH,9
            LEA     DX,NOPROB
            FSTSW   ST8087
            TEST    ST8087,MASK Z
            JZ      OK2
            LEA     DX,PROB
OK2:        INT     21H
            INT     20H
            END     ENTRY
```

To define the bit-by-bit flags in the status word, we use the RECORD directive again. As we saw earlier, the definition of a record has to fit on one line, so we make the abbreviation of each flag rather terse. Here's how the status word is stored in memory:

```
            .CODE
            .8087
            ORG     100H
ENTRY:      JMP     PROG
            OP1     DQ  10.0
            OP2     DQ  5.0
            OP3     DQ  0.0
            NOPROB  DB  'No '
            PROB    DB  'Divide by Zero',13,10,'$'
         →  ST8087  DW  0
         →  SW RECORD B:1,C3:1,TOP:3,C2:1,C1:1,C0:1,IT:1,X:1,P:1,U:1,O:1,Z:1,D:1,I:1
            :
            :
```

By defining dummy record named SW, we have given names to each bit, and the assembler will recognize these names when we use them again. To check the Zero bit, for instance, we use the 80×86 instruction TEST, along with the directive MASK Z. The assembler knows the place number of the Z bit from our RECORD definition. The MASK directive will make a mask for us. For example, if the Z bit was the third bit place, the mask would be 0000000000000100B, or 0004. Here's how we use MASK Z:

```
PROG:       FINIT
            FLD     OP1
            FDIV    OP2
            MOV     AH,9
            LEA     DX,NOPROB
            FSTSW   ST8087
         →  TEST    ST8087,MASK Z
            JZ      OK1
            LEA     DX,PROB
OK1:        INT     21H
            :
            :
```

We take the operand OP1 and first divide it by OP2. We then reload OP1 and divide by OP3:

352 ▶ Advanced Assembly Language

```
           .MODEL SMALL
           .CODE
           .8087
           ORG     100H
ENTRY:     JMP     PROG
       → OP1     DQ 10.0
       → OP2     DQ 5.0
       → OP3     DQ 0.0
         NOPROB  DB 'No '
         PROB    DB 'Divide by Zero',13,10,'$'
         ST8087  DW 0
         SW RECORD B:1,C3:1,TOP:3,C2:1,C1:1,C0:1,IT:1,X:1,P:1,U:1,O:1,Z:1,D:1,I:1
         :
         :
```

The first division is just 10.0 divided by 5.0, which will not lead to a division by zero. The second division, 10.0 divided by 0.0, however, will. In order to do these divisions, we start off with a FINIT to reset the 80×87 and clear all exception flags. We then load OP1 into ST with FLD and divide by OP2:

```
           .MODEL SMALL
           .CODE
           .8087
           ORG     100H
ENTRY:     JMP     PROG
           OP1     DQ 10.0
           OP2     DQ 5.0
           OP3     DQ 0.0
           NOPROB  DB 'No '
           PROB    DB 'Divide by Zero',13,10,'$'
           ST8087  DW 0
           SW RECORD B:1,C3:1,TOP:3,C2:1,C1:1,C0:1,IT:1,X:1,P:1,U:1,O:1,Z:1,D:1,I:1
PROG:      FINIT         ←
           FLD     OP1   ←
           FDIV    OP2   ←
           :
           :
```

We have to check the status word to make sure there was no divide by zero error. We will print out the results with the string printing function, Service 9 of INT 21H, so we start by optimistically loading DX with the address of the no error message, NOPROB:

```
           .MODEL SMALL
           .CODE
           .8087
           ORG     100H
ENTRY:     JMP     PROG
           OP1     DQ 10.0
           OP2     DQ 5.0
           OP3     DQ 0.0
       → NOPROB  DB 'No '
       → PROB    DB 'Divide by Zero',13,10,'$'
```

▶ Using the 80×87

```
             ST8087   DW    0
             SW RECORD B:1,C3:1,TOP:3,C2:1,C1:1,C0:1,IT:1,X:1,P:1,U:1,O:1,Z:1,D:1,I:1
    PROG:    FINIT
             FLD      OP1
             FDIV     OP2
          →  MOV      AH,9
          →  LEA      DX,NOPROB
             FSTSW    ST8087
             TEST     ST8087,MASK Z
             JZ       OK1
             LEA      DX,PROB
    OK1:     INT      21H
             :
             :
```

To check if there really was no error, we store the status word in a memory location we have set aside, ST8087, using the instruction FSTSW ST8087. We can check to see if the zero-divide bit was set with TEST ST8087, MASK Z:

```
             .MODEL SMALL
             .CODE
             .8087
             ORG      100H
    ENTRY:   JMP      PROG
             OP1      DQ    10.0
             OP2      DQ    5.0
             OP3      DQ    0.0
             NOPROB   DB    'No '
             PROB     DB    'Divide by Zero',13,10,'$'
          →  ST8087   DW    0
          →  SW RECORD B:1,C3:1,TOP:3,C2:1,C1:1,C0:1,IT:1,X:1,P:1,U:1,O:1,Z:1,D:1,I:1
    PROG:    FINIT
             FLD      OP1
             FDIV     OP2
             MOV      AH,9
             LEA      DX,NOPROB
          →  FSTSW    ST8087
          →  TEST     ST8087,MASK Z
             JZ       OK1
             LEA      DX,PROB
    OK1:     INT      21H
             :
             :
```

If the result of this TEST is zero, the zero-bit flag was not set. In that case, we want to print out the default message, NOPROB. Otherwise, of course, there has been an error, so we must load the address of the error message PROB into DX. We print out the results with INT 21H:

354 ▶ Advanced Assembly Language

```
                .MODEL  SMALL
                .CODE
                .8087
                ORG     100H
ENTRY:          JMP     PROG
                OP1     DQ      10.0
                OP2     DQ      5.0
                OP3     DQ      0.0
                NOPROB  DB      'No '
                PROB    DB      'Divide by Zero',13,10,'$'
                ST8087  DW      0
                SW      RECORD  B:1,C3:1,TOP:3,C2:1,C1:1,C0:1,IT:1,X:1,P:1,U:1,O:1,Z:1,D:1,I:1
PROG:           FINIT
                FLD     OP1
                FDIV    OP2
                MOV     AH,9
                LEA     DX,NOPROB
                FSTSW   ST8087
       →        TEST    ST8087,MASK Z
       →        JZ      OK1
       →        LEA     DX,PROB
OK1:            INT     21H
                :
                :
```

The code for the second division is the same as for the first. After using FCLEX, then FINIT to be sure, we divide OP1 by OP3 and print out the result in the same way:

```
                .MODEL  SMALL
                .CODE
                .8087
                ORG     100H
ENTRY:          JMP     PROG
                OP1     DQ      10.0
                OP2     DQ      5.0
                OP3     DQ      0.0
                NOPROB  DB      'No '
                PROB    DB      'Divide by Zero',13,10,'$'
                ST8087  DW      0
                SW      RECORD  B:1,C3:1,TOP:3,C2:1,C1:1,C0:1,IT:1,X:1,P:1,U:1,O:1,Z:1,D:1,I:1
PROG:           FINIT
                FLD     OP1
                FDIV    OP2
                MOV     AH,9
                LEA     DX,NOPROB
                FSTSW   ST8087
                TEST    ST8087,MASK Z
                JZ      OK1
                LEA     DX,PROB
OK1:            INT     21H
       →        FCLEX
       →        FINIT
       →        FLD     OP1
       →        FDIV    OP3
                MOV     AH,9
                LEA     DX,NOPROB
                FSTSW   ST8087
                TEST    ST8087,MASK Z
```

```
            JZ      OK2
            LEA     DX,PROB
OK2:        INT     21H
            INT     20H
            END     ENTRY
```

This second case is the one that does yield an error. In general, error checking on the 80×87 is not difficult, thanks to the status word. We've worked our way from doing things correctly to doing them incorrectly. That finishes our discussion of the 80×87. Next, let's turn to Microsoft Windows, a very popular programming topic.

▶ Chapter 12

Using Microsoft Windows

▶ Using Microsoft Windows 359

ONE OF THE hottest programming topics around is Microsoft Windows, and we'll take a look at that package in this chapter. Our object in this chapter will be to write a program that uses the Windows system to set up and maintain a window on the screen. We'll set up our own application that lets you make that window visible, draw lines, ellipses, or rectangles in it with the mouse, and print characters, all from an assembly language point of view.

In this chapter, we'll interface assembly language programming to Windows, but we will only be able to provide an introduction to Windows programming itself. There are many thick books on Windows, and, if you're interested, you should work through them after we cover the fundamentals of programming Windows in assembly language.

The reason those books are so thick is that programming a Windows application is not an easy task, as we'll see. The whole topic is involved and can become extremely complex, although not as complex as the OS/2 Presentation Manager, which will take two chapters later in this book.

Writing a program to handle Windows will be just like writing any other program, except that we have to name our program WinMain. This is the name that the Windows system will look for when we link it in. All our initialization — designing the windows, putting them on the screen and so on — will be done in WinMain.

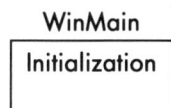

Figure 12-1.

When things happen that we should know about, such as the mouse being clicked in our window, another window covering ours up, or whatever, the Windows system will send us *messages*. We will handle these by setting up a *message loop* in WinMain:

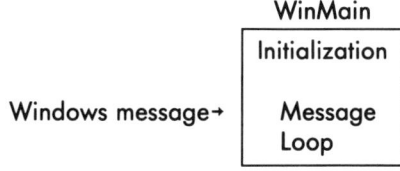

Figure 12-2.

However, the actual work of responding to the messages by adjusting our window will be done by a second function that we can name DecodeMessages (this is the way

Windows programs work: WinMain sends the messages it receives off to a new function that we'll have to *register* with Windows):

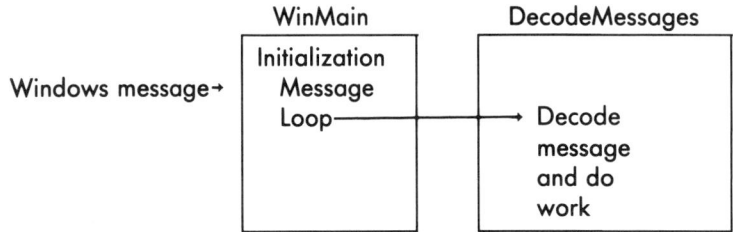

Figure 12-3.

DecodeMessages is where the action is. Every time something happens — the mouse is moved, a mouse button is pressed, or maybe a key is struck — a message is sent to our program. First it goes to WinMain and through the message loop, and on to us in DecodeMessages. We decode the message there and take the appropriate action.

It is DecodeMessages( ) that we're going to write in assembly language. However, we will also give a brief (and optional) discussion of how to write the function WinMain( ) in C for interested readers. (If you're not interested, just skip that section.)

We'll use Windows 3.0 in this chapter. The bad news is that you'll also need special library files from the Windows Software Development Kit (SDK) before writing your own applications. This kit is expensive, but it does contain the libraries we'll need to use (like SLIBCEW.LIB, LIBW.LIB, and SNOCRT.LIB).

Window Messages

The way Windows lets us know what's going on is by passing us messages. When our function DecodeMessages is called, the call looks like this:

```
DecodeMessages(Handle, Message, Wparam, Lparam);
```

where Handle is a word-long window handle (all handles in Windows are one word long, although in the OS/2 Presentation Manager, they are two words long), Message is the code value of the action that occurred, and Wparam and Lparam are one-word and two-word parameters associated with the message.

The message codes are defined in the Windows SDK file Windows.h. For example, if a key is typed, we'll get a WM_CHAR value for Message, the key's ASCII code will be in

Wparam, and other information, including the scan code, will be in Lparam. Here's a list of some of the messages we might receive.

Windows Messages

Message	Hex value
WM_NULL	0000H
WM_CREATE	0001H
WM_DESTROY	0002H
WM_MOVE	0003H
WM_SIZE	0005H
WM_ACTIVATE	0006H
WM_PAINT	000FH
WM_CLOSE	0010H
WM_QUIT	0012H
WM_ERASEBKGND	0014H
WM_SHOWWINDOW	0018H
WM_SETCURSOR	0020H
WM_MOUSEACTIVATE	0021H
WM_PAINTICON	0026H
WM_DRAWITEM	002BH
WM_DELETEITEM	002DH
WM_KEYFIRST	0100H
WM_KEYDOWN	0100H
WM_KEYUP	0101H
WM_CHAR	0102H
WM_DEADCHAR	0103H
WM_COMMAND	0111H
WM_TIMER	0113H
WM_HSCROLL	0114H
WM_VSCROLL	0115H
WM_INITMENU	0116H
WM_INITMENUPOPUP	0117H
WM_MENUSELECT	011FH
WM_MENUCHAR	0120H
WM_MOUSEFIRST	0200H
WM_MOUSEMOVE	0200H
WM_LBUTTONDOWN	0201H

362 ▶ Advanced Assembly Language

Text Value	Message
WM_LBUTTONUP	0202H
WM_LBUTTONDBLCLK	0203H
WM_RBUTTONDOWN	0204H
WM_RBUTTONUP	0205H
WM_RBUTTONDBLCLK	0206H
WM_MBUTTONDOWN	0207H
WM_MBUTTONUP	0208H
WM_MBUTTONDBLCLK	0209H
WM_MOUSELAST	0209H
WM_CUT	0300H
WM_COPY	0301H
WM_PASTE	0302H
WM_CLEAR	0303H
WM_UNDO	0304H

You should check the Windows SDK documentation to learn what messages correspond to what actions. For example, if the left mouse button is pushed, we'd get a WM_LBUTTONDOWN message (hex value 0201H) in DecodeMessages( ), and then we could take the appropriate action.

Now that we have an overview of the process, let's work through the WinMain( ) function. This section is optional and is included only for interested readers who want to get a headstart in programming Windows. We won't spend much time on the development of this program (what follows is just a standard version of WinMain( )).

WinMain — The Main Window Function

WinMain, as its name suggests, takes the place of a main procedure in a Windows application. As soon as our application is loaded, WinMain will be called (from the Windows package itself) this way:

```
int PASCAL WinMain(hInstance, hPrevInstance, lpCmdLine, nCmdShow)
```

The one word handle hInstance is the handle for this instance of our application program. Windows can run multiple copies of any application, and this handle specifies the current program. The one word handle hPrevInstance is 0, if this is the only instance of this application running in the current Windows session, and nonzero otherwise. This will be important for us in WinMain, if our application has run before, we won't need to design and initialize the kind of window we want to use. Windows will already have that information.

The long pointer lpCmdLine is a pointer to a string containing the command line text. Its type, defined in Windows.h, is LPSTR (just a far pointer to a char). For example, if our application is named MYWINDOW, and we started it like this: "MYWINDOW Hello there", lpCmdLine would be pointing to the C string " Hello there" (in C, strings are terminated with a 0, so this string is the same as DB " Hello there", 0).

The final parameter is the word long nCmdShow, which indicates how the program is initially going to be displayed under Windows. This number is usually 1. Note that WinMain( ) is a C function: it will return an integer value to Windows. Let's start writing WinMain immediately, like this:

```
#include <windows.h>
int PASCAL WinMain(HANDLE, HANDLE, LPSTR, int);
    :
```

Here we are using the Windows type definition LPSTR (as defined in Windows.h) to indicate a long pointer type. One interesting point is that even though the SDK is designed around C, it actually uses the more robust PASCAL calling convention, not the C calling convention.

For that reason, we have to include the keyword PASCAL in the definition of WinMain above. We are also leaving this function as a NEAR function. It is initialization code, so it will be called from the same code segment as the main Windows code.

We need to declare DecodeMessages( ) next. Since we're going to write DecodeMessages( ) in assembly language, it will be in a different file, so, as in the last chapter, we have to declare it EXTERN. Recall that DecodeMessages( ) is called like this:

```
DecodeMessages(Handle, Message, Wparam, Lparam);
```

So we can set it up like this in WinMain, where HWND is defined in Windows.h as the variable type for a main window:

```
#include <windows.h>

int PASCAL WinMain(HANDLE, HANDLE, LPSTR, int);
extern long FAR PASCAL DecodeMessages(HWND, unsigned, WORD, LONG);   ←
    :
```

364 ▶ Advanced Assembly Language

Notice that we're making DecodeMessages FAR, and that it is also a function, returning a long (doubleword) value. Windows expects this function to be FAR, so we'll have to plan accordingly when we write DecodeMessages. Next, we have to set up the types of Windows variables we'll need in WinMain itself:

```
#include <windows.h>

int PASCAL WinMain(HANDLE, HANDLE, LPSTR, int);
extern long FAR PASCAL DecodeMessages(HWND, unsigned, WORD, LONG);

int PASCAL WinMain(hInstance, hPrevInstance, lpCmdLine, nCmdShow)
HANDLE hInstance;
HANDLE hPrevInstance;
LPSTR  lpCmdLine;                   /* command line */
int    nCmdShow;                    /* show-window type (open/icon) */
{
    MSG      msg;                   /* message */
    WNDCLASS Our_class;
    HWND     hWnd;                  /* Main window handle. */
    :
```

The three types of variables we'll need are handles (HWND), which are one-word integers, messages (MSGs) and window classes (WNDCLASS). The message structure, MSG, is defined like this in Windows.h:

```
{
    HWND   Hwnd;
    WORD   Message;
    WORD   Wparam;
    LONG   Lparam;
    DWORD  Time;
    POINT  Pt;
} MSG;
```

Here, Message, Wparam, and Lparam are just the same values that passed to DecodeMessages. When we receive a message, we'll be able to read values either from this MSG structure, or as passed to DecodeMessages. The POINT structure is used to pass points on the screen and is defined like this:

```
{
  int x;
  int y;
} POINT;
```

The Window Class structure, which we'll need to define the type of window which we want to use, looks like this:

```
{
    WORD     style;
    LONG     (FAR PASCAL *lpfnWndProc)();
    int      cbClsExtra;
    int      cbWndExtra;
    HANDLE   hInstance;
    HICON    hIcon;
    HCURSOR  hCursor;
    HBRUSH   hbrBackground;
    LPSTR    lpszMenuName;
    LPSTR    lpszClassName;
} WNDCLASS;
```

Every object that begins with an "H" (e.g., HICON, HCURSOR, etc) is a handle, and we already know they are one word long. The LPSTR object is just a FAR pointer, defined like this:

```
typedef char far    *LPSTR;
```

Now that we have the types of variables and structures we'll need, let's start the WinMain code. The first thing we'll do is determine whether or not we have to set up the type of window we want, a process called *registering* a window lass. If our application is already running, then that job was done, so we check that with hPrevInstance, which is 0 if we're the first:

```
#include <windows.h>

int PASCAL WinMain(HANDLE, HANDLE, LPSTR, int);
extern long FAR PASCAL DecodeMessages(HWND, unsigned, WORD, LONG);

int PASCAL WinMain(hInstance, hPrevInstance, lpCmdLine, nCmdShow)
HANDLE hInstance;
HANDLE hPrevInstance;
LPSTR lpCmdLine;                     /* command line */
int nCmdShow;                        /* show-window type (open/icon) */
{
    MSG msg;                         /* message */
    WNDCLASS  Our_class;
    HWND hWnd;                       /* Main window handle.  */

    if (!hPrevInstance)
        {

        }
        :
```

If hPrevInstance is zero, we've got to register the class of window we want. We'll do that by first filling our Window Class structure with common default values (some of which are defined in Windows.h):

```c
#include <windows.h>

int PASCAL WinMain(HANDLE, HANDLE, LPSTR, int);
extern long FAR PASCAL DecodeMessages(HWND, unsigned, WORD, LONG);

int PASCAL WinMain(hInstance, hPrevInstance, lpCmdLine, nCmdShow)
HANDLE hInstance;
HANDLE hPrevInstance;
LPSTR lpCmdLine;                    /* command line */
int nCmdShow;                       /* show-window type (open/icon) */
{
    MSG msg;                        /* message */
    WNDCLASS Our_class;
    HWND hWnd;                      /* Main window handle. */

    if (!hPrevInstance)
    {
        Our_class.style = NULL;                     /* Class style.                  */
        Our_class.lpfnWndProc = DecodeMessages;     /* Function for messages         */
        Our_class.cbClsExtra = 0;                   /* No class extra data.          */
        Our_class.cbWndExtra = 0;                   /* No window extra data.         */
        Our_class.hInstance = hInstance;            /* App. that owns the class.     */
        Our_class.hIcon = LoadIcon(NULL, IDI_APPLICATION);
        Our_class.hCursor = LoadCursor(NULL, IDC_ARROW);
        Our_class.hbrBackground = GetStockObject(WHITE_BRUSH);
        Our_class.lpszMenuName = "";    /* Name of menu resource in .RC file. */
        Our_class.lpszClassName = "MyWClass"; /* Used CreateWindow call. */
        :
    }
    :
```

We'll call our class of window MyWClass, the "we-can-pass-this-structure-to-the-Windows-function-RegisterClass( )." If RegisterClass( ) returns a zero, the registration failed and we have to exit, returning a value of FALSE (defined as 0 in Windows.h) as the value of WinMain( ):

```c
#include <windows.h>

int PASCAL WinMain(HANDLE, HANDLE, LPSTR, int);
extern long FAR PASCAL DecodeMessages(HWND, unsigned, WORD, LONG);

int PASCAL WinMain(hInstance, hPrevInstance, lpCmdLine, nCmdShow)
HANDLE hInstance;
HANDLE hPrevInstance;
LPSTR lpCmdLine;                    /* command line */
int nCmdShow;                       /* show-window type (open/icon) */
{
    MSG msg;                        /* message */
    WNDCLASS Our_class;
    HWND hWnd;                      /* Main window handle. */
```

```c
    if (!hPrevInstance)
        {
        Our_class.style = NULL;                     /* Class style.                */
        Our_class.lpfnWndProc = DecodeMessages;     /* Function for messages       */
        Our_class.cbClsExtra = 0;                   /* No class extra data.        */
        Our_class.cbWndExtra = 0;                   /* No window extra data.       */
        Our_class.hInstance = hInstance;            /* App. that owns the class.   */
        Our_class.hIcon = LoadIcon(NULL, IDI_APPLICATION);
        Our_class.hCursor = LoadCursor(NULL, IDC_ARROW);
        Our_class.hbrBackground = GetStockObject(WHITE_BRUSH);
        Our_class.lpszMenuName = "";                /* Name of menu resource in .RC file. */
        Our_class.lpszClassName = "MyWClass";       /* Used CreateWindow call. */

←       if (!RegisterClass(&Our_class)) return (FALSE);
        }
```

If the registration was successful, we can put our registered class of window, MyWClass, to work with the Windows function CreateWindow( ). We call it like this:

```c
#include <windows.h>

int PASCAL WinMain(HANDLE, HANDLE, LPSTR, int);
extern long FAR PASCAL DecodeMessages(HWND, unsigned, WORD, LONG);

int PASCAL WinMain(hInstance, hPrevInstance, lpCmdLine, nCmdShow)
HANDLE hInstance;
HANDLE hPrevInstance;
LPSTR lpCmdLine;                        /* command line */
int nCmdShow;                           /* show-window type (open/icon) */
{
    MSG msg;                            /* message */
    WNDCLASS Our_class;
    HWND hWnd;                          /* Main window handle. */

    if (!hPrevInstance)
        {
        Our_class.style = NULL;                     /* Class style.                */
        Our_class.lpfnWndProc = DecodeMessages;     /* Function for messages       */
        Our_class.cbClsExtra = 0;                   /* No class extra data.        */
        Our_class.cbWndExtra = 0;                   /* No window extra data.       */
        Our_class.hInstance = hInstance;            /* App. that owns the class.   */
        Our_class.hIcon = LoadIcon(NULL, IDI_APPLICATION);
        Our_class.hCursor = LoadCursor(NULL, IDC_ARROW);
        Our_class.hbrBackground = GetStockObject(WHITE_BRUSH);
        Our_class.lpszMenuName = "";                /* Name of menu resource in .RC file. */
        Our_class.lpszClassName = "MyWClass";       /* Used CreateWindow call. */

        if (!RegisterClass(&Our_class)) return (FALSE);
        }

    hWnd = CreateWindow( ←
        "MyWClass",                     /* Class name.                 */
        "My Window",                    /* Window title bar.           */
        WS_OVERLAPPEDWINDOW,            /* Window style.               */
        CW_USEDEFAULT,                  /* Default horizontal position. */
        CW_USEDEFAULT,                  /* Default vertical position.  */
        CW_USEDEFAULT,                  /* Default width.              */
```

368 ▶ Advanced Assembly Language

```
            CW_USEDEFAULT,              /* Default height.                   */
            NULL,                       /* No parent.                        */
            NULL,                       /* Use the window class menu.        */
            hInstance,                  /* This instance owns this window.   */
            NULL                        /* Pointer not needed.               */
    );

    if (!hWnd) return (FALSE);
        :
```

Again, see the Windows SDK documentation for learning more about these options (all the constants are defined in Windows.h). CreateWindow( ) returns hWnd, the handle for our window. If this handle is 0, the creation was unsuccessful, and we have to return a value of FALSE and exit. If we were successful, however, we can show the window with the Windows function ShowWindow( ) and then "paint" it with UpdateWindow( ). ShowWindow( ) puts the window on the screen (in the default positon we specified to CreateWindow( )), and UpdateWindow( ) tells our function DecodeMessages( ) to fill in the window the way we want it:

```c
#include <windows.h>

int PASCAL WinMain(HANDLE, HANDLE, LPSTR, int);
extern long FAR PASCAL DecodeMessages(HWND, unsigned, WORD, LONG);

int PASCAL WinMain(hInstance, hPrevInstance, lpCmdLine, nCmdShow)
HANDLE hInstance;
HANDLE hPrevInstance;
LPSTR lpCmdLine;                    /* command line */
int nCmdShow;                       /* show-window type (open/icon) */
{
    MSG msg;                        /* message */
    WNDCLASS Our_class;
    HWND hWnd;                      /* Main window handle. */

    if (!hPrevInstance)
    {
        Our_class.style = NULL;                     /* Class style.                */
        Our_class.lpfnWndProc = DecodeMessages;     /* Function for messages       */
        Our_class.cbClsExtra = 0;                   /* No class extra data.        */
        Our_class.cbWndExtra = 0;                   /* No window extra data.       */
        Our_class.hInstance = hInstance;            /* App. that owns the class.   */
        Our_class.hIcon = LoadIcon(NULL, IDI_APPLICATION);
        Our_class.hCursor = LoadCursor(NULL, IDC_ARROW);
        Our_class.hbrBackground = GetStockObject(WHITE_BRUSH);
        Our_class.lpszMenuName = "";    /* Name of menu resource in .RC file. */
        Our_class.lpszClassName = "MyWClass"; /* Used CreateWindow call. */

        if (!RegisterClass(&Our_class)) return (FALSE);
    }
    hWnd = CreateWindow(
        "MyWClass",                 /* Class name.                       */
        "My Window",                /* Window title bar.                 */
        WS_OVERLAPPEDWINDOW,        /* Window style.                     */
        CW_USEDEFAULT,              /* Default horizontal position.      */
```

```
            CW_USEDEFAULT,              /* Default vertical position.      */
            CW_USEDEFAULT,              /* Default width.                  */
            CW_USEDEFAULT,              /* Default height.                 */
            NULL,                       /* No parent.                      */
            NULL,                       /* Use the window class menu.      */
            hInstance,                  /* This instance owns this window. */
            NULL                        /* Pointer not needed.             */
        );

        if (!hWnd) return (FALSE);

►       ShowWindow(hWnd, nCmdShow);     /* Show the window.        */
►       UpdateWindow(hWnd);             /* Sends WM_PAINT message. */
            :
```

At this point, the window is on the screen. Now we're ready to start receiving messages. We do that with the message loop, which looks like this:

```
#include <windows.h>

int PASCAL WinMain(HANDLE, HANDLE, LPSTR, int);
extern long FAR PASCAL DecodeMessages(HWND, unsigned, WORD, LONG);

int PASCAL WinMain(hInstance, hPrevInstance, lpCmdLine, nCmdShow)
HANDLE hInstance;
HANDLE hPrevInstance;
LPSTR lpCmdLine;                        /* command line */
int nCmdShow;                           /* show-window type (open/icon) */
{
    MSG msg;                            /* message */
    WNDCLASS Our_class;
    HWND hWnd;                          /* Main window handle. */

    if (!hPrevInstance)
        {
        Our_class.style = NULL;                  /* Class style.              */
        Our_class.lpfnWndProc = DecodeMessages;  /* Function for messages     */
        Our_class.cbClsExtra = 0;                /* No class extra data.      */
        Our_class.cbWndExtra = 0;                /* No window extra data.     */
        Our_class.hInstance = hInstance;         /* App. that owns the class. */
        Our_class.hIcon = LoadIcon(NULL, IDI_APPLICATION);
        Our_class.hCursor = LoadCursor(NULL, IDC_ARROW);
        Our_class.hbrBackground = GetStockObject(WHITE_BRUSH);
        Our_class.lpszMenuName = "";             /* Name of menu resource in .RC file. */
        Our_class.lpszClassName = "MyWClass";    /* Used CreateWindow call. */

        if (!RegisterClass(&Our_class)) return (FALSE);
        }
    hWnd = CreateWindow(
            "MyWClass",                 /* Class name.                     */
            "My Window",                /* Window title bar.               */
            WS_OVERLAPPEDWINDOW,        /* Window style.                   */
            CW_USEDEFAULT,              /* Default horizontal position.    */
            CW_USEDEFAULT,              /* Default vertical position.      */
            CW_USEDEFAULT,              /* Default width.                  */
            CW_USEDEFAULT,              /* Default height.                 */
            NULL,                       /* No parent.                      */
            NULL,                       /* Use the window class menu.      */
```

```
            hInstance,                  /* This instance owns this window.   */
            NULL                        /* Pointer not needed.               */
        );

        if (!hWnd) return (FALSE);

        ShowWindow(hWnd, nCmdShow);     /* Show the window.                  */
        UpdateWindow(hWnd);             /* Sends WM_PAINT message.           */

->      while (GetMessage(&msg,         /* the message structure */
:           NULL,                       /* handle of window receiving the message */
:           NULL,                       /* lowest message to accept */
            NULL))                      /* highest message to accept */
        {
            TranslateMessage(&msg);     /* Translates key codes */
            DispatchMessage(&msg);      /* Dispatches message to window function */
        }
        :
```

First, we call the function GetMessage( ). When a message is ready, control returns to us. Some of these messages, however, need further translation before we can work on them. For example, if a key was typed, we would only get the scan code after GetMessage( ). To "translate" the message fully, we call TranslateMessage(&msg), where msg is our message variable. In this case, the word parameter Wparam is filled with the ASCII code. Finally, we're ready to send the message off to DecodeMessages( ), which we do by calling the Windows function DispatchMessage( ). Now decoding the message and taking the correct action is up to DecodeMessages( ).

If GetMessage( ) returns a value of FALSE, the window is being destroyed, and we have to exit. In that case, we get a chance to return an exit code in WinMain with a function named PostQuitMessage( ). We also have to return the word long parameter as our final return value from WinMain. And that's it; the whole function is in Listing 12-1.

Listing 12-1. WINMAIN.C — Main Window Function.

```
#include <windows.h>

int PASCAL WinMain(HANDLE, HANDLE, LPSTR, int);
extern long FAR PASCAL DecodeMessages(HWND, unsigned, WORD, LONG);

int PASCAL WinMain(hInstance, hPrevInstance, lpCmdLine, nCmdShow)
HANDLE hInstance;
HANDLE hPrevInstance;
LPSTR lpCmdLine;                        /* command line */
int nCmdShow;                           /* show-window type (open/icon) */
{
    MSG msg;                            /* message */
    WNDCLASS Our_class;
    HWND hWnd;                          /* Main window handle.  */

    if (!hPrevInstance)
    {
        Our_class.style = NULL;                    /* Class style.         */
```

Listing 12-1. WINMAIN.C — Main Window Function.

```
    Our_class.lpfnWndProc = DecodeMessages; /* Function for messages   */
    Our_class.cbClsExtra = 0;                /* No class extra data.    */
    Our_class.cbWndExtra = 0;                /* No window extra data.   */
    Our_class.hInstance = hInstance;         /* App. that owns the class. */
    Our_class.hIcon = LoadIcon(NULL, IDI_APPLICATION);
    Our_class.hCursor = LoadCursor(NULL, IDC_ARROW);
    Our_class.hbrBackground = GetStockObject(WHITE_BRUSH);
    Our_class.lpszMenuName = "";    /* Name of menu resource in .RC file. */
    Our_class.lpszClassName = "MyWClass"; /* Used CreateWindow call. */

    if (!RegisterClass(&Our_class)) return (FALSE);
    }

    hWnd = CreateWindow(
        "MyWClass",             /* Class name.                          */
        "My Window",            /* Window title bar.                    */
        WS_OVERLAPPEDWINDOW,    /* Window style.                        */
        CW_USEDEFAULT,          /* Default horizontal position.         */
        CW_USEDEFAULT,          /* Default vertical position.           */
        CW_USEDEFAULT,          /* Default width.                       */
        CW_USEDEFAULT,          /* Default height.                      */
        NULL,                   /* No parent.                           */
        NULL,                   /* Use the window class menu.           */
        hInstance,              /* This instance owns this window.      */
        NULL                    /* Pointer not needed.                  */
    );

    if (!hWnd) return (FALSE);

    ShowWindow(hWnd, nCmdShow);  /* Show the window.           */
    UpdateWindow(hWnd);          /* Sends WM_PAINT message.    */

    while (GetMessage(&msg,      /* the message structure */
        NULL,                    /* handle of window receiving the message */
        NULL,                    /* lowest message to accept */
        NULL))                   /* highest message to accept */
    {
    TranslateMessage(&msg);      /* Translates key codes */
    DispatchMessage(&msg);       /* Dispatches message to window function */
    }
    return (msg.wParam);         /* Returns the value from PostQuitMessage */
}
```

DecodeMessages — Where the Action Is

Now that WinMain is done, we come at last to the real action, DecodeMessages( ), the part that we're going to write in assembly language. The task of this function will be to receive and decode Window messages. DecodeMessages( ) gets called when the window is being set up, or whenever it's supposed to be changed, and we've got to be ready to handle it. We can start by declaring the memory model we'll use, which will be the SMALL model (the model is determined by what Windows libraries we link to, and we'll use the SMALL model libraries):

372 ▶ Advanced Assembly Language

```
.MODEL  SMALL
.286
        :
```

We also enable the assembly of 80286 instructions because we'll need at least an 80286 to run Windows. Next we make our function PUBLIC so that we can link it in with WinMain:

```
.MODEL  SMALL
.286
        PUBLIC  DecodeMessages
        :
```

TIP If you're an experienced Windows programmer, you should note that making this procedure PUBLIC takes the place of listing it as EXPORTed in the .DEF file. There is no need to use EXPORT.

Now we can set up our data and code segments:

```
.MODEL  SMALL
.286
        PUBLIC  DecodeMessages
.DATA
        :
.CODE
DecodeMessages PROC FAR
        :
```

As mentioned before, we have to make this procedure FAR. For that reason, Windows may (and in fact does) call us with values in DS that do not correspond to our data segment. Therefore, our first action will be to set DS to .DATA:

```
.MODEL  SMALL
.286
        PUBLIC  DecodeMessages
.DATA
        OLD_DS          DW 0
.CODE
```

```
DecodeMessages PROC FAR
→       PUSH    DS          ;Use our data seg.
→       PUSH    @DATA
→       POP     DS
→       POP     OLD_DS
        :
```

Note that we save the old value of DS so that we can restore it before returning to Windows. Our function was called this way:

```
DecodeMessages(Handle, Message, Wparam, Lparam);
```

and we'll want to strip those values off the stack, particularly Message, which contains the message that we're supposed to decode. Unfortunately, we cannot use the extended PROC directive that we saw in the previous chapter. We won't be able to let the assembler handle all the details for us here because we'll have to do a little stack manipulation later. In fact, let's start DecodeMessages( ) by stripping all the parameters off the stack:

```
        .MODEL  SMALL
        .286
                PUBLIC  DecodeMessages
        .DATA
                OLD_DS          DW 0

                RET1            DW 0
                RET2            DW 0
                LPARAM_LO       DW 0
                LPARAM_HI       DW 0
                WPARAM          DW 0
                MSG             DW 0
                HWND            DW 0

        .CODE
DecodeMessages PROC FAR
                PUSH    DS          ;Use our data seg.
                PUSH    @DATA
                POP     DS
                POP     OLD_DS
→               POP     RET1        ;Pull params off stack
:               POP     RET2
                POP     LPARAM_LO
                POP     LPARAM_HI
                POP     WPARAM
                POP     MSG
                POP     HWND
```

```
              PUSH    RET2
              PUSH    RET1
              :
```

Notice that we pop the return address off the stack first and then push it back on the stack at the end. In that way, we've stripped off the parameters, and we're ready to return at the end of DecodeMessages( ) with a simple RET (which the assembler will make a FAR return, since this procedure is FAR).

Now we can examine the message passed to us in MSG and act accordingly. Let's start by seeing if our window is being closed. This is the one case we'll always have to handle. In this case, the normal way of finishing, we'll get a message (in MSG) of WM_DESTRY, which has a value of 2. This means (see the Windows SDK documentation) that we're supposed to call the special Windows function PostQuitMessage(Code), where Code is a one word exit Code (we'll use 0). We can do that like this (notice that we had to declare PostQuitMessage( ) as EXTRN):

```
.MODEL  SMALL

.286
        PUBLIC  DecodeMessages
        EXTRN   PostQuitMessage:FAR

.DATA

        OLD_DS          DW  0

        RET1            DW  0
        RET2            DW  0
        LPARAM_LO       DW  0
        LPARAM_HI       DW  0
        WPARAM          DW  0
        MSG             DW  0
        HWND            DW  0

.CODE

DecodeMessages PROC FAR

        PUSH    DS              ;Use our data seg.
        PUSH    @DATA
        POP     DS
        POP     OLD_DS

        POP     RET1            ;Pull params off stack
        POP     RET2
        POP     LPARAM_LO
        POP     LPARAM_HI
        POP     WPARAM
        POP     MSG
        POP     HWND
        PUSH    RET2
        PUSH    RET1
```

```
          →     CMP       MSG,2              ;Window destroyed?
          →     JNE       NOT_DESTROYED:
    DESTROYED:
          →     PUSH      0
          →     CALL      PostQuitMessage
          →     JMP       RET_0
          :     :
    NOT_DESTROYED:
                :
                :
    RET_0:

                PUSH      OLD_DS    ;Restore DS
                POP       DS

                MOV       AX,0      ;RETURN 0
                MOV       DX,0
                RET

    DecodeMessages    ENDP

                END
```

Notice at the end that we restore the old data segment value in DS before leaving and return a long value (i.e., DX and AX) of 0. So far, we're able to exit but nothing else. Let's add the ability to read keys from the keyboard. Our program is designed to read and print keys, as well as draw ellipses, lines, and rectangles. We can set it up so that, when you press "l," we turn on the line drawing function. "e" turns on the ellipse-drawing function and "r" the rectangle drawing function. Any other character should be printed in the window.

To begin, we'll receive a WM_CHAR message, value 102H as defined in Windows.h, when a character is typed (we cannot "include" Windows.h in our assembly language file, but we can use the values of those messages in our code):

```
    .MODEL   SMALL
    .286
             PUBLIC    DecodeMessages
             EXTRN     PostQuitMessage:FAR

    .DATA

             OLD_DS         DW 0

             RET1           DW 0
             RET2           DW 0
             LPARAM_LO      DW 0
             LPARAM_HI      DW 0
             WPARAM         DW 0
             MSG            DW 0
             HWND           DW 0

    .CODE
```

376 ▶ Advanced Assembly Language

```
DecodeMessages PROC FAR

        PUSH    DS          ;Use our data seg.
        PUSH    @DATA
        POP     DS
        POP     OLD_DS

        POP     RET1        ;Pull params off stack
        POP     RET2
        POP     LPARAM_LO
        POP     LPARAM_HI
        POP     WPARAM
        POP     MSG
        POP     HWND
        PUSH    RET2
        PUSH    RET1

        CMP     MSG,2       ;Window destroyed?
        JNE     KEY
DESTROYED:
        PUSH    0
        CALL    PostQuitMessage
        JMP     RET_0

KEY:    CMP     MSG,102H    ;Key pressed?
        JNE     NOT_KEY
        :
        :
RET_0:
```

At this point, we know that a key was typed. Now we have to determine if an "l," "e," or "r" was pressed (activating our line, ellipse, or rectangle functions). The Windows SDK documentation indicates that the ASCII code of the struck key is in WPARAM, so we can move it to a new memory location, CHAR_OUT. Now we've read the key.

The only keys we'll interpret are "l," "e," and "r." We can keep track of which one(s) have been typed with flags like LINE_FLAG, ELLIPSE_FLAG, and RECTANGLE_FLAG:

```
.MODEL  SMALL

.286
        PUBLIC  DecodeMessages
        EXTRN   PostQuitMessage:FAR
.DATA

        OLD_DS          DW 0

        RET1            DW 0
        RET2            DW 0
        LPARAM_LO       DW 0
        LPARAM_HI       DW 0
        WPARAM          DW 0
        MSG             DW 0
        HWND            DW 0
```

```
        +       LINE_FLAG       DW 0        ;Drawing flags
        +       ELLIPSE_FLAG    DW 0
        +       RECTANGLE_FLAG  DW 0

        .CODE

DecodeMessages PROC FAR

                PUSH    DS          ;Use our data seg.
                PUSH    @DATA
                POP     DS
                POP     OLD_DS

                POP     RET1        ;Pull params off stack
                POP     RET2
                POP     LPARAM_LO
                POP     LPARAM_HI
                POP     WPARAM
                POP     MSG
                POP     HWND
                PUSH    RET2
                PUSH    RET1

                CMP     MSG,2           ;Window destroyed?
                JNE     KEY
DESTROYED:
                PUSH    0
                CALL    PostQuitMessage
                JMP     RET_0

KEY:            CMP     MSG,102H        ;Key pressed?
                JNE     NOT_KEY
                PUSH    HWND

                MOV     LINE_FLAG, 0            ;Reset drawing flags
                MOV     ELLIPSE_FLAG, 0
                MOV     RECTANGLE_FLAG, 0

                PUSH    WPARAM      ;ASCII code of the key
                POP     CHAR_OUT

                CMP     CHAR_OUT, "l"           +
                JNE     NOT_l                   :
                MOV     LINE_FLAG, 1
                JMP     RET_0
NOT_l:
                CMP     CHAR_OUT, "e"
                JNE     NOT_e
                MOV     ELLIPSE_FLAG, 1
                JMP     RET_0
NOT_e:
                CMP     CHAR_OUT, "r"
                JNE     NOT_r
                MOV     RECTANGLE_FLAG, 1
                JMP     RET_0
NOT_r:
                   :
                   :
RET_0:
```

378 ▶ Advanced Assembly Language

If a character was typed that wasn't "l," "e," or "r," we'll want to print it out. To do that, we need a handle to the *device context* of this window. This is the handle that we'll pass to the character printing service. To get this new handle, we have to pass the handle of the window to a Windows function named GetDC( ) like this:

```
        .MODEL  SMALL

        .286
                PUBLIC  DecodeMessages
                EXTRN   GetDC:FAR
                EXTRN   PostQuitMessage:FAR
        .DATA

                OLD_DS          DW 0

                RET1            DW 0
                RET2            DW 0
                LPARAM_LO       DW 0
                LPARAM_HI       DW 0
                WPARAM          DW 0
                MSG             DW 0
                HWND            DW 0

                LINE_FLAG       DW 0    ;Drawing flags
                ELLIPSE_FLAG    DW 0
                RECTANGLE_FLAG  DW 0

        .CODE

        DecodeMessages PROC FAR

                PUSH    DS              ;Use our data seg.
                PUSH    @DATA
                POP     DS
                POP     OLD_DS
                POP     RET1            ;Pull params off stack
                POP     RET2
                POP     LPARAM_LO
                POP     LPARAM_HI
                POP     WPARAM
                POP     MSG
                POP     HWND
                PUSH    RET2
                PUSH    RET1

                CMP     MSG,2           ;Window destroyed?
                JNE     KEY
        DESTROYED:
                PUSH    0
                CALL    PostQuitMessage
                JMP     RET_0

        KEY:    CMP     MSG,102H        ;Key pressed?
                JNE     NOT_KEY
                PUSH    HWND

                MOV     LINE_FLAG, 0    ;Reset drawing flags
                MOV     ELLIPSE_FLAG, 0
```

Using Microsoft Windows

```
                MOV     RECTANGLE_FLAG, 0

                PUSH    WPARAM  ;ASCII code of the key
                POP     CHAR_OUT

                CMP     CHAR_OUT, "l"
                JNE     NOT_l
                MOV     LINE_FLAG, 1
                JMP     RET_0
        NOT_l:
                CMP     CHAR_OUT, "e"
                JNE     NOT_e
                MOV     ELLIPSE_FLAG, 1
                JMP     RET_0
        NOT_e:
                CMP     CHAR_OUT, "r"
                JNE     NOT_r
                MOV     RECTANGLE_FLAG, 1
                JMP     RET_0
        NOT_r:
            *   PUSH    HWND
            :   CALL    GetDC
                MOV     HDC, AX
                :
                :
        RET_0:
```

Now we can use the Windows service TextOut( ) to actually print on the screen. We have to call it like this:

```
        CALL    TextOut(HDC, x, y, CHAR_OUT, CHAR_LEN)
```

Where HDC is the device context handle that we just got from GetDC( ), (x, y) are the local window (pixel) coordinates to print the character at ((0,0) is the upper left of the window, and that's where we'll print out the character), CHAR_OUT is the string to print. In this case, a single character, and CHAR_LEN is the length of the string (1 here).

In the Pascal calling convention, you pass strings by reference, which means that we'll have to pass the address of CHAR_OUT when we call TextOut( ). Finally, we release the device context with ReleaseDC( ) like this:

```
        .MODEL  SMALL

        .286
                PUBLIC  DecodeMessages
                EXTRN   GetDC:FAR, ReleaseDC:FAR, TextOut:FAR
                EXTRN   PostQuitMessage:FAR
        .DATA

                OLD_DS          DW 0
```

```
                RET1            DW 0
                RET2            DW 0
                LPARAM_LO       DW 0
                LPARAM_HI       DW 0
                WPARAM          DW 0
                MSG             DW 0
                HWND            DW 0

                LINE_FLAG       DW 0    ;Drawing flags
                ELLIPSE_FLAG    DW 0
                RECTANGLE_FLAG  DW 0

                CHAR_OUT        DW 0

        .CODE

        DecodeMessages PROC FAR

                PUSH    DS          ;Use our data seg.
                PUSH    @DATA
                POP     DS
                POP     OLD_DS

                POP     RET1        ;Pull params off stack
                POP     RET2
                POP     LPARAM_LO
                POP     LPARAM_HI
                POP     WPARAM
                POP     MSG
                POP     HWND
                PUSH    RET2
                PUSH    RET1

                CMP     MSG,2           ;Window destroyed?
                JNE     KEY
        DESTROYED:
                PUSH    0
                CALL    PostQuitMessage
                JMP     RET_0

        KEY:    CMP     MSG,102H        ;Key pressed?
                JNE     NOT_KEY

                MOV     LINE_FLAG, 0        ;Reset drawing flags
                MOV     ELLIPSE_FLAG, 0
                MOV     RECTANGLE_FLAG, 0

                PUSH    WPARAM      ;ASCII code of the key
                POP     CHAR_OUT

                CMP     CHAR_OUT, "l"
                JNE     NOT_l
                MOV     LINE_FLAG, 1
                JMP     RET_0
        NOT_l:
                CMP     CHAR_OUT, "e"
                JNE     NOT_e
                MOV     ELLIPSE_FLAG, 1
                JMP     RET_0
        NOT_e:
                CMP     CHAR_OUT, "r"
```

```
            JNE        NOT_r
            MOV        RECTANGLE_FLAG, 1
            JMP        RET_0
NOT_r:
            PUSH       HWND
            CALL       GetDC
            MOV        HDC, AX

            PUSH       HDC
            PUSH       0          ;x
            PUSH       0          ;y
            PUSH       DS
            PUSH       OFFSET DS:CHAR_OUT
            PUSH       1          ;String length
            CALL       TextOut

            PUSH       HWND
            PUSH       HDC
            CALL       ReleaseDC
            JMP        RET_0
            ;
RET_0:
```

In addition, Windows may ask us at any time to update our window (in fact, it already has when we called UpdateWindow( ) in WinMain( )) by sending us a WM_PAINT message. This is where we set up our window ("paint" it) as we want, filling it with text or whatever. We use a service called BeginPaint( ) here, which is the second way to get a device context handle. If we get a WM_PAINT message, 23H, then we start off by getting HDC, the device context handle, by calling BeginPaint(HWND, PAINT_STRUC), where HWND is the handle of the window and PAINT_STRUC is a paint structure set up like this:

```
PAINT_STRUC   LABEL   WORD
HDC      DW 0
FERASE   DW 0
RCPAINT  LABEL WORD
    LEFT     DW 0
    TOP      DW 0
    RIGHT    DW 0
    BOTTOM   DW 0
FRESTORE    DW 0
FINCUPDATE DW 0
RESERVED    DB 0
```

We'll just make the barest use of the WM_PAINT message in this demonstration program. First, we get a device context handle for the window space, HDC:

```
.MODEL   SMALL
.286
        PUBLIC  DecodeMessages
```

382 ▶ Advanced Assembly Language

```
        EXTRN   GetDC:FAR, ReleaseDC:FAR, TextOut:FAR, BeginPaint:FAR,
        EXTRN   PostQuitMessage:FAR

.DATA

        OLD_DS          DW 0

        RET1            DW 0
        RET2            DW 0
        LPARAM_LO       DW 0
        LPARAM_HI       DW 0
        WPARAM          DW 0
        MSG             DW 0
        HWND            DW 0

        LINE_FLAG       DW 0    ;Drawing flags
        ELLIPSE_FLAG    DW 0
        RECTANGLE_FLAG  DW 0

        CHAR_OUT        DW 0

→       PAINT_STRUC     LABEL   WORD
:       HDC      DW 0
        FERASE   DW 0
        RCPAINT LABEL WORD
          LEFT   DW 0
          TOP    DW 0
          RIGHT  DW 0
          BOTTOM DW 0
        FRESTORE  DW 0
:       FINCUPDATE DW 0
→       RESERVED   DB 0

.CODE

DecodeMessages PROC FAR

        PUSH    DS          ;Use our data seg.
        PUSH    @DATA
        POP     DS
        POP     OLD_DS

        POP     RET1        ;Pull params off stack
        POP     RET2
        POP     LPARAM_LO
        POP     LPARAM_HI
        POP     WPARAM
        POP     MSG
        POP     HWND
        PUSH    RET2
        PUSH    RET1

        CMP     MSG,2           ;Window destroyed?
        JNE     KEY
DESTROYED:
        PUSH    0
        CALL    PostQuitMessage
        JMP     RET_0

KEY:    CMP     MSG,102H        ;Key pressed?
        JNE     NOT_KEY
```

```
                MOV     LINE_FLAG, 0            ;Reset drawing flags
                MOV     ELLIPSE_FLAG, 0
                MOV     RECTANGLE_FLAG, 0

                PUSH    WPARAM  ;ASCII code of the key
                POP     CHAR_OUT

                CMP     CHAR_OUT, "l"
                JNE     NOT_l
                MOV     LINE_FLAG, 1
                JMP     RET_0
        NOT_l:
                CMP     CHAR_OUT, "e"
                JNE     NOT_e
                MOV     ELLIPSE_FLAG, 1
                JMP     RET_0
        NOT_e:
                CMP     CHAR_OUT, "r"
                JNE     NOT_r
                MOV     RECTANGLE_FLAG, 1
                JMP     RET_0
        NOT_r:
                PUSH    HWND
                CALL    GetDC
                MOV     HDC, AX

                PUSH    HDC
                PUSH    0       ;x
                PUSH    0       ;y
                PUSH    DS
                PUSH    OFFSET DS:CHAR_OUT
                PUSH    1       ;String length
                CALL    TextOut

                PUSH    HWND
                PUSH    HDC
                CALL    ReleaseDC
                JMP     RET_0

        NOT_KEY:
                CMP     MSG,23H
                JNE     NOT_PAINT
        PAINT:  PUSH    HWND
                PUSH    DS
                PUSH    OFFSET DS:PAINT_STRUC
                CALL    BeginPaint
                MOV     HDC, AX

                ;Do work
                :
```

Then we just use a Windows service named ValidateRect( ) that tells Windows our window is *valid* (if another window is moved on top of ours or some other similar change is made, our window is made invalid). Finally, we release the device context handle with EndPaint:

```
        .MODEL  SMALL

        .286
                PUBLIC  DecodeMessages
                EXTRN   GetDC:FAR, ReleaseDC:FAR, TextOut:FAR, BeginPaint:FAR,
                EXTRN   ValidateRect:FAR, EndPaint:FAR, PostQuitMessage:FAR

        .DATA

                OLD_DS          DW 0

                RET1            DW 0
                RET2            DW 0
                LPARAM_LO       DW 0
                LPARAM_HI       DW 0
                WPARAM          DW 0
                MSG             DW 0
                HWND            DW 0

                LINE_FLAG       DW 0    ;Drawing flags
                ELLIPSE_FLAG    DW 0
                RECTANGLE_FLAG  DW 0

                CHAR_OUT        DW 0

                PAINT_STRUC     LABEL   WORD
                HDC     DW 0
                FERASE  DW 0
                RCPAINT LABEL WORD
                  LEFT    DW 0
                  TOP     DW 0
                  RIGHT   DW 0
                  BOTTOM  DW 0
                FRESTORE   DW 0
                FINCUPDATE DW 0
                RESERVED   DB 0

        .CODE

        DecodeMessages PROC FAR

                PUSH    DS      ;Use our data seg.
                PUSH    @DATA
                POP     DS
                POP     OLD_DS

                POP     RET1    ;Pull params off stack
                POP     RET2
                POP     LPARAM_LO
                POP     LPARAM_HI
                POP     WPARAM
                POP     MSG
                POP     HWND
                PUSH    RET2
                PUSH    RET1

                CMP     MSG,2           ;Window destroyed?
                JNE     KEY
        DESTROYED:
                PUSH    0
                CALL    PostQuitMessage
```

```
            JMP      RET_0
KEY:        CMP      MSG,102H          ;Key pressed?
            JNE      NOT_KEY

            MOV      LINE_FLAG, 0              ;Reset drawing flags
            MOV      ELLIPSE_FLAG, 0
            MOV      RECTANGLE_FLAG, 0
            PUSH     WPARAM   ;ASCII code of the key
            POP      CHAR_OUT

            CMP      CHAR_OUT, "l"
            JNE      NOT_l
            MOV      LINE_FLAG, 1
            JMP      RET_0
NOT_l:
            CMP      CHAR_OUT, "e"
            JNE      NOT_e
            MOV      ELLIPSE_FLAG, 1
            JMP      RET_0
NOT_e:
            CMP      CHAR_OUT, "r"
            JNE      NOT_r
            MOV      RECTANGLE_FLAG, 1
            JMP      RET_0
NOT_r:
            PUSH     HWND
            CALL     GetDC
            MOV      HDC, AX

            PUSH     HDC
            PUSH     0       ;x
            PUSH     0       ;y
            PUSH     DS
            PUSH     OFFSET DS:CHAR_OUT
            PUSH     1       ;String length
            CALL     TextOut

            PUSH     HWND
            PUSH     HDC
            CALL     ReleaseDC
            JMP      RET_0

NOT_KEY:
            CMP      MSG,23H
            JNE      NOT_PAINT
PAINT:      PUSH     HWND
            PUSH     DS
            PUSH     OFFSET DS:PAINT_STRUC
            CALL     BeginPaint
            MOV      HDC, AX

            ;Do work

     →      PUSH     HWND
     :      PUSH     0
     :      CALL     ValidateRect

            PUSH     HWND
            PUSH     DS
            PUSH     OFFSET DS:PAINT_STRUC
```

```
        CALL    EndPaint
        JMP     RET_0
        ;
RET_0:
```

And that's it for painting. Now we're ready to start drawing figures on the screen when one of the drawing instructions ("l," "e," or "r") is used. Let's say you press the left mouse button while the mouse cursor is in the window. That location defines one point in defining the figure (line, ellipse, or rectangle). Then you move the mouse cursor to another point and release the left mouse button. When you do, the figure is drawn, as defined by those two points.

That means that when the left mouse button is released, we can simply check which of the drawing flags (if any) are nonzero, and draw the appropriate figure. These are the two mouse messages we'll be interested in:

```
WM_LBUTTONDOWN          0201H
WM_LBUTTONUP            0202H
```

If the left mouse button is pressed in our window, we'll get a WM_LBUTTONDOWN message, 201H. In that case, the low word of Lparam will hold the (local window) X coordinate of the mouse cursor at that time, and the high word will hold the Y coordinate (as the Windows SDK documentation tells us). We want to save those coordinates as one anchor point of the figure we're supposed to draw (the other anchor point comes when the left mouse button is released, at which time we're supposed to actually draw the figure). We can store those coordinates in (X1, Y1) like this:

```
        .MODEL  SMALL
        .286
        PUBLIC  DecodeMessages
        EXTRN   GetDC:FAR, ReleaseDC:FAR, TextOut:FAR, BeginPaint:FAR,
        EXTRN   ValidateRect:FAR, EndPaint:FAR, PostQuitMessage:FAR

        .DATA

        OLD_DS          DW  0

        RET1            DW  0
        RET2            DW  0
        LPARAM_LO       DW  0
        LPARAM_HI       DW  0
        WPARAM          DW  0
        MSG             DW  0
        HWND            DW  0

        LINE_FLAG       DW  0       ;Drawing flags
        ELLIPSE_FLAG    DW  0
```

```
        RECTANGLE_FLAG DW 0

        CHAR_OUT     DW 0

        PAINT_STRUC   LABEL   WORD
        HDC     DW 0
        FERASE  DW 0
        RCPAINT LABEL WORD
          LEFT    DW 0
          TOP     DW 0
          RIGHT   DW 0
          BOTTOM  DW 0
        FRESTORE   DW 0
        FINCUPDATE DW 0
        RESERVED   DB 0

→       X1 DW 0
→       Y1 DW 0

.CODE

DecodeMessages PROC FAR

        PUSH    DS       ;Use our data seg.
        PUSH    @DATA
        POP     DS
        POP     OLD_DS

        POP     RET1     ;Pull params off stack
        POP     RET2
        POP     LPARAM_LO
        POP     LPARAM_HI
        POP     WPARAM
        POP     MSG
        POP     HWND
        PUSH    RET2
        PUSH    RET1

        CMP     MSG,2            ;Window destroyed?
        JNE     KEY
DESTROYED:
        PUSH    0
        CALL    PostQuitMessage
        JMP     RET_0

KEY:    CMP     MSG,102H         ;Key pressed?
        JNE     NOT_KEY

        MOV     LINE_FLAG, 0            ;Reset drawing flags
        MOV     ELLIPSE_FLAG, 0
        MOV     RECTANGLE_FLAG, 0

        PUSH    WPARAM   ;ASCII code of the key
        POP     CHAR_OUT

        CMP     CHAR_OUT, "L"
        JNE     NOT_L
        MOV     LINE_FLAG, 1
        JMP     RET_0
NOT_L:
        CMP     CHAR_OUT, "e"
```

```
                JNE         NOT_e
                MOV         ELLIPSE_FLAG, 1
                JMP         RET_0
        NOT_e:
                CMP         CHAR_OUT, "r"
                JNE         NOT_r
                MOV         RECTANGLE_FLAG, 1
                JMP         RET_0
        NOT_r:
                PUSH        HWND
                CALL        GetDC
                MOV         HDC, AX

                PUSH        HDC
                PUSH        0           ;x
                PUSH        0           ;y
                PUSH        DS
                PUSH        OFFSET DS:CHAR_OUT
                PUSH        1           ;String length
                CALL        TextOut

                PUSH        HWND
                PUSH        HDC
                CALL        ReleaseDC
                JMP         RET_0

        NOT_KEY:
                CMP         MSG,23H
                JNE         NOT_PAINT
        PAINT:  PUSH        HWND
                PUSH        DS
                PUSH        OFFSET DS:PAINT_STRUC
                CALL        BeginPaint
                MOV         HDC, AX

                ;Do work

                PUSH        HWND
                PUSH        0
                CALL        ValidateRect

                PUSH        HWND
                PUSH        DS
                PUSH        OFFSET DS:PAINT_STRUC
                CALL        EndPaint
                JMP         RET_0
        NOT_PAINT:
                CMP         MSG, 201H   ;Left button down?
                JNE         NOT_DOWN
        DOWN:   PUSH        LPARAM_LO   ;Left button went down -- save coords
                POP         X1
                PUSH        LPARAM_HI
                POP         Y1
                JMP         RET_0
                :
```

Now we've established one corner of the rectangle or end of the line, and we have to watch for the case when the left button is released, message 202H. When that happens, we first record the new position (X2, Y2) from Lparam. Then, we can check to see if LINE_FLAG is 1. If it is, we're supposed to draw a line.

Before we can actually draw lines or ellipses, we have to get a device context handle with GetDC( ). Then we can move to the first point, (X1, Y1), with a Windows service named MoveTo( ), draw the line with a the service named LineTo( ), and then release the device context handle with ReleaseDC( ) like this:

```
        .MODEL  SMALL
        .286
                PUBLIC  DecodeMessages
                EXTRN   GetDC:FAR, ReleaseDC:FAR, TextOut:FAR, BeginPaint:FAR,
                EXTRN   ValidateRect:FAR, EndPaint:FAR, PostQuitMessage:FAR
                EXTRN   MoveTo:FAR, LineTo:FAR
        .DATA

                OLD_DS          DW 0

                RET1            DW 0
                RET2            DW 0
                LPARAM_LO       DW 0
                LPARAM_HI       DW 0
                WPARAM          DW 0
                MSG             DW 0
                HWND            DW 0

                LINE_FLAG       DW 0    ;Drawing flags
                ELLIPSE_FLAG    DW 0
                RECTANGLE_FLAG  DW 0

                CHAR_OUT        DW 0

                PAINT_STRUC     LABEL   WORD
                HDC     DW 0
                FERASE  DW 0
                RCPAINT LABEL WORD
                  LEFT    DW 0
                  TOP     DW 0
                  RIGHT   DW 0
                  BOTTOM  DW 0
                FRESTORE   DW 0
                FINCUPDATE DW 0
                RESERVED   DB 0

                X1 DW 0
                Y1 DW 0
                X2 DW 0
                Y2 DW 0

        .CODE

        DecodeMessages PROC FAR

                PUSH    DS          ;Use our data seg.
                PUSH    @DATA
                POP     DS
                POP     OLD_DS
```

390 ▶ Advanced Assembly Language

```
        POP     RET1            ;Pull params off stack
        POP     RET2
        POP     LPARAM_LO
        POP     LPARAM_HI
        POP     WPARAM
        POP     MSG
        POP     HWND
        PUSH    RET2
        PUSH    RET1

        CMP     MSG,2           ;Window destroyed?
        JNE     KEY
DESTROYED:
        PUSH    0
        CALL    PostQuitMessage
        JMP     RET_0

KEY:    CMP     MSG,102H        ;Key pressed?
        JNE     NOT_KEY

        MOV     LINE_FLAG, 0            ;Reset drawing flags
        MOV     ELLIPSE_FLAG, 0
        MOV     RECTANGLE_FLAG, 0

        PUSH    WPARAM  ;ASCII code of the key
        POP     CHAR_OUT

        CMP     CHAR_OUT, "l"
        JNE     NOT_l
        MOV     LINE_FLAG, 1
        JMP     RET_0
NOT_l:
        CMP     CHAR_OUT, "e"
        JNE     NOT_e
        MOV     ELLIPSE_FLAG, 1
        JMP     RET_0
NOT_e:
        CMP     CHAR_OUT, "r"
        JNE     NOT_r
        MOV     RECTANGLE_FLAG, 1
        JMP     RET_0
NOT_r:
        PUSH    HWND
        CALL    GetDC
        MOV     HDC, AX

        PUSH    HDC
        PUSH    0       ;x
        PUSH    0       ;y
        PUSH    DS
        PUSH    OFFSET DS:CHAR_OUT
        PUSH    1       ;String length
        CALL    TextOut

        PUSH    HWND
        PUSH    HDC
        CALL    ReleaseDC
        JMP     RET_0

NOT_KEY:
        CMP     MSG,23H
```

```
            JNE     NOT_PAINT
PAINT:      PUSH    HWND
            PUSH    DS
            PUSH    OFFSET DS:PAINT_STRUC
            CALL    BeginPaint
            MOV     HDC, AX

            ;Do work

            PUSH    HWND
            PUSH    0
            CALL    ValidateRect

            PUSH    HWND
            PUSH    DS
            PUSH    OFFSET DS:PAINT_STRUC
            CALL    EndPaint
            JMP     RET_0

NOT_PAINT:
            CMP     MSG, 201H       ;Left button down?
            JNE     NOT_DOWN
DOWN:       PUSH    LPARAM_LO       ;Left button went down -- save coords
            POP     X1
            PUSH    LPARAM_HI
            POP     Y1
            JMP     RET_0

NOT_DOWN:
            CMP     MSG, 202H       ;Left button up?
            JE      UP
            JMP     NOT_UP
UP:         PUSH    LPARAM_LO
            POP     X2
            PUSH    LPARAM_HI
            POP     Y2

            CMP     LINE_FLAG, 1
            JNE     NOT_LINE

            PUSH    HWND
            CALL    GetDC

            PUSH    HDC
            PUSH    X1
            PUSH    Y1
            CALL    MoveTo

            PUSH    HDC
            PUSH    X2
            PUSH    Y2
            CALL    LineTo

            PUSH    HWND
            PUSH    HDC
            CALL    ReleaseDC
            JMP     RET_0
NOT_LINE:
            :
```

392 ▶ Advanced Assembly Language

And we've handled the line drawing case. Next, let's check for ellipses by looking at ELLIPSE_FLAG. If it's 1, we're supposed to draw an ellipse, which we can do by passing the two points (X1, Y1) and (X2, Y2) to Ellipse( ), like this:

```
.MODEL  SMALL

.286
        PUBLIC  DecodeMessages
        EXTRN   GetDC:FAR, ReleaseDC:FAR, TextOut:FAR, BeginPaint:FAR,
        EXTRN   ValidateRect:FAR, EndPaint:FAR, PostQuitMessage:FAR
        EXTRN   MoveTo:FAR, LineTo:FAR, Ellipse:FAR
.DATA
        OLD_DS          DW 0

        RET1            DW 0
        RET2            DW 0
        LPARAM_LO       DW 0
        LPARAM_HI       DW 0
        WPARAM          DW 0
        MSG             DW 0
        HWND            DW 0

        LINE_FLAG       DW 0    ;Drawing flags
        ELLIPSE_FLAG    DW 0
        RECTANGLE_FLAG  DW 0

        CHAR_OUT        DW 0

        PAINT_STRUC     LABEL   WORD
        HDC     DW 0
        FERASE  DW 0
        RCPAINT LABEL WORD
          LEFT    DW 0
          TOP     DW 0
          RIGHT   DW 0
          BOTTOM  DW 0
        FRESTORE   DW 0
        FINCUPDATE DW 0
        RESERVED   DB 0

        X1  DW 0
        Y1  DW 0
        X2  DW 0
        Y2  DW 0

.CODE

DecodeMessages PROC FAR

        PUSH    DS          ;Use our data seg.
        PUSH    @DATA
        POP     DS
        POP     OLD_DS

        POP     RET1        ;Pull params off stack
        POP     RET2
        POP     LPARAM_LO
        POP     LPARAM_HI
```

```
        POP     WPARAM
        POP     MSG
        POP     HWND
        PUSH    RET2
        PUSH    RET1

        CMP     MSG,2           ;Window destroyed?
        JNE     KEY
DESTROYED:
        PUSH    0
        CALL    PostQuitMessage
        JMP     RET_0

KEY:    CMP     MSG,102H        ;Key pressed?
        JNE     NOT_KEY

        MOV     LINE_FLAG, 0        ;Reset drawing flags
        MOV     ELLIPSE_FLAG, 0
        MOV     RECTANGLE_FLAG, 0

        PUSH    WPARAM  ;ASCII code of the key
        POP     CHAR_OUT
        CMP     CHAR_OUT, "l"
        JNE     NOT_l
        MOV     LINE_FLAG, 1
        JMP     RET_0
NOT_l:
        CMP     CHAR_OUT, "e"
        JNE     NOT_e
        MOV     ELLIPSE_FLAG, 1
        JMP     RET_0
NOT_e:
        CMP     CHAR_OUT, "r"
        JNE     NOT_r
        MOV     RECTANGLE_FLAG, 1
        JMP     RET_0
NOT_r:
        PUSH    HWND
        CALL    GetDC
        MOV     HDC, AX

        PUSH    HDC
        PUSH    0       ;x
        PUSH    0       ;y
        PUSH    DS
        PUSH    OFFSET DS:CHAR_OUT
        PUSH    1       ;String length
        CALL    TextOut

        PUSH    HWND
        PUSH    HDC
        CALL    ReleaseDC
        JMP     RET_0

NOT_KEY:
        CMP     MSG,23H
        JNE     NOT_PAINT
PAINT:  PUSH    HWND
        PUSH    DS
        PUSH    OFFSET DS:PAINT_STRUC
        CALL    BeginPaint
```

```
                MOV     HDC, AX

                ;Do work

                PUSH    HWND
                PUSH    0
                CALL    ValidateRect

                PUSH    HWND
                PUSH    DS
                PUSH    OFFSET DS:PAINT_STRUC
                CALL    EndPaint
                JMP     RET_0

NOT_PAINT:
                CMP     MSG, 201H           ;Left button down?
                JNE     NOT_DOWN
DOWN:           PUSH    LPARAM_LO           ;Left button went down -- save coords
                POP     X1
                PUSH    LPARAM_HI
                POP     Y1
                JMP     RET_0

NOT_DOWN:
                CMP     MSG, 202H           ;Left button up?
                JE      UP
                JMP     NOT_UP
UP:             PUSH    LPARAM_LO
                POP     X2
                PUSH    LPARAM_HI
                POP     Y2

                CMP     LINE_FLAG, 1
                JNE     NOT_LINE

                PUSH    HWND
                CALL    GetDC

                PUSH    HDC
                PUSH    X1
                PUSH    Y1
                CALL    MoveTo

                PUSH    HDC
                PUSH    X2
                PUSH    Y2
                CALL    LineTo

                PUSH    HWND
                PUSH    HDC
                CALL    ReleaseDC
                JMP     RET_0
NOT_LINE:
                CMP     ELLIPSE_FLAG, 1
                JNE     NOT_ELLIPSE
                PUSH    HWND
                CALL    GetDC

                PUSH    HDC
                PUSH    X1
                PUSH    Y1
```

```
            PUSH    X2
            PUSH    Y2
            CALL    Ellipse

            PUSH    HWND
            PUSH    HDC
            CALL    ReleaseDC
            JMP     RET_0
NOT_ELLIPSE:
            :
```

Finally, we can use the two points as the corners of a rectangle with the Rectangle( ) service like this:

```
        .MODEL  SMALL

        .286
                PUBLIC  DecodeMessages
                EXTRN   GetDC:FAR, ReleaseDC:FAR, TextOut:FAR, BeginPaint:FAR,
                EXTRN   ValidateRect:FAR, EndPaint:FAR, PostQuitMessage:FAR
                EXTRN   MoveTo:FAR, LineTo:FAR, Ellipse:FAR
                EXTRN   Rectangle:FAR

        .DATA

                OLD_DS          DW 0

                RET1            DW 0
                RET2            DW 0
                LPARAM_LO       DW 0
                LPARAM_HI       DW 0
                WPARAM          DW 0
                MSG             DW 0
                HWND            DW 0

                LINE_FLAG       DW 0    ;Drawing flags
                ELLIPSE_FLAG    DW 0
                RECTANGLE_FLAG  DW 0

                CHAR_OUT        DW 0

                PAINT_STRUC     LABEL   WORD
                HDC     DW 0
                FERASE  DW 0
                RCPAINT LABEL WORD
                    LEFT    DW 0
                    TOP     DW 0
                    RIGHT   DW 0
                    BOTTOM  DW 0
                FRESTORE   DW 0
                FINCUPDATE DW 0
                RESERVED   DB 0

                X1 DW 0
                Y1 DW 0
                X2 DW 0
                Y2 DW 0
```

396 ▶ Advanced Assembly Language

```
        .CODE

DecodeMessages PROC FAR

        PUSH    DS              ;Use our data seg.
        PUSH    @DATA
        POP     DS
        POP     OLD_DS

        POP     RET1            ;Pull params off stack
        POP     RET2
        POP     LPARAM_LO
        POP     LPARAM_HI
        POP     WPARAM
        POP     MSG
        POP     HWND
        PUSH    RET2
        PUSH    RET1

        CMP     MSG,2           ;Window destroyed?
        JNE     KEY
DESTROYED:
        PUSH    0
        CALL    PostQuitMessage
        JMP     RET_0

KEY:    CMP     MSG,102H        ;Key pressed?
        JNE     NOT_KEY

        MOV     LINE_FLAG, 0            ;Reset drawing flags
        MOV     ELLIPSE_FLAG, 0
        MOV     RECTANGLE_FLAG, 0

        PUSH    WPARAM  ;ASCII code of the key
        POP     CHAR_OUT

        CMP     CHAR_OUT, "l"
        JNE     NOT_l
        MOV     LINE_FLAG, 1
        JMP     RET_0
NOT_l:
        CMP     CHAR_OUT, "e"
        JNE     NOT_e
        MOV     ELLIPSE_FLAG, 1
        JMP     RET_0
NOT_e:
        CMP     CHAR_OUT, "r"
        JNE     NOT_r
        MOV     RECTANGLE_FLAG, 1
        JMP     RET_0
NOT_r:
        PUSH    HWND
        CALL    GetDC
        MOV     HDC, AX

        PUSH    HDC
        PUSH    0       ;x
        PUSH    0       ;y
        PUSH    DS
        PUSH    OFFSET DS:CHAR_OUT
        PUSH    1       ;String length
```

```
            CALL    TextOut

            PUSH    HWND
            PUSH    HDC
            CALL    ReleaseDC
            JMP     RET_0

NOT_KEY:
            CMP     MSG,23H
            JNE     NOT_PAINT
PAINT:      PUSH    HWND
            PUSH    DS
            PUSH    OFFSET DS:PAINT_STRUC
            CALL    BeginPaint
            MOV     HDC, AX

            ;Do work

            PUSH    HWND
            PUSH    0
            CALL    ValidateRect

            PUSH    HWND
            PUSH    DS
            PUSH    OFFSET DS:PAINT_STRUC
            CALL    EndPaint
            JMP     RET_0

NOT_PAINT:
            CMP     MSG, 201H       ;Left button down?
            JNE     NOT_DOWN
DOWN:       PUSH    LPARAM_LO       ;Left button went down -- save coords
            POP     X1
            PUSH    LPARAM_HI
            POP     Y1
            JMP     RET_0

NOT_DOWN:
            CMP     MSG, 202H       ;Left button up?
            JE      UP
            JMP     NOT_UP
UP:         PUSH    LPARAM_LO
            POP     X2
            PUSH    LPARAM_HI
            POP     Y2

            CMP     LINE_FLAG, 1
            JNE     NOT_LINE

            PUSH    HWND
            CALL    GetDC

            PUSH    HDC
            PUSH    X1
            PUSH    Y1
            CALL    MoveTo

            PUSH    HDC
            PUSH    X2
            PUSH    Y2
            CALL    LineTo
```

```
                PUSH        HWND
                PUSH        HDC
                CALL        ReleaseDC
                JMP         RET_0
NOT_LINE:

                CMP         ELLIPSE_FLAG, 1
                JNE         NOT_ELLIPSE
                PUSH        HWND
                CALL        GetDC

                PUSH        HDC
                PUSH        X1
                PUSH        Y1
                PUSH        X2
                PUSH        Y2
                CALL        Ellipse

                PUSH        HWND
                PUSH        HDC
                CALL        ReleaseDC
                JMP         RET_0
NOT_ELLIPSE:

                CMP         RECTANGLE_FLAG, 1
                JNE         NOT_RECTANGLE
                PUSH        HWND
                CALL        GetDC

                PUSH        HDC
                PUSH        X1
                PUSH        Y1
                PUSH        X2
                PUSH        Y2
                CALL        Rectangle

                PUSH        HWND
                PUSH        HDC
                CALL        ReleaseDC
                JMP         RET_0
NOT_RECTANGLE:
                :
```

Now our procedure is almost complete. All that remains is the default case, which will actually make up the majority of the cases we'll see in DecodeMessages( ). We will not handle most of the messages that DecodeMessages( ) gets. To handle them, Windows provides DefWindowsProc( ), and we can call it exactly as DecodeMessages( ) was called. In other words, we have to reconstruct the stack as we first got it by pushing the parameters back on, and then calling DefWindowProc( ).

When we return from DefWindowProc( ), we won't touch the return values in DX and AX, passing them on to Windows instead. The only item left on the stack will be the original return address (the one we would have normally returned to with the RET at the end of DecodeMessages( )), so we can simply return. That finishes DecodeMessages( ). The whole procedure is shown in Listing 12-2.

Listing 12-2. Window Function DecodeMessages( ).

```
.MODEL  SMALL

.286
        PUBLIC  DecodeMessages
        EXTRN   GetDC:FAR, ReleaseDC:FAR, TextOut:FAR, BeginPaint:FAR,
        EXTRN   ValidateRect:FAR, EndPaint:FAR, PostQuitMessage:FAR
        EXTRN   DefWindowProc:FAR, MoveTo:FAR, LineTo:FAR, Ellipse:FAR
        EXTRN   Rectangle:FAR
.DATA

        OLD_DS          DW 0

        RET1            DW 0
        RET2            DW 0
        LPARAM_LO       DW 0
        LPARAM_HI       DW 0
        WPARAM          DW 0
        MSG             DW 0
        HWND            DW 0

        LINE_FLAG       DW 0    ;Drawing flags
        ELLIPSE_FLAG    DW 0
        RECTANGLE_FLAG  DW 0

        CHAR_OUT        DW 0

        PAINT_STRUC     LABEL   WORD
        HDC     DW 0
        FERASE  DW 0
        RCPAINT LABEL WORD
          LEFT    DW 0
          TOP     DW 0
          RIGHT   DW 0
          BOTTOM  DW 0
        FRESTORE   DW 0
        FINCUPDATE DW 0
        RESERVED   DB 0

        X1 DW 0
        Y1 DW 0
        X2 DW 0
        Y2 DW 0

.CODE

DecodeMessages PROC FAR

        PUSH    DS      ;Use our data seg.
        PUSH    @DATA
        POP     DS
        POP     OLD_DS

        POP     RET1    ;Pull params off stack
        POP     RET2
```

Listing 12-2. Window Function DecodeMessages( ).

```
        POP     LPARAM_LO
        POP     LPARAM_HI
        POP     WPARAM
        POP     MSG
        POP     HWND
        PUSH    RET2
        PUSH    RET1

        CMP     MSG,2           ;Window destroyed?
        JNE     KEY
DESTROYED:
        PUSH    0
        CALL    PostQuitMessage
        JMP     RET_0

KEY:    CMP     MSG,102H        ;Key pressed?
        JNE     NOT_KEY

        MOV     LINE_FLAG, 0            ;Reset drawing flags
        MOV     ELLIPSE_FLAG, 0
        MOV     RECTANGLE_FLAG, 0

        PUSH    WPARAM  ;ASCII code of the key
        POP     CHAR_OUT

        CMP     CHAR_OUT, "l"
        JNE     NOT_l
        MOV     LINE_FLAG, 1
        JMP     RET_0
NOT_l:
        CMP     CHAR_OUT, "e"
        JNE     NOT_e
        MOV     ELLIPSE_FLAG, 1
        JMP     RET_0
NOT_e:
        CMP     CHAR_OUT, "r"
        JNE     NOT_r
        MOV     RECTANGLE_FLAG, 1
        JMP     RET_0
NOT_r:
        PUSH    HWND
        CALL    GetDC
        MOV     HDC, AX

        PUSH    HDC
        PUSH    0       ;x
        PUSH    0       ;y
        PUSH    DS
        PUSH    OFFSET DS:CHAR_OUT
        PUSH    1       ;String length
        CALL    TextOut

        PUSH    HWND
        PUSH    HDC
        CALL    ReleaseDC
        JMP     RET_0

NOT_KEY:
        CMP     MSG,23H
```

Listing 12-2. Window Function DecodeMessages( ).

```
        JNE     NOT_PAINT
PAINT:  PUSH    HWND
        PUSH    DS
        PUSH    OFFSET DS:PAINT_STRUC
        CALL    BeginPaint
        MOV     HDC, AX

        ;Do work

        PUSH    HWND
        PUSH    0
        CALL    ValidateRect

        PUSH    HWND
        PUSH    DS
        PUSH    OFFSET DS:PAINT_STRUC
        CALL    EndPaint
        JMP     RET_0

NOT_PAINT:
        CMP     MSG, 201H       ;Left button down?
        JNE     NOT_DOWN
DOWN:   PUSH    LPARAM_LO       ;Left button went down -- save coords
        POP     X1
        PUSH    LPARAM_HI
        POP     Y1
        JMP     RET_0

NOT_DOWN:
        CMP     MSG, 202H       ;Left button up?
        JE      UP
        JMP     NOT_UP
UP:     PUSH    LPARAM_LO
        POP     X2
        PUSH    LPARAM_HI
        POP     Y2

        CMP     LINE_FLAG, 1
        JNE     NOT_LINE

        PUSH    HWND
        CALL    GetDC

        PUSH    HDC
        PUSH    X1
        PUSH    Y1
        CALL    MoveTo

        PUSH    HDC
        PUSH    X2
        PUSH    Y2
        CALL    LineTo

        PUSH    HWND
        PUSH    HDC
        CALL    ReleaseDC
        JMP     RET_0
NOT_LINE:
```

Listing 12-2. Window Function DecodeMessages( ).

```
        CMP     ELLIPSE_FLAG, 1
        JNE     NOT_ELLIPSE
        PUSH    HWND
        CALL    GetDC

        PUSH    HDC
        PUSH    X1
        PUSH    Y1
        PUSH    X2
        PUSH    Y2
        CALL    Ellipse

        PUSH    HWND
        PUSH    HDC
        CALL    ReleaseDC
        JMP     RET_0
NOT_ELLIPSE:

        CMP     RECTANGLE_FLAG, 1
        JNE     NOT_RECTANGLE
        PUSH    HWND
        CALL    GetDC

        PUSH    HDC
        PUSH    X1
        PUSH    Y1
        PUSH    X2
        PUSH    Y2
        CALL    Rectangle

        PUSH    HWND
        PUSH    HDC
        CALL    ReleaseDC
        JMP     RET_0
NOT_RECTANGLE:

NOT_UP:

DEFAULT:
        PUSH    HWND
        PUSH    MSG
        PUSH    WPARAM
        PUSH    LPARAM_HI
        PUSH    LPARAM_LO

        PUSH    OLD_DS
        POP     DS

        CALL    DefWindowProc

        RET
RET_0:
        PUSH    OLD_DS   ;Restore DS
        POP     DS

        MOV     AX,0     ;RETURN 0
        MOV     DX,0
        RET
```

> **Listing 12-2.** Window Function DecodeMessages( ).

```
DecodeMessages    ENDP
                  END
```

Now we've put together WinMain (WINMAIN.C) and DecodeMessages (which we can call, say, DECODE.ASM). All we've got to do is to connect them, and we're set.

The Windows Definition File

Unfortunately, we cannot just compile, assemble, and link these files. Instead, we have to provide a *definition file* for the linker to make sure that our program will be made into a Windows program. That definition file, WINMAIN.DEF, looks like this:

```
NAME          My_Window
DESCRIPTION   'Example Application for Windows'
EXETYPE       WINDOWS
STUB          'WINSTUB.EXE' ; prints an error message if prog run w/o Windows
CODE    PRELOAD MOVEABLE DISCARDABLE
DATA    PRELOAD MOVEABLE MULTIPLE ;Make multiple since prog can be reloaded
HEAPSIZE      1024
STACKSIZE     5120
```

Here we specify that the program is designed to run under Windows, and we also load a *stub procedure*. This short procedure is designed to print out the message "This program requires Microsoft Windows" if you try to run the program under DOS. The stub is in the file WINSTUB.EXE, which is part of the Windows SDK. That's it for the definitions file, which we'll pass on to the linker when it's time to put the whole program together.

Making MYWINDOW.EXE

Now let's produce the .EXE files that we can run from Windows. We can compile WINMAIN.C like this using cl.exe:

```
F:\>cl -c -Gs WINMAIN.C
```

404 ▶ Advanced Assembly Language

Or like this, using the QuickC compiler:

```
F:\>qcl -c -Gs WINMAIN.C
```

The -c switch makes the compiler only compile WINMAIN.C, not attempt to link it. The -Gs switch is crucial — we are turning off stack checking, which is essential for Windows programs. Next, we assemble DECODE.ASM like this:

```
F:\>MASM -MX DECODE;
```

Where the -mx switch stops the assembler from capitalizing the labels in DECODE.ASM (particularly the label DecodeMessages) so that we can link it in with WINMAIN.OBJ.

The next step is to link it all together. Windows 3.0 provides its own versions of the C libraries, and we can link to the small model Windows C library (slibcew.lib) and the Windows library itself (libw.lib) like this:

```
F:\>link WINMAIN+DECODE ,,, /NOD slibcew libw, WINMAIN.DEF
```

> **TIP** Before Windows 3.0, the windows library libw.lib came in different versions for different models (e.g., slibw.lib for the small model), but now that library has been made model independent, which makes it much easier to use.

Notice that we had to include the definition file, WINMAIN.DEF, at the end of the command. We also include the /NOD switch (ignore default search records) to stop link.exe from searching for a default C library (such as slibce.lib). The linker produces WINMAIN.EXE, which you can run in Windows.

> **TIP** There's another way — new in Windows 3.0 — of producing WINMAIN.EXE that deserves mention. If our application does not explicitly call any runtime C routines, does not use _argc, _argv, or _environ, and does not call any runtime C routines implicitly (as stack checking would have done), we can use a quicker version of the C library in the SDK called snocrt.lib. This library links in routines that do not add startup code to the .EXE file, which makes the startup faster and more efficient. We can link to snocrt.lib like this: F:\>link WINMAIN+DECODE ,,, /NOD snocrt libw, WINMAIN.DEF.

And that's it. Our Windows program is ready to go: ready to draw ellipses, lines, rectangles, or just print characters. Give it a try. Windows offers many resources to the programmer and is well worth spending some time with. Now, however, it's time to move on to OS/2.

Chapter 13

Introduction to OS/2

Introduction to OS/2

COMPUTER MANUFACTURERS have always wondered where to go next with their products. This is always a gamble for them. What if their new machines are rejected by the public? On the other hand, several directions can always be followed with success if you're an established company, which would allow you more speed and less cost, for example. Also, the original PC had some deadly faults: the poor graphics capabilities, relatively slow microprocessors, and memory restrictions. So IBM brought out the PS/2.

The PS/2 itself is not such a departure from the PC. Largely, it simply follows the rule of more and faster: more disk space with faster access, more memory to expand into, faster processors, more keys on the keyboard, and faster clocks.

Usually, you can know where microcomputers are going simply by looking at mainframe computers. Mainframes represent an established, successful niche of the market. Over the years, they have taken their present forms, and every part of them has been proven in the marketplace. For example, it was clear even in 1981 that hard disks were on the way along with bigger memories. The development of the PC has followed this course within the confines of the microprocessor chips with which it works.

This means that Intel determines, to a large extent, where the PC line will go. The IBM microcomputer line is committed to Intel chips. And the Intel chips have not only gotten faster, they have also augmented the instruction set, and allowed for an altogether new ability — *multitasking*. And to handle that new capability, OS/2 was announced.

Being able to multitask is not an easy thing to accomplish. In fact, OS/2 brings with it most of the classical parts of a mainframe mulitasking operating system (which we'll examine soon) such as: hardware gates, protection rings, semaphores that programs can use to communicate with each other, pipes, queues, and other new concepts. Much of OS/2 is devoted to these new, and, to us, perhaps strange things.

OS/2 Is Not So Different

On the other hand, you shouldn't get the idea that programming in OS/2 is so different from what we have been doing. It's not. The writers of OS/2 went to great pains to include DOS compatibility. There is a *DOS compatibility mode* under OS/2, which you can select easily. For most purposes, this puts you back in DOS. Programs that will not run under OS/2 will run here — we'll have to run our macro assembler here. And many programs that will run under OS/2 have been specially designed to run under DOS as well.

Assembly language instructions like JMP, CMP, JAE, ADD, and so on have not changed. The chips used do not change when we use OS/2. They still use the same instruction set that they always have.

> **TIP** In fact, despite the attempt of OS/2 to break away from DOS, most of the DOS interrupt services that we have so carefully developed until now in this book are also available in OS/2 but under different names. This makes the transition to OS/2 easier.

Before, we used BIOS and DOS. Now, BIOS and DOS are no longer there. Instead, we will be calling OS/2. In fact, "calling" is the appropriate term for the way we will use OS/2. Under DOS and BIOS, we used system services by loading some registers and using INT. Under OS/2, we will push the values we used to load into registers onto the stack and then call OS/2. Here's an example. If we wanted to print the message "No Worries." under DOS, here is how we could do it:

```
MESSAGE         DB      "No Worries.$"
       :
       MOV      DX,OFFSET MESSAGE
       MOV      AH,9
       INT      21H
```

We would just use service 9 of interrupt 21H, the major DOS interrupt. We load AH with the number of the service we want, load the data's address into DS:DX, and we're off.

OS/2 is different in this regard. Here you call services by name, not as services under an INT. Here is how we would print out the same message under OS/2:

```
MESSAGE         DB      "No Worries."
MESSAGELENGTH   EQU     $-MESSAGE

       PUSH     DS
       PUSH     OFFSET MESSAGE
       PUSH     MESSAGELENGTH
       PUSH     0               ;Video handle
       CALL     VioWrtTTY
```

Instead of loading the address into DS:DX, we push DS and then push MESSAGE's offset address. Instead of terminating the string with $, we explicitly tell OS/2 how long the string to print is by pushing MESSAGELENGTH. Then we push 0 to make sure we use the standard video handle (the "video handle" will always be 0 for us), and CALL a routine named VioWrtTTY.

> **TIP** Notice the quick way we found the length of MESSAGE in this example: with MESSAGELENGTH EQU $-MESSAGE. Keep in mind that $ refers to

> the offset from the beginning of the current segment (here the code segment).

This is how it's done: with a CALL not an INT. VioWrtTTY is the OS/2 service that prints a character string at the current cursor position. Notice that since it is a call, and the procedure for VioWrtTTY is not present in our program, we will have to declare VioWrtTTY as EXTRN. Somewhere in the program, we will have to have the line: EXTRN VioWrtTTY:FAR.

This is the case for all OS/2 services. They will all have to be declared EXTRN, and these references will be picked up at link time. This does not mean that the full code for VioWrtTTY will be linked into your program, as would be normal for linking (that would make all OS/2 programs prohibitively large). Instead, what is linked is a reference to VioWrtTTY, not the whole thing. This is called *dynamic linking*, which we'll see in a moment. When your program is loaded to run, and only then, the rest of VioWrtTTY will be attached.

Despite the similar setup, to understand OS/2, we'll have to become familiar with a new way of looking at the computer, and a new set of concepts (such as the idea of "threads," which is central to OS/2). This will take some examination on our part of just what is going on. To start understanding OS/2, we'll examine the chip that fathered it, the 80×86.

The 80×86

The 80×86 chip has two modes of operating, real and protected. The two operating systems for the PS/2 match these modes, DOS (real) and OS/2 (protected). Real mode is what we have been working in until now. The memory, all 1 MB of it, is available to the user (minus the BIOS 360K at the top, leaving 640K for general use). Here we use segments, and interrupts, and only one program runs at a time.

Protected mode is, as its name suggests, a mode in which multiple programs can run, protected from each other. There are various levels of hierarchy in the computer. And, in protected mode, we no longer use segments. Instead, we use segment *selectors*.

Segment Selectors

Segment selectors look to our programs just like real segment addresses. That is, they are 16-bit numbers which fit into the segment registers. We will work with them here in the same way we used to work with segments. What they really are is a different story;

in reality, a segment selector points to a table called the segment descriptor table. The segment descriptor pointed to in the table holds the real information about the real segment in memory.

This means that we could have 1343H in the CS register when our program is loaded, and we could think that we are dealing with segment 1343H — that is, 1343:0000 in memory — but we are not. This selector points to an entry in the segment descriptor table, where the real segment address is stored. And this real address does not use the 20 bits we are used to but 24. This means that we can now address up to 16MB of memory.

The reason selectors are useful for multitasking is that OS/2 can move the real segment in memory around wherever it wanted to put it, and the same selector (in a register like CS or DS) would still point to it (although indirectly). If some program finished, segments in memory could be moved around until memory was compacted. Keep in mind that these segments can be of various lengths. They are not necessarily 64K (which is their maximum length).

If the memory is available, OS/2 is a wizard at it. And, as if that weren't enough, you can use what is called *virtual memory*. This means that if OS/2 runs out of memory in the machine, it will take the least frequently used sections of memory and send them out to the disk. They will wait until there is either room for them again, or they are specifically referenced by a program then running.

When a section of memory is sent out to the disk, it is *swapped out*. This is a common occurrence in mainframe machines. In the PS/2, however, the disk-acccess time is slow (compared to mainframe hard disks), so it will be noticeable if your program starts to swap out very much. What this means, in practice, is that the 16 MB limit is not truly exceeded by using virtual (disk) memory but just softened.

In addition to selectors and virtual memory, the 80×86 uses almost all the normal tools for multitasking. A complete description of them is beyond this book (a complete description is beyond almost any book). But we can mention a few more things that will be important.

Hardware Gates

The 80×86 uses hardware *gates* in protected mode. When you call a far location, you have to go through a gate before you can access memory in that location. The 80×86 maintains a table that tells it whether or not you are qualified to pass through that gate, and, if not, access is denied. All this is done on a hardware level. This means that each program will stay in its own area of memory, although it can ask for more, or even set up memory to share with other programs.

What is important for us is that if a program attempts to go through an "illegal" gate by making a memory access outside its own memory space, OS/2 terminates the program. A screen will come up, telling you that the program was terminated.

Security Rings

In addition, there are *rings* of protection. Ring 0 is the highest priority ring, and the innermost OS/2 procedures (the OS/2 *kernel*) run there. We progress outward to I/O handlers in ring 2, and then to normal application programs, which are always in ring 3, the ring with the least priority. Depending on which ring your process is in, you will be granted access or denied access to certain parts of memory.

Time sharing depends on the rings. Inside the same ring, time is allocated equally. However, a program with a lower ring number (and therefore higher priority) will always get time before a program with a higher number (that is, lower priority).

If all this sounds like a hierarchy is being set up in your computer, it is. The 80×86 chip enforces rings of priority, isolation of programs, gates for far calls, and other things. No longer is all memory open to you, nor I/O devices, nor the screen buffer (nor interrupts). Although this can take some of the "personal" out of the computer, there are advantages to this scheme, too, and the primary advantage one is multitasking.

How Multitasking Works

Now that we have seen a little of the chip, we can see that it was built with multitasking in mind. And OS/2 exploits that capability. To make a machine truly multitasking is a demanding problem, and it brings with it new conceptions of how programs will run. Central to multitasking are what OS/2 refers to as *threads*.

A thread is an important concept in OS/2. It is what runs through programs that are active. For example, let's say that you have a notepad pop-up program installed under DOS, and are currently running an editor. The notepad is not running because it has no thread. Under DOS, there is only a single thread, and, here, the editor has it. When you pop up the notepad, it gets the thread.

In OS/2, you can have multiple threads running at once. This is like the voices in a speaker system. If the speaker has only one voice, like the PC or PS/2 speaker, then even if you emulate a fine instrument, you can only play one at a time. Multiple voices mean that multiple instruments can play at the same time, as in an orchestra. What voices are to a symphony, threads are to OS/2. Saying that OS/2 supports multiple threads means that many programs can be active at once.

Communication between Programs

OS/2 allows programs to pass data and signals back and forth. Although we are not going to examine those services here, you can allocate shared segments. Such a segment can then be reached by multiple programs. In addition, you can ask the system to put aside an open segment that all programs can access.

Besides shared segments, *semaphores* are used to communicate between programs. A semaphore is used by two programs as a flag. One program can tell the other that it is using, for example, a certain part of memory, and that the memory is not available until the semaphore has been *cleared*.

> **NOTE** Semaphores are the basis of multitasking in many ways, and you can learn more about them in any book on mainframe operating systems.

Other types of communication can take place through OS/2 constructions like queues and pipes. You are probably familiar with the idea of queues from the PRINT command in DOS. When you queue a number of files to printed, PRINT takes the one that was first and starts to print it. The next one in line has to wait (in the queue) until the first one is finished. In the same way, programs in OS/2 can set up queues for use between themselves.

Pipes are a similar idea. Data can be put into a pipe from the output of one program and read as the input of another. Pipes can accept data from one program at a rate that may be faster than the rate at which the other program can accept it. In this way, they can act as a buffer between programs. Even so, pipes are not inexhaustible. When a pipe fills up, OS/2 will then block the program that fills it until it is at least partially cleared.

With these tools built into it, OS/2 has good support for interprogram (or intraprogram) communication. What we've said here only serves as the briefest of introductions to them. For more details, you should consult an OS/2 book (such as OS/2 Assembly Language from Brady Books).

Writing an OS/2 Program

To use OS/2 services instead of the DOS and BIOS ones, we have to know how to reach them. There are four groups of OS/2 services (excluding the Presentation Manager services) that we can call from our assembly language programs — that is, link to — and each of them starts with a particular three letter combination.

▶ Introduction to OS/2   415

The first group is the Vio group, which means video Input/Output, and it is the way that you will write to the screen. It replaces BIOS INT 10H. Examples of the Vio services are VioWrtTTY, VioWrtCharStr, and VioScrollUp. You can get an idea of what they do just from their names. Mou is the prefix for services that deal with the mouse. An example is MouGetPtrPos. Kbd means Keyboard. These services are used for reading what has been typed. Two examples of Kbd services are KbdPeek and KbdCharIn.

Dos may be a prefix that you were not expecting. In fact, the commands prefixed with Dos make up most of OS/2. All memory management services (a big consideration under a multitasking operating system) are in the Dos group, as are the file management services. In fact, everything that is not I/O-related begins with Dos. Some examples are: DosWrite, DosRead, DosOpen, DosMKDir, and DosGetMachineMode.

> **NOTE** It may be worth noting that IBMBIO and IBMDOS still exist on the disk, just as they do under DOS (see Chapter 6). IBMBIO is now tiny, and IBMDOS is huge.

In many cases, the use of named procedures makes code easier to read. After all, what is INT 21H service 3FH? It is better to call the similar OS/2 service DosRead.

> **TIP** The reason you call a procedure in OS/2 rather than use INT to access system services is primarily so that it's easier for high-level languages to interface directly to the operating system. This means that you may not have to drop into assembly language at all for some problems.

As we'll see later, the way OS/2 returns errors is similar to the DOS interrupts too. It uses the AX register. Before, we could check AX for an error code. If AX was zero, this meant there was no error (although some services returned data in AX or some value that was not zero was returned to indicate no error). Under OS/2, the error code will also be returned in AX, and, if it is zero, there was no error. If it was not zero, we will have to track the error down.

When you've filled your program with the Vio, Mou, Dos, and Kbd services, you can link your .OBJ files to OS/2 libraries to make a running .EXE file. As mentioned, this does not link in the routines at that time. OS/2 uses a different method.

Dynamic Linking

This new aspect of OS/2 is called *dynamic linking*. What we have developed so far in this book, OS/2 refers to as *static linking*. In static linking, the .EXE or .COM file is complete. Everything that is necessary to run it is in it. All the code that needs to do the job is there.

Dynamic linking is different. Here is how it works: you run your .ASM file through MASM as you used to do under DOS. In fact, since MASM won't work under OS/2, you'll have to run it under DOS compatibility mode. Then you use the OS/2 linker, LINK (which can also be run under DOS if you wish).

LINK will ask for the name of the .OBJ file and the names of any libraries you want to give it. One such library — the library we'll use — is called DOSCALLS.LIB. This library (which is supplied on the OS/2 disks) is set up to satisfy references to external calls to the OS/2 services. What usually happens at this point is that the procedure that satisfies the external call in the .ASM file is read in from the library and included in the .EXE file. Here, however, is where the difference comes in.

Instead of procedures, OS/2 .LIB files hold the names of *dynamic link library files* and the locations in those dynamic link library files of the called procedure.

NOTE Dynamic link library files have the extension .DLL.

Let's take an example. One OS/2 service is named DosOpen, and it is used to open or create files. If we were linking in a call to DosOpen, there would be a reference in DOSCALLS.LIB for DosOpen. It would indicate that DosOpen exists in a .DLL file (actually DOSCALL1.DLL) and give its location there.

When the .EXE file was loaded into memory to run, the loader would see that Dos-Read is indicated as being found in a .DLL file, and the appropriate .DLL file is read in. The procedure is placed in memory, and its address is placed into the call instruction in the program being loaded. (If DosRead had already been installed in memory by another program, it is not read in again.)

This is what is meant by dynamic linking: the actual linking of the call to the called procedure is not done until the program is loaded in and run.

An OS/2 EXE File Shell with DosExit

Now we know something about the OS/2 services and how to create an .EXE file by using LINK under OS/2. We're ready to see what an .EXE file will look like. Our OS/2

.EXE file shell isn't so different from what we are used to. In fact, it's quite similar, as we can see in Listing 13-1.

Listing 13-1. An .EXE File Shell under OS/2.

```
        .286
        .MODEL  SMALL
        .STACK  200H

        .DATA

        .CODE
                EXTRN   DOSEXIT:FAR

ENTRY:          ;Program goes here.

EXIT:           PUSH    1               ;A Normal Exit.
                PUSH    0
                CALL    DOSEXIT

                END     ENTRY
```

At the top is the directive .286. This enables the assembler to assemble instructions for the 80×86 chip, in lowest priority mode. To assemble instructions that will need higher authority (and manipulate privileged tables and registers), the .286P directive is used. Next, we set up the memory model and the segments we'll use:

```
        .286
        .MODEL  SMALL           ←
        .STACK  200H            ←

        .DATA                   ←

        .CODE                   ←
                EXTRN   DOSEXIT:FAR

ENTRY:          ;Program goes here.

EXIT:           PUSH    1               ;A Normal Exit.
                PUSH    0
                CALL    DOSEXIT

                END     ENTRY
```

We'll have to match segment and group names with the ones already in DOS-CALLS.LIB when we link to it. When we use the simplified directives this is all taken care of automatically. Also, note that we no longer set up the stack at the beginning of the program. With DOS .EXE files, we had to push a two word address onto the stack because, when the program ended, control would go to DS:0000 where an INT 20H instruction waited. This is no longer necessary under OS/2.

At the end of the program, we use call DosExit. This is how you end a program under OS/2. To use it, you have to push two words, and then CALL DosExit. The first word pushed is either 0 or 1, and tells DosExit whether or not you want to terminate all threads. It is possible for a program to have numerous threads executing at the same time. A 0 here means that DosExit should terminate only the current thread; a 1 means that all threads should be terminated. We will always set this word to 1, since we are not going to deal with multithreaded processes.

The second word pushed is a *termination code*, which can be passed back to a program that started the current one. We'll always use a code of 0:

```
        .286
        .MODEL  SMALL
        .STACK  200H

        .DATA

        .CODE
                EXTRN   DOSEXIT:FAR

ENTRY:          ;Program goes here.

EXIT:           PUSH    1
                PUSH    0
                CALL    DOSEXIT

                END     ENTRY
```

Note that DosExit is also declared as EXTRN FAR in the beginning of the program, as all service calls will have to be from now on. Now that we are familiar with the stack loading (as opposed to register loading) calls of OS/2, we have to look at the type of items that can be loaded onto the stack. There are three such stack objects in OS/2 as shown below.

Stack Objects in OS/2

Type	Explanation
WORD	Just a 16-bit value.
DWORD	A value held in two words, like DX:AX. The high word of a register pair (DX here) is pushed first.
PTR	An address pointer. Here you just push values like DS:BX or ES:DI onto the stack. The selector value is pushed first, followed by the offset (like DS and then BX).

▶ Introduction to OS/2 419

Because of the nature of the OS/2 Applications Programming Interface (API), and its heavy reliance on pushing values on the stack, we will become quite familiar with these types. We'll see how they work when we start filling out our .EXE file shell later.

We should also cover one more point about .EXE files under OS/2. That is the default values in the registers when the program begins. When the .EXE file is first loaded, the registers are set to specific values. CS:IP is set to the entry point of the program, as expected. SS:SP points to the top of the stack. DS holds the selector for the data segment. But AX holds something a little new — the selector for the environment. This is much like the PSP (program segment prefix) under DOS, in that we will be able to find all the characters typed after the program's name on the command line in the environment.

If you are going to use information from the environment, it is usual to move AX into DS (having preserved the data segment's selector, usually in ES). Then DS:0000 is the beginning of the enviroment. At this location, you will find an ASCIIZ string (ASCII terminated with a 0 byte) that gives the current program's full name, including path. For example, if you adapted the .EXE file shell into a program named GO.ASM, you could produce the .EXE file GO.EXE using MASM in the DOS mode:

```
C:\>MASM GO;
```

When we link, we'll have to use OS/2's linker and include the library that will resolve the EXTRN references for us, DOSCALLS.LIB. Here is the LINK command for GO.OBJ:

```
C:\>LINK GO        ← Type this
IBM Linker/2 Version 1.00
Copyright (C) IBM Corporation 1987
Copyright (C) Microsoft Corp 1983-1987. All rights reserved.

Run File [GO.EXE]:
List File [NUL.MAP]:
Libraries [.LIB]: DOSCALLS       ← And this
Definitions File [NUL .DEF]:
```

Now let's say that you moved to the subdirectory C:\SUB› and started GO.EXE like this:

```
C:\SUB>GO
```

In this case, the character appearing at the beginning of the enviroment would be "C:\SUB\GO.EXE",0. The BX register holds the offset, in the environment, of the string of characters typed after the program's name on the command line. If we had typed

```
C:\SUB>GO Hello
```

(and had moved the environment selector into DS), we would find this at DS:BX: " Hello",0. In addition, when the .EXE file is first loaded, DX holds the size of the stack, and CX holds the actual length of the data segment. This information can be useful to a program as it is running.

That's our OS/2 .EXE file shell. It's not much different than its DOS counterpart. In fact, almost everything we examine will have some close DOS or BIOS counterpart, beginning with the first OS/2 programming topic we take up: OS/2 Output.

OS/2 Output (Vio and DosWrite)

Character output is always done in strings in OS/2. If you just want to type out one character, that's a string of length 1. Also, you pass the length of strings to OS/2. You don't terminate them, as you do under DOS (with "$").

You may recall that the BIOS treatment of the cursor when typing out characters was sometimes disappointing because the cursor was not updated. OS/2 is even worse than that (unfortunately) in the majority of its string printing services. It ignores the cursor altogether. You have to specify a row and column at which printout will start. This awkward method takes some getting used to in your programs.

The DosWrite Service

        PUSH   WORD   A file or device handle (=1 to print on screen).
        PUSH   PTR   Address of data to be printed.
        PUSH   WORD   Number of bytes to print.
        PUSH   PTR   Address at which OS/2 is to return the number of bytes
                                  it actually wrote (more useful for files than typing
                                  on the screen).
        CALL   DOSWRITE

Before we get into the Vio services, let's look at DosWrite, similar to the all-purpose DOS INT 21H output service (40H). You simply give DosWrite a handle to write to, the location of the data, the length of the data, and you're off. This handle could be a handle to a file, which you got when opening or creating a file, or it could be one of the predefined handles.

In OS/2, the predefined handles are Standard Input (STDIN = keyboard for all our purposes) = 0; Standard Output (STDOUT = the screen for us) = 1; and Standard Error (STDERR) = 2. These handles are always available (unless you are running under OS/2 detached mode; see the end of this chapter). They do not have to be opened with something like DosOpen, as you have to do for files.

To send output to the screen, we select a handle of 1 (STDOUT). We also have to give DosWrite these things on the stack, in order:

WORD   A file or device handle (=1 to print on screen).
PTR   Address of data to be printed.
WORD   Number of bytes to print.
PTR   Address at which OS/2 is to return the number of bytes it actually wrote (more useful for files than typing on the screen).

Let's make this clear with an example. Here is a small program, DOSWRITE.ASM, from beginning to end. All it does is to print out the message "No Worries.":

```
        .286
        .MODEL  SMALL
        .STACK  200H

        .DATA
MESSAGE         DB      "No Worries."
MESSAGELEN      EQU     $-MESSAGE
NUMBER_BYTES    DW      0

        .CODE

        EXTRN   DOSWRITE:FAR, DOSEXIT:FAR

ENTRY:  PUSH    1
        PUSH    DS
        PUSH    OFFSET MESSAGE
        PUSH    MESSAGELEN
        PUSH    DS
        PUSH    OFFSET NUMBER_BYTES
        CALL    DOSWRITE

        PUSH    1                       ;Exit normally.
        PUSH    0
        CALL    DOSEXIT

        END     ENTRY
```

422 ▶ Advanced Assembly Language

We simply set up the message in the data segment like this:

```
.DATA
MESSAGE         DB      "No Worries."   ←
MESSAGELEN      EQU     $-MESSAGE       ←
NUMBER_BYTES    DW      0
```

We find the message length with MESSAGELEN EQU $-MESSAGE, right after the definition of MESSAGE. This just fills MESSAGELEN with the length of message. Now we add these instructions to the .EXE file shell:

```
.286
.MODEL  SMALL
.STACK  200H

.DATA
MESSAGE         DB      "No Worries."
MESSAGELEN      EQU     $-MESSAGE
NUMBER_BYTES    DW      0

.CODE
        EXTRN   DOSWRITE:FAR, DOSEXIT:FAR

ENTRY:  PUSH    1                           ←
        PUSH    DS                          ←
        PUSH    OFFSET MESSAGE              ←
        PUSH    MESSAGELEN                  ←
        PUSH    DS                          ←
        PUSH    OFFSET NUMBER_BYTES         ←
        CALL    DOSWRITE                    ←

        PUSH    1               ;Exit normally.
        PUSH    0
        CALL    DOSEXIT

        END     ENTRY
```

In particular, notice that we are are now pushing immediate values such as:

```
→ PUSH    1
         :
  PUSH    OFFSET MESSAGE
  PUSH    MESSAGELEN
```

This is the first time we have seen this immediate method of pushing values, and it will come in handy with the enormous number of pushes you have to do in the average OS/2 program. Note that immediate pushing will not work on the 8088 or 8086 chips (and OS/2 will not work with 8088s or 8086s either).

> **TIP** In fact, it is common in OS/2 programming to define macros that will do all the pushing for you and then to pass the values to be pushed as parameters. Often, OS/2 programs are simply masses of macros.

In our program, we push the video handle (1), the address of MESSAGE, the length of MESSAGE, and the address of the location where OS/2 will return the number of bytes actually typed to the screen.

```
        .286
        .MODEL  SMALL
        .STACK  200H

        .DATA
MESSAGE         DB      "No Worries."
MESSAGELEN      EQU     $-MESSAGE
NUMBER_BYTES    DW      0

        .CODE
        EXTRN   DOSWRITE:FAR, DOSEXIT:FAR
ENTRY:  PUSH    1                       ←
        PUSH    DS                      ←
        PUSH    OFFSET  MESSAGE         ←
        PUSH    MESSAGELEN              ←
        PUSH    DS                      ←
        PUSH    OFFSET  NUMBER_BYTES    ←
        CALL    DOSWRITE                ←
        :
        :
```

And then end with DosExit:

```
        .286
        .MODEL  SMALL
        .STACK  200H

        .DATA
MESSAGE         DB      "No Worries."
MESSAGELEN      EQU     $-MESSAGE
NUMBER_BYTES    DW      0

        .CODE
        EXTRN   DOSWRITE:FAR, DOSEXIT:FAR

ENTRY:  PUSH    1
        PUSH    DS
        PUSH    OFFSET  MESSAGE
        PUSH    MESSAGELEN
        PUSH    DS
        PUSH    OFFSET  NUMBER_BYTES
        CALL    DOSWRITE

←       PUSH    1                       ;Exit normally.
←       PUSH    0
←       CALL    DOSEXIT

        END     ENTRY
```

Give this program a try if you want to see the message, "No Worries." appear under OS/2. Our first OS/2 program works, and it wasn't hard to write. DosWrite types out the bytes that you have selected starting at the current cursor position, as does the next OS/2 service, VioWrtTTY.

VioWrtTTY — TTY Output to Screen (Uses and Updates Cursor)

PUSH	PTR	Pointer to the ASCII string to print on the screen.
PUSH	WORD	Length of the string.
PUSH	WORD	The VIO handle (must be 0).
CALL	VIOWRTTTY	

The first Vio service we will work on is VioWrtTTY. Again, you pass the address of the data to be printed, and then the number of bytes to print. The Vio handle for the screen, however, is not 1, but 0. We'll see that you have to pass the Vio handle for virtually every Vio service, and it will always be 0.

VioWrtTTY starts printing at the cursor location, unlike all the following Vio services. It treats screen control characters like <cr> (ASCII 13) or <lf> (ASCII 10) as control characters. It does not print them out as symbols as some of the BIOS services do. Instead, <cr> will generate a carriage return, <lf> will generate a line feed, and so forth.

Also, the string to be printed is only ASCII. No screen display attributes are included. You may recall that characters can be typed to the screen can sometimes be specified as ASCII with a particular attribute under BIOS. This same thing can be done a number of ways under OS/2.

VioWrtCellStr — Write a Cell String

PUSH	PTR	Address of cell string (attribute, character, attribute, character...) to be printed.
PUSH	WORD	The number of bytes to be printed
PUSH	WORD	Screen Row where the string will be printed
PUSH	WORD	Screen Column where the string will be printed
PUSH	WORD	Vio Handle (must be 0).
CALL	VIOWRTCELLSTR	

▶ Introduction to OS/2   425

This is the first of the normal Vio printing services. VioWrtCellStr is an improvement on its BIOS counterpart in that you can specify different attributes for each character to be printed.

> **TIP** To make the Vio services (which print at a specifed row and column position) print out at the cursor position, you can use another OS/2 service named VioGetCursorPos. See Appendix B for more details.

The combination of ASCII character and screen attribute (two bytes) is referred to as a *character cell*. This Vio service will let you print out a whole string of such cells. The screen attributes that can be used in the Vio services that print attributes work as shown in Figure 13-1.

```
XRGBIRGB
 | |  | |_____Color of Character
 | |  |_____If = 1, makes character intense
 | |_____Color of Background
 |_____The meaning of "X" is set with VioSetState. If "Blink" is enabled, then X=1
              means the character will blink. If "Intensity" is enabled, then X=1 means
              the background will be intense.
```
Figure 13-1. Screen Attributes for Vio Services

An example would be 01110100B = 74H, red on a white background, or 00001111 = FH, high intensity white on a black background. For example, if you wanted to print out four red A's (ASCII 41H) on a white background (attribute 74H), followed by three blue B's (ASCII 42H) on a white background (attribute 71H), then you could define a *cell string* like this (with attribute first, then ASCII, attribute, ASCII, etc):

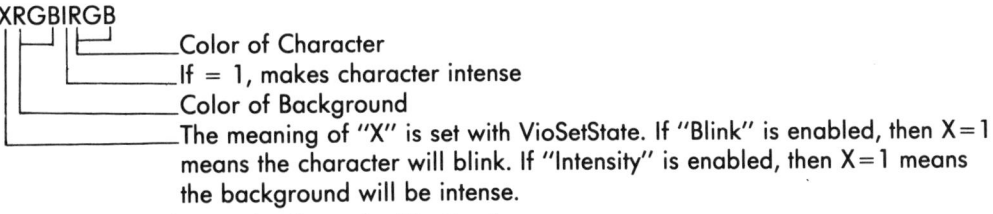

This service is one of the ones where you have to specify row and column at which your cell string will be printed.

> **NOTE** When you specify row and column, remember that (0,0) is the upper left-hand corner of the screen.

If you wanted to use a service more like the old BIOS, where you specify what to type and only one attribute, the next service, VioWrtCharStrAtt, will let you do so.

VioWrtCharStrAttr — Write Character String with Attribute

    PUSH PTR   Address of the character string to print on screen.
    PUSH WORD The length in bytes of the character string.
    PUSH WORD Screen Row at which printout will start.
    PUSH WORD Screen Column at which printout will start.
    PUSH PTR   Address of the attribute byte.
    PUSH WORD The Vio handle (must be 0).
    CALL VIOWRTCHARSTRATTR

This service prints out a character string (specified as a string of ASCII bytes) with a single attribute. Instead of loading the attribute byte into a word (in, say, the lower byte) and pushing that, you pass the address (two words) of the attribute byte as stored in memory. Let's give VioWrtStrAttr a try ourselves and print out the "No Worries." message with some dramatic attribute, say blue on black, attribute 1. First, we'd start with the .EXE file shell:

```
.286
.MODEL   SMALL
.STACK   200H

.DATA

.CODE
         EXTRN    DosExit:FAR

ENTRY:

         PUSH     1                       ;Exit normally.
         PUSH     0
         CALL     DOSEXIT

         END      ENTRY
```

Then we can add the data we'll need: the string itself, the string's length, and the attribute byte (which we'll call ATTRIBYTE):

```
.286
.MODEL   SMALL
.STACK   200H

.DATA
MESSAGE          DB       "No Worries."
```

▶ Introduction to OS/2

```
MESSAGELEN      EQU     $-MESSAGE
ATTRIBYTE       DB      1       ;Use a blue-on-black attribute.

.CODE

        EXTRN   DosExit:FAR

ENTRY:

        PUSH    1               ;Exit normally.
        PUSH    0
        CALL    DOSEXIT

        END     ENTRY
```

Now we have to set up for VioWrtCharStrAtt. To begin, we have to push a pointer to MESSAGE. Pointers are pushed with the selector register first, like this:

```
.286
.MODEL  SMALL
.STACK  200H

.DATA
MESSAGE         DB      "No Worries."
MESSAGELEN      EQU     $-MESSAGE
ATTRIBYTE       DB      1       ;Use a blue-on-black attribute.

.CODE
        EXTRN   VioWrtCharStrAtt:FAR, DosExit:FAR

ENTRY:  PUSH    DS
        PUSH    OFFSET MESSAGE
        PUSH    MESSAGELEN

        PUSH    1               ;Exit normally.
        PUSH    0
        CALL    DOSEXIT

        END     ENTRY
```

We follow it with the message's length, as required. Next, we have to select the row and column location of our message on the screen. Let's choose row 10, column 30, near the middle of the screen:

```
.286
.MODEL  SMALL
.STACK  200H

.DATA
MESSAGE         DB      "No Worries."
MESSAGELEN      EQU     $-MESSAGE
ATTRIBYTE       DB      1       ;Use a blue-on-black attribute.

.CODE
```

```
            EXTRN    VioWrtCharStrAtt:FAR, DosExit:FAR

ENTRY:      PUSH     DS
            PUSH     OFFSET MESSAGE
            PUSH     MESSAGELEN
            PUSH     10                    ←
            PUSH     30                    ←

            PUSH     1                    ;Exit normally.
            PUSH     0
            CALL     DOSEXIT

            END      ENTRY
```

Finally, we push a pointer to the attribute byte ATTRIBYTE, and the Vio handle (0). The whole program is shown in Listing 13-2.

Listing 13-2. OS/2 VioWrtCharStrAtt Example.

```
            .286
            .MODEL   SMALL
            .STACK   200H

            .DATA
MESSAGE              DB       "No Worries."
MESSAGELEN           EQU      $-MESSAGE
ATTRIBYTE            DB       1           ;Use a blue-on-black attribute.

            .CODE
            EXTRN    VioWrtCharStrAtt:FAR, DosExit:FAR

ENTRY:      PUSH     DS
            PUSH     OFFSET MESSAGE
            PUSH     MESSAGELEN
            PUSH     10
            PUSH     30
            PUSH     DS                    ←
            PUSH     OFFSET ATTRIBYTE      ←
            PUSH     0                     ←
            CALL     VioWrtCharStrAtt      ←
            PUSH     1                    ;Exit normally.
            PUSH     0
            CALL     DOSEXIT

            END      ENTRY
```

VioPopUp — Pop-Ups under OS/2

One additional Vio call deserves notice here, VioPopUp. VioPopUp is not to be used in the way that you might think: it is not supposed to be used for normal "popup" utilities. Instead, it is used by programs that are normally cut off from using the screen when they need to grab screen control to report some sort of problem or emergency.

▶ **Introduction to OS/2** 429

Under OS/2, you can *detach* a program and that program will continue to run. DETACH is a common mainframe command; however, the program can no longer accept input from the keyboard or print out to the screen unless it takes special action, and that action is calling VioPopUp. The parameters you push for VioPopUp are these:

                PUSH   PTR   Address of a one word option field:
                                rrrrrrrr rrrrrrXW (r = reserved).
                                X = 0 → Nontransparent pop-up (screen cleared).
                                  = 1 → Transparent pop-up.
                                W = 0 → Return with error if pop-up cannot be made.
                                  = 1 → Wait for pop-up.
                PUSH   WORD   Vio handle (must be 0).
                CALL   VIOPOPUP

Selecting a nontransparent pop-up means that the screen will be cleared before your program starts to type on it. If you were in graphics mode, the screen is reset to text mode. If you ask for a transparent pop-up, the screen is not reset, and the call will fail if the screen is currently in graphics mode.

TAKE5.EXE — An OS/2 TSR

Let's write a program called TAKE5 that you can DETACH, and that will grab the screen and clear it after 5 minutes are up with the message: "Time Is Up!" It will wait until you type a key and then reliniquish the screen.

After making TAKE5.EXE, just type DETACH TAKE5. In a way, this is like the DOS memory-resident programs we developed in Chapter 7, but only slightly. TAKE5 cannot read what is being typed in the main session, it cannot print on the screen (except via VioPopUp), and it is isolated from every other program.

In TAKE5, we'll use a service called DosSleep. If you pass DosSleep a number of milliseconds as a double word (push high word first, then low word), it will suspend the program for that long. Since we want to suspend TAKE5 for 5 minutes, we need to know how many milliseconds there are in those 5 minutes. That is 5 (minutes) × 60 (seconds/minute) × 1,000 (milliseconds/second) = 300,000 milliseconds. In hex, this is 493E0H. That means that we can execute these instructions and then call DosSleep:

430 ▶ Advanced Assembly Language

```
                        ;493E0H = 300,000 = no. of millisec.s in 5 minutes.
ENTRY:  PUSH    4       ;Push high word
        PUSH    93E0H   ;Push low word
        CALL    DosSleep
          :
          :
        END     ENTRY
```

After we return, we have to grab the screen with VioPopUp. To do that, we add this code:

```
.286
.MODEL  SMALL
.STACK  200H

.DATA

.CODE
        EXTRN   DOSEXIT:FAR
                        ;493E0H = 300,000 = no. of millisec.s in 5 minutes.
ENTRY:  PUSH    4       ;Push high word
        PUSH    93E0H   ;Push low word
        CALL    DosSleep
        PUSH    DS
        PUSH    OFFSET POPUP_OPTIONS
        PUSH    0
        CALL    VioPopUp
          :
          :
        END     ENTRY
```

Where POPUP_OPTIONS is defined in the data area to request a nontransparent popup that will wait:

```
.286
.MODEL  SMALL
.STACK  200H

.DATA
        POPUP_OPTIONS   DB 1

.CODE
        EXTRN   DOSEXIT:FAR
                        ;493E0H = 300,000 = no. of millisec.s in 5 minutes.
ENTRY:  PUSH    4       ;Push high word
        PUSH    93E0H   ;Push low word
        CALL    DosSleep

        PUSH    DS
        PUSH    OFFSET POPUP_OPTIONS
        PUSH    0
        CALL    VioPopUp
          :
          :
        END     ENTRY
```

▶ **Introduction to OS/2** 431

After we have control of the screen, we have to print out our message. We can put the message into the data segment like this:

```
        .286
        .MODEL  SMALL
        .STACK  200H

        .DATA
                MESSAGE DB "Time Is Up!"            ←
                MESSAGELEN EQU $ - MESSAGE          ←
                POPUP_OPTIONS   DB 1

        .CODE
                EXTRN   DOSEXIT:FAR
                                ;493E0H = 300,000 = no. of millisec.s in 5 minutes.
        ENTRY:  PUSH    4           ;Push high word
                PUSH    93E0H       ;Push low word
                CALL    DosSleep

                PUSH    DS
                PUSH    OFFSET POPUP_OPTIONS
                PUSH    0
                CALL    VioPopUp
                    :
                    :
                END     ENTRY
```

NOTE VioPopUp gives a program control of the screen, keyboard, and mouse.

And print it out like this:

```
        .286
        .MODEL  SMALL
        .STACK  200H

        .DATA
                MESSAGE DB "Time Is Up!"
                MESSAGELEN EQU $ - MESSAGE
                POPUP_OPTIONS   DB 1

        .CODE
                EXTRN   DOSEXIT:FAR
                                ;493E0H = 300,000 = no. of millisec.s in 5 minutes.
        ENTRY:  PUSH    4           ;Push high word
                PUSH    93E0H       ;Push low word
                CALL    DosSleep

                PUSH    DS
                PUSH    OFFSET POPUP_OPTIONS
                PUSH    0
                CALL    VioPopUp

                PUSH    DS              ←
                PUSH    OFFSET MESSAGE  ←
```

432 ▶ Advanced Assembly Language

```
        PUSH    MESSAGELEN         ←
        PUSH    0                  ←
        CALL    VioWrtTTY          ←
          :
          :
        END     ENTRY
```

Next we will wait for a key to be struck with the Kbd service KbdCharIn. Reading keys is not an easy process under OS/2, but it will be easier when we work with the Presentation Manager in the next chapter. Here, we are instructing OS/2 to read a key, and, if no keys are ready, to wait for one:

```
        .286
        .MODEL  SMALL
        .STACK  200H
        .DATA
                MESSAGE DB "Time Is Up!"
                MESSAGELEN EQU $ - MESSAGE
                POPUP_OPTIONS   DB 1
                CHAR_DATA       DB 0
                        SCAN    DB 0
                        STATUS  DB 0
                        NSHIFT  DB 0
                        SHIFT   DW 0
                        TSTAMP  DD 0

        .CODE
                EXTRN   DOSEXIT:FAR
                                ;493E0H = 300,000 = no. of millisec.s in 5 minutes.
ENTRY:  PUSH    4               ;Push high word
        PUSH    93E0H           ;Push low word
        CALL    DosSleep

        PUSH    DS
        PUSH    OFFSET POPUP_OPTIONS
        PUSH    0
        CALL    VioPopUp

        PUSH    DS
        PUSH    OFFSET MESSAGE
        PUSH    MESSAGELEN
        PUSH    0
        CALL    VioWrtTTY

        PUSH    DS                          ←
        PUSH    OFFSET CHAR_DATA            ←
        PUSH    0                           ←
        PUSH    0                           ←
        CALL    KbdCharIn                   ←
          :
          :
        END     ENTRY
```

▶ Introduction to OS/2 433

You might note in passing the data area we had to set up for KbdCharIn, just to read in a single key. After we receive a key, we just end the pop-up with VioEndPopUp:

```
        .286
        .MODEL  SMALL
        .STACK  200H

        .DATA
                MESSAGE DB "Time Is Up!"
                MESSAGELEN EQU $ - MESSAGE
                POPUP_OPTIONS   DB 1
                CHAR_DATA       DB 0
                    SCAN        DB 0
                    STATUS      DB 0
                    NSHIFT      DB 0
                    SHIFT       DW 0
                    TSTAMP      DD 0

        .CODE
                EXTRN   DOSEXIT:FAR
                            ;493E0H = 300,000 = no. of millisec.s in 5 minutes.
ENTRY:          PUSH    4           ;Push high word
                PUSH    93E0H       ;Push low word
                CALL    DosSleep

                PUSH    DS
                PUSH    OFFSET POPUP_OPTIONS
                PUSH    0
                CALL    VioPopUp

                PUSH    DS
                PUSH    OFFSET MESSAGE
                PUSH    MESSAGELEN
                PUSH    0
                CALL    VioWrtTTY

                PUSH    DS
                PUSH    OFFSET CHAR_DATA
                PUSH    0
                PUSH    0
                CALL    KbdCharIn

                PUSH    0
                CALL    VioEndPopUp
                :
                :
                END     ENTRY
```

Now we're ready to exit with DosExit. The whole TAKE5.ASM program, including all the EXTRNs, is shown in Listing 13-3.

Listing 13-3. TAKE5.ASM — Waits Five Minutes and Grabs the Screen.

```
        .286
        .MODEL  SMALL
        .STACK  200H

        .DATA
                MESSAGE DB "Time Is Up!"
                MESSAGELEN EQU $ - MESSAGE
                POPUP_OPTIONS   DB 1
                CHAR_DATA       DB 0
                        SCAN    DB 0
                        STATUS  DB 0
                        NSHIFT  DB 0
                        SHIFT   DW 0
                        TSTAMP  DD 0

        .CODE
                EXTRN   DosExit:FAR,DosSleep:FAR,VioPopUp:FAR,
                EXTRN   VioEndPopUp:FAR,VioWrtTTY:FAR,KbdCharIn:FAR

                        ;493E0H = 300,000 = no. of millisec.s in 5 minutes.
        ENTRY:  PUSH    4       ;Push high word
                PUSH    93E0H   ;Push low word
                CALL    DosSleep

                PUSH    DS
                PUSH    OFFSET POPUP_OPTIONS
                PUSH    0
                CALL    VioPopUp

                PUSH    DS
                PUSH    OFFSET MESSAGE
                PUSH    MESSAGELEN
                PUSH    0
                CALL    VioWrtTTY

                PUSH    DS
                PUSH    OFFSET CHAR_DATA
                PUSH    0
                PUSH    0
                CALL    KbdCharIn

                PUSH    0
                CALL    VioEndPopUp

        EXIT:   PUSH    1               ;A Normal Exit.
                PUSH    0
                CALL    DosExit

                END     ENTRY
```

Give it a try. Just type DETACH TAKE5. Five minutes later, TAKE5 will let you know that the time's up, stopping the program, and then running. Our first multitasking example! Now that we have the basics of OS/2 down, we're ready to turn to the most popular OS/2 topic, the Presentation Manager.

Chapter 14

OS/2 Presentation Manager Primer

Welcome to the Presentation Manager

The big news about OS/2 1.1 was the release of Presentation Manager. This was a long-awaited event in PC–PS/2 history. For the first time, the primary interface with the machine made use of windows and of the mouse.

When you boot under OS/2 1.1 or 1.2, you are faced with the Presentation Manager screen, which is a collection of icons and windows. Although it is possible to use the keyboard with Presentation Manager, it is uncompromisingly awkward. Similiar actions can require very different keystrokes, and the use of nonintuitive keycodes (like Alt-F4 or Cntrl-F5) make them hard to remember. To use the Presentation Manager fully, you must have a mouse.

OS/2 and the Mouse

This was a big switch, but a big improvement. The Presentation Manager is a graphical interface, designed for easy screen manipulation (on the user's part, anyway). You just point and shoot. Windows open, scroll, or shrink into icons at the click of the mouse.

The use of the mouse has allowed the introduction of the desktop metaphor to the IBM line. The Macintosh has used the desktop metaphor from the beginning, and its introduction by IBM is a measure of its success. The idea is to think of computer tasks as being represented on pieces of paper on a desktop. Papers can overlap, be moved, or even be thrown out. It is a very effective way to handle multiple tasks.

Presentation Manager (PM) programs simply open another window on the display and the user interacts with them primarily through the use of the mouse. Occasionally, you may have to type text commands (to name files, for example). For this purpose, you can open *dialog boxes*, which accept keystrokes. The use of the mouse was also made easier by introducing *buttons* (actually a special type of window), which allow you to make easy choices on the screen. Another concept we will meet is the *menu*. If you've used PM, you're familiar with menus. You can click the mouse on the menu bar at the top of most windows, and various options appear, allowing you to select them.

The last new item on your screen is the *icon*. This is an easy handle representing a program or file, ready to spring into action as soon as it's clicked or selected. When you *minimize* a program's window, it becomes an icon on the lower part of the screen. To open that window up again, all you have to do is select it with mouse or keyboard.

With all these improvements, using Presentation Manager programs is easy. From the programmer's point of view, however, writing them has become more difficult.

Programming the Presentation Manager

The number of functions available in the Win group of function calls — the central functions of PM programs — is enormous. That doesn't simply mean that the programmer has the luxury of choosing among hundreds of options; it means that he or she will have to be conversant with a large number of functions before even starting.

Programming PM is not easy. It is a whole world by itself. As we progress through this chapter, you'll get an indication of the complexity involved. When the Macintosh was introduced and became popular, programmers were dismayed with the extraordinary amount of material they had to learn to put together even the most rudimentary program.

Presentation Manager programs should adhere to the basic PM philosophy: use the mouse, icons, and buttons, and avoid excessive use of the keyboard. PM program windows should look much like other PM program windows. If you've programmed on the Mac, you know that very heavy stress is laid on making programs conform to the norm. That means that the programmer has to supply code to handle many tasks that the user expects, from the ability to import "clipboard" graphics from other programs to making sure your window has and can use scroll bars.

Some Unpleasant Presentation Manager Surprises

The emphasis is so heavy on "nonamateur" programming, that you can't even write Presentation Manager programs without purchasing either the expensive OS/2 Software Developer's Kit, or the OS/2 Presentation Manager Toolkit.

Until now, all the programs we have written could be compiled under simple OS/2 1.0. To create links to the OS/2 functions in the dynamic link libraries, we have linked in the DOSCALLS.LIB library when we have used LINK. DOSCALLS.LIB comes with OS/2, so there is no problem.

On the other hand, you cannot use any Win or Gpi functions if you only have DOSCALLS.LIB. All Presentation Manager functions are in a library named OS2.LIB. This library also includes all the functions we have been using up to now, the Mou, Kbd, Dos, and Vio groups.

However, simple OS/2 itself does not include OS2.LIB. You have to buy this library in one of the two software packages listed above (the Software Developer's Kit or the Programmer's Toolkit). In this and the following chapter, we will be using OS2.LIB when we link, not DOSCALLS.LIB:

```
D:\>LINK PROG,,,OS2;
```

There's more bad news. The Presentation Manager is a graphical interface, and, until now in OS/2, we've only been dealing with text I/O. That means that the Vio functions will no longer work (except some of them and under certain circumstances). In addition, PM programs receive input through *messages*. Neither the Kbd nor the Mou functions will work here. Instead, we'll see how to process messages (which include keystrokes and mouse movements) sent to our particular window.

Of course, the Mou, Kbd, and Vio functions are not useless. PM is only one OS/2 session. In all the other sessions, they will work as expected. However, if you want to produce PM programs, you'll have to learn a new way of accepting input and displaying output.

> **NOTE** The Dos group, however, is unaffected.

However, the advantages of PM clearly outweigh the disadvantages, and, with all this preparation, we are ready to begin. In this chapter, we're going to develop a Presentation Manager progam named WIN.ASM. When you run WIN the screen snaps to the Presentation Manager display, and a window will appear that you can shrink or enlarge, maximize, or minimize (i.e., make into an icon).

Getting Started with the Presentation Manager

We can start with the usual .EXE file skeleton:

```
        .MODEL  SMALL
        .286

        .STACK  20000

        .DATA

        .CODE
ENTRY:

        END     ENTRY
```

> **TIP** One thing you might notice immediately is that the stack is larger here — 20,000 bytes. This size is more than ample; however, Presentation Manager programs are fond of using the stack, and you should not go below 4K of stack space. If you do, you risk crashing your program.

The first thing we must do is to initialize the window system with a call to WinInitialize. We pass a value of 0 to that function call like this:

```
    .MODEL  SMALL
    .286

    .STACK  20000

    .DATA

    .CODE
        EXTRN   WinInitialize:FAR

ENTRY   PROC FAR

→       PUSH    0                       ;Get Anchor Block Handle
→       CALL    WinInitialize
                :
                :
```

This function returns a 32-bit handle to something called an *anchor block*. This anchor block is an area of memory where OS/2 keeps track of much of the information associated with the window we are going to produce. This is where it's easier in C: there, you can just say ANCHOR_BLOCK_HANDLE = WinInitialize(0);. The way the handle is really returned is in the register pair DX:AX. The C compiler takes care of the details for you if you are using C, but the actual value is returned in those registers and we can make use of them.

NOTE If the handle was a 16-bit one, it would have been returned in AX alone.

We have to put aside storage for the full 32-bit handle, which we can do with two words, ANCHOR_LOW and ANCHOR_HIGH, like this:

```
    .MODEL  SMALL
    .286

    .STACK  20000

    .DATA
→       ANCHOR_LOW      DW 0            ;Anchor block handle
→       ANCHOR_HIGH     DW 0

    .CODE
        EXTRN   WinInitialize:FAR

ENTRY   PROC FAR

        PUSH    0                       ;Get Anchor Block Handle
        CALL    WinInitialize
→       MOV     ANCHOR_LOW,AX
→       MOV     ANCHOR_HIGH,DX
```

▶ OS/2 Presentation Manager Primer

We now have the 32-bit anchor block handle in custody. The next step is to set up a message queue. It is during this step that the screen switches to the Presentation Manager display (and graphics mode). All input to our program (like keyboard or mouse input) will be handled through this queue, so you can see that it is important. We can set it up using WinCreateMsgQueue. First, we have to push the anchor block handle. To push a 32-bit value, we first push the high word and then the low word. Since these numbers are still in DX and AX respectively, we can push those like this:

```
        .MODEL  SMALL
        .286

        .STACK  20000

        .DATA
                ANCHOR_LOW      DW 0            ;Anchor block handle
                ANCHOR_HIGH     DW 0

        .CODE
                EXTRN   WinInitialize:FAR, WinCreateMsgQueue:FAR

ENTRY   PROC FAR
        PUSH    0                               ;Get Anchor Block Handle
        CALL    WinInitialize
        MOV     ANCHOR_LOW,AX
        MOV     ANCHOR_HIGH,DX

→       PUSH    DX      ;Set up message queue -- Anchor high
→       PUSH    AX      ;Anchor low
                :
                :
```

Next we have to push the size of the message queue in bytes and then call WinCreateMsgQueue. If we push a value of 0, OS/2 will use the default size, which is fine for us:

```
        .MODEL  SMALL
        .286

        .STACK  20000

        .DATA
                ANCHOR_LOW      DW 0            ;Anchor block handle
                ANCHOR_HIGH     DW 0

        .CODE
                EXTRN   WinInitialize:FAR, WinCreateMsgQueue:FAR

ENTRY   PROC FAR
```

442 ▶ Advanced Assembly Language

```
        PUSH    0                       ;Get Anchor Block Handle
        CALL    WinInitialize
        MOV     ANCHOR_LOW,AX
        MOV     ANCHOR_HIGH,DX

        PUSH    DX      ;Set up message queue -- Anchor high
        PUSH    AX      ;Anchor low
→       PUSH    0       ;Use default size
→       CALL    WinCreateMsgQueue
                :
                :
```

WinCreateMsgQueue returns a 32-bit message queue handle that we'll need later. This handle is also returned in DX:AX. We can store it in the two words QUEUE_LOW and QUEUE_HIGH:

```
        .MODEL  SMALL
        .286

        .STACK  20000

        .DATA
                ANCHOR_LOW      DW 0            ;Anchor block handle
                ANCHOR_HIGH     DW 0
→               QUEUE_LOW       DW 0            ;Queue handle
→               QUEUE_HIGH      DW 0

        .CODE
                EXTRN   WinInitialize:FAR, WinCreateMsgQueue:FAR

ENTRY   PROC FAR

        PUSH    0                       ;Get Anchor Block Handle
        CALL    WinInitialize
        MOV     ANCHOR_LOW,AX
        MOV     ANCHOR_HIGH,DX

        PUSH    DX      ;Set up message queue -- Anchor high
        PUSH    AX      ;Anchor low
        PUSH    0       ;Use default size
        CALL    WinCreateMsgQueue
→       MOV     QUEUE_LOW,AX
→       MOV     QUEUE_HIGH,DX
                :
                :
```

The message queue has been set up. The following step is to do some window work. We need to *register* the kind of window we are going to produce before we create it, just as we did with MS Windows.

The main purpose of registering a window is to set up a *window function*. The window function answers any questions OS/2 has about the window and handles keyboard and mouse messages. We called this function DecodeMessages when we used Windows.

▶ OS/2 Presentation Manager Primer 443

When an action occurs (e.g., the mouse was moved or your window was covered up), OS/2 uses the window function to query your program about what it should do. The window function that we are going to write checks the message that was sent to it and returns appropriate values to OS/2. Let's just call our window function WINDOW_FUNC.

To use the function WinRegisterClass and register our window, we have to push the anchor block handle:

```
        .MODEL  SMALL
        .286

        .STACK  20000
        .DATA
                ANCHOR_LOW      DW 0            ;Anchor block handle
                ANCHOR_HIGH     DW 0
                QUEUE_LOW       DW 0            ;Queue handle
                QUEUE_HIGH      DW 0

        .CODE
                EXTRN   WinInitialize:FAR, WinCreateMsgQueue:FAR

ENTRY   PROC FAR

                PUSH    0                       ;Get Anchor Block Handle
                CALL    WinInitialize
                MOV     ANCHOR_LOW,AX
                MOV     ANCHOR_HIGH,DX

                PUSH    DX      ;Set up message queue -- Anchor high
                PUSH    AX      ;Anchor low
                PUSH    0       ;Use default size
                CALL    WinCreateMsgQueue
                MOV     QUEUE_LOW,AX
                MOV     QUEUE_HIGH,DX

     *          PUSH    ANCHOR_HIGH     ;Register class so we can get messages
     *          PUSH    ANCHOR_LOW
                        :
                        :
```

Next, we have to give a name to the class of windows we are registering. We don't need to name the class if we don't want to register the window, but, to receive messages, we have to register it (unregistered windows exit but can't accept messages). We'll call the class of windows FRANK. We set up a string in memory, and push the address onto the stack in preparation for WinRegisterClass:

444 ▶ Advanced Assembly Language

```
        .MODEL  SMALL
        .286

        .STACK  20000

        .DATA
                ANCHOR_LOW      DW  0           ;Anchor block handle
                ANCHOR_HIGH     DW  0
                QUEUE_LOW       DW  0           ;Queue handle
                QUEUE_HIGH      DW  0
→               CLASS_NAME      DB  'FRANK',0   ;Private window class name

        .CODE
                EXTRN   WinInitialize:FAR, WinCreateMsgQueue:FAR, DosExit:FAR

ENTRY   PROC FAR

                PUSH    0                       ;Get Anchor Block Handle
                CALL    WinInitialize
                MOV     ANCHOR_LOW,AX
                MOV     ANCHOR_HIGH,DX

                PUSH    DX      ;Set up message queue -- Anchor high
                PUSH    AX      ;Anchor low
                PUSH    0       ;Use default size
                CALL    WinCreateMsgQueue
                MOV     QUEUE_LOW,AX
                MOV     QUEUE_HIGH,DX

                PUSH    ANCHOR_HIGH     ;Register class so we can get messages
                PUSH    ANCHOR_LOW
→               PUSH    DS              ;Register this name for class
→               PUSH    OFFSET CLASS_NAME
                        :
                        :
```

Next we have to specify the class of window. We will use the most common user window, style 4. If you read the Presentation Manager documentation, you'll see that this style specifies that the window be redrawn when it is moved. The style is a double word, so we push the high word first, followed by the low word:

```
        .MODEL  SMALL
        .286

        .STACK  20000

        .DATA
                ANCHOR_LOW      DW  0           ;Anchor block handle
                ANCHOR_HIGH     DW  0
                QUEUE_LOW       DW  0           ;Queue handle
                QUEUE_HIGH      DW  0
                CLASS_NAME      DB  'FRANK',0   ;Private window class name

        .CODE
                EXTRN   WinInitialize:FAR, WinCreateMsgQueue:FAR, DosExit:FAR

ENTRY   PROC FAR

                PUSH    0                       ;Get Anchor Block Handle
                CALL    WinInitialize
                MOV     ANCHOR_LOW,AX
                MOV     ANCHOR_HIGH,DX
```

```
            PUSH    DX      ;Set up message queue -- Anchor high
            PUSH    AX      ;Anchor low
            PUSH    0       ;Use default size
            CALL    WinCreateMsgQueue
            MOV     QUEUE_LOW,AX
            MOV     QUEUE_HIGH,DX

            PUSH    ANCHOR_HIGH     ;Register class so we can get messages
            PUSH    ANCHOR_LOW
            PUSH    DS              ;Register this name for class
            PUSH    OFFSET CLASS_NAME
            PUSH    CS              ;Set up window function
            PUSH    OFFSET CS:WINDOW_FUNC
→           PUSH    0       ;High style -- use style 00000004H
→           PUSH    4       ;Low style
                  :
                  :
```

The final parameter is the amount of extra storage we are requesting in bytes. We won't take advantage of that extra memory here, so we set that value to 0 and call WinRegisterClass:

```
        .MODEL  SMALL
        .286

        .STACK  20000

        .DATA
            ANCHOR_LOW      DW 0            ;Anchor block handle
            ANCHOR_HIGH     DW 0
            QUEUE_LOW       DW 0            ;Queue handle
            QUEUE_HIGH      DW 0
            CLASS_NAME      DB 'FRANK',0    ;Private window class name

        .CODE
            EXTRN   WinInitialize:FAR, WinCreateMsgQueue:FAR, DosExit:FAR
            EXTRN   WinRegisterClass:FAR

ENTRY   PROC FAR

            PUSH    0               ;Get Anchor Block Handle
            CALL    WinInitialize
            MOV     ANCHOR_LOW,AX
            MOV     ANCHOR_HIGH,DX

            PUSH    DX      ;Set up message queue -- Anchor high
            PUSH    AX      ;Anchor low
            PUSH    0       ;Use default size
            CALL    WinCreateMsgQueue
            MOV     QUEUE_LOW,AX
            MOV     QUEUE_HIGH,DX

            PUSH    ANCHOR_HIGH     ;Register class so we can get messages
            PUSH    ANCHOR_LOW
            PUSH    DS              ;Register this name for class
            PUSH    OFFSET CLASS_NAME
            PUSH    CS              ;Set up window function
```

446 ▶ Advanced Assembly Language

```
            PUSH    OFFSET CS:WINDOW_FUNC
            PUSH    0       ;High style -- use style 00000004H
            PUSH    4       ;Low style
→           PUSH    0       ;No additional storage space
→           CALL    WinRegisterClass
                    :
                    :
```

Now when we start to request messages, OS/2 will know that WINDOW_FUNC is our message handler.

So far, nothing has appeared on the screen. We have gone to graphics mode, and the Presentation Manager display has appeared, but there is no window yet. The next call, WinCreateStdWindow, will make the window visible. We have to begin by pushing the handle of the parent window. In practice, the parent window is treated as the screen itself for a user window like ours with a 32-bit handle of 1. You can also pass 0 here for the same effect. Here we push the parent handle (high word followed by low word), which means that our window will appear as a PM window:

```
        .MODEL  SMALL
        .286

        .STACK  20000

        .DATA
                ANCHOR_LOW      DW 0            ;Anchor block handle
                ANCHOR_HIGH     DW 0
                QUEUE_LOW       DW 0            ;Queue handle
                QUEUE_HIGH      DW 0
                FLAGS           DW 0C3BH        ;Window flags
                                DW 8000H
                CLASS_NAME      DB 'FRANK',0    ;Private window class name

        .CODE
                EXTRN   WinInitialize:FAR, WinCreateMsgQueue:FAR, DosExit:FAR
                EXTRN   WinRegisterClass:FAR

ENTRY   PROC FAR

                PUSH    0                       ;Get Anchor Block Handle
                CALL    WinInitialize
                MOV     ANCHOR_LOW,AX
                MOV     ANCHOR_HIGH,DX

                PUSH    DX      ;Set up message queue -- Anchor high
                PUSH    AX      ;Anchor low
                PUSH    0       ;Use default size
                CALL    WinCreateMsgQueue
                MOV     QUEUE_LOW,AX
                MOV     QUEUE_HIGH,DX

                PUSH    ANCHOR_HIGH     ;Register class so we can get messages
                PUSH    ANCHOR_LOW
                PUSH    DS              ;Register this name for class
```

OS/2 Presentation Manager Primer 447

```
        PUSH    OFFSET CLASS_NAME
        PUSH    CS                      ;Set up window function
        PUSH    OFFSET CS:WINDOW_FUNC
        PUSH    0       ;High style -- use style 00000004H
        PUSH    4       ;Low style
        PUSH    0       ;No additional storage space
        CALL    WinRegisterClass

→       PUSH    0
→       PUSH    1
                :
                :
```

Next, we push the style of the window. In our case, we want to make the window visible, so we push the corresponding value, 800000000H. That is pushed high word first, low word second:

```
        .MODEL  SMALL
        .286

        .STACK  20000

        .DATA
        ANCHOR_LOW      DW 0            ;Anchor block handle
        ANCHOR_HIGH     DW 0
        QUEUE_LOW       DW 0            ;Queue handle
        QUEUE_HIGH      DW 0
        FLAGS           DW 0C3BH        ;Window flags
                        DW 8000H
        CLASS_NAME      DB 'FRANK',0    ;Private window class name

        .CODE
        EXTRN   WinInitialize:FAR, WinCreateMsgQueue:FAR, DosExit:FAR
        EXTRN   WinRegisterClass:FAR

ENTRY   PROC FAR

        PUSH    0                       ;Get Anchor Block Handle
        CALL    WinInitialize
        MOV     ANCHOR_LOW,AX
        MOV     ANCHOR_HIGH,DX

        PUSH    DX      ;Set up message queue -- Anchor high
        PUSH    AX      ;Anchor low
        PUSH    0       ;Use default size
        CALL    WinCreateMsgQueue
        MOV     QUEUE_LOW,AX
        MOV     QUEUE_HIGH,DX

        PUSH    ANCHOR_HIGH     ;Register class so we can get messages
        PUSH    ANCHOR_LOW
        PUSH    DS              ;Register this name for class
        PUSH    OFFSET CLASS_NAME
        PUSH    CS              ;Set up window function
        PUSH    OFFSET CS:WINDOW_FUNC
        PUSH    0       ;High style -- use style 00000004H
        PUSH    4       ;Low style
```

```
        PUSH    0               ;No additional storage space
        CALL    WinRegisterClass

        PUSH    0               ;Parent window handle
        PUSH    1
→       PUSH    8000H           ;Make window visible -- Style high
→       PUSH    0000H           ;Style low
        :
        :
```

Now we have to specify what type of window we want. You can do that by pushing the address of a double word of window flags, which we'll call FLAGS:

```
        .MODEL  SMALL
        .286

        .STACK  20000

        .DATA
            ANCHOR_LOW      DW 0            ;Anchor block handle
            ANCHOR_HIGH     DW 0
            QUEUE_LOW       DW 0            ;Queue handle
            QUEUE_HIGH      DW 0
→           FLAGS           DW 0C3BH        ;Window flags
→                           DW 8000H
            CLASS_NAME      DB 'FRANK',0    ;Private window class name

        .CODE
            EXTRN   WinInitialize:FAR, WinCreateMsgQueue:FAR, DosExit:FAR
            EXTRN   WinRegisterClass:FAR

ENTRY   PROC FAR

        PUSH    0                       ;Get Anchor Block Handle
        CALL    WinInitialize
        MOV     ANCHOR_LOW,AX
        MOV     ANCHOR_HIGH,DX

        PUSH    DX      ;Set up message queue -- Anchor high
        PUSH    AX      ;Anchor low
        PUSH    0       ;Use default size
        CALL    WinCreateMsgQueue
        MOV     QUEUE_LOW,AX
        MOV     QUEUE_HIGH,DX

        PUSH    ANCHOR_HIGH     ;Register class so we can get messages
        PUSH    ANCHOR_LOW
        PUSH    DS              ;Register this name for class
        PUSH    OFFSET CLASS_NAME
        PUSH    CS              ;Set up window function
        PUSH    OFFSET CS:WINDOW_FUNC
        PUSH    0               ;High style -- use style 00000004H
        PUSH    4               ;Low style
        PUSH    0               ;No additional storage space
        CALL    WinRegisterClass

        PUSH    0               ;Parent window handle
        PUSH    1
```

```
            PUSH      8000H        ;Make window visible -- Style high
            PUSH      0000H        ;Style low
            PUSH      DS           ;Point to window flags
            PUSH      OFFSET FLAGS
                      :
                      :
```

Here are some of the flags you can use, specifying the types of windows you want to use:

Visible	80000000H
Minimized	01000000H
Maximixed	00800000H
Titlebar	00000001H
SysMenu	00000002H
Vert. scroll	00000010H
Horiz. scroll	00000020H
Side border	00000040H
Border	00000200H
Minbutton	00001000H
Maxbutton	00002000H
Minmax	00003000H

You can OR these together to form a window that you like. In our case, we will include a title bar, the system menu, and a minmax button (which lets you expand or contract the window). We take the individual values from the list above, OR these options together ourselves, place the result (low word first) at FLAGS, and then pass the address to WinCreateStdWindow:

```
.MODEL  SMALL
.286

.STACK  20000

.DATA
        ANCHOR_LOW          DW 0
        ANCHOR_HIGH         DW 0
        QUEUE_LOW           DW 0              ;Queue handle
        QUEUE_HIGH          DW 0
        FLAGS               DW 0C3BH          ;Window flags
                            DW 8000H
        CLASS_NAME          DB 'FRANK',0      ;Private window class name

.CODE
        EXTRN   WinInitialize:FAR, WinCreateMsgQueue:FAR, DosExit:FAR
        EXTRN   WinRegisterClass:FAR
```

```
ENTRY    PROC FAR

         PUSH    0                       ;Get Anchor Block Handle
         CALL    WinInitialize
         MOV     ANCHOR_LOW,AX
         MOV     ANCHOR_HIGH,DX

         PUSH    DX      ;Set up message queue -- Anchor high
         PUSH    AX      ;Anchor low
         PUSH    0       ;Use default size
         CALL    WinCreateMsgQueue
         MOV     QUEUE_LOW,AX
         MOV     QUEUE_HIGH,DX

         PUSH    ANCHOR_HIGH     ;Register class so we can get messages
         PUSH    ANCHOR_LOW
         PUSH    DS              ;Register this name for class
         PUSH    OFFSET CLASS_NAME
         PUSH    CS              ;Set up window function
         PUSH    OFFSET CS:WINDOW_FUNC
         PUSH    0       ;High style -- use style 00000004H
         PUSH    4       ;Low style
         PUSH    0       ;No additional storage space
         CALL    WinRegisterClass

         PUSH    0       ;Parent window handle
         PUSH    1
         PUSH    8000H   ;Make window visible -- Style high
         PUSH    0000H   ;Style low
→        PUSH    DS      ;Point to window flags
→        PUSH    OFFSET FLAGS
                :
                :
```

Next we push the address of the class name. This allows OS/2 to call our function WINDOW_FUNC since we registered WINDOW_FUNC under a specific class name ("FRANK") before. To specify the window class, and therefore WINDOW_FUNC, we point to the class name in memory:

```
         .MODEL  SMALL
         .286

         .STACK  20000

         .DATA
         ANCHOR_LOW      DW 0            ;Anchor block handle
         ANCHOR_HIGH     DW 0
         QUEUE_LOW       DW 0            ;Queue handle
         QUEUE_HIGH      DW 0
         FLAGS           DW 0C3H         ;Window flags
                         DW 8000H
         CLASS_NAME      DB 'FRANK',0    ;Private window class name

         .CODE
         EXTRN   WinInitialize:FAR, WinCreateMsgQueue:FAR, DosExit:FAR
         EXTRN   WinRegisterClass:FAR
```

```
ENTRY   PROC FAR

        PUSH    0                       ;Get Anchor Block Handle
        CALL    WinInitialize
        MOV     ANCHOR_LOW,AX
        MOV     ANCHOR_HIGH,DX

        PUSH    DX      ;Set up message queue -- Anchor high
        PUSH    AX      ;Anchor low
        PUSH    0       ;Use default size
        CALL    WinCreateMsgQueue
        MOV     QUEUE_LOW,AX
        MOV     QUEUE_HIGH,DX

        PUSH    ANCHOR_HIGH     ;Register class so we can get messages
        PUSH    ANCHOR_LOW
        PUSH    DS              ;Register this name for class
        PUSH    OFFSET CLASS_NAME
        PUSH    CS              ;Set up window function
        PUSH    OFFSET CS:WINDOW_FUNC
        PUSH    0       ;High style -- use style 00000004H
        PUSH    4       ;Low style
        PUSH    0       ;No additional storage space
        CALL    WinRegisterClass

        PUSH    0       ;Parent window handle
        PUSH    1
        PUSH    8000H   ;Make window visible -- Style high
        PUSH    0000H   ;Style low
        PUSH    DS      ;Point to window flags
        PUSH    OFFSET FLAGS
→       PUSH    DS                      ;← make 0 for default window
→       PUSH    OFFSET CLASS_NAME ;← make 0 for default window
                :
                :
```

If we had passed a NULL address — that is, both words were zero — we would have gotten the default window. However, we could not receive messages then, since we need a registered window class to receive messages. There is no way of setting up a window function for an unregistered window.

Now we have the option of giving our window a title. We need to pass the address of an ASCIIZ string here. If we pass 0000:0000, the default title will hold only the name of the program (WIN.EXE). We can add our own string here, however, like this:

```
.MODEL SMALL
.286

.STACK  20000

.DATA
        ANCHOR_LOW      DW 0            ;Anchor block handle
        ANCHOR_HIGH     DW 0
        QUEUE_LOW       DW 0            ;Queue handle
        QUEUE_HIGH      DW 0
        FLAGS           DW 0C38H        ;Window flags
```

452 ▶ Advanced Assembly Language

```
                    DW    8000H
        CLASS_NAME  DB    'FRANK',0        ;Private window class name
        TITLE_BAR   DB    'Welcome to PM',0   ;Window title bar

.CODE
        EXTRN   WinInitialize:FAR, WinCreateMsgQueue:FAR, DosExit:FAR
        EXTRN   WinRegisterClass:FAR

ENTRY   PROC FAR

        PUSH    0                       ;Get Anchor Block Handle
        CALL    WinInitialize
        MOV     ANCHOR_LOW,AX
        MOV     ANCHOR_HIGH,DX

        PUSH    DX      ;Set up message queue -- Anchor high
        PUSH    AX      ;Anchor low
        PUSH    0       ;Use default size
        CALL    WinCreateMsgQueue
        MOV     QUEUE_LOW,AX
        MOV     QUEUE_HIGH,DX

        PUSH    ANCHOR_HIGH     ;Register class so we can get messages
        PUSH    ANCHOR_LOW
        PUSH    DS              ;Register this name for class
        PUSH    OFFSET CLASS_NAME
        PUSH    CS              ;Set up window function
        PUSH    OFFSET CS:WINDOW_FUNC
        PUSH    0       ;High style -- use style 00000004H
        PUSH    4       ;Low style
        PUSH    0       ;No additional storage space
        CALL    WinRegisterClass

        PUSH    0       ;Parent window handle
        PUSH    1
        PUSH    8000H   ;Make window visible -- Style high
        PUSH    0000H   ;Style low
        PUSH    DS      ;Point to window flags
        PUSH    OFFSET FLAGS
        PUSH    DS              ;- make 0 for default window
        PUSH    OFFSET CLASS_NAME ;- make 0 for default window
        PUSH    DS      ;Point to title bar text
        PUSH    OFFSET TITLE_BAR
                :
                :
```

Then we have to push the style of the client window, which we will make 0; a "module handle," which we will also leave at zero (you can specify additional *resources* in a module, which we will not do here); and a resource id, which we will also leave at 0:

```
.MODEL  SMALL
.286

.STACK  20000

.DATA
        ANCHOR_LOW      DW  0           ;Anchor block handle
```

```
                ANCHOR_HIGH     DW  0
                QUEUE_LOW       DW  0               ;Queue handle
                QUEUE_HIGH      DW  0
                FLAGS           DW  0C3BH           ;Window flags
                                DW  8000H
                CLASS_NAME      DB  'FRANK',0       ;Private window class name
                TITLE_BAR       DB  'Welcome to PM',0   ;Window title bar

        .CODE
                EXTRN   WinInitialize:FAR, WinCreateMsgQueue:FAR, DosExit:FAR
                EXTRN   WinRegisterClass:FAR

        ENTRY   PROC FAR

                PUSH    0                   ;Get Anchor Block Handle
                CALL    WinInitialize
                MOV     ANCHOR_LOW,AX
                MOV     ANCHOR_HIGH,DX

                PUSH    DX      ;Set up message queue -- Anchor high
                PUSH    AX      ;Anchor low
                PUSH    0       ;Use default size
                CALL    WinCreateMsgQueue
                MOV     QUEUE_LOW,AX
                MOV     QUEUE_HIGH,DX

                PUSH    ANCHOR_HIGH     ;Register class so we can get messages
                PUSH    ANCHOR_LOW
                PUSH    DS              ;Register this name for class
                PUSH    OFFSET CLASS_NAME
                PUSH    CS              ;Set up window function
                PUSH    OFFSET CS:WINDOW_FUNC
                PUSH    0       ;High style -- use style 00000004H
                PUSH    4       ;Low style
                PUSH    0       ;No additional storage space
                CALL    WinRegisterClass

                PUSH    0       ;Parent window handle
                PUSH    1
                PUSH    8000H   ;Make window visible -- Style high
                PUSH    0000H   ;Style low
                PUSH    DS      ;Point to window flags
                PUSH    OFFSET FLAGS
                PUSH    DS              ;- make 0 for default window
                PUSH    OFFSET CLASS_NAME ;- make 0 for default window
                PUSH    DS      ;Point to title bar text
                PUSH    OFFSET TITLE_BAR
        →       PUSH    0
        →       PUSH    0
        →       PUSH    0
        →       PUSH    0
                        :
                        :
```

WinCreateStdWindow returns a handle to the client window. The space we will draw on makes up the center of the window (excluding scroll bars and title bar). We have to push the address of a double word to receive that handle:

454 ▶ Advanced Assembly Language

```
    .MODEL  SMALL
    .286

    .STACK  20000
    .DATA
        ANCHOR_LOW      DW 0            ;Anchor block handle
        ANCHOR_HIGH     DW 0
        QUEUE_LOW       DW 0            ;Queue handle
        QUEUE_HIGH      DW 0
        FLAGS           DW 0C3BH        ;Window flags
                        DW 8000H
        CLASS_NAME      DB 'FRANK',0    ;Private window class name
        TITLE_BAR       DB 'Welcome to PM',0  ;Window title bar
→       CLIENT_LOW      DW 0            ;Client window handle
→       CLIENT_HIGH     DW 0

    .CODE
        EXTRN   WinInitialize:FAR, WinCreateMsgQueue:FAR, DosExit:FAR
        EXTRN   WinRegisterClass:FAR, WinCreateStdWindow:FAR

ENTRY   PROC FAR

        PUSH    0                       ;Get Anchor Block Handle
        CALL    WinInitialize
        MOV     ANCHOR_LOW,AX
        MOV     ANCHOR_HIGH,DX

        PUSH    DX      ;Set up message queue -- Anchor high
        PUSH    AX      ;Anchor low
        PUSH    0       ;Use default size
        CALL    WinCreateMsgQueue
        MOV     QUEUE_LOW,AX
        MOV     QUEUE_HIGH,DX

        PUSH    ANCHOR_HIGH     ;Register class so we can get messages
        PUSH    ANCHOR_LOW
        PUSH    DS              ;Register this name for class
        PUSH    OFFSET CLASS_NAME
        PUSH    CS              ;Set up window function
        PUSH    OFFSET CS:WINDOW_FUNC
        PUSH    0       ;High style -- use style 00000004H
        PUSH    4       ;Low style
        PUSH    0       ;No additional storage space
        CALL    WinRegisterClass

        PUSH    0       ;Parent window handle
        PUSH    1
        PUSH    8000H   ;Make window visible -- Style high
        PUSH    0000H   ;Style low
        PUSH    DS      ;Point to window flags
        PUSH    OFFSET FLAGS
        PUSH    DS                      ;← make 0 for default window
        PUSH    OFFSET CLASS_NAME       ;← make 0 for default window
        PUSH    DS      ;Point to title bar text
        PUSH    OFFSET TITLE_BAR
        PUSH    0
        PUSH    0
        PUSH    0
```

▶ OS/2 Presentation Manager Primer 455

```
        PUSH    0
        PUSH    DS          ;Get client handle
→       PUSH    OFFSET CLIENT_LOW
→       CALL    WinCreateStdWindow
                :
                :
```

And the window appears on the screen at this point. WinCreateStdWindow returns a handle to the main window in DX:AX, and we will store that handle in FRAME_HIGH and FRAME_LOW for later use. Already, WINDOW_FUNC (which we have yet to write) has been called five times by OS/2. In it, we have specified that our window should be solid, and then let OS/2 itself handle most of the defaults.

Next, we have to set up a loop for continually receiving messages from the Presentation Manager, just as we did in Windows. We start by setting up a message area to receive *message packets* from the queue. That format looks like this:

```
    .DATA
        ANCHOR_LOW      DW 0            ;Anchor block handle
        ANCHOR_HIGH     DW 0
        QUEUE_LOW       DW 0            ;Queue handle
        QUEUE_HIGH      DW 0
        FLAGS           DW 0C3BH        ;Window flags
                        DW 8000H
        CLASS_NAME      DB 'FRANK',0    ;Private window class name
        TITLE_BAR       DB 'Welcome to PM',0   ;Window title bar
        CLIENT_LOW      DW 0            ;Client window handle
        CLIENT_HIGH     DW 0
        FRAME_LOW       DW 0            ;Main window handle
        FRAME_HIGH      DW 0
→       QUEUE_MSG       DW 0            ;Queue Message will go here
→                       DW 0
→       MSG             DW 0
→       MP1             DW 0
→                       DW 0
→       MP2             DW 0
→                       DW 0
→       TIME            DW 0
→                       DW 0
→       MOUSE_LOW_X     DW 0
→       MOUSE_HIGH_X    DW 0
→       MOUSE_LOW_Y     DW 0
→       MOUSE_HIGH_Y    DW 0
```

To fill this data area, we have to call WinGetMsg. We'll continually loop, waiting for messages. When one comes, we'll check to see if WinGetMsg returned 0. If it did, we should exit. Some common QUEUE_MSG messages, returned in MSG in QUEUE_MSG, are shown below:

456 ▶ Advanced Assembly Language

Common QUEUE_MSG Messages

Refresh window request	0023H
Button 1 down	0071H
Button 1 up	0072H
Button 1 double click	0073H
Button 2 down	0074H
Button 2 up	0075H
Button 2 double click	0076H
Key was hit	007AH
Window was created	0001H
Window destroyed	0002H
OK to erase background?	004FH
Horizontal scroll	0032H
Mouse moved	0070H
Vertical scroll	0031H
Window terminated	002AH

To use WinGetMsg, we have to push in order: the handle of the anchor block; the address of the QUEUE_MSG data area; a window handle (NULL — that is, zero — specifies that we should receive all messages); and two parameters that specify how many messages we can accept (specifying 0 for both means we'll get all messages). Here's what it looks like:

```
.MODEL  SMALL
.286

.STACK  20000

.DATA
        ANCHOR_LOW      DW 0            ;Anchor block handle
        ANCHOR_HIGH     DW 0
        QUEUE_LOW       DW 0            ;Queue handle
        QUEUE_HIGH      DW 0
        FLAGS           DW 0C3BH        ;Window flags
                        DW 8000H
        CLASS_NAME      DB 'FRANK',0    ;Private window class name
        TITLE_BAR       DB 'Welcome to PM',0   ;Window title bar
        CLIENT_LOW      DW 0            ;Client window handle
        CLIENT_HIGH     DW 0
        FRAME_LOW       DW 0            ;Main window handle
        FRAME_HIGH      DW 0
        QUEUE_MSG       DW 0            ;Queue Message will go here
                        DW 0
        MSG             DW 0
        MP1             DW 0
                        DW 0
```

```
            MP2             DW 0
                            DW 0
            TIME            DW 0
                            DW 0
            MOUSE_LOW_X     DW 0
            MOUSE_HIGH_X    DW 0
            MOUSE_LOW_Y     DW 0
            MOUSE_HIGH_Y    DW 0

    .CODE
            EXTRN   WinInitialize:FAR, WinCreateMsgQueue:FAR, DosExit:FAR
            EXTRN   WinRegisterClass:FAR, WinCreateStdWindow:FAR

    ENTRY   PROC FAR

            PUSH    0                       ;Get Anchor Block Handle
            CALL    WinInitialize
            MOV     ANCHOR_LOW,AX
            MOV     ANCHOR_HIGH,DX

            PUSH    DX      ;Set up message queue -- Anchor high
            PUSH    AX      ;Anchor low
            PUSH    0       ;Use default size
            CALL    WinCreateMsgQueue
            MOV     QUEUE_LOW,AX
            MOV     QUEUE_HIGH,DX

            PUSH    ANCHOR_HIGH     ;Register class so we can get messages
            PUSH    ANCHOR_LOW
            PUSH    DS              ;Register this name for class
            PUSH    OFFSET CLASS_NAME
            PUSH    CS              ;Set up window function
            PUSH    OFFSET CS:WINDOW_FUNC
            PUSH    0       ;High style -- use style 00000004H
            PUSH    4       ;Low style
            PUSH    0       ;No additional storage space
            CALL    WinRegisterClass

            PUSH    0       ;Parent window handle
            PUSH    1
            PUSH    8000H   ;Make window visible -- Style high
            PUSH    0000H   ;Style low
            PUSH    DS      ;Point to window flags
            PUSH    OFFSET FLAGS
            PUSH    DS              ;- make 0 for default window
            PUSH    OFFSET CLASS_NAME ;- make 0 for default window
            PUSH    DS      ;Point to title bar text
            PUSH    OFFSET TITLE_BAR
            PUSH    0
            PUSH    0
            PUSH    0
            PUSH    0
            PUSH    DS      ;Get client handle
            PUSH    OFFSET CLIENT_LOW
            CALL    WinCreateStdWindow

            MOV     FRAME_HIGH,DX   ;Save main handle
            MOV     FRAME_LOW,AX

    GET_MSG:        ;Main message loop
            PUSH    ANCHOR_HIGH     ;Push anchor block handle
```

458 ▶ Advanced Assembly Language

```
→       PUSH    ANCHOR_LOW
→       PUSH    DS                      ;Push our data area for queue messages
→       PUSH    OFFSET QUEUE_MSG
→       PUSH    0
→       PUSH    0
→       PUSH    0
→       PUSH    0
→       CALL    WinGetMsg
                :
                :
```

When control returns from WinGetMsg, QUEUE_MSG has been filled. Some of those messages are intended for OS/2, some for us; we'll see how to handle messages in the next chapter. The next step is to send the messages off to a dispatcher named WinDispatchMsg. This function call interprets the message and calls our WINDOW_FUNC to handle it if needed. To use WinDispatchMsg, push the anchor block handle, and the address of QUEUE_MSG, like this:

```
        .MODEL  SMALL
        .286

        .STACK  20000

        .DATA
        ANCHOR_LOW      DW 0            ;Anchor block handle
        ANCHOR_HIGH     DW 0
        QUEUE_LOW       DW 0            ;Queue handle
        QUEUE_HIGH      DW 0
        FLAGS           DW 0C3BH        ;Window flags
                        DW 8000H
        CLASS_NAME      DB 'FRANK',0    ;Private window class name
        TITLE_BAR       DB 'Welcome to PM',0    ;Window title bar
        CLIENT_LOW      DW 0            ;Client window handle
        CLIENT_HIGH     DW 0
        FRAME_LOW       DW 0            ;Main window handle
        FRAME_HIGH      DW 0
        QUEUE_MSG       DW 0            ;Queue Message will go here
                        DW 0
          MSG           DW 0
          MP1           DW 0
                        DW 0
          MP2           DW 0
                        DW 0
          TIME          DW 0
                        DW 0
          MOUSE_LOW_X   DW 0
          MOUSE_HIGH_X  DW 0
          MOUSE_LOW_Y   DW 0
          MOUSE_HIGH_Y  DW 0

        .CODE
        EXTRN   WinInitialize:FAR, WinCreateMsgQueue:FAR, DosExit:FAR
        EXTRN   WinRegisterClass:FAR, WinCreateStdWindow:FAR, WinGetMsg:FAR

ENTRY   PROC FAR
```

```
            PUSH    0                       ;Get Anchor Block Handle
            CALL    WinInitialize
            MOV     ANCHOR_LOW,AX
            MOV     ANCHOR_HIGH,DX

            PUSH    DX      ;Set up message queue -- Anchor high
            PUSH    AX      ;Anchor low
            PUSH    0       ;Use default size
            CALL    WinCreateMsgQueue
            MOV     QUEUE_LOW,AX
            MOV     QUEUE_HIGH,DX

            PUSH    ANCHOR_HIGH     ;Register class so we can get messages
            PUSH    ANCHOR_LOW
            PUSH    DS              ;Register this name for class
            PUSH    OFFSET CLASS_NAME
            PUSH    CS              ;Set up window function
            PUSH    OFFSET CS:WINDOW_FUNC
            PUSH    0       ;High style -- use style 00000004H
            PUSH    4       ;Low style
            PUSH    0       ;No additional storage space
            CALL    WinRegisterClass

            PUSH    0       ;Parent window handle
            PUSH    1
            PUSH    8000H   ;Make window visible -- Style high
            PUSH    0000H   ;Style low
            PUSH    DS      ;Point to window flags
            PUSH    OFFSET FLAGS
            PUSH    DS              ;- make 0 for default window
            PUSH    OFFSET CLASS_NAME ;- make 0 for default window
            PUSH    DS      ;Point to title bar text
            PUSH    OFFSET TITLE_BAR
            PUSH    0
            PUSH    0
            PUSH    0
            PUSH    0
            PUSH    DS      ;Get client handle
            PUSH    OFFSET CLIENT_LOW
            CALL    WinCreateStdWindow

            MOV     FRAME_HIGH,DX   ;Save main handle
            MOV     FRAME_LOW,AX

GET_MSG:            ;Main message loop
            PUSH    ANCHOR_HIGH     ;Push anchor block handle
            PUSH    ANCHOR_LOW
            PUSH    DS              ;Push our data area for queue messages
            PUSH    OFFSET QUEUE_MSG
            PUSH    0
            PUSH    0
            PUSH    0
            CALL    WinGetMsg

            CMP     AX,0            ;If null recieved, Exit has been selected
            JE      FINISH

            PUSH    ANCHOR_HIGH     ;No exit message recieved -- dispatch message
            PUSH    ANCHOR_LOW
            PUSH    DS              ;Point to message itself
```

460 ▶ **Advanced Assembly Language**

```
→       PUSH    OFFSET QUEUE_MSG
→       CALL    WinDispatchMsg

        JMP     GET_MSG         ;Loop again for another message
                :
                :
```

The message has been handled now. All that remains is to loop and wait for another message from WinGetMsg. Notice that the first thing we did after getting the message was to check AX. If it were zero, the Close option would be selected with the mouse from the system menu in our window. If it were selected, we would jump to the label FINISH.

At FINISH, we handle the process of shutting the window down. To begin, we call WinDestroyWindow and WinDestroyMsgQueue. To call those functions, you only need to pass the correct handles like this:

```
.MODEL  SMALL
.286

.STACK  20000

.DATA
        ANCHOR_LOW      DW 0            ;Anchor block handle
        ANCHOR_HIGH     DW 0
        QUEUE_LOW       DW 0            ;Queue handle
        QUEUE_HIGH      DW 0
        FLAGS           DW 0C3BH        ;Window flags
                        DW 8000H
        CLASS_NAME      DB 'FRANK',0    ;Private window class name
        TITLE_BAR       DB 'Welcome to PM',0  ;Window title bar
        CLIENT_LOW      DW 0            ;Client window handle
        CLIENT_HIGH     DW 0
        FRAME_LOW       DW 0            ;Main window handle
        FRAME_HIGH      DW 0
        QUEUE_MSG       DW 0            ;Queue Message will go here
                        DW 0
        MSG             DW 0
        MP1             DW 0
                        DW 0
        MP2             DW 0
                        DW 0
        TIME            DW 0
                        DW 0
        MOUSE_LOW_X     DW 0
        MOUSE_HIGH_X    DW 0
        MOUSE_LOW_Y     DW 0
        MOUSE_HIGH_Y    DW 0

.CODE
        EXTRN   WinInitialize:FAR, WinCreateMsgQueue:FAR, DosExit:FAR
        EXTRN   WinRegisterClass:FAR, WinCreateStdWindow:FAR, WinGetMsg:FAR
        EXTRN   WinDispatchMsg:FAR, WinDestroyWindow:FAR
        EXTRN   WinDestroyMsgQueue:FAR
```

```
ENTRY     PROC FAR

          PUSH    0                       ;Get Anchor Block Handle
          CALL    WinInitialize
          MOV     ANCHOR_LOW,AX
          MOV     ANCHOR_HIGH,DX

          PUSH    DX      ;Set up message queue -- Anchor high
          PUSH    AX      ;Anchor low
          PUSH    0       ;Use default size
          CALL    WinCreateMsgQueue
          MOV     QUEUE_LOW,AX
          MOV     QUEUE_HIGH,DX

          PUSH    ANCHOR_HIGH     ;Register class so we can get messages
          PUSH    ANCHOR_LOW
          PUSH    DS              ;Register this name for class
          PUSH    OFFSET CLASS_NAME
          PUSH    CS                      ;Set up window function
          PUSH    OFFSET CS:WINDOW_FUNC
          PUSH    0       ;High style -- use style 00000004H
          PUSH    4       ;Low style
          PUSH    0       ;No additional storage space
          CALL    WinRegisterClass

          PUSH    0       ;Parent window handle
          PUSH    1
          PUSH    8000H   ;Make window visible -- Style high
          PUSH    0000H   ;Style low
          PUSH    DS      ;Point to window flags
          PUSH    OFFSET FLAGS
          PUSH    DS              ;- make 0 for default window
          PUSH    OFFSET CLASS_NAME ;- make 0 for default window
          PUSH    DS      ;Point to title bar text
          PUSH    OFFSET TITLE_BAR
          PUSH    0
          PUSH    0
          PUSH    0
          PUSH    0
          PUSH    DS      ;Get client handle
          PUSH    OFFSET CLIENT_LOW
          CALL    WinCreateStdWindow

          MOV     FRAME_HIGH,DX   ;Save main handle
          MOV     FRAME_LOW,AX

GET_MSG:          ;Main message loop
          PUSH    ANCHOR_HIGH     ;Push anchor block handle
          PUSH    ANCHOR_LOW
          PUSH    DS              ;Push our data area for queue messages
          PUSH    OFFSET QUEUE_MSG
          PUSH    0
          PUSH    0
          PUSH    0
          PUSH    0
          CALL    WinGetMsg

          CMP     AX,0            ;If null recieved, Exit has been selected
          JE      FINISH

          PUSH    ANCHOR_HIGH     ;No exit message recieved -- dispatch message
```

462 ▶ Advanced Assembly Language

```
            PUSH    ANCHOR_LOW
            PUSH    DS                  ;Point to message itself
            PUSH    OFFSET QUEUE_MSG
            CALL    WinDispatchMsg

            JMP     GET_MSG             ;Loop again for another message
FINISH:
    →       PUSH    FRAME_HIGH          ;Exit here -- get rid of window
    →       PUSH    FRAME_LOW
    →       CALL    WinDestroyWindow

    →       PUSH    QUEUE_HIGH          ;Get rid of message queue
    →       PUSH    QUEUE_LOW
    →       CALL    WinDestroyMsgQueue
                :
                :
```

Finally, we call the final function, WinTerminate, passing it the window handle, and use DosExit to end the procedure ENTRY:

```
.MODEL  SMALL
.286

.STACK  20000

.DATA
        ANCHOR_LOW      DW 0                ;Anchor block handle
        ANCHOR_HIGH     DW 0
        QUEUE_LOW       DW 0                ;Queue handle
        QUEUE_HIGH      DW 0
        FLAGS           DW 0C3BH            ;Window flags
                        DW 8000H
        CLASS_NAME      DB 'FRANK',0        ;Private window class name
        TITLE_BAR       DB 'Welcome to PM',0    ;Window title bar
        CLIENT_LOW      DW 0                ;Client window handle
        CLIENT_HIGH     DW 0
        FRAME_LOW       DW 0                ;Main window handle
        FRAME_HIGH      DW 0
        QUEUE_MSG       DW 0                ;Queue Message will go here
                        DW 0
        MSG             DW 0
        MP1             DW 0
                        DW 0
        MP2             DW 0
                        DW 0
        TIME            DW 0
                        DW 0
        MOUSE_LOW_X     DW 0
        MOUSE_HIGH_X    DW 0
        MOUSE_LOW_Y     DW 0
        MOUSE_HIGH_Y    DW 0
        RET1            DW 0                ;Return values on stack in WINDOW_FUNC
        RET2            DW 0
        P1              DW 0                ;Parameters on stack in WINDOW_FUNC
        P2              DW 0
        P3              DW 0
        P4              DW 0
```

```
            P5      DW 0
            P6      DW 0
            P7      DW 0

    .CODE
            EXTRN   WinInitialize:FAR, WinCreateMsgQueue:FAR, DosExit:FAR
            EXTRN   WinRegisterClass:FAR, WinCreateStdWindow:FAR, WinGetMsg:FAR
            EXTRN   WinDispatchMsg:FAR, WinDestroyWindow:FAR, DosBeep:FAR
            EXTRN   WinDestroyMsgQueue:FAR, WinTerminate:FAR, WinDefWindowProc:FAR

ENTRY       PROC FAR

            PUSH    0                       ;Get Anchor Block Handle
            CALL    WinInitialize
            MOV     ANCHOR_LOW,AX
            MOV     ANCHOR_HIGH,DX

            PUSH    DX      ;Set up message queue -- Anchor high
            PUSH    AX      ;Anchor low
            PUSH    0       ;Use default size
            CALL    WinCreateMsgQueue
            MOV     QUEUE_LOW,AX
            MOV     QUEUE_HIGH,DX

            PUSH    ANCHOR_HIGH     ;Register class so we can get messages
            PUSH    ANCHOR_LOW
            PUSH    DS              ;Register this name for class
            PUSH    OFFSET CLASS_NAME
            PUSH    CS              ;Set up window function
            PUSH    OFFSET CS:WINDOW_FUNC
            PUSH    0       ;High style -- use style 00000004H
            PUSH    4       ;Low style
            PUSH    0       ;No additional storage space
            CALL    WinRegisterClass

            PUSH    0       ;Parent window handle
            PUSH    1
            PUSH    8000H   ;Make window visible -- Style high
            PUSH    0000H   ;Style low
            PUSH    DS      ;Point to window flags
            PUSH    OFFSET FLAGS
            PUSH    DS                      ;← make 0 for default window
            PUSH    OFFSET CLASS_NAME ;← make 0 for default window
            PUSH    DS      ;Point to title bar text
            PUSH    OFFSET TITLE_BAR
            PUSH    0
            PUSH    0
            PUSH    0
            PUSH    0
            PUSH    DS      ;Get client handle
            PUSH    OFFSET CLIENT_LOW
            CALL    WinCreateStdWindow

            MOV     FRAME_HIGH,DX   ;Save main handle
            MOV     FRAME_LOW,AX

GET_MSG:            ;Main message loop
            PUSH    ANCHOR_HIGH     ;Push anchor block handle
            PUSH    ANCHOR_LOW
            PUSH    DS              ;Push our data area for queue messages
            PUSH    OFFSET QUEUE_MSG
```

464 ▶ Advanced Assembly Language

```
            PUSH    0
            PUSH    0
            PUSH    0
            PUSH    0
            CALL    WinGetMsg

            CMP     AX,0            ;If null recieved, Exit has been selected
            JE      FINISH

            PUSH    ANCHOR_HIGH     ;No exit message recieved -- dispatch message
            PUSH    ANCHOR_LOW
            PUSH    DS              ;Point to message itself
            PUSH    OFFSET QUEUE_MSG
            CALL    WinDispatchMsg

            JMP     GET_MSG         ;Loop again for another message
FINISH:
            PUSH    FRAME_HIGH      ;Exit here -- get rid of window
            PUSH    FRAME_LOW
            CALL    WinDestroyWindow

            PUSH    QUEUE_HIGH      ;Get rid of message queue
            PUSH    QUEUE_LOW
            CALL    WinDestroyMsgQueue

→           PUSH    ANCHOR_HIGH     ;Finish up with window
→           PUSH    ANCHOR_LOW
→           CALL    WinTerminate

EXIT:       PUSH    1               ;A Normal Exit.
→           PUSH    0
→           CALL    DosExit
ENTRY       ENDP
```

Everything is ready now, except the window function that handles messages from OS/2, WINDOW_FUNC, and we'll put that together next.

The Window Function

As mentioned, the window function handles messages passed to us from the Presentation Manager. We will receive different codes depending on what action has occurred, and it's up to us to tell OS/2 what to do when it asks. We can begin with a normal outline for a FAR procedure:

```
WINDOW_FUNC     PROC FAR
                :
                :
                RET
WINDOW_FUNC     ENDP

→               END     ENTRY
```

▶ OS/2 Presentation Manager Primer 465

Because this procedure finishes off our file WIN.ASM, we have placed the line END ENTRY at the end to let the assembler know what our intended entry point is. When OS/2 calls our function, it will have pushed these parameters (just as under Windows):

Double Word	Handle of window message is for.
Word	The message itself.
Far Address	Address of first message parameter.
Far Address	Address of second message parameter.

Some messages come with extra parameters, and the final two addresses point to them. We will not use those extra parameters. After those seven words, OS/2 has pushed the two word return address normal to any call. It is our responsibility to read the data from the stack and act accordingly.

Our first impulse might be to pop the words off the stack and store them in memory. Already, we're in trouble if we do that. WINDOW_FUNC has to be *reenterable*, and our program will crash unless we write it in a certain way.

Reentrant Code in OS/2

One facet of multitasking is reentrant code. For example, imagine that we are just setting our window up. WINDOW_FUNC is called for the first time, and we pop the parameters off the stack and into memory locations in order to work with them. Most of the time, we will pass control on to PM's default message handler, WinDefWindowProc. While we're still waiting for control to return from WinDefWindowProc, it won't hesitate to call WINDOW_PROC again to learn some other piece of information:

```
WINDOW_PROC  PROC FAR  ◄─────┐
             :                │
[Store parameters from stack] │
             :                │
   CALL   WinDefWindowProc → WinDefWindowProc
             :
             :
             RET
WINDOW_PROC  ENDP
```

Figure 14-1.

When this happens, the first thing that we do with the new call is to pick parameters off the stack as before and store them in memory, overwriting what was stored from the first call which is still being processed. In this case, WinDefWindowProc has called WINDOW_FUNC again while we are still waiting inside WINDOW_FUNC for it to return the first time.

Not only are the parameters (like the message itself) overwritten when we start to process the second call, but the original return address is also overwritten. When the second call finishes and WinDefWindowProc returns, we have lost the original parameters and return address. Our program will stop.

To handle this problem, let's take a look at what the stack holds when we get it:

| HANDLE1 |
| HANDLE2 |
| MESSAGE |
| PARM1HI |
| PARM1LO |
| PARM2HI |
| PARM2LO |
| PMRETHI |
| PMRETLO |

Figure 14-2.

Where PMRETHI and PMRETLO stand for PM's return address. The trouble comes when we call WinDefWindowProc. Since we have to pass the same parameters to it that we have received, the stack would look like this:

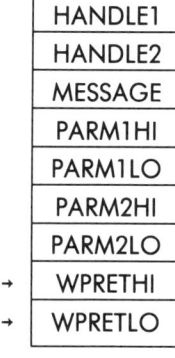

Figure 14-3.

Where WPRETHI and WPRETLO are our return address (so control returns to us), and we have stored PMRETHI and PMRETLO. If WinDefWindowProc calls WINDOW_FUNC again, PMRETHI and PMRETLO, the original return address, will be destroyed. The trick is to store them on the stack, not in memory. When we call WinDefWindowProc, we will have set the stack up this way:

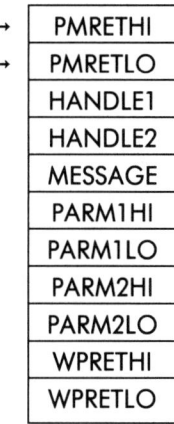

Figure 14-4.

WinDefWindowProc will pop off our return address and the parameters, but no more than that. When we return from WinDefWindowProc, everything will be popped, except for the two words we need most. The orignal return address:

| PMRETHI |
| PMRETLO |

Figure 14-5.

Now that the call to WinDefWindowProc has returned, these words are next on the stack, so we can just execute a RET ourselves and return from WINDOW_FUNC.

Let's see all this in code. In WINDOW_FUNC, we can't even assume that DS is set correctly when we get control, so we first set it to our data segment:

```
WINDOW_FUNC     PROC FAR
     →    PUSH    @DATA    ;Set DS to our data segment
     →    POP     DS
               :
               :
          RET
WINDOW_FUNC     ENDP

          END     ENTRY
```

Now we will store the parameters from the stack in memory. If we have to call WinDefWindowProc, we will push them back on the stack, so they will not be damaged. The important thing is to preserve the return address. Here's how we pop the values:

```
WINDOW_FUNC     PROC FAR

        PUSH    @DATA       ;Set DS to our data segment
        POP     DS
        POP     RET1        ;Save return values
        POP     RET2
        POP     P1          ;Get all parameters
        POP     P2
        POP     P3
        POP     P4
        POP     P5
        POP     P6
        POP     P7
        PUSH    RET2        ;Put return values back on stack for return
        PUSH    RET1
            :
            :
        RET
WINDOW_FUNC     ENDP

        END     ENTRY
```

Notice that we put the two return words PMRETHI and PMRETLO back on the stack. We must add all those words to the data segment:

```
.MODEL SMALL
.286

.STACK 20000

.DATA
        ANCHOR_LOW      DW 0            ;Anchor block handle
        ANCHOR_HIGH     DW 0
        QUEUE_LOW       DW 0            ;Queue handle
        QUEUE_HIGH      DW 0
        FLAGS           DW 0C3BH        ;Window flags
                        DW 8000H
        CLASS_NAME      DB 'FRANK',0    ;Private window class name
        TITLE_BAR       DB 'Welcome to PM',0  ;Window title bar
        CLIENT_LOW      DW 0            ;Client window handle
        CLIENT_HIGH     DW 0
        FRAME_LOW       DW 0            ;Main window handle
        FRAME_HIGH      DW 0
        QUEUE_MSG       DW 0            ;Queue Message will go here
```

OS/2 Presentation Manager Primer

```
                        DW 0
        MSG             DW 0
        MP1             DW 0
                        DW 0
        MP2             DW 0
                        DW 0
        TIME            DW 0
                        DW 0
        MOUSE_LOW_X     DW 0
        MOUSE_HIGH_X    DW 0
        MOUSE_LOW_Y     DW 0
        MOUSE_HIGH_Y    DW 0
→       RET1            DW 0    ;Return values on stack in WINDOW_FUNC
→       RET2            DW 0
→       P1              DW 0    ;Parameters on stack in WINDOW_FUNC
→       P2              DW 0
→       P3              DW 0
→       P4              DW 0
→       P5              DW 0
→       P6              DW 0
→       P7              DW 0
```

The stack looks like this now:

PMRETHI
PMRETLO

Figure 14-6.

All set for a return from WINDOW_PROC to Presentation Manager. If we have to call WinDefWindowProc (which takes the same parameters in the same order as WINDOW_FUNC), we will push the parameters on the stack again, and the CALL instruction will push our return address, leaving the stack like this:

PMRETHI
PMRETLO
HANDLE1
HANDLE2
MESSAGE
PARM1HI
PARM1LO
PARM2HI
PARM2LO
WPRETHI
WPRETLO

Figure 14-7.

470 ▶ Advanced Assembly Language

When we return from WinDefWindowProc, everything will be cleared from the stack but the top two words. The return address we need to return to OS/2, so we can just execute a RET.

Now we have to check for various messages from Presentation Manager. Let's start off by checking for a keystroke. With the way we've stored the parameters, the message is in P5, so we can check that against 7AH (the message meaning that a key was pushed). Let's beep if a key was typed with DosBeep:

```
WINDOW_FUNC     PROC FAR

                PUSH    @DATA       ;Set DS to our data segment
                POP     DS
                POP     RET1        ;Save return values
                POP     RET2
                POP     P1          ;Get all parameters
                POP     P2
                POP     P3
                POP     P4
                POP     P5
                POP     P6
                POP     P7
                PUSH    RET2        ;Put return values back on stack for return
                PUSH    RET1
                PUSH    BP          ;Save stack base pointer
                PUSH    SP
                POP     BP          ;Can use for stack manipulations
KEY:
→               CMP     P5,7AH      ;Keystroke?
→               JNE     NOT_KEY     ;No
→               PUSH    1500        ;Yes -- beep
→               PUSH    1
→               CALL    DOSBEEP
→               JMP     RET_0       ;Return 0

NOT_KEY:
                            :
                            :
RET_0:          MOV     AX,0        ;Return 0 for OK
                MOV     DX,0
OVER:           POP     BP
                RET
WINDOW_FUNC     ENDP

                END     ENTRY
```

If it was a key, we call DosBeep and then exit. Before we exit, we fill DX and AX with 0 for OS/2. The most common return value for us will be 0. We can cover other possibilities besides just a struck key:

```
WINDOW_FUNC      PROC FAR

        PUSH    @DATA       ;Set DS to our data segment
        POP     DS
        POP     RET1        ;Save return values
        POP     RET2
        POP     P1          ;Get all parameters
        POP     P2
        POP     P3
        POP     P4
        POP     P5
        POP     P6
        POP     P7
        PUSH    RET2        ;Put return values back on stack for return
        PUSH    RET1
        PUSH    BP          ;Save stack base pointer
        PUSH    SP
        POP     BP          ;Can use for stack manipulations
KEY:
        CMP     P5,7AH      ;Keystroke?
        JNE     NOT_KEY     ;No
        PUSH    1500        ;Yes -- beep
        PUSH    1
        CALL    DOSBEEP
        JMP     RET_0       ;Return 0

NOT_KEY:
        CMP     P5,1        ;Window created?
        JNE     NOT_CREATE  ;No
                            ;Yes -- do initialization
        JMP     RET_0
NOT_CREATE:
        CMP     P5,23H      ;Have to paint?
        JNE     NOT_PAINT   ;No
                            ;Yes -- do paint here
        JMP     RET_0       ;Return 0
NOT_PAINT:
        CMP     P5,71H      ;Button 1 pushed?
        JNE     NOT_BUTTON_1 ;No
                            ;Yes -- handle button 1
        JMP     RET_0       ;Return 0
NOT_BUTTON_1:
        CMP     P5,70H      ;Did the mouse move?
        JNE     NOT_MOUSE_MOVE ;No
                            ;Yes -- handle new mouse position
        JMP     RET_0       ;Return 0
NOT_MOUSE_MOVE:
        CMP     P5,31H      ;Vertical scroll?
        JNE     NOT_VSCROLL ;No
                            ;Yes -- scroll window
        JMP     RET_0       ;Return 0
NOT_VSCROLL:
        CMP     P5,32H      ;Horizontal scroll?
        JNE     NOT_HSCROLL ;No
                            ;Yes -- scroll window
NOT_HSCROLL:
                :
                :
RET_0:  MOV     AX,0        ;Return 0 for OK
        MOV     DX,0
OVER:   POP     BP
        RET
WINDOW_FUNC     ENDP

        END     ENTRY
```

One important case is the erase background request from OS/2, message 4FH. If we see this message, PM is asking whether it is alright to erase the background behind the window.

> **TIP** Unless you return TRUE in response to message 4FH from Presentation Manager, your window will remain a transparent box with borders.

In this case, we return TRUE (DX=0, AX=1), and our window becomes solid (white):

```
WINDOW_FUNC     PROC FAR
        PUSH    @DATA       ;Set DS to our data segment
        POP     DS
        POP     RET1        ;Save return values
        POP     RET2
        POP     P1          ;Get all parameters
        POP     P2
        POP     P3
        POP     P4
        POP     P5
        POP     P6
        POP     P7
        PUSH    RET2        ;Put return values back on stack for return
        PUSH    RET1
        PUSH    BP          ;Save stack base pointer
        PUSH    SP
        POP     BP          ;Can use for stack manipulations
KEY:
        CMP     P5,7AH      ;Keystroke?
        JNE     NOT_KEY     ;No
        PUSH    1500        ;Yes -- beep
        PUSH    1
        CALL    DOSBEEP
        JMP     RET_0       ;Return 0

NOT_KEY:
        CMP     P5,1        ;Window created?
        JNE     NOT_CREATE  ;No
                            ;Yes -- do initialization
        JMP     RET_0
NOT_CREATE:
        CMP     P5,23H      ;Have to paint?
        JNE     NOT_PAINT   ;No
                            ;Yes -- do paint here
        JMP     RET_0       ;Return 0
NOT_PAINT:
        CMP     P5,71H      ;Button 1 pushed?
        JNE     NOT_BUTTON_1 ;No
                            ;Yes -- handle button 1
        JMP     RET_0       ;Return 0
NOT_BUTTON_1:
        CMP     P5,70H      ;Did the mouse move?
```

```
                JNE         NOT_MOUSE_MOVE  ;No
                                            ;Yes -- handle new mouse position
                JMP         RET_0           ;Return 0
NOT_MOUSE_MOVE:
                CMP         P5,31H          ;Vertical scroll?
                JNE         NOT_VSCROLL     ;No
                                            ;Yes -- scroll window
                JMP         RET_0           ;Return 0
NOT_VSCROLL:
                CMP         P5,32H          ;Horizontal scroll?
                JNE         NOT_HSCROLL     ;No
                                            ;Yes -- scroll window
NOT_HSCROLL:
    →           CMP         P5,4FH          ;Make window solid?
    →           JNE         NOT_ERASE_BKGND ;Not this time
    →           MOV         DX,0            ;Yes -- return 1 for true
    →           MOV         AX,1
    →           JMP         OVER
                            :
                            :
RET_0:          MOV         AX,0            ;Return 0 for OK
                MOV         DX,0
OVER:           POP         BP
                RET
WINDOW_FUNC     ENDP

                END         ENTRY
```

We've handled all the cases we're going to handle here. Now we have to pass the rest on to OS/2 for default handling by WinDefWindowProc. We do that by pushing the parameters again, and calling WinDefWindowProc. After the call, we simply return, and that completes WIN.ASM, which can be seen in Listing 14-1.

Listing 14-1. WIN.ASM — A Presentation Manager Window Program.

```
WINDOW_FUNC     PROC FAR

                PUSH        @DATA           ;Set DS to our data segment
                POP         DS
                POP         RET1            ;Save return values
                POP         RET2
                POP         P1              ;Get all parameters
                POP         P2
                POP         P3
                POP         P4
                POP         P5
                POP         P6
                POP         P7
                PUSH        RET2            ;Put return values back on stack for return
                PUSH        RET1
                PUSH        BP              ;Save stack base pointer
                PUSH        SP
                POP         BP              ;Can use for stack manipulations
KEY:
```

Listing 14-1. WIN.ASM — A Presentation Manager Window Program.

```
        CMP     P5,7AH      ;Keystroke?
        JNE     NOT_KEY     ;No
        PUSH    1500        ;Yes -- beep
        PUSH    1
        CALL    DOSBEEP
        JMP     RET_0       ;Return 0

NOT_KEY:
        CMP     P5,1        ;Window created?
        JNE     NOT_CREATE  ;No
                            ;Yes -- do initialization
        JMP     RET_0
NOT_CREATE:
        CMP     P5,23H      ;Have to paint?
        JNE     NOT_PAINT   ;No
                            ;Yes -- do paint here
        JMP     RET_0       ;Return 0
NOT_PAINT:
        CMP     P5,71H      ;Button 1 pushed?
        JNE     NOT_BUTTON_1 ;No
                            ;Yes -- handle button 1
        JMP     RET_0       ;Return 0
NOT_BUTTON_1:
        CMP     P5,70H      ;Did the mouse move?
        JNE     NOT_MOUSE_MOVE ;No
                            ;Yes -- handle new mouse position
        JMP     RET_0       ;Return 0
NOT_MOUSE_MOVE:
        CMP     P5,31H      ;Vertical scroll?
        JNE     NOT_VSCROLL ;No
                            ;Yes -- scroll window
        JMP     RET_0       ;Return 0
NOT_VSCROLL:
        CMP     P5,32H      ;Horizontal scroll?
        JNE     NOT_HSCROLL ;No
                            ;Yes -- scroll window

NOT_HSCROLL:
        CMP     P5,4FH      ;Make window solid?
        JNE     NOT_ERASE_BKGND ;Not this time
        MOV     DX,0        ;Yes -- return 1 for true
        MOV     AX,1
        JMP     OVER
NOT_ERASE_BKGND:
                            ;Handle other cases here
DEFAULT:
→       POP     BP          ;Let WinDefWindowProc handle defaults
→       PUSH    P7          ;Push parameters back on stack
→       PUSH    P6
→       PUSH    P5
→       PUSH    P4
→       PUSH    P3
→       PUSH    P2
→       PUSH    P1

→       CALL    WinDefWindowProc    ;Call for default handling
```

Listing 14-1. WIN.ASM — A Presentation Manager Window Program.

```
        RET
RET_0:  MOV    AX,0     ;Return 0 for OK
        MOV    DX,0
OVER:   POP    BP
        RET
WINDOW_FUNC    ENDP

        END    ENTRY
```

That's it. When you assemble and run WIN.ASM, the screen will snap to the Presentation Manager display, and our window will appear. You can move the window around the screen, maximize or minimize it, switch to other windows, and close it using the system menu. And when you type a key, WINDOW_FUNC will process the keystroke and beep.

On the other hand, we've just begun with Presentation Manager. Let's turn to the next chapter for more in-depth information.

Chapter 15

The Presentation Manager in Action

▶ **The Presentation Manager in Action** 479

THERE IS AN enormous number of Presentation Manager functions, and we'll see some of them in action in this chapter. So far, we have put a window on the screen. You can resize that window, open and close it, and move it around. But you can't type characters and watch them appear; draw points, lines, and boxes; or resize the window and have the program react accordingly. We'll do all that in this chapter.

This chapter explores the graphical interface function group — the Gpi group. It is by using these functions that you will be able to draw on the screen. We'll also start dissecting message packets from the keyboard in order to place typed keys in our particular window.

The Gpi Functions

The unfortunate thing is that you can't use the Vio functions (except for a small subgroup) here. Those functions are text based, and the screen is in graphics mode when you are using windows.

Instead, a whole new function group was written for Presentation Manager use, the Gpi functions. The ones we'll see in this chapter include: GpiCharStringAt, GpiSetBackColor, GpiSetColor, GpiSetCurrentPosition, GpiSetPel, and GpiPolyLine, among others. There are some strengths to the Gpi functions (graphics) and some weaknesses (cursor control). We'll see both aspects. To begin, let's send a character string that says "This is it!" to our window.

GpiCharStringAt

The most important function in our program for this chapter is going to be the window function, WINDOW_FUNC. So far, it looks like this:

```
WINDOW_FUNC     PROC FAR

        PUSH    @DATA
        POP     DS
        POP     RET1
        POP     RET2
        POP     P1
        POP     P2
        POP     P3
        POP     P4
        POP     P5
        POP     P6
        POP     P7
        PUSH    RET2
        PUSH    RET1
        PUSH    BP
```

```
        PUSH    SP
        POP     BP
KEY:
        CMP     P5,7AH
        JNE     NOT_KEY
        PUSH    1500
        PUSH    1
        CALL    DOSBEEP
        JMP     RET_0

NOT_KEY:
        CMP     P5,1
        JNE     NOT_CREATE
        ;
        JMP     RET_0
NOT_CREATE:
        CMP     P5,23H
        JNE     NOT_PAINT
        ;
        JMP     RET_0
NOT_PAINT:
        CMP     P5,71H
        JNE     NOT_BUTTON_1
        ;
        JMP     RET_0
NOT_BUTTON_1:
        CMP     P5,70H
        JNE     NOT_MOUSE_MOVE
        ;
        JMP     RET_0
NOT_MOUSE_MOVE:
        CMP     P5,31H
        JNE     NOT_VSCROLL
        ;
        JMP     RET_0
NOT_VSCROLL:
        CMP     P5,32H
        JNE     NOT_HSCROLL
        ;
NOT_HSCROLL:
        CMP     P5,4FH
        JNE     NOT_ERASE_BKGND
        MOV     DX,0
        MOV     AX,1            ;RETURN TRUE
        JMP     OVER
NOT_ERASE_BKGND:
        ;
DEFAULT:
        POP     BP
        PUSH    P7
        PUSH    P6
        PUSH    P5
        PUSH    P4
        PUSH    P3
        PUSH    P2
        PUSH    P1

        CALL    WinDefWindowProc

        RET
```

```
RET_0:      MOV     AX,0    ;RETURN 0
            MOV     DX,0
OVER:       POP     BP
            RET
WINDOW_FUNC ENDP
```

We are capable of handling many cases with this function, and we'll add one or two more. One important case is when we receive a message from Presentation Manager that our window needs to be *repainted*. This occurs when the window is resized, or moved, partially covered or uncovered. In that case, we have to redraw (or draw for the first time) what is supposed to be in the window. Let's print out the message "This is it!" in this case. We will use the Gpi function GpiCharStringAt.

This function is the primary string printing function, but it has a number of prominent problems. Like almost all Vio functions, it does not advance the cursor (in fact, there is no cursor). Here, however, that is a much more significant problem because in graphics mode, we are dealing with individual dots on the screen, called *pels* (for picture elements), not orderly columns of text, and the font used by PM varies in width character by character. When we are done printing our string, we don't know exactly where to start printing again since the length of the string depends on the widths of the characters we've used.

However, GpiCharStringAt does print on the screen, and we'll use it here. If you have been following our progress so far, you are probably sick of handles, but there is one more we need before we can actually print, and that is a presentation space, or PS, handle.

The presentation space need not be the screen (although for us it always will be). There are three kinds of presentation spaces: normal, micro, and cached micro. The first two can send output to any device (actually referred to as a device context), and the last one, which is much simpler to use, can only send output to the screen. We will restrict ourselves to cached micro presentation spaces.

We need a handle to a cached micro PS, and we can get it with WinBeginPaint. We have to push the handle of the current window (which is passed to us as parameters six and seven when WINDOW_FUNC is called), a preexisting PS handle if we have one (if NULL — two words of zeroes — the function will return one), and the address of a structure detailing the region in the window we want to update. If that last address is NULL, as it will be for us, it means we will be updating the whole window. The handle to the PS is returned, as usual, in DX:AX. Here's what it looks like so far:

482 ▶ Advanced Assembly Language

```
WINDOW_FUNC     PROC FAR
                        :
                        :
NOT_CREATE:
                CMP     PS,23H
                JNE     NOT_PAINT
        →       PUSH    P7
        →       PUSH    P6
        →       PUSH    0
        →       PUSH    0
        →       PUSH    0
        →       CALL    WinBeginPaint

        →       MOV     PS_HANDLE_HIGH,DX
        →       MOV     PS_HANDLE_LOW,AX
                        :
                        :
                JMP     RET_0
NOT_PAINT:
                        :
                        :
WINDOW_FUNC     ENDP
```

Now that we have the PS handle, we are free to print on the screen with GpiCharStringAt. First, we set up screen coordinates and a message in our data segment:

```
.DATA
        ANCHOR_LOW      DW  0
        ANCHOR_HIGH     DW  0
        QUEUE_LOW       DW  0
        QUEUE_HIGH      DW  0
        FLAGS           DW  0C3BH
                        DW  8000H
        CLASS_NAME      DB  'FRANK',0
        TITLE_BAR       DB  'Welcome to PM',0
        CLIENT_LOW      DW  0
        CLIENT_HIGH     DW  0
        FRAME_LOW       DW  0
        FRAME_HIGH      DW  0
        QUEUE_MSG       DW  0
                        DW  0
        MSG             DW  0
        MP1             DW  0
                        DW  0
        MP2             DW  0
                        DW  0
        TIME            DW  0
                        DW  0
        MOUSE_LOW_X     DW  0
        MOUSE_HIGH_X    DW  0
        MOUSE_LOW_Y     DW  0
        MOUSE_HIGH_Y    DW  0
        HANDLE_LOW      DW  0
        HANDLE_HIGH     DW  0
        MESSAGE         DW  0
        PARM1_LOW       DW  0
        PARM1_HIGH      DW  0
        PARM2_LOW       DW  0
        PARM2_HIGH      DW  0
        RET1    DW  0
```

The Presentation Manager in Action 483

```
            RET2         DW  0
            OLD_DS       DW  0
            P1           DW  0
            P2           DW  0
            P3           DW  0
            P4           DW  0
            P5           DW  0
            P6           DW  0
            P7           DW  0
            PS_HANDLE_LOW    DW  0
            PS_HANDLE_HIGH   DW  0
→           SCREEN_COORDS    DW  0
→                            DW  0
→           Y                DW  0
→                            DW  0
→           MSSG         DB  "This is it!",0
→           MSSG_LEN     DW  $ - MSSG
```

Note that each of the screen coordinates (X first, then Y) is made up of a double word. The low word is stored first. To use GpiCharStringAt, we have to push the handle of the PS, the address of the screen coordinates, the message length (a double word value), and then the address of the message itself.

The window coordinates work like this: the bottom left corner of the window is defined as (0,0), and the coordinates then increase pel by pel as you move up or to the right:

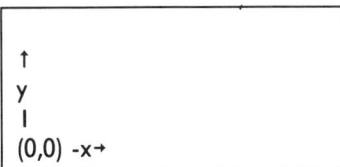

Figure 15–1.

We will leave the coordinates at (0,0), so the message will be printed out in the lower left-hand corner of our window. Here's what it looks like in code:

```
WINDOW_FUNC      PROC FAR
                 :
                 :
NOT_CREATE:
        CMP      P5,23H
        JNE      NOT_PAINT
        PUSH     P7
        PUSH     P6
        PUSH     0
        PUSH     0
        PUSH     0
        PUSH     0
```

484 ▶ Advanced Assembly Language

```
                CALL    WinBeginPaint

                MOV     PS_HANDLE_HIGH,DX
                MOV     PS_HANDLE_LOW,AX

        →       PUSH    PS_HANDLE_HIGH
        →       PUSH    PS_HANDLE_LOW
        →       PUSH    DS
        →       PUSH    OFFSET SCREEN_COORDS
        →       PUSH    0
        →       PUSH    MSSG_LEN
        →       PUSH    DS
        →       PUSH    OFFSET MSSG
        →       CALL    GpiCharStringAt
                        :
                        :
                JMP     RET_0
NOT_PAINT:
                        :
                        :
WINDOW_FUNC     ENDP
```

Finally, we have to close the PS handle, and we do that with WinEndPaint. All we have to do is to push the PS handle and call it:

```
WINDOW_FUNC     PROC FAR
                        :
                        :
NOT_CREATE:
                CMP     P5,23H
                JNE     NOT_PAINT
                PUSH    P7
                PUSH    P6
                PUSH    0
                PUSH    0
                PUSH    0
                CALL    WinBeginPaint

                MOV     PS_HANDLE_HIGH,DX
                MOV     PS_HANDLE_LOW,AX

                PUSH    PS_HANDLE_HIGH
                PUSH    PS_HANDLE_LOW
                PUSH    DS
                PUSH    OFFSET SCREEN_COORDS
                PUSH    0
                PUSH    MSSG_LEN
                PUSH    DS
                PUSH    OFFSET MSSG
                CALL    GpiCharStringAt

        →       PUSH    PS_HANDLE_HIGH
        →       PUSH    PS_HANDLE_LOW
        →       CALL    WinEndPaint

                JMP     RET_0
NOT_PAINT:
                        :
                        :
WINDOW_FUNC     ENDP
```

That's it. Our WINDOW_FUNC is ready. What it looks like in the full program is shown in Listing 15-1.

Listing 15-1. WIN.ASM Capable of Printing in the Window.

```
.MODEL   SMALL
.286

.STACK   20000

.DATA
         ANCHOR_LOW      DW 0
         ANCHOR_HIGH     DW 0
         QUEUE_LOW       DW 0
         QUEUE_HIGH      DW 0
         FLAGS           DW 0C3BH
                         DW 8000H
         CLASS_NAME      DB 'FRANK',0
         TITLE_BAR       DB 'Welcome to PM',0
         CLIENT_LOW      DW 0
         CLIENT_HIGH     DW 0
         FRAME_LOW       DW 0
         FRAME_HIGH      DW 0
         QUEUE_MSG       DW 0
                         DW 0
         MSG             DW 0
         MP1             DW 0
                         DW 0
         MP2             DW 0
                         DW 0
         TIME            DW 0
                         DW 0
         MOUSE_LOW_X     DW 0
         MOUSE_HIGH_X    DW 0
         MOUSE_LOW_Y     DW 0
         MOUSE_HIGH_Y    DW 0
         HANDLE_LOW      DW 0
         HANDLE_HIGH     DW 0
         MESSAGE         DW 0
         PARM1_LOW       DW 0
         PARM1_HIGH      DW 0
         PARM2_LOW       DW 0
         PARM2_HIGH      DW 0
         RET1     DW 0
         RET2     DW 0
         OLD_DS   DW 0
         P1       DW 0
         P2       DW 0
         P3       DW 0
         P4       DW 0
         P5       DW 0
         P6       DW 0
         P7       DW 0
         PS_HANDLE_LOW   DW 0
```

Listing 15-1. WIN.ASM Capable of Printing in the Window. 2 of 5

```
        PS_HANDLE_HIGH  DW  0
        SCREEN_COORDS   DW  0
                        DW  0
                        DW  0
                        DW  0
        MSSG            DB  "This is it!",0
        MSSG_LEN        DW  $ - MSSG

    .CODE
        EXTRN   WinInitialize:FAR, WinCreateMsgQueue:FAR, DosExit:FAR
        EXTRN   WinRegisterClass:FAR, WinCreateStdWindow:FAR, WinGetMsg:FAR
        EXTRN   WinDispatchMsg:FAR, WinDestroyWindow:FAR, DosBeep:FAR
        EXTRN   WinDestroyMsgQueue:FAR, WinTerminate:FAR, WinDefWindowProc:FAR
        EXTRN   WinBeginPaint:FAR, GpiCharStringAt:FAR, WinEndPaint:FAR

ENTRY   PROC FAR

        PUSH    0
        CALL    WinInitialize
        MOV     ANCHOR_LOW,AX
        MOV     ANCHOR_HIGH,DX

        PUSH    DX      ;ANCHOR HIGH
        PUSH    AX      ;ANCHOR LOW
        PUSH    0       ;DEFAULT SIZE
        CALL    WinCreateMsgQueue
        MOV     QUEUE_LOW,AX
        MOV     QUEUE_HIGH,DX

        PUSH    ANCHOR_HIGH
        PUSH    ANCHOR_LOW
        PUSH    DS
        PUSH    OFFSET CLASS_NAME
        PUSH    CS
        PUSH    OFFSET CS:WINDOW_FUNC
        PUSH    0       ;HIGH STYLE
        PUSH    4       ;LOW STYLE
        PUSH    0       ;NO EXTRA STORAGE
        CALL    WinRegisterClass

        PUSH    0       ;HWND_DESKTOP
        PUSH    1
        PUSH    8000H   ;STYLE HIGH
        PUSH    0000H   ;STYLE LOW
        PUSH    DS
        PUSH    OFFSET FLAGS
        PUSH    DS                  ;- make 0 for default window
        PUSH    OFFSET CLASS_NAME   ;- make 0 for default window
        PUSH    DS
        PUSH    OFFSET TITLE_BAR
        PUSH    0
        PUSH    0
        PUSH    0
        PUSH    0
        PUSH    DS
        PUSH    OFFSET CLIENT_LOW
        CALL    WinCreateStdWindow

        MOV     FRAME_HIGH,DX
```

Listing 15-1. WIN.ASM Capable of Printing in the Window.

```
        MOV     FRAME_LOW,AX
GET_MSG:
        PUSH    ANCHOR_HIGH
        PUSH    ANCHOR_LOW
        PUSH    DS
        PUSH    OFFSET QUEUE_MSG
        PUSH    0
        PUSH    0
        PUSH    0
        PUSH    0
        CALL    WinGetMsg

        CMP     AX,0
        JE      FINISH

        PUSH    ANCHOR_HIGH
        PUSH    ANCHOR_LOW
        PUSH    DS
        PUSH    OFFSET QUEUE_MSG
        CALL    WinDispatchMsg

        JMP     GET_MSG
FINISH:
        PUSH    FRAME_HIGH
        PUSH    FRAME_LOW
        CALL    WinDestroyWindow

        PUSH    QUEUE_HIGH
        PUSH    QUEUE_LOW
        CALL    WinDestroyMsgQueue

        PUSH    ANCHOR_HIGH
        PUSH    ANCHOR_LOW
        CALL    WinTerminate

EXIT:   PUSH    1               ;A Normal Exit.
        PUSH    0
        CALL    DosExit
ENTRY   ENDP

WINDOW_FUNC     PROC FAR

        PUSH    @DATA
        POP     DS
        POP     RET1
        POP     RET2
        POP     P1
        POP     P2
        POP     P3
        POP     P4
        POP     P5
        POP     P6
        POP     P7
        PUSH    RET2
        PUSH    RET1
        PUSH    BP
        PUSH    SP
```

Listing 15-1. WIN.ASM Capable of Printing in the Window.

```
        POP     BP
KEY:
        CMP     P5,7AH
        JNE     NOT_KEY
        PUSH    1500
        PUSH    1
        CALL    DOSBEEP
        JMP     RET_0

NOT_KEY:
        CMP     P5,1
        JNE     NOT_CREATE
        ;
        JMP     RET_0
NOT_CREATE:
        CMP     P5,23H
        JNE     NOT_PAINT
        PUSH    P7
        PUSH    P6
        PUSH    0
        PUSH    0
        PUSH    0
        PUSH    0
        CALL    WinBeginPaint

        MOV     PS_HANDLE_HIGH,DX
        MOV     PS_HANDLE_LOW,AX

        PUSH    PS_HANDLE_HIGH
        PUSH    PS_HANDLE_LOW
        PUSH    DS
        PUSH    OFFSET SCREEN_COORDS
        PUSH    0
        PUSH    MSSG_LEN
        PUSH    DS
        PUSH    OFFSET MSSG
        CALL    GpiCharStringAt

        PUSH    PS_HANDLE_HIGH
        PUSH    PS_HANDLE_LOW
        CALL    WinEndPaint

        JMP     RET_0
NOT_PAINT:
        CMP     P5,71H
        JNE     NOT_BUTTON_1
        ;
        JMP     RET_0
NOT_BUTTON_1:
        CMP     P5,70H
        JNE     NOT_MOUSE_MOVE
        ;
        JMP     RET_0
NOT_MOUSE_MOVE:
        CMP     P5,31H
        JNE     NOT_VSCROLL
        ;
        JMP     RET_0
NOT_VSCROLL:
```

Listing 15-1. WIN.ASM Capable of Printing in the Window.

```
              CMP       P5,32H
              JNE       NOT_HSCROLL
              ;
NOT_HSCROLL:
              CMP       P5,4FH
              JNE       NOT_ERASE_BKGND
              MOV       DX,0
              MOV       AX,1
              JMP       OVER
NOT_ERASE_BKGND:
              ;
DEFAULT:
              POP       BP
              PUSH      P7
              PUSH      P6
              PUSH      P5
              PUSH      P4
              PUSH      P3
              PUSH      P2
              PUSH      P1

              CALL      WinDefWindowProc

              RET

RET_0:        MOV       AX,0      ;RETURN 0
              MOV       DX,0
OVER:         POP       BP
              RET
WINDOW_FUNC   ENDP

              END       ENTRY
```

If you execute this program, the window will appear and "This is it!" will be printed at the lower left. Now we've sent output to our window. Of course, there are other options as well. We can print out in color.

GpiSetColor

We can set the foreground (drawing) color, as well as the background color. A list of colors that we can use with the functions GpiSetColor and GpiSetBackColor is shown below.

Colors to Use with GpiSetColor and GpiSetBackColor

Default	-3
White	-2
Black	-1
Background	0

Blue	1
Red	2
Pink	3
Green	4
Cyan	5
Yellow	6
Neutral grey	7
Dark grey	8
Dark blue	9
Dark red	10
Dark pink	11
Dark green	12
Dark cyan	13
Brown	14
Light grey	15

Each of these colors is passed as a double-word value, which means the high word is 0 for positive numbers and 0FFFFH for negative ones. Let's print out our message in yellow letters on a blue background. We begin by setting the background to blue by pushing the PS handle and the code for blue, which is 00000001H, and calling GpiSetBackColor:

```
WINDOW_FUNC     PROC FAR
                :
                :
NOT_CREATE:
        CMP     P5,23H
        JNE     NOT_PAINT
        PUSH    P7
        PUSH    P6
        PUSH    0
        PUSH    0
        PUSH    0
        PUSH    0
        CALL    WinBeginPaint

        MOV     PS_HANDLE_HIGH,DX
        MOV     PS_HANDLE_LOW,AX
     →  PUSH    PS_HANDLE_HIGH
     →  PUSH    PS_HANDLE_LOW
     →  PUSH    0           ;Blue background
     →  PUSH    1
     →  CALL    GpiSetBackColor
                :
                :
        PUSH    PS_HANDLE_HIGH
        PUSH    PS_HANDLE_LOW
```

The Presentation Manager in Action 491

```
            PUSH    DS
            PUSH    OFFSET SCREEN_COORDS
            PUSH    0
            PUSH    MSSG_LEN
            PUSH    DS
            PUSH    OFFSET MSSG
            CALL    GpiCharStringAt

            PUSH    PS_HANDLE_HIGH
            PUSH    PS_HANDLE_LOW
            CALL    WinEndPaint

            JMP     RET_0
NOT_PAINT:
                    :
                    :
WINDOW_FUNC ENDP
```

Next, we specify "overwrite" mode. When we do so, our text will overwrite what is there already. To do that, we pass the PS handle and an option to GpiSetBackMix. That option is 00000000H if we want to use the system default, 00000002H if we want to overwrite the current color, and 00000005H if we want to leave the current background color untouched:

```
WINDOW_FUNC PROC FAR
                    :
                    :
NOT_CREATE:
            CMP     P5,23H
            JNE     NOT_PAINT
            PUSH    P7
            PUSH    P6
            PUSH    0
            PUSH    0
            PUSH    0
            PUSH    0
            CALL    WinBeginPaint

            MOV     PS_HANDLE_HIGH,DX
            MOV     PS_HANDLE_LOW,AX

            PUSH    PS_HANDLE_HIGH
            PUSH    PS_HANDLE_LOW
            PUSH    0       ;Blue background
            PUSH    1
            CALL    GpiSetBackColor

*           PUSH    PS_HANDLE_HIGH
*           PUSH    PS_HANDLE_LOW
*           PUSH    0       ;Overwrite current bkgnd color
*           PUSH    2
*           CALL    GpiSetBackMix
                    :
                    :
            PUSH    PS_HANDLE_HIGH
            PUSH    PS_HANDLE_LOW
```

492 ▶ Advanced Assembly Language

```
            PUSH      DS
            PUSH      OFFSET SCREEN_COORDS
            PUSH      0
            PUSH      MSSG_LEN
            PUSH      DS
            PUSH      OFFSET MSSG
            CALL      GpiCharStringAt

            PUSH      PS_HANDLE_HIGH
            PUSH      PS_HANDLE_LOW
            CALL      WinEndPaint

            JMP       RET_0
NOT_PAINT:
            :
            :
WINDOW_FUNC  ENDP
```

Finally, we call GpiSetColor, specifying yellow for our text, and that's it:

```
            WINDOW_FUNC    PROC FAR
            :
            :
NOT_CREATE:

            CMP       P5,23H
            JNE       NOT_PAINT
            PUSH      P7
            PUSH      P6
            PUSH      0
            PUSH      0
            PUSH      0
            PUSH      0
            CALL      WinBeginPaint

            MOV       PS_HANDLE_HIGH,DX
            MOV       PS_HANDLE_LOW,AX

            PUSH      PS_HANDLE_HIGH
            PUSH      PS_HANDLE_LOW
            PUSH      0       ;Blue background
            PUSH      1
            CALL      GpiSetBackColor

            PUSH      PS_HANDLE_HIGH
            PUSH      PS_HANDLE_LOW
            PUSH      0       ;Overwrite current bkgnd color
            PUSH      2
            CALL      GpiSetBackMix

→           PUSH      PS_HANDLE_HIGH
→           PUSH      PS_HANDLE_LOW
→           PUSH      0       ;Yellow letters
→           PUSH      6
→           CALL      GpiSetColor

            PUSH      PS_HANDLE_HIGH
            PUSH      PS_HANDLE_LOW
```

```
             PUSH     DS
             PUSH     OFFSET SCREEN_COORDS
             PUSH     0
             PUSH     MSSG_LEN
             PUSH     DS
             PUSH     OFFSET MSSG
             CALL     GpiCharStringAt

             PUSH     PS_HANDLE_HIGH
             PUSH     PS_HANDLE_LOW
             CALL     WinEndPaint

             JMP      RET_0
NOT_PAINT:
                      :
                      :
WINDOW_FUNC  ENDP
```

Now our message appears in yellow letters on a blue background. The whole program, printing in color, appears in Listing 15-2.

Listing 15-2. WIN.ASM Capable of Printing in Color.   1 of 6

```
.MODEL  SMALL
.286

.STACK  20000

.DATA
        ANCHOR_LOW      DW 0
        ANCHOR_HIGH     DW 0
        QUEUE_LOW       DW 0
        QUEUE_HIGH      DW 0
        FLAGS           DW 0C3BH
                        DW 8000H
        CLASS_NAME      DB 'FRANK',0
        TITLE_BAR       DB 'Welcome to PM',0
        CLIENT_LOW      DW 0
        CLIENT_HIGH     DW 0
        FRAME_LOW       DW 0
        FRAME_HIGH      DW 0
        QUEUE_MSG       DW 0
                        DW 0
        MSG             DW 0
        MP1             DW 0
                        DW 0
        MP2             DW 0
                        DW 0
        TIME            DW 0
                        DW 0
        MOUSE_LOW_X     DW 0
        MOUSE_HIGH_X    DW 0
        MOUSE_LOW_Y     DW 0
        MOUSE_HIGH_Y    DW 0
        HANDLE_LOW      DW 0
        HANDLE_HIGH     DW 0
        MESSAGE         DW 0
        PARM1_LOW       DW 0
```

Listing 15-2. WIN.ASM Capable of Printing in Color.

```
            PARM1_HIGH      DW 0
            PARM2_LOW       DW 0
            PARM2_HIGH      DW 0
            RET1    DW 0
            RET2    DW 0
            OLD_DS  DW 0
            P1      DW 0
            P2      DW 0
            P3      DW 0
            P4      DW 0
            P5      DW 0
            P6      DW 0
            P7      DW 0
            PS_HANDLE_LOW   DW 0
            PS_HANDLE_HIGH  DW 0
            SCREEN_COORDS   DW 0
                            DW 0
                            DW 0
                            DW 0
            MSSG            DB "This is it!",0
            MSSG_LEN        DW $ - MSSG

    .CODE
            EXTRN   WinInitialize:FAR, WinCreateMsgQueue:FAR, DosExit:FAR
            EXTRN   WinRegisterClass:FAR, WinCreateStdWindow:FAR, WinGetMsg:FAR
            EXTRN   WinDispatchMsg:FAR, WinDestroyWindow:FAR, DosBeep:FAR
            EXTRN   WinDestroyMsgQueue:FAR, WinTerminate:FAR, WinDefWindowProc:FAR
            EXTRN   WinBeginPaint:FAR, GpiCharStringAt:FAR, WinEndPaint:FAR
            EXTRN   GpiSetBackColor:FAR, GpiSetBackMix:FAR, GpiSetColor:FAR

    ENTRY   PROC FAR

            PUSH    0
            CALL    WinInitialize
            MOV     ANCHOR_LOW,AX
            MOV     ANCHOR_HIGH,DX
            PUSH    DX      ;ANCHOR HIGH
            PUSH    AX      ;ANCHOR LOW
            PUSH    0       ;DEFAULT SIZE
            CALL    WinCreateMsgQueue
            MOV     QUEUE_LOW,AX
            MOV     QUEUE_HIGH,DX

            PUSH    ANCHOR_HIGH
            PUSH    ANCHOR_LOW
            PUSH    DS
            PUSH    OFFSET CLASS_NAME
            PUSH    CS
            PUSH    OFFSET CS:WINDOW_FUNC
            PUSH    0       ;HIGH STYLE
            PUSH    4       ;LOW STYLE
            PUSH    0       ;NO EXTRA STORAGE
            CALL    WinRegisterClass

            PUSH    0       ;HWND_DESKTOP
            PUSH    1
            PUSH    8000H   ;STYLE HIGH
            PUSH    0000H   ;STYLE LOW
            PUSH    DS
```

Listing 15-2. WIN.ASM Capable of Printing in Color.

```
        PUSH    OFFSET FLAGS
        PUSH    DS                      ;= make 0 for default window
        PUSH    OFFSET CLASS_NAME       ;= make 0 for default window
        PUSH    DS
        PUSH    OFFSET TITLE_BAR
        PUSH    0
        PUSH    0
        PUSH    0
        PUSH    0
        PUSH    DS
        PUSH    OFFSET CLIENT_LOW
        CALL    WinCreateStdWindow

        MOV     FRAME_HIGH,DX
        MOV     FRAME_LOW,AX

GET_MSG:
        PUSH    ANCHOR_HIGH
        PUSH    ANCHOR_LOW
        PUSH    DS
        PUSH    OFFSET QUEUE_MSG
        PUSH    0
        PUSH    0
        PUSH    0
        PUSH    0
        CALL    WinGetMsg

        CMP     AX,0
        JE      FINISH

        PUSH    ANCHOR_HIGH
        PUSH    ANCHOR_LOW
        PUSH    DS
        PUSH    OFFSET QUEUE_MSG
        CALL    WinDispatchMsg
        JMP     GET_MSG

FINISH:
        PUSH    FRAME_HIGH
        PUSH    FRAME_LOW
        CALL    WinDestroyWindow

        PUSH    QUEUE_HIGH
        PUSH    QUEUE_LOW
        CALL    WinDestroyMsgQueue

        PUSH    ANCHOR_HIGH
        PUSH    ANCHOR_LOW
        CALL    WinTerminate

EXIT:   PUSH    1                       ;A Normal Exit.
        PUSH    0
        CALL    DosExit
ENTRY   ENDP

WINDOW_FUNC     PROC FAR

        PUSH    BDATA
```

Listing 15-2. WIN.ASM Capable of Printing in Color.

```
            POP     DS
            POP     RET1
            POP     RET2
            POP     P1
            POP     P2
            POP     P3
            POP     P4
            POP     P5
            POP     P6
            POP     P7
            PUSH    RET2
            PUSH    RET1
            PUSH    BP
            PUSH    SP
            POP     BP
KEY:
            CMP     P5,7AH
            JNE     NOT_KEY
            PUSH    1500
            PUSH    1
            CALL    DOSBEEP
            JMP     RET_0

NOT_KEY:
            CMP     P5,1
            JNE     NOT_CREATE
            ;
            JMP     RET_0
NOT_CREATE:
            CMP     P5,23H
            JNE     NOT_PAINT
            PUSH    P7
            PUSH    P6
            PUSH    0
            PUSH    0
            PUSH    0
            PUSH    0
            CALL    WinBeginPaint

            MOV     PS_HANDLE_HIGH,DX
            MOV     PS_HANDLE_LOW,AX

            PUSH    PS_HANDLE_HIGH
            PUSH    PS_HANDLE_LOW
            PUSH    0       ;Blue background
            PUSH    1
            CALL    GpiSetBackColor

            PUSH    PS_HANDLE_HIGH
            PUSH    PS_HANDLE_LOW
            PUSH    0       ;Overwrite current bkgnd color
            PUSH    2
            CALL    GpiSetBackMix

            PUSH    PS_HANDLE_HIGH
            PUSH    PS_HANDLE_LOW
            PUSH    0       ;Yellow letters
            PUSH    6
            CALL    GpiSetColor
```

Listing 15-2. WIN.ASM Capable of Printing in Color.

```
            PUSH    PS_HANDLE_HIGH
            PUSH    PS_HANDLE_LOW
            PUSH    DS
            PUSH    OFFSET SCREEN_COORDS
            PUSH    0
            PUSH    MSSG_LEN
            PUSH    DS
            PUSH    OFFSET MSSG
            CALL    GpiCharStringAt

            PUSH    PS_HANDLE_HIGH
            PUSH    PS_HANDLE_LOW
            CALL    WinEndPaint

            JMP     RET_0
NOT_PAINT:
            CMP     P5,71H
            JNE     NOT_BUTTON_1
            ;
            JMP     RET_0
NOT_BUTTON_1:
            CMP     P5,70H
            JNE     NOT_MOUSE_MOVE
            ;
            JMP     RET_0
NOT_MOUSE_MOVE:
            CMP     P5,31H
            JNE     NOT_VSCROLL
            ;
            JMP     RET_0
NOT_VSCROLL:
            CMP     P5,32H
            JNE     NOT_HSCROLL
            ;
NOT_HSCROLL:
            CMP     P5,4FH
            JNE     NOT_ERASE_BKGND
            MOV     DX,0
            MOV     AX,1            ;RETURN TRUE
            JMP     OVER
NOT_ERASE_BKGND:
            ;
DEFAULT:
            POP     BP
            PUSH    P7
            PUSH    P6
            PUSH    P5
            PUSH    P4
            PUSH    P3
            PUSH    P2
            PUSH    P1

            CALL    WinDefWindowProc

            RET

RET_0:      MOV     AX,0    ;RETURN 0
            MOV     DX,0
OVER:       POP     BP
```

Listing 15-2. WIN.ASM Capable of Printing in Color.

```
            RET
WINDOW_FUNC ENDP

        END     ENTRY
```

Our next improvement has to do with reading keys. For the first time, we'll start accepting input to our Presentation Manager program.

Reading Keys in Presentation Manager

As you know, we receive a variety of messages from OS/2 in WINDOW_FUNC. One of them, 7AH, has to do with keystrokes. Now that we can display output on the screen, let's see if we can't read a typed key and display that.

When we receive a keystroke message (the message parameter passed to WINDOW_FUNC, P5, will equal 7AH), a number of things may have happened. The key may have been pressed, or released (we get messages for both). It may be a control key or a character. We have to find out what occurred.

If a key has been typed, the lower word of MP1 in our message queue (as defined in our data segment) will hold information about the struck key. Bits will be set according to what type of key it was as shown below.

The Lower Word of MP1

Character	Bit 0	(1)
Special key	Bit 1	(2)
Scan code	Bit 2	(4)
Shift key	Bit 3	(8)
Control key	Bit 4	(16)
Alt key	Bit 5	(32)
Key up	Bit 6	(64)
Key was down	Bit 7	(128)
Single key	Bit 8	(256)
Unused key	Bit 9	(512)
Composite key	Bit 10	(1,024)
Invalid	Bit 11	(2,048)
Toggle key	Bit 12	(4,096)

The Presentation Manager in Action 499

In our case, we are looking for a character (bit 0 set), and we want to read the character only when the key was released (bit 6 set also). In WINDOW_FUNC, we check bit 6 first to make sure a character was typed:

```
          WINDOW_FUNC    PROC FAR
                 :
                 :
KEY:
          CMP       P5,7AH
          JE        POSS_KEY
          JMP       NOT_KEY

POSS_KEY:
          MOV       AX,MP1      ←
          AND       AX,64       ←
          JZ        KEY_IN      ←
          JMP       RET_0       ←

KEY_IN:
                 :
                 :
          JMP       RET_0

NOT_KEY:
                 :
                 :
          WINDOW_FUNC    ENDP
```

Next, we make sure the key is being released:

```
          WINDOW_FUNC    PROC FAR
                 :
                 :
KEY:
          CMP       P5,7AH
          JE        POSS_KEY
          JMP       NOT_KEY

POSS_KEY:
          MOV       AX,MP1
          AND       AX,64
          JZ        KEY_IN
          JMP       RET_0

KEY_IN:   MOV       AX,MP1      ←
          AND       AX,1        ←
          JNZ       CHAR_IN     ←
          JMP       RET_0       ←

CHAR_IN:
                 :
                 :
          JMP       RET_0

NOT_KEY:
                 :
                 :
          WINDOW_FUNC    ENDP
```

500 ▶ Advanced Assembly Language

Now we know that a key has been typed. The ASCII code itself is in the low word of MP2. To print it out, we will use GpiCharStringAt as before. First, we have to get a PS handle.

It turns out that we don't have to use WinBeginPaint, although we could, to get a PS handle. There is a quicker function named WinGetPS, and we only have to push the window's handle that has already been passed to us in WINDOW_FUNC. We get the handle, save it, and also set overstrike mode like this:

```
            WINDOW_FUNC     PROC FAR
                            :
                            :
KEY:
            CMP     P5,7AH
            JE      POSS_KEY
            JMP     NOT_KEY


POSS_KEY:
            MOV     AX,MP1
            AND     AX,64
            JZ      KEY_IN
            JMP     RET_0


KEY_IN:     MOV     AX,MP1
            AND     AX,1
            JNZ     CHAR_IN
            JMP     RET_0


CHAR_IN:
      →     PUSH    P7
      →     PUSH    P6
      →     CALL    WinGetPS

      →     MOV     PS_HANDLE_HIGH,DX
      →     MOV     PS_HANDLE_LOW,AX

      →     PUSH    PS_HANDLE_HIGH
      →     PUSH    PS_HANDLE_LOW
      →     PUSH    0
      →     PUSH    2
      →     CALL    GpiSetBackMix
                            :
                            :
            JMP     RET_0

NOT_KEY:
                            :
                            :
            WINDOW_FUNC     ENDP
```

The next step is to get the character and print it. Since it is just the bottom 16 bits of MP2, we can load those bits into a word named CHAR_1 and print them with GpiCharStringAt:

```
          WINDOW_FUNC    PROC FAR
                  :
                  :
KEY:
          CMP     P5,7AH
          JE      POSS_KEY
          JMP     NOT_KEY

POSS_KEY:
          MOV     AX,MP1
          AND     AX,64
          JZ      KEY_IN
          JMP     RET_0

KEY_IN:   MOV     AX,MP1
          AND     AX,1
          JNZ     CHAR_IN
          JMP     RET_0

CHAR_IN:
          PUSH    P7
          PUSH    P6
          CALL    WinGetPS

          MOV     PS_HANDLE_HIGH,DX
          MOV     PS_HANDLE_LOW,AX

          PUSH    PS_HANDLE_HIGH
          PUSH    PS_HANDLE_LOW
          PUSH    0
          PUSH    2
          CALL    GpiSetBackMix

*         MOV     AX, MP2
*         MOV     CHAR_1, AX

*         PUSH    PS_HANDLE_HIGH
*         PUSH    PS_HANDLE_LOW
*         PUSH    DS
*         PUSH    OFFSET SCREEN_COORDS
*         PUSH    0
*         PUSH    1
*         PUSH    DS
*         PUSH    OFFSET CHAR_1
*         CALL    GpiCharStringAt
                  :
                  :
          JMP     RET_0

NOT_KEY:
                  :
                  :
WINDOW_FUNC    ENDP
```

Now we still have to release the PS handle, which we can do with WinReleasePS (not WinEndPaint), like this:

```
            WINDOW_FUNC     PROC FAR
                  :
                  :
KEY:
            CMP     P5,7AH
            JE      POSS_KEY
            JMP     NOT_KEY

POSS_KEY:
            MOV     AX,MP1
            AND     AX,64
            JZ      KEY_IN
            JMP     RET_0

KEY_IN:     MOV     AX,MP1
            AND     AX,1
            JNZ     CHAR_IN
            JMP     RET_0

CHAR_IN:
            PUSH    P7
            PUSH    P6
            CALL    WinGetPS

            MOV     PS_HANDLE_HIGH,DX
            MOV     PS_HANDLE_LOW,AX

            PUSH    PS_HANDLE_HIGH
            PUSH    PS_HANDLE_LOW
            PUSH    0
            PUSH    2
            CALL    GpiSetBackMix

            MOV     AX, MP2
            MOV     CHAR_1, AX

            PUSH    PS_HANDLE_HIGH
            PUSH    PS_HANDLE_LOW
            PUSH    DS
            PUSH    OFFSET SCREEN_COORDS
            PUSH    0
            PUSH    1
            PUSH    DS
            PUSH    OFFSET CHAR_1
            CALL    GpiCharStringAt

→           PUSH    PS_HANDLE_HIGH
→           PUSH    PS_HANDLE_LOW
→           CALL    WinReleasePS

            JMP     RET_0

NOT_KEY:
                  :
                  :
WINDOW_FUNC       ENDP
```

And that's all there is to it: We have read a character and printed it on the screen. The whole program is in Listing 15-3.

Listing 15-3. WIN.ASM Capable of Reading and Printing Struck Keys.

```
.MODEL  SMALL
.286

.STACK  20000

.DATA
        ANCHOR_LOW       DW 0
        ANCHOR_HIGH      DW 0
        QUEUE_LOW        DW 0
        QUEUE_HIGH       DW 0
        FLAGS            DW 0C3BH
                         DW 8000H
        CLASS_NAME       DB 'FRANK',0
        TITLE_BAR        DB 'Welcome to PM',0
        CLIENT_LOW       DW 0
        CLIENT_HIGH      DW 0
        FRAME_LOW        DW 0
        FRAME_HIGH       DW 0
        QUEUE_MSG        DW 0
                         DW 0
        MSG              DW 0
        MP1              DW 0
                         DW 0
        MP2              DW 0
                         DW 0
        TIME             DW 0
                         DW 0
        MOUSE_LOW_X      DW 0
        MOUSE_HIGH_X     DW 0
        MOUSE_LOW_Y      DW 0
        MOUSE_HIGH_Y     DW 0
        HANDLE_LOW       DW 0
        HANDLE_HIGH      DW 0
        MESSAGE          DW 0
        PARM1_LOW        DW 0
        PARM1_HIGH       DW 0
        PARM2_LOW        DW 0
        PARM2_HIGH       DW 0
        RET1    DW 0
        RET2    DW 0
        OLD_DS  DW 0
        P1      DW 0
        P2      DW 0
        P3      DW 0
        P4      DW 0
        P5      DW 0
        P6      DW 0
        P7      DW 0
```

Listing 15-3. WIN.ASM Capable of Reading and Printing Struck Keys.

```
            PS_HANDLE_LOW      DW 0
            PS_HANDLE_HIGH     DW 0
            P1_LOW             DW 0
            P1_HIGH            DW 0
            P2_LOW             DW 0
            P2_HIGH            DW 0
            SCREEN_COORDS      DW 0
                               DW 0
                               DW 0
                               DW 0
            CHAR_1             DW 0

    .CODE
            EXTRN   WinInitialize:FAR, WinCreateMsgQueue:FAR, DosExit:FAR
            EXTRN   WinRegisterClass:FAR, WinCreateStdWindow:FAR, WinGetMsg:FAR
            EXTRN   WinDispatchMsg:FAR, WinDestroyWindow:FAR, DosBeep:FAR
            EXTRN   WinDestroyMsgQueue:FAR, WinTerminate:FAR, WinDefWindowProc:FAR
            EXTRN   WinGetPS:FAR, WinReleasePS:FAR, GpiCharStringAt:FAR
            EXTRN   GpiSetBackMix:FAR

    ENTRY   PROC FAR
            PUSH    0
            CALL    WinInitialize
            MOV     ANCHOR_LOW,AX
            MOV     ANCHOR_HIGH,DX

            PUSH    DX      ;ANCHOR HIGH
            PUSH    AX      ;ANCHOR LOW
            PUSH    0       ;DEFAULT SIZE
            CALL    WinCreateMsgQueue
            MOV     QUEUE_LOW,AX
            MOV     QUEUE_HIGH,DX

            PUSH    ANCHOR_HIGH
            PUSH    ANCHOR_LOW
            PUSH    DS
            PUSH    OFFSET CLASS_NAME
            PUSH    CS
            PUSH    OFFSET CS:WINDOW_FUNC
            PUSH    0       ;HIGH STYLE
            PUSH    4       ;LOW STYLE
            PUSH    0       ;NO EXTRA STORAGE
            CALL    WinRegisterClass

            PUSH    0       ;HWND_DESKTOP
            PUSH    1
            PUSH    8000H   ;STYLE HIGH
            PUSH    0000H   ;STYLE LOW
            PUSH    DS
            PUSH    OFFSET FLAGS
            PUSH    DS                    ;- make 0 for default window
            PUSH    OFFSET CLASS_NAME     ;- make 0 for default window
            PUSH    DS
            PUSH    OFFSET TITLE_BAR
            PUSH    0
            PUSH    0
            PUSH    0
            PUSH    0
```

Listing 15-3. WIN.ASM Capable of Reading and Printing Struck Keys.

```
            PUSH    DS
            PUSH    OFFSET CLIENT_LOW
            CALL    WinCreateStdWindow

            MOV     FRAME_HIGH,DX
            MOV     FRAME_LOW,AX

GET_MSG:
            PUSH    ANCHOR_HIGH
            PUSH    ANCHOR_LOW
            PUSH    DS
            PUSH    OFFSET QUEUE_MSG
            PUSH    0
            PUSH    0
            PUSH    0
            PUSH    0
            CALL    WinGetMsg

            CMP     AX,0
            JE      FINISH
            PUSH    ANCHOR_HIGH
            PUSH    ANCHOR_LOW
            PUSH    DS
            PUSH    OFFSET QUEUE_MSG
            CALL    WinDispatchMsg

            JMP     GET_MSG
FINISH:
            PUSH    FRAME_HIGH
            PUSH    FRAME_LOW
            CALL    WinDestroyWindow

            PUSH    QUEUE_HIGH
            PUSH    QUEUE_LOW
            CALL    WinDestroyMsgQueue

            PUSH    ANCHOR_HIGH
            PUSH    ANCHOR_LOW
            CALL    WinTerminate

EXIT:       PUSH    1               ;A Normal Exit.
            PUSH    0
            CALL    DosExit
ENTRY       ENDP

WINDOW_FUNC PROC FAR

            PUSH    @DATA
            POP     DS
            POP     RET1
            POP     RET2
            POP     P1
            POP     P2
            POP     P3
            POP     P4
            POP     P5
            POP     P6
```

Listing 15-3. WIN.ASM Capable of Reading and Printing Struck Keys.

```
        POP     P7
        PUSH    RET2
        PUSH    RET1
        PUSH    BP
        PUSH    SP
        POP     BP
KEY:
        CMP     P5,7AH
        JE      POSS_KEY
        JMP     NOT_KEY

POSS_KEY:
        MOV     AX,MP1
        AND     AX,64
        JZ      KEY_IN
        JMP     RET_0

KEY_IN: MOV     AX,MP1
        AND     AX,1
        JNZ     CHAR_IN
        JMP     RET_0

CHAR_IN:
        PUSH    P7
        PUSH    P6
        CALL    WinGetPS

        MOV     PS_HANDLE_HIGH,DX
        MOV     PS_HANDLE_LOW,AX

        PUSH    PS_HANDLE_HIGH
        PUSH    PS_HANDLE_LOW
        PUSH    0
        PUSH    2
        CALL    GpiSetBackMix

        MOV     AX, MP2
        MOV     CHAR_1, AX

        PUSH    PS_HANDLE_HIGH
        PUSH    PS_HANDLE_LOW
        PUSH    DS
        PUSH    OFFSET SCREEN_COORDS
        PUSH    0
        PUSH    1
        PUSH    DS
        PUSH    OFFSET CHAR_1
        CALL    GpiCharStringAt

        PUSH    PS_HANDLE_HIGH
        PUSH    PS_HANDLE_LOW
        CALL    WinReleasePS

        JMP     RET_0

NOT_KEY:
        CMP     P5,1
```

Listing 15-3. WIN.ASM Capable of Reading and Printing Struck Keys.

```
        JNE     NOT_CREATE
        ;
        JMP     RET_0
NOT_CREATE:
        CMP     P5,23H
        JNE     NOT_PAINT
        ;
        JMP     RET_0
NOT_PAINT:
        CMP     P5,71H
        JNE     NOT_BUTTON_1
        ;
        JMP     RET_0
NOT_BUTTON_1:
        CMP     P5,70H
        JNE     NOT_MOUSE_MOVE
        ;
        JMP     RET_0
NOT_MOUSE_MOVE:
        CMP     P5,31H
        JNE     NOT_VSCROLL
        ;
        JMP     RET_0
NOT_VSCROLL:
        CMP     P5,32H
        JNE     NOT_HSCROLL
        ;
NOT_HSCROLL:
        CMP     P5,4FH
        JNE     NOT_ERASE_BKGND
        MOV     DX,0
        MOV     AX,1            ;RETURN TRUE
        JMP     OVER
NOT_ERASE_BKGND:
        ;
DEFAULT:
        POP     BP
        PUSH    P7
        PUSH    P6
        PUSH    P5
        PUSH    P4
        PUSH    P3
        PUSH    P2
        PUSH    P1

        CALL    WinDefWindowProc

        RET

RET_0:  MOV     AX,0    ;RETURN 0
        MOV     DX,0
OVER:   POP     BP
        RET
WINDOW_FUNC     ENDP

        END     ENTRY
```

Now our PM program can both accept input and display output, the fundamentals of any real program. You can see that it took quite an amount of preparation before we were able to reach this point.

> **TIP** Although this program prints out the character in the lower left-hand corner of the window, you can specify the location for text output yourself using the Presentation Manager function GpiCharStringAt. You can also accept a number of characters and make up a string before printing them out all at once.

The next step is graphics. Presentation Manager is the first part of the OS/2 operating system to support graphics.

Presentation Manager Graphics

There are a number of graphics functions supported, and we will make use of them when we get a repaint message. As before, this message means that we have to refresh the window or draw it for the first time. Let's start off by getting a PS handle and setting the drawing colors to yellow on blue:

```
WINDOW_FUNC     PROC FAR
                :
                :
PAINT:  PUSH    P7
        PUSH    P6
        PUSH    0
        PUSH    0
        PUSH    0
        PUSH    0
        CALL    WinBeginPaint

        MOV     PS_HANDLE_HIGH,DX
        MOV     PS_HANDLE_LOW,AX

        PUSH    PS_HANDLE_HIGH
        PUSH    PS_HANDLE_LOW
        PUSH    0          ;Blue background
        PUSH    1
        CALL    GpiSetBackColor

        PUSH    PS_HANDLE_HIGH
        PUSH    PS_HANDLE_LOW
        PUSH    0          ;Overwrite current bkgnd color
        PUSH    2
        CALL    GpiSetBackMix

        PUSH    PS_HANDLE_HIGH
        PUSH    PS_HANDLE_LOW
```

```
                PUSH      0              ;Yellow letters
                PUSH      6
                CALL      GpiSetColor
                          :
                          :
                JMP       RET_0
NOT_PAINT:
                          :
                          :
WINDOW_FUNC     ENDP
```

Our first action will be to draw a line from (0,0) to (30,30). The GpiLine function draws lines from the *current graphics position* to a specified point. To set that current graphics position to (0,0), we only need to set the location in SCREEN_COORDS, push the PS handle, point to SCREEN_COORDS, and call GpiSetCurrentPosition. GpiLine will then draw a line from there to a specified new set of coordinates, which we set to (30,30), and is measured in pels from the lower left-hand corner of our window. To use GpiLine, we just push the PS handle and the address of the new screen coordinates:

```
WINDOW_FUNC     PROC FAR
                          :
                          :
PAINT:  PUSH    P7
        PUSH    P6
        PUSH    0
        PUSH    0
        PUSH    0
        PUSH    0
        CALL    WinBeginPaint

        MOV     PS_HANDLE_HIGH,DX
        MOV     PS_HANDLE_LOW,AX

        PUSH    PS_HANDLE_HIGH
        PUSH    PS_HANDLE_LOW
        PUSH    0              ;Blue background
        PUSH    1
        CALL    GpiSetBackColor

        PUSH    PS_HANDLE_HIGH
        PUSH    PS_HANDLE_LOW
        PUSH    0              ;Overwrite current bkgnd color
        PUSH    2
        CALL    GpiSetBackMix

        PUSH    PS_HANDLE_HIGH
        PUSH    PS_HANDLE_LOW
        PUSH    0              ;Yellow letters
        PUSH    6
        CALL    GpiSetColor

→       PUSH    PS_HANDLE_HIGH
→       PUSH    PS_HANDLE_LOW
→       PUSH    DS
→       PUSH    OFFSET SCREEN_COORDS
```

510 ▶ Advanced Assembly Language

```
→           CALL    GpiSetCurrentPosition
→           MOV     SCREEN_COORDS,30
→           MOV     Y,30

→           PUSH    PS_HANDLE_HIGH
→           PUSH    PS_HANDLE_LOW
→           PUSH    DS
→           PUSH    OFFSET SCREEN_COORDS
→           CALL    GpiLine
                    :
                    :
            JMP     RET_0
NOT_PAINT:
                    :
                    :
WINDOW_FUNC ENDP
```

At this point, a line has been drawn on the window. It was that easy. We can also set pels on the screen with GpiSetPel. We only need to push the PS handle and set SCREEN_COORDS like this:

```
WINDOW_FUNC     PROC FAR
                :
                :
PAINT:  PUSH    P7
        PUSH    P6
        PUSH    0
        PUSH    0
        PUSH    0
        PUSH    0
        CALL    WinBeginPaint

        MOV     PS_HANDLE_HIGH,DX
        MOV     PS_HANDLE_LOW,AX

        PUSH    PS_HANDLE_HIGH
        PUSH    PS_HANDLE_LOW
        PUSH    0       ;Blue background
        PUSH    1
        CALL    GpiSetBackColor

        PUSH    PS_HANDLE_HIGH
        PUSH    PS_HANDLE_LOW
        PUSH    0       ;Overwrite current bkgnd color
        PUSH    2
        CALL    GpiSetBackMix

        PUSH    PS_HANDLE_HIGH
        PUSH    PS_HANDLE_LOW
        PUSH    0       ;Yellow letters
        PUSH    6
        CALL    GpiSetColor

        PUSH    PS_HANDLE_HIGH
        PUSH    PS_HANDLE_LOW
        PUSH    DS
```

▶ The Presentation Manager in Action 511

```
              PUSH      OFFSET SCREEN_COORDS
              CALL      GpiSetCurrentPosition

              MOV       SCREEN_COORDS,30
              MOV       Y,30

              PUSH      PS_HANDLE_HIGH
              PUSH      PS_HANDLE_LOW
              PUSH      DS
              PUSH      OFFSET SCREEN_COORDS
              CALL      GpiLine

        →     MOV       Screen_Coords, 50
        →     MOV       Y, 50

        →     PUSH      PS_HANDLE_HIGH
        →     PUSH      PS_HANDLE_LOW
        →     PUSH      DS
        →     PUSH      OFFSET SCREEN_COORDS
        →     CALL      GpiSetPel
                         :
                         :
              JMP       RET_0
NOT_PAINT:
                         :
                         :
WINDOW_FUNC   ENDP
```

Here, the dot at (50,50) is turned on and becomes the current drawing color. Now that you have control over the individual pels, you can (in theory) draw any figure you require.

We can draw boxes too. To do that, set the current position, specify new screen coordinates, and call GpiBox. You push the PS handle, a double word style, the address of the new screen coordinates, and two double words having to do with rounding the corners (that we will set to 0 for sharp corners). The style parameter can be 1 to fill the box, 2 to outline the box, and 3 to do both. Here's how it would look to draw a box from (200,200) to (300,300):

```
WINDOW_FUNC   PROC FAR
                         :
                         :
PAINT:        PUSH      P7
              PUSH      P6
              PUSH      0
              PUSH      0
              PUSH      0
              PUSH      0
              CALL      WinBeginPaint

              MOV       PS_HANDLE_HIGH,DX
              MOV       PS_HANDLE_LOW,AX

              PUSH      PS_HANDLE_HIGH
```

```
        PUSH    PS_HANDLE_LOW
        PUSH    0       ;Blue background
        PUSH    1
        CALL    GpiSetBackColor

        PUSH    PS_HANDLE_HIGH
        PUSH    PS_HANDLE_LOW
        PUSH    0       ;Overwrite current bkgnd color
        PUSH    2
        CALL    GpiSetBackMix

        PUSH    PS_HANDLE_HIGH
        PUSH    PS_HANDLE_LOW
        PUSH    0       ;Yellow letters
        PUSH    6
        CALL    GpiSetColor

        PUSH    PS_HANDLE_HIGH
        PUSH    PS_HANDLE_LOW
        PUSH    DS
        PUSH    OFFSET SCREEN_COORDS
        CALL    GpiSetCurrentPosition

        MOV     SCREEN_COORDS,30
        MOV     Y,30

        PUSH    PS_HANDLE_HIGH
        PUSH    PS_HANDLE_LOW
        PUSH    DS
        PUSH    OFFSET SCREEN_COORDS
        CALL    GpiLine

        MOV     Screen_Coords, 50
        MOV     Y, 50

        PUSH    PS_HANDLE_HIGH
        PUSH    PS_HANDLE_LOW
        PUSH    DS
        PUSH    OFFSET SCREEN_COORDS
        CALL    GpiSetPel

→       MOV     Screen_Coords, 200
→       MOV     Y, 200

→       PUSH    PS_HANDLE_HIGH
→       PUSH    PS_HANDLE_LOW
→       PUSH    DS
→       PUSH    OFFSET SCREEN_COORDS
→       CALL    GpiSetCurrentPosition

→       MOV     Screen_Coords, 300
→       MOV     Y, 300

→       PUSH    PS_HANDLE_HIGH
→       PUSH    PS_HANDLE_LOW
→       PUSH    0
→       PUSH    2
→       PUSH    DS
→       PUSH    OFFSET SCREEN_COORDS
→       PUSH    0
→       PUSH    0
```

```
      →        PUSH      0
      →        PUSH      0
      →        CALL      GpiBox

      →        PUSH      PS_HANDLE_HIGH
      →        PUSH      PS_HANDLE_LOW
      →        CALL      WinEndPaint

               JMP       RET_0
NOT_PAINT:
                         :
                         :
WINDOW_FUNC    ENDP
```

Notice at the end that we used WinEndPaint to release the PS handle. In order to produce these graphics figures, you have to put this into the whole program and run it. That program appears in Listing 15-4.

Listing 15-4. WIN.ASM with Graphics.

```
.MODEL SMALL
.286

.STACK 20000

.DATA
        ANCHOR_LOW         DW 0
        ANCHOR_HIGH        DW 0
        QUEUE_LOW          DW 0
        QUEUE_HIGH         DW 0
        FLAGS              DW 0C3BH
                           DW 8000H
        CLASS_NAME         DB 'FRANK',0
        TITLE_BAR          DB 'Welcome to PM',0
        CLIENT_LOW         DW 0
        CLIENT_HIGH        DW 0
        FRAME_LOW          DW 0
        FRAME_HIGH         DW 0
        QUEUE_MSG          DW 0
                           DW 0
        MSG                DW 0
        MP1                DW 0
                           DW 0
        MP2                DW 0
                           DW 0
        TIME               DW 0
                           DW 0
        MOUSE_LOW_X        DW 0
        MOUSE_HIGH_X       DW 0
        MOUSE_LOW_Y        DW 0
        MOUSE_HIGH_Y       DW 0
        HANDLE_LOW         DW 0
        HANDLE_HIGH        DW 0
        MESSAGE            DW 0
        PARM1_LOW          DW 0
        PARM1_HIGH         DW 0
        PARM2_LOW          DW 0
```

Listing 15-4. WIN.ASM with Graphics.

```
        PARM2_HIGH      DW  0
        RET1       DW   0
        RET2       DW   0
        OLD_DS     DW   0
        P1         DW   0
        P2         DW   0
        P3         DW   0
        P4         DW   0
        P5         DW   0
        P6         DW   0
        P7         DW   0
        PS_HANDLE_LOW    DW  0
        PS_HANDLE_HIGH   DW  0
        SCREEN_COORDS    DW  0
                         DW  0
        Y                DW  0
                         DW  0
        MSSG       DB  "This is it!",0
        MSSG_LEN   DW  $ - MSSG

.CODE
        EXTRN   WinInitialize:FAR, WinCreateMsgQueue:FAR, DosExit:FAR
        EXTRN   WinRegisterClass:FAR, WinCreateStdWindow:FAR, WinGetMsg:FAR
        EXTRN   WinDispatchMsg:FAR, WinDestroyWindow:FAR, DosBeep:FAR
        EXTRN   WinDestroyMsgQueue:FAR, WinTerminate:FAR, WinDefWindowProc:FAR
        EXTRN   WinBeginPaint:FAR, GpiCharStringAt:FAR, WinEndPaint:FAR
        EXTRN   GpiSetBackColor:FAR, GpiSetBackMix:FAR, GpiSetColor:FAR
        EXTRN   GpiSetCurrentPosition:FAR, GpiLine:FAR, GpiSetPel:FAR
        EXTRN   GpiBox:FAR

ENTRY   PROC FAR

        PUSH    0
        CALL    WinInitialize
        MOV     ANCHOR_LOW,AX
        MOV     ANCHOR_HIGH,DX

        PUSH    DX          ;ANCHOR HIGH
        PUSH    AX          ;ANCHOR LOW
        PUSH    0           ;DEFAULT SIZE
        CALL    WinCreateMsgQueue
        MOV     QUEUE_LOW,AX
        MOV     QUEUE_HIGH,DX

        PUSH    ANCHOR_HIGH
        PUSH    ANCHOR_LOW
        PUSH    DS
        PUSH    OFFSET CLASS_NAME
        PUSH    CS
        PUSH    OFFSET CS:WINDOW_FUNC
        PUSH    0           ;HIGH STYLE
        PUSH    4           ;LOW STYLE
        PUSH    0           ;NO EXTRA STORAGE
        CALL    WinRegisterClass

        PUSH    0           ;HWND_DESKTOP
        PUSH    1
        PUSH    8000H       ;STYLE HIGH
        PUSH    0000H       ;STYLE LOW
```

Listing 15-4. WIN.ASM with Graphics.

```
        PUSH    DS
        PUSH    OFFSET FLAGS
        PUSH    DS                       ;← make 0 for default window
        PUSH    OFFSET CLASS_NAME        ;← make 0 for default window
        PUSH    DS
        PUSH    OFFSET TITLE_BAR
        PUSH    0
        PUSH    0
        PUSH    0
        PUSH    0
        PUSH    DS
        PUSH    OFFSET CLIENT_LOW
        CALL    WinCreateStdWindow

        MOV     FRAME_HIGH,DX
        MOV     FRAME_LOW,AX

GET_MSG:
        PUSH    ANCHOR_HIGH
        PUSH    ANCHOR_LOW
        PUSH    DS
        PUSH    OFFSET QUEUE_MSG
        PUSH    0
        PUSH    0
        PUSH    0
        PUSH    0
        CALL    WinGetMsg

        CMP     AX,0
        JE      FINISH

        PUSH    ANCHOR_HIGH
        PUSH    ANCHOR_LOW
        PUSH    DS
        PUSH    OFFSET QUEUE_MSG
        CALL    WinDispatchMsg

        JMP     GET_MSG

FINISH:
        PUSH    FRAME_HIGH
        PUSH    FRAME_LOW
        CALL    WinDestroyWindow

        PUSH    QUEUE_HIGH
        PUSH    QUEUE_LOW
        CALL    WinDestroyMsgQueue

        PUSH    ANCHOR_HIGH
        PUSH    ANCHOR_LOW
        CALL    WinTerminate

EXIT:   PUSH    1                        ;A Normal Exit.
        PUSH    0
        CALL    DosExit
ENTRY   ENDP

WINDOW_FUNC     PROC FAR
```

Listing 15-4. WIN.ASM with Graphics.

```
        PUSH    @DATA
        POP     DS
        POP     RET1
        POP     RET2
        POP     P1
        POP     P2
        POP     P3
        POP     P4
        POP     P5
        POP     P6
        POP     P7
        PUSH    RET2
        PUSH    RET1
        PUSH    BP
        PUSH    SP
        POP     BP
KEY:
        CMP     P5,7AH
        JNE     NOT_KEY
        PUSH    1500
        PUSH    1
        CALL    DOSBEEP
        JMP     RET_0

NOT_KEY:
        CMP     P5,1
        JNE     NOT_CREATE
        ;
        JMP     RET_0
NOT_CREATE:
        CMP     P5,23H
        JE      PAINT
        JMP     NOT_PAINT
PAINT:  PUSH    P7
        PUSH    P6
        PUSH    0
        PUSH    0
        PUSH    0
        PUSH    0
        CALL    WinBeginPaint

        MOV     PS_HANDLE_HIGH,DX
        MOV     PS_HANDLE_LOW,AX

        PUSH    PS_HANDLE_HIGH
        PUSH    PS_HANDLE_LOW
        PUSH    0       ;Blue background
        PUSH    1
        CALL    GpiSetBackColor

        PUSH    PS_HANDLE_HIGH
        PUSH    PS_HANDLE_LOW
        PUSH    0       ;Overwrite current bkgnd color
        PUSH    2
        CALL    GpiSetBackMix

        PUSH    PS_HANDLE_HIGH
        PUSH    PS_HANDLE_LOW
        PUSH    0       ;Yellow letters
```

Listing 15-4. WIN.ASM with Graphics. 5 of 6

```
            PUSH    6
            CALL    GpiSetColor

            PUSH    PS_HANDLE_HIGH
            PUSH    PS_HANDLE_LOW
            PUSH    DS
            PUSH    OFFSET SCREEN_COORDS
            CALL    GpiSetCurrentPosition

            MOV     SCREEN_COORDS,30
            MOV     Y,30

            PUSH    PS_HANDLE_HIGH
            PUSH    PS_HANDLE_LOW
            PUSH    DS
            PUSH    OFFSET SCREEN_COORDS
            CALL    GpiLine

            MOV     Screen_Coords, 50
            MOV     Y, 50

            PUSH    PS_HANDLE_HIGH
            PUSH    PS_HANDLE_LOW
            PUSH    DS
            PUSH    OFFSET SCREEN_COORDS
            CALL    GpiSetPel

            MOV     Screen_Coords, 200
            MOV     Y, 200

            PUSH    PS_HANDLE_HIGH
            PUSH    PS_HANDLE_LOW
            PUSH    DS
            PUSH    OFFSET SCREEN_COORDS
            CALL    GpiSetCurrentPosition

            MOV     Screen_Coords, 300
            MOV     Y, 300

            PUSH    PS_HANDLE_HIGH
            PUSH    PS_HANDLE_LOW
            PUSH    0
            PUSH    2
            PUSH    DS
            PUSH    OFFSET SCREEN_COORDS
            PUSH    0
            PUSH    0
            PUSH    0
            PUSH    0
            CALL    GpiBox

            PUSH    PS_HANDLE_HIGH
            PUSH    PS_HANDLE_LOW
            CALL    WinEndPaint

            JMP     RET_0
NOT_PAINT:
            CMP     P5,71H
            JNE     NOT_BUTTON_1
```

Listing 15-4. WIN.ASM with Graphics.

```
        ;
        JMP         RET_0
NOT_BUTTON_1:
        CMP         P5,70H
        JNE         NOT_MOUSE_MOVE
        ;
        JMP         RET_0
NOT_MOUSE_MOVE:
        CMP         P5,31H
        JNE         NOT_VSCROLL
        ;
        JMP         RET_0
NOT_VSCROLL:
        CMP         P5,32H
        JNE         NOT_HSCROLL
        ;
NOT_HSCROLL:
        CMP         P5,4FH
        JNE         NOT_ERASE_BKGND
        MOV         DX,0
        MOV         AX,1            ;RETURN TRUE
        JMP         OVER
NOT_ERASE_BKGND:
        ;
DEFAULT:
        POP         BP
        PUSH        P7
        PUSH        P6
        PUSH        P5
        PUSH        P4
        PUSH        P3
        PUSH        P2
        PUSH        P1

        CALL        WinDefWindowProc

        RET

RET_0:  MOV         AX,0    ;RETURN 0
        MOV         DX,0
OVER:   POP         BP
        RET
WINDOW_FUNC ENDP

        END         ENTRY
```

GpiPolyLine

Now that we have some familiarity with graphics, let's take a look at a function that makes drawing multiple lines a little easier. We can adapt our program to draw multiple lines with the GpiPolyLine function. We just supply a series of coordinates (double word X followed by double word Y) like these five pairs:

```
SCREEN_COORDS   DW 0        ← X 1
                DW 0
Y               DW 0        ← Y 1
                DW 0
                DW 50       ← X 2
                DW 0
                DW 50       ← Y 2
                DW 0
                DW 200      ← X 3
                DW 0
                DW 120      ← Y 3
                DW 0
                DW 90       ← X 4
                DW 0
                DW 240      ← Y 4
                DW 0
                DW 210      ← X 5
                DW 0
                DW 10       ← Y 5
                DW 0
```

Then we can point to the first pair of coordinates and use GpiPolyLine. We pass the PS handle, the number of coordinate pairs in a double word value, and the address of the coordinates in memory. GpiPolyLine draws lines from one pair of coordinates to the next. The modified program appears in Listing 15-5 below.

Listing 15-5. WIN.ASM Using GpiPolyLine.

```
.MODEL   SMALL
.286

.STACK   20000
.DATA
        ANCHOR_LOW      DW 0
        ANCHOR_HIGH     DW 0
        QUEUE_LOW       DW 0
        QUEUE_HIGH      DW 0
        FLAGS           DW 0C3BH
                        DW 8000H
        CLASS_NAME      DB 'FRANK',0
        TITLE_BAR       DB 'Welcome to PM',0
        CLIENT_LOW      DW 0
        CLIENT_HIGH     DW 0
        FRAME_LOW       DW 0
        FRAME_HIGH      DW 0
```

Listing 15-5. WIN.ASM Using GpiPolyLine.

```
            QUEUE_MSG       DW 0
                            DW 0
            MSG             DW 0
            MP1             DW 0
                            DW 0
            MP2             DW 0
                            DW 0
            TIME            DW 0
                            DW 0
            MOUSE_LOW_X     DW 0
            MOUSE_HIGH_X    DW 0
            MOUSE_LOW_Y     DW 0
            MOUSE_HIGH_Y    DW 0
        HANDLE_LOW          DW 0
        HANDLE_HIGH         DW 0
        MESSAGE             DW 0
        PARM1_LOW           DW 0
        PARM1_HIGH          DW 0
        PARM2_LOW           DW 0
        PARM2_HIGH          DW 0
        RET1    DW 0
        RET2    DW 0
        OLD_DS  DW 0
        P1      DW 0
        P2      DW 0
        P3      DW 0
        P4      DW 0
        P5      DW 0
        P6      DW 0
        P7      DW 0
        PS_HANDLE_LOW   DW 0
        PS_HANDLE_HIGH  DW 0
        SCREEN_COORDS   DW 0
                        DW 0
        Y               DW 0
                        DW 0
                        DW 50
                        DW 0
                        DW 50
                        DW 0
                        DW 200
                        DW 0
                        DW 120
                        DW 0
                        DW 90
                        DW 0
                        DW 240
                        DW 0
                        DW 210
                        DW 0
                        DW 10
                        DW 0
        MSSG            DB "This is it!",0
        MSSG_LEN        DW $ - MSSG

.CODE
        EXTRN   WinInitialize:FAR, WinCreateMsgQueue:FAR, DosExit:FAR
        EXTRN   WinRegisterClass:FAR, WinCreateStdWindow:FAR, WinGetMsg:FAR
        EXTRN   WinDispatchMsg:FAR, WinDestroyWindow:FAR, DosBeep:FAR
```

Listing 15-5. WIN.ASM Using GpiPolyLine.

```
        EXTRN   WinDestroyMsgQueue:FAR, WinTerminate:FAR, WinDefWindowProc:FAR
        EXTRN   WinBeginPaint:FAR, GpiCharStringAt:FAR, WinEndPaint:FAR
        EXTRN   GpiSetBackColor:FAR, GpiSetBackMix:FAR, GpiSetColor:FAR
        EXTRN   GpiSetCurrentPosition:FAR, GpiPolyLine:FAR

ENTRY   PROC FAR

        PUSH    0
        CALL    WinInitialize
        MOV     ANCHOR_LOW,AX
        MOV     ANCHOR_HIGH,DX

        PUSH    DX      ;ANCHOR HIGH
        PUSH    AX      ;ANCHOR LOW
        PUSH    0       ;DEFAULT SIZE
        CALL    WinCreateMsgQueue
        MOV     QUEUE_LOW,AX
        MOV     QUEUE_HIGH,DX

        PUSH    ANCHOR_HIGH
        PUSH    ANCHOR_LOW
        PUSH    DS
        PUSH    OFFSET CLASS_NAME
        PUSH    CS
        PUSH    OFFSET CS:WINDOW_FUNC
        PUSH    0       ;HIGH STYLE
        PUSH    4       ;LOW STYLE
        PUSH    0       ;NO EXTRA STORAGE
        CALL    WinRegisterClass

        PUSH    0       ;HWND_DESKTOP
        PUSH    1
        PUSH    8000H   ;STYLE HIGH
        PUSH    0000H   ;STYLE LOW
        PUSH    DS
        PUSH    OFFSET FLAGS
        PUSH    DS                      ;- make 0 for default window
        PUSH    OFFSET CLASS_NAME ;- make 0 for default window
        PUSH    DS
        PUSH    OFFSET TITLE_BAR
        PUSH    0
        PUSH    0
        PUSH    0
        PUSH    DS
        PUSH    OFFSET CLIENT_LOW
        CALL    WinCreateStdWindow

        MOV     FRAME_HIGH,DX
        MOV     FRAME_LOW,AX

GET_MSG:
        PUSH    ANCHOR_HIGH
        PUSH    ANCHOR_LOW
        PUSH    DS
        PUSH    OFFSET QUEUE_MSG
        PUSH    0
        PUSH    0
        PUSH    0
```

Listing 15-5. WIN.ASM Using GpiPolyLine.

```
            PUSH    0
            CALL    WinGetMsg

            CMP     AX,0
            JE      FINISH

            PUSH    ANCHOR_HIGH
            PUSH    ANCHOR_LOW
            PUSH    DS
            PUSH    OFFSET QUEUE_MSG
            CALL    WinDispatchMsg

            JMP     GET_MSG

FINISH:
            PUSH    FRAME_HIGH
            PUSH    FRAME_LOW
            CALL    WinDestroyWindow

            PUSH    QUEUE_HIGH
            PUSH    QUEUE_LOW
            CALL    WinDestroyMsgQueue

            PUSH    ANCHOR_HIGH
            PUSH    ANCHOR_LOW
            CALL    WinTerminate

EXIT:       PUSH    1                       ;A Normal Exit.
            PUSH    0
            CALL    DosExit
ENTRY       ENDP

WINDOW_FUNC PROC FAR

            PUSH    @DATA
            POP     DS
            POP     RET1
            POP     RET2
            POP     P1
            POP     P2
            POP     P3
            POP     P4
            POP     P5
            POP     P6
            POP     P7
            PUSH    RET2
            PUSH    RET1
            PUSH    BP
            PUSH    SP
            POP     BP
KEY:
            CMP     P5,7AH
            JNE     NOT_KEY
            PUSH    1500
            PUSH    1
            CALL    DOSBEEP
            JMP     RET_0

NOT_KEY:
```

Listing 15-5. WIN.ASM Using GpiPolyLine.

```
            CMP     P5,1
            JNE     NOT_CREATE
            ;
            JMP     RET_0
NOT_CREATE:
            CMP     P5,23H
            JE      PAINT
            JMP     NOT_PAINT
PAINT:      PUSH    P7
            PUSH    P6
            PUSH    0
            PUSH    0
            PUSH    0
            CALL    WinBeginPaint

            MOV     PS_HANDLE_HIGH,DX
            MOV     PS_HANDLE_LOW,AX

            PUSH    PS_HANDLE_HIGH
            PUSH    PS_HANDLE_LOW
            PUSH    0       ;Blue background
            PUSH    1
            CALL    GpiSetBackColor

            PUSH    PS_HANDLE_HIGH
            PUSH    PS_HANDLE_LOW
            PUSH    0       ;Overwrite current bkgnd color
            PUSH    2
            CALL    GpiSetBackMix

            PUSH    PS_HANDLE_HIGH
            PUSH    PS_HANDLE_LOW
            PUSH    0       ;Yellow letters
            PUSH    6
            CALL    GpiSetColor

*           PUSH    PS_HANDLE_HIGH
*           PUSH    PS_HANDLE_LOW
*           PUSH    DS
*           PUSH    OFFSET SCREEN_COORDS
*           CALL    GpiSetCurrentPosition

*           PUSH    PS_HANDLE_HIGH
*           PUSH    PS_HANDLE_LOW
*           PUSH    0
*           PUSH    5
*           PUSH    DS
*           PUSH    OFFSET SCREEN_COORDS
*           CALL    GpiPolyLine

            PUSH    PS_HANDLE_HIGH
            PUSH    PS_HANDLE_LOW
            CALL    WinEndPaint

            JMP     RET_0
NOT_PAINT:
            CMP     P5,71H
            JNE     NOT_BUTTON_1
```

Listing 15-5. WIN.ASM Using GpiPolyLine.

```
        ;
        JMP     RET_0
NOT_BUTTON_1:
        CMP     P5,70H
        JNE     NOT_MOUSE_MOVE
        ;
        JMP     RET_0
NOT_MOUSE_MOVE:
        CMP     P5,31H
        JNE     NOT_VSCROLL
        ;
        JMP     RET_0
NOT_VSCROLL:
        CMP     P5,32H
        JNE     NOT_HSCROLL
        ;
NOT_HSCROLL:
        CMP     P5,4FH
        JNE     NOT_ERASE_BKGND
        MOV     DX,0
        MOV     AX,1            ;RETURN TRUE
        JMP     OVER
NOT_ERASE_BKGND:
        ;
DEFAULT:
        POP     BP
        PUSH    P7
        PUSH    P6
        PUSH    P5
        PUSH    P4
        PUSH    P3
        PUSH    P2
        PUSH    P1

        CALL    WinDefWindowProc

        RET

RET_0:  MOV     AX,0    ;RETURN 0
        MOV     DX,0
OVER:   POP     BP
        RET
WINDOW_FUNC     ENDP

        END     ENTRY
```

> **TIP** It's a good idea to break your graphics into geometrical figures to draw, or anything that can be illustrated by connecting the dots. At that point, all you have to do is set up the coordinates in memory and call GpiPolyLine.

Resizing the Window

There is even a resizing message sent to WINDOW_FUNC when the window is resized. In that case, the resizing message number (in P5) is 7, so we can put it to use immediately by adding another case to WINDOW_FUNC. The new size of the window is in the parameters passed to WINDOW_FUNC. The new height (in pels) is in P2, and the new width is in P1.

It is important to respond to such a message: If the window is resized, programs should adjust their output accordingly, perhaps shrinking their displays to fit into the new window.

Let's write an example program to print an "X" in the center of the window and keep it there, even as the window is being resized. This way, as the window shrinks or enlarges, the "X" will stay in the center. We start off by checking for message 7:

```
WINDOW_FUNC      PROC FAR
                   :
                   :
NOT_PAINT:
→       CMP        P5,7              ;Resized window
→       JE         SIZED
→       JMP        NOT_SIZE

SIZED:
                   :
                   :
        JMP        RET_0
NOT_SIZE:
                   :
                   :
WINDOW_FUNC      ENDP
```

If the window is indeed being resized, we will first get a PS handle:

```
WINDOW_FUNC      PROC FAR
                   :
                   :
NOT_PAINT:
        CMP        P5,7              ;Resized window
        JE         SIZED
        JMP        NOT_SIZE

SIZED:  PUSH       P7                        ←
        PUSH       P6                        ←
        CALL       WinGetPS                  ←

        MOV        PS_HANDLE_HIGH,DX         ←
        MOV        PS_HANDLE_LOW,AX          ←
                   :
                   :
        JMP        RET_0
```

526 ▶ Advanced Assembly Language

```
NOT_SIZE:
                    :
                    :
WINDOW_FUNC     ENDP
```

Next we want to set up the SCREEN_COORDS to point to the center of the window. If the vertical height is H and the horizontal width is W, then the center of the window is at (H/2,W/2).

Let's put our "X" there by setting up SCREEN_COORDS to match. First, we get the x position by dividing P1 by 2 (using SHR):

```
WINDOW_FUNC     PROC FAR
                    :
                    :
NOT_PAINT:
        CMP     P5,7            ;Resized window
        JE      SIZED
        JMP     NOT_SIZE

SIZED:  PUSH    P7
        PUSH    P6
        CALL    WinGetPS

        MOV     PS_HANDLE_HIGH,DX
        MOV     PS_HANDLE_LOW,AX
→       MOV     AX,P1
→       SHR     AX,1
→       MOV     SCREEN_COORDS,AX
                    :
                    :
        JMP     RET_0
NOT_SIZE:
                    :
                    :
WINDOW_FUNC     ENDP
```

And then the Y coordinates by doing the same to P2:

```
WINDOW_FUNC     PROC FAR
                    :
                    :
NOT_PAINT:
        CMP     P5,7            ;Resized window
        JE      SIZED
        JMP     NOT_SIZE

SIZED:  PUSH    P7
        PUSH    P6
        CALL    WinGetPS

        MOV     PS_HANDLE_HIGH,DX
        MOV     PS_HANDLE_LOW,AX
```

```
                MOV     AX,P1    ;MP2
                SHR     AX,1
                MOV     SCREEN_COORDS,AX

        →       MOV     AX,P2    ;MP2_HIGH
        →       SHR     AX,1
        →       MOV     Y,AX
                        :
                        :
                JMP     RET_0
NOT_SIZE:
                        :
                        :
WINDOW_FUNC     ENDP
```

All that remains now is to print out the "X" with GpiCharStringAt and quit:

```
WINDOW_FUNC     PROC FAR
                        :
                        :
NOT_PAINT:
                CMP     P5,7            ;Resized window
                JE      SIZED
                JMP     NOT_SIZE

SIZED:  PUSH    P7
        PUSH    P6
        CALL    WinGetPS

                MOV     PS_HANDLE_HIGH,DX
                MOV     PS_HANDLE_LOW,AX

                MOV     AX,P1    ;MP2
                SHR     AX,1
                MOV     SCREEN_COORDS,AX

                MOV     AX,P2    ;MP2_HIGH
                SHR     AX,1
                MOV     Y,AX

        →       PUSH    PS_HANDLE_HIGH
        →       PUSH    PS_HANDLE_LOW
        →       PUSH    DS
        →       PUSH    OFFSET SCREEN_COORDS
        →       PUSH    0
        →       PUSH    1
        →       PUSH    DS
        →       PUSH    OFFSET XCHAR
        →       CALL    GpiCharStringAt

        →       PUSH    PS_HANDLE_HIGH
        →       PUSH    PS_HANDLE_LOW
        →       CALL    WinReleasePS

                JMP     RET_0
NOT_SIZE:
                        :
                        :
WINDOW_FUNC     ENDP
```

We're done. The whole resizing program is in Listing 15-6.

Listing 15-6. WIN.ASM Capable of Resizing the Window.

```
.MODEL  SMALL
.286

.STACK  20000

.DATA
        ANCHOR_LOW       DW 0
        ANCHOR_HIGH      DW 0
        QUEUE_LOW        DW 0
        QUEUE_HIGH       DW 0
        FLAGS            DW 0C3BH
                         DW 8000H
        CLASS_NAME       DB 'FRANK',0
        TITLE_BAR        DB 'Welcome to PM',0
        CLIENT_LOW       DW 0
        CLIENT_HIGH      DW 0
        FRAME_LOW        DW 0
        FRAME_HIGH       DW 0
        QUEUE_MSG        DW 0
                         DW 0
          MSG            DW 0
          MP1            DW 0
                         DW 0
          MP2            DW 0
          MP2_HIGH       DW 0
          TIME           DW 0
                         DW 0
          MOUSE_LOW_X    DW 0
          MOUSE_HIGH_X   DW 0
          MOUSE_LOW_Y    DW 0
          MOUSE_HIGH_Y   DW 0
        HANDLE_LOW       DW 0
        HANDLE_HIGH      DW 0
        MESSAGE          DW 0
        PARM1_LOW        DW 0
        PARM1_HIGH       DW 0
        PARM2_LOW        DW 0
        PARM2_HIGH       DW 0
        RET1     DW 0
        RET2     DW 0
        OLD_DS   DW 0
        P1       DW 0
        P2       DW 0
        P3       DW 0
        P4       DW 0
        P5       DW 0
        P6       DW 0
        P7       DW 0
        PS_HANDLE_LOW    DW 0
        PS_HANDLE_HIGH   DW 0
        SCREEN_COORDS    DW 0
                         DW 0
        Y                DW 0
                         DW 0
```

Listing 15-6. WIN.ASM Capable of Resizing the Window.

```
        XCHAR           DB  "X",0

.CODE
        EXTRN    WinInitialize:FAR, WinCreateMsgQueue:FAR, DosExit:FAR
        EXTRN    WinRegisterClass:FAR, WinCreateStdWindow:FAR, WinGetMsg:FAR
        EXTRN    WinDispatchMsg:FAR, WinDestroyWindow:FAR, DosBeep:FAR
        EXTRN    WinDestroyMsgQueue:FAR, WinTerminate:FAR, WinDefWindowProc:FAR
        EXTRN    WinGetPS:FAR, GpiCharStringAt:FAR, WinReleasePS:FAR
        EXTRN    GpiSetBackMix:FAR

ENTRY   PROC FAR

        PUSH     0
        CALL     WinInitialize
        MOV      ANCHOR_LOW,AX
        MOV      ANCHOR_HIGH,DX

        PUSH     DX      ;ANCHOR HIGH
        PUSH     AX      ;ANCHOR LOW
        PUSH     0       ;DEFAULT SIZE
        CALL     WinCreateMsgQueue
        MOV      QUEUE_LOW,AX
        MOV      QUEUE_HIGH,DX

        PUSH     ANCHOR_HIGH
        PUSH     ANCHOR_LOW
        PUSH     DS
        PUSH     OFFSET CLASS_NAME
        PUSH     CS
        PUSH     OFFSET CS:WINDOW_FUNC
        PUSH     0       ;HIGH STYLE
        PUSH     4       ;LOW STYLE
        PUSH     0       ;NO EXTRA STORAGE
        CALL     WinRegisterClass

        PUSH     0       ;HWND_DESKTOP
        PUSH     1
        PUSH     8000H   ;STYLE HIGH
        PUSH     0000H   ;STYLE LOW
        PUSH     DS
        PUSH     OFFSET FLAGS
        PUSH     DS                      ;← make 0 for default window
        PUSH     OFFSET CLASS_NAME       ;← make 0 for default window
        PUSH     DS
        PUSH     OFFSET TITLE_BAR
        PUSH     0
        PUSH     0
        PUSH     0
        PUSH     0
        PUSH     DS
        PUSH     OFFSET CLIENT_LOW
        CALL     WinCreateStdWindow

        MOV      FRAME_HIGH,DX
        MOV      FRAME_LOW,AX

GET_MSG:
        PUSH     ANCHOR_HIGH
```

Listing 15-6. WIN.ASM Capable of Resizing the Window.

```
                PUSH    ANCHOR_LOW
                PUSH    DS
                PUSH    OFFSET QUEUE_MSG
                PUSH    0
                PUSH    0
                PUSH    0
                PUSH    0
                CALL    WinGetMsg

                CMP     AX,0
                JE      FINISH

                PUSH    ANCHOR_HIGH
                PUSH    ANCHOR_LOW
                PUSH    DS
                PUSH    OFFSET QUEUE_MSG
                CALL    WinDispatchMsg

                JMP     GET_MSG
FINISH:
                PUSH    FRAME_HIGH
                PUSH    FRAME_LOW
                CALL    WinDestroyWindow

                PUSH    QUEUE_HIGH
                PUSH    QUEUE_LOW
                CALL    WinDestroyMsgQueue

                PUSH    ANCHOR_HIGH
                PUSH    ANCHOR_LOW
                CALL    WinTerminate

EXIT:           PUSH    1                       ;A Normal Exit.
                PUSH    0
                CALL    DosExit
ENTRY           ENDP

WINDOW_FUNC     PROC FAR

                PUSH    @DATA
                POP     DS
                POP     RET1
                POP     RET2
                POP     P1
                POP     P2
                POP     P3
                POP     P4
                POP     P5
                POP     P6
                POP     P7
                PUSH    RET2
                PUSH    RET1
                PUSH    BP
                PUSH    SP
                POP     BP
KEY:
                CMP     P5,7AH
                JNE     NOT_KEY
```

Listing 15-6. WIN.ASM Capable of Resizing the Window. 4 of 5

```
            PUSH    1500
            PUSH    1
            CALL    DOSBEEP
            JMP     RET_0

NOT_KEY:
            CMP     P5,1
            JNE     NOT_CREATE
            ;
            JMP     RET_0
NOT_CREATE:
            CMP     P5,23H
            JNE     NOT_PAINT
            ;
            JMP     RET_0
NOT_PAINT:
            CMP     P5,7              ;Resized window
            JE      SIZED
            JMP     NOT_SIZE

SIZED:      PUSH    P7
            PUSH    P6
            CALL    WinGetPS

            MOV     PS_HANDLE_HIGH,DX
            MOV     PS_HANDLE_LOW,AX

            MOV     AX,P1   ;MP2
            SHR     AX,1
            MOV     SCREEN_COORDS,AX

            MOV     AX,P2   ;MP2_HIGH
            SHR     AX,1
            MOV     Y,AX

            PUSH    PS_HANDLE_HIGH
            PUSH    PS_HANDLE_LOW
            PUSH    DS
            PUSH    OFFSET SCREEN_COORDS
            PUSH    0
            PUSH    1
            PUSH    DS
            PUSH    OFFSET XCHAR
            CALL    GpiCharStringAt

            PUSH    PS_HANDLE_HIGH
            PUSH    PS_HANDLE_LOW
            CALL    WinReleasePS

            JMP     RET_0
NOT_SIZE:
            CMP     P5,71H
            JNE     NOT_BUTTON_1
            ;
            JMP     RET_0
NOT_BUTTON_1:
            CMP     P5,70H
            JNE     NOT_MOUSE_MOVE
            ;
```

Listing 15-6. WIN.ASM Capable of Resizing the Window.   5 of 5

```
        JMP     RET_0
NOT_MOUSE_MOVE:
        CMP     P5,31H
        JNE     NOT_VSCROLL
        ;
        JMP     RET_0
NOT_VSCROLL:
        CMP     P5,32H
        JNE     NOT_HSCROLL
        ;
NOT_HSCROLL:
        CMP     P5,4FH
        JNE     NOT_ERASE_BKGND
        MOV     DX,0
        MOV     AX,1            ;RETURN TRUE
        JMP     OVER
NOT_ERASE_BKGND:
        ;
DEFAULT:
        POP     BP
        PUSH    P7
        PUSH    P6
        PUSH    P5
        PUSH    P4
        PUSH    P3
        PUSH    P2
        PUSH    P1

        CALL    WinDefWindowProc

        RET
RET_0:  MOV     AX,0    ;RETURN 0
        MOV     DX,0
OVER:   POP     BP
        RET
WINDOW_FUNC     ENDP

        END     ENTRY
```

That's it for our demonstration programs, and that's it for our coverage of the OS/2 Presentation Manager. As you can see, it's not a terribly simple programming environment, and there are hundreds of other functions we did not cover. Still, PM is a rich resource, and with care it can be an extremely powerful tool.

And that finishes our book. The Presentation Manager is the last topic we'll cover. We ranged far and wide over the PC during our discussion. We've seen how to use video buffers or the keyboard buffer directly; how to work with disks at the lowest levels; how to use Windows, the Presentation Manager, the mouse, macros, math coprocessors; and many other topics. All that remains now is to put all this expertise to work — happy programming!

Appendix A

The BIOS and DOS Reference

The BIOS and DOS Reference

THIS APPENDIX IS intended for use as a reference. We will work through all the interrupts that are available, from 0 to FFH, reviewing the ones that are useful.

Interrupt 0 Divide by 0

This is the first of the BIOS interrupts. BIOS uses interrupts 0 to 1FH, and DOS continues from 20H upward. Interrupt 0 is the divide by zero routine. If a divide by zero occurs, then this interrupt is called. It prints out its message, "Divide Overflow," and usually stops program execution.

Interrupt 1 Single Step

No one, except a debugger, uses this interrupt. It is used to single step through code with a call to this interrupt between executed instructions.

Interrupt 2 Nonmaskable Interrupt (NMI)

This is a hardware interrupt. This interrupt cannot be blocked off by using STI and CLI. It always gets executed when called.

Interrupt 3 Breakpoint

This is another debugger interrupt. DEBUG uses this interrupt with the Go command. If you want to execute all the code up to a particular address and then stop, DEBUG will insert an INT 3 into the code at that point and then give control to the program. When the INT 3 is reached, DEBUG can take control again.

Interrupt 4 Overflow

This is similar to INT 0. If there is an overflow condition, this interrupt is called. Usually, though, no action is called for, and BIOS simply returns.

Interrupt 5 Print Screen

This interrupt was chosen by BIOS to print the screen out. If you use the PrtSc key on the keyboard, this is the interrupt that gets called. Needless to say, your program can also issue an INT 5 by just including that instruction in the program. There are no arguments to be passed.

Interrupts 6 and 7 Reserved

Interrupt 8 Time of Day

This is another hardware interrupt. This interrupt is called to update the internal time of day (stored in the BIOS data area) 18.2 times a second. If the date needs to be changed, this interrupt will handle that too.

This interrupt calls INT 1CH as well. If you want to intercept the timer and do something 18.2 times a second, it is recommended you intercept INT 1CH instead of this one.

Interrupt 9 Keyboard

This hardware interrupt may be intercepted by memory-resident programs.

Interrupt 0AH Reserved

Interrupts 0BH-0FH

These interrupts point to the BIOS routine D_EOI, which is BIOS' End of Interrupt routine. All this routine does is to reset the interrupt handler at port 20H and return.

INT 10H Service 0 Set Screen Mode

Input
AH = 0
AL = Mode

Mode (in AL)	Display Lines	Number of Colors	Adapters	Maximum Pages
0	40 × 25	B&W text	CGA, EGA, VGA	8
1	40 × 25	Color text	CGA, EGA, VGA	8
2	80 × 25	B&W text	CGA, EGA, VGA	4 (CGA) 8 (EGA, VGA)
3	80 × 25	Color text	CGA, EGA, VGA	4 (CGA) 8 (EGA, VGA)
4	320 × 200	4	CGA, EGA, VGA	1
5	320 × 200	B&W	CGA, EGA, VGA	1

6	640×200	2 (on or off)	CGA, EGA, VGA	1
7	80×25	Monochrome	MDA, EGA, VGA	1 (MDA)
				8 (EGA, VGA)
8	160×200	16	PCjr	1
9	320×200	16	PCjr	1
A	640×200	1	PCjr	1
B	Reserved for future use.			
C	Reserved fod future use.			
D	320×200	16	EGA, VGA	8
E	640×200	16	EGA, VGA	4
F	640×350	monochrome	EGA, VGA	2
10H	640×350	16	EGA, VGA	2
11H	640×480	2	VGA	1
12H	640×480	16	VGA	1
13H	320×200	256	VGA	1

INT 10H Service 1 Set Cursor Type

Input
AH = 1
CH = Cursor Start Line
CL = Cursor End Line

Output
New Cursor

INT 10H Service 2 Set Cursor Position

Input
DH,DL = Row, column
BH = Page number
AH = 2

Note: DH,DL = 0,0 = Upper left.

Output
Cursor position changed.

INT 10H Service 3 Find Cursor Position

Input
BH = Page number
AH = 3

Output
DH,DL = Row, Column of cursor.
CH,CL = Cursor mode currently set.

INT 10H Service 4 Read Light Pen Position

Input
AH = 4

Output
AH = 0→Light pen switch not down.
AL = 1→DH,DL = Row, column of light pen position.
       CH raster line (vertical) 0–199.
       BX pixel column (horizontal) 0–319,639

INT 10H Service 5 Set Active Display Page

Input
AL = 0–7 (Screen modes 0,1)
     0–3 (Screen modes 2,3)
AH = 5

Output
Active page changed.

Note: Different pages available in alphanumeric modes only (graphics adapters).

INT 10H Service 6 Scroll Active Page Up

Input
AL = #Lines blanked at bottom (0→blank whole area).
CH,CL = Upper left row,column of area to scroll.
DH,DL = Lower right row,column of area to scroll.
BH = Attribute used on blank line.
AH = 6

INT 10H Service 7 Scroll Active Page Down

Input
AL = #Lines blanked at bottom (0→blank whole area).
CH,CL = Upper left row,column of area to scroll.
DH,DL = Lower right row,column of area to scroll.
BH = Attribute used on blank line.
AH = 7

INT 10H Service 8 Read Attribute and Character at Cursor Position

Input
BH = Page number.
AH = 8

Output
AL = Character read (ASCII).
AH = Attribute of character (alphanumerics only).

INT 10H Service 9 Write Attribute and Character at Cursor Position

Input
BH = Page number.
BL→Alpha modes = Attribute.
 Graphics modes = Color.
CX = Count of characters to write.
AL = IBM ASCII code.
AH = 9

Output
Character written on screen at cursor position.

INT 10H Service A Write Character ONLY at Cursor Position

Input
BH = Page number.
CX = Count of characters to write.
AL = IBM ASCII code.
AH = 0AH

Output
Character written on screen at cursor position.

INT 10H Service B Set Color Palette

Input
BH = Palette color ID
BL   BH = 0→BL = Background color
      BH = 1→BL = Palette number
           (0 = Green/red/yellow)
           (1 = Cyan/magenta/white)
AH = 11

INT 10H Service C Write Dot

Input
DX = Row number(0–199).   [0,0] is upper left.
CX = Column Number(0–319,639)
AL = Color value (0–3)
AH = 12

Note: If bit 7 of AL is 1, the color value is XORed with the current value of the dot.

INT 10H Service D Read Dot

Input
DX = Row number(0–199)
CX = Column number(0–319,639)
AH = 13
[0,0] is upper left.

Output
AL = Color value (0–3)

Note: If bit 7 of AL is 1, the color value is XORed with the current value of the dot.

INT 10H Service E Teletype Write to Active Page

Input
AL = IBM ASCII code.
BL = Foreground color
      (Graphics mode).

AH = 14

INT 10H Service FH Return Video State

Input
AH = 15

Output
AH = Number of alphanumeric columns on screen.
AL = Current mode (See INT 10H Service 0).
BH = Active display page.

INT 10H Service 10H Set Palette Registers

Default Palette Colors (0–15) on EGA

Color value	Color	rgbRGB
0	Black	000000
1	Blue	000001
2	Green	000010
3	Cyan	000011
4	Red	00 100
5	Magenta	000101
6	Brown	010100
7	White	000111
8	Dark gray	111000
9	Light blue	111001
10	Light green	111010
11	Light cyan	111011
12	Light red	111100
13	Light magenta	111101
14	Yellow	111110
15	Intense white	111111

INT 10H Service 10H Function 0 Set Individual Palette Register

Input
AH = 10H
AL = 0
BL = Palette register to set (0–15).
BH = value to set (0–63).

INT 10H Service 10H Function 1—Set Overscan (Border) Register

Input
AH = 10H
BH = Value to set (0–63).

INT 10H Service 10H Function 2—Set All Palette Registers

Input
AH = 10H
AL = 2
ES:BX = Address of a 17-byte table holding color selections (0–63).
        Bytes 0 – 15 hold color selections for palette registers 0 – 15.
        Byte 16 holds the new overscan (border) color.

INT 10H Service 10H Function 7—Read Individual Palette Register

Input
AH = 10H
AL = 7
BL = Register to read (color value).

Output
BH = Register setting.

INT 10H Service 10H Function 8—Read Overscan (Border) Register

Input
AH = 10H
AL = 8

Output
BH = Overscan setting.

INT 10H Service 10H Function 10H—Set DAC Register

Input
AH = 10H
AL = 10H
BX = Register to set (0–255).
CH = Green intensity.

CL = Blue intensity.
DH = Red intensity.

INT 10H Service 10H Function 12H—Set DAC Registers

Input
AH = 10H
AL = 12H
BX = First register to set (0 – 255).
CX = Number of registers to set (1 – 256).
ES:DX = Address of a table of color intensities. 3 bytes are used for each DAC register (use only lower 6 bits of each byte). Table is set up: red, green, blue, red, green, blue....

INT 10H Service 10H Function 13H—Select Color Page Mode

Input
AH = 10H
AL = 13H
BL = 0 Select color paging mode
    BH = 0 Selects 4 DAC register pages of 64 registers each.
    BH = 1 Selects 16 DAC register pages of 16 registers each.
BL = 1 Select Active Color Page
    For use with 4 page mode:
    BH = 0 Selects the first block of 64 DAC registers.
    BH = 1 Selects the second block of 64 DAC registers.
    BH = 2 Selects the third block of 64 DAC registers.
    BH = 3 Selects the fourth block of 64 DAC registers.
    For use with 16 page setting:
    BH = 0 Selects the first block of 16 DAC registers.
    BH = 1 Selects the second block of 16 DAC registers.
            ⋮
    BH = 2 Selects the 15th block of 16 DAC registers.
    BH = 3 Selects the 16th block of 16 DAC registers.

INT 10H Service 11H—Character Generator

INT 10H Service 12H—Alternate Select

Input
AH = 12H
BL = 30H
AL = 0 → 200 screen scan lines
 = 1 → 350 screen scan lines
 = 2 → 400 screen scan lines

INT 11H Equipment Determination

Output
Bits of AX
15,14 = Number of printers.
13 Not used.
12 Game adapter attached.
11,10,9 Number of RS232 cards installed.
8 Unused.
7,6 Number of Diskette drives.
 (00→1;01→2;10→3;11→4 If Bit 0 = 1)
5,4 Video Mode.
 (00 Unused, 01 = 40 × 25 Color card
 10 = 80 × 25 Color Card, 11 = 80 × 25 Monochrome).
3,2 Motherboard RAM
 (00 = 16K, 01 = 32K, 10 = 48K, 11 = 64K).
1 Not used.
0 = 1 if there are diskette drives attached.

INT 12H Determine Memory Size

Output
AX = Number of contiguous 1K memory blocks.

INT 13H Service 0 Reset Disk

Input
AH = 0

Output
No carry → AH = 0, success.
Carry → AH = Error code (See Service 1).

Note: Hard disk systems: DL=80H→reset diskette(s);
DL=81H→reset hard disk.

INT 13H Service 1 Read Status of Last Operation

Input
AH = 1

Output
Disk error codes:
AL = 00   No error.
AL = 01   Bad command passed to controller.
AL = 02   Address mark not found.
AL = 03   Diskette is write protected.
AL = 04   Sector not found.
AL = 05   Reset failed.
AL = 07   Drive parameters wrong.
AL = 09   DMA across segment end.
AL = 0BH   Bad track flag seen.
AL = 10H   Bad error check seen.
AL = 11H   Data is error corrected.
AL = 20H   Controller failure.
AL = 40H   Seek operation has failed.
AL = 80H   No response from disk.
AL = 0BBH   Undefined error.
AL = 0FFH   Sense operation failed.

Note: DL = Drive number; set bit 7 to 1 for hard disks. For hard disks, drive number in DL can range from 80H to 87H.

INT 13H Service 2 Read Sectors into Memory

Input
AH = 2
DL = Drive number.
DH = Head number.
CH = Cylinder or track (floppies) number.
CL = bits 7,6 high 2 bits of 10-bit cylinder number.
CL = Sector number (bit 0–5).

AL = Number of sectors to read (floppies 1–8
                                Hard disks 1–80H
                                Hard disks read/write long 1–79H).
ES:BX = Address of buffer for reads and writes.

Output
No Carry→ AL = No. of sectors read (diskette).
Carry→AH = Disk error code. (See Service 1.)

Note: DL = Drive number; set bit 7 to 1 for hard disks. For hard disks, drive number in DL can range from 80H to 87H.

INT 13H Service 3 Write Sectors to Disk

Input
AH = 3
DL = Drive number.
DH = Head number.
CH = Cylinder or track (floppies) number.
CL = bits 7,6 high 2 bits of 10-bit cylinder number.
CL = Sector number (bits 0–5).
AL = Number of sectors to write (floppies 1–8
                                 Hard disks 1–80H
                                 Hard disks read/write long 1–79H).
ES:BX = Address of buffer for reads and writes.

Output
No Carry→AL = no. sectors written (diskette).
Carry→AH = Disk Error Code. (See Service 1.)

Note: DL = Drive number; set bit 7 to 1 for hard disks. For hard disks, drive number in DL can range from 80H to 87H.

INT 13H Service 4 Verify Sectors

Input
AH = 4
DL = Drive number.
DH = Head number.
CH = Cylinder or track (floppies) number.

CL = Bits 7,6 high 2 bits of 10-bit cylinder number.
CL = Sector number (bits 0–5).
AL = Number of sectors.   (Floppies 1–8
                           Hard disks 1–80H
                           Hard disks read/write long 1–79H).

Output
No carry→AH = 0, Success.
Carry→AH = Disk error code. (See Service 1)

Note: DL = Drive number; set bit 7 to 1 for hard disks. For hard disks, drive number in DL can range from 80H to 87H.

INT 13H Service 8 Return Drive Parameters

This service works ONLY on hard disks and PS/2s.

Input
AH = 8
DL = Drive number (0 based).

Output
DL = Number of drives attached to controller.
DH = Maximum value for head number.
CH = Maximum cylinder value.
CL = Bits 7,6 high 2 bits of 10-bit cylinder no.
CL = Maximum value for sector number (bits 0–5)
BL (For PS/2 diskettes only)
    = 1 → 360K drive
    = 2 → 1.2 Mbyte drive
    = 3 → 720K drive
    = 4 → 1.44 Mbyte drive.

Note: DL = Drive number; set bit 7 to 1 for hard disks. For hard disks, drive number in DL can range from 80H to 87H.

INT 13H Services 0AH and 0BH Reserved

INT 13H Service 0CH Seek

This service works ONLY on hard disks.

Input
AH = 0CH
DH = Head number.
DL = Drive number. (80H–87H allowed)
CH = Cylinder number.
CL = Sector number; bits 7,6 of CL = high 2 bits of 10-bit cylinder no.

Output
No carry→AH = 0, success.
Carry→AH = Disk error code (see Service 1).

Note: DL = Drive number; set bit 7 to 1 for hard disks. For hard disks, drive number in DL can range from 80H to 87H.

INT 13H Service 0DH Alternate Disk Reset

INT 13H Services 0EH and 0FH Reserved

INT 13H Service 10H Test Drive Ready

INT 13H Service 11H Recalibrate Hard Drive

This service works ONLY on hard disks.

Input
AH = 11H (Read)
DL = Drive number (80H–87H allowed).

Output
No carry→AH = 0, success.
Carry→AH = Disk error code (see Service 1).

Note: DL = Drive number; set bit 7 to 1 for hard disks. For hard disks, drive number in DL can range from 80H to 87H.

INT 13H Diagnostic Services

These services work ONLY on hard disks.

Input
AH = 12H (RAM diagnostic).

AH = 13H (Drive diagnostic).
AH = 14H (Controller diagnostic).
DL = Drive number. (80H–87H allowed).

Output
No carry→AH = 0, success.
Carry→AH = Disk error code (see Service 1).

Note: DL = Drive number; set bit 7 to 1 for hard disks. For hard disks, drive number in DL can range from 80H to 87H.

INT 13H Service 19H Park Heads PS/2 Only

Input (PS/2)
DL = Drive number

Output
Carry = 1 → Error, AH = Error code
     = 0 → Success

Note: DL = Drive number; set bit 7 to 1 for hard disks. For hard disks, drive number in DL can range from 80H to 87H.

INT 14H, AH = 0 Initialize RS232 Port

Input
AH = 0
Bits of AL:
0,1 Word length. 01→7 bits, 11→8 bits.
2   Stop bits. 0→1, 1→2 stop bits.
3,4 Parity. 00→none, 01→odd, 11→even.
5,6,7 Baud rate. 000→ 110
                 001→ 150
                 010→ 300
                 011→ 600
                 100→1,200
                 101→2,400
                 110→4,800
                 111→9,600

INT 14H, AH=1 Send Character through Serial Port

Input
AH=1
AL=Character to send.

Output
If bit 7 of AH is set, failure.
If bit 7 is not set, bits 0–6 hold status (see INT 14H, AH=3).

INT 14H, AH=2 Receive Character from Serial Port

Input
AH=2

Output
AL=Character received.
AH=0, success.
   Otherwise, AH holds an error code (see INT 14H, AH=3).

INT 14H, AH=3 Return Serial Port's Status

Input
AH=3

Output
AH Bits set:
7→Time out.
6→Shift register empty.
5→Holding register empty.
4→Break detected.
3→Framing error.
2→Parity error.
1→Overrun error.
0→Data ready.
AL Bits set:
7→Received line signal detect.
6→Ring indicator.
5→Data set ready.
4→Clear to send.
3→Delta receive line signal detect.

2→Trailing edge ring detector.
1→Delta data set ready.
0→Delta clear to send.

INT 15H Cassette I/O

Input
AH=0 → Turn cassette motor on.
AH=1 → Turn cassette motor off.
AH=2 → Read 1 or more 256-byte blocks. Store data at ES:BX.
    CX=Count of bytes to read.
AH=3 → Write 1 or more 256-byte blocks from ES:BX. Count of bytes to write in CX.

Output
DX=Number of bytes actually read.
Carry flag set if error.
If Carry, AH=01→CRC Error.
        =02→Data transitions lost.
        =04→No data found.

In recent BIOS versions, new items have been added to this interrupt, such as joystick support, the ability to switch processor mode (protected or not), mouse support, and some BIOS parameters.

INT 16H, Service 0 Read Key from Keyboard

Input
AH = 0

Output
AH = Scan code AL = ASCII code

INT 16H, Service 1 Check if Key Ready to be Read

Input
AH = 1

Output
Zero flag=1 → Buffer empty
Zero flag=0 → AH=Scan code
           AL=ASCII code

INT 16H, Service 2 Find Keyboard Status

Input
AH = 2

Output
AL = Keyboard status byte.

INT 17H Service 0 Print character in AL

Input
AH = 0
AL = Character to be printed.
DX = Printer number (0,1,2)

Output
AH = 1→ Printer time out.

INT 17H Service 1 Initialize Printer Port

Input
AH = 1
DX = Printer number (0,1,2).

Output
AH = Printer status:
Bits set of AH:
   7→Printer not busy.
   6→Acknowledge.
   5→Out of paper.
   4→Selected.
   3→I/O error.
   2→Unused.
   1→Also unused.
   0→Time out.

INT 17H Service 2 Read Printer Status into AH

Input
AH = 2
DX = Printer number (0,1,2).

Output
AH Set to status byte as in INT 17H, AH = 1.

INT 18H Resident BASIC

This interrupt starts up ROM resident BASIC in the PC.

INT 19H Bootstrap

This interrupt is the one that boots the machine (try it with DEBUG).

INT 1AH Service 0 Read Time of Day

Input
AH = 0

Output
CX = High word of timer count.
DX = Low word of timer count.
AL = 0 If timer has not passed 24 hours since last read.

Note: Timer count increases by 65,536 in one hour.

INT 1AH Service 1 Set Time of Day

Input
AH = 1
CX = High word of timer count.
DX = Low word of timer count.

Note: Timer count increases by 65,536 in one hour.

INT 1BH Keyboard Break Address

INT 1CH Timer Tick Interrupt

INT 1DH Video Parameter Tables

INT 1EH Diskette Parameters

INT 1FH Graphics Character Definitions

DOS Interrupts

Interrupt 1FH is the last BIOS Interrupt, and DOS starts with INT 20H.

INT 20H Terminate

Programs are usually ended with an INT 20H.

Interrupt 21H

Interrupt 21H is the DOS service interrupt. To call one of these services, load AH with the service number, and the other registers as shown.

INT 21H Service 0 Program Terminate

Input
AH = 0

INT 21H Service 1 Keyboard Input

Input
AH = 1

Output
AL = ASCII code of struck key does echo on screen.

This service checks for ^C or ^Break.

INT 21H Service 2 Character Output on Screen

Input
DL = IBM ASCII character.
AH = 2

INT 21H Service 3 Standard Auxiliary Device Input

Input
AH = 3

Output
Character in AL

INT 21H Service 4 Standard Auxiliary Device Output

Input
AH = 4
DL = Character to output.

INT 21H Service 5 Printer Output

Input
AH = 5
DL = Character to output.

INT 21H Service 6 Console I/O

Input		Output
AH = 6		
DL = FF	→	AL holds character. If one ready,
DL < FF	→	type ASCII code in DL out. Does NOT echo on screen.

This service does NOT check for ^C or ^Break.

INT 21H Service 7 Console Input without Echo

Input
AH = 7

Output
AL = ASCII code of struck key
NO echo on screen.

This service does NOT Check for ^C or ^Break.

INT 21H Service 8 Console Input without Echo with ^C Check

Input
AH = 8

Output
AL = ASCII code of struck key.
Does NOT echo the typed key.

This service checks for ^C or ^Break.

DOS INT 21H Service 9 String Print

Input
DS:DX point to a string that ends in '$'.
AH = 9

INT 21H Service A String Input

Input
AH = 0AH
[DS:DX] = Length of buffer.

Output
Buffer at DS:DX filled.
Echo the typed keys.

This service checks for ^C or ^Break.

INT 21H Service 0BH Check Input Status

Input
AH = 0BH

Output
AL = FF → Character ready.
AL = 00 → Nothing to read in.

^Break is checked for.

INT 21H Service 0CH Clear Keyboard Buffer and Invoke Service

Input
AH = 0CH
AL = Keyboard function #

Output
Standard output from the selected service.

^Break is checked for.

INT 21H Service 0DH Disk Reset

Input
AH = 0DH

INT 21H Service 0EH Select Disk

Input
AH = 0EH
DL = Drive number
    (DL = 0 → A
    DL = 1 → B
    and so on).

INT 21H Service 0FH Open Preexisting File

Input
DS:DX points to an FCB.
AH = 0FH

Output
AL = 0 → Success
AL = FF → Failure

INT 21H Service 10H Close File

Input
DS:DX points to an FCB.
AH = 10H

Output
AL = 0 → Success
AL = FF → Failure

INT 21H Service 11H Search for First Matching File

Input
DS:DX points to an unopened FCB
AH = 11H

Output
AL = FF → Failure
AL = 0 → Success DTA holds FCB for match.

Note: DTA is at CS:0080 in .COM files on startup.

INT 21H Service 12H Search for Next Matching File

Input
DS:DX points to an unopened FCB.
AH = 12H

Output
AL = FF → Failure
AL = 0 → Success DTA holds FCB for match.

Note: Use this service after Service 11H.

INT 21H Service 13H Delete Files

Input
DS:DX points to an unopened FCB.
AH = 13H

Output
AL = FF → Failure
AL = 0 → Success

INT 21H Service 14H Sequential Read

Input
DS:DX points to an opened FCB.
AH = 14H
Current block and record set in FCB.

Output
Requested record put in DTA.
AL = 0 Success.
    1 End of File, no data in record.
    2 DTA Segment too small for record.
    3 End of file; record padded with 0.

Note: Record address increased.

INT 21H Service 15H Sequential Write

Input
DS:DX points to an opened FCB.
AH = 15H
Current block & record set in FCB.

Output
One record read from DTA and written.
AL = 0 Success.
    1 Disk full.
    2 DTA Segment too small for record.
Record address increased.

INT 21H Service 16H Create File

Input
DS:DX points to an unopened FCB.
AH = 16H

Output
AL = 0 Success.
    = FF Directory full.

INT 21H Service 17H Rename File

Input
DS:DX points to a MODIFIED FCB.
AH = 17H

Output
AL = 0 Success.
    = FF Failure.

Note: Modified FCB → Second file name starts 6 bytes after the end of the first file name, at DS:DX+11H.

INT 21H Service 18H Internal to DOS

INT 21H Service 19H Find Current Disk

Input
AH = 19H

Output
AL = Current disk (0 = A, 1 = B, and so on).

INT 21H Service 1AH Set the DTA Location

Input
DS:DX points to new DTA address.
AH = 1AH

Note: DTA = Disk transfer address, the data area used with FCB services. Default DTA is 128 bytes long, starting at CS:0080 in the PSP.

INT 21H Service 1BH FAT Information for Default Drive

Input
AH = 1BH

Output
DS:BX points to the "FAT Byte."
DX = Number of clusters.
AL = Number of sectors/cluster.
CX = Size of a sector (512 bytes).

Note: Files are stored in clusters, the smallest allocatable unit on a disk.

INT 21H Service 1CH FAT Information for Specified Drive

Input
AH = 1CH
DL = Drive number (0 = default
     1 = A...)

Output
DS:BX points to the "FAT Byte."
DX = Number of clusters.
AL = Number of sectors/cluster.
CX = Size of a sector (512).

Note: Files are stored in clusters, the smallest allocatable unit on a disk.

INT 21H Services 1DH–20H Internal to DOS

INT 21H Service 21H Random Read

Input
DS:DX points to an opened FCB.
Set FCB's Random Record field at DS:DX+33 and DS:DX+35.
AH=21H

Output
AL=00 Success.
   =01 End of file, no more data.
   =02 Not enough space in DTA segment.
   =03 End of file, partial record padded with 0s.

INT 21H Service 22H Random Write

Input
DS:DX points to an opened FCB.
Set FCB's random record field at DS:DX+33 and DS:DX+35.
AH=21H

Output
AL=00 Success.
   =01 Disk is full.
   =02 Not enough space in DTA segment.

INT 21H Service 23H File Size

Input
DS:DX points to an unopened FCB.
AH=23H

Output
AL=00 Success.
   =FF No file found that matched FCB.
Random record field set to file length in records, rounded up.

INT 21H Service 24H Set Random Record Field

Input
DS:DX points to an opened FCB.
AH=24H

Output
Random record field set to match current record and current block.

INT 21H Service 25H Set Interrupt Vector

Input
AH = 25H
AL = Interrupt number.
DS:DX = New address.

Note: This service can help you intercept an interrupt vector.

INT 21H Service 26H Create a New Program Segment (PSP)

INT 21H Service 27H Random Block Read

Input
DS:DX points to an opened FCB.
Set FCB's random record field at DS:DX + 33 and DS:DX + 35.
AH = 27H

Output
AL = 00 Success.
  = 01 End of file, no more data.
  = 02 Not enough space in DTA segment.
  = 03 End of file, partial record padded with 0s.
CX = Number of records read.
Random record fields set to access next record.

Note: The data buffer used in FCB services is the DTA, or disk transfer area.

INT 21H Service 28H Random Block Write

Input
DS:DX points to an opened FCB.
Set FCB's random record field at DS:DX + 33 and DS:DX + 35.
CX = Number of records to write.
AH = 28H

Output
AL = 00 Success.
  = 01 Disk is full.

         =02 Not enough space in DTA segment.
         Random record fields set to access next record.

   CX=0 → File set to the size indicated by the Random Record field

   Note: The data buffer used in FCB services is the DTA, or disk transfer area.

INT 21H Service 29H Parse File name

   Input
   DS:SI = Command line to parse.
   ES:DI = Address to put FCB at.
   AL = Bit 0=1 → Leading separators are scanned off command line.
         Bit 1=1 → Drive ID in final FCB will be changed ONLY if a drive was specified.
         Bit 2=1 → File name in FCB changed ONLY if command line includes file name.
         Bit 3=1 → File name extension in FCB will be changed ONLY if command line contains a file name extension.
   AH=29H

   Output
   DS:SI = 1st character after file name.
   ES:DI = Valid FCB

   Note: If the command line does not contain a valid file name, ES:[DI+1] will be a blank.

INT 21H Service 2AH Get Date

   Input
   AH=2AH

   Output
   CX = Year - 1980
   DH = Month (1=January, etc.)
   DL = Day of the month.

INT 21H Service 2BH Set Date

   Input
   CX = Year - 1980

DH = Month (1=January, etc.)
DL = Day of the month.
AH=2BH

Output
AL = 0 Success.
AL = FF Date not valid.

INT 21H Service 2CH Get Time

Input
AH=2CH

Output
CH = Hours (0–23)
CL = Minutes (0–59)
DH = Seconds (0–59)
DL = Hundredths of seconds (0–99)

INT 21H Service 2DH Set Time

Input
AH=2DH
CH = Hours (0–23)
CL = Minutes (0–59)
DH = Seconds (0–59)
DL = Hundreds of seconds (0–99)

Output
AL = 0 Success.
AL = FF Time is invalid.

INT 21H Service 2EH Set or Reset Verify Switch

Input
AH=2EH
DL=0
AL=1 → Turn verify on.
   =0 → Turn verify off.

INT 21H Service 2FH Get Current DTA

Input
AH = 2FH

Output
ES:BX = Current DTA address.

Note: The data buffer used in FCB services is the DTA, or disk transfer area.

INT 21H Service 30H Get DOS Version Number

Input
AH = 30H

Output
AL = Major version number (3 in DOS 3.10)
AH = Minor version number (10 in DOS 3.10)
BX = 0
CX = 0

Note: If AL returns 0, you are working with a version of DOS before 2.0.

INT 21H Service 31H Terminate Process and Keep Resident

Input
AH = 31H
AL = Binary exit code
DX = Size of memory request in paragraphs.

Note: Exit code can be read by a parent program with Service 4DH. It can also be tested by ERRORLEVEL commands in batch files.

INT 21H Service 32H Internal to DOS

INT 21H Service 33H Control-Break Check

Input
AH = 33H
AL = 0 → Check state of ^Break checking.
   = 1 → Set the state of ^Break checking.
      (DL = 0→ Turn it off.

566 ▶ Advanced Assembly Language

DL=1→ Turn it on.)

Output
DL=0 → Off.
DL=1 → On.

INT 21H Service 34H Internal to DOS

INT 21H Service 35H Get Interrupt Vector

Input
AH=35H
AL=Interrupt number.

Output
ES:BX = Interrupt's vector.

INT 21H Service 36H Get Free Disk Space

Input
AH=36H
DL=Drive number (0=Default
                 1=A...)

Output
AX=0FFFH→Drive number invalid.
AX=Number of sectors/cluster.
BX=Number of available clusters.
CX=Size of a sector (512).
DX=Number of clusters.

Note: Files are stored in clusters, the smallest allocatable unit on a disk.

INT 21H Service 37H Internal to DOS

INT 21H Service 38H Returns Country Dependent Information

Input
AH=38H
DS:DX = address of 32-byte block.
AL=0

The BIOS and DOS Reference

Output
Filled in 32-byte block (see below).

The 32-byte block looks like this:

```
2 bytes DATE/TIME Format.
1 byte of currency symbol (ASCII)
1 byte set to 0.
1 byte thousands separator (ASCII)
1 byte set to 0.
1 byte decimal separator (ASCII)
1 byte set to 0.
24 bytes used internally.
```

The DATE/TIME format has these values:

```
0 = USA (H:M:S M/D/Y)
1 = EUROPE (H:M:S D/M/Y)
2 = JAPAN (H:M:S D:M:Y)
```

Note: In DOS 3+ you can set, as well as read, these values.

INT 21H Service 39H Create a Subdirectory

Input
AH = 39H
DS:DX point to ASCIIZ string with directory name.

Output
No carry → Success.
Carry → AH has error value.
    AH = 3 Path not found.
    AH = 5 Access denied.

INT 21H Service 3AH Delete a Subdirectory

Input
AH = 3AH
DS:DX point to ASCIIZ string with directory name.

Output
No Carry→ Success.
Carry→AH has error value.
    AH=3 Path not found.
    AH=5 Access denied or subdirectory not empty.

INT 21H Service 3BH Change Current Directory

Input
AH=3BH
DS:DX point to ASCIIZ string with directory name.

Output
No Carry→ Success.
Carry→AH has error value.
    AH=3 Path not found.

INT 21H Service 3CH Create a File

Input
DS:DX points to ASCIIZ file name.
CX=Attribute of file.
AH=3CH

Output
No carry → AX=File handle.
Carry → AL=3 Path not found.
        =4 Too many files open.
        =5 Dir full, or previous Read-Only file exists.

INT 21H Service 3DH Open a File

Input
DS:DX points to ASCIIZ file name.
AL=Access code.
AH=3DH

Access codes: AL=0   File opened for reading.
               AL=1   File opened for writing.
               AL=2   File opened for reading and writing.
Access Code DOS 3+: isssraaa

The BIOS and DOS Reference 569

        i = 1 → file is not to be inherited by child processes
        i = 0 → file handle will be inherited
        sss = 000 → Compatibility mode
        sss = 001 → Deny all
        sss = 010 → Deny write
        sss = 011 → Deny read
        sss = 100 → Deny none
        r = reserved
        aaa = 000 → Read access
        aaa = 001 → Write access
        aaa = 010 → Read/write access

Output
No carry → AX = File handle.
Carry → AL = Error code
(Check error table).

INT 21H Service 3EH Close a File Handle

Input
BX holds a valid file handle.
AH = 3EH

Output
Carry → AL = 6 → Invalid handle.

INT 21H Service 3FH Read from File or Device

Input
DS:DX = Data buffer address.
CX = Number of bytes to read.
BX = File handle.
AH = 3FH

Output
No Carry → AX = Number of bytes read.
Carry → AL = 5 Access denied.
       AL = 6 Invalid handle.

INT 21H Service 40H Write to File or Device

Input
DS:DX = Data buffer address.
CX = Number of bytes to write.
BX = File handle.
AH = 40H

Output
No Carry→ AX = Number of bytes written.
Carry→ AL = 5 Access denied.
　　　　AL = 6 Invalid handle.

Note: Full disk is NOT considered an error: check the number of bytes you wanted to write (CX) against the number actually written (returned in AX). If they do not match, the disk is probably full.

INT 21H Service 41H Delete a File

Input
DS:DX = ASCIIZ file name.
AH = 41H

Output
No carry→ Success.
Carry→ AL = 2　File not found.
　　　　AL = 5　Access denied.

Note: No wildcards allowed in file name.

INT 21H Service 42H Move Read/Write Pointer

Input
BX = File handle
CX:DX = Desired offset.
AL = Method value
AH = 42H

Method values (AL):
　　AL = 0　Read/write pointer moved to CX:DX from the start of the file.

     AL=1 Pointer increased CX:DX bytes.
     AL=2 Pointer moved to end-of-file plus offset (CX:DX).

Output
No Carry→DX:AX = New location of pointer.
Carry→AL = 1 Illegal function number.
   AL = 6 Invalid Handle.

INT 21H Service 43H Change File's Attribute

Input
DS:DX = ASCIIZ Filestring.
AL = 1→ File attribute changed.
    CX holds new attribute.
AL = 0→ File's current attribute returned in CX.
AH = 43H

Output
No Carry →Success.
Carry→ AL = 2 File not found.
    AL = 3 Path not found.
    AL = 5 Access denied.
    If AL was 0, CX returns the attribute.

INT 21H Service 44H I/O Control

INT 21H Service 45H Duplicate a File Handle

Input
BX = File handle to duplicate.
AH = 45H

Output
No carry →AX = New, duplicated handle.
Carry→ AL = 4 Too many files open.
    AL = 6 Invalid handle.

INT 21H Service 46H Force Duplication of a File Handle

Input
BX = File handle to duplicate.
CX = Second file handle.

AH = 46H

Output
No carry→Handles refer to same "stream."
Carry→AL = 6 Invalid handle.

INT 21H Service 47H Get Current Directory on Specified Drive

Input
AH = 47H
DS:SI point to 64 byte buffer.
DL = Drive number.

Output
No Carry→ Success, ASCIIZ at DS:SI
Carry→AH = 15 Invalid drive specified.

-Note: Drive letter is NOT included in returned ASCIIZ string.

INT 21H Service 48H Allocate Memory

Input
AH = 48H
BX = Number of paragraphs requested.

Output
No carry→AX :0000 memory block address.
Carry→AL = 7 Memory control blocks destroyed.
       AL = 8 Insufficient memory, BX contains maximum allowable request.

INT 21H Service 49H Free Allocated Memory

Input
AH = 49H
ES = Segment of block being freed.

Output
No carry → Success.
Carry → AL = 7 Memory control blocks destroyed.
        = 9 Incorrect memory block address.

INT 21H Service 4AH SETBLOCK

Input
AH = 4AH
ES = Segment of block to modify.
BX = Requested size in paragraphs.

Output
No Carry → Success.
Carry → AL = 7 Memory control blocks destroyed.
    = 8 Insufficient memory; BX holds maximum possible request.
    = 9 Invalid memory block address.

INT 21H Service 4BH Load or Execute a program—EXEC

Input
AH = 4BH
DS:DX = ASCIIZ string with drive, path name, file name.
ES:BX = Parameter block address (see below).
AL = 0 → Load and execute the program.
    3 → Load but create no PSP, don't run. (Overlay.)

Parameter block for AL = 0:

  Segment address of environment to pass (word).
  Address of command to put at PSP+80H (DWord).
  Address of default FCB to put at PSP+5CH (DWord).
  Address of 2nd default FCB to put at PSP+6CH (DWord).

Parameter Block for AL = 3:

  Segment address to load file at (Word).
  Relocation factor for image (Word).

Output
No carry → Success
Carry:
    AL = 1 Invalid function number
       2 File not found on disk.

5 Access denied.
8 Insufficient memory for requested operation.
10 Invalid environment.
11 Invalid format.

INT 21H Service 4CH Exit

Input
AH = 4CH
AL = Binary return code.

Note: This service can end a program.

INT 21H Service 4DH Get Return Code of Subprocess

Input
AH = 4DH

Output
AL = Binary return code from subprocess.
AH = 0 If subprocess ended normally.
    1 If subprocess ended with a ^Break.
    2 If it ended with a critical device error.
    3 If it ended with Service 31H.

INT 21H Service 4EH Find First Matching File

Input
DS:DX→ASCIIZ filestring.
CX = Attribute to match.
AH = 4EH

Output
Carry→AL = 2 No match found.
       AL = 18 No more files.
No Carry→DTA filled as follows:
    21 bytes reserved.
    1 byte found attribute.
    2 bytes file's time.
    2 bytes file's date.
    2 bytes low word of size.

2 bytes high word of size.
13 bytes name and extension of found file in ASCIIZ form (NO path name).

Note: The data buffer used in FCB services is the DTA, or disk transfer area. See earlier services.

INT 21H Service 4FH Find Next Matching File

Input
Use Service 4EH BEFORE 4FH.
AH = 4FH

Output
Carry→AL = 18 No more files.
No carry→DTA filled as follows:
    21 bytes reserved.
    1 byte found attribute.
    2 bytes file's time.
    2 bytes file's date.
    2 bytes low word of size.
    2 bytes high word of size.
    13 bytes name and extension of found file in ASCIIZ form (NO path name).

Note: The data buffer used in FCB services is the DTA, or disk transfer area. See earlier services.

INT 21H Services 50H-53H Internal to DOS

INT 21H Service 54H Get Verify State

Input
AH = 54H

Output
AL = 0→ Verify is OFF.
    1→ Verify is ON.

INT 21H Service 55H Internal to DOS

INT 21H Service 56H Rename File

Input
DS:DX = ASCIIZ filestring to be renamed.
ES:DI = ASCIIZ filestring that holds the new name.
AH = 56H

Output
No carry → Success.
Carry → AL = 3 Path not found.
         AL = 5 Access denied.
         AL = 17 Not same device.

Note: File CANNOT be renamed to another drive.

INT 21H Service 57H Get or Set a File's Date & Time

Input
BX = File handle.
AL = 0 → Get date & time ───────→ CX returns time.
                                        DX returns date.
AL = 1 → Set time to CX ───────→ File's date and time set.
       Set date to DX.

Output
No carry:
    CX returns time.
    DX returns date.
    File's date and time set.

Carry → AL = 1 Invalid function number.
              6 Invalid handle.

The time and date of a file are stored like this:

$$\text{Time} = 2048 \times \text{Hours} + 32 \times \text{Minutes} + \text{Seconds}/2$$

$$\text{Date} = 512 \times (\text{Year-1980}) + 32 \times \text{Month} + \text{Day}$$

INT 21H Service 58H Internal to DOS

INT 21H Service 59H Get Extended Error DOS 3+

Input
AH = 59H

BX = 0

Output
AX = Extended error
BH = Error class
BL = Suggested action
CH = Locus

This error handling service is very lengthy and involves the many DOS 3+ extended errors.

INT 21H Service 5AH Create Unique File DOS 3+

Input
AH = 5AH
DS:DX = Address of an ASCIIZ path (ending with "/").
CX = File's attribute.

Output
AX = Error if carry is set.
DS:DX = ASCIIZ path and file name.

INT 21H Service 5BH Create a New File DOS 3+

Input
AH = 5BH
DS:DX = Address of an ASCIIZ path (ending with "/").
CX = File's attribute.

Output
AX = Error if carry is set
   = Handle if carry is not set.

INT 21H Service 5CH Lock and Unlock Access to a File DOS 3+

Input
AH = 5CH
AL = 0 → Lock byte range.
     1 → Unlock byte range.
BX = File handle.
CX = Byte range start (high word).
DX = Byte range start (low word).

SI = No. bytes to (un)lock (high word).
DI = No. bytes to (un)lock (low word).

Output
If carry = 1, AX = error

INT 21H Service 5E00H Get Machine Name DOS 3+

Input
AX = 5E00H
DS:DX = Buffer for computer name.

Output
DS:DX = ASCIIZ computer name.
CH = 0 → Name not defined.
CL = NETBIOS number.
AX = Error if carry set.

INT 21H Service 5E02 Set Printer Setup DOS 3+

Input
AX = 5E02H
BX = Redirection list index.
CX = Length of setup string.
DS:DI = Pointer to printer setup buffer.

Output
AX = Error if carry is set.

INT 21H Service 5E03 Get Printer Setup DOS 3+

Input
AX = 5E03H
BX = Redirection list index.
ES:DI = Pointer to printer setup buffer.

Output
AX = Error if carry is set.
CX = Length of data returned.
ES:DI = Filled with printer setup string.

INT 21H Service 5F03 Redirect Device DOS 3+

Input
AX = 5F03H
BL = Device type
    = 3 → Printer device.
    = 4 → File device.
CX = Value to save for caller.
DS:SI = Source ASCIIZ device name.
ES:DI = Destination ASCIIZ network path with password.

Output
AX = Error if carry is set

INT 21H Service 5F04H Cancel Redirection DOS 3+

Input
AX = 5F04H
DS:SI = ASCIIZ device name or path.

Output
AX = Error if carry is set.

INT 21H Service 62H Get Program Segment Prefix DOS 3+

Input
AX = 62H

Output
BX = Segment of currently executing program.

INT 21H Service 67H Set Handle Count DOS 3.30

Input
AX = 67H
BX = Number of allowed open handles (up to 255).

Output
AX = Error if carry is set.

INT 21H Service 68H Commit File (Write Buffers) DOS 3.30

Input
AX = 68H

Output
BX = File handle

Note: 68H is the last of the DOS 3.3 INT 21H services.

INT 22H Terminate Address

INT 23H Control Break Exit Address

INT 24H Critical Error Handler

AH filled this way:
- 0 Diskette is write protected.
- 1 Unknown Unit.
- 2 The requested drive is not ready.
- 3 Unknown command.
- 4 Cyclic redundancy check error in the data.
- 5 Bad request structure length.
- 6 Seek error.
- 7 Media type unknown.
- 8 Sector not found.
- 9 The printer is out of paper.
- A Write fault.
- B Read fault.
- C General failure.

If you just execute an IRET, DOS will take an action based on the contents of AL. If AL=0, the error will be ignored. If AL=1, the operation will be retried. If AL=2, the program will be terminated through INT 23H.

INT 25H Absolute Disk Read

Input
AL = Drive number.
CX = Number of sectors to read.
DX = First logical sector.
DS:BX = Buffer address.

Output
No carry → Success.

Carry→AH=80H Disk didn't respond.
AH=40H Seek failed.
AH=20H Controller failure.
AH=10H Bad CRC error check.
AH=08 DMA overrun.
AH=04 Sector not found.
AH=03 Write protect error.
AH=02 Address mark missing.
AH=00 Error unknown.

Note: Flags left on stack after this INT call because information is returned in current flags. After you check the flags that were returned, make sure you do a POPF. Also, this INT destroys the contents of ALL registers.

INT 26H Absolute Disk Write

Input
AL=Drive number.
CX=Number of sectors to write.
DX=First logical sector.
DS:BX=Buffer address.

Output
No carry→ Success.
Carry→AH=80H Disk didn't respond.
AH=40H Seek failed.
AH=20H Controller failure.
AH=10H Bad CRC error check.
AH=08 DMA overrun.
AH=04 Sector not found.
AH=03 Write protect error.
AH=02 Address mark missing.
AH=00 Error unknown.

Note: Flags left on stack after this INT call because information is returned in current flags. After you check the flags that were returned, make sure you do a POPF. Also, this INT destroys the contents of ALL registers.

INT 27H Terminate and Stay Resident

Input
DS:DX = Point directly after end of code which is to stay resident.

INTs 28H-2EH Internal to DOS

INT 2FH Multiplex Interrupt

INT 30H-3FH DOS Reserved

INT 40H-5FH Reserved

INT 60H-67H Reserved for User Software

INTs 68H-7FH Not Used

INTs 80H-85H Reserved by BASIC

INTs 86H-F0H Used by BASIC Interpreter

INTs F1H-FFH Not Used

Appendix B

The OS/2 Reference

NOTE: Push address pointers (PTR) selector first, followed by offset. Push DWORDs high word first. Double word values are returned with high word in DX, low word in AX. Addresses are returned with selector in DX, offset in AX.

DosAllocHuge

PUSH	WORD	Number of whole segments to allocate.
PUSH	WORD	Length of the last segment.
PUSH	PTR	Address of memory word to receive allocated memory selector.
PUSH	WORD	Maximum number of segments to which allocated memory will grow.
PUSH	WORD	OR these values: 1 → Shareable with DosGiveSeg.
		2 → Shareable with DosGetSeg.
		4 → Segment may be discarded.

DosAllocShrSeg

PUSH	WORD	Size of the segment requested.
PUSH	PTR	Pointer to the ASCIIZ name of the shared memory.
PUSH	PTR	Pointer to memory word for returned memory selector.

DosBeep

| PUSH | WORD | Frequency (25–32K) |
| PUSH | WORD | Duration (milliseconds) |

DosChgFilePtr

PUSH	WORD	Open file handle.
PUSH	DWORD	Distance to move file pointer.
PUSH	WORD	Method: 0 → move from start of file.
		1 → move from current location.
		2 → move from end of file.
PUSH	PTR	Address of memory dword to receive new file pointer location in file.

DosClose

| PUSH | WORD | File handle to close. |

DosCloseSem

    PUSH DWORD   Semaphore handle returned by DosOpenSem or DosCreateSem.

DosCreateSem

    PUSH WORD   Type of semaphore: 0 → not shared.
                                                  1 → shared.
    PUSH PTR   Pointer to dword field to receive semaphore handle.
    PUSH PTR   Pointer to ASCIIZ name of sem, must begin with "\SEM\".

DosCreateThread

    PUSH PTR   Pointer to thread procedure.
    PUSH PTR   Pointer to dword field to receive thread ID.
    PUSH PTR   Pointer to top of stack set aside for thread.

DosEnterCritSec

(No PUSHes)

DosExecPgm

    PUSH PTR   Address of fail buffer (128 or so bytes long).
    PUSH WORD   Length of fail buffer.
    PUSH WORD   Flags: 0 → synchronous execution.
                                      1 → Asynchronous execution (don't save child's result).
                                      2 → Asynchronous execution (save child's result).
                                      3 → Run program in debug mode.
                                      4 → Detached—use different session.
    PUSH PTR   Address of two ASCIIZ strings, one after the other. First is program name (omitting extension), next is command line input.
    PUSH PTR   ASCIIZ environment block. May be a NULL string

PUSH	PTR	Address of a dword area for termination information Asynchronous execution → first word is process ID of terminating process. Synchronous Execution → first word is: 0 → normal 1 → hard error exit 2 → trap 3 → DosKillProcess used Second word is always child's termination code.
PUSH	PTR	Address of full ASCIIZ file name to execute (include file's extension).

DosExit

PUSH	WORD	Action code: 0 → stop this thread only. 1 → stop all threads.
PUSH	WORD	Termination code, passed to parent.

DosExitCritSec

(No PUSHes)

DosGetHugeShift

PUSH	PTR	Address of word to receive huge shift count.

DosGetInfoSeg

PUSH	PTR	Pointer to word to receive selector of global information segment.
PUSH	PTR	Pointer to word to receive selector of local information segment.

DosGetPrty

PUSH	WORD	Scope of request: 0 → priority of first thread. 2 → priority of specified thread.
PUSH	PTR	Address of word which will receive the priority value.
PUSH	WORD	ID of process (if scope is 0) or thread (if scope is 2) that priority is requested for.

DosGetShrSeg

PUSH	PTR	Address of ASCIIZ string holding the name of the segment.
PUSH	PTR	Address of memory word to receive segment selector.

DosKillProcess

PUSH	WORD	Action code: 0 → kill specified process and its descendents. 1 → kill only indicated process
PUSH	WORD	Process ID of process to kill.

DosMakePipe

PUSH	PTR	Address of word to receive pipe read handle
PUSH	PTR	Address of word to receive pipe write handle
PUSH	WORD	Size of pipe in bytes

DosMonClose

PUSH	WORD	Device monitor handle to close.

DosMonOpen

PUSH	PTR	Address of ASCIIZ device name.
PUSH	PTR	Address of memory word to receive monitor handle.

DosMonRead

PUSH	PTR	Address of monitor input buffer (set up with DosMonReg).
PUSH	WORD	0 → Wait for data 1 → Do not wait for data.
PUSH	PTR	Address of data buffer for monitor input record.
PUSH	PTR	Address of word to receive size of read bytes in data record.

DosMonReg

PUSH	WORD	Device monitor handle.
PUSH	PTR	Address of input buffer to register.
PUSH	PTR	Address of output buffer to register.

PUSH	WORD	I/O chain location: 0 → no preference
		1 → install at head of chain
		2 → install at end of chain.
PUSH	WORD	Depends on device (see chapter on monitors).

DosMonWrite

PUSH	PTR	Address of monitor output buffer (set up with DosMonReg).
PUSH	PTR	Address of buffer that will hold monitor output record.
PUSH	WORD	Length of data record in output buffer.

DosOpen

PUSH	PTR	Address of ASCIIZ file name
PUSH	PTR	Address of word to receive the file handle
PUSH	PTR	Address of word to receive action code:
		1 → file existed
		2 → was created
		3 → was replaced.
PUSH	DWORD	Initial file size (valid only when file is opened or created).
PUSH	WORD	File attribute
PUSH	WORD	Open flag
		If file does not already exist:
		0000 nnnn fail
		0001 nnnn create file.
		If file does exist already:
		nnnn 0000 fail
		nnnn 0001 open file
		nnnn 0010 create file.
PUSH	WORD	Open mode: dwfrrrrrisssraaa (see file handling chapter)
PUSH	DWORD	Both words must be 0

DosOpenSem

PUSH	PTR	Address of dword to receive semaphore handle.
PUSH	PTR	Address of ASCIIZ semaphore name (begin with "\SEM\").

DosRead

PUSH	WORD	File handle.
PUSH	PTR	Address of input buffer to use.
PUSH	WORD	Length of input buffer.
PUSH	PTR	Address of word to receive number of bytes read.

DosSemClear

| PUSH | DWORD | Semaphore handle |

DosSemRequest

| PUSH | DWORD | Semaphore handle |
| PUSH | DWORD | Timeout value:
    0FFFFH → wait forever
    00000H → return immediately if cannot get semaphore
    nnnnnH → milliseconds to timeout. |

DosSemSet

| PUSH | DWORD | Semaphore handle |

DosSetPrty

PUSH	WORD	Scope:
		    0 → the process and all threads
		    1 → process and all decendents
		    2 → single thread in current process.

PUSH	WORD	New priority class:
		    0 → do not change class
		    *1 → idle
		    2 → regular
		    3 → time-critical.

PUSH	WORD	Change in priority (-31 to 31).
PUSH	WORD	(scope = 0 or 1) ID of process; (scope = 2) ID of thread.

DosSleep

| PUSH | DWORD | Number of milliseconds to suspend execution. |

DosStartSession

PUSH	PTR	Address of start session record:
		    DW 24
		    DW relation: 0 → new session is independent
		                       1 → new session is child.
		    DW 0 → start session in foreground
		          1 → start session in background.
		    DW 0 → session is not traceable
		          1 → session is traceable.
		    DD address of ASCIIZ session title.
		    DD address of program to run.
		    DD address of parameter list passed to program.
		    DD address of termination queue (can be NULL).

PUSH	PTR	Address of word to receive new session ID.
PUSH	PTR	Address of word to receive ID of process in new session.

DosSuspendThread

PUSH	WORD	Thread ID

DosWrite

PUSH	WORD	File handle.
PUSH	PTR	Address of output buffer to use.
PUSH	WORD	Length of output buffer.
PUSH	PTR	Address of word to receive number of bytes written.

GpiBox

PUSH	DWORD	Presentation space handle.

PUSH	DWORD	Style: 0 → fill box
		          1 → outline box
		          2 → fill and outline.

PUSH	PTR	Address of screen coordinates for one corner.
PUSH	DWORD	Horizontal rounding (0 in this book).
PUSH	DWORD	Vertical rounding (0 in this book).

GpiCharStringAt

PUSH	DWORD	Presentation space handle.
PUSH	PTR	Address of screen coordinates.
PUSH	DWORD	Length of string.
PUSH	PTR	Address of the string.

GpiLine

PUSH	DWORD	Presentation space handle.
PUSH	PTR	Address of screen coordinates to draw to.

GpiPolyLine

PUSH	DWORD	Presentation space handle.
PUSH	DWORD	Number of coordinates to connect on screen.
PUSH	PTR	Address of first pair of screen coordinates.

GpiSetBackColor

PUSH	DWORD	Presentation space handle
PUSH	DWORD	Color:

Color	Value
Default	-3
White	-2
Black	-1
Background	0
Blue	1
Red	2
Pink	3
Green	4
Cyan	5
Yellow	6
Neutral grey	7
Dark grey	8
Dark blue	9
Dark red	10
Dark pink	11
Dark green	12
Dark cyan	13
Brown	14
Light grey	15

GpiSetBackMix

    PUSH DWORD Presentation space handle.
    PUSH DWORD Option: 0 → Default.
                                1 → Overwrite current color.
                                2 → Leave curent background unchanged.

GpiSetColor

    PUSH DWORD Presentation space handle.
    PUSH DWORD Color:

Default	-3
White	-2
Black	-1
Background	0
Blue	1
Red	2
Pink	3
Green	4
Cyan	5
Yellow	6
Neutral grey	7
Dark grey	8
Dark blue	9
Dark red	10
Dark pink	11
Dark green	12
Dark cyan	13
Brown	14
Light grey	15

GpiSetCurrentPosition

    PUSH DWORD Presentation space handle.
    PUSH PTR   Address of screen coordinates.

GpiSetPel

    PUSH DWORD Presentation space handle.
    PUSH PTR   Address of screen coordinates.

KbdCharIn

PUSH	PTR	Address of kbd input structure:
		DB ASCII character code.
		DB scan code.
		DB character status.
		DB NLS shift status.
		DW shift state.
		DD time stamp (milliseconds).
PUSH	WORD	0 → wait for character
		1 → do not wait
PUSH	WORD	Kbd handle (default = 0).

KbdStringIn

PUSH	PTR	Address of input buffer.
PUSH	PTR	Address of structure: DW Input buffer length
		DW Returned data length.
PUSH	WORD	0 → Wait until buffer is full.
		1 → Return immediately.
PUSH	WORD	Kbd handle (default = 0).

MouClose

PUSH	WORD	Mouse handle

MouDrawPtr

PUSH	WORD	Mouse handle

MouGetPtrPos

PUSH	PTR	Pointer to structure to return data:
		DW row
		DW column
PUSH	WORD	Mouse handle

MouOpen

PUSH	PTR	Address of ASCIIZ name of mouse.
PUSH	PTR	Address of word to receive mouse handle.

MouReadEventQueue

PUSH	PTR	Address of structure for returned data:
		DW mouse state (see input chapter)
		DD time tamp (milliseconds)
		DW absolute or relative row
		DW absolute or relative column.
PUSH	PTR	Address of word which holds: 0 → do not wait.
		1 → wait for data.
PUSH	WORD	Mouse handle

VioEndPopUp

PUSH	WORD	Vio handle (0)

VioPopUp

PUSH	PTR	Option flags, OR these: 2 → transparent
		1 → wait for pop-up
PUSH	WORD	Vio handle (0)

VioWrtCellStr

PUSH	PTR	Address of cell string (attribute, character)
PUSH	WORD	Length of string
PUSH	WORD	Row on screen
PUSH	WORD	Column on screen
PUSH	WORD	Vio handle (0)

VioWrtCharStr

PUSH	PTR	Address of character string
PUSH	WORD	Length of string
PUSH	WORD	Row on screen
PUSH	WORD	Column on screen
PUSH	WORD	Vio handle (0)

VioWrtCharStrAtt

PUSH	PTR	Address of character string
PUSH	WORD	Length of string
PUSH	WORD	Row on screen

596 ▶ Advanced Assembly Language

	PUSH	WORD	Column on screen
	PUSH	PTR	Address of attribute byte to use
	PUSH	WORD	Vio handle (0)

VioWrtTTY

	PUSH	PTR	Address of character string
	PUSH	WORD	Length of string
	PUSH	WORD	Vio handle (0)

WinBeginPaint

	PUSH	DWORD	Window handle (passed to window function).
	PUSH	DWORD	If NULL, returns a Presentation Space handle.
	PUSH	PTR	Address of a region structure (left NULL in this book).

RETURNS: 32-bit presentation space handle.

WinCreateMsgQueue

| | PUSH | DWORD | Anchor block handle |
| | PUSH | WORD | Size (0 = default) |

RETURNS: Queue handle

WinCreateStdWindow

	PUSH	DWORD	Parent window handle (0000 0001).
	PUSH	DWORD	Style: 8000 000H to make visible).
	PUSH	PTR	Address of window flags (see window chapter).
	PUSH	PTR	Address of class name (set up with WinRegisterClass).
	PUSH	PTR	Address of title bar text.
	PUSH	DWORD	Resource handle (set to 0 in this book).
	PUSH	DWORD	Resource ID (set to 0 in this book).
	PUSH	PTR	Address of dword to receive client window handle.

RETURNS: 32-bit frame handle.

WinDefWindowProc

PUSH 7 WORDS PASSED WINDOW FUNCTION

WinDestroyMsgQueue

| | PUSH | DWORD | Queue handle |

WinDestroyWindow

    PUSH   DWORD   Frame handle (returned by WinCreateStdWindow)

WinDispatchMsg

    PUSH   DWORD   Anchor block handle.
    PUSH   PTR   Address of queue buffer.

WinEndPaint

    PUSH   DWORD   Presentation space handle

WinGetMsg

    PUSH   DWORD   Anchor block handle.
    PUSH   PTR   Address of queue buffer.
    PUSH   DWORD   Handle of window that you want to get messages for (NULL → receive all messages).
    PUSH   WORD   Set to 0.
    PUSH   WORD   Set to 0.

WinGetPS

    PUSH   DWORD   Window handle (passed to window function).
    RETURNS: 32-bit presentation space handle.

WinInitialize

    PUSH   WORD   Set to 0.
    RETURNS: 32-bit anchor block handle.

WinRegisterClass

    PUSH   DWORD   Anchor block handle.
    PUSH   PTR   Address of ASCIIZ window class name to register.
    PUSH   PTR   Address of window function.
    PUSH   DWORD   Set to 4 to have window redrawn when resized.
    PUSH   WORD   Extra memory requested (default = 0).

WinReleasePS

    PUSH   DWORD   Presentation space handle

WinTerminate

    PUSH   DWORD   Anchor block handle

Appendix C

Device Drivers and IOCTL

▶ **Device Drivers and IOCTL** 601

IT'S POSSIBLE TO connect your own, custom-designed peripherals to the PC. For example, you might build your own (nonstandard) diskette drive, or your own printer, even a laser printer. The question you would be faced with then is connecting it up to your computer so that the PC could run standard, commercial programs and still use your devices, even though the programs use DOS interupts.

This used to be quite difficult, but possible, by intercepting interrupts. But now it is much easier to connect a device using DOS itself by using *device drivers*.

What Is a Device Driver?

A device driver handles the interface between the PC and the device you want to attach. What this means in the case of a disk drive, for example, is that DOS is able to treat your disk drive as it would one of its own. By requesting information from the device driver, DOS can find out how many sectors you are using on a track, whether you are using the standard IBM format (FAT followed by directory and so on), or whether you've changed a disk.

Block and Character Devices

There are two kinds of devices: block and character devices. Block devices are devices that work in blocks of data, in particular, disk drives. These types of devices are not given names, only letters. The first such device DOS loads from device drivers will be A, the next B, and so on.

Character devices, the other type, can have names. Typical character devices are CON, AUX, and PRN. If you put in a device driver, you can redefine any of these devices from the default simply by giving your devices these names (in the name field of the device header).

The Device Header

Device drivers are .EXE files that have a specific device driver header. To install a device driver named MYDISK, put the line DEVICE=MYDISK in your CONFIG.SYS file to be read at boot time. DOS will read in the file and examine the device header in it. Such a header looks like this in the beginning of the .EXE file:

DWORD	Pointer to next device header.
WORD	Attribute word.
WORD	Pointer to strategy routine in this .EXE file.
WORD	Pointer to interrupt rountine in this .EXE file.
8 BYTES	Name or Unit field.

Figure C-1.

The first two words are an address (offset, segment) of the location of the next device driver header in this .EXE file. The last device driver header should have a -1 in this field so that DOS can chain all the devices together. If this is the only device in this .EXE file, use a -1 here.

The attribute word tells the PC something about your device: whether it is a block or character device, whether it supports IBM format, or whether it should be treated as the standard input or output device. Here is a breakdown of this word:

Bit	Meaning
15	1 This device is a character device.
	0 This device is a block device.
14	1 Supports the I/O control Int, IOCTL (DOS Service 44H).
	0 Does NOT support IOCTL.
13	1 For block devices only: Non-IBM format.
	0 For block devices only: IBM format.
11	1 Has removable media.
	0 Does not support removable media.
10-4	Reserved.
3	1 This device is the clock device.
	0 This device is NOT the clock device.
2	1 This device is the NUL device.
	0 This device is NOT the NUL device.
1	1 This device is the standard output device.
	0 This device is NOT the standard output device.
0	1 This device is the standard input device.
	0 This device is NOT the standard input device.

Note: As you will see at the end of this appendix, if this device supports I/O control — IOCTL (DOS Service 44H) — you can do such things as change baud rate and so forth with this interrupt.

▶ Device Drivers and IOCTL   603

If a block device uses an IBM format, a FAT with a FAT byte, standard directory structure and so on, it should set bit 13 to zero. If this bit is zero, DOS will later send a request to the device driver to build a BIOS Parameter Block (BPB) for it, so that the BIOS calls will function. This parameter block (reviewed later) includes such information as the number of FATs, the number of root directory entries and so on.

If the device can handle "removable media" — diskettes or disk cartridges — the driver should set bit 11 in the device header to 1. In this case, DOS will be aware of the fact that you may have changed diskettes, and the new diskette may not even be the same format as the last one (for example, double sided instead of single sided). Whenever it needs to check if the disk has been changed, therefore, it reads in the first FAT sector and compares it to the old version.

The next word in the device header is the pointer to the strategy routine. This pointer is only a word long, so the strategy routine must start in the same segment as the device header itself. Device drivers are broken up into two parts: one that queues and sets things up for requests (the strategy routine), and one that actually executes the request (the interrupt routine).

The way DOS asks the device to do something is with a device request. DOS calls the strategy routine first, and at that time ES:BX holds the address of the request header. The strategy routine stores the address of the request header on a queue. Immediately after the strategy routine returns, the interrupt routine is called (without parameters) so that the request can be fulfilled. The interrupt routine reads the request header address from the queue and performs the request. We will examine the structure of various requests shortly.

Character devices can have names (CON, AUX, PRN, etc.), but block devices can only be "mapped" to drive letters: A, B, C, up to Z. For instance, if you want to install your device as the printer, give it the name PRN (left-hand justified and padded with spaces), making it the standard printer. To use it, you can then send data to the printer, or the device's handle (in this case, 4 is the handle for the standard printer). The standard devices all have handles already assigned: standard input device is 0, standard output is 1, standard error device is 2, standard AUX device (for serial data) is 3, and the standard printer is 4.

Block devices have unit numbers: drive A is unit 1, drive B is unit 2 and so on. DOS itself fills in the unit number here for block devices after you have filled its "INIT" request, so you don't put any name for the block device in this field at all. To reach this drive, you have to specify the correct drive number when using a system interrupt.

The Request Header

All requests have the same header. The device driver learns what it is supposed to do — initialize, I/O, etc — by the command code in the request header. Here is the request header's format:

BYTE	Length of request header and data to follow.
BYTE	Block devices: Unit Code.
BYTE	Command code — tells the device what to do.
WORD	Status (returned by device).
8 BYTES	Reserved.
: :	Additional data as needed for the specific request.

Figure C-2.

The first byte is the Length of Request Header and Data to Follow byte, which is self-explanatory. It tells the device driver how long the request header and data are together so that, if necessary, the device driver can copy it for its own use.

The next byte is the unit code for block devices. Block devices can have several subunits. This means that one device driver can be responsible for several disk drives. The number of drives the driver addresses is returned to DOS when DOS initializes the driver (with an INIT request). The "subunit" — that is, drive number — that this request is for is stored in this byte.

Next, the 1-byte command code tells the driver what the device is supposed to do. Here are some values for the command code. We will not cover all possible command codes in this discussion (they are all listed in the DOS Technical Reference Manual):

Value	Meaning
0	INIT — initialize the device.
1	Media check for block devices (Has the disk been changed?).
2	Make a BPB — BIOS Parameter Block — so the BIOS calls will work.
3	IOCTL Input (see below).
4	Input — do a read.
8	Output — write data.
9	Output with verify.
12	IOCTL output (see below).

13	Device open.
14	Device close.
15	Removable media.
23	Get logical device.
24	Set logical device.

The status word, the next word in the request header, is returned by the device to DOS. Bit 15 of this word is set if there was an error of some type in performing the request. If there was an error, the bottom byte of this word holds the error code so that DOS will know what's going on. Here are some error codes:

Code	Meaning
00	Write protect attempt.
02	Device not ready.
04	CRC error.
06	Seek error.
08	Sector not found.
09	Printer out of paper.
0C	General failure.
0F	Invalid disk change.

From the type of error returned, DOS can treat your device like any normal device and inform the user that there has been an error of a specific type. This is a powerful utility — DOS is treating your disk drive as it would any IBM-standard drive.

Bit 9 in the status word is the busy bit. If a request was made and the device is busy, it can set this bit. Bit 8 is the "done" bit. If it is set to 1, the operation requested by this request header was completed successfully.

The next 8 bytes of the request header are reserved for DOS's use. At the end, the request header is followed by the data that is needed to fill the request. For example, if the request header is requesting an I/O operation, one of the data items that will follow the request header is the address of the data buffer to be used.

INIT (Command Code 1)

Let's work through a number of requests to see what they look like. Here is what the request for an initialization looks like:

13 BYTE	Request header
BYTE	Number of units (set by block devices only).
DWORD	End of memory-resident code.
DWORD	Pointer to BPB (BIOS parameter block).
BYTE	Drive Number (DOS 3+).
WORD	CONFIG.SYS Error Message control flag (DOS 4+).

Figure C-3.

When the device is first installed, DOS sends an INIT request. The device driver performs whatever initialization is needed in the device, and then sets a number of bytes in the request area. In particular, it sets (1) the number of units (drives) it is responsible for (if it is a block device); (2) the location of the top of the code it wants to keep memory-resident; (3) the status word from the request header; and (4) a pointer to an appropriate BIOS Parameter Block. The BPB looks like this (you can use command code 2 to build a BPB):

8 BYTES	Product name and version.
WORD	Bytes per sector.
BYTE	Sectors per cluster.
WORD	Number of reserved sectors (for partitioning).
BYTE	Number of FATs.
WORD	Number of root directory entries.
WORD	Total number of sectors in this device.
BYTE	Media descriptor (see below).
WORD	FAT length in sectors.
WORD	Sectors per track (DOS 3+).
WORD	Number of heads (DOS 3+).
WORD	Number of hidden sectors (DOS 3+).

Figure C-4.

The media descriptor byte always has bits 3–7 set to 1, and bit 2 is set to 1 if the medium is removable. Bit 1 is set if the medium is 8 sector, and bit 0 is set if the medium is two-sided. Under DOS 3+, DOS will fill in the drive letter of the first drive in the last field of the request.

I/O (Command Code 3)

For actually performing I/O, the request looks like this:

13 BYTE	Request header.
BYTE	Media descriptor byte.
DWORD	Transfer address — the location of the buffer.
WORD	Number of bytes or sectors.
WORD	Starting sector number.
DWORD	DOS 3+: Pointer to volume identification if error code OFH is returned.
DWORD	DOS 4+: Starting 32-bit sector number.

Figure C-5.

The command code in the request header tells the device whether Input or Output is required. For block devices, I/O is specified in sectors, for character devices, in bytes. The number of bytes or sectors requested is found from the word above, and the device is responsible for setting that word to the number of actual bytes or sectors read or written.

The location of the buffer, or data transfer address, is given in the request as well, as is the starting sector number (although this has no meaning for character devices). After the device is finished, it must set the status word in the request header.

If your device specifies (in the device header) that it can support IOCTL control, some of the I/O requests it receives may actually be IOCTL requests. If the command code specifies an IOCTL read or IOCTL write, for example, then DS:DX points to the bytes that should be read from or written to the device's control channel. These bytes can be in your own format, as long as your device understands them. Any time your program wants to change the baud rate of a device, it can send along a control string to the device in this manner.

IOCTL — INT 21H Service 44H

If your device can support IOCTL requests, you can control it through the use of DOS INT 21H, Service 44H. With IOCTL, you can change the nature of the I/O undertaken by the device. For example, you can reset it or set parity bits. This service sends information to the device that is not for I/O, but rather controls the I/O that does occur.

IOCTL is used to send control strings that the device can interpret to its "control channel." Here is the way the registers are set for an IOCTL call (i.e., to interrupt 21H):

Register	Value
AH	44H
AL	Function value.
BX	File or device handle.
CX	Byte count (to be read or written).
DS:DX	Data buffer.

Here are some possible function values (placed in AL):

AL	Meaning
0	Get device information and return it in DX.
1	Set device information from DX.
2	Read CX bytes from DS:DX into device control channel.
3	Write CX bytes from device control channel into buffer at DS:DX.
4	Use drive number in BL and execute function 2.
5	Use drive number in BL and execute function 3.
8	Determine if drive can use removable media.
0CH	Request a device driver to perform code page switching.

If your program, using IOCTL, requests function 0 of a device that you have installed with a device driver, DOS can take the information about the device from the device header and code it in the DX register. This coded information includes such information as whether or not this device is the CLOCK, NUL, or console output device, and whether or not this device can process control strings under functions 2 and 3.

DOS knows whether or not the device can process control strings by examining bit 14 of the attribute byte in the device header. If the answer is yes, then your program can send control strings to the device by using IOCTL. When the strategy routine receives this request, it knows that the string waiting at address DS:DX is a control string, and not just normal data by checking the command code in the request header.

Command code 3 means that CX bytes should be read from the buffer at DS:DX and written to the control channel. Command code 12 means that CX bytes should be written to the buffer from the control channel. This way, you can communicate with your device.

For character devices, you should use device handles and functions 2 and 3 to control your device. For block devices, which are mapped to drive letters, use Functions 4 and 5, which specify drive numbers in BL. Again, for more details, refer to the DOS Technical Reference Manual.

Index

A

ADC instruction, 226, 227, 236
ADD instruction, 227, 239
adding integers with the 80 × 87, 320-323
adding with carries, 225-228
addresses, 6, 9, 16
AH register, 33
alphanumeric characters, 61
alphanumeric modes, 63, 66, 74
alphanumeric mouse cursor, 156
Alt key, 53
Alt-S key, 211
analog display, 84
anchor block, 440
AND/OR register, 102, 103, 104
ANDing, 102, 103, 104, 156
ASCII arguments, 10
ASCII characters, 10, 156, 158
ASCII codes, 10, 33, 34, 49, 156, 500
ASCII strings, 244, 245
ASCII values, 157
ASCIIZ string, 113, 116, 451
assembling programs, 3-4
ASSUME directive, 22, 263
AT and .COM files, 21-23
AT directive, 22
attribute bytes, 63, 64, 66-68

B

BACK.COM program, 121-131
backing up files, 121-131
.BAK extension, 121, 122
BASIC program, 49, 287
BASIC–Assembly Interface, 297-302
BAT extension, 168
BeginPaint () service, 381
binary coded decimals, 330-331
BIOS data area, 21, 22, 50, 53
BIOS disk support, 177-181
BIOS Interface Technical Reference Manual, 186
BIOS parameter block, 606
BIOS interrupts, 33, 48-51, 535-553
    Interrupt 0, 535
    Interrupt 1, 535
    Interrupt 2, 535
    Interrupt 3, 535
    Interrupt 4, 535
    Interrupt 5, 535
    Interrupt 6, 536
    Interrupt 7, 536
    Interrupt 8, 536
    Interrupt 9, 536
    Interrupt 0AH, 536
    Interrupts 0BH–0FH, 536
    INT 10H Service 0, 536
    INT 10H Service 1, 537
    INT 10H Service 2, 537
    INT 10H Service 3, 538
    INT 10H Service 4, 538
    INT 10H Service 5, 538
    INT 10H Service 6, 538
    INT 10H Service 7, 539
    INT 10H Service 8, 539
    INT 10H Service 9, 539
    INT 10H Service A, 539
    INT 10H Service B, 540
    INT 10H Service C, 540
    INT 10H Service D, 540
    INT 10H Service E, 540
    INT 10H Service FH, 541
    INT 10H Service 10H, 541
    INT 10H Service 10H Function 0, 541
    INT 10H Service 10H Function 1, 542
    INT 10H Service 10H Function 2, 542
    INT 10H Service 10H Function 7, 542
    INT 10H Service 10H Function 8, 542
    INT 10H Service 10H Function 10H, 542
    INT 10H Service 10H Function 12H, 543
    INT 10H Service 10H Function 13H, 543
    INT 10H Service 11H, 543
    INT 10H Service 12H, 544
    INT 11H, 544
    INT 12H, 544
    INT 13H Service 0, 544
    INT 13H Service 1, 545
    INT 13H Service 2, 545
    INT 13H Service 3, 546
    INT 13H Service 4, 546
    INT 13H Service 8, 547
    INT 13H Services 0AH and 0BH, 547
    INT 13H Service 0CH, 547
    INT 13H Service 0DH, 548
    INT 13H Services 0EH and 0FH, 548
    INT 13H Service 10H, 548
    INT 13H Service 11H, 548
    INT 13H, 548
    INT 13H Service 19H, 549
    INT 14H, AH=0, 549
    INT 14H, AH=1, 550
    INT 14H, AH=2, 550
    INT 14H, AH=3, 550
    INT 15H Cassette I/O, 551
    INT 16H Service 0, 551
    INT 16H Service 1, 551

INT 16H Service 2, 552
INT 17H Service 0, 552
INT 17H Service 1, 552
INT 17H Service 2, 552
INT 18H, 553
INT 19H, 553
INT 1AH Service 0, 553
INT 1AH Service 1, 553
INT 1BH, 553
INT 1CH, 553
INT 1DH, 553
INT 1EH, 553
INT 1FH, 553
BIOS parameter block, 606
bit planes, 101, 102
bit test instructions, 238
bit-by-bit manipulations, 238-244
bits, 66, 86
black and white monitors, 75
block devices, 601
boot record, 161, 162-163, 171
border flag, 449
BP register, 289
^Break character, 33, 36, 37, 38, 47
buttons, 437
byte 0, 25
byte 2, 25
bytes 5-9, 25
byte 2CH, 26
byte 5CH, 26
byte 6CH, 26
byte 12H, 26
byte 16H, 26
byte 50H, 26
byte 80H, 27
byte OAH, 25
byte OEH, 26
bytes, 8, 9, 10, 16, 17, 22, 27, 66

C

^C character, 33, 36, 37, 38
C compiler, 440
C program, 287
C–Assembly Interface, 307-312
calling, 255, 410
calling convention table, 287, 288
calling conventions at work, 287-288
calls, 15
Caps-Lock key, 23
carriage return, 29, 44, 46, 53, 133
carry flag, 118, 119, 150, 218, 220, 226, 239, 243
cell string, 425

CGA background color, 78-80
CGA buffer, 61, 92
CGA card, 63
CGA memory blocks, 92, 93
CGA video controller, 96
changing directories, 114
character cell, 425
character devices, 601
character input, 33-34
checking for bootable partitions, 172-174
checking the keyboard buffer, 47
circular buffers, 53-54
Clear Direction flag, 40
Clear Interrupt flag, 190
clearing the keyboard buffer, 47-48
clipboard graphics, 438
closing files, 114, 130
clusters, 162, 164
CMPS operation, 42-43
CMPSB operation, 42-43
CMPSW operation, 42-43
@ CODE, 200
code in .COM files, 29-30
code segments, 6, 7, 14
CodeView program, 25
coding long division, 235-236
Color Graphics Adapter (CGA), 61, 66, 91
COM files, 3, 5-7, 8-11, 14, 15-23, 36, 258, 260, 323, 416
comparing bytes, 44-46
comparing strings, 42-43
COMSPEC string, 26
condition codes, 348
conditional jumps, 237
Control Break Exit address, 26
Control Break handler, 26
Control key, 53
Control Shift key, 23
control packet, 183
CONVERT.ASM program, 244-249
converting between bases, 244-249
converting hex numbers to decimals, 249
converting uppercase to lowercase, 34-36
coping files, 121-131
Create Window () function, 367
creating files, 114, 125
creating signed numbers, 218
creating subdirectories, 114
Critical Error Exit address, 26
cursor mask, 156
cursor mask attribute, 156
cursor mask character, 156

▶ **Index** **613**

cursors, 51, 62, 63
cylinders, 161

D

DAC registers, 84, 85, 86-87
data area in .COM files, 8-11
.DATA directive, 18
Data Segment register, 18
data segments, 6, 7, 18, 20
data storage, 9
@ DATA value, 18, 200
DD directives, 201-203
DEBUG program, 22, 34, 66, 224, 241, 323
DecodeMessages function, 359, 360, 364, 371-403
Define Doubleword directive, 10
Define Quadword directive, 10, 328
Define Tenbytes directive, 10
Define Word directive, 10
definition files, 403
DefWindowsProc service, 398
DEL command, 116
deleting files, 115, 116-118
deleting subdirectories, 114
Destination Index, 40
DETACH command, 429
determining video equipment, 89-90
device context, 378
device drivers, 601
device header, 601-603
dialog boxes, 437
Digital to Analog converter, 84
direct CGA buffer use, 93-98
direct EGA buffer use, 99-110
disk directory, 161, 168-169
disk drives, 51, 161-170
disk formats, 161
Disk Full message, 9, 10
disk partitions, 163
Disk Transfer Area, 27-29
diskette change signal, 181
diskette controller, 51
diskette motor, 51
display code, 89
display mode, 51
displaying the mouse cursor, 150-151
DIV command, 231, 245
divide algorithm, 231
dividing integers with 80 × 87, 325
.DLL extension, 416
DOS, 5, 7, 16
DOS compatibility mode, 409
DOS disk services, 181-186

DOS error codes, 119-120
DOS function dispatcher, 25
DOS Interrupts, 5, 9, 13, 33-34, 554-582
INT 20H, 554
INT 21H, 554
INT 21H Service 0, 554
INT 21H Service 1, 554
INT 21H Service 2, 554
INY 21H Service 3, 554
INT 21H Service 4, 555
INT 21H Service 5, 555
INT 21H Service 6, 555
INT 21H Service 7, 555
INT 21H Service 8, 555
INT 21H Service 9, 556
INT 21H Service A, 556
INT 21H Service OBH, 556
INT 21H Service OCH, 556
INT 21H Service ODH, 557
INT 21H Service OEH, 557
INT 21H Service OFH, 557
INT 21H Service 10H, 557
INT 21H Service 11H, 557
INT 21H Service 12H, 558
INT 21H Service 13H, 558
INT 21H Service 14H, 558
INT 21H Service 15H, 559
INT 21H Service 16H, 559
INT 21H Service 17H, 559
INT 21H Service 18H, 559
INT 21H Service 19H, 559
INT 21H Service 1AH, 560
INT 21H Service 1BH, 560
INT 21H Service 1CH, 560
INT 21H Services 1DH–20H, 560
INT 21H Service 21H, 561
INT 21H Service 22H, 561
INT 21H Service 23H, 561
INT 21H Service 24H, 561
INT 21H Service 25H, 562
INT 21H Service 26H, 562
INT 21H Service 27H, 562
INT 21H Service 28H, 562
INT 21H Service 29H, 563
INT 21H Service 2AH, 563
INT 21H Service 2BH, 563
INR 21H Service 2CH, 564
INT 21H Service 2DH, 564
INT 21H Service 2EH, 564
INT 21H Service 2FH, 565
INT 21H Service 30H, 565
INT 21H Service 31H, 565

614 ▶ Advanced Assembly Language

INT 21H Service 32H, 565
INT 21H Service 33H, 565
INT 21H Service 34H, 566
INT 21H Service 35H, 566
INT 21H Service 36H, 566
INT 21H Service 37H, 566
INT 21H Service 38H, 566
INT 21H Service 39H, 567
INT 21H Service 3AH, 567
INT 21H Service 3BH, 568
INT 21H Service 3CH, 568
INT 21H Service 3DH, 568
INT 21H Service 3EH, 569
INT 21H Service 3FH, 569
INT 21H Service 40H, 570
INT 21H Service 41H, 570
INT 21H Service 42H, 570
INT 21H Service 43H, 571
INT 21H Service 44H, 571
INT 21H Service 45H, 571
INT 21H Service 46H, 571
INT 21H Service 47H, 572
INT 21H Service 48H, 572
INT 21H Service 49H, 572
INT 21H Service 4AH, 573
INT 21H Service 4BH, 573
INT 21H Service 4CH, 574
INT 21H Service 4DH, 574
INT 21H Service 4EH, 574
INT 21H Service 4FH, 575
INT 21H Services 50H–53H, 575
INT 21H Service 54H, 575
INT 21H Service 55H, 576
INT 21H Service 56H, 576
INT 21H Service 57H, 576
INT 21H Service 58H, 576
INT 21H Service 59H, 576
INT 21H Service 5AH, 577
INT 21H Service 5BH, 577
INT 21H Service 5CH, 577
INT 21H Service 5E00H, 578
INT 21H Service 5E02, 578
INT 21H Service 5E03, 578
INT 21H Service 5F03, 579
INT 21H Service 5F04H, 579
INT 21H Service 62H, 579
INT 21H Service 67H, 579
INT 21H Service 68H, 579
INT 22H, 580
INT 23H, 580
INT 24H, 580
INT 25H, 580

INT 26H, 581
INT 27H, 582
INTs 28H–2EH, 582
INT 2FH, 582
INT 30H–3FH, 582
INT 40H–5FH, 582
INT 60H–67H, 582
INTs 68H–7FH, 582
INTs 80H–85H, 582
INTs 86H–F0H, 582
INTs F1H–FFH, 582
DOS string printing service, 9
DOS Technical Reference Manual, 119, 186, 609
DosBeep service, 470
DosExit service, 416, 418, 433, 462
DosOpen service, 416
DosRead service, 416
DosSleep service, 429
DosWrite service, 420-424
double-sided diskettes, 161, 162
dragging the mouse, 154
drawing flags, 386
drawing instructions, 386
DUMMY.ASM program, 266
Dump instruction, 53
dynamic link library files, 416
dynamic linking, 411, 416

E

echoing to the screen, 33, 36, 37, 38
EGA/VGA bit planes, 98-99
EGA/VGA buffer, 61, 66
80 × 86 chip, 411-412
80 × 86 math coprocessor, 319
80 × 87 commands, 319
80 × 87 error checking, 348-355
80 × 87 floating point formats, 328-331
80 × 87 instructions, 331-348
    F2 × M1—2^x Minus 1, 331-332
    FABS, 332
    FADD, 332
    FBLD, 333
    FBSTP, 333
    FCHS, 334
    FCLEX, 334
    FCOM, 334
    FDIV, 338
    FIADD, 338
    FICOM, 339
    FIDIV, 339
    FILD, 339
    FIMUL, 340

Index 615

FINIT, 340, 352
FIST, 340
FISTP, 340
FISUB, 341
FLD, 341, 352
FMUL, 341
FNCLEX, 342
FNOP, 342
FNSTSW, 343
FPATAN, 343
FPREM, 343
FPTAN, 344
FSQRT, 344
FST, 345
FSTSW, 345
FSUB, 345
FTST, 346
FWAIT, 346
FXAM, 346
FXCH, 347
FXTRACT, 347
FYL2X YLog$_2$X, 347-348
80 × 87 integer formats, 327-328
80 × 87 math coprocessor, 319
Ellipse () service, 392
ellipse drawing instruction, 386
ellipses, 386, 392
empty buffers, 54
END directive, 14
END ENTRY directive, 265
end-of-file markers, 132
end-of-record markers, 133
end-of-string marker, 10
ending programs, 12-13
ENDM directive, 268, 279
ENDP directive, 11, 12, 36
Enhanced Graphics Adapter (EGA), 61, 81-83, 91
ENTRY label, 14
entry points, 18, 19
environment string, 26
equipment flag, 50, 211
error flags, 348
error handler, 26
error handling, 119-120
exception flags, 348, 349
.EXE files, 3, 7, 12, 13, 14, 15-23, 403, 415
.EXE file shells, 17-19
.EXE files versus .COM files, 15-23
EXITM directive, 279, 280
extended ASCII codes, 49-50
EXTRN label, 265

F

F2 × M1—2^x Minus 1 instruction, 331-332
FADD instruction, 332
FAR instructions, 15, 16, 19
FAR labels, 11, 12, 254
FASB instruction, 332
fast mathematical calculations, 215-249
FAT byte, 603
FBLD instruction, 333
FBSTP instruction, 333
FCHS instruction, 334
FCLEX instruction, 334
FCOM instruction, 334
FDIV instruction, 327
FIADD instruction, 323, 338
FIDIV instruction, 325, 327, 339
fields, 133
FILD instruction, 320, 339
file access mode, 123
File Allocation Table (FAT), 161, 162, 164-165, 176, 184
FILE.ASM program, 266
File Cannot Be Converted message, 15
file control blocks, 27, 113, 132
file error checking, 118-119
file handles, 27, 113-114, 124, 132
file manipulation, 111-145
file names, 29
file records, 132-134
File Searcher Outline, 13
filled buffers, 54
FIMUL instruction, 325, 340, 341
FIND procedure, 14
finding matching files, 115
finishing code segments, 14-15
FINIT instruction, 340, 352, 354
FIST instruction, 340
FISTP instruction, 340
FISUB instruction, 323, 338, 341
FLD instruction, 320, 339, 341, 352
floating point addition, 321
floating point load, 320
floating point notation, 10
floating point numbers, 319
FNCLEX instruction, 342, 354
FNOP instruction, 342
FNSTSW instruction, 343
FORTRAN program, 13, 287
FORTRAN–Assembly Interface, 302-307
FPATAN instruction, 343
FPREM instruction, 343
FPTAN instruction, 344

616 ▶ Advanced Assembly Language

FSQRT instruction, 344
FST instruction, 345
FSTSW instruction, 345
FSUB instruction, 345
FTST instruction, 346
FUNCTIONs, 13
FXAM instruction, 346
FXCH instruction, 347
FXTRACT instruction, 347
FYL2X Y—Log$_2$X instruction, 347-348

G

GET_FILE subroutine, 14
get interrupt vector services, 194
get extended error service, 120
GetMessage function, 370
getting free disk space, 185-186
getting mouse information, 151-152
getting the cursor, 62-63
GO command, 523
Gpi functions, 479-498
    GpiBox, 511
    GpiCharStringAt, 479-489, 501, 508, 527
    GpiLine, 509
    GpiPolyLine, 479, 518-524
    GpiSetBackColor, 489-498
    GpiSetBackMix, 491
    GpiSetColor, 479, 489, 492
    GpiSetCurrentPosition, 479, 509
    GpiSetPel, 479, 510
graphics, 61, 73-81
graphics mode, 66, 75
graphics monitors, 63
graphics video controller, 77, 96
GROUP directive, 262
groups, 261, 262
groups collecting segments, 265

H

handling the keyboard, 31-58
handling the mouse cursor, 154-156
hard disks, 161, 170-174
hard platters, 161
hardware gates, 412-413
headers, 15, 16, 19, 30
Hex notation, 34
high resolution CGA mode, 80-81
high resolution mode, 76, 77
high-level functions, 293
high-level languages, 13, 16, 287, 315
high-level subroutines, 293
hInstance handle, 262

HOLD.COM program, 37
Horizontal Scroll flag, 449
hot keys, 190
hPrevInstance handle, 362, 365, 366

I

IBM chips, 61
icons, 437
IDIV command, 223, 225
IF statements, 273, 279
illegal gates, 413
IMUL command, 223, 224, 225
indirect calls, 201-203
INIT request, 605-606
initializing the mouse, 150
initiating the math coprocessor, 319-320
I/O call, 36, 607
I/O channel memory, 50
I/O port, 51, 606
IOCTL call, 607-609
Insert key, 23
integer load procedure, 320
integer point addition, 321
integers, 364
intercepting interrupt vectors, 192-193
intercepting the keyboard interrupt, 207-214
internal timer, 22
Interrupt 9, 51-53
Interrupt 10H, 70, 72, 73, 74-75, 92
Interrupt 16H, 34, 48, 50
Interrupt 20H, 113
Interrupt 21H, 5, 9, 13, 33-34
Interrupt 27H, 13
Interrupt 31H, 13
Interrupt 33H, 149
interrupt vector, 51
interrupt vector table, 23, 191, 192
interrupts at work, 191-195
IRP directive, 280
IRPC directive, 280
intrasegment labels, 12

J

JMP instruction, 35
jumps, 15

K

kbd services, 415, 432
kbdCharIn service, 432, 433
key-intercepting TSR .COM file shell, 208, 209-210
keyboard buffer, 36, 44, 47, 48, 49, 54, 55, 56, 57, 200, 208

Index 617

keyboard buffer head, 51, 53
keyboard buffer tail, 51, 53
keyboard flags, 50
keyboard input, 33-39

L

LABEL directive, 201-203
labels, 9, 11
latches, 102
Left Shift key, 23
.LIB files, 268
libraries, 266-268
library commands, 267-268
    add, 267
    delete, 267
    Extract, 267
    Del & Extract, 267
line drawing instruction, 386
LINK command, 259
LINK program, 4
linking files, 256-261
linking subroutines, 259-261
linking to high-level languages, 285-315
Load command, 176
load module, 17, 19
loaders, 19
loading strings, 46-47
LOCAL directive, 278
LODS operation, 46-47
LODSB operation, 46
LODSW operation, 46
logical sectors, 169-170
Logitech mouse, 149
long division, 230-233
long integer, 327
long integer format, 327
loop index 68, 69, 235
loop instruction, 41
low intensity, 81
low resolution mode, 76, 77
Lparam parameter, 360, 364
lpCmdLine pointer, 363

M

machine code, 40
macro assembler, 4
MACRO directive, 268
macro libraries, 278-279
macros, 268
macros at work, 268-284
mainframe computers, 409
making code memory-resident, 196-198

making .COM files, 5-7
manufacturer's test mark, 50
MASK directive, 335-338, 351
MASKZ directive, 351
Maxbutton flag, 449
Maxmized flag, 449
McIntosh computer, 73
medium intensity, 81
medium resolution mode, 76
memory, 9, 17, 22, 25
memory models, 6, 55
memory-resident program, 49
menus, 437
message 4FH, 472
message loops, 359, 369
message packets, 455
messages, 359, 364
Microsoft Assembler, 300
Microsoft mouse, 149
Microsoft Windows, 58, 288, 355, 359
Minbutton flag, 449
Minimized flag, 449
Minmax flag, 449
Monochrome Display Adapter (MDA), 61, 75
monochrome monitors, 66
monochrome screen, 61
monochrome video buffer, 66
motherboard memory, 50
Mou services, 415
mouse, 149, 443
mouse button, 152, 153
mouse cursor, 150, 153
MOUSE.COM program, 149
mouse driver, 149, 150
mouse driver software, 149
Mouse Systems mouse, 149
MOUSESYS.COM program, 149
MoveTo () service, 389
moving read/write pointer, 115
moving strings, 40-42
MOVS operation, 40-42
MOVSB operation, 40-42
MOVSW operation, 40-42
MUL instruction, 229, 239
multiplying integers with 80 × 87, 325
multiplying large numbers, 229-230
multitasking, 409, 412
multitasking at work, 413-414

N

NEAR labels, 11, 12, 254, 257
NEAR procedures, 19

NEAR subroutine, 255
NEG instruction, 220
negative numbers, 218, 219, 221
no operands form, 345
No Worries message, 424, 426
nonmatching bytes, 42, 43
nontransparent pop-ups, 429
normalized 80 × 87 format, 328-331
NOT instruction, 220
NULL address, 451
Num-Lock key, 23

O

.OBJ files, 4, 10, 266
offset addresses, 15, 294
OFFSET directive, 45
offset register, 6, 10
opening files, 114, 123
operands, 43, 46
ORG 100H directive, 7, 258
ORG statements, 258
ORing, 102, 103, 449
OS/2 and the mouse
OS/2 services, 583-598
    DosAllocHuge, 585
    DosAllocShrSeg585
    DosBeep, 585
    DosChgFilePtr, 585
    DosClose, 585
    DosCloseSem, 586
    DosCreateSem, 586
    DosCreateThread, 586
    DosEnter CritSec, 586
    DosExecPgm, 586
    DosExit, 587
    DosExitCritSec, 587
    DosGetHugeShift, 587
    DosGetInfoSeg, 587
    DosGetPrty, 587
    DosGetShrSeg, 588
    DosKillProcess, 588
    Dos MakePipe, 588
    DosMonClose, 588
    DosMonOpen, 588
    DosMonRead, 588
    DosMonReg, 588
    DosMonWrite, 589
    DosOpen, 589
    DosOpenSem, 589
    DosRead, 590
    DosSemClear, 590
    DosSemRequest, 590
    DosSemSet, 590
    DosSetPrty, 590
    DosSleep, 590
    DosStartSession, 591
    DosSuspendThread, 591
    DosWrite, 591
    GpiBox, 591
    GpiCharStringAt, 592
    GpiLine, 592
    GpiPolyLine, 592
    GpiSetBackColor, 592
    GpiSetBackMix, 593
    GpiSetColor, 593
    GpiSetCurrentPosition, 593
    GpiSetPel, 593
    KbdCharIn, 594
    KbdStringIn, 594
    MouClose, 594
    MouDrawPtr, 594
    MouGetPtrPos, 594
    MouOpen, 594
    MouReadEventQueue, 595
    VioEndPopUp, 595
    VioPopUp, 595
    VioWrtCellStr, 595
    VioWrtCharStr, 595
    VioWrtCharStrAtt, 595
    VioWrtTTy, 596
    WinBeginPaint, 596
    WinCreateMsgQueue, 596
    WinCreateStdWindow, 596
    WinDefWindowProc, 596
    WinDestroyMsgQueue, 596
    WinDestroyWindow, 597
    WinDispatchMsg, 597
    WinEndpaint, 597
    WinGetMsg, 597
    WinGetPS, 597
    WinInitialize, 597
    WinRegisterClass, 597
    WinReleasePS, 598
    WinTerminate, 598
OS/2 computer, 49, 58, 149
OS/2 EXE file shell, 416-420
OS/s libraries, 415
OS/2 output, 420-429
OS/2 Presentation Manager, 288, 359, 360, 435-475
OS/2 TSR program, 429-434
Overflow flag, 222-223

P

page numbers, 63

Index

palette registers, 82, 83, 84
palettes, 77-78
painting windows, 381-385
paragraphs, 196
partition table, 171
partitioning the disk, 163
partitions, 170-174
Pascal calling convention, 287
Pascal program, 287
Pascal–Assembly Interface, 312-315
passing parameters, 288
passing parameters in BASIC, 299-300
passing parameters in C, 309-311
passing parameters in FORTRAN, 304-306
passing parameters in Pascal, 313-314
passing parameters to a macro, 274
passwords, 37-38
PATH commands, 26
pels, 481
phase error, 272
PHONE.ASM program, 137-145
pipes, 414
pixel ranges, 153, 155
pixels, 61, 73, 77, 91, 94, 95
plane register, 101
POINT structure, 364
polling, 152
pop-up programs, 63
pop-ups under OS/2, 428-429
port 60H, 51
positive numbers, 219, 221
PostQuitMessage () function, 370, 374
Presentation Manager at work, 439-464, 477-532
Presentation Manager graphics, 508-524
PRINT command, 414
PRINT.MSG procedure, 255
printing trial messages, 253-256
PRINTOUT command, 268, 269
PROC directive, 11, 12, 36
PROCEDUREs, 13
procedures in .COM files, 11-12
program segment prefix (PSP), 3, 7-8, 16, 20, 24-30
programming the Presentation Manager, 438
PROTECT.ASM file, 3
PROTECT .COM file, 4, 7
protect disk files, 3-4
PROTECT.EXE file, 4
PROTECT.OBJ file, 4
PS handle, 481, 482, 491, 502, 508, 510, 511, 513
PS/2 computer, 61, 74, 409
PUBLIC label, 265
PURGE directive, 282

pushing parameters, 288

R

random access formatting, 133
RCL instruction, 240, 243, 244
RCR instruction, 240, 243, 244
read-only attribute, 3
reading disks, 181-183
reading from files, 115, 127
reading from the keyboard buffer, 55-58
reading keys, 50
reading keys in Presentation Manager, 498-508
reading sectors into memory, 178-179
reading status bytes, 50
reading the mouse queue, 152-154
reading the video state, 90
read/write pointer, 135,-137, 141, 142-145
RECORD directive, 335-338, 351
rectangle drawing instruction, 386
Rectangle () service, 395
reentrant code in OS/2, 465-475
registers, 6
RELEASE.ASM file, 4
RELEASE.COM file, 5
Release DC (), 389
relocating .EXE files, 16-17
relocation table, 17
renaming files, 115
REP operation, 40-42
REPE operation, 42-43
REPEATER.COM service, 36
REPNE operation, 42-43
REPT directive, 280-281
request header, 604-605
resetting the interrupt vector, 195-196
resident programs, 13
resizing the window, 525-532
RET instruction, 12, 14
retrieving data from files, 134-135
return code, 196
returning disk parameters, 180-181
returning values from functions, 293-294
returning values in BASIC, 294-295
returning values in C, 294
returning values in FORTRAN, 294-295
returning values in Pascal, 294-295
rgbRGB setting, 82, 86
Right Shift key, 23
ROL instruction, 240, 242, 244
ROR instruction, 240, 242, 244
rotating bytes, 240-243
rotating through carry, 242-243

S

rotating words, 240-243
RUBOUT.COM program, 116-118
running programs, 4-5

.SAL instruction, 239
SAR instruction, 239, 240
SBB instruction, 228-229
scan codes, 49, 53
scan string instructions, 44
SCAS operation, 44-46
SCASP operation, 44-46
SCASW operation, 44-46
screen buffer, 23
screen attributes, 64-65
screen buffer, 66-68
screen displays, 61
screen flicker, 96-98
screen handling, 59-110
screen mask, 156
screen mask attribute, 156
screen mask character, 156
scrolling, 63, 64
sectors, 161, 164, 169-170
security rings, 413
segment registers, 6, 22, 28, 40
segment selectors, 411-412
self-defining macros, 282-284
semaphores, 414
sequential access, 134
Set Direction flag, 41
Set Interrupt flag, 190
set interrupt vector services, 194
setting the cursor, 62-63
setting the read/write pointer, 142-145
setting the video mode, 73-75
Shift key, 53
SHL instruction, 238, 240
short integer, 327
shortcut parameter passing in BASIC, 300-302
shortcut parameter passing in C, 311-312
shortcut parameter passing in FORTRAN, 306-307
shortcut parameter passing in Pascal, 314-315
SHR instruction, 238, 240
ShowWindow () function, 368
Side Border flag, 449
sign bit, 217-218
signed jumps, 221-222
signed multiplication, 223-225
signed numbers at work, 217-237
significand, 328
single-sided disks, 161

Source Index, 40
SP register, 289
SS register, 289
.STACK directive, 21
stack in .EXE files, 19-21
stack objects in OS/2, 418
stack-oriented chips, 319
stack pointer, 12, 289
stack segments, 4
start segment, 17, 19
status bytes, 50, 51
static linking, 416
storing data, 8-11
storing strings, 46-47
STOS operation, 46-47
STOSB operation, 46
STOSW operation, 46
string input, 38
string instructions, 39-48
string searches, 29
strings, 10, 13
stub procedures, 403
SUB instruction, 229
subdirectories, 13, 174-177
SUBROUTINEs, 13, 255
Subtracting integers with 80 × 87, 323-325
SWITCH.ASM program, 211-214
SysMenu flag, 449

T

TAKE5.EXE program, 429-434
terminate address, 25
terminate-but-stay-resident interrupts, 13
terminate-but-stay-resident (TSR) programs, 13, 183, 189
terminate-but-stay-resident shell, 204-207
termination code, 418
text modes, 75, 156
TextOut service, 379
threads, 411, 413
Titlebar flag, 449
toolbox, 73
tracks, 161, 169-170
Translate Message function, 370
transparent pop-ups, 429
two's complement numbers, 219-220, 221, 228
two-pass assemblers, 272
two-word addresses, 6, 10, 17, 22
Turbo Assembler, 6, 300

U

U instruction, 35

unprotect disk files, 4
unsigned jumps, 221-222
unsigned numbers, 220
Update Window () function, 368, 381
using advanced directives, 251-284
using & in macros, 275-277
using BP and stack frames, 291-292
using groups, 262-265
using macros, 251-284
using Microsoft Windows, 357-405
using multiple procedures in .COM files, 13-14
using % in macros, 275-277
using the disks, 159-186
using the 80 × 87, 317-355
using the mouse, 147-186

V

valid windows, 383
Validate Rect () service, 383
vertical scroll, 449
video buffer, 67, 81
Video Graphics Adapter (VGA), 61, 66, 84-91
video memory, 63
video modes, 63, 74
Vio services, 415, 425
VioEndPopUp service, 433
VioGetCursorPos service, 425
VioPopUp service, 428-429, 430, 436
VioWrtCellStr service, 424
VioWrtCharStrAttr service, 426-428
VioWrtTTY service, 411, 424
virtual memory, 412

W

W instruction, 35
WIN.ASM program, 473-475
WinBegin Paint function, 500
WinCreateMsgQueue function, 441, 442
WinCreateStdWindow function, 446, 449, 453, 455
WinDefWindowProc function, 465, 466, 467, 468, 469, 470

WinDestroyMsgQueue functions, 460
WinDestroyWindow function, 460
WinDispatchMsg function, 458
window class structure, 364
window classes, 364
window flags, 448
window function, 442, 464-475
window lass, 365
window messages, 360-362
windows definition file, 403
windows library, 404
Windows Software Development kit, 360
WinEndPaint function, 484, 502, 513
WinGetMsg function, 455, 456, 458, 460
WinGetPS function, 500
WinInitialize function, 440
WinMain program, 359, 362-371, 372
WinRegisterClass function, 443, 445
WinTerminate function, 462
Wparam parameter, 360, 364
write command, 176
write dot service, 81, 92
writing an OS/2 program, 414-416
writing graphic images, 91
writing memory resident code, 189-190
writing pop-up programs, 187-214
writing programs, 1-30
writing programs to handle interrupts, 198-203
writing sectors to disk, 180
writing to disks, 181-183
writing to files, 115, 128-129
writing to the buffer, 91-92

X

XOR A, AX instruction, 20
XORing, 20

Z

zero flag, 36, 50

////BradyLine

**Insights into
tomorrow's technology from the
authors and editors of Brady**

You rely on Brady's bestselling computer books for up-to-date information about high technology. Now turn to *BradyLine* for the details behind the titles.

Find out what new trends in technology spark Brady's authors and editors. Read about what they're working on, and predicting, for the future. Get to know the authors through interviews and profiles, and get to know each other through your questions and comments.

BradyLine keeps you ahead of the trends with the stories behind the latest computer developments. Informative previews of forthcoming books and excerpts from new titles keep you apprised of what's going on in the fields that interest you most.

- Peter Norton on operating systems
- Winn Rosch on hardware
- Jerry Daniels, Mary Jane Mara, Robert Eckhardt, and Cynthia Harriman on Macintosh development, productivity, and connectivity

Get the Spark. Get *BradyLine*.

Published quarterly, beginning with the Summer 1990 issue. Free exclusively to our customers.
Just check the box on the Warranty/Registration card and mail it to begin your subscription now.

CUSTOMER SUPPORT

It is important that you register your purchase of any Simon & Schuster software package. By completing and returning your Owner Registration Card, you become eligible for:

- Software support directly from S & S.
- Diskette replacement when applicable.
- Purchase of future product upgrades at special prices.
- Subscriptions to Hint Books and newsletters where applicable.

Software Support

S & S will provide support to registered owners. Our technical support number is (900) 990-2778. It is staffed on working days during normal business hours, 10:00 am to 6:00 pm, Eastern time. There is a charge of $1.00 per minute charged to your phone for each minute after the first.

Mail-in Support Service—Registered owners may write to us with questions. We will respond in writing. There is no additional charge for this service.

We realize that our software packages are put to a wide variety of uses, however, we can only answer questions about the software package itself. We cannot support the hardware and operating system required to run our software packages.

Before Calling Customer Support

Before calling our Technical Support Department, please make sure you have followed the steps in the "Pre-call Checklist" below.

Pre-call Checklist

1. If you are having difficulty understanding the program, have you read and performed the suggestions listed in the manual?
2. If you are not sure how to operate the program, have you used the help system (where available) to find the answer?
3. If there seems to be a problem in the software, can you reproduce the problem by following your steps again?
4. If the program displayed an error message, please write down the exact message.
5. You should be familiar with the hardware configuration you are using. We may need to know the brand/model of your computer, printer, the total amount of memory available, what video adaptor(s) you have in the system, the operating system version, etc.
6. When you call our Technical Support Department, please be at your computer or be prepared to repeat the sequence of steps leading up to the problem.

Services and Prices

The above services and prices are subject to change without prior notice.

Important! Read before Opening Sealed Diskette
END USER LICENSE AGREEMENT

The software in this package is provided to You on the condition that You agree with SIMON & SCHUSTER, INC. ("S&S") to the terms and conditions set forth below. **Read this End User Agreement carefully. You will be bound by the terms of this agreement if you open the sealed diskette.** If You do not agree to the terms contained in this End User License Agreement, return the entire product, along with your receipt, to *Brady, Simon & Schuster, Inc.,* 15 Columbus Circle,14th floor, New York, NY 10023, *Attn: Refunds,* and your purchase price will be refunded.

S&S grants, and You hereby accept, a personal, nonexclusive license to use this software program and associated documentation in this package, or any part of it ("Licensed Product"), subject to the following terms and conditions:

1. License
The license granted to You hereunder authorizes You to use the Licensed Product on any single computer system. A separate license, pursuant to a separate End User License Agreement, is required for any other computer system on which You intend to use the Licensed Product.

2. Term
This End User License Agreement is effective from the date of purchase by You of the Licensed Product and shall remain in force until terminated. You may terminate this End User License at any time by destroying the Licensed Product together with all copies in any form made by You or received by You. Your right to use or copy the Licensed Product will terminate if You fail to comply with any of the terms or conditions of this End User License Agreement. Upon such termination, You shall destroy the copies of the Licensed Product in your possession.

3. Restriction against Transfer
This End User License Agreement, and the Licensed Product, may not be assigned, sublicensed, or otherwise transferred by You to another party unless the other party agrees to accept the terms and conditions of the End User License Agreement. If You transfer the Licensed Product, You must at the same time either transfer all copies, whether in printed or machine-readable form, to the same party or destroy any copies not transferred.

4. Restrictions against Copying or Modifying the Licensed Product
The Licensed Product is copyrighted and except for certain limited uses as noted on the copyright page, may not be further copied without the prior written approval of S&S. You may make one copy for backup purposes provided You reproduce and include the complete copyright notice on the backup copy. Any unauthorized coyping is in violation of this Agreement and may also constitute a violation of the United States Copyright Law for which You could be liable in a civil or criminal lawsuit. **You may not use, transfer, copy, or otherwise reproduce the Licensed Product, or any part of it, except as expressly permitted in this End User License Agreement.**

5. Protection and Security
You shall take all reasonable steps to safeguard the Licensed Product and to ensure that no unauthorized person shall have access to it and that no unauthorized copy of any part of it in any form shall be made.

6. Limited Warranty
If You are the original consumer purchaser of a diskette and it is found to be defective in materials or workmanship (which shall not include problems relating to the nature or operation of the Licensed Product) under normal use, S&S will replace it free of charge (or, at S&S's option, refund your purchase price) within 30 days following the date of purchase. Following the 30-day period, and up to one year ofter purchase, S&S will replace any such defective diskette upon payment of a $5 charge (or, at S&S's option, refund your purchase price), provided that the Limited Warranty Registration Card has been filed within 30 days following the date of purchase. Any request for replacement of a defective diskette must be accompanied by the original defective diskette and proof of date of purchase and purchase price. S&S shall have no obligation to replace a diskette (or refund your purchase price based on claims of defects in the nature or operation of the Licensed Product.

The software program is provided "as is" without warranty of any kind, either expressed or implied, including but not limited to the implied warranties of merchantability and fitness for a particular purpose. The entire risk as to the quality and performance of the program is with You. Should the program prove defective, You (and not S&S) assume the entire cost of necessary servicing, repair or correction.

Some states do not allow the exclusion of implied waraanties, so the above exclusion may not apply to You. This warrant gives you specific legal rights, and You may also have other rights which vary from state to satate.

S&S does not warrant that the functions contained in the program will meet your requirements or that the operation of the program will be uninterrupted or error free. Neither S&S nor anyone else who has been involved in the creation of production of this product shall be liable for any direct, indirect, incidental, special, or consequential damages, whether arising out of the use or inability to use the product, or any breach of a warranty, and S&S shall have no responsibility except to replace the diskette pursuant to this limited warranty (or, at its option, provide a refund of the purchase price).

No sales personnel or other representative of any party involved in the distribution of the Licensed Product is authorized by S&S to make any warranties with respect to the diskette or the Licensed Product beyond those contained in this Agreement. **Oral statements do not constitute warranties,** shall not be relied upon by You, and are not part of this Agreement. The entire agreement between S&S and You is embodied in this Agreement.

7. General
If any provision of this End User License Agreement is determined to be invalid under any applicable statute of rule of law, it shall be deemed omitted and the remaining provisions shall continue in full force and effect. This End User License Agreement is to be governed by the construed in accordance with the laws of the State of New York.

Simon & Schuster, Inc. and the authors make no warranties, express or implied in connection with the software, and expressly exclude all warranties of fitness for a particular purpose. Simon & Schuster, Inc. and the authors shall have no liability for consequential, incidental, or exemplary damages.

Advanced Assembly Language
REPLACEMENT ORDER FORM

Please use this form when ordering a 3.5-inch disk or a replacement for a defective diskette.

A. If Ordering within Thirty Days of Purchase
If a diskette is reported defective within thirty days of purchase, a replacement diskette will be provided free of charge. *The back of this card must be totally filled out and accompanied by the defective diskette and a copy of the dated sales receipt.* In addition, please complete and return the Limited Warranty Registration Card.

B. If Ordering after Thirty Days of Purchase but within One Year
If a diskette is reported defective after thirty days, but within one year of purchase and the Warranty Registration Card has been properly filed, a replacement diskette will be provided to you for a nominal fee of $5.00 (send check or money order only). *The back of this card must be totally filled out and accompanied by the defective diskette, a copy of the dated sales receipt, and a $5.00 check or money order made payable to Simon & Schuster, Inc.*

C. If ordering 3.5 inch replacement disks
If you wish to order 3.5-inch disks for this product, please complete the back of this card and mail it with your original 5.25-inch diskettes along with a nominal fee of $5.00 to cover shipping and handling (send check or money order only). In addition, please complete and return the Limited Warranty Registration Card.

Advanced Assembly Language
LIMITED WARRANTY REGISTRATION CARD

In order to preserve your rights as provided in the limited warranty, this card must be on file with Simon & Schuster within thirty days of purchase.

Please fill in the information requested:

NAME _____ PHONE NUMBER ( ) _____
ADDRESS _____
CITY _____ STATE _____ ZIP _____
COMPUTER BRAND & MODEL _____ DOS VERSION _____ MEMORY _____ K

Where did you purchase this product?
DEALER NAME? _____ PHONE NUMBER ( ) _____
ADDRESS _____
CITY _____ STATE _____ ZIP _____
PURCHASE DATE _____ PURCHASE PRICE _____

How did you learn about this product? (Check as many as applicable.)
STORE DISPLAY _____ SALESPERSON _____ MAGAZINE ARTICLE _____ ADVERTISEMENT _____
OTHER (Please explain) _____

How long have you owned or used this computer?
LESS THAN 30 DAYS _____ LESS THAN 6 MONTHS _____ 6 MONTHS TO A YEAR _____ OVER 1 YEAR _____

What is your primary use for the computer?
BUSINESS _____ PERSONAL _____ EDUCATION _____ OTHER (Please explain) _____

Where is your computer located?
HOME _____ OFFICE _____ SCHOOL _____ OTHER (Please explain) _____

67-65877

Get the Spark. Get *BradyLine*.
Published quarterly, beginning with the Summer 1990 issue. Free exclusively to our customers.
☐ Check here to begin your subscription.

Advanced Assembly Language

Please fill out the information below and return it to the address listed with your *original* 5.25-inch diskettes. Please print clearly.

☐ I am ordering replacement diskettes within 30 days. I have enclosed my original diskettes and a copy of the dated sales receipt.   ISBN 0-13-658774-4

☐ I am ordering replacement diskettes after 30 days but within one year. I have enclosed my original diskettes, a copy of the dated sales receipt and check or money order for $5.00 made out to Simon & Schuster, Inc.   ISBN 0-13-658774-4

☐ I am ordering 3.5-inch disks. I have enclosed my original 5.25-inch diskettes along with a check or money order for $5.00 made out to Simon & Schuster, Inc.
   ISBN 0-13-663113-4

NAME _____ PHONE NUMBER ( ) _____
ADDRESS _____
CITY _____ STATE _____ ZIP _____

Please mail this request to: MICROSERVICES, 200 Old Tappan Road, Old Tappan, NJ 07675. For more information, call (201) 767-5054.

PUT FIRST CLASS STAMP HERE

College Marketing Group
50 Cross Street
Winchester, MA 01890

ATTN: **CHERYL READ**